Readings in Deviant Behavior

READINGS IN DEVIANT BEHAVIOR

THIRD EDITION

ALEX THIO

Ohio University

THOMAS C. CALHOUN

Southern Illinois University at Carbondale

Boston ■ New York ■ San Francisco
Mexico City ■ Montreal ■ Toronto ■ London ■ Madrid ■ Munich ■ Paris
Hong Kong ■ Singapore ■ Tokyo ■ Cape Town ■ Sydney

Series Editor: Jennifer Jacobson
Series Editorial Assistant: Amy Holborow
Senior Marketing Manager: Krista Groshong
Editorial-Production Service: Omegatype Typography, Inc.
Manufacturing Buyer: JoAnne Sweeney
Composition and Prepress Buyer: Linda Cox
Cover Administrator: Joel Gendron
Electronic Composition: Omegatype Typography, Inc.

For related titles and support materials, visit our online catalogue at www.ablongman.com.

Between the time Website information is gathered and then published, it is not unusual for some sites to have closed. Also, the transcription of URLs can result in typographical errors. The publishers would appreciate notification where these errors occur so that they may be corrected in subsequent editions.

Library of Congress Cataloging-in-Publication Data

Readings in deviant behavior / [edited by] Alex Thio, Thomas C. Calhoun.—3rd ed.
    p. cm.
  Includes bibliographical references and index.
  ISBN 0-205-38915-5 (alk. paper)
  1. Deviant behavior. I. Thio, Alex. II. Calhoun, Thomas C.

HM811.R4 2004
302.5'42—dc21

                                       2003041868

Printed in the United States of America

10 9 8 7 6 5 4   08 07 06 05 04

CONTENTS

PREFACE

In this edition of *Readings in Deviant Behavior,* more than half of all the articles are new. They reflect current trends in the sociology of deviance. The inclusion of many more studies on non-criminal deviance—such as tattooing, hyperactivity, nude dancing, binge drinking, smoking, and online sex—represents a significant shift from criminal deviance such as murder and rape. Some of the noncriminal deviances, such as the proliferation of cyberdeviance, have only recently emerged on the scene; others, such as cockfighting and tattooing, have been around for a long time but have only recently become the subject of research by sociologists. On the theoretical front there is a change in emphasis from the positivist perspective to the constructionist one. In research methodology there is greater use of ethnography at the expense of the traditional use of surveys. All these new developments are showcased in the current edition of this reader.

Like its previous editions, this anthology offers comprehensive coverage. Unlike many other editors, we decided against taking a single theoretical approach when selecting articles for our book. Instead, we present a great variety of readings that represent the full range of deviance sociology. We believe that students should be exposed to different theories of deviance. Students should also know different kinds of data collected with different research methodologies.

This reader covers all the major theories in deviance sociology, from classic ones such as Merton's anomie-strain theory, and Becker's labeling theory, to modern ones such as shaming, phenomenological, feminist, and postmodernist theories. In addition, this anthology encompasses a wide spectrum of deviant behaviors. There are articles about deviances that have long attracted sociological attention, such as homicide, burglary, drug abuse, and homosexuality. There are also articles on deviances that in recent years have leapt into public and sociological consciousness, such as suicide bombing, sex tourism, binge drinking, cigarette smoking, and cyberdeviance. Analyses of these subjects rely on data from theory-informed research that runs the gamut from survey to ethnographic studies. All these analyses are multidisciplinary, coming not only from sociologists but also from scholars and researchers in other fields. They all effectively reflect what the sociology of deviance is like today: diverse, wide-ranging, and exciting.

This is a user-friendly reader, put together with students in mind. The articles are not only authoritative but also interesting. Many were chosen from a diversity of books, journals, and magazines. Some were solicited from well-known or well-qualified sociologists and researchers. Most important, unique to this anthology, nearly all these articles were carefully edited for clarity, conciseness, and forcefulness. Students will therefore find them easy and enjoyable to read while learning what deviance is all about.

We want to thank our colleagues who specifically wrote for this reader. Our deep gratitude also goes to all those writers whose published works are presented here. Further deserving our thanks are the following reviewers, who contributed greatly to preparation of a truly useful and student-oriented reader: James Nolan, West Virginia University, and James T. Oleson, Old Dominion University. Last but not least, we thank Addrain Conyers, sociology graduate student at Southern Illinois University at Carbondale, for his significant contribution to this project.

ABOUT THE EDITORS

ALEX THIO

Alex Thio is Professor of Sociology at Ohio University. Born of Chinese parentage in Malaysia, he grew up in a multicultural environment. He acquired fluency in Mandarin (modern standard Chinese), Malay, and Indonesian. He also picked up a smattering of English and Dutch. He further took French and German in high school and college.

Professor Thio attended primary school in Malaysia and high school in Indonesia. He then came to the United States and worked his way through Central Methodist College in Missouri. Later, he studied sociology as a graduate student and received his Ph.D. at the State University of New York at Buffalo.

Dr. Thio regularly teaches courses in deviance, introductory sociology, social problems, and criminology. In addition to teaching, he enjoys writing. Aside from this book, he is the author of the popular texts *Deviant Behavior,* seventh edition (2004), and *Sociology: A Brief Introduction,* fifth edition (2003), and has written many articles.

THOMAS C. CALHOUN

Thomas Calhoun is Professor of Sociology at Southern Illinois University at Carbondale. Born and reared in rural Mississippi, he attended segregated schools and witnessed many civil rights activities in the 1960s. He received his B.A. in sociology from Texas Wesleyan College, M.A. from Texas Tech University, and Ph.D. from the University of Kentucky.

Dr. Calhoun teaches courses in deviant behavior, juvenile delinquency, and race relations. His articles have appeared in journals such as *Deviant Behavior, Sociological Spectrum,* and *Sociological Inquiry,* and he co-authored *Readings in Delinquency and Juvenile Justice* (2003). He is currently President of the North Central Sociological Association and is a former President of the Association of Social and Behavioral Scientists.

Readings in Deviant Behavior

What is deviant behavior? Why ask what it is? Doesn't everybody know it has to do with weirdos and perverts? Not at all. There is, in fact, a great deal of disagreement among people about what they consider deviant. In a classic study, sociologist Jerry Simmons asked a sample of the general public who they thought was deviant. They mentioned 252 different kinds of people as deviants, including homosexuals, prostitutes, alcoholics, drug addicts, murderers, the mentally ill, communists, atheists, liars, Democrats, reckless drivers, self-pitiers, the retired, career women, divorcées, Christians, suburbanites, movie stars, perpetual bridge players, prudes, pacifists, psychiatrists, priests, liberals, conservatives, junior executives, girls who wear makeup, smart-aleck students, and know-it-all professors. If you are surprised that some of these people are considered deviant, your surprise simply adds to the fact that a good deal of disagreement exists among the public about what deviant behavior is.

There is a similar lack of consensus among sociologists. We could say that the study of deviant behavior is probably the most "deviant" of all the subjects in sociology. Sociologists disagree more about the definition of deviant behavior than they do on any other subject.

CONFLICTING DEFINITIONS

Some sociologists simply say that deviance is a violation of any social rule, but others argue that deviance involves more than rule violation—it also has the quality of provoking disapproval, anger, or indignation. Some advocate a broader definition, arguing that a person can be a deviant without violating any rule or doing something that rubs others the wrong way. According to this argument, individuals who are afflicted with some unfortunate condition for which they cannot be held responsible are deviant. Examples include psychotics, paraplegics, the mentally challenged, and other people with physical or mental disabilities. These people are considered deviant because they are disvalued by society. In contrast, some sociologists contend that deviance does not have to be negative. To these sociologists, deviance can be positive, such as being a genius, reformer, creative artist, or glamorous celebrity. Other sociologists disagree, considering "positive deviance" to be an oxymoron—a contradiction in terms.

All these sociologists apparently assume that, whether it is a positive or a negative, disturbing, or disvalued behavior, deviance is real in and of itself. The logic behind this assumption is that if it is not real in the first place, it cannot be considered positive, negative, disturbing, or disvalued. Other sociologists disagree, arguing that deviance does not have to be real behavior for it to be labeled deviant. People can be falsely accused of being criminal, erroneously diagnosed as mentally ill, stereotyped as dangerous because of their skin color, and so on. Conversely, committing a deviant act does not necessarily make a person a deviant, especially when the act is kept secret. It is, therefore, the label *deviant*—a mental construction or image of an act as deviant, rather than the act itself—that makes an individual deviant.

Some sociologists go beyond the notion of labeling to define deviance by stressing the importance of power. They observe that relatively powerful people are capable of avoiding the fate suffered by the powerless—being falsely, erroneously, or unjustly labeled deviant. The key reason is that the powerful, either by themselves or through influencing public opinion or both, hold more power for labeling others' behavior as deviant. Understandably, sociologists who hold this view define deviance as any act considered by the powerful at a given time and place to be a violation of some social rule.

From this welter of conflicting definitions we can nonetheless discern the influence of two opposing perspectives: positivism and social constructionism. The positivist perspective is associated with the sciences, such as physics, chemistry, or biology. It influences how scientists see and study their subject. On the other hand, the constructionist perspective has more to do with the humanities, such as art, language, or philosophy. It affects how scholars in these fields see and study their subject. These two perspectives can be found in sociology; some sociologists are more influenced by the positivist perspective and others by the constructionist. Positivist sociologists tend to define deviance in one way, whereas constructionist sociologists pursue another way. The two perspectives further influence the use of certain theory and methodology for producing knowledge about deviant behavior. The conflicting definitions that we have discussed can be couched in terms of these two perspectives. The definitions that focus on deviance as rule-breaking behavior are essentially positivist, whereas those that center on labeling and power are constructionist. Let us delve more deeply into the meanings and implications of these two conflicting perspectives.

CONFLICTING PERSPECTIVES

The knowledge about deviance basically consists of answers to three questions: (1) What to study?

(2) How to study it? (3) What does the result of the study mean? The first question deals with the subject of study, the second has to do with the method of study, and the third concerns the data-based theory about the subject. Positivism and constructionism provide conflicting answers to each question.

Subject: What to Study?

Positivism suggests that we study deviance or deviants. The reason deals with the positivist's absolutist definition of deviance. According to this definition, deviance is absolutely or intrinsically real in that it possesses some qualities that distinguish it from conventionality. Similarly, deviants are thought to have certain attributes that make them different from conventional individuals. By contrast, social constructionism suggests that we study law enforcers and other such people who are influenced by society to construct an image of certain others as deviants and then label them as such, or how the process of such labeling takes place and affects the labeled. This is because the constructionist assumes the relativist stance in defining deviance as a socially constructed label imposed on some behavior. Such a definition can be said to be relativist by implying that the deviancy of a behavior is relative to—dependent on—the socially constructed negative reaction to the behavior.

Absolutism: Deviance as Absolutely Real. Around the turn of the twentieth century, criminologists believed that criminals possessed certain biological traits that were absent in noncriminals. Those biological traits included defective genes, bumps on the head, a long lower jaw, a scanty beard, an unattractive face, and a tough body build. Because all these traits are inherited, people were believed to be criminals simply because they were born criminals. If they were born criminals, they would always be criminals. As the saying goes, "If you've had it, you've had it." No matter where they might go—they could go anywhere in the world—they would still be criminals.

Then the criminologists shifted their attention from biological to psychological traits. Criminals were thought to have certain mental characteristics that noncriminals did not have. More specifically, criminals were believed to be feeble-minded, psychotic, neurotic, psychopathic, or otherwise mentally disturbed. Like biological traits, these mental characteristics were seen as inherent in individual criminals. Also like biological traits, mental characteristics would stay with the criminals, no matter where they went. Again, because of these psychological traits, criminals would always remain criminals.

Today's positivist sociologists, however, have largely abandoned the use of biological and psychological traits to differentiate criminals from noncriminals. They recognize the important role of social factors in determining a person's status as a criminal. Such status does not remain the same across time and space; instead, it changes in different periods and with different societies. A polygamist may be a criminal in Western society but a law-abider in Moslem countries. A person who sees things invisible to others may be a psychotic in Western society but may become a spiritual leader among some South Pacific tribes. Nevertheless, positivist sociologists still largely regard deviance as intrinsically real. Countering the relativist notion of deviance as basically a social construction in the form of a label imposed on an act, positivist Travis Hirschi (1973) argues: "The person may not have committed a 'deviant' act, but he did (in many cases) do *something*. And it is just possible that what he did was a result of things that had happened to him in the past; it is also possible that the past in some inscrutable way remains with him and that if he were left alone he would *do it again*." Moreover, countering the relativist notion of mental illness as a label imputed to some people's behavior, positivist Gwynn Nettler (1974) explicitly voices his absolutist stance: "Some people *are* more crazy than others; we can tell the difference; and calling lunacy a name does not *cause* it." These

positivist sociologists seem to say that just as a rose by any other name would smell as sweet, so deviance by any other label is just as real.

Relativism: Deviance as a Label. Social constructionists hold the relativist view that deviant behavior by itself does not have any intrinsic characteristics unless it is thought to have those characteristics. The so-called intrinsically deviant characteristics do not come from the behavior itself; they originate instead from some people's minds. To put it simply, an act appears deviant only because some people think it so. As Howard Becker (1963) says, "Deviant behavior is behavior that people so label." Therefore, no deviant label, no deviant behavior. The existence of deviance depends on the label. Deviance, then, is a mental construct (an idea, thought, or image) expressed in the form of a label.

Because they effectively consider deviance unreal, constructionists understandably stay away from studying it. They are more interested in the questions of whether and why a given act is defined by society as deviant. This leads to studying people who label others as deviant—such as the police and other law-enforcing agents. If constructionists study so-called deviants, they do so by focusing on the nature of labeling and its consequences.

In studying law-enforcing agents, constructionists have found a huge lack of consensus on whether a certain person should be treated as a criminal. The police often disagree among themselves about whether a suspect should be arrested, and judges often disagree about whether those arrested should be convicted or acquitted. In addition, because laws vary from one state to another, the same type of behavior may be defined as criminal in one state but not in another. Prostitution, for example, is legal in Nevada but not in other states. There is, then, a *relativity* principle in deviant behavior; behavior gets defined as deviant relative to a given norm, standard of behavior, or the way people react to it. If it is not related to the norm or to the reaction of other people, a given behavior is in itself meaningless—it is impossible to say whether it is deviant or conforming. Constructionists strongly emphasize this relativistic view, according to which, deviance, like beauty, is in the eye of the beholder.

Method: How to Study It?

Positivism suggests that we use objective methods such as survey, experiment, or detached observation. The subject is treated like an object, forced, for example, to answer the same questions as presented to everybody else with the same value-free, emotionless demeanor. This is because positivists define deviance as a largely objective fact, namely, a publicly observable, outward aspect of human behavior. By contrast, social constructionism suggests that we study individuals with more subjective methods, such as ethnography, participant observation, or open-ended, in-depth interviews. With these methods, subjects are treated as unique, whole persons and are encouraged to freely express their feelings in any way they want. This is because constructionists define deviance as a mostly personal experience—a hidden, inner aspect of human behavior.

Objectivism: Deviance as an Objective Fact.   By focusing on the outward aspect of deviance, positivists assume that sociologists can be as objective in studying deviance as natural scientists can be in studying physical phenomena. The trick is to treat deviants as if they are objects, like those studied by natural scientists. Nonetheless, positivist sociologists cannot help being aware of the basic difference between their subject, human beings, and that of natural scientists, inanimate objects. As human beings themselves, positivist sociologists must have certain feelings about their subject. However, they try to control their personal biases by forcing themselves not to pass moral judgment on deviant behavior or share the deviant person's feelings. Instead, they try to concentrate on the subject matter as it outwardly appears. Further, these sociologists have tried hard to follow the scientific rule that all their ideas about deviant be-

havior should be subject to public scrutiny. This means that other sociologists should be able to check out the ideas to see whether they are supported by facts.

Such a drive to achieve scientific objectivity has produced substantial knowledge about deviant behavior. No longer popular today are such value-loaded and subjective notions as maladjustment, moral failing, debauchery, demoralization, sickness, pathology, and abnormality. Replacing these outdated notions are such value-free and objective concepts as innovation, retreatism, ritualism, rebellion, culture conflict, subcultural behavior, white-collar crime, norm violation, learned behavior, and reinforced behavior.

To demonstrate the objective reality of these concepts, positivist sociologists have used official reports and statistics, clinical reports, surveys of self-reported behavior, and surveys of victimization. Positivists recognize the unfortunate fact that the sample of deviants in the studies—especially in official statistics—does not accurately represent the entire population of deviants. Nevertheless, positivists believe that the quality of information obtained by these methods can be improved and refined. In the meantime, they consider the data, though inadequate, useful for revealing at least some aspect of the totality of deviant behavior.

Subjectivism: Deviance as a Personal Experience.   To positivists, the supposedly deviant behavior is a personal experience and the supposedly deviant person is a conscious, feeling, thinking, and reflective subject. Social constructionists insist that there is a world of difference between humans (as active subjects) and nonhuman beings and things (as passive objects). Humans feel and reflect, but animals, plants, things, and the others do not. It is proper and useful for natural scientists to assume and then study nature as an object, because this study can produce objective knowledge for controlling the natural world. It may also be useful for social scientists to assume and then study humans as objects, because it may produce objective knowledge for controlling humans.

However, this violates the constructionist's humanist values and sensibilities.

Constructionists are opposed to the control of humans; instead, they advocate the protection and expansion of human worth, dignity, and freedom. One result of this humanist ideology is the observation that so-called objective knowledge about human behavior is inevitably superficial whenever it is used to control people. In order for the former white racist government in South Africa to control blacks, for example, it needed only the superficial knowledge that blacks were identifiable and separable from whites. However, to achieve the humanist goal of protecting and expanding blacks' human worth, dignity, and freedom, a deeper understanding of blacks is needed. This understanding requires appreciating and empathizing with them, experiencing what they experience as blacks, and seeing blacks' lives and the world around them from their perspective. We must look at the black experience from the inside as a participant rather than from the outside as a spectator. In a word, we must adopt the internal, subjective view instead of the external, objective one.

The same principle, according to constructionists, should hold for understanding deviants and their deviant behavior. Constructionists contrast this subjective approach with the positivists' objective one. To constructionists, positivists treat deviance as if it were an immoral, unpleasant, or repulsive phenomenon that should be controlled, corrected, or eliminated. In consequence, positivists have used the objective approach by staying aloof from deviants, studying the external aspects of their deviant behavior and relying on a set of preconceived ideas to guide their study. The result is a collection of surface facts about deviants, such as their poverty, lack of schooling, poor self-image, and low aspirations. All this may be used to control and eliminate deviance, but it does not tell us, in Howard Becker's (1963) words, "what a deviant does in his daily round of activity, and what he thinks about himself, society, and his activities." To understand the life of a deviant, constructionists believe, we need to use the relatively subjective approach, which requires our appreciation for and empathy with the deviant. The aim of this subjective approach, according to David Matza (1969), "is to comprehend and to illuminate the subject's view and to interpret the world *as it appears to him.*"

As a result of their subjective and empathetic approach, constructionists often present an image of deviants as basically the same as conventional people. People who are deaf, for example, are the same as those who hear in being able to communicate and live a normal life. They should, therefore, be respected rather than pitied. This implies that so-called deviant behavior, because it is like so-called conventional behavior, should not be controlled, cured, or eradicated by society.

Theory: What Does It Mean?

Positivism suggests that we use etiological, causal, or explanatory theories to make sense of what research has found out about deviant behavior because positivists favor the determinist view that deviance is determined by forces beyond the individual's control. By contrast, constructionism suggests that we go for largely noncausal, descriptive, or analytical theories. Such theories provide detailed analyses of the subjective, experiential world of deviance. Constructionists feel at home with these analyses because they regard most deviance as a voluntary act, an expression of free will.

Determinism: Deviance as "Determined" Behavior. Overly enthusiastic about the prospect of turning their discipline into a science, early sociologists argued that, like animals, plants, and material objects that natural scientists study, humans do not have any free will. The reason is that acknowledgment of free will would contradict the scientific principle of determinism. If a killer is thought to will, cause, or determine a murderous act, then it does not make sense to say that the murderous act is caused by such things as the individual's physical characteristics, mental condition, family background, or some social experience. Therefore, in defending their scientific principle of determinism, the early sociologists maintained their denial of

6   INTRODUCTION

free will. However, today's positivist sociologists assume that humans do possess free will. Still, this assumption, they argue, does not undermine the scientific principle of determinism. No matter how much a person exercises free will by making choices and decisions, the choices and decisions do not simply happen but are determined by some causes. If a woman chooses to kill her husband rather than continue to live with him, she certainly has free will or freedom of choice so long as nobody forces her to do what she does. However, some factor may determine the woman's choice of one alternative over another, or the way she exercises her free will. One such factor, as research has suggested, may be a long history of abuse at the hands of her husband. Thus, according to today's positivists, there is no inconsistency between freedom and causality.

Although they allow for human freedom of choice, positivists do not use it to explain why people behave in a certain way. They will not, for example, explain why the woman kills by saying "because she chooses to kill." This is no explanation at all, because the idea of choice can also be used to explain why another woman does *not* kill her husband—by saying "because she chooses not to." According to positivists, killing and not killing (or, more generally, deviant and conventional behavior), being two contrary phenomena, cannot be explained by the same thing, such as choice. The idea of choice simply cannot explain the difference between deviance and conventionality; it cannot explain why one man chooses to kill when another chooses not to. Therefore, although positivists do believe in human choice, they will not attribute deviance to human choice. They will instead explain deviance by using such concepts as wife abuse, broken homes, unhappy homes, lower-class background, economic deprivation, social disorganization, rapid social change, differential association, differential reinforcement, and lack of social control. Any one of these causes of deviance can be used to illustrate what positivists consider a real explanation of deviance, because, for example, wife abuse is more likely to cause a woman to kill her husband than not. Etio-

logical theories essentially point out factors like those as the causes of deviance.

Voluntarism: Deviance as a Voluntary Act. To social constructionists, the supposedly deviant behavior is a voluntary act or an expression of human volition, will, or choice. Constructionists take this stance because they are disturbed by what they claim to be the dehumanizing implication of the positivist view of deviant behavior. The positivist view is said to imply that a human being is like "a robot, a senseless and purposeless machine reacting to every fortuitous change in the external and internal environment." Constructionists emphasize that human beings, because they possess free will and choice-making ability, determine or cause their own behavior.

To support this voluntarist assumption, constructionists tend to analyze how social control agencies define some people as deviant and carry out the sanctions against them. Such analyses often accent, as Edwin Lemert (1972) has observed, "the arbitrariness of official action, stereotyped decision-making in bureaucratic contexts, bias in the administration of law, and the general preemptive nature of society's controls over deviants." All this conveys the strong impression that control agents, being in positions of power, exercise their free will by actively, intentionally, and purposefully controlling the "deviants."

Constructionists also analyze people who have been labeled deviant. The "deviants" are not presented as if they are robots, passively and senselessly developing a poor self-image as conventional society expects. Instead, they are described as actively seeking positive meanings in their deviant activities. In Jack Katz's (1988) analysis, murderers see themselves as morally superior to their victims. The killing is said to give the murderers the self-righteous feeling of defending their dignity and respectability because their victims have unjustly humiliated them by taunting or insulting them. Katz also portrays robbers as feeling themselves morally superior to their victims—regarding their victims as fools or suckers who deserve to be robbed. If robbers want to hold up somebody on the street, they first ask a potential victim for the time, for directions, for a cigarette light, or for change. Each of these requests is intended to determine whether the person is a fool. The request for the time, for example, gives the robber the opportunity to know whether the prospective victim has an expensive watch. Complying with the request, then, is taken to establish the person as a fool and hence the right victim.

SUMMARY AND CONCLUSION

Each of the positivist and social constructionist perspectives consists of three related assumptions, and each assumption suggests a strategy for contributing to the sociology of deviance. For the positivist perspective, the first is the absolutist assumption that deviant behavior is absolutely real. This suggests that we study deviance or deviants. Second is the objectivist assumption that deviant behavior is an objective, publicly observable fact. This suggests that we use objective research methods such as survey, experiment, or detached observation. Third is the determinist assumption that deviance is determined or caused by certain social forces. This suggests that we use causal theories to make sense of research data. With the social constructionist perspective, the first assumption is that deviant behavior is basically a label, mental construct, or social construction. This suggests that we study law enforcers and other labelers, the process of labeling, and the consequences of labeling. The second assumption is that the supposedly deviant behavior is a personal experience. This suggests that we use less objective research methods such as ethnography, participant observation, or open-ended, in-depth interviews. The third assumption is that the so-called deviance is a voluntary, self-willed act. This suggests that we develop noncausal, descriptive theories. (See Table I.1 for a quick review.)

The diverse definitions, theories, methodologies, and data we have discussed reflect many different aspects of deviant behavior. Although they appear to conflict, they actually complement each other. They may be compared with the different views of a house. From the front, the house has a door, windows, and a chimney on top. From the back, it has a door and a chimney on top but fewer windows. From the side, it has no doors, but it has windows and a chimney on top. From the top, it has no doors or windows, but a chimney in the middle. It is the same house, but it looks different, depending on one's position. Taking in the

---

Table I.1   A Summary of Two Perspectives

POSITIVIST PERSPECTIVE	CONSTRUCTIONIST PERSPECTIVE
Absolutism Deviance is absolutely, intrinsically real; hence, deviance or deviants are the subjects of study.	*Relativism* Deviance is a label, a social construction; hence, labelers, labeling, and the impacts of labeling are the subject of study.
Objectivism Deviance is an objective, observable fact; hence, objective research methods are used.	*Subjectivism* Deviance is a personal experience; hence, subjective research methods are used.
Determinism Deviance is a determined behavior, a product of causation; hence, casual, explanatory theory is developed.	*Voluntarism* Deviance is a voluntary act, an expression of free will; hence, noncausal, descriptive theory is developed.

different views on the house ensures a fuller knowledge of what the house actually looks like. Similarly, knowing the different views on deviant behavior ensures a fuller understanding of deviance. This reader is intended to make that possible.

REFERENCES

Becker, Howard S. 1963. *Outsiders: Studies in the Sociology of Deviance.* New York: Free Press.

Hirschi, Travis. 1973. "Procedural Rules and the Study of Deviant Behavior." *Social Problems,* 21, 166–171.

Katz, Jack. 1988. *Seductions of Crime: Moral and Sensual Attractions in Doing Evil.* New York: Basic Books.

Lemert, Edwin M. 1972. *Human Deviance, Social Problems, and Social Control,* 2d ed. Englewood Cliffs, N.J.: Prentice Hall.

Matza, David. 1969. *Becoming Deviant.* Englewood Cliffs, N.J.: Prentice Hall.

Nettler, Gwynn. 1974. "On Telling Who's Crazy." *American Sociological Review,* 39, 893–894.

PART ONE

DEFINING AND RESEARCHING DEVIANCE

Charles Farnham is a software writer who has an enormous collection of commercial programs for his computer. Like millions of other people, he has not bought most of the programs; he has simply copied them from his friends' software. Federal law prohibits this kind of behavior, but many computer users who would not steal a library book or cheat on a test have no qualms about copying software illegally. Farnham explains that most software is too expensive and that there is nothing wrong with sampling a program before spending $500 or more.[1]

On the other hand, Aleta Walker, an obese 36-year-old woman, has a different kind of experience. Throughout her life, she has been ridiculed and abused for her weight. What she suffered during childhood and adolescence was particularly poignant. Every day, when she walked down the halls at school, boys would step back and yell, "Wide load!" It was worse at lunchtime. As she said, "Every day there was this production of watching me eat lunch." One day, schoolmates threw food at her. Spaghetti splashed on her head and face, and the long greasy strands dripped onto her clothes. "Everyone was laughing and pointing. They were making pig noises. I just sat there," she said.[2]

Is Farnham deviant for copying software illegally? Some people would say yes, but others would say no. Is Walker deviant for being overweight? Again, some people would say yes, but others would say no. In fact, some would claim that it is her tormentors—the so-called normal people—who are deviant because they are grossly insensitive, nasty, or cruel. Given this disagreement, who determines what constitutes deviance? Stephen Pfohl deals with this issue in the first article here, "Images of Deviance." In the second article, "Defining Deviancy Down," Daniel Patrick Moynihan shows how our society today no longer defines many harmful behaviors as deviant. In Moynihan's words, many people define deviance down by accepting or tolerating a large amount of it as normal, but more conservative Americans define deviance up by demonizing it, condemning it, or advocating a harsh penalty for it. In the third article, "Strategies for Researching Street Deviance," Leon Anderson and Thomas Calhoun show how opportunities for researching street deviants—homeless persons and male prostitutes—can be used to maximize the efficiency and quality of field research with deviant populations. Finally, in "Pleasures and Perils in Deviance Research," Erich Goode discusses the benefits and problems that researchers have if they have sex with their subjects.

1. John Markoff, "Though Illegal, Copied Software Is Now Common," *New York Times,* July 27, 1992, pp. A1, C4.

2. Gina Kolata, "The Burdens of Being Overweight: Mistreatment and Misconceptions," *New York Times,* November 22, 1992, pp. 1, 18.

IMAGES OF DEVIANCE

STEPHEN PFOHL

The scene is a crowded church during the American Civil War. "It was a time of great and exalting excitement. The country was up in arms, the war was on, in every breast burned the holy fire of patriotism." So says Mark Twain in his short and searing parable—*The War Prayer.* Amidst the clamor of beating drums, marching bands, and toy pistols popping, Twain describes an emotional church service. A passionate minister stirs the gallant hearts of eager volunteers; bronzed returning heroes; and their families, friends, and neighbors. The inspired congregation await their minister's every word.

> And with one impulse the house rose, with glowing eyes and beating hearts, and poured out that tremendous invocation—
>
> > God the all-terrible!
> > Thou who ordainest,
> > Thunder thy clarion
> > and lightning thy sword!

Then came the "long" prayer. None could remember the like of it for passionate pleading and moving and beautiful language. The burden of its supplication was that an ever-merciful and benignant Father of us all would watch over our noble young soldiers and aid, comfort, and encourage them in their patriotic work; bless them, shield them in the day of battle and the hour of peril, bear them in His mighty hand, make them strong and confident, invincible in the bloody onset; help them to crush the foe, grant to them and to their flag and country imperishable honor and glory.

Wars come and go. Words vary. Nonetheless, the essential message of this sermon remains alarmingly the same: "God is on our side." Before continuing with Twain's story, I ask you to consider a more contemporary version of this age-old narrative—the 1991 Gulf War between Iraq and the United States–led coalition of "New World Order" forces demanding an Iraqi withdrawal from Kuwait. Claiming it to be its moral imperative to repel an act of international aggression, the United States pictured Iraqi President Saddam Hussein as a Hitler-like character bent on world domination. Iraq in turn cited contradictions in the U.S. position (its long-term support for Israeli occupation of Palestinian territories, for example) as evidence of both U.S. hypocrisy and what Iraq alleged to be the true motives for the attack on Iraq—namely, "American" efforts to police the price of oil. Each side in this conflict represented the other as evil, treacherous, and power-mongering. Each side claimed to be righteous and blessed by God. This is typical of societies engaged in war.

Returning to Twain's story, what is untypical about this thoughtful tale is what happens next. It is not only untypical, but "deviant." After the minister completes his moving prayer, an "unnaturally pale," aged stranger enters the church. He is adorned with long hair and dressed in a full-length robe. The stranger motions the startled minister aside and informs the shocked parishioners that he is a messenger from Almighty God. He tells the

Source: Stephen Pfohl, *Images of Deviance and Social Control,* 2nd ed. (New York: McGraw-Hill, 1994), pp. 1–6.
Reprinted with permission.

congregation that God has heard their prayer and will grant it, but only after they consider the full import of their request. In rephrasing the original sermon the mysterious messenger reveals a more troubling side to the congregation's prayer. When they ask blessing for themselves they are, at the same time, praying for the merciless destruction of other humans (their enemies). In direct and graphic language the old man portrays the unspoken implications of their request, as follows:

> help us to tear their soldiers to bloody shreds with our shells;
>
> help us to cover their smiling fields with the pale forms of their patriotic dead;
>
> help us to draw the thunder of the guns with shrieks of their wounded, writhing in pain;
>
> help us to lay waste their humble homes with a hurricane of fire;
>
> help us to wring the hearts of their unoffending widows to unavailing grief;
>
> help us to turn them out roofless with their little children to wander unbefriended the wastes of their desolated land.

The strange old man continues—talking about blighting their lives, bringing tears, and staining the snow with blood. He completes his war prayer with a statement about the humble and contrite hearts of those who ask God's blessings. The congregation pauses in silence. He asks if they still desire what they have prayed for. "Ye have prayed it; if ye still desire it, speak! The messenger of the Most High waits." We are now at the final page of Twain's book. The congregation's response is simple and abrupt. As suggested previously, the old stranger was clearly a social deviant. In Twain's words: "It was believed afterward that the man was a lunatic, because there was no sense in what he said."

The stranger in *The War Prayer* directly threatens the normal, healthy, patriotic, and blood-lusting beliefs of the embattled congregation. Yet it is with ease that they contain and control this threat. They do not have to take seriously the chilling implications of his sermon. Their religious and patriotic senses are protected from his disturbing assault. Why? The reason is as simple as their response. They believe that he is a lunatic. They believe that he is a deviant. By classifying the old man as a deviant they need not listen to him. The congregation's beliefs are protected, even strengthened. The lunatic's beliefs are safely controlled. *The War Prayer* is thus a story of how some people imagine other people to be "deviant" and thereby protect or isolate themselves from those whom they fear and from that which challenges the way in which "normal" social life is organized. It is a story of how people convince themselves of what is normal by condemning those who disagree. It is a story of both deviance and social control. . . .

The story of deviance and social control is a battle story. It is a story of the battle to control the ways people think, feel, and behave. It is a story of winners and losers and of the strategies people use in struggles with one another. Winners in the battle to control "deviant acts" are crowned with a halo of goodness, acceptability, normality. Losers are viewed as living outside the boundaries of social life as it ought to be, outside the "common sense" of society itself. They may be seen by others as evil, sleazy, dirty, dangerous, sick, immoral, crazy, or just plain deviant. They may even come to see themselves in such negative imagery, to see themselves as *deviants*.

Deviants are only one part of the story of deviance and social control. Deviants never exist except in relation to those who attempt to control them. Deviants exist only in opposition to those whom they threaten and those who have enough power to control against such threats. The outcome of the battle of deviance and social control is this. Winners obtain the privilege of organizing social life as they see fit. Losers are trapped within the vision of others. They are labeled deviant and subjected to an array of current social control practices. Depending upon the controlling wisdom at a particular moment in history, deviants may be executed, brutally beaten, fined, shamed, incarcerated, drugged, hospitalized, or even treated to heavy doses of tender loving care. But first and foremost they are prohibited from passing as normal women or men. They are branded with the image of being deviant.

When we think of losers in the battle to control acceptable images of social life, it may seem natural to think of juvenile gang members, serial killers, illegal drug users, homosexuals, and burglars. Indeed, common sense may tell us that such people are simply deviant. But where does this common sense come from? How do we come to know that certain actions or certain people are deviant, while others are "normal"? Do people categorized as deviants really behave in a more dangerous fashion than others? Some people think so. Is this true?

Think of the so-called deviants mentioned above. Are their actions truly more harmful than the actions of people not labeled as deviants? In many cases the answer is no. Consider the juvenile gang. In recent years the organized drug dealing and violent activities of gangs have terrorized people living in poverty-stricken and racially segregated urban neighborhoods. Gang-related deviance has also been the focal point for sensational media stories and for social control policies ranging from selective "stop-and-search" police tactics to the building of new prisons and (in Los Angeles) even the criminalization of alleged gang members' parents.

But what about the people most responsible for the oppressive inner-city conditions that lie at the root of many gang-related activities? What about the "gangs" of bankers whose illegal redlining of mortgage loans blocks the investment of money in inner-city neighborhoods? What about the "gangs" of corporate executives whose greed for short-term profits has led to the "offshoring" of industrial jobs to "underdeveloped" countries where labor is cheap and more easily exploitable? Aren't the actions of such respectable people as costly as, if less visible than, the activities of most inner-city gangs? Yet, there is an important difference: unlike gangs of elite deviants, inner-city youths have little or no real access to dominant institutions in which contemporary power is concentrated.

A related question may be posed concerning serial killers. The violence of serial killers haunts our nightly news broadcasts. Indeed, the seemingly random character of serial killings—although they are most commonly directed against women and children—instills a deep and alarming sense of dread within society as a whole. Nevertheless, the sporadic violence of serial murderers, no matter how fearful, is incomparable in terms of both scope and number to the much less publicized "serial killings" perpetrated by U.S.-supported *death squads* in countries such as El Salvador and Guatemala. The targets of such death squads are typically people who dare to speak out in the name of social justice. From 1980 to 1991, for instance, approximately 75,000 Salvadoran civilians were secretly killed or made to "disappear" by paramilitary executioners. Why is it that such systematic murders are rarely acknowledged as true serial killings? Why, moreover, do such cold-blooded killings provoke so little U.S. public outrage in comparison to the attention given to the isolated violence of individual murderers, such as Ted Bundy or Jeffrey Dahmer? Is it because the people who authorize them are respectable persons, sometimes even publicly elected officials? Is it because, though we feel vulnerable to other serial killers, we ourselves—at least those of us who are white, male, North American, and economically privileged to live at a distance from the violence that historically envelops the daily lives of others—feel protected from death squads?

Similar questions might be raised about drug users. When we speak of the abuse of drugs, why do we often think only of the "controlled substances" that some people use as a means of achieving psychic escape, altered consciousness, and/or bodily pleasure? True, we as individuals and as a society may pay a heavy price for the abuse of such drugs as cocaine and heroin. But what about other—legal—substances that many of us are "on" much of the time? Some of these drugs are even more dangerous than their illicit counterparts. In addition to alcohol, tobacco, chemical food additives, and meat from animals that have been fed antibiotics and hormones, our society openly promotes the use of prescription and over-the-counter drugs for everything from losing weight, curing acne, and overcoming anxiety to

building strong bodies, fighting depression, and al-
leviating allergies caused by industrial pollution.
Certainly many of these substances have their salu-
tary effects and may help us adjust to the world in
which we live. However, even legal substances can
be abused; they too can be dangerous. The effects
can be direct, jeopardizing an individual's health or
fostering addiction, or they can be indirect and more
insidious. For example, consider the role drugs play
in creating and sustaining our excessively image-
conscious, age-conscious environment and in promoting our tendency to avoid dealing with personal
conflicts and everyday problems in a thoughtful
and responsible manner. Also—not to belabor the
issue—just think of what we are doing to our
planet, to our future, with our use of pesticides,
fertilizers, and other industrial products and by-
products. To raise such concerns is not to claim that
legal drugs are more dangerous than illegal drugs,
but simply to suggest that what is officially labeled
illegal or deviant often has more to do with what
society economically values than with whether the
thing is physically harmful per se.

Further consider the actions of sexist heterosexuals. Such persons may routinely mix various
forms of sexual harassment with manipulative patriarchal power and an intolerance of alternative
forms of sexual intimacy. Despite the harm these
heterosexist individuals cause, they are far less
likely to be labeled deviant than are gay, lesbian,
or bisexual lovers who caress one another with affection. The same goes for corporate criminals,
such as the executives recently implicated in the
savings and loan scandal. The stealthy acts of such
white-collar criminals have cost the U.S. public as
much as $500 billion. Yet the elite deviance of the
upper echelon of rule breakers is commonly less
feared than are the street crimes of ordinary burglars and robbers.

From the preceding examples it should be evident that many forms of labeled deviance are not
more costly to society than the behaviors of people
who are less likely to be labeled deviant. Why?
The answer . . . is that labeled deviants are viewed
as such because they threaten the control of people
who have enough power to shape the way society
imagines the boundary between good and bad,
normal and pathological, acceptable and deviant.
This is the crux of the effort to understand the battle between deviance and social control. Deviance
is always the flip side of the coin used to maintain
social control.

REVIEW QUESTIONS

1. Explain what the author means when he says, "Deviants never exist except in relation to those who attempt to control them."
2. Why did the congregation dismiss what the "strange old man" had to say?

2

DEFINING DEVIANCY DOWN

DANIEL PATRICK MOYNIHAN

In one of the founding texts of sociology, *The Rules of Sociological Method* (1895), Emile Durkheim set it down that "crime is normal." "It is," he wrote, "completely impossible for any society entirely free of it to exist." By defining what is deviant, we are enabled to know what is not, and hence to live by shared standards.

The matter was pretty much left at that until seventy years later when, in 1965, Kai T. Erikson published *Wayward Puritans,* a study of "crime rates" in the Massachusetts Bay Colony. The plan behind the book, as Erikson put it, was "to test [Durkheim's] notion that the number of deviant offenders a community can afford to recognize is likely to remain stable over time." The notion proved out very well indeed. Despite occasional crime waves, as when itinerant Quakers refused to take off their hats in the presence of magistrates, the amount of deviance in this corner of seventeenth-century New England fitted nicely with the supply of stocks and whipping posts. Erikson remarks:

The agencies of control often seem to define their job as that of keeping deviance within bounds rather than that of obliterating it altogether. Many judges, for example, assume that severe punishments are a greater deterrent to crime than moderate ones, and so it is important to note that many of them are apt to impose harder penalties when crime seems to be on the increase and more lenient ones when it does not, almost as if the power of the bench were being used to keep the crime rate from getting out of hand.... Hence "the number of deviant offenders

a community can afford *to recognize is likely to remain stable over time." [My emphasis]*

Social scientists are said to be on the lookout for poor fellows getting a bum rap. But here is a theory that clearly implies that there are circumstances in which society will choose *not* to notice behavior that would be otherwise controlled, or disapproved, or even punished.

It appears to me that this is in fact what we in the United States have been doing of late. I proffer the thesis that, over the past generation, since the time Erikson wrote, the amount of deviant behavior in American society has increased beyond the levels the community can "afford to recognize" and that, accordingly, we have been re-defining deviancy so as to exempt much conduct previously stigmatized, and also quietly raising the "normal" level in categories where behavior is now abnormal by any earlier standard....

[In today's normalization of deviance] we are dealing with the popular psychological notion of "denial." In 1965, having reached the conclusion that there would be a dramatic increase in single-parent families, I reached the further conclusion that this would in turn lead to a dramatic increase in crime. In an article in *America,* I wrote:

From the wild Irish slums of the 19th century Eastern seaboard to the riot-torn suburbs of Los Angeles, there is one unmistakable lesson in American history: a community that allows a large number of young men to grow up in broken families, dominated

Source: Daniel Patrick Moynihan, "Defining Deviancy Down," *The American Scholar,* vol. 62, no. 1 (Winter 1993), pp. 17–30. © 1992 by the author. Reprinted with permission.

by women, never acquiring any stable relationship to male authority, never acquiring any set of rational expectations about the future—that community asks for and gets chaos. Crime, violence, unrest, unrestrained lashing out at the whole social structure—that is not only to be expected; it is very near to inevitable.

The inevitable, as we now know, has come to pass, but here again our response is curiously passive. Crime is a more or less continuous subject of political pronouncement, and from time to time it will be at or near the top of opinion polls as a matter of public concern. But it never gets much further than that. In the words spoken from the bench, Judge Edwin Torres of the New York State Supreme Court, Twelfth Judicial District, described how "the slaughter of the innocent marches unabated: subway riders, bodega owners, cab drivers, babies; in laundromats, at cash machines, on elevators, in hallways." In personal communication, he writes: "This numbness, this near narcoleptic state can diminish the human condition to the level of combat infantrymen, who, in protracted campaigns, can eat their battlefield rations seated on the bodies of the fallen, friend and foe alike. A society that loses its sense of outrage is doomed to extinction." There is no expectation that this will change, nor any efficacious public insistence that it do so. The crime level has been *normalized.*

Consider the St. Valentine's Day Massacre. In 1929 in Chicago during Prohibition, four gangsters killed seven gangsters on February 14. The nation was shocked. The event became legend. It merits not one but two entries in the *World Book Encyclopedia.* I leave it to others to judge, but it would appear that the society in the 1920s was simply not willing to put up with this degree of deviancy. In the end, the Constitution was amended, and Prohibition, which lay behind so much gangster violence, ended.

In recent years, again in the context of illegal traffic in controlled substances, this form of murder has returned. But it has done so at a level that induces denial. James Q. Wilson comments that Los Angeles has the equivalent of a St. Valentine's

Day Massacre every weekend. Even the most ghastly reenactments of such human slaughter produce only moderate responses. On the morning after the close of the Democratic National Convention in New York City in July, there was such an account in the second section of the *New York Times.* It was not a big story; bottom of the page, but with a headline that got your attention. "3 Slain in Bronx Apartment, but a Baby is Saved." A subhead continued: "A mother's last act was to hide her little girl under the bed." The article described a drug execution; the now-routine blindfolds made from duct tape; a man and a woman and a teenager involved. "Each had been shot once in the head." The police had found them a day later. They also found, under a bed, a three-month-old baby, dehydrated but alive. A lieutenant remarked of the mother, "In her last dying act she protected her baby. She probably knew she was going to die, so she stuffed the baby where she knew it would be safe." But the matter was left there. The police would do their best. But the event passed quickly; forgotten by the next day, it will never make *World Book.*

Nor is it likely that any great heed will be paid to an uncanny reenactment of the Prohibition drama a few months later, also in the Bronx. The *Times* story, page B3, reported:

9 Men Posing as Police Are Indicted in 3 Murders

DRUG DEALERS WERE KIDNAPPED FOR RANSOM

The *Daily News* story, same day, page 17, made it *four* murders, adding nice details about torture techniques. The gang members posed as federal Drug Enforcement Administration agents, real badges and all. The victims were drug dealers, whose families were uneasy about calling the police. Ransom seems generally to have been set in the $650,000 range. Some paid. Some got it in the back of the head. So it goes.

Yet, violent killings, often random, go on unabated. Peaks continue to attract some notice. But these are peaks above "average" levels that thirty years ago would have been thought epidemic. . . . A Kai Erikson of the future will surely need to know that the Department of Justice in 1990 found that Americans reported only about 38 percent of all crimes and 48 percent of violent crimes. This, too, can be seen as a means of *normalizing* crime. In much the same way, the vocabulary of crime reporting can be seen to move toward the normal-seeming. A teacher is shot on her way to class. The *Times* subhead reads: "Struck in the Shoulder in the Year's First Shooting Inside a School." First of the season. . . .

The hope—if there be such—of this essay has been twofold. It is, first, to suggest that the Durkheim constant, as I put it, is maintained by a dynamic process which adjusts upwards and *downwards*. Liberals have traditionally been alert for upward redefining that does injustice to individuals. Conservatives have been correspondingly sensitive to downward redefining that weakens societal standards. Might it not help if we could all agree that there is a dynamic at work here? It is not revealed truth, nor yet a scientifically derived formula. It is simply a pattern we observe in our-

selves. Nor is it rigid. There may once have been an unchanging supply of jail cells which more or less determined the number of prisoners. No longer. We are building new prisons at a prodigious rate. Similarly, the executioner is back. There is something of a competition in Congress to think up new offenses for which the death penalty is seen the only available deterrent. Possibly also modes of execution, as in "fry the kingpins." Even so, we are getting used to a lot of behavior that is not good for us.

As noted earlier, Durkheim states that there is "nothing desirable" about pain. . . . Pain, even so, is an indispensable warning signal. But societies under stress, much like individuals, will turn to pain killers of various kinds that end up concealing real damage. There is surely nothing desirable about *this*. If our analysis wins general acceptance, if, for example, more of us came to share Judge Torres's genuine alarm at "the trivialization of the lunatic crime rate" in his city (and mine), we might surprise ourselves how well we respond to the manifest decline of the American civic order. Might.

REVIEW QUESTIONS

1. Defend this statement: "we have been re-defining deviancy so as to exempt much conduct previously stigmatized. . . ."
2. What is (are) the theme(s) of the Moyniham article "Defining Deviancy Down"?

STRATEGIES FOR RESEARCHING STREET DEVIANCE

LEON ANDERSON
THOMAS C. CALHOUN

Deviant individuals and groups have historically comprised a large portion of the field studies conducted by sociologists. . . . Fieldworkers must overcome [certain dilemmas] to study these deviant populations. As Douglas . . . observes:

> [B]ecause those considered deviant in our society are commonly so distrustful and so concerned with managing their own self-presentations, including hiding their identities, there is great need to analyze and solve the special methodological problems involved [in researching them]. (1972, pp. 4–5)

Specifically, researchers have . . . suggested that the collection of such data is more difficult with deviant populations than more conventional ones. . . .

[But] fieldworkers have failed to address systematically the ways in which field research may be facilitated rather than hampered by characteristics and dynamics associated with deviant populations. A large number of scattered observations consistent with our argument have been made over the past three decades, but these observations have never been pulled together. The goal of this discussion is to examine ways in which ethnographic research can take advantage of special opportunities in conducting fieldwork with those deviant individuals and groups whose deviance occurs largely in public settings, and whose lives are characterized by stigmatization and powerlessness.

METHOD

We explore the facilitative aspects of participant observation with deviant populations by drawing on two field studies. One is a year-long team field study of homelessness in a Sunbelt city conducted in the mid-1980s. Contact was made with homeless individuals almost daily in a variety of settings, such as at meal and shelter lines, under bridges, at day-labor pickup sites, and by following homeless persons through their daily routines. Over a twelve-month period, more than 400 hours were involved observing 168 homeless people in a variety of settings.

The second study, which involved male street prostitutes, was conducted over a three-month period during 1984. The project involved systematic observation on a daily basis in a setting known as "the Block" that served as a pick-up site for hustlers. In addition, interviews were conducted with eighteen male prostitutes between the ages of thirteen and twenty-two.

The researchers engaged in a modified version of the "observer as participant" role (Gold 1958) in which observation is more important

Source: Leon Anderson and Thomas C. Calhoun, "Facilitative Aspects of Field Research with Deviant Street Populations," *Sociological Inquiry,* vol. 62, no. 4 (1992), pp. 490–498. Reprinted with permission.

than actual participation. The goal was to gather observational data from natural settings and the personal accounts of members, rather than to "learn from doing." This was particularly the case for the study of male street prostitutes, in which observation was limited to hustling activities on the streets, rather than including more intimate illegal acts with "tricks."

Field observations were recorded in the two-stage process described by Lofland and Lofland (1984, pp. 62–68) of compiling mental and jotted field notes, which are elaborated immediately upon leaving the research settings. Both studies utilized inductive filing and coding procedures appropriate for the development of grounded theory (Glaser and Strauss 1967). In keeping with grounded theory techniques, insights from earlier observations were used to set data collection goals in later stages of the research.

FACILITATIVE ASPECTS AND STIGMATIZED POPULATIONS

Four categories were identified in which fieldwork with deviant populations can present strategic research opportunities: (1) access to research settings, (2) establishing relationships, (3) acquisition of information, and (4) researcher interest. Each of these categories is discussed below.

Access to Research Settings

To do field research one must have access to the particular settings in which members conduct their lives (Weppner 1977; Burgess 1984; Lofland and Lofland 1984). Deviant street populations conduct their daily activities in what Lofland (1987) has referred to as the "public realm." By virtue of this, they are often readily accessible for observation. Homeless people live in public space and, therefore, are unable to shelter themselves from probing individuals. In fieldwork with the homeless, initial access was available simply by showing up at the Salvation Army dinner line, observing people, and waiting for conversational openings. Similarly, street hustlers were observed within a public

setting that, although restricted, required no special qualifications to enter. In each case, easy access clearly facilitated the research process.

Establishing Relationships

Perhaps the most widespread assumption regarding deviant populations is that they are suspicious groups with whom it is particularly difficult to establish rapport (Douglas 1972; Kelly 1990). Even though traditional notions of rapport have come under considerable attack in recent years (Johnson 1975; Pollner and Emerson 1983), it is generally agreed that trust is a necessary component of field research in general, and research on deviants in particular. This view is exemplified in Warren's (1972) observation that "trust is necessary to gain access to any world, and particularly necessary in the case of gaining access to a world . . . whose members tend to perceive any alien as a threat" (1972, p. 157).

This assumption is only partially justified. Deviant groups also present special opportunities for developing rapport. Rapport can develop through the researcher's willingness to accept stigma by association, or what Goffman (1963a) referred to as a "courtesy stigma." An example of this stigma was experienced when one of the authors protested the arrest of two homeless men with whom he had been drinking beer under a bridge. When the police offered to let him go, despite the fact that he had been engaged in the same drinking behavior as the other two men, the researcher argued that the other men should be let go as well. The police responded by arresting him. As they walked to the police station one of the officers commented, "This guy isn't very bright, or he wouldn't have argued with us." One of the homeless men replied, "No, he's just a guy who sticks up for his friends." Such experiences strengthen trust in the researcher; the two men ultimately became key informants and introduced the researcher to other homeless individuals.

The second author experienced a similar incident when he was accosted by the police and questioned about a rock-throwing incident that had taken place earlier. When he denied any knowl-edge about the incident, the police informed him, "You should be careful about being seen in this area because people might get the wrong idea about you." Witnessing this encounter a young hustler said, "I was glad you didn't squeal." The researcher's willingness to accept the courtesy stigma increased the inclination of several street hustlers to share information.

Acquisition of Information

Other aspects of research with deviant populations may facilitate access to members' insider infor-mation. Three such aspects are social roles, desire for attention, and opportunities for observing problematic situations.

Social Roles.   Snow, Benford, and Anderson (1986, p. 377) observed that " . . . by virtue of their attendant rights and obligations, [social roles] function as avenues and barriers to other roles and their information bases and per-spectives." Two particular roles seem useful with deviant populations: the anonymous stranger and the "wise" person. Paul Cressey, in a posthu-mously published article (1983), noted that the anonymous stranger role provides an opportunity for gaining information that is difficult for some-one who is personally known to the informant to obtain. "The transitory character of contact in the anonymous relationship" (p. 114), Cressey ob-served, presents no threat of disclosure of poten-tially damaging information to socially significant others. This anonymous relationship offers infor-mants the opportunity to gain "catharsis and sym-pathy through impersonal confession" (p. 110).

Most social contexts do not support communi-cation among anonymous strangers (Goffman 1963b, 1971). However, some settings involving stigmatized individuals do support such communi-cation. Alcoholics Anonymous meetings, for exam-ple, provide a social setting where individuals are encouraged to share intimate details of their personal lives. While not providing direct sharing among strangers, the homeless subculture entails anonymity and is accepting of intimate revelations shared among strangers as they pass time at soup kitchens, labor corners, and dinner lines. This allowed the gathering of intimate details of many homeless in-dividuals' lives. Often such information was offered during the first or second encounter with a homeless person without probing questions being posed. While these personal narratives must be accepted with caution, since they may contain considerable distortion, they do provide important data.

A second role, the wise person, enhances op-portunities for relationships with members of stigmatized populations. Erving Goffman (1963a, p. 28) referred to wise persons as "persons who are normal, but whose special situation has made them intimately privy to the secret life of the stig-matized individual and sympathetic with it, and who find themselves accorded a measure of ac-ceptance." Acceptance evolves largely from the perceived sympathy wise persons have for the stigmatized and the fact that they "are ready to adopt his standpoint in the world and to share with him the feeling that he is human and 'es-sentially' normal in spite of appearances and in spite of his own self-doubts" (pp. 19–20). The wise individual may be a socially valued com-modity, providing deviants with social validation. The wise person also functions as a sounding board for the stigmatized individual's experi-ences, trials, and tribulations. The social position occupied by the wise person may be useful for those seeking to collect data on many deviant populations, ranging from homosexuals (Warren 1972) to drug dealers (Adler 1985, Adler and Adler 1991).

Need for Attention.   The anonymous stranger and the wise individual roles are of particular util-ity in field research with deviant populations be-cause they allow the researcher to become a focus of potential informants' needs for attention. As Derber (1979) demonstrated, attention is a funda-mental human need that is differentially distrib-uted in society. Attention deprivation is common among such relatively powerless social categories as women and members of stigmatized deviant groups. Some deviant individuals seek attention from almost any available source, thus providing a special opportunity for the responsive and strategic field researcher.

Both research projects presented occasions when informants' desires for attention led to increased opportunities for the collection of both life history data and direct observations, although over-rapport (Miller 1952) had to be avoided. Once street hustlers developed trust, some became so interested in the attention received that they would stop hustling and talk to the researcher. Several began taking the researcher's field schedule into consideration when planning their trips to the cruising area. Socializing became so extensive that it threatened the natural flow of activities in the area and the researcher was forced to randomize visits.

In particular, some subjects want to counter what they view as negative stereotypes about people with their particular stigma. Polsky (1967) noted this potential motivation among criminals, as did Agar (1973) among drug addicts. We observed it as well. For instance, a 49-year-old female who sat on a curb by the Salvation Army reading a newspaper article on the homeless angrily shoved the paper toward the researcher while exclaiming, "Can you believe the way they talk about us transients?" For forty-five minutes she went about "setting the record straight," admonishing the researcher to "be sure to get the truth about us in your book!"

Opportunity in Problematic Situations. In field research analytic insights can be prompted by the fact that the researcher finds the setting and actors new and unusual. In situations where the observed activities are taken for granted by all participants (including the researcher), it may be difficult to discover the socially constructed dimensions of the activity. As Patton (1990, p. 204) observed, "participants in . . . routines may take them so much for granted that they cease to be aware of important nuances that are apparent only

to an observer who has not become fully immersed in those routines." Given this, it is understandable why sociological fieldwork has been conducted so often with exotic and deviant populations. Such populations create an analytically productive distance between the researcher and the social world which he or she is investigating. This logic of discovery has at least implicitly guided such works as Goffman's (1961) research on the dilemmas of the self in total institutions and Garfinkel's (1967) study of the construction of a transsexual identity.

One example illustrates how theoretical insights may come more easily in the study of deviant populations. During the early months of fieldwork, the researcher was surprised by the frequency of identity statements by the homeless. These comments were so salient because talk about personal identity seemed to be only weakly related to the essence of homeless existence: physical deprivation. It was difficult for the researcher to understand why individuals who lack such basic survival requisites as stable housing spent considerable time making assertions about who they were. Recognizing this discrepancy between researcher assumptions about homeless life and field observations led to a systematic focus on "identity work among the homeless." The resulting analysis (Snow and Anderson 1987) elucidated the ways in which the homeless fashion and assert personal identities and how those identities change over time. The more focused analysis was relevant to broader social psychological theories as well, in that it challenged some of the prevailing principles of role-identity theory developed by Stryker (1980) and Maslow's (1962) hierarchy of needs.

Researcher Interest

The final aspect of research with deviant groups is in many ways emotional rather than cognitive or social relational. Deviant groups are very compelling populations. The nature of their collective and individual situations may well keep the researcher both emotionally and intellectually interested in research long after his or her interest might have faded in other social groups. As Lofland and Lofland (1984, p. 10) wrote, "Unless you are emotionally engaged in your work, the inevitable boredom, confusion, and frustration of rigorous scholarship will make even the completion—much less the quality—of the project problematic."

One important research activity jeopardized by a lack of interest and emotional involvement in the research topic, Lofland and Lofland note, is the tenacious data logging necessary to produce substantial field notes. Both authors found their experiences in the field to be so powerful that they were motivated to detail their observations in extensive notes. Furthermore, their field experiences made them want to return to the field as soon as possible so as not to miss the action. The compelling character of these groups resulted in more time being in the field and recording more complete field notes than otherwise might have been the case.

CONCLUSION

This discussion has examined facilitative aspects of fieldwork with deviant street populations. Strategic research opportunities were delineated into four areas: access to settings, social relationships, acquisition of information, and the maintenance of researcher interest. As current problems in American society spur a new wave of street ethnography (Kotarba 1990; Calhoun 1992; Koegel, 1992), the foregoing analysis may help to improve the efficiency and quality of street-based fieldwork by enabling researchers to rely less on serendipitous accidents in the field and more on conscious efforts informed by previous experience. Several suggestions for research with deviant street populations that emerge from this discussion are:

1. Access to street deviants in situ tends not to be blocked by powerful official gatekeepers, as is often the case with more formal settings. For this reason, researchers may find it useful to begin their work in these settings directly, rather than by attempting to gain familiarization with street settings and groups through more formal channels such as police departments or social service agencies.

2. Some of the best opportunities for collecting information about street informants are likely to occur in early anonymous encounters before the researcher has established more enduring relationships with the individuals. Researchers need to be aware of this dynamic and prepared to receive a considerable amount of such data in early encounters.

3. Occasional situations in which the researcher has the opportunity to make visible a willingness to accept courtesy stigma may be anticipated and used to enhance rapport.

4. Among street deviants and other stigmatized populations, the researcher is likely to be used by informants to fulfill needs for attention. The researcher should expect to be a confidante for informants and use this role to gather substantial data.

5. The researcher should be particularly attentive to problematic or conflictful situations in the field since these may lead to analytic insights.

6. Within bounds, researchers should welcome the chance to become personally engaged in the social world of their informants, rather than struggling to maximize their emotional distance. Such emotional involvement need not involve a loss of objectivity. In fact, such involvement may well enhance objectivity by eliciting greater rigor and attention to detail in data collection and analysis than would otherwise be the case.

These suggestions obviously do not apply equally to all field research, even with deviant street populations. Indeed, fieldworkers must always assess new settings and groups largely in terms of their uniqueness. Nonetheless, on the basis of the authors' experiences and those of other researchers cited in this paper, the preceding suggestions should be useful in sensitizing those engaged in a street ethnography of deviant populations.

ENDNOTE

An earlier version of this paper was presented at the Qualitative Research Conference in Toronto, Canada, in May 1990. The homelessness research described in this paper was facilitated by a grant from the Hogg Foundation for Mental Health and directed by David A. Snow. The authors wish to thank Mara Holt, Mike Polioudakis, and the anonymous reviewers for helpful comments and suggestions. Editor's Note: The reviewers were J. Kenneth Davidson, Nanette J. Davis, and Joseph Harry.

REFERENCES

Adler, Patricia A. 1985. *Wheeling and Dealing.* New York: Columbia University Press.

Adler, Patricia A., and Peter Adler. 1991. "Stability and Flexibility: Maintaining Relations with Organized and Unorganized Groups." Pp. 173–83 in *Experiencing Fieldwork,* edited by William B. Shaffir and Robert A. Stebbins. Newbury Park, CA: Sage.

Agar, Michael H. 1973. *Ripping and Running.* New York: Academic Press.

———. 1980. *The Professional Stranger.* New York: Academic Press.

Burgess, Robert C. 1984. *In the Field: An Introduction to Field Research.* Boston: George Allen and Unwin.

Calhoun, Thomas C. 1992. "Male Street Hustling: Introduction Processes and Stigma Containment." *Sociological Spectrum* 12:35–52.

Cressey, Paul. 1983. "A Comparison of the Roles of the 'Sociological Stranger' and the 'Anonymous Stranger' in Field Research." *Urban Life* 12:102–20.

Derber, Charles. 1979. *The Pursuit of Attention: Power and Individualism in Everyday Life.* New York: Oxford University Press.

Douglas, Jack, ed. 1972. *Research on Deviance.* New York: Random House.

Garfinkel, Harold. 1967. *Studies in Ethnomethodology.* Englewood Cliffs, NJ: Prentice-Hall.

Glaser, Barney, and Anselm Strauss. 1967. *The Discovery of Grounded Theory.* Chicago: Aldine.

Goffman, Erving. 1961. *Asylums.* New York: Doubleday Anchor.

———. 1963a. *Stigma.* Englewood Cliffs, N.J.: Prentice-Hall.

———. 1963b. *Behavior in Public Places.* New York: The Free Press.

———. 1971. *Relations in Public.* New York: Harper and Row.

Gold, Raymond. 1958. "Roles in Sociological Field Observation." *Social Forces* 36:217–23.

Johnson, John M. 1975. *Doing Field Research.* New York: Free Press.

Kelly, Robert. 1990. "Field Research among Deviants: A Consideration of Some Methodological Recommendations." Pp. 148–56 in *Deviant Behavior,* edited by Clifton D. Bryant. New York: Hemisphere.

Koegel, Paul. (1992). "Understanding Homelessness: An Ethnographic Approach," in *Homelessness: A Prevention Oriented Approach,* edited by Rene Jahid. Baltimore: Johns Hopkins Press.

Kotarba, Joseph A. 1990. "Ethnography and AIDS: Returning to the Streets." *Journal of Contemporary Ethnography* 19:259–70.

Lofland, John, and Lyn Lofland. 1984. *Analyzing Social Settings: A Guide to Qualitative Observation and Analysis.* 2nd ed. Belmont, CA: Wadsworth.

Lofland, Lyn, 1987. "Social Life in the Public Realm: A Review." *Journal of Contemporary Ethnography* 17:453–82.

Maslow, Abraham. 1962. *Toward a Psychology of Being.* New York: Van Nostrand.

Miller, S. M. 1952. "The Participant Observer and Over-Rapport." *American Sociological Review* 17:97–9.

Patton, Michael Quinn. 1990. *Qualitative Evaluation and Research Methods.* Beverly Hills, CA.: Sage.

Pollner, Melvin, and Robert M. Emerson. 1983. "The Dynamics of Inclusion and Distance in Fieldwork Relations." Pp. 235–52 in *Contemporary Field Research,* edited by Robert M. Emerson. Boston: Little, Brown and Company.

Polsky, Ned. 1967. *Hustlers, Beats, and Others.* New York: Aldine.

Snow, David A., and Leon Anderson. 1987. "Identity Work Among the Homeless: The Verbal Construction and Avowal of Personal Identities." *American Journal of Sociology* 92:1336–71.

Snow, David A., Robert D. Benford, and Leon Anderson. 1986. "Fieldwork Roles and Informational

Yield: A Comparison of Alternative Settings and Roles." *Urban Life* 14:377–408.

Stryker, Sheldon. 1980. *Symbolic Interactionism: A Social Structural Version.* Menlo Park, CA: Benjamin-Cummings.

Warren, Carol. 1972. "Observing the Gay Community." Pp. 139–63 in *Research on Deviance,* edited by Jack D. Douglas. New York: Random House.

Weppner, Robert S., ed. 1977. *Street Ethnography.* Beverly Hills, CA: Sage.

REVIEW QUESTIONS

1. What is the difference between the two concepts, *wise person* and *courtesy stigma*?
2. How might the *wise person* role enhance the quality of one's research?

PLEASURES AND PERILS
IN DEVIANCE RESEARCH

ERICH GOODE

Sociologists very rarely discuss their own emotional or physical intimacy with their subjects, informants, and interviewees. Do they avoid the subject because it is unimportant, because their own emotional or physical intimacy does not impinge on how they think about the issue, what they see, or what they write about in their books and articles? We cannot know the answers, for we are not given the full story on the participation of most social science observers in the behaviors they examine and involvements with the people they study.

Gary Alan Fine (1993) discusses ten "lies" of ethnography, myths that are widely disseminated in print as true but that insiders know to be false. One of these lies is that the researcher is sexually chaste. But the reality is far from it. As Fine says, "humans are attracted to one another in all domains. They look, they leer, they flirt, and they fantasize." And yet, he remarks, the "written record inscribes little of this rough and hot humanity" (p. 284).

Tobias Schneebaum's experiences (1988) with self-disclosure go a long way in explaining why such revelations tend to be rare. According to James Wafer (1996) Schneebaum "breaks the ultimate taboo by being explicit about the fact that he had sex with the natives" whom he studied. A colleague accuses Schneebaum of conducting his research just "to get screwed," thereby dismissing him and his work.

Nevertheless, a few researchers do boldly reveal their intimate involvement with their subjects. Bolton (1992), for example, expresses what is very close to an outright endorsement of sex in the field. In order to study sexual behavior as it takes place, he tells us, "we must go beyond the narrow concept of participant observation," that is, mere observation without participation. Indeed, he argues, "some of the very best cross-cultural work on homosexuality has benefited from insights gained through participation" (p. 132). As for engaging in his ethnography of sexual practices among gay males and how they impact on the transmission of AIDS, Bolton says, "I did not merely observe but participated fully in all aspects of gay life. . . . In my casual sexual encounters with men I picked up in gay cruising situations, my approach during sex was to allow my partner to take the lead in determining which sexual behaviors to engage in" (high-risk activities—unprotected anal intercourse—excepted) (pp. 134, 135). His activities were consonant with the norms of the gay community he investigated, and hence, he feels, his sexual activity while engaged in research was perfectly ethical.

In spite of this remarkable revelation, the fact remains that, of the thousands of ethnographers who have spent uncountable hours in close proximity with the people whose lives they shared and

Source: Specifically written for this reader, with portions drawn from the author's "Sex with Informants as Deviant Behavior: An Account and Commentary," *Deviant Behavior,* vol. 20 (1999), pp. 301–324.

behavior they observed, engaging in almost every imaginable activity with them, only a few dozen have had the courage to step forward and tell the world about their more intimate moments. Informal consensus has it that most ethnographers have remained chaste in the field, and my guess is that assessment is correct. But vastly more sexual behavior has taken place than is reported, and that disparity is worthy of discussion. Clearly, then, extremely strong norms within the academic community govern the construction of self-revelations, and those norms are, for the most part, obeyed.

SEX WITH INFORMANTS: BENEFIT AND RISK

I decided to defy this taboo on sexual self-revelation by writing an account of my intimate experiences with informants in three research endeavors: marijuana use (the research was conducted in 1967 and culminated in a book published in 1970), personals-generated courtship (in which I participated between 1979 and 1983 for the purpose of dating, and which I studied more systematically in the 1990s), and NAAFA (then, the National Association to Aid Fat Americans), a kind of "Love Boat" for fat women and for men who were sexually and romantically attracted to fat women (where I conducted field research, and dated, between 1980 and 1983).

Was it necessary to have sex with my informants to learn what I found out? Of course not, although, at the times when I did so, it seemed perfectly natural; in fact, to have done otherwise would have felt awkward and out of step with everything that was going on. By doing so, I felt a natural and organic part of the tribes I was studying, much as the handful of anthropologists who discussed it openly did. Does sharing intimate moments with informants lend an authenticity to the researcher's vision that might otherwise have been less authoritative? Discounting the social disruption that such experiences may cause, yes, I believe so. Is it worth the risk? That's a separate issue. Manda Cesara claims that a sexual and emotional relationship

with an informant permits "laying hold of the culture in its entirety through that particular individual" (1982, p. 60).

Many commentators have argued against becoming too involved in the lives of one's informants because it is likely to lead to a loss of objectivity. In my experience, it's difficult to sentimentalize and romanticize the people you're studying if you are in their face—and they are in yours—all the time. This is especially the case if you engage in intimate relations with them over an extended period of time. The fact is, you are acquainted with details of their lives that range from the spiritual to the mundane, from the way they express their most heartfelt emotions to the way they trim their toenails. For me, unabashed advocacy of my subjects was impossible precisely because I knew too much about them.

The issue of my intimate relations was central to the work I conducted and the research reports I was, and was not, able to write. Permit me to spell out how.

First of all, in all three of my investigations, sex was a centrally relevant topic. In the marijuana research, the conjunction between sex and marijuana use was a major component; and in the personals ad and the NAAFA studies, sex and romance were more or less what they were all about. Ignoring my own sexual experiences during the course of these studies now seems inconceivable to me.

Second, intimacy generates access to information and usually more information and better information. Sex has a way of riveting one's attention to the matter at hand; what one learns in bed is not likely to be forgotten. At the very least, establishing an intimate liaison with an insider does influence access and rapport, whether for better or for worse. Moreover, this is likely to be gender related.

Third, having romantic and sexual relations with informants is likely to influence one's view of the reality of the scene or behavior under discussion. One's vision of how things are and how they work cannot but be shaped by sharing one's most intimate moments with an insider, who is likely to see things a certain way.

Fourth, the fact that one has shared an informant's bed necessarily alters how the researcher–author writes up the report. In my case, not only did I change inconsequential details to protect the identity of my sexual partners, but I also left out certain details for fear those partners would feel that I had betrayed them even though their identities were disguised. The very intimacy that grants access to information often results in inhibiting public revelations.

Fifth, sex represented my unconditional entry into NAAFA, and it was sex that proved to be my undoing in it. Only by dating was I seen as a full-fledged member of the organization; and as a result of dating (admittedly, recklessly and promiscuously), I found it impossible to continue my research. Sex was the central fact of my investigation in that setting, and any honest account had to take note of it.

Sixth—and here we come to the issue at hand—sexual intimacy with informants raises a host of ethical questions that demand discussion. At the very least, admissions of sexual liaisons will force researchers to account for their actions, since, in the academic environments in which we move, such behavior tends to be frowned on. More on this momentarily.

And seventh, sexual liaisons present risk, especially for women. For all researchers, they may make a research enterprise less viable, close off avenues of information, upset and anger participants in a given scene. My own, extremely poorly thought-out, involvements in NAAFA made it impossible for me to continue with my research. I have no doubt that for most researchers, sex on the job traverses much of the same land-mined territory offered by sex off the job. The wrong partner or partners, too many partners, partners under inappropriate times or circumstances, too much time with one partner or not enough time with another—or, for that matter, spurning someone who wants to be a partner: we all know the perils that lie in wait for us when we make the wrong decision.

For women, as I said, these risks are far more perilous, manifold, and painful, in fact, are om-nipresent even whether they engage in sex or not. In one study, 7 percent of the female anthropologists who responded reported rape or attempted rape against them in the field (Howell, 1990); it's possible that was an underestimation. In all likelihood, most of these women in this study were completely celibate. At the same time, it is highly likely that sex with a number of men increases the odds of sexual violence. If a woman becomes known in the community as someone who is sexually accessible to more than a small number of men, she may become a target for unwanted attention, including violence. But again, even if she is celibate, she could become a victim of sexual violence. This is not true of all communities, as we've seen. Female researchers studying more than a handful of communities have found informants more relaxed and accessible after their affair with a local became known (Cesara, 1982). Unfortunately, this is atypical.

Far from endorsing sex between researchers and informants, I am arguing that, under certain circumstances, it is likely to be a terrible thing to do. But under others, it may yield insight. Moreover, I am not arguing that discussing it is a relevant issue in every research project; again, this depends on the study under investigation.

THE ETHICS OF SEX WITH INFORMANTS

To be frank, during none of the three research efforts in which I engaged did I give the matter of the ethics of sex with informants a great deal of thought. In fact, it never occurred to me that sex with informants was ethically improper or methodologically questionable.

In 1967, when I conducted the marijuana interviews, I didn't even know about the existence of "human subjects committees." (In 1967, neither New York University, where I taught during the spring semester, nor Stony Brook, where I began teaching that fall, even had a human subjects committee.) Even if I had, I would have regarded them as yet another hurdle in a gauntlet of bureaucratic restrictions. I had never been told by an academic adviser or older colleague that researchers were required to treat their subjects in specified ways—and must not treat them in specific other ways—as spelled out in a clearly articulated code of ethics. Did the American Sociological Association promulgate a code of ethics before 1967? At the time, I simply had no idea. The possibility of the very *existence* of an ethics code never entered my mind. As it turns out, the ASA did not formulate one until 1968.

To me, in interactions with my marijuana informants in 1967, the relationship seemed completely nonhierarchical. In my interviews, it was I who was invading the user's turf, begging them for their time and words. If anything, I reasoned, I was the subordinate party in this transaction, not the other way around. Any intimate relations that fortuitously transpired seemed to me to have nothing to do with my status as a researcher or a university instructor, I figured. In the social settings in which I moved, I assumed I was as free as a bird and so were my informants. In 1967, I gave little or no thought to the ethical, moral, or ideological implications of what I was doing. At the time, it seemed absolutely inconceivable that any single, under-thirty researcher—male or female—who was undertaking a naturalistic or an interview study of marijuana use in 1967 would have abstained from either marijuana use or sex with informants. As I saw things then, I was simply doing what came naturally, what seemed most comfortable. In fact, it would have been prudish, unseemly, and out of place to have abstained from joining the party, much like refusing to take off one's clothes at a nudist camp. Having conducted fieldwork among an extremely sexually permissive people, Cesara states categorically that it is inevitable that certain anthropologists would experience sexual relations with informants (1982, p. 59). I agree. None of this justifies or excuses my behavior, but it does help explain it.

What about the issue of my dating women by using the personal ads (1979–1983)? Under "Ethical Standards," subsection 7, "Harassment," the American Sociological Association (1997) states that sociologists are not to engage in "harassment of any person." Sexual harassment, the ASA states, "May include sexual solicitation, physical advance, or verbal or non-verbal conduct that is sexual in nature" (p. 4). Or it may not. From the wording of this declaration, it's not clear that such actions are *by their very nature* or *by definition* sexual harassment. My behavior *could* represent a violation of this principle.

Or could it? In answering personal ads, perhaps 90 percent of my motive was for the purpose of dating, while only 10 percent was to gather information. In fact, for all three of these projects, personal and research motives intertwined; I found it impossible to separate them. (I still do.) The politically engaged social scientist informs us that all of us express our ideology in our research, that pure objectivity is a myth, that all science is personal. I'm sure that no one who espouses that position has in mind anything like the sort of behavior I'm detailing here, but drawing a line in the sand between acceptable and unacceptable personal involvements cannot be an easy task. The fact is, when I answered and placed personal ads, I wasn't certain that I would ever study such behavior more systematically or publish anything from it. In writing about dating via the personals in the 1990s, I was simply drawing on my own biographical experiences to enrich my vision of a given social phenomenon, much the same way a pool player, an ex-convict, or a poker player would have done.

My feelings about my personal involvements in NAAFA (1980–1983) are a great deal more complex, ambivalent, and conflicted than they were for the other two studies because my motives were more mixed; I never clarified for myself or for others exactly what it was I was doing there, what my primary role was. Eventually, I fell off the tightrope because I simply couldn't maintain the dual role I was attempting to play. I do not think that such a role is inherently impossible to maintain. However, I do know that I played it extremely badly. Looking back from the perspective of two decades, it seems almost redundant for me to admit that I should have handled things quite differently.

Are there sexual actions in the field and revelations of them about which I would be horrified? Of course. Force, sex with minors, and sex with the mentally incompetent are crimes, crimes of violence, crimes that truly horrify me. Whenever gross disparities in power exist between the researcher and the subject, my sense of ethical disapproval would begin kicking in, sex between faculty and student being the most salient example. In addition, sex between researcher and welfare moms, heroin or crack addicts, residents of a battered women's shelter—in short, weak and vulnerable parties. Since the scenes I looked at were inhabited by nonindigent, fairly middle-class informants, to me, none of this seemed to enter into the picture.

CONCLUSIONS

In the first volume of Michel Foucault's *The History of Sexuality,* we are told that in Western society, sex is *the* secret. To most of us, sex remains private, a sphere of life over which a veil of secrecy must be drawn. Its enactment is special to us. When this veil is ripped away and the intimate doings of one of us are forced into the public consciousness—as we saw with President Bill Clinton, whose lies about an affair with a White House intern resulted in his impeachment—much of the public is simultaneously embarrassed by and riveted on the details.

Sex has played a unique and distinctive role in the study of social life, yet we have thrown a veil of secrecy around not merely sex but its possible role in social research. "Throughout all the decades of concern with the sex lives of others, anthropologists [and, I would add, other social scientists as well] have remained very tightlipped about their own sexuality" (Kulick, 1995, p. 3). Commenting on what the researcher is expected—and expected not—to do with subjects, Dubisch (1995, p. 31) points out:

> We do almost everything else with our "informants": share their lives, eat with them, attend their rituals, become part of their families, even become close friends, and sometimes establish life-long relationships. At the same time, we "use" them to further our goals, writing and speaking about personal and even intimate aspects of their lives, appropriating these lives for our own professional purposes. Could a sexual relationship be any more intimate, committing, or exploitative than our normal relations with the "natives"? (In some societies, it might even be less so).

Why? one wonders. Does sex play the same "special" and enshrouded role in the professional lives of social researchers that it plays in the everyday lives of all of us? Is it only sex—that is, this Foucaudian "secret" realm—to them? Or is there something more to it than that?

Is it possible that this veil over the sex life of the researcher is even more crucial for the social scientist than it is for the ordinary man and woman? Might this "secret" to which Foucault refers function to maintain an even deeper secret, the secret of research intersubjectivity? What better means of maintaining the traditional social science fiction of objectivity than to pretend that all ethnographers remain completely celibate when they conduct their research? And what more effective means of emphasizing the fact that sociology and anthropology are deeply social, deeply human, and therefore deeply flawed enterprises than to report, explore, and discuss the subject of sex with the people whose behavior we study?

Kulick and Willson (1995, p. xiii) found heterosexual men not only the most "elusive" about their own sexual activities in the field but also the ones who discouraged them most emphatically about doing their book *Taboo,* which focuses on that selfsame topic. Why? they ask. Is it possible, Kulick and Willson suggest, that such discussion not only would reveal that sex between male researchers and female informants is vastly more common than that between female researchers and male informants, but also would cast a bright beam of light on the sexism and racism inherent in such practices, which are woven into the very fabric of anthropology? The "disciplinary silence about desire in the field is a way for anthropologists to avoid confronting the issues of positionality, hierarchy, exploitation, and racism" (Kulick, 1995, p. 19).

Once the secret is revealed, the social science pose of objectivity will be more difficult to sustain. How long can we validate the "onstage" pose of ourselves as disembodied, disinterested, and uninvolved social scientists acting out the dictates of a methodology textbook? Is the topic of researchers' entanglements in the lives of their subjects of study not worthy of discussion? Is the simple admonition "Don't do it!" enough? Contrarily, is the fact that most of us are *not* entangled in their lives as revealing—and as damning—as the fact that some of us are? Are the implications of erotic subjectivity so obvious and banal as to merit no discussion whatsoever?

I do not see intersubjectivity as inherently poisonous to the task of unlocking the secrets of social life. Like almost everything else in life, intimacy between researcher and subject poses a host of dilemmas. Carefully cultivated, it can be a resource; if permitted to run rampant, it makes the researcher's mission impossible. I fear a too-detached relationship with informants because that means I will remain so utterly out of touch with their lives that anything they say, however fanciful, will seem plausible to me. At the same time, I fear a too-cozy relationship with informants because I want to be free to tell the truth about them. The closer we come to the lives of the people we study, the more we touch them, physically and emotionally, the more we will know about them, yet the greater the likelihood that resentments will be stirred up. There is no way out of this dilemma.

REFERENCES

American Sociological Association. 1968. "Toward a Code of Ethics for Sociologists." *The American Sociologist* 3 (November):316–318.

American Sociological Association. 1997. "Code of Ethics" (pamphlet). Washington, D.C.: ASA.

Bolton, Ralph. 1992. "Mapping Terra Incognita: Sex Research for AIDS Prevention—An Urgent Agenda for the 1990s," pp. 124–158 in *The Time of AIDS: Social Analysis, Theory, and Method,* edited by Gilbert Herdt and Shirley Lindenbaum. Thousand Oaks, Calif: Sage.

Cesara, Manda. 1982. *Reflections of a Woman Anthropologist: No Hiding Place.* New York: Academic Press.

Dubisch, Jill. 1995. "Lovers in the Field: Sex, Dominance, and the Female Anthropologist," pp. 29–50 in *Taboo: Sex, Identity and Erotic Subjectivity in Anthropological Fieldwork,* edited by Don Kulick and Margaret Willson. London: Routledge.

Fine, Gary Alan. 1993. "Ten Lies of Ethnography: Moral Dilemmas of Field Research." *Journal of Contemporary Ethnography* 22 (October):267–294.

Goode, Erich. 2002. "Sexual Involvement and Social Research in a Fat Civil Rights Organization." *Qualitative Sociology,* 25 (Summer).

Howell, Nancy. 1990. *Surviving Fieldwork. A Report of the Advisory Panel on Health and Safety in Field-work.* Washington, D.C.: American Anthropological Association.

Kulick, Don. 1995. "Introduction: The Sexual Life of Anthropologists: Erotic Subjectivity and Ethnographic Work," pp. 1–28 in *Identity and Erotic Subjectivity in Anthropological Fieldwork,* edited by Don Kulick and Margaret Willson. London: Routledge.

Kulick, Don, and Margaret Willson (editors). 1995. *Taboo: Sex, Identity and Erotic Subjectivity in Anthropological Fieldwork.* London: Routledge.

Lewin, Ellen, and William L. Leap (editors). 1996. *Out in the Field: Reflections of Lesbian and Gay Anthropologists.* Urbana: University of Illinois Press.

Schneebaum, Tobias. 1988. *Where the Spirits Dwell: An Odyssey in the New Guinea Jungle.* New York: Grove Press.

Styles, Joseph. 1979. "Outsider/Insider: Researching Gay Baths." *Urban Life 8* (July):135–152.

Wafer, James. 1996. "Out of the Closet and into Print: Sexual Identity in the Textual Field," pp. 261–273 in *Out in the Field: Reflections of Lesbian and Gay Anthropologists,* edited by Ellen Lewin and William L. Leap. Urbana: University of Illinois Press.

REVIEW QUESTIONS_____

1. What are the benefits and liabilities of having sex with informants while conducting research?
2. Do you agree or disagree with the statement "Having sex with informants is acceptable"? Defend your answer.

PART TWO

POSITIVIST THEORIES

In October 2002, two men terrorized the residents of the national capital's suburbs for nearly three weeks. They drove around in their car and shot at people whom they picked out randomly. Ten of the victims died instantly, and three were critically wounded. During the siege by the serial killers, residents were afraid to go out, causing restaurants, retail stores, and other businesses to suffer sharp declines in patronage. Schoolchildren ran for cover as soon as they got off the bus, and they were "locked down" and not allowed to romp in the playground. High-school homecoming games were played at undisclosed places away from the Washington area. Owners of gas stations put up large tarps to shield customers from the snipers. In fact, thanks to daily reports on national television about the sniping, Americans all over the country couldn't help feeling less safe than before.[1]

Soon after the alleged snipers were caught, it was reported that before their killing spree in the Washington suburbs they had murdered two people in Louisiana and Alabama. The alleged killers were identified as John Muhammad, 41, and Lee Malvo, 17. Muhammad was said to have treated the teenager as his son, and Malvo was said to be deferential and obedient to the older man. Muhammad was also reported to be "singularly unsuccessful at life," "a two-time loser at money and love." He was twice divorced and had lost custody of his children to his ex-wives, who accused him of being abusive. He had opened a martial-arts school, which went under, and then a car-repair business, which also failed. He was also arrogant and bad-tempered. When he was in the National Guard, he was court-martialed twice, for disobeying an order and for striking an officer.[2] All these experiences were presented by the media as if they had caused Muhammad to go on the killing spree. The focus on the causes of behavior like Muhammad's rampage characterizes the positivist theory of deviance.

Positivist theories differ from each other in explaining what causes deviance. The well-known examples are shown in four articles here. In the first, "Anomie-Strain Theory," Robert Merton explains how a lack of opportunity to achieve success pressures individuals toward deviance. In the second article, "Differential Association Theory," Edwin Sutherland and Donald Cressey attribute deviance to an excess of deviant associations over conventional associations. In the third selection, "Control Theory," Travis Hirschi blames deviance on a lack of control in the individual's life. In the final piece, "Shaming Theory," John Braithwaite shows how disintegrative shaming causes deviance to flourish.

---

1. Evan Thomas, "Descent into Evil," *Newsweek,* November 4, 2002, pp. 21–38.
2. Brian Duffy and Angie Cannon, "The End of the Road," *U.S. News & World Report,* November 4, 2002, pp. 19–30.

ANOMIE-STRAIN THEORY

ROBERT K. MERTON

The framework set out in this essay is designed to provide one systematic approach to the analysis of social and cultural sources of deviant behavior. Our primary aim is to discover how some *social structures exert a definite pressure upon certain persons in the society to engage in nonconforming rather than conforming conduct.* If we can locate groups peculiarly subject to such pressures, we should expect to find fairly high rates of deviant behavior in these groups, not because the human beings comprising them are compounded of distinctive biological tendencies but because they are responding normally to the social situation in which they find themselves. Our perspective is sociological. We look at variations in the *rates* of deviant behavior, not at its incidence. Should our quest be at all successful, some forms of deviant behavior will be found to be as psychologically normal as conformist behavior, and the equation of deviation and psychological abnormality will be put in question.

PATTERNS OF CULTURAL GOALS AND INSTITUTIONAL NORMS

Among the several elements of social and cultural structures, two are of immediate importance. These are analytically separable although they merge in concrete situations. The first consists of culturally defined goals, purposes and interests, held out as legitimate objectives for all or for diversely located members of the society. The goals are more or less integrated—the degree is a question of empirical fact—and roughly ordered in some hierarchy of value. Involving various degrees of sentiment and significance, the prevailing goals comprise a frame of aspirational reference. They are the things "worth striving for." They are a basic, though not the exclusive, component of what Linton has called "designs for group living." And though some, not all, of these cultural goals are directly related to the biological drives of man, they are not determined by them.

A second element of the cultural structure defines, regulates, and controls the acceptable modes of reaching out for these goals. Every social group invariably couples its cultural objectives with regulations, rooted in the mores or institutions, of allowable procedures for moving toward these objectives. These regulatory norms are not necessarily identical with technical or efficiency norms. Many procedures which from the standpoint of particular individuals would be most efficient in securing desired values—the exercise of force, fraud, power—are ruled out of the institutional area of permitted conduct. At times, the disallowed procedures include some which would be efficient for the group itself—for example, historic taboos on vivisection, on medical experimentation, on the sociological analysis of "sacred" norms—since the criterion of acceptability is not technical efficiency but value-laden sentiments (supported by most

Source: Robert K. Merton, *Social Theory and Social Structure* (New York: The Free Press, a division of Simon & Schuster, 1957), pp. 131–160. Reprinted with permission of The Free Press, an imprint of Simon & Schuster Adult Publishing Group.

members of the group or by those able to promote these sentiments through the composite use of power and propaganda). In all instances, the choice of expedients for striving toward cultural goals is limited by institutionalized norms.

We shall be primarily concerned with the first—a society in which there is an exceptionally strong emphasis upon specific goals without a corresponding emphasis upon institutional procedures. If it is not to be misunderstood, this statement must be elaborated. No society lacks norms governing conduct. But societies do differ in the degree to which the folkways, mores and institutional controls are effectively integrated with the goals which stand high in the hierarchy of cultural values. The culture may be such as to lead individuals to center their emotional convictions upon the complex of culturally acclaimed ends, with far less emotional support for prescribed methods of reaching out for these ends. With such differential emphases upon goals and institutional procedures, the latter may be so vitiated by the stress on goals as to have the behavior of many individuals limited only by considerations of technical expediency. In this context, the sole significant question becomes: Which of the available procedures is most efficient in netting the culturally approved value? The technically most effective procedure, whether culturally legitimate or not, becomes typically preferred to institutionally prescribed conduct. As this process of attenuation continues, the society becomes unstable and there develops what Durkheim called "anomie" (or normlessness).

The working of this process eventuating in anomie can be easily glimpsed in a series of familiar and instructive, though perhaps trivial, episodes. Thus, in competitive athletics, when the aim of victory is shorn of its institutional trappings and success becomes construed as "winning the game" rather than "winning under the rules of the game," a premium is implicitly set upon the use of illegitimate but technically efficient means. The star of the opposing football team is surreptitiously slugged; the wrestler incapacitates his opponent through ingenious but illicit techniques;

university alumni covertly subsidize "students" whose talents are confined to the athletic field. The emphasis on the goal has so attenuated the satisfactions deriving from sheer participation in the competitive activity that only a successful outcome provides gratification. Through the same process, tension generated by the desire to win in a poker game is relieved by successfully dealing one's self four aces or, when the cult of success has truly flowered, by sagaciously shuffling the cards in a game of solitaire. The faint twinge of uneasiness in the last instance and the surreptitious nature of public delicts indicate clearly that the institutional rules of the game are *known* to those who evade them. But cultural (or idiosyncratic) exaggeration of the success-goal leads men to withdraw emotional support from the rules.

This process is of course not restricted to the realm of competitive sport, which has simply provided us with microcosmic images of the social macrocosm. The process whereby exaltation of the end generates a literal *demoralization,* that is, a de-institutionalization, of the means occurs in many groups where the two components of the social structure are not highly integrated.

Contemporary American culture appears to approximate the polar type in which great emphasis upon certain success-goals occurs without equivalent emphasis upon institutional means. It would of course be fanciful to assert that accumulated wealth stands alone as a symbol of success, just as it would be fanciful to deny that Americans assign it a place high in their scale of values. In some large measure, money has been consecrated as a value in itself, over and above its expenditure for articles of consumption or its use for the enhancement of power. "Money" is peculiarly well adapted to become a symbol of prestige. As Simmel emphasized, money is highly abstract and impersonal. However acquired, fraudulently or institutionally, it can be used to purchase the same goods and services. The anonymity of an urban society, in conjunction with these peculiarities of money, permits wealth, the sources of which may be unknown to the community in which the plutocrat lives or, if known, to become purified in the course of time, to serve as a symbol of high status. Moreover, in the American Dream there is no final stopping point. The measure of "monetary success" is conveniently indefinite and relative. At each income level, as H. F. Clark found, Americans want just about 25 percent more (but of course this "just a bit more" continues to operate once it is obtained). In this flux of shifting standards, there is no stable resting point, or rather, it is the point which manages always to be "just ahead." An observer of a community in which annual salaries in six figures are not uncommon reports the anguished words of one victim of the American Dream: "In this town, I'm snubbed socially because I only get a thousand a week. That hurts."

To say that the goal of monetary success is entrenched in American culture is only to say that Americans are bombarded on every side by precepts which affirm the right or, often, the duty of retaining the goal even in the face of repeated frustration. Prestigeful representatives of the society reinforce the cultural emphasis. The family, the school and the workplace—the major agencies shaping the personality structure and goal formation of Americans—join to provide the intensive disciplining required if an individual is to retain intact a goal that remains elusively beyond reach, if he is to be motivated by the promise of a gratification which is not redeemed. As we shall presently see, parents serve as a transmission belt for the values and goals of the groups of which the are a part—above all, of their social class or of the class with which they identify themselves. And the schools are of course the official agency for the passing on of the prevailing values, with a large proportion of the textbooks used in city schools implying or stating explicitly "that education leads to intelligence and consequently to job and money success." Central to this process of disciplining people to maintain their unfulfilled aspirations are the cultural prototypes of success, the living documents testifying that the American Dream can be realized if one but has the requisite abilities.

Coupled with this positive emphasis upon the obligation to maintain lofty goals is a correlative emphasis upon the penalizing of those who draw in their ambitions. Americans are admonished "not to be a quitter" for in the dictionary of American culture, as in the lexicon of youth, "there is no such word as 'fail.' " The cultural manifesto is clear: one must not quit, must not cease striving, must not lessen his goals, for "not failure, but low aim, is crime."

Thus the culture enjoins the acceptance of three cultural axioms: First, all should strive for the same lofty goals since these are open to all; second, present seeming failure is but a way-station to ultimate success; and third, genuine failure consists only in the lessening or withdrawal of ambition.

In rough psychological paraphrase, these axioms represent, first a symbolic secondary reinforcement of incentive; second, curbing the threatened extinction of a response through an associated stimulus; third, increasing the motive strength to evoke continued responses despite the continued absence of reward.

In sociological paraphrase, these axioms represent, first, the deflection of criticism of the social structure onto one's self among those so situated in the society that they do not have full and equal access to opportunity; second, the preservation of a structure of social power by having individuals in the lower social strata identify themselves, not with their compeers, but with those at the top (whom they will ultimately join); and third, providing pressures for conformity with the cultural dictates of unslackened ambition by the threat of less than full membership in the society for those who fail to conform.

It is in these terms and through these processes that contemporary American culture continues to be characterized by a heavy emphasis on wealth as a basic symbol of success, without a corresponding emphasis upon the legitimate avenues on which to march toward this goal. How do individuals living in this cultural context respond? And how do our observations bear upon the doctrine that deviant behavior typically derives from biological impulses breaking through the restraints imposed by culture? What, in short, are the consequences for the behavior of people variously situated in a social structure of a culture in which the emphasis on dominant success goals has become increasingly separated from an equivalent emphasis on institutionalized procedures for seeking these goals?

TYPES OF INDIVIDUAL ADAPTATION

Turning from these culture patterns, we now examine types of adaptation by individuals within the culture-bearing society. Though our focus is still the cultural and social genesis of varying rates and types of deviant behavior, our perspective shifts from the plane of patterns of cultural values to the plane of types of adaptation to these values among those occupying different positions in the social structure.

We here consider five types of adaptation (see Table 5.1), as these are schematically set out in the following table, where (+) signifies "acceptance," (–) signifies "rejection," and (±) signifies "rejection of prevailing values and substitution of new values."

A Typology of Modes of Individual Adaptation

MODES OF ADAPTATION	CULTURE GOALS	INSTITUTIONALIZED MEANS
I. Conformity	+	+
II. Innovation	+	–
III. Ritualism	–	+
IV. Retreatism	–	–
V. Rebellion	±	±

I. Conformity

To the extent that a society is stable, adaptation type I—conformity to both cultural goals and institutionalized means—is the most common and widely diffused. Were this not so, the stability and continuity of the society could not be maintained. . . .

II. Innovation

Great cultural emphasis upon the success-goal invites this mode of adaptation through the use of institutionally proscribed but often effective means of attaining at least the simulacra of success—wealth and power. This response occurs when the individual has assimilated the cultural emphasis upon the goal without equally internalizing the institutional norms governing ways and means for its attainment. . . .

It appears from our analysis that the greatest pressures toward deviation are exerted upon the lower strata. Cases in point permit us to detect the sociological mechanisms involved in producing these pressures. Several researches have shown that specialized areas of vice and crime constitute a "normal" response to a situation where the cultural emphasis upon pecuniary success has been absorbed, but where there is little access to conventional and legitimate means for becoming successful. The occupational opportunities of people in these areas are largely confined to manual labor and the lesser white-collar jobs. Given the American stigmatization of manual labor *which has been found to hold rather uniformly in all social classes,* and the absence of realistic opportunities for advancement beyond this level, the result is a marked tendency toward deviant behavior. The status of unskilled labor and the consequent low income cannot readily compete *in terms of established standards of worth* with the promises of power and high income from organized vice, rackets and crime.

For our purposes, these situations exhibit two salient features. First, incentives for success are provided by the established values of the culture *and* second, the avenues available for moving toward this goal are largely limited by the class structure to those of deviant behavior. It is the *combination* of the cultural emphasis and the social structure which produces intense pressure for deviation. . . .

III. Ritualism

The ritualistic type of adaptation can be readily identified. It involves the abandoning or scaling down of the lofty cultural goals of great pecuniary success and rapid social mobility to the point where one's aspirations can be satisfied. But though one rejects the cultural obligation to attempt "to get ahead in the world," though one draws in one's horizons, one continues to abide almost compulsively by institutional norms. . . .

We should expect this type of adaptation to be fairly frequent in a society which makes one's social status largely dependent upon one's achievements. For, as has so often been observed, this ceaseless competitive struggle produces acute status anxiety. One device for allaying these anxieties is to lower one's level of aspiration—permanently. Fear produces inaction, or, more accurately, routinized action.

The syndrome of the social ritualist is both familiar and instructive. His implicit life-philosophy finds expression in a series of cultural clichés: "I'm not sticking my neck out," "I'm playing it safe," "I'm satisfied with what I've got," "Don't aim high and you won't be disappointed." The theme threaded through these attitudes is that high ambitions invite frustration and danger whereas lower aspirations produce satisfaction and security. It is the perspective of the frightened employee, the zealously conformist bureaucrat in the teller's cage of the private banking enterprise, or in the front office of the public works enterprise.

IV. Retreatism

Just as Adaptation I (conformity) remains the most frequent, Adaptation IV (the rejection of cultural goals and institutional means) is probably the least common. People who adapt (or maladapt) in this fashion are, strictly speaking, *in* the society but not *of* it. Sociologically these constitute the true aliens. Not sharing the common frame of values, they can be included as members of the *society* (in distinction from the *population*) only in a fictional sense.

In this category fall some of the adaptive activities of psychotics, autists, pariahs, outcasts, vagrants, vagabonds, tramps, chronic drunkards and drug addicts. They have relinquished culturally

prescribed goals and their behavior does not accord with institutional norms. The competitive order is maintained but the frustrated and handicapped individual who cannot cope with this order drops out. Defeatism, quietism and resignation are manifested in escape mechanisms which ultimately lead him to "escape" from the requirements of the society. It is thus an expedient which arises from continued failure to near the goal by legitimate measures and from an inability to use the illegitimate route because of internalized prohibitions.

V. Rebellion

This adaptation leads men outside the environing social structure to envisage and seek to bring into being a new, that is to say, a greatly modified social structure. It presupposes alienation from reigning goals and standards. These come to be regarded as purely arbitrary. And the arbitrary is precisely that which can neither exact allegiance nor possess legitimacy, for it might as well be otherwise. In our society, organized movements for rebellion apparently aim to introduce a social structure in which the cultural standards of success would be sharply modified and provision would be made for a closer correspondence between merit, effort and reward.

THE STRAIN TOWARD ANOMIE

The social structure we have examined produces a strain toward anomie and deviant behavior. The pressure of such a social order is upon outdoing one's competitors. So long as the sentiments supporting this competitive system are distributed throughout the entire range of activities and are not confined to the final result of "success," the choice of means will remain largely within the ambit of institutional control. When, however, the cultural emphasis shifts from the satisfactions deriving from competition itself to almost exclusive concern with the outcome, the resultant stress makes for the breakdown of the regulatory structure.

REVIEW QUESTIONS_____

1. Identify a situation in which an individual could use two of Merton's modes of adaptation simultaneously.
2. What are at least two weaknesses of this theory?

DIFFERENTIAL ASSOCIATION THEORY

EDWIN H. SUTHERLAND
DONALD R. CRESSEY

The following statements refer to the process by which a particular person comes to engage in criminal behavior.

1. *Criminal behavior is learned.* Negatively, this means that criminal behavior is not inherited, as such; also, the person who is not already trained in crime does not invent criminal behavior, just as a person does not make mechanical inventions unless he has had training in mechanics.
2. *Criminal behavior is learned in interaction with other persons in a process of communication.* This communication is verbal in many respects but includes also "the communication of gestures."
3. *The principal part of the learning of criminal behavior occurs within intimate personal groups.* Negatively, this means that the impersonal agencies of communication, such as movies and newspapers, play a relatively unimportant part in the genesis of criminal behavior.
4. *When criminal behavior is learned, the learning includes (a) techniques of committing the crime, which are sometimes very complicated, sometimes very simple; and (b) the specific direction of motives, drives, rationalizations, and attitudes.*
5. *The specific direction of motives and drives is learned from definitions of the legal codes as favorable or unfavorable.* In some societies an individual is surrounded by persons who invariably define the legal codes as rules to be observed, while in others he is surrounded by persons whose definitions are favorable to the violation of the legal codes. In our American society these definitions are almost always mixed, with the consequence that we have culture conflict in relation to the legal codes.
6. *A person becomes delinquent because of an excess of definitions favorable to violation of law over definitions unfavorable to violation of law.* This is the principle of differential association. It refers to both criminal and anticriminal associations and has to do with counteracting forces. When persons become criminal, they do so because of contacts with criminal patterns and also because of isolation from anticriminal patterns. Any person inevitably assimilates the surrounding culture unless other patterns are in conflict; a southerner does not pronounce *r* because other Southerners do not pronounce *r.* Negatively, this proposition of differential association means that associations which are neutral so far as crime is concerned have little or no effect on the genesis of criminal behavior. Much of the experience of a person is neutral in this sense, for example, learning to brush one's teeth. This behavior has no negative or positive effect on criminal behavior except as

Source: Edwin H. Sutherland and Donald R. Cressey, *Criminology,* 9th ed. (Philadelphia: Lippincott, 1977), pp. 75–77. Reprinted with permission.

it may be related to associations which are concerned with the legal codes. This neutral behavior is important especially as an occupier of the time of a child so that he is not in contact with criminal behavior during the time he is so engaged in the neutral behavior.

7. *Differential associations may vary in frequency, duration, priority, and intensity.* This means that associations with criminal behavior and also associations with anticriminal behavior vary in those respects. "Frequency" and "duration" as modalities of associations are obvious and need no explanation. "Priority' is assumed to be important in the sense that lawful behavior developed in early childhood may persist throughout life, and also that delinquent behavior developed in early childhood may persist throughout life. This tendency, however, has not been adequately demonstrated, and priority seems to be important principally through its selective influence. "Intensity" is not precisely defined, but it has to do with such things as the prestige of the source of a criminal or anticriminal pattern and with emotional reactions related to the associations. In a precise description of the criminal behavior of a person, these modalities would be rated in quantitative form and a mathematical ratio reached. A formula in this sense has not been developed, and the development of such a formula would be extremely difficult.

8. *The process of learning criminal behavior by association with criminal and anticriminal patterns involves all of the mechanisms that are involved in any other learning.* Negatively, this means that the learning of criminal behavior is not restricted to the process of imitation. A person who is seduced, for instance, learns criminal behavior by association, but this process would not ordinarily be described as imitation.

9. *While criminal behavior is an expression of general needs and values, it is not explained by those general needs and values, since non-criminal behavior is an expression of the same needs and values.* Thieves generally steal in order to secure money, but likewise honest laborers work in order to secure money. The attempts by many scholars to explain criminal behavior by general drives and values, such as the happiness principle, striving for social status, the money motive, or frustration, have been, and must continue to be, futile, since they explain lawful behavior as completely as they explain criminal behavior. They are similar to respiration, which is necessary for any behavior, but which does not differentiate criminal from noncriminal behavior.

It is not necessary, at this level of explanation, to explain why a person has the associations he has; this certainly involves a complex of many things. In an area where the delinquency rate is high, a boy who is sociable, gregarious, active, and athletic is very likely to come in contact with the other boys in the neighborhood, learn delinquent behavior patterns from them, and become a criminal; in the same neighborhood the psychopathic boy who is isolated, introverted, and inert may remain at home, not become acquainted with the other boys in the neighborhood, and not become delinquent. In another situation, the sociable, athletic, aggressive boy may become a member of a scout troop and not become involved in delinquent behavior. The person's associations are determined in a general context of social organization. A child is ordinarily reared in a family; the place of residence of the family is determined largely by family income; and the delinquency rate is in many respects related to the rental value of the houses. Many other aspects of social organization affect the kinds of associations a person has.

The preceding explanation of criminal behavior purports to explain the criminal and noncriminal behavior of individual persons. It is possible to state sociological theories of criminal behavior which explain the criminality of a community, nation, or other group. The problem, when thus stated, is to account for variations in crime rates and involves a comparison of the crime rates of various groups or the crime rates of a particular group at different times. The explanation of a crime rate must be consistent with the explanation of the criminal behavior of the person, since the crime rate is a summary statement of the number of persons in the group who commit crimes and the frequency with which they commit crimes. One of the best explanations of crime rates from this point of view is that a high crime rate is due to social disorganization. The term *social disorganization* is not entirely satisfactory, and it seems preferable to substitute for it the term *differential social organiza-* *tion.* The postulate on which this theory is based, regardless of the name, is that crime is rooted in the social organization and is an expression of that social organization. A group may be organized for criminal behavior or organized against criminal behavior. Most communities are organized for both criminal and anticriminal behavior, and, in that sense the crime rate is an expression of the differential group organization. Differential group organization as an explanation of variations in crime rates is consistent with the differential association theory of the processes by which persons become criminals.

REVIEW QUESTIONS

1. Using differential association theory, explain how a person could become a drug user, prostitute, or insurance con man.
2. What is the basic premise of differential association theory?

CONTROL THEORY

TRAVIS HIRSCHI

Control theories assume that delinquent acts result when an individual's bond to society is weak or broken. . . . [Elements of the bond are as follows.]

ATTACHMENT

It can be argued that all of the characteristics attributed to the psychopath follow from, are effects of, his lack of attachment to others. To say that to lack attachment to others is to be free from moral restraints is to use lack of attachment to explain the guiltlessness of the psychopath, the fact that he apparently has no conscience or superego. In this view, lack of attachment to others is not merely a symptom of psychopathy, it *is* psychopathy; lack of conscience is just another way of saying the same thing; and the violation of norms is (or may be) a consequence.

For that matter, given that man is an animal, "impulsivity" and "aggressiveness" can also be seen as natural consequences of freedom from moral restraints. However, since the view of man as endowed with natural propensities and capacities like other animals is peculiarly unpalatable to sociologists, we need not fall back on such a view to explain the amoral man's aggressiveness. The process of becoming alienated from others often involves or is based on active interpersonal conflict. Such conflict could easily supply a reservoir of *socially derived* hostility sufficient to account for the aggressiveness of those whose attachments to others have been weakened.

Durkheim said it many years ago: "We are moral beings to the extent that we are social beings." This may be interpreted to mean that we are moral beings to the extent that we have "internalized the norms" of society. But what does it mean to say that a person has internalized the norms of society? The norms of society are by definition shared by the members of society. To violate a norm is, therefore, to act contrary to the wishes and expectations of other people. If a person does not care about the wishes and expectations of other people—that is, if he is insensitive to the opinion of others—then he is to that extent not bound by the norms. He is free to deviate.

The essence of internalization of norms, conscience, or superego thus lies in the attachment of the individual to others. This view has several advantages over the concept of internalization. For one, explanations of deviant behavior based on attachment do not beg the question, since the extent to which a person is attached to others can be measured independently of his deviant behavior. Furthermore, change or variation in behavior is explainable in a way that it is not when notions of interaction or superego are used. For example, the divorced man is more likely after divorce to commit a number of deviant acts, such as suicide or forgery. If we explain these acts by reference to the super-ego (or internal control), we are forced to say that the man "lost his conscience" when he got a divorce; and, of course, if he remarries, we have to conclude that he gets his conscience back. . . .

Source: Travis Hirschi, *Causes of Delinquency,* (Berkeley: University of California Press, 1969), pp. 16–26. Reprinted by permission of the author.

COMMITMENT

"Of all passions, that which inclineth men least to break the laws, is fear. Nay, excepting some generous natures, it is the only thing, when there is the appearance of profit or pleasure by breaking the laws, that makes men keep them." Few would deny that men on occasion obey the rules simply from fear of the consequences. This rational component in conformity we label commitment. What does it mean to say that a person is committed to conformity? . . . [It means] that the person invests time, energy, himself, in a certain line of activity—say, getting an education, building up a business, acquiring a reputation for virtue. When or whenever he considers deviant behavior, he must consider the costs of this deviant behavior, the risk he runs of losing the investment he has made in conventional behavior.

If attachment to others is the sociological counterpart of the superego or conscience, commitment is the counterpart of the ego or common sense. To the person committed to conventional lines of action, risking one to ten years in prison for a ten-dollar holdup is stupidity, because to the committed person the costs and risks obviously exceed ten dollars in value. (To the psychoanalyst, such an act exhibits failure to be governed by the "reality-principle.") In the sociological control theory, it can be and is generally assumed that the decision to commit a criminal act may well be rationally determined—that the actor's decision was not irrational given the risks and costs he faces. . . .

INVOLVEMENT

Many persons undoubtedly owe a life of virtue to a lack of opportunity to do otherwise. Time and energy are inherently limited: "Not that I would not, if I could, be both handsome and fat and well dressed, and a great athlete, and make a million a year, be a wit, a bon vivant, and a lady killer, as well as a philosopher, a philanthropist, a statesman, warrior, and African explorer, as well as a 'tone-poet' and saint. But the thing is simply impossible." The things that William James here says

he would like to be or do are all, I suppose, within the realm of conventionality, but if he were to include illicit actions he would still have to eliminate some of them as simply impossible.

Involvement or engrossment in conventional activities is thus often part of a control theory. The assumption, widely shared, is that a person may be simply too busy doing conventional things to find time to engage in deviant behavior. The person involved in conventional activities is tied to appointments, deadlines, working hours, plans, and the like, so the opportunity to commit deviant acts rarely arises. To the extent that he is engrossed in conventional activities, he cannot even think about deviant acts, let alone act out his inclinations. . . .

BELIEF

The control theory assumes the existence of a common value system within the society or group whose norms are being violated. If the deviant is committed to a value system different from that of conventional society, there is, within the context of the theory, nothing to explain. The question is, "Why does a man violate the rules in which he believes?" It is not, "Why do men differ in their beliefs about what constitutes good and desirable conduct?" The person is assumed to have been socialized (perhaps imperfectly) into the group whose rules he is violating; deviance is not a question of one group imposing its rules on the members of another group. In other words, we not only assume the deviant *has* believed the rules, we assume he believes the rules even as he violates them.

How can a person believe it is wrong to steal at the same time he is stealing? In the strain theory, this is not a difficult problem. (In fact, the strain theory was devised specifically to deal with this question.) The motivation to deviance adduced by the strain theorist is so strong that we can well understand the deviant act even assuming the deviator believes strongly that it is wrong. However, given the control theory's assumptions about motivation, if both the deviant and the nondeviant believe the deviant act is wrong, how do we account for the fact that one commits it and the other does not?

Control theories have taken two approaches to this problem. In one approach, beliefs are treated as mere words that mean little or nothing. . . . The second approach argues that the deviant rationalizes his behavior so that he can at once violate the rule and maintain his belief in it. . . . We assume, however, that there is *variation* in the extent to which people believe they should obey the rules of society, and, furthermore, that the less a person believes he should obey the rules, the more likely he is to violate them.

REVIEW QUESTIONS

1. Using control theory as a frame of reference, explain why a city would implement a program that includes midnight football and other programs for those who do not want to play football; a kitchen where an entire family can work together with other families preparing a meal; and a short simple movie, which plays while people are eating, whose theme reinforces some positive aspect of American life such as respecting others' property and treating all people with dignity and respect.
2. What is the difference between control theory and differential association theory?

SHAMING THEORY

JOHN BRAITHWAITE

Cultural commitments to shaming are the key to controlling all types of crime. However, for all types of crime, shaming runs the risk of counter-productivity when it shades into stigmatization.

The crucial distinction is between shaming that is reintegrative and shaming that is disintegrative (stigmatization). Reintegrative shaming means that expressions of community disapproval, which may range from mild rebuke to degradation ceremonies, are followed by gestures of reacceptance into the community of law-abiding citizens. These gestures of reacceptance will vary from a simple smile expressing forgiveness and love to quite formal ceremonies to decertify the offender as deviant. Disintegrative shaming (stigmatization), in contrast, divides the community by creating a class of outcasts. Much effort is directed at labeling deviance, while little attention is paid to delabeling, to signifying forgiveness and reintegration, to ensuring that the deviance label is applied to the behavior rather than the person, and that this is done under the assumption that the disapproved behavior is transient, performed by an essentially good person. . . .

The best place to see reintegrative shaming at work is in loving families. . . . Family life teaches us that shaming and punishment are possible while maintaining bonds of respect. Two hypotheses are suggested: first, families are the most effective agents of social control in most societies partly because of this characteristic; second, those families that are disintegrative rather than reintegrative in their punishment processes, that have not learnt the trick of punishing within a continuum of love, are the families that fail at socializing their children.

KEY CONCEPTS

Interdependency is a condition of individuals. It means the extent to which individuals participate in networks wherein they are dependent on others to achieve valued ends and others are dependent on them. We could describe an individual as in a state of interdependency even if the individuals who are dependent on him are different from the individuals on whom he is dependent. Interdependency is approximately equivalent to the social bonding, attachment and commitment of control theory.

Communitarianism is a condition of societies. In communitarian societies individuals are densely enmeshed in interdependencies which have the special qualities of mutual help and trust. The interdependencies have symbolic significance in the culture of group loyalties which take precedence over individual interests. The interdependencies also have symbolic significance as attachments which invoke personal obligation to others in a community of concern, rather than simply interdependencies of convenience as between a bank and a small depositor. A communitarian culture

Source: John Braithwaite, *Crime, Shame, and Reintegration* (New York: Cambridge University Press, 1989), pp. 55–56. Reprinted with permission.

rejects any pejorative connotation of dependency as threatening individual autonomy. Communitarian cultures resist interpretations of dependency as weakness and emphasize the need for mutuality of obligation in interdependency (to be both dependent and dependable). The Japanese are said to be socialized not only to *amaeru* (to be succored by others) but also to *amayakasu* (to be nurturing to others).

Shaming means all social processes of expressing disapproval which have the intention or effect of invoking remorse in the person being shamed and/or condemnation by others who become aware of the shaming. When associated with appropriate symbols, formal punishment often shames. But societies vary enormously in the extent to which formal punishment is associated with shaming or in the extent to which the social meaning of punishment is no more than to inflict pain to tip reward-cost calculations in favor of certain outcomes. Shaming, unlike purely deterrent punishment, sets out to moralize with the offender to communicate reasons for the evil of her actions. Most shaming is neither associated with formal punishment nor perpetrated by the state, though both shaming by the state and shaming with punishment are important types of shaming. Most shaming is by individuals within interdependent communities of concern.

Reintegrative shaming is shaming which is followed by efforts to reintegrate the offender back into the community of law-abiding or respectable citizens through words or gestures of forgiveness or ceremonies to decertify the offender as deviant. Shaming and reintegration do not occur simultaneously but sequentially, with reintegration occurring before deviance becomes a master status. It is shaming which labels the act as evil while striving to preserve the identity of the offender as essentially good. It is directed at signifying evil deeds rather than evil persons in the Christian tradition of "hate the sin and love the sinner." Specific disapproval is expressed within relationships characterized by general social approval; shaming criminal behavior is complemented by ongoing social rewarding of alternative behavior patterns. Reintegrative shaming is not necessarily weak; it can be cruel, even vicious. It is not distinguished from stigmatization by its potency, but by (a) a finite rather than open-ended duration which is terminated by forgiveness; and by (b) efforts to maintain bonds of love or respect throughout the finite period of suffering shame.

Stigmatization is disintegrative shaming in which no effort is made to reconcile the offender with the community. The offender is outcast, her deviance is allowed to become a master status, degradation ceremonies are not followed by ceremonies to decertify deviance.

Criminal subcultures are sets of rationalizations and conduct norms which cluster together to support criminal behavior. The clustering is usually facilitated by subcultural groups which provide systematic social support for crime in any of a number of ways—supplying members with criminal opportunities, criminal values, attitudes which weaken conventional values of law-abidingness, or techniques of neutralizing conventional values.

SHORT SUMMARY OF THE THEORY

The following might serve as the briefest possible summary of the theory. A variety of life circumstances increase the chances that individuals will be in situations of greater interdependency, the most important being age (under 15 and over 25), being married, female, employed, and having high employment and educational aspirations. Interdependent persons are more susceptible to shaming. More important, societies in which individuals are subject to extensive interdependencies are more likely to be communitarian, and shaming is much more widespread and potent in communitarian societies. Urbanization and high residential mobility are societal characteristics which undermine communitarianism.

The shaming produced by interdependency and communitarianism can be either of two types—shaming that becomes stigmatization or shaming that is followed by reintegration. The shaming engendered is more likely to become reintegrative in societies that are communitarian. In societies where shaming does become reintegrative, low crime rates are the result because disapproval is dispensed without eliciting a rejection of the disapprovers, so that the potentialities for future disapproval are not dismantled. . . .

Shaming that is stigmatizing, in contrast, makes criminal subcultures more attractive because these are in some sense subcultures which reject the rejectors. Thus, when shaming is allowed to become stigmatization for want of reintegrative gestures or ceremonies which decertify deviance, the deviant is both attracted to criminal subcultures and cut off from other interdependencies (with family, neighbors, church, etc.). Participation in subcultural groups supplies criminal role models, training in techniques of crime and techniques of neutralizing crime (or other forms of social support) that make choices to engage in crime more attractive. Thus, to the extent that shaming is of the stigmatizing rather than the reintegrative sort, and that criminal subcultures are widespread and accessible in the society, higher crime rates will be the result. While societies characterized by high levels of stigmatization will have, higher crime rates than societies characterized by reintegrative shaming, the former will have higher or lower crime rates than societies with little shaming at all depending largely on the availability of criminal subcultures.

Yet a high level of stigmatization in the society is one of the very factors that encourages criminal subculture formation by creating populations of outcasts with no stake in conformity, no chance of self-esteem within the terms of conventional society—individuals in search of an alternative culture that allows them self-esteem. A communitarian culture, on the other hand, nurtures deviants within a network of attachments to conventional society, thus inhibiting the widespread outcasting that is the stuff of subculture formation.

REVIEW QUESTIONS

1. There has been a tremendous amount of media coverage of the behavior of some Catholic priests and their interaction with children. Given the coverage, do you think reintegrative or disintegrative shaming should be applied? Defend your answer.
2. What is the value of having a communitarian culture as it relates to the treatment of deviants in a given society? Explain your response in detail.

PART THREE

CONSTRUCTIONIST THEORIES

In January 2000, Richard Pitcher, 35, and Kimberly Henry, 31, began a romance that led to talk of marriage three weeks later. But the sting of his second divorce was still fresh, and her first marriage had also been a disaster. So they decided to move in together as a trial run instead of rushing into marriage. About a month after enjoying their lives as a couple, they suddenly found a summons in the mail charging them with violating Article 30-10-2 of the New Mexico criminal code, also known as unlawful cohabitation. They were told that first offenders get a warning and repeat offenders could be sent to jail for six months. "I couldn't believe it," Pitcher said. "I was shocked." Later Pitcher found out that his second former wife had filed a complaint with the police. She had just been married for the fourth time, but as a newly born-again Christian she did not want her 5-year-old daughter to see her dad living in sin. The local district attorney said he would dismiss the case, calling the unlawful-cohabitation law "weird."[1]

Is living together really deviant? Positivist sociologists assume that it is because it involves breaking the legal norm that prohibits cohabitation. Because they regard that law-breaking behavior as really deviant, positivists are inclined to find out the causes of cohabitation. Constructionist sociologists, however, are not interested in studying cohabitation because they do not consider it really deviant behavior. They are more interested in finding out who thinks of cohabitation as deviant and why. To constructionists, cohabitation is not deviant as an act and appears deviant only as a mental construction, a figment of human imagination. Thus constructionists have developed theories about how people impute the notion of "deviance" to behaviors like cohabitation and what consequences this attribution has for themselves and others.

In this part of our reader we present various constructionist theories. In the first article, "Labeling Theory," Howard Becker shows how the meaning of deviance derives not from the act a person commits but from society's labeling of an act as deviant. In the second selection, "Phenomenological Theory," Jack Katz provides a tour into the experiential world of deviants, revealing how they feel about their so-called deviant activities. In the third reading, "Conflict Theory," Richard Quinney describes what he calls "the social reality of crime." The reality is said to comprise the meanings of criminal laws, enforcement of these laws, their violations by relatively powerless people, and the dominant class' crime ideology that supports the enforcement of laws against lower-class criminals.

---

1. Jim Yardley, "Unmarried and Living Together till the Sheriff Do Us Part," *New York Times,* March 25, 2000, p. A7.

In the fourth article, "Feminist Theory," Kathleen Daly discusses how women differ from men in lawbreaking. Finally, in "Postmodernist Theory," David Friedrichs and Jessica Friedrichs present the major points of the newest constructionist theory in the sociology of deviance.

LABELING THEORY

HOWARD S. BECKER

A sociological view . . . defines deviance as the infraction of some agreed-upon rule. It then goes on to ask who breaks rules, and to search for the factors in their personalities and life situations that might account for the infractions. This assumes that those who have broken a rule constitute a homogeneous category, because they have committed the same deviant act.

Such an assumption seems to me to ignore the central fact about deviance: it is created by society. I do not mean this in the way it is ordinarily understood, in which the causes of deviance are located in the social situation of the deviant or in "social factors" which prompt his action. I mean, rather, that *social groups create deviance by making the rules whose infraction constitutes deviance,* and by applying those rules to particular people and labeling them as outsiders. From this point of view, deviance is *not* a quality of the act the person commits, but rather a consequence of the application by others of rules and sanctions to an "offender." The deviant is one to whom that label has successfully been applied; deviant behavior is behavior that people so label.

Since deviance is, among other things, a consequence of the responses of others to a person's act, students of deviance cannot assume that they are dealing with a homogeneous category when they study people who have been labeled deviant. That is, they cannot assume that these people have actually committed a deviant act or broken some rule, because the process of labeling may not be infallible; some people may be labeled deviant who in fact have not broken a rule. Furthermore, they cannot assume that the category of those labeled deviant will contain all those who actually have broken a rule, for many offenders may escape apprehension and thus fail to be included in the population of "deviants" they study. Insofar as the category lacks homogeneity and fails to include all the cases that belong in it, one cannot reasonably expect to find common factors of personality or life situation that will account for the supposed deviance.

What, then, do people who have been labeled deviant have in common? At the least, they share the label and the experience of being labeled as outsiders. I will begin my analysis with this basic similarity and view deviance as the product of a transaction that takes place between some social group and one who is viewed by that group as a rule-breaker. I will be less concerned with the personal and social characteristics of deviants than with the process by which they come to be thought of as outsiders and their reactions to that judgment.

The point is that the response of other people has to be regarded as problematic. Just because one has committed an infraction of a rule does not mean that others will respond as though this had happened. (Conversely, just because one has not violated a rule does not mean that he may not be treated, in some circumstances, as though he had.)

Source: Howard S. Becker, *Outsiders: Studies in the Sociology of Deviance* (New York: The Free Press, a division of Simon & Schuster, 1963), pp. 8–14, 31–35. Reprinted with permission of The Free Press, an imprint of Simon & Schuster Adult Publishing Group.

The degree to which other people will respond to a given act as deviant varies greatly. Several kinds of variation seem worth noting. First of all, there is variation over time. A person believed to have committed a given "deviant" act may at one time be responded to much more leniently than he would be at some other time. The occurrence of "drives" against various kinds of deviance illustrates this clearly. At various times, enforcement officials may decide to make an all-out attack on some particular kind of deviance, such as gambling, drug addiction, or homosexuality. It is obviously much more dangerous to engage in one of these activities when a drive is on than at any other time. (In a very interesting study of crime news in Colorado newspapers, Davis found that the amount of crime reported in Colorado newspapers showed very little association with actual changes in the amount of crime taking place in Colorado. And, further, that peoples' estimate of how much increase there had been in crime in Colorado was associated with the increase in the amount of crime news but not with any increase in the amount of crime.)

The degree to which an act will be treated as deviant depends also on who commits the act and who feels he has been harmed by it. Rules tend to be applied more to some persons than others. Studies of juvenile delinquency make the point clearly. Boys from middle-class areas do not get as far in the legal process when they are apprehended as do boys from slum areas. The middle-class boy is less likely, when picked up by the police, to be taken to the station; less likely when taken to the station to be booked; and it is extremely unlikely that he will be convicted and sentenced. This variation occurs even though the original infraction of the rule is the same in the two cases.

Why repeat these commonplace observations? Because, taken together, they support the proposition that deviance is not a simple quality, present in some kinds of behavior and absent in others. Rather, it is the product of a process which involves responses of other people to the behavior. The same behavior may be an infraction of the rules at one time and not at another; may be an infraction when committed by one person, but not when committed by another; some rules are broken with impunity, others are not. In short, whether a given act is deviant or not depends in part on the nature of the act (that is, whether or not it violates some rule) and in part on what other people do about it.

Some people may object that this is merely a terminological quibble, that one can, after all, define terms any way he wants to and that if some people want to speak of rule-breaking behavior as *deviant* without reference to the reactions of others they are free to do so. This, of course, is true. Yet it might be worthwhile to refer to such behavior as *rule-breaking behavior* and reserve the term *deviant* for those labeled as deviant by some segment of society. I do not insist that this usage be followed. But it should be clear that insofar as a scientist uses "deviant" to refer to any rule-breaking behavior and takes as his subject of study only those who have been *labeled* deviant, he will be hampered by the disparities between the two categories.

If we take as the object of our attention behavior which comes to be labeled as deviant, we must recognize that we cannot know whether a given act will be categorized as deviant until the response of others has occurred. Deviance is not a quality that lies in behavior itself, but in the interaction between the person who commits an act and those who respond to it....

In any case, being caught and branded as deviant has important consequences for one's further social participation and self-image. The most important consequence is a drastic change in the individual's public identity. Committing the improper act and being publicly caught at it place him in a new status. He has been revealed as a different kind of person from the kind he was supposed to be. He is labeled a "fairy," "dope fiend," "nut," or "lunatic," and treated accordingly....

To be labeled a criminal one need only commit a single criminal offense, and this is all the term formally refers to. Yet the word carries a number of connotations specifying auxiliary traits characteristic of anyone bearing the label. A man who has been convicted of housebreaking and thereby labeled criminal is presumed to be a person likely to break into other houses; the police, in rounding up known offenders for investigation after a crime has been committed, operate on this premise. Further, he is considered likely to commit other kinds of crimes as well, because he has shown himself to be a person without "respect for the law." Thus, apprehension for one deviant act exposes a person to the likelihood that he will be regarded as deviant or undesirable in other respects....

Treating a person as though he were generally rather than specifically deviant produces a self-fulfilling prophecy. It sets in motion several mechanisms which conspire to shape the person in the image people have of him. In the first place, one tends to be cut off, after being identified as deviant, from participation in more conventional groups, even though the specific consequences of the particular deviant activity might never of themselves have caused the isolation had there not also been the public knowledge and reaction to it. . . .Though the effects of opiate drugs may not impair one's

working ability, to be known as an addict will probably lead to losing one's job. In such cases, the individual finds it difficult to conform to other rules which he had no intention or desire to break, and perforce finds himself deviant in these areas as well. The drug addict finds himself forced into other illegitimate kinds of activity, such as robbery and theft, by the refusal of respectable employers to have him around.

When the deviant is caught, he is treated in accordance with the popular diagnosis of why he is that way, and the treatment itself may likewise produce increasing deviance. The drug addict, popularly considered to be a weakwilled individual who cannot forego the indecent pleasures afforded him by opiates, is treated repressively. He is forbidden to use drugs. Since he cannot get drugs legally, he must get them illegally. This forces the market underground and pushes the price of drugs up far beyond the current legitimate market price into a bracket that few can afford on an ordinary salary. Hence the treatment of the addict's deviance places him in a position where it will probably be necessary to resort to deceit and crime in order to support his habit. The behavior is a consequence of the public reaction to the deviance rather than a consequence of the inherent qualities of the deviant act.

REVIEW QUESTIONS

1. Mary, a college freshman, has gained a reputation for being loose and easy, willing to have sex with just about anyone, although in reality she is a virgin. How would a labeling theorist like Becker explain this situation?
2. People break the law all the time, yet not all are defined as deviant. After reading Becker's article, explain how this can be so.

10

PHENOMENOLOGICAL THEORY

JACK KATZ

The study of crime has been preoccupied with a search for background forces, usually defects in the offenders' psychological backgrounds or social environments, to the neglect of the positive, often wonderful attractions within the lived experience of criminality. The novelty of this [theory] is its focus on the seductive qualities of crimes: those aspects in the foreground of criminality that make its various forms sensible, even sensually compelling, ways of being.

The social science literature contains only scattered evidence of what it means, feels, sounds, tastes, or looks like to commit a particular crime. Readers of research on homicide and assault do not hear the slaps and curses, see the pushes and shoves, or feel the humiliation and rage that may build toward the attack, sometimes persisting after the victim's death. How adolescents manage to make the shoplifting or vandalism of cheap and commonplace things a thrilling experience has not been intriguing to many students of delinquency. Researchers of adolescent gangs have never grasped why their subjects so often stubbornly refuse to accept the outsider's insistence that they wear the "gang" label. The description of "cold-blooded, senseless murders" has been left to writers outside the social sciences. Neither academic methods nor academic theories seem to be able to grasp why such killers may have been courteous to their victims just moments before the killing, why they often wait until they have dominated victims in sealed-off environments before coldly ex-

ecuting them, or how it makes sense to them to kill when only petty cash is at stake. Sociological and psychological studies of robbery rarely focus on the *distinctive* attractions of robbery, even though research has now clearly documented that alternative forms of criminality are available and familiar to many career robbers. In sum, only rarely have sociologists taken up the challenge of explaining the qualities of deviant experience.

The statistical and correlational findings of positivist criminology provide the following irritations to inquiry: (1) whatever the validity of the hereditary, psychological, and social-ecological conditions of crime, many of those in the supposedly causal categories do not commit the crime at issue, (2) many who do commit the crime do not fit the causal categories, and (3) and what is most provocative, many who do fit the background categories and later commit the predicted crime go for long stretches without committing the crimes to which theory directs them. Why are people who were not determined to commit a crime one moment determined to do so the next?

I propose that empirical research turn the direction of inquiry around to focus initially on the foreground, rather than the background of crime. Let us for once make it our first priority to understand the qualities of experience that distinguish different forms of criminality. . . .

A sense of being determined by the environment, of being pushed away from one line of action and pulled toward another, is natural to everyday,

Source: Jack Katz, *Seductions of Crime* (New York: Basic Books, 1988), pp. 3–5, 8–10. © 1988 by Jack Katz. Reprinted by permission of Basic Books, a member of Perseus Books, L.L.C.

routine human experience. We are always moving away from and toward different objects of consciousness, taking account of this and ignoring that, and moving in one direction or the other between the extremes of involvement and boredom. In this constant movement of consciousness, we do not perceive that we are controlling the movement. Instead, to one degree or another, we are always being seduced and repelled by the world. "This *is* fascinating (interesting, beautiful, sexy, dull, ugly, disgusting)," we know (without having to say), as if the thing itself possessed the designated quality independent of us and somehow controlled our understanding of it. Indeed, the very nature of mundane being is emotional; attention is feeling, and consciousness is sensual.

Only rarely do we actually experience ourselves as subjects directing our conduct. How often, when you speak, do you actually sense that you are choosing the words you utter? As the words come out, they reveal the thought behind them even to the speaker whose lips gave them shape. Similarly, we talk, walk, and write in a sense of natural competence governed by moods of determinism. We rest our subjectivity on rhythmic sensibilities, feelings for directions, and visions of unfolding patterns, allowing esthetics to guide us. Self-reflexive postures, in which one creates a distance between the self and the world and pointedly directs the self into the world, occur typically in an exceptional mood of recognizing a malapropism, after a misstep, or at the slip of the pen. With a slight shock, we recognize that it was not the things in themselves but our perspective that temporarily gave things outside of us the power to seduce or repel.

Among the forms of crime, the range of sensual dynamics runs from enticements that may draw a person into shoplifting to furies that can compel him to murder. If, as social researchers, we are to be able to explain more variation in criminality than background correlations allow, it appears that we must respect these sensual dynamics and honor them as authentic. . . .

Approaching criminality from the inside, social research takes as its subject the morally ex-

ceptional conduct that the persons themselves regard as criminally sanctionable in official eyes. Since there is an enormous variety of criminal phenomena, how can one demarcate and set up for explanation a limited number of subjectively homogeneous offenses? I suggest that a seemingly simple question be asked persistently in detailed application to the facts of criminal experience: What are people trying to do when they commit a crime?

The resulting topics will not necessarily follow official crime categories. Crimes, as defined in statutes, surveys of citizens, and police records, take definitional shape from the interests of victims and from practical problems of detection and punishment, not necessarily from the experience of those committing the crimes. But if one begins with rough conventional or folk categories, such as hot-blooded murder, gang violence, adolescent property crime, commercial robbery, and "senseless" and "cold-blooded" murder, and refines the concepts to fit homogeneous forms of experience, one can arrive at a significant range of criminal projects: committing righteous slaughter, mobilizing the spirit of a street elite, constructing sneaky thrills, persisting in the practice of stickup as a hardman, and embodying primordial evil.

By way of explanation, I will propose for each type of crime a different set of individually necessary and jointly sufficient conditions, each set containing (1) a path of action—distinctive practical requirements for successfully committing the crime, (2) a line of interpretation—unique ways of understanding how one is and will be seen by others, and (3) an emotional process—seductions and compulsions that have special dynamics. Raising the spirit of criminality requires practical attention to a mode of executing action, symbolic creativity in defining the situation, and esthetic finesse in recognizing and elaborating on the sensual possibilities.

Central to all these experiences in deviance is a member of the family of moral emotions: humiliation, righteousness, arrogance, ridicule, cynicism, defilement, and vengeance. In each, the attraction that proves to be most fundamentally compelling is that of overcoming a personal challenge to moral—not to material—existence. For the impassioned killer, the challenge is to escape a situation that has come to seem otherwise inexorably humiliating. Unable to sense how he or she can move with self-respect from the current situation, now, to any mundane-time relationship that might be reengaged, then, the would-be killer leaps at the possibility of embodying, through the practice of "righteous" slaughter, some eternal, universal form of the Good.

For many adolescents, shoplifting and vandalism offer the attractions of a thrilling melodrama about the self as seen from within and from without. Quite apart from what is taken, they may regard "getting away with it" as a thrilling demonstration of personal competence, especially if it is accomplished under the eyes of adults.

Specifically "bad" forms of criminality are essentially addressed to a moral challenge experienced in a spatial metaphor. Whether by intimidating others' efforts to take him into their worlds ("Who you lookin' at?") or by treating artificial geographic boundaries as sacred and defending local "turf" with relentless "heart," "badasses" and *barrio* warriors celebrate an indifference to modern society's expectation that a person should demonstrate a sensibility to reshape himself as he moves from here to there.

To make a habit of doing stickups, I will argue, one must become a "hardman." It is only smart to avoid injuring victims unnecessarily, but if one becomes too calculating about the application of violence, the inherent uncertainties of face-to-face interaction in robberies will be emotionally forbidding. Beneath the surface, there may be, to paraphrase Nietzsche, a ball of snakes in chaotic struggle. But the stickup man denies any uncertainty and any possibility of change with a personal style that ubiquitously negates social pressures toward a malleable self.

Perhaps the ultimate criminal project is mounted by men who culminate a social life organized around the symbolism of deviance with a cold-blooded, "senseless" murder. Mimicking the ways of primordial gods as they kill, they proudly appear to the world as astonishingly evil. Through a killing only superficially justified by the context of robbery, they emerge from a dizzying alternation between affiliation with the great symbolic powers of deviant identity and a nagging disease that conformity means cowardice.

Overall, my objective is to demonstrate that a theory of moral self-transcendence can make comprehensible the minutia of experiential details in the phenomenal foreground, as well as explain the general conditions that are most commonly found in the social backgrounds of these forms of criminality.

REVIEW QUESTIONS

1. Do you support Katz's contention that we should focus on the foreground rather than the background of crime? If yes, why? If no, why not?
2. Katz argues that participation in some forms of behavior, most notably shoplifting and vandalism, can be seductive to the individual. How does he arrive at this conclusion?

CONFLICT THEORY

RICHARD QUINNEY

A theory that helps us begin to examine the legal order critically is the one I call the *social reality of crime.* Applying this theory, we think of crime as it is affected by the dynamics that mold the society's social, economic, and political structure. First, we recognize how criminal law fits into capitalist society. The legal order gives reality to the crime problem in the United States. Everything that makes up crime's social reality, including the application of criminal law, the behavior patterns of those who are defined as criminal, and the construction of an ideology of crime, is related to the established legal order. The social reality of crime is constructed on conflict in our society. The theory of the social reality of crime is formulated as follows.

I. THE OFFICIAL DEFINITION OF CRIME:

Crime as a legal definition of human conduct is created by agents of the dominant class in a politically organized society.

The essential starting point is a definition of crime that itself is based on the legal definition. Crime, as *officially* determined, is a *definition* of behavior that is conferred on some people by those in power. Agents of the law (such as legislators, police, prosecutors, and judges) are responsible for formulating and administering criminal law. Upon *formulation* and *application* of these definitions of crime, persons and behaviors become criminal.

Crime, according to this first proposition, is not inherent in behavior, but is a judgment made by some about the actions and characteristics of others. This proposition allows us to focus on the formulation and administration of the criminal law as it applies to the behaviors that become defined as criminal. Crime is seen as a result of the class-dynamic process that culminates in defining persons and behaviors as criminal. It follows, then, that the greater the number of definitions of crime that are formulated and applied, the greater the amount of crime.

II. FORMULATING DEFINITIONS OF CRIME:

Definitions of crime are composed of behaviors that conflict with the interests of the dominant class.

Definitions of crime are formulated according to the interests of those who have the power to translate their interests into public policy. Those definitions are ultimately incorporated into the criminal law. Furthermore, definitions of crime in a society change as the interests of the dominant class change. In other words, those who are able to have their interests represented in public policy regulate the formulation of definitions of crime.

The powerful interests are reflected not only in the definitions of crime and the kinds of penal sanctions attached to them, but also in the *legal policies* on handling those defined as criminals. Procedural rules are created for enforcing and administering the criminal law. Policies are also established on programs for treating and punishing the criminally defined and programs for controlling

Source: Richard Quinney, *Criminology* (Boston: Little, Brown, 1975), pp. 37–41. Reprinted with permission.

and preventing crime. From the initial definitions of crime to the subsequent procedures, correctional and penal programs, and policies for controlling and preventing crime, those who have the power regulate the behavior of those without power.

III. APPLYING DEFINITIONS OF CRIME:

Definitions of crime are applied by the class that has the power to shape the enforcement and administration of criminal law.

The dominant interests intervene in all the stages at which definitions of crime are created. Because class interests cannot be effectively protected merely by formulating criminal law, the law must be enforced and administered. The interests of the powerful, therefore, also operate where the definitions of crime reach the *application* stage. As Vold has argued, crime is "political behavior and the criminal becomes in fact a member of a 'minority group' without sufficient public support to dominate the control of the police power of the state." Those whose interests conflict with the ones represented in the law must either change their behavior or possibly find it defined as criminal.

The probability that definitions of crime will be applied varies according to how much the behaviors of the powerless conflict with the interests of those in power. Law enforcement efforts and judicial activity are likely to increase when the interests of the dominant class are threatened. Fluctuations and variations in applying definitions of crime reflect shifts in class relations.

Obviously, the criminal law is not applied directly by those in power; its enforcement and administration are delegated to authorized *legal agents*. Because the groups responsible for creating the definitions of crime are physically separated from the groups that have the authority to enforce and administer law, local conditions determine how the definitions will be applied. In particular, communities vary in their expectations of law enforcement and the administration of justice.

The application of definitions is also influenced by the visibility of offenses in a community and by the public's norms about reporting possible violations. And especially important in enforcing and administering the criminal law are the legal agents' occupational organization and ideology.

The probability that these definitions will be applied depends on the actions of the legal agents who have the authority to enforce and administer the law. A definition of crime is applied depending on their evaluation. Turk has argued that during "criminalization," a criminal label may be affixed to people because of real or fancied attributes: "Indeed, a person is evaluated, either favorably or unfavorably, not because he *does* something, or even because he is something, but because others react to their perceptions of him as offensive or inoffensive." Evaluation by the definers is affected by the way in which the suspect handles the situation, but ultimately the legal agents' evaluations and subsequent decisions are the crucial factors in determining the criminality of human acts. As legal agents evaluate more behaviors and persons as worthy of being defined as crimes, the probability that definitions of crime will be applied grows.

IV. HOW BEHAVIOR PATTERNS DEVELOP IN RELATION TO DEFINITIONS OF CRIME:

Behavior patterns are structured in relation to definitions of crime, and within this context people engage in actions that have relative probabilities of being defined as criminal.

Although behavior varies, all behaviors are similar in that they represent patterns within the society. All persons—whether they create definitions of crime or are the objects of these definitions—act in reference to *normative systems* learned in relative social and cultural settings. Because it is not the quality of the behavior but the action taken against the behavior that gives it the character of criminality, that which is defined as criminal is relative to the behavior patterns of the class that formulates and applies definitions. Consequently, people whose behavior patterns are not represented when the definitions of crime are formulated and applied are more likely to act in ways that will be defined as criminal than those who formulate and apply the definitions.

Once behavior patterns become established with some regularity within the segments of society, individuals have a framework for creating *personal action patterns*. These continually develop for each person as he moves from one experience to another. Specific action patterns give behavior an individual substance in relation to the definitions of crime.

People construct their own patterns of action in participating with others. It follows, then, that the probability that persons will develop action patterns with a high potential for being defined as criminal depends on (1) structured opportunities, (2) learning experiences, (3) interpersonal associations and identifications, and (4) self-conceptions. Throughout the experiences, each person creates a conception of self as a human social being. Thus prepared, he behaves according to the anticipated consequences of his actions.

In the experiences shared by the definers of crime and the criminally defined, personal-action patterns develop among the latter because they are so defined. After they have had continued experience in being defined as criminal, they learn to manipulate the application of criminal definitions.

Furthermore, those who have been defined as criminal begin to conceive of themselves as criminal. As they adjust to the definitions imposed upon them, they learn to play the criminal role. As a result of others' reactions, therefore, people may develop personal action patterns that increase the likelihood of their being defined as criminal in the future. That is, increased experience with definitions of crime increases the probability of their developing actions that may be subsequently defined as criminal.

Thus, both the definers of crime and the criminally defined are involved in reciprocal action patterns. The personal-action patterns of both the definers and the defined are shaped by their common, continued, and related experiences. The fate of each is bound to that of the other.

V. CONSTRUCTING AN IDEOLOGY OF CRIME:

An ideology of crime is constructed and diffused by the dominant class to secure its hegemony.

This ideology is created in the kinds of ideas people are exposed to, the manner in which they select information to fit the world they are shaping, and their way of interpreting this information. People behave in reference to the *social meanings* they attach to their experiences.

Among the conceptions that develop in a society are those relating to what people regard as crime. The concept of crime must of course be accompanied by ideas about the nature of crime. Images develop about the relevance of crime, the offender's characteristics, the appropriate reaction to crime, and the relation of crime to the social order. These conceptions are constructed by communication, and, in fact, an ideology of crime depends on the portrayal of crime in all personal and mass communication. This ideology is thus diffused throughout the society.

One of the most concrete ways by which an ideology of crime is formed and transmitted is the official investigation of crime. The President's Commission on Law Enforcement and Administration of Justice is the best contemporary example of the state's role in shaping an ideology of crime. Not only are we as citizens more aware of crime today because of the President's Commission, but official policy on crime has been established in a crime bill, the Omnibus Crime Control and Safe Streets Act of 1968. The crime bill, itself a reaction to the growing fears of class conflict in American society, creates an image of a severe crime problem and, in so doing, threatens to negate some of our basic constitutional guarantees in the name of controlling crime.

Consequently, the conceptions that are most critical in actually formulating and applying the definitions of crime are those held by the dominant class. These conceptions are certain to be incorporated into the social reality of crime. The more the government acts in reference to crime, the more probable it is that definitions of crime will be created and that behavior patterns will develop in opposition to those definitions. The formulation of definitions of crime, their application, and the development of behavior patterns in relation to the definitions, are thus joined in full circle by the construction of an ideological hegemony toward crime.

VI. CONSTRUCTING THE SOCIAL REALITY OF CRIME:

The social reality of crime is constructed by the formulation and application of definitions of crime, the development of behavior patterns in relation to these definitions, and the construction of an ideology of crime.

The first five propositions are collected here into a final composition proposition. The theory of the social reality of crime, accordingly, postulates creating a series of phenomena that increase the probability of crime. The result, holistically, is the social reality of crime.

Because the first proposition of the theory is a definition and the sixth is a composite, the body of the theory consists of the four middle propositions. These form a model of crime's social reality. The model, as diagrammed, relates the proposition units into a theoretical system (Figure 11.1). Each unit is related to the others. The theory is thus a system of interacting developmental propositions. The phenomena denoted in the propositions and their relationships culminate in what is regarded as the amount and character of crime at any time—that is, in the social reality of crime.

The theory of the social reality of crime as I have formulated it is inspired by a change that is occurring in our view of the world. This change, pervading all levels of society, pertains to the world that we all construct and from which, at the same time, we pretend to separate ourselves in our human experiences. For the study of crime, a revision in thought has directed attention to the criminal process: All relevant phenomena contribute to creating definitions of crime, development of behaviors by those involved in criminal-defining situations, and constructing an ideology of crime. The result is the social reality of crime that is constantly being constructed in society.

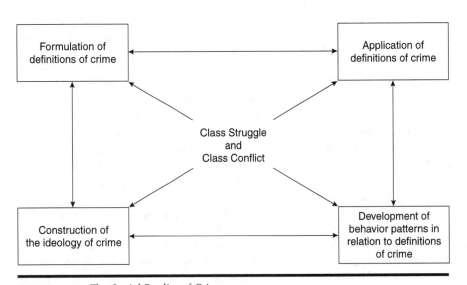

FIGURE 11.1   The Social Reality of Crime

REVIEW QUESTIONS_____

1. Identify one type of behavior that can be explained by using conflict theory.
2. How might you argue, from a conflict perspective, that changes in marijuana laws are not a reflection of the opinions of the average American but a reflection of the views of those with the capacity to make laws?

FEMINIST THEORY

KATHLEEN DALY

The [feminist] research literature on women and gender differences in lawbreaking can be divided into two categories. The first is concerned with aggregate patterns and trends from a variety of data sources, and the second addresses the qualities of offenses committed and the life worlds of lawbreakers.

PATTERNS AND TRENDS [OF LAWBREAKING]

First, self-report studies of lawbreaking show higher rates of prevalence (committing an offense) and incidence (number of times) for boys than girls. From the Denver Youth Survey (1976–1980), boys' prevalence rates were higher than girls' for eighteen of twenty offenses. Girls' prevalence rates were slightly higher for "running away from home" and "hitting a parent" (Chesney-Lind and Shelden 1992; Tripplet and Myers 1995). In general, as offense seriousness increases, the gender gap widens in measures of prevalence and incidence. A 1988–1991 survey of self-reported crime by Denver youths in "high-risk" neighborhoods (Esbensen and Huizinga 1993, p. 574) found higher prevalence rates for nongang boys than nongang girls for street crime, drug sales, and "serious offenses" but not for minor offenses or alcohol or drug use. (Incidence rates were also higher for the boys than the girls for street crime, drug sales, and alcohol use.) Not surprisingly, for both groups, prevalence rates were greater for those boys and

girls who were involved in gangs, and especially so for the girls. This "gang effect" in enhancing crime involvement was stronger, however, for the boys than for the girls in reported incidence rates.

Second, arrest data show larger gender ratios of lawbreaking than self-report studies, although a similar structure of offending is apparent. Specifically, gender gaps in lawbreaking are largest for the more serious offenses (such as violent offenses) and smaller for minor forms of property offenses. The structure of offenses for which men and women are arrested is similar: the most typical are substance abuse offenses (alcohol or drug-related) and larceny-theft (Steffensmeier and Allan 1996, p. 461).

Third, trend data for arrests from 1960 to 1990 show that the female share of all arrests rose from 10 to 20 percent; these shifts are evident for younger (under eighteen) and older women. For both age-groups, increases were greatest for larceny-theft; for older women, increases were also apparent for fraud and forgery (Steffensmeier 1993, pp. 415–21). For the thirty-year period, Darrell Steffensmeier (1993, p. 419) sees a shift in the offenses for which both men and women are arrested: today a larger share are arrested for driving under the influence, larceny-theft, and drug law violations, with a comparatively smaller share arrested for public drunkenness and disorderly conduct. Trends from the National Crime Victimization Survey (1975–1990) for the perceived sex of offenders in robbery, simple and aggravated assault, burglary, and motor vehicle theft show that

Source: Kathleen Daly, "Gender, Crime, and Criminology," in Michael Tonry (ed.), *The Handbook of Crime and Punishment* (New York: Oxford University Press, 1998), pp. 85–108. Used by permission of Oxford University Press, Inc.

the female share has remained the same over time (Steffensmeier and Allan 1996, p. 463).

Fourth, arrest data suggest that in societies and groups where there are high male arrest rates, there are high female arrest rates; where there are low male rates, there are low female rates. Over time, male and female arrest rates will rise and fall in parallel fashion, suggesting roughly similar responses to broader socioeconomic and legal forces (Steffensmeier and Allan 1996, p. 465). With such a pattern, we would expect that the profile of men and women accused, prosecuted, and imprisoned for crime would have a similar class- and race-based structure. And indeed the profile is similar: compared with their proportions in the general population, criminalized men and women are more likely to be economically marginalized and to be members of racial/ethnic minority groups; they are less likely to have completed high school.

Fifth, gender differences in arrest rates cannot be understood apart from race, ethnicity, and class. Analyses of victimization, self-report, and arrest data show major racial differences in the likelihood of involvement in crime, especially in violent offenses. For example, arrest rates for black, white, and Hispanic women for three violent offenses in New York City during 1987–1990 show significant differences: 1,670 per 100,000 for black women compared with 503 and 126, respectively, for Hispanic and white women (Sommers and Baskin 1992, p. 194). These racial/ethnic differences may be explained, in part, by where the women lived: those who lived in high-poverty neighborhoods had the highest arrest rates for violent crime compared with those who lived in low- or moderate-poverty areas. Substantially higher proportions of arrested black women lived in high-poverty neighborhoods (69 percent) than did arrested Hispanic or white women (20 and 11 percent, respectively; Sommers and Baskin 1992, p. 199).

QUALITIES OF OFFENSES AND LIFE WORLDS OF OFFENDERS

First, female involvement in gangs is more varied than earlier research (from the 1940s to the 1960s)

had revealed. . . . In surveys of gangs, estimates of female involvement range from 10 to 38 percent (Miller 1996). Esbensen and Huizinga (1993, p. 581) say that their survey-based estimate—that girls or women constitute 25 percent of gang members—is consistent with the gender composition of gangs in other research on urban areas in the late 1980s. But saying that you are "in" a gang and that you participate in criminal activities may not mean the same thing for male and female gang members. Esbensen and Huizinga (1993, pp. 572, 574) found that offending rates were twice as high for gang boys as for gang girls across a range of delinquent acts; the differences were greatest for serious forms of delinquency. It should be emphasized that even in "high-risk" areas in Denver, recent surveys suggest that the percentage of youths reporting gang membership is small, ranging from 3 to 7 percent (Esbensen and Huizinga 1993, p. 572).

Second, little is known about women's involvement or gender differences in white-collar crime. Beginning with Edwin Sutherland ([1949] 1983), researchers have assumed that *the* white-collar offender is male (e.g., Mann, Wheeler, and Sarat 1980), a not unreasonable assumption when one examines the profile of those convicted of white-collar crime (Daly 1989). For those offenses considered to be "real" forms of white-collar lawbreaking (i.e., committed by those in occupational positions of power, such as antitrust violations and securities fraud), an analysis of federal court convictions in the late 1970s shows the female share of convictions to be very low (0.5 to 2 percent). The female share of convictions for bank embezzlement was higher (45 percent); but when the specific job that convicted embezzlers held was examined, few women were bank officers or managers (7 percent), whereas just over half of the men were (Daly 1989).

An obvious explanation for gender differences in white-collar crime is to say that there are fewer workplace opportunities for women to engage in such crime. Less obvious but better explanations focus on the gendered structure of opportunities. Such explanations draw linkages between men's sexism toward women in the "upperworld" and "underworld" that may serve to exclude women from men's crime groups (Messerschmidt 1993; Steffensmeier 1983). They may also include attention to gender-based variability in motive, the size of the crime group, and offense roles that would defy a simple "workplace opportunities" argument (Daly 1989). Analyses of drug markets suggest that "opportunities" are circumscribed by particular masculine qualities thought necessary for selling and distributing drugs (Maher and Daly 1996). Gang research reveals that women themselves ratify gender hierarchies and female devaluation, even as they claim to be the equals of men (Miller 1996). Elucidating the *gendered* [emphasis added] structures of illegitimate and workplace opportunities for crime will prove a more fruitful strategy than one which makes the glib assumption that "men and women will behave in like manner when occupying similar positions in the social structure" (Simon and Landis 1991, p. 14). Indeed, this assumption cannot be sustained in explaining the lawbreaking of poor or marginalized men and women, as we have already seen. Why would we ever assume that gender divisions are less salient for more affluent men and women or those in the paid labor force?

Third, women's roles in offenses are varied. In their review of the literature, Leanne Alarid and colleagues (1996) found that in eleven of nineteen studies, women played minor or secondary roles. Alarid et al. also interviewed 104 young women (average age, twenty years) in boot camp, asking them what part they played in the crime for which they were incarcerated. They found that 15 percent of the women said they acted alone, whereas identical proportions of about 42 percent each said they had primary (or equal) and secondary roles. When the women acted with others, two sources of variability in their offense roles were noted: the woman's race-ethnicity and the offense she committed. A somewhat higher proportion of African-American (48 percent) and Hispanic women (45 percent) played primary or equal offense roles, compared with Anglo women (36 percent). Women were more likely to play primary or

equal roles (56 percent) for drug offenses than for property (36 percent) or violent (31 percent) offenses. The women were asked who influenced them to become involved in crime during the past year. While just over half of the Anglo and Hispanic women said they were "influenced by men," only 20 percent of the African-American women said they were influenced by men. But when the women were asked whether they acted as a "leader or a follower when with [their] friends," a similar proportion of both Anglo (38 percent) and African-American (33 percent) women said they were followers. My interpretation of these data is that a larger portion of African-American women are influenced by other African-American women to become involved in crime than are Anglo women, whose deviant pathways appear to be related more to men's influences. Such Anglo and African-American differences were also found in Lisa Maher's (1995) research on New York City women's initiation into drug use.

Fourth, research on gender, offense contexts, and motives is most developed for homicide (see reviews by Ogle, Maier-Katkin, and Bernard 1995; Wilson and Daly 1992). From this research we find that women represent a small share (about 10–12 percent) of homicide arrests. They are more likely to kill intimates (spouses or partners) than are men, who are more likely to kill acquaintances or strangers. The victims of women's homicides are more likely to have initiated the violence than are the victims of men's homicides. Women's homicides generally occur in their own or the victim's residence, while men's homicides occur more frequently outside residential settings. The situational and relational differences in men's and women's homicides can be explained, in part, by the fact that fewer women's homicides occur in the course of robberies, burglaries, or rapes. Ogle, Maier-Katkin, and Bernard report that the "consistency of the pattern of homicides by women, as well as the differences from the patterns of homicides by men, suggests the need for a separate theoretical explanation of female homicide" (1995, p. 174). I am not persuaded that homicide requires a separate theory from, say, aggravated or simple assault. More important, it is not clear that homicide patterns for women are "consistent" when one considers data from other countries. Margo Wilson and Martin Daly (1992, p. 191) show that U.S. women (especially black women) are far more likely to kill male spouses or cohabitants than are women in Canada, England and Wales, Scotland, Australia, or other countries. They argue against a simple "underclass" or "black" explanation for this pattern and instead suggest a focus on structured and situational sources of marital conflict: the social and economic devaluation of minority group men, which [increases] the men's desire to coerce female partners; residential and kin patterns, which may empower some women to retaliate; and the incidence of step-relationships, which may increase the frequency with which women need to defend their children.

Fifth, girls' and women's pathways to lawbreaking are many and varied. Drawing from U.S. and non-U.S. studies, I identified what I termed the "leading feminist scenario" of women's lawbreaking, that of street women (Daly 1994). These women may have run from abusive households to the street, or they may have been attracted to the "fast money" of a deviant lifestyle. Once on the street, young women engage in petty hustles or prostitution. Life on the street may lead to drug use and addiction, which may lead to more frequent lawbreaking to support a drug habit.

Interview studies by Arnold (1990), Chesney-Lind and Shelden (1992, chap. 9), and Gilfus (1992) have centered attention on girls' sexual and physical victimization while growing up, their efforts to escape abuse and violence, and the consequent "criminalizing of girls' survival" (Chesney-Lind 1989) on the streets. Eleanor Miller (1986) identified several routes for Milwaukee street women: those running away from home to the streets, and those whose households were connected to the streets via "domestic networks." In my analysis of the biographies of forty women prosecuted in the New Haven felony court, I found that street women characterized about a third of my sample. As frequent was a second group I termed "harmed and harming women." These women had chaotic and difficult experiences growing up, with violent or "out of control" behavior evinced in childhood or adolescence. Other groups of New Haven women had associates who used or sold drugs (drug-connected women, about 15 percent) or were fending off and fighting abusive partners (battered women, about 10 percent; Daly 1994).

EXPLAINING PATTERNS OF LAWBREAKING

A decade ago, Meda Chesney-Lind and I identified two related, though distinct, theoretical problems for . . . the study of women, gender, and crime. They are the gender ratio problem (why are men more likely involved in or arrested for crime than women?) and the generalizability problem (do theories of crime based on boys' or men's lives apply to girls or women?; Daly and Chesney-Lind 1988). For most nonfeminist scholars, interest remains in addressing the gender ratio problem, with the working assumption that a "gender-neutral" theory is preferable. Here we see a clash in theoretical objectives.

On the one hand, Darrell Steffensmeier and Emilie Allan suggest that "the traditional gender-neutral theories [derived from male samples] provide reasonable explanations of less serious forms of [crime]" for men and women (1996, p. 473). Such thinking is common in nonfeminist and liberal feminist analyses of gender and crime (e.g., Smith and Paternoster 1987; Simon and Landis 1991). On the other hand, feminist scholars, including myself, find it illogical to say that traditional theories derived from male samples are gender-neutral. Traditional theories are more appropriately labeled *male-specific,* not gender-neutral. Such theories may, of course, be relevant to girls and women: we would expect that elements of social control, learning, labeling, and opportunity would be applicable in a general sense. However, even if particular elements are applicable, they may not be applicable in the same ways or to the same degree. Likewise, elements from theories developed from all-female samples may be applicable to boys and men, but not necessarily in the same ways or to the same degree.

We should abandon the concept of, and the quest for, gender-neutral criminological theories. Instead, we should use terms that better describe the theoretical enterprise: to identify variables, factors, or conceptual elements that have similar and different influences on lawbreaking for boys/men and girls/women. This is just one potential focus of theoretical work; there are others, as follows.

Gender ratio of crime. What is the nature of, and what explains the "gender gap" in, lawbreaking and arrests for crime? What is the nature of, and what explains variation in, the kinds of offenses that girls/women and boys/men get involved with (or arrested for), in terms of both prevalence and incidence? What is the nature of, and what explains gender-based variation in, arrest rates across nations, including developed and developing countries?

Gendered crime. What are the contexts and qualities of boys'/men's and girls'/women's illegal acts? What is the social organization of specific offenses (e.g., drug dealing, prostitution, and credit frauds)?

Gendered pathways to lawbreaking. What is the nature of, and what explains the character of, girls'/women's and boys'/men's pathways to lawbreaking? What brings people to the street, to use illegal drugs, to become involved in workplace crime, or to be arrested and prosecuted for crime? How do boys/men and girls/women move in and out of foster homes, conventional work, jails and prisons, hospitals, and halfway houses?

Gendered lives. How does gender organize the ways in which men and women survive, take care of themselves and their children, and find shelter and food? How does gender structure thinkable courses of action and identities?

Researchers may address these thematics with a focus on class, racial-ethnic, age, regional, or other sources of variability. Or they may decide to analyze one particular group, such as black women. Using Don Gibbons's (1994) categories, the gender ratio of crime and gendered crime address "the rates question," gendered crime and gendered pathways attend to questions of "why they did it," and gendered lives examines general life course trajectories that may or may not include lawbreaking. . . . Nonfeminist inquiries on gender and crime are principally focused on the gender ratio and gendered crime problems; they attempt to measure rates of involvement in crime/delinquency and to explain [gender] "gaps" in such involvement. Scholars in this tradition may draw from a nascent understanding of feminist theories, but their guiding metaphors and concepts come largely from [traditional] criminology. By comparison, feminist inquiries on gender and crime are principally focused on demonstrating the ways in which the social organization of gender shapes women's and men's lives on the streets and in neighborhoods, workplaces, and households. [Feminist] research tends to focus on gendered crime, gendered pathways, and gendered lives,

REFERENCES

Alarid, Leanne Fiftal, James W. Marquart, Veliner S. Burston Jr., Francis T. Cullen, and Steven J. Cuvelier. 1996. "Women's Roles in Serious Offenses: A Study of Adult Felons." *Justice Quarterly* 13:431–54.

Arnold, Regina. 1990. "Processes of Victimization and Criminalization of Black Women." *Social Justice* 17:153–66.

Chesney-Lind, Meda. 1989. "Girls' Crime and Woman's Place: Toward a Feminist Model of Female Delinquency." *Crime and Delinquency* 35:5–29.

Chesney-Lind, Meda, and Randall G. Shelden. 1992. *Girls, Delinquency, and Juvenile Justice.* Pacific Grove. Calif.: Brooks/Cole.

Daly, Kathleen. 1989. "Gender and Varieties of White-Collar Crime." *Criminology* 27:769–94.

———. 1994. *Gender, Crime, and Punishment.* New Haven, Conn.: Yale University Press.

Daly, Kathleen, and Meda Chesney-Lind. 1988. "Feminism and Criminology." *Justice Quarterly* 5:497–538.

Esbensen, Finn-Aage, and David Huizinga. 1993. "Gangs, Drugs, and Delinquency in a Survey of Urban Youth." *Criminology* 31:565–87.

Gibbons, Don C. 1994. *Talking about Crime and Criminals: Problems and Issues in Theory Development in Criminology.* Englewood Cliffs, N.J.: Prentice-Hall.

Gilfus, Mary E. 1992. "From Victims to Survivors to Offenders: Women's Routes of Entry and Immersion into Street Crime." *Women and Criminal Justice* 4:63–89.

Maher, Lisa. 1995. "In the Name of Love: Women and Initiation to Illicit Drugs." In *Gender and Crime,* edited by R. Emerson Dobash, Russell P. Dobash, and Lesley Noakes. Cardiff: University of Wales Press.

Maher, Lisa, and Kathleen Daly. 1996. "Women in the Street-Level Drug Economy: Continuity or Change?" *Criminology* 34:465–91.

Mann, Kenneth, Stanton Wheeler, and Austin Sarat. 1980. "Sentencing the White-Collar Offender." *American Criminal Law Review* 17:479–500.

Messerschmidt, James W. 1993. *Masculinities and Crime: Critique and Reconceptualization of Theory.* Lanham, Md.: Rowman and Littlefield.

Miller, Eleanor. 1986. *Street Woman.* Philadelphia: Temple University Press.

Miller, Jody. 1996. "Female Gang Involvement in a Midwestern City: Correlates, Nature, and Meanings." Ph.D. diss., University of Southern California, Department of Sociology.

Ogle, Robbin, Daniel Maher-Katkin, and Thomas J. Bernard. 1995. "A Theory of Homicidal Behavior among Women." *Criminology* 33:173–93.

Simon, Rita, and Jean Landis. 1991. *The Crimes Women Commit, the Punishments They Receive.* Lexington, Mass.: Lexington Books.

Smith, Douglas A., and Raymond Paternoster. 1987. "The Gender Gap in Theories of Deviance: Issues and Evidence." *Journal of Research in Crime and Delinquency* 24:140–72:

Sommers, Ira, and Deborah Baskin. 1992. "Sex, Race, Age, and Violent Offending." *Violence and Victims* 7:191–201.

Steffensmeier, Darrell. 1983. "Organization Properties and Sex-Segregation in the Underworld: Building a Sociological Theory of Sex Differences in Crime." *Social Forces* 61:1010–32.

———. 1993. "National Trends in Female Arrests, 1960–1990: Assessment and Recommendations for Research." *Journal of Quantitative Criminology* 9:411–41.

Steffensmeier, Darrell, and Emilie Allan. 1996. "Gender and Crime: Toward a Gendered Theory of Female Offending." *Annual Review of Sociology* 22:459–87.

Sutherland, Edwin H. [1949] 1983. *White Collar Crime: The Uncut Version.* New Haven, Conn.: Yale University Press.

Tripplet, Ruth, and Laura B. Myers. 1995. "Evaluating Contextual Patterns of Delinquency: Gender-Based Differences." *Justice Quarterly* 12:59–84.

Wilson, Margo, and Martin Daly. 1992. "Who Kills Whom in Spouse Killings? On the Exceptional Sex Ratio of Spousal Homicides in the United States." *Criminology* 30:189–215.

REVIEW QUESTIONS

1. What are the patterns and trends of the gender differences in lawbreaking? How would you explain these differences?
2. What is the distinctive nature of the offenses committed by females?

POSTMODERNIST THEORY

DAVID O. FRIEDRICHS
JESSICA FRIEDRICHS

WHAT IS POSTMODERNISM?

The premise for this article is simple: The student of deviance should have at least some understanding of the meaning of postmodernism and its relevance for the study of deviance. The term *postmodern,* although invoked much earlier, only began to be widely used in the final two decades of the twentieth century (B. Smart, 1993). By century's end a vast literature, cutting across many different disciplines, was adopting a postmodernist perspective in one way or another. A subject search on postmodernism in *Books in Print,* for example, comes up with 839 titles. Accordingly, most if not all readers of this article will have encountered the term postmodern in some form. But to what does this term refer? It does not have a single, fixed meaning. In fact, it has been used in so many ways some scholars have called for its abandonment. Nevertheless, whether we like it or not, postmodernism is surely here to stay, so it makes sense to try to identify some of the principal ways in which the term is invoked. The "post" in postmodernism reflects both the notion of "after" (or a time following the modern) and "against" (in opposition to modern sensibilities and assumptions). The term has also been used in more specific ways. First, postmodernism deals with postmodernity. This term is used to refer to a period in human history that follows the period designated as the modern. The modern era is generally thought to have begun to emerge in the fifteenth or sixteenth century, with the beginnings of

capitalism and colonialism and eventually the effects of the Enlightenment period and the Industrial Revolution (Lembcke, 1993). This "modern" way of life accelerated and expanded until about the 1960s. Since then the Western world has undergone a basic transformation and thus entered the postmodern era. In this new era we have seen the collapse of the Euro-American colonial system around the globe, which has left the world without a dominating center and has produced widespread repudiation of the Euro-American value system (Lemert, 1997). In this postmodern era, globalization has also emerged, with various societies powerfully influencing each other and threatening the native culture and way of life in those societies (Benhabib, 1999).

Our postmodern society seems to be changing rapidly in many different ways. Our communities are fragmented, complex, and increasingly "virtual," for example, linking people via the Internet. We are in the heart of a global community, simultaneously transmitting and receiving materials and ideas to and from other societies. Conventional forms of bureaucracy are giving way to more flexible, adaptable "adhocracies," with constant changing of institutional arrangements and roles to fit specific situations. The computer has rapidly been replacing industrial machinery as the core of our technological existence. Mass communication is evolving with almost lightning speed into a form of interactive communication, as exemplified by cable television, the Internet,

Source: Written specifically for this reader, with substantial editing and condensing by Alex Thio.

and home shopping. Growing "fluidity" is taking place in residence and career, with people moving back and forth between different residential locations and in and out of different careers. All these changes inevitably affect deviant behavior and societal responses to deviance. For example, in the increasingly market-dependent economy of our postmodern era, the poor are less and less needed as cheap labor and are turning in growing numbers to criminal behavior (Bauman, 1997). It is therefore important to understand postmodernity in order to understand deviance.

Postmodernism also reflects postmodern thought. This term has been applied to a collection of ideas from a number of late-twentieth-century French philosophers. These ideas include: there is no absolute truth nor stable, fixed meaning in the world; differences of ideas should be celebrated; any attempt to explain the whole of human social existence should be rejected; local action as opposed to collective or centralized action should be used to transform society; and positivism, such as the scientific method, should be repudiated as a means of understanding the human condition (Rosenau, 1992).

Postmodern thought challenges conventional conceptions of the individual or the human subject as a real, independent entity and instead espouses the idea that the individual is knowable only through the language used in interaction with others. Skeptical postmodernists offer a largely negative, hopeless view of the social world with an emphasis on oppression, fragmentation, meaninglessness, vanishing morals, and social chaos (Rosenau, 1992). Some skeptical postmodernists even question the relevance of the social sciences for interpreting the social world, insofar as there is no objective truth about that world. Other postmodern thinkers—affirmative postmodernists—provide a more hopeful, optimistic view, being open to positive action as long as such action is tentative, nondogmatic, and nonideological (Rosenau, 1992). For both strains of postmodernists, language plays a central role in the human experience of reality, so the key to understanding human behavior and events is through an analysis of language.

In sum, college students, including those who study deviance, can benefit from knowing about postmodernism. This does not necessarily mean that students need to undertake a rigorous, intense, and comprehensive study of postmodernism (Friedrichs, 1999). It is, however, an aspect of being culturally literate today to have at least some familiarity with postmodernism. It offers an alternative to conventional perspectives on social reality, including deviance. In the next section we will see how a postmodern criminology has emerged and how it can be applied to the understanding of deviant behavior.

POSTMODERN CRIMINOLOGY AND THE STUDY OF DEVIANCE

Long after postmodern thought had become a significant presence in many areas of intellectual inquiry, it remained little represented in the fields of criminology and deviance (Schwartz and Friedrichs, 1994; Russell, 1997; South, 1997). In the final decade of the twentieth century this began to change. Leading promoters of a postmodern criminology among U.S. criminologists have looked to French postmodern thinkers for inspiration and for perspectives and concepts applicable to crime and deviance. However, their work also reflects the influence of other theoretical perspectives within sociology and criminology, such as conflict, critical, or radical criminology (Arrigo, 1999; MacLean and Milovanovic, 1997). On the other hand, postmodern criminology does not emphasize the larger issues of social conflict and power. It focuses more on the day-to-day struggles and problems of the human subject, which distinguishes postmodern criminology from conflict or radical theory (Arrigo and Bernard, 1997). In short, postmodern criminology has some parallels and intersecting concerns with other theoretical perspectives but also has its own unique dimensions.

Postmodern criminologists generally have a keen appreciation for human diversity and differences, including those shown by deviants. Compared with other perspectives, postmodernism pays more attention to the outlook and voice of deviants as the marginalized or outsiders of society.

Postmodern criminologists challenge the basic claim of the dominant social "discourse" and seek to "replace" that discourse with the voices of those who are different or powerless, such as criminals and deviants. Revolutionaries who fight for a better society, for example, are considered deviants in the dominant discourse, but they can be considered merely different or powerless according to one postmodernist view. The power of language to do harm, such as a school authority who labels hyperactive pupils as troublemakers who need to be punished, is one core thesis of postmodern criminology. Such a criminology focuses on how language is used not only to control but also to destroy those who are different. Language is central, then, to the process of transforming some members of society into deviants, and postmodern criminology is committed to revealing more fully how this transformation works.

At least two postmodern concepts are arguably useful in the understanding of deviance. First the notion of *intertextuality* refers to the idea that there is a complex and infinite set of interwoven relationships, comparable to an endless conversation among different individuals without any prospect of achieving an agreement or final resolution (Bauman, 1990; Graham, 1992). This suggests the need to explore the complex interrelationships among many different forms of deviant behavior—for example, how domestic violence, mental illness, sexual perversion, substance abuse, and corporate crime interact with each other. The concept of intertextuality further suggests that we must attend to the complex ways in which convention and deviation define each other, with ambiguous lines of demarcation between them, so that what is conventional (say, worshiping God) may sometimes be considered deviant (if one is seen as part of a religious cult). The postmodern approach challenges the popular tendency to draw a clear-cut and fixed boundary between convention and deviance.

Another postmodern concept, *hyperreality,* is also useful for understanding deviance (Baudrillard, 1994). We live in a world in which we are inundated with simulations of the real, as can be seen in the pervasive presence of television in our lives. A postmodern, hyperreal world is also perceivable through contemporary advertising, gangsta rap, karaoke, and cybersex (Appignanesi and Garratt, 1995). When we can no longer tell the difference between simulation and reality, when simulation becomes autonomous, and when we are no longer able to verify simulation against reality, then we have entered the realm of the hyperreal. Of course, not everybody is sucked totally into the hyperreal (King, 1998). However, most people cannot escape hyperreality, which inevitably influences many lives to one degree or another. Because the concept of hyperreality usefully captures the erosion of the boundaries between the real and the unreal, it may broaden our understanding of deviance. Consider Las Vegas, America's fastest growing city in the 1990s. In Las Vegas, simulation displaces a reality rooted in the conditions of a natural environment and authentic human experiences. It reeks with the celebration of money as an end in itself (rather than simply as a means), of a world divided into winners and losers, of materialistic excess, of conflict, of sexism and exploitation, of artificiality and inauthenticity, of "amusing ourselves to death," and of excitement over the clatter of slot machine payouts. All these reflect the simulated, unreal quality of human life. Not surprisingly, all manner of deviance, as conventionally defined, thrives in the Las Vegas environment: rates of homicide and suicide in Las Vegas are exceptionally high; sex workers of all types are ubiquitous; substance abuse is a runaway problem; and, of course, compulsive and self-destructive gamblers are all over (Friedrichs, 1996).

On the other hand, hyperreality can also convey a false impression of a totally conventional world with no apparent deviance. Consider Disneyland/ Disney World. In sharp contrast with Las Vegas, Disney promotes a wholesome, fun-filled, thoroughly controlled environment where nothing bad or painful happens, where there is no crime or substance abuse or even sex in any recognizable form (Ritzer, 1999). For that matter, some isolated college campuses and college towns have also turned into "unreal" environments vis-à-vis the outside world, but they are not simply similar to Disney World in creating a simulated, unreal, and idealized conventional milieu. They are also similar to Las Vegas in having drinking problems, wild parties, and other deviant activities on campus.

The link between simulation and reality that may lead to deviance also appears in some contemporary films. In *The Truman Show* and *Pleasantville,* idealized simulated communities replace real-life experiences, which raises complicated questions about such experiences. The films *Natural Born Killers* and *Pulp Fiction* explore the complex, interactive relationship between contemporary violence as reality and the media representations of violence. On television, the cult show *Twin Peaks* exemplified the hyperreal phenomena, whereas many television shows create unreal worlds either pervaded with deviance like Las Vegas or reflecting a totally sanitized environment à la Disney World. Video games, too, draw young people into a simulated world in a powerful way. The simulated violence of television and video games tends to lead to violence among troubled teenagers, as has been suggested by a series of school shootings in recent years. This has caused some to ask: Are such teenagers unable to discriminate between the virtual reality of violence and the actual violence in real life that truly hurts people?

Postmodern criminology has quite a number of distinctive strains, but we here consider several that are especially applicable to understanding deviance. One is deconstructionist criminology (Pfohl, 1990; 1994). This suggests that, like crime, deviance can best be understood through deconstruction, or destruction of a conventional way of looking at deviance that is biased by an author's attempt to control powerless deviants. More positively, better understanding can come from analyzing deviance from the perspective of deviants, from knowing what deviants think and feel about themselves and others. A deconstructionist criminology breaks with conventional forms of communicating knowledge by using a multimedia approach with a complex mixture of images and observations.

A second type of postmodern criminology is constitutive criminology (Henry and Milovanovic, 1996). It regards crime (and by extension, deviance) as involving the power to do harm. It further proposes that social beings, such as members of groups and society, as well as social entities, such as groups, institutions, and society, work together in some complex ways to produce crime and deviance. According to constitutive criminology, then, individuals do not by themselves engage in criminal and deviant activities but coproduce what is defined as deviance in the course of their interaction with others. New forms of dialogue, then, can foster greater justice.

A third type of postmodern criminology is cultural criminology (Ferrell and Sanders, 1995). It exposes "crime as culture," emphasizing how crime or deviance can be understood in a cultural context, as a particular way of life, in relation to such forms of behavior as involvement with illicit drugs, posting graffiti, and skinhead violence. The media is viewed as often distorting images of crime and deviance and accordingly promoting inappropriate responses to it. The media generates drug scares and helps foster the image of serial killers as "mythic monsters."

A fourth type of postmodern criminology is postmodern feminist criminology (C. Smart, 1990, 1995). To postmodern feminists, the self does not have a fixed, unchangeable identity but instead varies from one situation to another (Benhabib, 1999; Carrington, 1994). This fluid and changing nature of a woman's self can be applied to deviance: like the woman's self, deviance varies from situation to situation. A postmodern feminist criminology, for example, questions such categories as "wife" and "lesbian"; it suggests more tolerance for ambiguity.

THE CRITIQUE OF POSTMODERNISM

Postmodernist theory has been widely criticized for a variety of reasons. The most common criticism is that the proponents of the theory do not write clearly. As a result, their convoluted, confusing writing often makes the reader unsure of what the postmodernists are talking about. Another criticism is that postmodernists do not have any special training in physics and mathematics and yet some postmodernists try to use quantum mechanics, chaos theory, and other esoteric physical sciences to explain human behavior. Not surprisingly, according to scientists such as Nobel Prize–winning physicist Steven Weinberg (1996), postmodernists get the science wrong and apply scientific concepts incoherently. Most directly relevant to the study of deviance, however, is the criticism that the postmodernist ideas about deviance are not unique or new because they can be found in conflict and symbolic interactionist theories.

Postmodern thought has also been criticized as being inherently conservative and defeatist (Handler, 1992; Taylor-Gooby, 1994). Postmodernism repudiates the assignment of people to categories, but women, minority groups and marginalized deviants (e.g., homosexuals) who are still establishing their "selves" are not necessarily prepared to reject their group identity (Rosenau, 1992). Critics would argue that conditions such as discrimination against homosexuals are best confronted directly, rather than in terms of a postmodernist perspective.

No matter how postmodernism is judged, it does enhance in its own way our understanding of deviance, and reinforces what we already know from other older theories. However, it requires patience to cut through the thick brambles of postmodernist prose to get at what is being said.

THE FUTURE OF POSTMODERNISM

What will the status of postmodernist theory be in the new century? One possible scenario is that postmodernism may be largely discredited, disparaged, forgotten, or written off as a pretentious late-twentieth-century intellectual fad. It could meet the same fate as phrenology (the nineteenth-century pseudoscience that human character could be determined by feeling the bumps on the head), which fell into disrepute in the twentieth century. On the other hand, postmodernism could hypothetically become the dominant form of intellectual discourse, to be hailed as the pathbreaking perspective for making sense of the human world, including deviant behavior. The most likely scenario probably falls somewhere between those two extremes. Postmodernist theory will likely evolve, with some of its ideas falling by the wayside and others being refined and becoming more widely accepted. When applied to the study of deviance, postmodernist theory will probably co-exist with other approaches more rooted in traditional and modern thought. But the serious student of deviance should surely be open to the usefulness of some postmodern concepts and metaphors for more fully understanding the production and control of deviant behavior in a rapidly changing world.

APPENDIX: A BRIEF GUIDE TO THE LITERATURE ON POSTMODERNISM

The literature on postmodernist theory is vast, and the original works of the French philosophers who have pioneered this approach are especially difficult. If you are interested in some general guidance on postmodernism and postmodern thought, going beyond what has been provided in this article, you may want to consult works by the following authors, listed in the References section: Anderson (1995); Appignanesi and Garratt (1995); Crook, Pakulski, and Waters (1992); Dickens and Fontana (1994); Doherty, Graham, and Malek (1992); Grenz (1996); Harvey (1989); Hollinger (1994); Kumar (1995); Rosenau (1992); Sarap (1993); Sim (1999); Barry Smart (1993); and Turner (1990).

ACKNOWLEDGMENTS

The support of a University of Scranton Faculty Research grant is gratefully acknowledged. David Friedrichs would like to thank Martin D. Schwartz, as this article draws significantly from our collaborative work on postmodern criminology. He would also like to note that over the years he has learned much about postmodern criminology from Bruce Arrigo, Stuart Henry, and Dragan Milovanovic, esteemed professional colleagues and friends. Jessica Friedrichs would like to thank Greg Lawless and Matt Fagerberg for helpful discussions. Both David and Jessica Friedrichs thank Jeanne and Bryan Friedrichs for putting up with us while we worked on this article.

REFERENCES

Anderson, Walter Truett, ed. 1995. *The Truth about the Truth: De-Confusing and Re-Constructing the Postmodern World.* New York: Tarcher/Putnam Books.

Appignanesi, Richard, and Chris Garratt. 1995. *Introducing Postmodernism.* New York: Totem Books.

Arrigo, Bruce, ed. 1999. *Social Justice/Criminal Justice: The Maturation of Critical Theory in Law, Crime, and Deviance.* Belmont, CA: ITP/Wadsworth.

Arrigo, Bruce, and Thomas J. Bernard. 1997. "Postmodern Criminology in Relation to Radical and Conflict Criminology." *Critical Criminology: An International Journal* 8:39–60.

Baudrillard, J. 1994. *Simulacra and Simulation.* Ann Arbor: University of Michigan Press.

Bauman, Zygmunt. 1990. "Philosophical Affinities of Postmodern Sociology." *Sociological Review* 38: 411–444.

Bauman, Zygmunt. 1997. *Postmodernity and Its Discontents.* New York: New York University Press.

Benhabib, Seyla. 1999. "Sexual Difference and Collective Identities: The New Global Constellation." *Signs: Journal of Women in Culture and Society* 24: 335–361.

Carrington, Kerry. 1994. "Postmodernism and Feminist Criminologies: Disconnecting Discourses?" *International Journal of the Sociology of Law* 22:261–277.

Crook, Stephen, Jan Pakulski, and Malcolm Waters. 1992. *Postmodernization: Change in Advanced Society.* London: Sage.

Dickens, David R., and Andrea Fontana, eds. 1994. *Postmodernism and Social Inquiry.* New York: Guilford Press.

Doherty, Joe, Elspeth Graham, and Mo Malek, eds. 1992. *Postmodernism and the Social Sciences.* New York: St. Martin's.

Ferrell, Jeff, and Clinton R. Sanders, eds. 1995. *Cultural Criminology.* Boston, MA: Northeastern University Press.

Friedrichs, David O. 1996. "Critical Criminology and Progressive Pluralism: Strength in Diversity for These Times." *Critical Criminology: An International Journal* 7:121–128.

Friedrichs, David O. 1999. "Can Students Benefit from an Intensive Engagement with Postmodern Criminology? No." Pp. 159–164 in *Controversial Issues in Criminology,* edited by John R. Fuller and Eric W. Hickey. Boston: Allyn & Bacon.

Graham, Elspeth. 1992. "Postmodernism and Paradox." Pp. 197–211 in *Postmodernism and the Social Sciences,* edited by Joe Doherty, Elspeth Graham and Mo Malek. New York: St. Martin's.

Grenz, S. J. 1996. *A Primer on Postmodernism.* Grand Rapids, MI: Eardmans.

Handler, Joel F. 1992. "Postmodernism, Protest, and the New Social Movements." *Law & Society Review* 26:697–732.

Harvey, David. 1989. *The Condition of Postmodernity.* Cambridge, MA: Blackwell.

Henry, Stuart, and Dragan Milovanovic. 1996. *Constitutive Criminology: Beyond Postmodernism.* London: Sage.

Hollinger, Robert. 1994. *Postmodernism and the Social Sciences.* Thousand Oaks, CA: Sage.

King, Anthony. 1998. "A Critique of Baudrillard's Hyperreality: Towards a Sociology of Postmodernism." *Philosophy & Social Criticism* 6:47–66.

Kumar, Krishan. 1995. *From Post-Industrial to Post-Modern Society: New Theories of the Contemporary World.* Oxford, UK: Blackwell.

Lembcke, Jerry Lee. 1993. "Classical Theory, Post-modernism, and the Sociology Liberal Arts Curriculum." *The American Sociologist* 24:55–68.

Lemert, Charles. 1997. *Postmodernism Is Not What You Think.* Oxford, UK: Blackwell.

MacLean, Brian D., and Dragan Milovanovic. 1997. *Thinking Critically about Crime.* Vancouver, BC: Collective Press.

Pfohl, Stephen C. 1990. "Welcome to the PARASITE CAFE: Postmodernity as a Social Problem." *Social Problems* 37:421–442.

Pfohl, Stephen C. 1994. *Images of Deviance and Social Control,* 2nd ed. New York: McGraw-Hill.

Ritzer, George. 1999. *Enchanting a Disenchanted World: Revolutionizing the Means of Consumption.* Thousand Oaks, CA: Pine Forge Press.

Rosenau, Pauline Marie. 1992. *Post-Modernism and the Social Sciences: Insights, Inroads, and Intrusions.* Princeton, NJ: Princeton University Press.

Russell, Stuart. 1997. "The Failure of Postmodern Criminology." *Critical Criminology: An International Journal* 8:61–90.

Sarap, Madan. 1993. *An Introductory Guide to Post-Structuralism and Post-Modernism,* 2nd ed. Athens: University of Georgia Press.

Schwartz, Martin D., and David O. Friedrichs. 1994. "Postmodern Thought and Criminological Discontent: New Metaphors for Understanding Violence." *Criminology* 32:221–246.

Sim, Stuart, ed. 1999. *Critical Dictionary of Postmodern Thought.* New York: Routledge.

Smart, Barry. 1993. *Postmodernity.* London: Routledge.

Smart, Carol. 1990. "Feminist Approaches to Criminology, or Postmodern Woman Meets Atavistic Man." Pp. 70–84 in *Feminist Perspectives in Criminology,* edited by A. Morris. Buckingham, UK: Open University Press.

Smart, Carol. 1995. *Law, Crime, and Sexuality.* London: Sage.

South, Nigel. 1997. "Late-Modern Criminology: 'Late' as in 'Dead' or 'Modern' as in 'New.' " Pp. 81–102 in *Sociology after Postmodernism,* edited by David Owen. London: Sage.

Taylor-Gooby, Peter. 1994. "Postmodernism and Social Policy: A Great Leap Backwards?" *Journal of Social Policy* 23:385–404.

Turner, Bryan S. 1990. *Theories of Modernity and Postmodernity.* London: Sage.

Weinberg, Steven. 1996. "Sokal's Hoax." *New York Review of Books* August 8, pp. 11–15.

REVIEW QUESTIONS

1. According to the authors of this article, college students "can benefit from knowing postmodernism." How do the authors arrive at this conclusion?

2. What do the authors mean when discussing the concept "hyperreality"? Cite an example of this concept *not* identified in the article.

PART FOUR

PHYSICAL VIOLENCE

In March 2002, a Palestinian suicide bomber blew himself up at a café in Jerusalem, taking eleven Israelis with him to the hereafter. Shalita, 25, a member of Israel's Disaster Victims Identification team, arrived at the restaurant a few minutes after the explosion. He saw that "the walls were covered with blood. There were broken tables, plates, salads all over the floor, total chaos. People were lying in a pile, one on top of the other, in a pool of blood."[1] The Israeli government retaliated by having its soldiers destroy the home of the Palestinian assailant. In August 2002, one day after his 17-year-old son blew himself up in a Jerusalem suicide attack, the Palestinian schoolteacher Ata Sarasra saw his seven-bedroom home reduced to rubble by Israeli soldiers. He mourned for his house, which he had built with savings from wages he had earned working for two decades in the United Arab Emirates. He also mourned for his son but was proud of him for having "died a martyr, thank God." The cycle of violence between the Israelis and the Palestinians cost the lives of 607 Israelis and 1,702 Palestinians between August 2000 and August 2002.[2]

What is the nature of that physical violence in Israel? Does it have something in common with other forms of violence? What causes violence in general? And what are the similarities and differences among the causes of various forms of violence? We may get the answers by reading and pondering the articles presented here. In the first article, "Men and Violence: Is the Pattern Universal?" Dane Archer and Patricia McDaniel offer research evidence to settle the issue of whether men in other societies are as violent as their counterparts in the United States. In the second article, "Serial Murder: Popular Myths and Empirical Realities," James Alan Fox and Jack Levin critically examine a number of popular beliefs about serial killers. In the third reading, "The Violence of Hate," Jack Levin analyzes the nature of hate crime. In the fourth selection, "What Makes Suicide Bombers Tick?" Eyad Sarraj and Ehud Sprinzak offer the Palestinian and Israeli views on the causes of suicide bombing.

1. Larry Derfner, "After a Suicide Bomb," *U.S. News & World Report,* August 19, 2002, pp. 24–26.
2. Matt Rees, "Where to Now?" *Time,* August 19, 2002, pp. 28–31.

MEN AND VIOLENCE:
IS THE PATTERN UNIVERSAL?

DANE ARCHER
PATRICIA McDANIEL

Men are more likely than women to commit virtually all types of violent crimes in the United States. This male-female difference is one of the best-known findings in American criminology. On closer inspection, however, this apparently "obvious" finding turns out to be poorly understood. Is the link between gender and violence strictly an American phenomenon, or is the pattern also found in other, very different societies? Also, how well do we understand the *reasons* for the maleness–violence link—does this pattern reflect socialization patterns, cultural factors, or biological differences between the sexes?

Questions about violence have a special urgency in American society. Although violence and aggression are considered important social problems in many societies, the United States leads the industrial world in lethal violence. In any given year, out of every hundred thousand Americans, ten will die from homicide. This homicide rate is 50 times as high as the rate in New Zealand, 30 times as high as the rate in Great Britain, and 10 times as high as the rate in France (Archer and Gartner, 1984). In fact, the American homicide rate is grossly higher than the rate in *any* other industrial nation. This difference is so large that even societies undergoing civil wars—such as the periodic factional strife in Northern Ireland—do not reach the normal, everyday, *av-erage* homicide rate of the United States. Clearly, then, violence constitutes an urgent social agenda for American society.

THEORIES ABOUT GENDER AND VIOLENCE

The research literature on violence and aggression is enormous. Any exhaustive review requires a book-length treatment (e.g., Goldstein, 1986), and thus will not be attempted here. Instead, exemplars of different theoretical traditions will be used to contrast the very different perspectives embedded in research on biological, social, and cultural factors that may cause violence and aggression.

Biological theories have provided intriguing but inconclusive findings. For example, Christiansen and Knussman (1987) compared self-ratings of aggressiveness in 117 individuals with actual levels of serum testosterone. The researchers found a positive correlation—that is, individuals with higher self-ratings tended to have higher levels of serum testosterone—but the relationship was not strong. Rada, Laws, and Kellner (1976) compared 52 men imprisoned for rape with a control group of 12 nonviolent prisoners. In general, the two groups did not differ in testosterone levels, but the most violent rapists (those who committed additional, brutal violence during the rape) did have significantly higher testosterone levels.

Source: Written specifically for this reader, with some shortening by Alex Thio. The research was supported by a grant from the H. F. Guggenheim Foundation and by the University of California.

[Research on social factors has shown] that parental socialization tended to foster greater levels of aggression in boys (Sears, Maccoby, and Levin, 1957). Parents are more likely to encourage boys to fight back if they are challenged and—at least in American society—this encouragement reflects a widespread parental belief that some aggression is a natural, even desirable aspect of masculinity. The picture is quite different for girls. Parents tend to discourage female aggression, or they simply ignore it. In either case, the net effect is the same: female aggression is simply not reinforced. Research by Bardwick (1971) suggested, though, that although girls were socialized away from using direct physical aggression (the province of boys), they were socialized *toward* other forms of aggression: verbal aggression, subtle interpersonal rejection, manipulation, and so on. Still, it is precisely *physical* aggression that has become urgently problematic. After all, physical aggression—homicide, assault, or rape—wreaks a much greater toll than verbal unpleasantness.

Much of the research sketched thus far reflects American society. . . . It is obviously critical to include in our discussion *cultural* factors by asking how aggression and the male-violence link differ across societies. Clearly, there are vast societal differences, including the provocative finding that lethal violence is pandemic in some societies but relatively unknown in others (Archer and Gartner, 1984). Much of the research on cultural differences derives from anthropology. For example, Rohner (1976) coded published ethnographic accounts of children's behavior in 14 traditional societies. He found large intersocietal differences in fostering aggressive behavior among children—for some societies, high levels of aggression were the norm; for others, aggression was relatively unacceptable.

The question of the link between maleness and violence also has cultural implications. It may be that boys and girls are socialized for different adult roles—that is, a sexual division of labor. Perhaps many societies socialize boys for adult roles that require greater levels of aggression, such as hunting or intergroup conflict. This "differential gender socialization" hypothesis has been invoked to account for the higher levels of male aggression observed in many societies studied by anthropologists (Tieger, 1980; Segall, 1983).

NEW CROSS-CULTURAL RESEARCH

Since the late 1980s we have begun a program of work to try to illuminate cultural aspects of violence. The catalyst for this work was the finding by Archer and Gartner (1984) of large, problematic, and intriguing differences in the levels of violence across societies. This new work complements their use of aggregate statistics on national rates of violent crime by examining social psychological differences across cultures. The basic method used in this new research presents individuals aged 16 to 18 with a series of twelve standardized "problem-solving" tasks. Each task involves a different conflict or problem (an unfaithful spouse, a romantic triangle, disciplining a child, a public dispute, a rejected lover, conflict at work, a quarrel between two nations, etc.). The individual is asked to write an imaginative story about how characters in these situations will respond to the conflict.

In each case, potential solutions range from nonviolent to violent. The research focus is on the *quantities and qualities of violence in the stories as a reflection of attitudes toward, expectations about, and justifications for violence as a means of solving conflicts.* The approach can be illustrated here with a conflict situation involving a woman (Mary) and her unfaithful husband (William). The problem is presented to participants, who are asked to write a story about how Mary would respond:

William and Mary have been married for two years. They both leave the house during the day, but they have different schedules. A friend of Mary's tells her that her husband has been seen with another woman while Mary is away from the house. Mary decides to see for herself. After pre-

tending to leave the house as usual, Mary parks her car half a block from her house. Twenty minutes later, Mary sees a woman drive up to the house. Mary sees William come out of the house. He gives the woman a long, intimate kiss, and they go inside the house together. What will Mary do?

The twelve problem-solving situations used in the study are:

Unfaithful Mary—a husband discovers his wife is unfaithful

Unfaithful William—a wife discovers her husband is unfaithful

Unhappy Ann—a depressed young woman confronts school failure

Demonstrators—an extended protest occurs at a factory

Catherine Leaves James—a young woman tells boyfriend she loves another

James Leaves Catherine—a young man tells girlfriend he loves another

Coworker Dispute—a person steals work and credit from a coworker

Mark the Policeman—a policeman confronts two thieves

Roger and His Son—a father disciplines five-year-old son

Big and Small Nation—two nations are in conflict

Mary Denies Richard—a woman refuses the sexual advances of male friend

John in the Pub—a man is confronted by an aggressive drunk

For each of three of these twelve conflicts (four different test booklets are used, each containing three problems), participants in the study generate an imaginative story about how the characters will respond to or attempt to solve the conflict described. In every case, the problem can be solved by either nonviolent or violent means. For example, the previous problem ("Unfaithful William") generates a wide variety of solutions, including the two examples given here. The first

was written by a Swedish high school student; the second by an American high school student.

SWEDISH EXAMPLE (Female Subject, 23095): Mary runs into the house and catches them red-handed. Mary is very unhappy. She yells at William and runs out of the house. William runs after her. Mary calms down. They decide to talk about it in peace and quiet. The other woman drives home. William and Mary take a seat on the sofa. William explains that he loves the other woman and wants a divorce. Mary says that she agrees. She will not live with a man who does not love her.

AMERICAN EXAMPLE (Male Subject, 01128): Mary feels a sudden surge of anger deep from within her innermost self. Mary vows revenge. She slams the car into gear and races out to the hardware store where she purchases a 33-inch McCulloch chainsaw. When she arrives at the house most of the lights are out, so she creeps around back only to discover that William and his mistress are in back on the deck, dining with fine food over candlelight. Seeing this, Mary pulls the rip cord on her chainsaw. The chainsaw whines to life as William jumps up and screams, "What the fuck is going on?" Mary springs up on to the deck and buries the chainsaw deep into the other woman's head. Her body convulses as blood, flesh, gray matter, and bone fragments fly everywhere. William screams with terror as Mary cuts the motor and pulls the chainsaw out of the shaking lump of flesh which used to be a human. William is cornered as Mary fires up the saw. "Don't Mary, I can explain, please wait, don't!" Mary's eyes are glazed over and she seems possessed. She screams, "Rot in hell you stinking motherfucker!" as she slams the roaring chainsaw into William's mouth.

By themselves, of course, two isolated stories tell us little. The important questions involve the possibility of *general* and *systematic differences* in large samples obtained from different societies. Stories written in response to the twelve problem-solving stimuli were obtained from secondary-level schools in several societies. Data were collected from eleven nations. These nations vary with respect to the prevalence of violence—with some characterized by low rates of violent crime and others by high rates.

Within each of the societies included in the study, efforts were made to identify secondary schools diverse in parental social class, academic ability, and probable educational future. Secondary schools were chosen, rather than colleges and universities, because secondary schools are much more likely to be representative of all levels of class and ability. In most societies, tertiary education is highly stratified, drawing overwhelmingly from the highest financial and ability strata. In each case, a knowledgeable local scholar was asked to identify schools that were likely to draw from populations diverse in social class. In each national sample, approximately 600 to 750 stories were obtained from 200 to 250 individuals—that is, each individual wrote three stories. The general instructions were as follows:

> SOLVING PROBLEMS. In each of the following situations, a specific problem is described. After reading each description, make up a *detailed* story about how the characters in the story will try to solve this problem. In your story, describe *what* the characters do and *what happens* as a result. PLEASE MAKE YOUR STORIES AS *DETAILED* AS POSSIBLE.

A "Violence Code" was created using the method of content analysis to summarize the quantities of violence in the stories from each national sample. Although the Violence Code permits the systematic enumeration of the *quantities* of violence in the stories, qualitative differences between the national samples are also extremely important, because these differences are often subtle and elude simple tabulation. The two methods, quantitative and qualitative, are complementary rather than redundant because they tap very different facets of the data set.*

*The methodology is too briefly presented here; a fully detailed description is available from Professor Dane Archer, Department of Sociology, University of California at Santa Cruz, Santa Cruz, CA 95064.

RESULTS: QUANTITATIVE DATA

A comparison of eleven national data sets reveals large differences in quantities of violence contained in the stories. . . . The overall incidence of violence shows low values for the Korean (18.6 percent), Swedish (19.3 percent), and Mexican samples (19.9 percent); much higher values for the New Zealand (38.7 percent), Australian (37.7 percent) and American (29.8 percent) samples. . . . The eleven national samples can be ranked from high to low in the following order on the frequency of any form of violence in the stories: New Zealand, Australia, Northern Ireland, United States, Japan, England, Canada, France, Mexico, Sweden, and Korea.

Gender Differences

Stories written by men are more likely to contain violence than those written by women. This pattern is consistent (1) across all eleven societies and (2) across all twelve problem-solving situations. . . . A higher proportion of male stories (35 percent overall) contained violence than female stories (22.5 percent) for all eleven national samples. This indicates that male stories were 1.56 times more likely to contain violence than female stories.

The differential for stories containing homicides was even greater; compared with women's stories, men's stories were 2.40 times more likely to contain a homicide. The differential for stories containing firearms was roughly 2.13. [In short,] men were more likely than women to write violent stories.

RESULTS: QUALITATIVE DATA

The eleven national data sets vary dramatically not only in the frequency of violent acts—something quantification does a reasonable job of summarizing—but also in the nuances that make the eleven data sets so dissimilar. These nuances defy quantification, and they reflect some of the most important qualities that make the Swedish stories unlike the American stories, and that make both unlike the English stories, and so on. Many themes, patterns, and outcomes found frequently in the stories from one nation were infrequent or even unknown in the stories from another society. Quantification therefore leaves unanswered many subtle questions regarding cultural differences, and a close reading of the stories is required.

With so many stories to choose from, it is possible here only to illustrate some of their diversity and cultural uniqueness. The examples are all from the "Unfaithful William" and "Unfaithful Mary" conflicts. In American stories written in response to these two problems, reactions generally involve anger and rage. When violence takes place in these stories, it is frequently fatal, occurs rapidly in hot blood, and often involves firearms. There was a gender difference in the frequency of violence in American stories about "Unfaithful Mary" (36.8 percent of male stories contained violence; 9.6 percent of female stories contained violence) and, to a lesser degree, about "Unfaithful William" (22.6 percent of male stories; 14.6 percent of female stories). The following six examples come from the American sample; the first three were written by men and the next three by women.

American Male, 01049: William waits for three hours. Then finally the man comes out of the house tucking his shirt. By this time, William is outraged, so he starts up his car and drives casually over toward the man and parks right in the way of the man's car. William steps out very casually and reaches under the seat and pulls out his service .45 and chambers a round. In the meantime the man steps out of the car and is walking toward William. William sees him coming toward him so he just points it toward the man and pulls the trigger. The shock of the slug to the man's chest was so great it broke all his ribs and put a hole through him that you could stick a baseball through.

American Male, 03102: First, William hit the dashboard as hard as he could and nearly broke his hand doing so. William starts to get an angry look

on his face and all of a sudden, pulls out a .357 Magnum, the most powerful in the world. . . . When William began the third knock, the man answered the door. William asked if Mary was there, the man said that he doesn't know any Mary and so she wasn't there. William then blew off his head and took Mary home and romped on her.

American Male, 12180: William is going to go kick some ass on this dude. First thing William does is wait 15 minutes so he can barge into the house and catch this man fucking the brains out of his wife. Then William fucks this dude up, beats his head in and gets a gun and shoots his ass. Then he goes and fucks Mary's pussy all the rest of the day to make sure she won't want any more dick for a while.

American Female, 12085: William should talk to Mary about what's going on. He should ask her what kind of problem is going on between them, and ask her if there is a problem (and) why she can't tell him instead of sleeping around with other guys. Maybe they should see a marriage counselor.

American Female, 03106: At the door to the bedroom he stops and listens carefully. His blood is pounding so loudly through his ears that it is hard to hear. Taking a deep breath, he opens the door and stalks into the bedroom. Mary is undressed in bed with a man William has never seen before. She jumps up and the blood rushes from her face. "What the hell is going on here?!" William shouts. Mary breaks down and starts crying as the stranger hurriedly gets dressed and runs out the door. . . . Mary rambles on and on, not seeing what Will is doing, then out of nowhere William pulls out a gun and says, "If I can't have you neither can he!" and with that he proceeds to shoot Mary in the head and, only seconds later, to shoot himself.

American Female, 11012: Mary will probably sit there and think "I want to kill them both." But obviously she won't hurt him. The other woman would yell at him for not getting rid of Mary and the two women will end up fighting and, at the end, the other woman will probably just give up and say something to William like, "You'll be sorry."

The following stories are drawn from some of the other national samples. These examples vary in the quantities and qualities of violence they contain. They also reflect some degree of cultural uniqueness, containing themes and solutions encountered rarely if at all in the American stories.

Swedish Male, 23194: William, a bit sexually frustrated himself, is extremely jealous. He finds however that this jealousy provokes an erotic feeling. His loins tingled as he watched them kiss. His normal uncreative mind starts to burn with new and exciting ideas. He decides to cut loose from his inhibitions and join them. Once in the house, he can hear their laughter in the bathroom. He begins to unbutton his shirt as he approaches the door. As he turns the knob, he can hear the couple gasp. "It's OK," he whispers, "I've come to join you." The couple is noticeably apprehensive but, as he undresses, they begin to relax. Their innovative afternoon has begun.

Swedish Female, 23127: William will go into the house and call for an explanation, (and) ask what the other man is doing in his house with his wife and so on. If it just was a temporary romance, they can be friends again. Or perhaps William will sue for a divorce.

English Female, 28066: After a very hard morning at work, she returns home. William by this time would have gone to work. Mary, in her hunt for evidence, finds an article of the woman's clothing under the bed. Later when her husband returns she confronts him. They don't argue about it but talk sensibly, deciding the best course of action calmly among the two of themselves. Agreeing eventually that she, Mary, is willing to give him a second chance if he gives his word to forget that woman.

English Male, 28015: William sat in his car trying to decide what to do. Should he burst in on them, should he kill them both, should he go to a lawyer or ignore what was happening? William drove up to his house, walked up to the door. He goes inside. Giggles can be heard upstairs. He goes up to the bedroom and Mary and her lover are lying on the bed, semi-naked. Both try to cover themselves up.

Mary gets out of bed and tries to calm William down. William pushes her away over a chair. Her lover gets up to defend her and receives a fist in the face. William leaves the house and drives off at high speed to the nearest bar.

Australian Female, 26018: Mary is stunned. Slowly she walks to her car and in a daze drives off. Images of the woman kissing her husband flash through her mind. Resolutely, she parks her car near a deserted beach and goes for a walk. She is in a turmoil. Should she confront her husband and demand an explanation or should she bide her time and hope that he tells her himself? Direct confrontation is best, so slowly Mary gets back into her car and drives back home. She is just in time to see the lady leaving. . . . Guilt is written all over William's face as he sees Mary. "It was nothing," he stutters desperately. Mary doesn't say anything. She walks determinedly to their bedroom, pulls out her suitcase and starts packing her belongings. For a moment her eyes fall upon their wedding picture, but she turns away. At the door, she turns one last time to take a look at what was her home and at the man she once loved. Then she turns and purposefully walks toward her car.

Australian Male, 26109: There were noises coming from the bedroom so she moved down the passage slowly and then she peered around the corner. Her friend was right. Then Mary quickly moved to the passage closet and pulled out a handgun. She then returned to the bedroom with the loaded gun, shooting her husband first and then his little playmate. Then turning the gun on herself, after shooting everybody. They had all died instantly.

Korean Female, 25043: Mary investigates their relationship with suspicion. She tries to find out whether their relationship is unclean or just friendship, or has to do with business. If the relationship turns out to be serious (unclean), Mary will suffer deeply from agony and anguish. Since Mary loves William very much, she will leave him for his happiness. Mary's life will be filled with joy thinking that William, the one whom she loves the most, is living a happy life by her sacrifice.

Korean Male, 25149: When William gets home, he asks Mary with a smiling face, "Did you have fun while I was gone?" Mary looks surprised, "How did you know?" If I were William, I'd go to the man and hit him a few times, then give my wife (Mary) to the man.

AN ATTEMPT AT THEORETICAL SYNTHESIS

The large gender differences reported in this paper have implications for three different theoretical explanations that emphasize respectively, biological, social, and cultural factors. Each explanation can be examined in light of the new findings presented here.

First, biology. Given the large and highly consistent gender differences obtained in these data, biological factors cannot in our view be discounted—males wrote more violent stories than women in every national sample and for almost every conflict. In our view, this cross-national finding is apparently consistent with the proposition that gender differences in violence are influenced by biological factors. In the data reported here, the maleness-violence link is both large and apparently universal.

Second, social factors. In all the societies studied here males are consistently more violent than women, but the specific amount of gender difference in violence varies from one society to another. For example, the male–female difference in violence is greater in the United States than in Canada or Japan. Similarly, the amount of male violence per se varies from one society to another. Such societal variations can be attributed to socialization, with some societies being more energetic than others in socializing males toward aggression. Socialization does not operate in a social vacuum, though. It seems to work hand in glove with culture.

Third, cultural factors. Gender differences aside, there are dramatic intersocietal differences. Samples from some societies show much higher levels of overall violence and aggression than those from other societies. This finding is consistent with the view that differences in violence are culturally constructed, and that this process varies

in significant ways across societies. Standing alone, however, cultural factors appear unable to account for the gender differences found. Given the diversity of cultural practices and variation in child rearing in different societies, universal gender differences in violence and aggression are relatively unexpected. Again, however, the large aggregate differences across national samples are perfectly consistent with the notion that different cultures produce aggression and violence in different quantities.

CONCLUSION

As noted earlier, there is evident overlap in the predictions implied by social and cultural theories; these perspectives could be referred to collectively as "social-cultural" explanations. Although in this study the surprisingly *consistent* pattern of gender differences (men being more violent than women in all societies) lends apparent credibility to biological explanations, the large *differences* across nations just as strongly support "social-cultural" explanations.

The gender differentials are consistent with biological models. Because the pattern of these gender differences is largely the same *within* each of the national data sets, biology—or at least universals that transcend national boundaries—may be implicated. However, the different levels of violence between nations are difficult to explain without "social-cultural" models. The enormous differences *between* national data sets in the prevalence of violence in the stories cannot be explained by biological factors and, instead, require consideration of social and cultural variables that vary across these societies. The precise nature of these social and cultural variables remains unknown at this point, but the huge cross-national differences reported here appear to provide a "smoking gun" proving that these variables exist.

The data reported here therefore provide support for the role of very different types of etiological explanations. Both "social-cultural" and biological explanations can claim support in these data because both *differences* (the variation in aggregate violence levels across samples) and *similarities* (the almost universally higher levels of male violence) are found in this cross-cultural comparison.

REFERENCES

Archer, Dane, and Rosemary Gartner. 1984. *Violence and Crime in Cross-National Perspective.* New Haven: Yale University Press.

Bardwick, Judith. 1971. *The Psychology of Women: A Study of Bio-Cultural Conflicts.* New York: Harper and Row.

Christiansen, Kerrin, and Rainer Knussman. 1987. "Androgen Levels and Components of Aggressive Behavior in Man." *Hormones and Behavior* 21:170–180.

Goldstein, Jeffrey. 1986. *Aggression and Crimes of Violence.* New York: Oxford University Press.

Maccoby, Eleanor, and Carol Jacklin. 1974. *The Psychology of Sex Differences.* Stanford: Stanford University Press.

Rada, Richard, D. Laws, and Robert Kellner. 1976. "Plasma Testosterone Levels in the Rapist." *Psychosomatic Medicine* 38:257–268.

Rohner, Ronald P. 1976. "Sex Differences in Aggression: Phylogenetic and Enculturation Perspectives." *Ethos* 4:57–72.

Sears, Robert, Eleanor Maccoby, and Harry Levin. 1957. *Patterns of Child Rearing.* Stanford: Stanford University Press, 1957.

Segall, Marshall. 1983. "Aggression in Global Perspective," in *Aggression in Global Perspective,* edited by Arnold P. Goldstein and Marshall Segall. New York: Pergamon Press.

Tieger, Todd. 1980. "On the Biological Bases of Sex Differences in Aggression." *Child Development* 51:943–963.

REVIEW QUESTIONS

1. What are two major conclusions reached in this article?
2. Given the conclusions reached in this article, what theoretical explorations do the authors offer to explain the gender differences observed?

SERIAL MURDER: POPULAR MYTHS AND EMPIRICAL REALITIES

JAMES ALAN FOX
JACK LEVIN

Since the early 1980s, Americans have become more aware of and concerned about a particularly dangerous class of murderers, known as serial killers. Characterized by the tendency to kill repeatedly (at least three or four victims) and often with increasing brutality, serial killers stalk their victims, one at a time, for weeks, months, or years, generally not stopping until they are caught.

The term *serial killer* was first used in the early 1980s (see Jenkins, 1994), although the phenomenon of repeat killing existed, of course, throughout recorded history. In the late 1800s, for example, Hermann Webster Mudgett (aka H. H. Holmes) murdered dozens of attractive young women in his Chicago "house of death," and the infamous Jack the Ripper stalked the streets of London, killing five prostitutes. Prior to the 1980s, repeat killers such as Mudgett and Jack the Ripper were generally described as mass murderers. The need for a special classification for repeat killers was later recognized because of the important differences between multiple murderers who kill simultaneously and those who kill serially (Levin & Fox, 1985). *Mass killers*—those who slaughter their victims in one event—tend to target people they know (e.g., family members or coworkers), often for the sake of revenge, using an efficient weapon of mass destruction (e.g., a high-powered firearm). As we shall describe below, serial murderers are different in all these respects, typically killing total strangers with their hands to achieve a sense of power and control over others.

A rising concern with serial killing has spawned a number of media presentations, resulting in the perpetrators of this type of murder becoming a regular staple of U.S. popular culture. A steady diet of television and movie productions could lead viewers to believe that serial killing is a common type of homicide. An increasing interest in serial homicide, however, has not been limited solely to the lay public. During the past two decades, the number, as well as the mix, of scholars devoting their attention to this crime has dramatically changed. Until the early 1980s, the literature exploring aspects of multiple homicide consisted almost exclusively of bizarre and atypical case studies contributed by forensic psychiatrists pertaining to their court-assigned clients. More recently, there has been a significant shift toward social scientists examining the cultural and social forces underlying the late 20th-century rise in serial murder as well as law enforcement operatives developing research-based investigative tools for tracking and apprehending serial offenders.

Author's Note: We contributed equally to this work; the order of authorship was determined alphabetically. We wish to acknowledge the able assistance of Stephanie Flagg.

Source: M. Dwayne Smith and Margaret A. Zahn (eds.), *Homicide: A Sourcebook of Social Research* (Thousand Oaks, CA: Sage, 1999), pp. 167–175. Reprinted by permission of Sage Publications Inc.

Despite the shift in disciplinary focus, some basic assumptions of psychiatry appear to remain strong in the public mind. In particular, it is widely believed that the serial killer acts as a result of some individual pathology produced by traumatic childhood experiences. At the same time, a developing law enforcement perspective holds that the serial killer is a nomadic, sexual sadist who operates with a strict pattern to victim selection and crime scene behavior; this model has also contributed to myopic thinking in responding to serial murder. Unfortunately, these assumptions from both psychiatry and law enforcement may have retarded the development of new and more effective approaches to understanding this phenomenon. In an attempt to present a more balanced view, this chapter examines (serially, of course) several myths about serial killing/killers, some long-standing and others of recent origin, that have been embraced more on faith than on hard evidence.

MYTH 1: THERE IS AN EPIDEMIC OF SERIAL MURDER IN THE UNITED STATES

Although interest in serial murder has unquestionably grown, the same may not necessarily be true for the incidence of this crime itself. Curiously enough, there may actually be more scholars studying serial murder than there are offenders committing it. Regrettably, it is virtually impossible to measure with any degree of precision the prevalence of serial murder today, or even less so to trace its long-term trends (see Egger, 1990, 1998; Kiger, 1990). One thing for certain, however, is that the problem is nowhere near epidemic proportions (Jenkins, 1994). . . .

The lack of any hard evidence concerning the prevalence of serial homicide has not prevented speculation within both academic and law enforcement fields. The "serial killer panic of 1983–85," as it has been described by Jenkins (1988), was fueled by some outrageous and unsupportable statistics promulgated by the U.S. Department of Justice to buttress its claim that the extent of serial murder was on the rise. Apparently, some government officials reasoned that because the number of unsolved homicides had surged from several hundred per year in the early 1960s to several thousand per year in the 1980s, the aggregate body count produced by serial killers could be as high as 5,000 annually (Fox & Levin, 1985). Unfortunately, this gross exaggeration was endorsed in some academic publications as well (see Egger, 1984; Holmes & DeBurger, 1988).

More sober thinking on the prevalence issue has occurred in recent years (Egger, 1990, 1998; Holmes & Holmes, 1998). Although still subject to the methodological limitations noted above in the identification of serial crimes, Hickey (1997) has attempted the most exhaustive measurement of the prevalence and trends in serial murder. In contrast to the Justice Department's estimate of thousands of victims annually, Hickey (1997) enumerated only 2,526 to 3,860 victims slain by 399 serial killers between 1800 and 1995. Moreover, between 1975 and 1995, the highest levels in the two centuries, Hickey identified only 153 perpetrators and as many as 1,400 victims, for an average annual tally of far less than 100 victims. Although Hickey's data collection strategy obviously ignored undetected cases, the extent of the problem is likely less than 1% of homicides in the country. Of course, that as much as 1% of the nation's murder problem can potentially be traced to but a few dozen individuals reminds us of the extreme deadliness of their predatory behavior.

MYTH 2: SERIAL KILLERS ARE UNUSUAL IN APPEARANCE AND LIFESTYLE

As typically portrayed, television and cinematic versions of serial killers are either sinister-appearing creatures of the night or brilliant-but-evil master criminals. In reality, however, most tend to fit neither of these descriptions. Serial killers are generally White males in their late 20s or 30s who span a broad range of human qualities including appearance and intelligence.

Some serial killers are high school dropouts, and others might indeed be regarded as unappealing by conventional standards. At the same time, a few actually possess brilliance, charm, and attractiveness. Most serial killers, however, are fairly average, at least to the casual observer. In short, they are "extraordinarily ordinary"; ironically, part of the secret of their success is that they do not stand out in a crowd or attract negative attention to themselves. Instead, many of them look and act much like "the boy next door"; they hold full-time jobs, are married or involved in some other stable relationship, and are members of various local community groups. The one trait that tends to separate prolific serial killers from the norm is that they are exceptionally skillful in their presentation of self so that they appear beyond suspicion. This is part of the reason why they are so difficult to apprehend (Levin & Fox, 1985).

A related misconception is that serial killers, lacking stable employment or family responsibilities, are full-time predators who roam far and wide, often crossing state and regional boundaries in their quest for victims. Evidence to the contrary notwithstanding, serial killers have frequently been characterized as nomads whose compulsion to kill carries them hundreds of thousands of miles a year as they drift from state to state and region to region leaving scores of victims in their wake. This may be true of a few well-known and well-traveled individuals, but not for the vast majority of serial killers (Levin & Fox, 1985). According to Hickey (1997), only about a third of the serial killers in his database crossed state lines in their murder sprees. John Wayne Gacy, for example, killed all of his 33 young male victims at his Des Plaines, Illinois, home, conveniently burying most of them there as well. Gacy had a job, friends, and family but secretly killed on a part-time, opportunistic basis.

MYTH 3: SERIAL KILLERS ARE ALL INSANE

What makes serial killers so enigmatic—so irrational to many casual observers—is that they generally kill not for love, money, or revenge but for the fun of it. That is, they delight in the thrill, the sexual satisfaction, or the dominance that they achieve as they squeeze the last breath of life from their victims. At a purely superficial level, killing for the sake of pleasure seems nothing less than "crazy."

The basis for the serial killer's pursuit of pleasure is found in a strong tendency toward sexual sadism (Hazelwood, Dietz, & Warren, 1992) and an interest reflected in detailed fantasies of domination (Prentky, Burgess, & Rokous,1989). Serial killers tie up their victims to watch them squirm and torture their victims to hear them scream. They rape, mutilate, sodomize, and degrade their victims to feel powerful, dominant, and superior.

Many individuals may have fantasies about torture and murder but are able to restrain themselves from ever translating their sadistic dreams into reality. Those who do not contain their urges to kill repeatedly for no apparent motive are assumed to suffer from some extreme form of mental illness. Indeed, some serial killers have clearly been driven by psychosis, such as Herbert Mullen of Santa Cruz, California, who killed 13 people during a 4-month period to avert an earthquake—at least that is what the voices commanded him to do (the voices also ordered him to burn his penis with a cigarette).

In either a legal or a medical sense, however, most serial killers are not insane or psychotic (see Levin & Fox, 1985; Leyton, 1986). They know right from wrong, know exactly what they are doing, and can control their desire to kill—but choose not to. They are more cruel than crazy. Their crimes may be sickening, but their minds are not necessarily sick. Most apparently do not suffer from hallucinations, a profound thought disorder, or major depression. Indeed, those assailants who are deeply confused or disoriented are generally not capable of the level of planning and organization necessary to conceal their identity from the authorities and, therefore, do not amass a large victim count.

Many serial killers seem instead to possess a personality disorder known as sociopathy (or antisocial personality). They lack a conscience, are remorseless, and care exclusively for their own needs and desires. Other people are regarded merely as tools to be manipulated for the purpose of maximizing their personal pleasure (see Harrington, 1972; Magid & McKelvey, 1988). Thus, if given to perverse sexual fantasy, sociopaths simply feel uninhibited by societal rules or by conscience from literally chasing their dreams in any way necessary for their fulfillment (see Fox, 1989; Levin & Fox, 1985; Vetter, 1990). . . .

MYTH 4: ALL SERIAL KILLERS ARE SOCIOPATHS

Although many serial killers tend to be sociopaths, totally lacking in concern for their victims, some actually do have a conscience but are able to neutralize or negate their feelings of remorse by rationalizing their behavior. They feel as though they are doing something good for society, or at least nothing that bad.

Milwaukee's cannibalistic killer, Jeffrey Dahmer, for example, actually viewed his crimes as a sign of love and affection. He told Tracy Edwards, a victim who managed to escape, that if he played his cards right, he too could give his heart to Jeff. Dahmer meant it quite literally, of course, but according to Edwards, he said it affectionately, not threateningly.

The powerful psychological process of *dehumanization* allows many serial killers to slaughter scores of innocent people by viewing them as worthless and therefore expendable. To the dehumanizer, prostitutes are seen as mere sex machines, gays are AIDS carriers, nursing home patients are vegetables, and homeless alcoholics are nothing more than human trash.

In a process related to this concept of dehumanization, many serial killers compartmentalize the world into two groups—those whom they care about versus everyone else. "Hillside Strangler" Kenneth Bianchi, for example, could be kind and loving to his wife and child as well as to his mother and friends yet be vicious and cruel to those he considered meaningless. He and his cousin started with prostitutes, but later, when they grew comfortable with killing, branched out to middle-class targets.

MYTH 5: SERIAL KILLERS ARE INSPIRED BY PORNOGRAPHY

Could Theodore Bundy have been right in his death row claim that pornography turned him into a vicious killer, or was he just making excuses to deflect blame? It should be no surprise that the vast majority of serial killers do have a keen interest in pornography, particularly sadistic magazines and films (Ressler, Burgess, & Douglas, 1988). Sadism is the source of their greatest pleasure, and so, of course, they experience it vicariously in their spare time, when not on the prowl themselves. That is, a preoccupation with pornography is a reflection, not the cause, of their own sexual desires. At most, pornography may reinforce sadistic impulses, but it cannot create them.

There is experimental evidence that frequent and prolonged exposure to violent pornography tends to desensitize "normal" men to the plight of victims of sexual abuse (Malamuth & Donnerstein, 1984). In the case of serial killers, however, it takes much more than pornography to create such an extreme and vicious personality.

MYTH 6: SERIAL KILLERS ARE PRODUCTS OF BAD CHILDHOODS

Whenever the case of an infamous serial killer is uncovered, journalists and behavioral scientists alike tend to search for clues in the killer's childhood that might explain the seemingly senseless or excessively brutal murders. Many writers have emphasized, for example, Theodore Bundy's concerns about being illegitimate, and biographers of Hillside Strangler Kenneth Bianchi capitalized on his having been adopted. . . .

It is true that the biographies of most serial killers reveal significant physical and psychological trauma at an early age. For example, based on in-depth interviews with 36 incarcerated murderers, Ressler et al. (1988) found evidence of psychological abuse (e.g., public humiliation) in 23 cases and physical trauma in 13 cases. Hickey (1997) reported that among a group of 62 male serial killers, 48% had been rejected as children by a parent or some other important person in their lives. Of course, these same types of experiences can be found in the biographies of many "normal" people as well. More specifically, although useful for characterizing the backgrounds of serial killers, the findings presented by Ressler at al. and Hickey lack a comparison group drawn from nonoffending populations for which the same operational definitions of trauma have been applied. Therefore, it is impossible to conclude that serial killers have suffered as children to any greater extent than others. . . .

Some neurologists and a growing number of psychiatrists suggest that serial killers have incurred serious injury to the limbic region of the brain resulting from severe or repeated head trauma, generally during childhood. As an example, psychiatrist Dorothy Lewis and neurologist Jonathan Pincus, along with other colleagues, examined 15 murderers on Florida's death row and found that all showed signs of neurological irregularities (Lewis, Pincus, Feldman, Jackson, & Bard, 1986). In addition, psychologist Joel Norris (1988) reported excessive spinal fluid found in the brain scan of serial killer Henry Lee Lucas. Norris argued that this abnormality reflected the possible damage caused by an earlier blow or a series of blows to Lucas's head.

It is critical that we place in some perspective the many case studies that have been used in an attempt to connect extreme violence to neurological impairment. Absent from the case study approach is any indication of the prevalence of individuals who did not act violently despite a history of trauma. Indeed, if head trauma were as strong a contributor to serial murder as some suggest, then we would have many times more of these killers than we actually do.

It is also important to recognize that neurological impairment must occur in combination with a host of environmental conditions to place an individual at risk for extreme acts of brutality. Dorothy Lewis cautions, "The neuropsychiatric problems alone don't make you violent. Probably the environmental factors in and of themselves don't make you a violent person. But when you put them together, you create a very dangerous character" ("Serial Killers," 1992). Similarly, Ressler asserts that no single childhood problem indicates future criminality: "There are a whole pot of conditions that have to be met" for violence to be predictable (quoted in Meddis, 1987, p. 3A). Head trauma and abuse, therefore, may be important risk factors, but they are neither necessary nor sufficient to make someone a serial killer. Rather, they are part of a long list of circumstances—including adoption, shyness, disfigurement, speech impediments, learning and physical disabilities, abandonment, death of a parent, academic and athletic inadequacies—that may make a child feel frustrated and rejected enough to predispose, but not predestine, him or her toward extreme violence.

Because so much emphasis has been placed on early childhood, developmental factors in making the transition into adulthood and middle age are often overlooked. Serial killers tend to be in their late 20s and 30s, if not older, when they first show outward signs of murderous behavior. If only early childhood and biological predisposition were involved, why do they not begin killing as adolescents or young adults? Many individuals suffer as children, but only some of them continue to experience profound disappointment and detachment regarding family, friends, and work. For example, Danny Rolling, who murdered several college students in Gainesville, Florida, may have had a childhood filled with frustration and abuse, but his eight-victim murder spree did not commence until he was 36 years old. After experiencing a painful divorce, he drifted from job to job, from state to state, from prison to prison, and finally from murder to murder (Fox & Levin, 1996).

MYTH 7: SERIAL KILLERS CAN BE IDENTIFIED IN ADVANCE

Predicting dangerousness, particularly in an extreme form such as serial homicide, has been an elusive goal for those investigators who have attempted it. For example, Lewis, Lovely, Yeager, and Femina (1989) suggest that the interaction of neurological/psychiatric impairment and a history of abuse predicts violent crime, better even than previous violence itself. Unfortunately, this conclusion was based on retrospective "postdiction" with a sample of serious offenders, rather than a prospective attempt to predict violence within a general cross section.

It is often said that "hindsight is 20/20." This is especially true for serial murder. Following the apprehension of a serial killer, we often hear mixed reports that "he seemed like a nice guy, but there was something about him that wasn't quite right." Of course, there is often something about most people that may not seem "quite right." When such a person is exposed to be a serial murderer, however, we tend to focus on those warning signs in character and biography that were previously ignored. Even the stench emanating from Jeffrey Dahmer's apartment, which he had convincingly explained to the neighbors as the odor of spoiled meat from his broken freezer, was unexceptional until after the fact.

The methodological problems in predicting violence in advance are well known (Chaiken, Chaiken, & Rhodes, 1994). For a category of violence as rare as serial murder, however, the low base rate and consequent false-positive dilemma are overwhelming. Simply put, there are thousands of White males in their late 20s or 30s who thirst for power, are sadistic, and lack strong internal controls; most emphatically, however, the vast majority of them will never kill anyone.

MYTH 8: ALL SERIAL KILLERS ARE SEXUAL SADISTS

Serial killers who rape, torture, sodomize, and mutilate their victims attract an inordinate amount of attention from the press, the public, and professionals as well. Although they may be the most fascinating type of serial killer, they are hardly the only type.

Expanding their analysis beyond the sexual sadist, Holmes and DeBurger (1988) were among the first to assemble a motivational typology of serial killing, classifying serial murderers into four broad categories: visionary (e.g., voices from God), mission-oriented (e.g., ridding the world of evil), hedonistic (e.g., killing for pleasure), and power/control-oriented (e.g., killing for dominance). Holmes and DeBurger further divided the hedonistic type into three subtypes: lust, thrill, and comfort (see also Holmes & Holmes, 1998). . . .

Modifying the Holmes-DeBurger framework, we suggest that serial murders can be reclassified into three categories, each with two subtypes:

1. Thrill
   a. Sexual sadism
   b. Dominance
2. Mission
   a. Reformist
   b. Visionary
3. Expedience
   a. Profit
   b. Protection

Most serial killings can be classified as thrill motivated, and the *sexual sadist* is the most common of all. In addition, a growing number of murders committed by hospital caretakers have been exposed in recent years; although not sexual in motivation, these acts of murder are perpetrated for the sake of *dominance* nevertheless.

A less common form of serial killing consists of mission-oriented killers who murder to further a cause. Through killing, the *reformist* attempts to rid the world of filth and evil, such as by killing prostitutes, gays, or homeless persons. Most self-proclaimed reformists are also motivated by thrill seeking but try to rationalize their murderous behavior. For example, Donald Harvey, who worked as an orderly in Cincinnati-area hospitals, confessed to killing 80 or more patients through the years. Although he was termed a mercy killer, Harvey actually enjoyed the dominance he achieved by playing God with the lives of other people.

In contrast to pseudoreformists, *visionary* killers, as rare as they may be, genuinely believe in their missions. They hear the voice of the devil or God instructing them to kill. Driven by these delusions, visionary killers tend to be psychotic, confused, and disorganized. Because their killings are impulsive and even frenzied, visionaries rarely remain on the street long enough to become prolific serial killers.

The final category of serial murder includes those who are motivated by the expedience of either profit or protection. The *profit-oriented* serial killer systematically murders as a critical element of the overall plan to dispose of victims to make money (e.g., Sacramento landlady Dorothea Puente murdered 9 elderly tenants to cash their social security checks). By contrast, the *protection-oriented* killer uses murder to cover up criminal activity (e.g., the Lewington brothers systematically robbed and murdered 10 people throughout Central Ohio).

MYTH 9: SERIAL KILLERS SELECT VICTIMS WHO SOMEHOW RESEMBLE THEIR MOTHERS

Shortly after the capture of Hillside Strangler Kenneth Bianchi, psychiatrists speculated that he tortured and murdered young women as an expression of hatred toward his mother, who had allegedly brutalized him as a youngster (Fox & Levin, 1994). Similarly, the execution of Theodore Bundy gave psychiatrists occasion to suggest that

his victims served as surrogates for the real target he sought, his mother.

Although unresolved family conflicts may in some cases be a significant source of frustration, most serial killers have a more opportunistic or pragmatic basis for selecting their victims. Quite simply, they tend to prey on the most vulnerable targets—prostitutes, drug users, hitchhikers, and runaways, as well as older hospital patients (Levin & Fox, 1985). Part of the vulnerability concerns the ease with which these groups can be abducted or overtaken. Children and older persons are defenseless because of physical stature or disability; hitchhikers and prostitutes become vulnerable as soon as they enter the killer's vehicle; hospital patients are vulnerable in their total dependency on their caretakers.

Vulnerability is most acute in the case of prostitutes, which explains their relatively high rate of victimization by serial killers. A sexual sadist can cruise a red-light district, seeking out the woman who best fits his deadly sexual fantasies. When he finds her, she willingly complies with his wishes—until it is too late.

Another aspect of vulnerability is the ease with which the killers can avoid being detected following a murder. Serial killers of our time are often sly and crafty, fully realizing the ease with which they can prey on streetwalkers and escape detection, much less arrest. Because the disappearance of a prostitute is more likely to be considered by the police, at least initially, as a missing person rather than a victim of homicide, the search for the body can be delayed weeks or months. Also, potential witnesses to abductions in red-light districts tend to be unreliable sources of information or distrustful of the police.

Frail older persons, particularly those in hospitals and nursing homes, represent a class of victims that is at the mercy of a different type of serial killer, called "angels of death." Revelations by a Long Island nurse who poisoned his patients in a failed attempt to be a hero by resuscitating them and of two Grand Rapids nurses aides who murdered older patients to form a lovers' pact have horrified even the most jaded observers of crime.

Not only are persons who are old and infirm vulnerable to the misdeeds of their caretakers who may have a particularly warped sense of mercy, but hospital homicides are particularly difficult to detect and solve. Death among older patients is not uncommon, and suspicions are rarely aroused. Furthermore, should a curiously large volume of deaths occur within a short time on a particular nurse's shift, hospital administrators feel in a quandary. Not only are they reluctant to bring scandal and perhaps lawsuits to their own facility without sufficient proof, but most of the potentially incriminating evidence against a suspected employee is long buried with the victim.

MYTH 10: SERIAL KILLERS REALLY WANT TO GET CAUGHT

Despite the notion that serial killers are typically lacking in empathy and remorse, some observers insist that deeply repressed feelings of guilt may subconsciously motivate them to leave telltale clues for the police. Although this premise may be popular in media portrayals, most serial killers go to great lengths to avoid detection, such as carefully destroying crime scene evidence or disposing of their victims' bodies in hard-to-find dump sites.

There is an element of self-selection in defining serial killing. Only those offenders who have sufficient cunning and guile are able to avoid capture long enough to accumulate the number of victims necessary to be classified as serial killers. Most serial killers are careful, clever, and, to use the FBI's typology (see Ressler et al., 1988), organized. Of course, disorganized killers, because of their carelessness, tend to be caught quickly, often before they surpass the serial killer threshold of victim count.

Murders committed by a serial killer are typically difficult to solve because of lack of both motive and physical evidence. Unlike the usual homicide that involves an offender and a victim who know one another, serial murders are almost exclusively committed by strangers. Thus, the usual police strategy of identifying suspects by considering their possible motive, be it jealousy, revenge, or greed, is typically fruitless.

Another conventional approach to investigating homicides involves gathering forensic evidence—fibers, hairs, blood, and prints—from the scene of the crime. In the case of many serial murders, however, this can be rather difficult, if not impossible. The bodies of the victims are often found at desolate roadsides or in makeshift graves, exposed to rain, wind, and snow. Most of the potentially revealing crime scene evidence remains in the unknown killer's house or car.

Another part of the problem is that unlike those shown in the media, many serial killers do not leave unmistakable and unique "signatures" at their crime scenes. As a result, the police may not recognize multiple homicides as the work of the same perpetrator. Moreover, some serial killings, even if consistent in style, traverse jurisdictional boundaries. Thus, "linkage blindness" is a significant barrier to solving many cases of serial murder (Egger, 1984). . . .

FROM MYTH TO REALITY

The study of serial homicide is in its infancy, less than two decades old (O'Reilly-Fleming, 1996). The pioneering scholars noted the pervasiveness and inaccuracy of long-standing psychiatric misconceptions regarding the state of mind of the serial killer (see Levin & Fox, 1985; Leyton, 1986; Ressler et al., 1988). More recently, these unfounded images have been supplanted by newer myths, including those concerning the prevalence and apprehension of serial killers.

The mythology of serial killing has developed from a pervasive fascination with a crime about which so little is known. Most of the scholarly literature is based on conjecture, anecdote, and small samples, rather than rigorous and controlled research. The future credibility of this area of study will depend on the ability of criminologists to up-grade the standards of research on serial homicide.

Only then will myths about serial murder give way to a reliable foundation of knowledge.

REFERENCES

American Psychiatric Association. (1994). *Diagnostic and statistical manual of mental disorders* (4th ed.). Washington, DC: American Psychiatric Association.

Chaiken, J., Chaiken, M., & Rhodes, W. (1994). Predicting violent behavior and classifying violent offenders. In A. J. Reiss Jr. & J. A. Roth (Eds.), *Understanding and preventing violence* (Vol. 4, pp. 217–295). Washington, DC: National Academy Press.

Egger, S. A. (1984). A working definition of serial murder and the reduction of linkage blindness. *Journal of Police Science and Administration, 12,* 348–357.

Egger, S. A. (1990). *Serial murder: An elusive phenomenon.* Westport, CT: Praeger.

Egger, S. A. (1998). *The killers among us: An examination of serial murder and its investigation.* Upper Saddle River, NJ: Prentice Hall.

Fox, J. A. (1989, January 29). The mind of a murderer. *Palm Beach Post,* p. 1E.

Fox, J. A., & Levin. J. (1985, December 1). Serial killers: How statistics mislead us. *Boston Herald,* p. 45.

Fox, J. A., & Levin, J. (1994). *Overkill. Mass murder and serial killing exposed.* New York: Plenum.

Fox, J. A., & Levin, J. (1996). *Killer on campus.* New York: Avon Books.

Harrington, A. (1972). *Psychopaths.* New York: Simon & Schuster.

Hazelwood, R. R., Dietz, P. E., & Warren, J. (1992). The criminal sexual sadist. *FBI Law Enforcement Bulletin, 61,* 12–20.

Hazelwood, R. R., & Douglas, J. E. (1980). The lust murderer. *FBI Law Enforcement Bulletin, 49,* 1–5.

Hickey, E. W. (1997). *Serial murderers and their victims* (2nd ed.). Belmont, CA: Wadsworth.

Holmes, R. M., & DeBurger, J. (1988). *Serial murder.* Newbury Park, CA: Sage.

Holmes, R. M., & Holmes, S. T. (1998). *Serial murder* (2nd ed.). Thousand Oaks, CA: Sage.

Howlett, J. B., Haufland, K. A., & Ressler, R. J. (1986). The violent criminal apprehension program—VICAP: A progress report. *FBI Law Enforcement Bulletin, 55,* 14–22.

Jenkins, P. (1988). Myth and murder. The serial killer panic of 1983–85. *Criminal Justice Research Bulletin* (No. 3). Huntsville, TX: Sam Houston State University.

Jenkins, P. (1994). *Using murder: The social construction of serial homicide.* New York: Walter de Gruyter.

Kiger, K. (1990). The darker figure of crime: The serial murder enigma. In S. A. Egger (Ed.), *Serial murder: An elusive phenomenon* (pp. 35–52). New York: Praeger.

Kirschner, D. (1990). The adopted child syndrome: Considerations for psychotherapy. *Psychotherapy in Private Practice, 8,* 93–100.

Kirschner, D. (1992). Understanding adoptees who kill: Dissociation, patricide, and the psychodynamics of adoption. *International Journal of Offender Therapy & Comparative Criminology, 36,* 323–333.

Levin, J., & Fox, J. A. (1985). *Mass murder: America's growing menace.* New York: Plenum.

Lewis, D. O., Lovely, R., Yeager, C., & Femina, D. D. (1989). Toward a theory of the genesis of violence: A follow-up study of delinquents. *Journal of the American Academy of Child and Adolescent Psychiatry, 28,* 431–436.

Lewis, D. O., Pincus, J. H., Feldman, M., Jackson, L., & Bard, B. (1986). Psychiatric, neurological, and psychoeducational characteristics of 15 death row inmates in the United States. *American Journal of Psychiatry, 143,* 838–845.

Leyton, E. (1986). *Compulsive killers: The story of modern multiple murderers.* New York: New York University Press.

Macdonald, J. M. (1963). The threat to kill. *American Journal of Psychiatry, 120,* 125–130.

Macdonald, J. M. (1968). *Homicidal threats.* Springfield, IL: Charles C Thomas.

Magid, K., & McKelvey, C. A. (1988). *High risk: Children without a conscience.* New York: Bantam.

Malamuth, N. M., & Donnerstein, E. (1984). *Pornography and sexual aggression.* Orlando, FL: Academic Press.

Meddis, S. (1987, March 31). FBI: Possible to spot, help serial killers early. *USA Today,* p. 3A.

Norris, J. (1988). *Serial killers: The growing menace.* New York: Doubleday.

O'Reilly-Fleming, T. (1996). *Serial and mass murder: Theory, research and policy.* Toronto, Ontario: Canadian Scholars' Press.

Prentky, R. A., Burgess, A. W., & Rokous, F. (1989). The presumptive role of fantasy in serial sexual homicide. *American Journal of Psychiatry, 146,* 887–891.

Ressler, R. K., Burgess, A. W., & Douglas, J. E. (1988). *Sexual homicide: Patterns and motives.* Lexington, MA: Lexington Books.

Sears, D. J. (1991). *To kill again.* Wilmington, DE: Scholarly Resources Books.

Serial killers. (1992, October 18). *NOVA.* Boston: WGBH-TV.

Vetter, H. (1990). Dissociation, psychopathy, and the serial murderer. In S. A. Egger (Ed.), *Serial murder: An elusive phenomenon* (pp. 73–92). New York: Praeger.

REVIEW QUESTIONS

1. Identify and discuss five myths about serial killers.
2. Distinguish between mass killers and serial killers.

THE VIOLENCE OF HATE

JACK LEVIN

When a sadistic offense is committed because a victim is different, there seems to be much reason to suggest that the motivation contains important elements of hate. Sadism is essentially designed to give a perpetrator a sense of power, control, and dominance, but at the expense of a set of victims. The three White supremacists who were charged with James Byrd's murder in Jasper, Texas—John King, Lawrence Brewer, and Shawn Berry—beat the Black hitchhiker until he was unconscious, chained him to their pickup truck and then dragged him down the road on his back for almost three miles to his death. For the first two miles, not only was Byrd alive, but he was also conscious. Only when he was decapitated by a boulder at the side of the road was the victim's suffering ended and his life mercifully taken.

THE ROLE OF ORGANIZED HATE

Investigators discovered a Ku Klux Klan manual among the possessions carried by one of the suspects; and two of the suspects wore White supremacist body tattoos depicting the Confederate Knights of America. King, Brewer, and Berry were definitely ardent admirers of the Klan who used White supremacist propaganda and enjoyed being identified with White supremacy symbols of power.

In addition to the murder of James Byrd, there have been several high-profile hate crimes over the last few years committed by the members of White supremacist organizations (Fox and Levin, 2001). In August 1999, Buford Furrow walked into a Jewish Community Center in the Los Angeles area where he opened fire on a group of children as they played. Although he failed in his attempt to kill his young victims, Furrow then shot to death a Filipino letter carrier who just happened to be in the wrong place at the wrong time. A photograph later released to the public showed Furrow a few years earlier dressed in a Nazi uniform at the Hayden, Idaho, compound of the racist organization known as Aryan Nations. A few weeks after Furrow went on his shooting spree in Los Angeles, Larry Gene Ashbrooke went on a rampage with an AK-47 at Fort Worth's Wedgewood Baptist Church, where he killed seven people as they prayed. It turned out that Ashbrooke was a member of Phineas Priesthood, an organized hate group whose members preach that Jews are the children of Satan. Why then had Ashbrooke targeted Baptists? The answer involves a proclamation by the Southern Baptist Conference urging its members to convert as many Jews as possible. For Ashbrooke, this would have been the ultimate blasphemy. If Jews are the offspring of the devil, then the last thing you would want is to convert them to your cause (Lamy, 1996).

As a cultural phenomenon, there are literally millions of Americans who, in varying degrees, dislike the members of various minority groups in society. Most of them would, however, never even think of committing an act of violence against someone because they are different. The relationship between hate and violence is far from perfect. Hate can and does occur without violence; violence

Source: Jack Levin, *The Violence of Hate* (Boston: Allyn and Bacon, 2002), pp. 30–38. Reprinted with permission.

against outsiders can and does occur in the absence of hate.

Organized hate groups provide the situational facilitators in whose presence hate violence becomes more likely to occur. Not unlike a gang or a cult, the organized hate group comes to represent the family of a newly recruited member. Typically, the members of organized hate groups have lacked a sense of belonging. They aren't getting along with their parents, can't make it at school with their peers, and are forced to take dead-end jobs, at best. But in Posse Comitatus, Aryan Nations, White Aryan Resistance, World Church of the Creator, or the Klan, they gain what has been missing in their lives, a sense of belonging and a vague feeling of their own importance. Hatemongers espouse hate and violence, but their underlying motivation is more complex (Ezekiel, 1995).

In social psychology it is well known that the group can make the difference between attitude and action, between thinking about violence and actually perpetrating it. Acting in a group rather than alone reduces any feeling of personal responsibility. Because blame or responsibility is shared, it is also weakened. Individuals may be willing to take more risks, to engage in dangerous behavior, simply because they don't feel that they can be held accountable for their actions.

HATE FROM A DISTANCE

No more than 5% of all hate crimes nationally are committed by the members of organizations like the Ku Klux Klan, Aryan Nations, or the White Aryan Resistance. Still, groups of White supremacists continue behind the scenes to inspire murder, assault, and vandalism. They encourage and support much larger numbers of violent offenses committed by nonmembers who may be totally unsophisticated with respect to the ideology of hate—racist skinheads, alienated teenagers, hate-filled young men looking to have a good time at someone else's expense (Levin and McDevitt, 1993).

While serving time behind bars for burglary convictions, two of the suspects in Jasper apparently had links with the Aryan Brotherhood, a prison hate group whose members are often recruited by White supremacists after they have been released. Established in many states around the country, the Aryan Brotherhood introduces inmates to the theology of the Identity Church, according to which a race war is inevitable. Prison may be a school for crime, but it is also a crash course in hatred and a training ground for leaders of the most dangerous White supremacist groups in our society.

Hatemongers often retaliate in an organized fashion. They want more than just to stop a particular event from happening or a particular individual from intruding; they believe that the very presence of certain groups of people in *their* town, *their* state, *their* country represents an intolerable threat to their personal well-being and to the survival of their group's way of life. Hatemongers provide propaganda to individuals looking to justify their own hateful behavior; they train youngsters in the art of bashing minorities; they recruit on college campuses and in prisons and workplaces; and they operate cable-access television programs featuring interviews with one another. These are the Americans who join Posse Comitatus, The Identity Church, The White Aryan Resistance, the Ku Klux Klan, the American Nazi Party, or the like. There aren't many who qualify as hatemongers, but the few who do are responsible for some of the most vicious acts of violence perpetrated against citizens (Levin and McDevitt, 1993).

BIBLICAL BIGOTRY

The underlying religious inspiration for many organized hate groups is provided by the Christian Identity Church, a world-wide movement whose ministers preach that those who call themselves Jews are actually the children of the devil and that Blacks, Latinos and Asians are "mud people" whose spiritual development remains at the level of animals rather than human beings. According to the Identity Church, the true Israelites in the Bible are the ancestors of Americans who came from Northern European countries.

White Aryan hatemongers are not the only ones who preach biblical bigotry. The beliefs of the Black Hebrew Israelites bear a remarkable resemblance to the theology of Christian Identity practiced by many White supremacists. Members of the Black movement depict themselves as divinely blessed by God with moral superiority; they are God's authentic chosen people of the Old Testament. They see Whites as blue-eyed devils and conventional Jews as imposters.

Black Hebrew Israelites who have migrated from the United States to Israel are usually peaceful. In America, however, they are known by the police for their violence and criminal activities, due in large part to the Miami-based Nation of Yahweh headed by Yahweh Ben Yahweh. In the 1980s, members of the Nation of Yahweh, under the direction of the man they thought of as the Messiah, committed several homicides (Levin and Fox, 1991).

Also like Christian Identity as well as certain civilian militia groups, Black Hebrew Israelites draw on the Khazarian legend in order to explain why those who refer to themselves as Jews are actually imposters. The Kingdom of Khazaria, one of the most diverse countries of medieval Europe, existed in an area of what is known now as southern Russia. In the eighth century, Bulan, who was the king of Khazaria, adopted Judaism. In one version of the story, he was forced to become Jewish after his kingdom was invaded by Jewish tribes from the Crimean Peninsula. In another version, Bulan voluntarily converted to Judaism only after carefully considering the relative merits of Islam, Christianity, and Judaism. Soon afterwards, Khazarian aristocrats also converted and Judaism became the official religion of the kingdom of Khazaria, although other religions were also tolerated. Most Khazarians became Jews, but some converted to Islam or Christianity. The appeal of Judaism may have been enhanced by the fact that Khazaria had, at the same time, become a destina-

tion for substantial numbers of persecuted Jews from Europe and Asia who sought a safe haven (Brook, 1999).

After 250 years, the medieval kingdom of Khazaria was overrun by Russian soldiers. Those Jews who remained in Khazaria were forcibly baptized. The remainder fled to Hungary, Ukraine, Lithuania, Belarus, Slovakia, Romania, Poland, and parts of Russia (Brook, 1999).

The existence of the Kingdom of Khazaria is an indisputable historical fact. Yet most of the details surrounding the association of Eastern European Jews with Khazaria and the dissolution of the Kingdom constitute unsubstantiated legend wholeheartedly adopted by organizations and individuals—members of the Black Hebrew Israelites, Christian Identity, and some militia groups—eager to discredit Judaism and to substantiate their conspiratorial views concerning the Jewish people. They argue that the origins of most of European or Ashkenazi Jewry can be traced back to the Kingdom of Khazarian and not to Jerusalem. Thus, European Jews were converted and therefore cannot make claims to the land of Israel.

One part of the legend supports the notion that Jews seek to control the world's peoples. Their claim is that for more than 1000 years, ever since the dissolution of the Khazarian kingdom and the dispersion of European Jews throughout the world, Khazarians have passed along to their offspring a secret plot to amass great wealth and political power and ultimately to take over all of the countries around the world.

For anti-Semites both Black and White, the term Khazarian serves more than one purpose. First, the Khazarian legend traces in detail the historical basis for the centuries old charge that Jews represent an international conspiracy to gain control over the world's economic resources. Second, the term "Khazarian" (as a replacement for "Jew") has become a codeword for those who do not wish to be accused of anti-Semitism. They are not anti-Jewish, only anti-Khazarian. Third, the term Khazarian has greater scope than Ashkenazi Jew, including within it not only all Jews of European descent but also certain Christians and Moslems who are considered the enemies of freedom and whose ancestry can be traced back to Eastern Europe (remember that some Khazarians converted to Christianity and Islam). Thus, some opponents of the concept of a "one-world order" identify the Rockefeller family and former President George Bush as non-Jewish Khazarians. Finally, focusing on Khazarians also lends credibility to the accusation that Jews, especially Ashkenazi Jews, represent a racial group rather than just a religion. Treating Jews as a race becomes important to those who argue that they are a breed apart from the rest of humanity and must be eliminated rather than converted to Christianity.

THE MILITIA MOVEMENT AND WHITE SUPREMACY

A couple of years ago, I spent the day in a small town north of Boston at a "Patriot Potluck" attended by 75 members of the so-called Patriot movement, militia members, survivalists, and other political discontents who listened attentively to the words of a long list of speakers. The first and featured speaker was a leader of the militia movement in New Hampshire, Ed Brown, who spoke among other things about the evils of the Khazarians. As he warned the audience to be on guard, a voice in the audience could clearly be heard to agree with Brown's cautionary words. "Right, Ed," said the man in the crowd, "It's the Ashkenazi." Brown immediately admonished him about using the word Ashkenazi. "Stick to the term Khazarian," he advised. "They are the true source of evil."

Militias have been linked, at least in the public mind, with everything from the Oklahoma City massacre in which 168 people lost their lives to Atlanta's Olympics pipebomb murder. According to the stereotyped version, militia members are nothing more than a collection of gun-loving hatemongers and thugs who preach first and second

amendment rights as an excuse for waging war against the federal government. And I am certain that there are some militia members who fit the image. But that is also why I was so surprised when the 75 men, women, and children at the Patriot potluck I attended seemed so hospitable and friendly, even innocuous.

The first thing that struck me about this gathering was its diversity in terms of age, social class, and geography. They were men, women, and children from several states who hardly resembled the image I had expected to see. From a distance, in fact, they could easily have been mistaken for a group of bridge players or a convention of social workers.

I was also surprised by the utter boredom of their speeches. Through a five-hour procession, I heard almost nothing about guns and bombs and a great deal about financial hardship and economic disaster. Speaker after speaker after speaker talked about money and how to keep it or make more of it—about how to defeat the IRS through Common Law Courts, about how to withdraw from the Social Security system, about the effect of free trade on the unemployment rate, and about how to avoid going into debt. I got the strong impression that these were Americans who had suffered through hard times and were looking for some way to survive. Their response was to blame the federal government, the UN, the so-called one-world order, the communists, and international bankers. Some, but by no means all of them, also blamed Jews, Blacks, Asians, and Latinos (Levin, 1997).

If there is a bit of overlap between militia groups and White supremacists, it is because both believe that the federal government has let them down. Both have committed themselves to the defense of their version of America. The militia movement gained dramatically in both membership and publicity during the deep recession of the early 1980s, at a time when much of the attention of the nation was on big city problems. Some militia members came from the ranks of automobile workers who lost their jobs in Detroit's massive layoffs, but many more had been miners, farmers, ranchers, and people in the timber business who had been put of business, who simply could no longer make ends meet, and who were looking for help from government officials—help that never came or came too late to make a difference. In addition, some militia groups were convinced that communists had taken over all branches of the federal government and that the United Nations and one-world order types were conspiring to rob the United States of its sovereignty.

So concerned are militia members about the erosion of their constitutional rights that they stand ready and willing to defend our country against itself. They often cite what they regard as a federally instigated conflagration at Waco, Texas, and before that the killing by federal agents of the wife and son of a White supremacist at Ruby Ridge, Idaho, as proof that the government is out to get its citizens. They refuse to give up their firearms, believing that they might very well need all the weapons they can get in order to resist the coming onslaught by foreign and communist forces. Some hate Jews and Blacks, but there are also Jewish and Black militia members.

Not unlike militia groups, the members of organized hate groups like the Klan, Posse Comitatus, Aryan Nations, World Church of the Creator, and White Aryan Resistance also despise the federal government, but for different if overlapping reasons. They refer to the federal government as ZOG (Zionist Occupied Government) and they emphasize their belief that Jews and Blacks have conspired with other enemies of the Republic to benefit themselves at the expense of White Christian Americans.

According to Ezekiel (1995), the leaders of White supremacist organizations are motivated less by sheer hate than by a burning desire to assume a position of power and to be important in the eyes of others. Their followers are recruited from the ranks of marginalized and alienated Americans, many poorly educated and financially troubled, who are searching for a sense of belonging that they never had at home, but they find readily available in organized hate (Langer, 1990).

EXPANDING THE INFLUENCE OF ORGANIZED HATE

At the same time, marginality and alienation do not always depend on impoverishment. Although most White supremacists are from working class backgrounds, there are also some who seem to be well-educated and wealthy. One of the most tragic examples of the appeal of racism and anti-Semitism to an economically advantaged White supremacist can be found in the July 1999 three-day rampage of 21-year-old Benjamin Smith, in which the Indiana University student murdered a Korean graduate student and a Black basketball coach at Northwestern University. He also fired bullets at a group of Orthodox Jews, injuring six of them before taking his own life.

Smith, whose father was a physician, grew up in an affluent suburb northwest of Chicago. His mentor was, however, not his father, but 27-year-old Matthew Hale, the son of a police officer and law-school graduate from East Peoria who, based on his racist beliefs and practices, had been denied the privilege of practicing law by the state of Illinois. In his role as head of the White supremacist group World Church of the Creator, Hale was able to express his racist views to a group of followers who were eager to hear them. He had been in contact with Smith for several days prior to the young man's murderous rampage through Illinois and Indiana and considered Smith a martyr and a friend. Some questioned whether Hale had inspired Smith's killing spree.

The leader of World Church of the Creator also preached Ra-Ho-Wa—the inevitability of a racial holy war from which Whites would ultimately emerge the winners. He despised Jews, Blacks, Latinos, and Asians, considering them to be subhumans at the same level as animals. He also argued that Christianity was merely a tool of deception used by power-hungry Jews to nurture a mindset that would allow them to take over the world. Smith was reportedly furious when he learned that the state of Illinois had denied Hale's bid to practice law. This may have been the catalyst for initiating his killing spree.

Peer pressure may also have been a factor. Smith's girlfriend, 20-year-old Christine Weiss, was also a member of Hale's World Church of the Creator. Like her boyfriend, Weiss had grown up in a wealthy Chicago suburb. She had played soccer and classical music for 11 years and had attended the same high school as Smith, one of the best in the country. Then, Weiss learned on the internet about World Church of the Creator and Matthew Hale. After graduating from high school, she disavowed her Episcopalian roots and joined up. She now talks about preparing for the racial holy war espoused by Hale and about caring only for "her own kind"—the White people of the world (CNN, 2000).

The internet and its thousands of hate websites give to hatemongers a degree of influence well beyond their small numbers. Thanks to the internet, Mat Hale's World Church of the Creator has reached thousands of young people around the country who may have racist and anti-Semitic feelings and are thrilled to learn that they are not alone in these beliefs.

According to former racist Tom Leyden, the internet is probably the best thing ever to happen to the White supremacist movement. Any child with a computer can access hundreds of hate websites, including that of Matthew Hale's organization. In fact, 6-year-olds can even visit the website called World Church of the Creator for Kids, where they can find a crossword puzzle to solve and a White power coloring book to download.

Leyden should know about hate. He preaches tolerance for the Simon Wiesenthal Center in Los Angeles, but he's not Jewish. For 15 years, he was a Neo Nazi skinhead whose body was covered with racist and anti-Semitic tattoos. In his younger days, when he wasn't in jail, Leyden was in the streets, fighting, attacking, and beating up people he considered to be his enemies.

Leyden later married another White supremacist. But when he had children, he felt it was time to make a profound change in his life. There was no way, he reasoned, that he was going to raise his sons in the image of the Nazi movement. There was no way that he was going to contribute to the making of the next generation of hatemongers. Now, he works for the other side, seeking to make up for the time he lost in his early years when they were filled with hate and prejudice.

Leyden's reference to the internet should not be taken lightly. As he suggested in a CNN (2000) interview with correspondent Art Harris, there are youngsters in small towns and big cities around the country who feel alone in their racism. They don't have friends; they have trouble getting along with their peers. But when they boot up their computers and log onto the internet, they've got good friends literally around the world who love them and who agree with their racist views.

Because of the internet, hate websites originating in the United States have also had a powerful impact on youngsters in other countries where the restrictions on hate are more rigorously applied. According to German law, for example, the dissemination of Nazi propaganda is strictly forbidden. Yet German laws banning hate on the internet have been easily circumvented by the spread of websites in the United States operated by neo-Nazi extremists and accessible in the German language to German youths. Protected by the First Amendment to the Constitution, U.S. sites offer propaganda, insignias, music, and computer games that have been officially outlawed from German society but are nevertheless within easy reach of German youths. There are many computer hate games available from American sources, including Concentration Camp Manager, an extremely popular game among German teenagers in which players choose who lives and who dies in the gas chambers. Other computer games have been modified by American Nazis who add an element of hate to what would otherwise be an innocuous form of high tech entertainment. In the game Grouse Hunt, for example, the virtual pheasants to be shot were replaced by yamulkes (Jewish prayer caps) and Stars of David. According to a German Interior Ministry estimate, the number of Nazi sites outside Germany that are directed at German citizens has recently soared (Finn, 2000).

REFERENCES

Brook, Kevin Alan. 1999. *The Jews of Khazaria.* Northvale, NJ: Jason Aronson.

CNN. 2000. "True Believers; Hot Rocks; Breach of Faith." August 6.

Ezekiel, Raphael S. 1995. *The Racist Mind: Portraits of American NeoNazis and Klansmen.* New York: Viking.

Finn, Peter. 2000. "NeoNazis Spreading Hate Chat from U.S.," *The Boston Globe,* December 22, p. A19.

Fox, James, and Jack Levin. 2001. *The Will to Kill: Making Sense of Senseless Murder.* Boston: Allyn and Bacon.

Lamy, Philip. 1996. *Millennium Rage.* New York: Plenum.

Langer, Elinor. 1990. "The American NeoNazi Movement Today," *The Nation,* July 16/23, pp. 82–87.

Levin, Jack. 1997. "Visit to a Patriot Potluck." *USA Today,* March 1, p. 6A.

Levin, Jack, and James A. Fox. 1991. *Mass Murder: America's Growing Menace.* New York: Berkley Books.

Levin, Jack, and Jack McDevitt. 1993. *Hate Crimes: The Rising Tide of Bigotry and Bloodshed.* New York: Plenum.

REVIEW QUESTIONS

1. Is there an overlap between militia groups and white supremacists? Defend your answer.
2. How is the influence of organized hate spread throughout the world?

WHAT MAKES SUICIDE
BOMBERS TICK?

EYAD SARRAJ
EHUD SPRINZAK

A PALESTINIAN VIEW*

A few weeks ago, my sister, a professional and a mother of four, was visibly shaken as she watched, on television, Israeli tanks torturing the streets of a refugee camp and soldiers raping its homes. She shocked us all when she declared that she would like to become a martyr. A few hours later, a young Palestinian woman stunned the world when she turned herself into a human bomb and exploded in Jerusalem, killing one Israeli and wounding 150 others. In the weeks after, more women joined the queue of suicide bombers as the world stood alarmed and bewildered.

To understand why Palestinian men, and now women, are blowing themselves up in Israeli restaurants and buses is to understand the Arab–Israeli conflict. Ours is a nation of anger and defiance. The struggle today is how not to become a suicide bomber. We are told that there are long queues of people willing to join the road to heaven, and I believe it.

What propels people into such action is a long history of humiliation and a desire for revenge that every Arab harbors. Since the establishment of Israel in 1948 and the resultant uprooting of Palestinians, a deep-seated feeling of shame has taken root in the Arab psyche. Shame is the most painful

*From Eyad Sarraj, "Why We Blow Ourselves Up," *Time Atlantic,* vol. 159, no. 14 (April 8, 2002), p. 28. © 2002 TIME Inc. Reprinted with permission.

emotion in the Arab culture, producing the feeling that one is unworthy to live. The honorable Arab is the one who refuses to suffer shame and dies in dignity.

The 35 years of Israeli military occupation of the West Bank and the Gaza Strip has served as a continuous reminder of Arab weakness. But it was the destruction of the P.L.O. in Lebanon by Ariel Sharon that decisively shifted the Palestinian–Israeli confrontation to the occupied territories and Israel. Helplessness and shame gave way to anger that later poured into the streets as defiance. That was the first intifadeh.

Suddenly Palestinians felt that they were restoring their honor by fighting the aggressor, by not being helpless victims. Facing a superior Israeli army with its formidable arsenal, they felt morally victorious as the children of the stones became heroes of defiance. While that sense of victory served Arafat as a psychological platform to launch his peace initiative and recognition of Israel, it was the Oslo agreement and the peace process that followed that disillusioned the Palestinians and threw them into a new episode of confrontation. The reluctance of Israeli governments to implement promised withdrawals from Palestinian land, and then the catastrophic failure of the Camp David talks, prepared the fertile soil for a new breed of militants and suicide bombers.

It was the re-entry of Sharon to the political scene that sparked the new intifadeh. Scores of

Palestinians were killed and maimed as Sharon declared his intention to cause as many casualties as possible. This time around, however, Israeli soldiers were not on foot and not even visible as they shot from their tanks. Palestinian militants shifted their target to the exposed Israeli civilians in markets and cafes. For the extremist militant, there is no difference between Israelis. They are the enemy; they are all the same.

In every case of martyrdom, there is a personal story of tragedy and trauma. A curious journalist once asked me to introduce him to a potential martyr. When the journalist asked, "Why would you do it?" he was told, "Would you fight for your country or not? Of course you would. You would be respected in your country as a brave man, and I would be remembered as a martyr."

This is the influence of the teaching of the Koran, the most potent and powerful book in Arabia for the past 14 centuries. In the holy book, God promised Muslims who sacrificed themselves for the sake of Islam that they would not die. They would live on in paradise. Muslims, men and women, even secularists, hold to the promise literally. Heaven is then the ultimate reward of the devout who have the courage to take the ultimate test of faith.

What the young man did not say was that he was burning with a desire for revenge. He was a tearful witness, at the age of six, to his father's beating by Israeli soldiers. He would never forget seeing his father taken away, bleeding from the nose.

As Sharon was taking Arafat hostage and grinding the salt of humiliation into the sour wounds, he was taking us into a new horrific level of madness. Another Palestinian girl blew herself up in Jerusalem last week, killing two Israelis and wounding more. She will not be the last.

AN ISRAELI VIEW*

October 23, 1983, was one of the most horrific days in the history of modern terrorism. Two massive explosions destroyed the barracks of the U.S. and French contingents of the multinational peacekeeping force in Beirut, Lebanon, killing 241 American servicemen and 58 French paratroopers. Both explosions were carried out by Muslim extremists who drove to the heart of the target area and detonated bombs with no intention of escaping. Subsequent suicide attacks against Israeli and U.S. targets in Lebanon and Kuwait made it clear that a new type of killing had entered the repertoire of modern terrorism: a suicide operation in which the success of the attack depends on the death of the perpetrator.

This tactic stunned security experts. Two centuries of experience suggested that terrorists, though ready to risk their lives, wished to live after the terrorist act in order to benefit from its accomplishments. But this new terrorism defied that belief. It seemed qualitatively different, appearing almost supernatural, extremely lethal, and impossible to stop. Within six months, French and U.S. Presidents François Mitterrand and Ronald Reagan pulled their troops out of Lebanon—a tacit admission that the new terrorism rendered all known counterterrorist measures useless. Government officials erected concrete barriers around the White House and sealed the Pentagon's underground bus tunnels. Nobody was reassured. As *Time* magazine skeptically observed in 1983: "No security expert thinks such defensive measures will stop a determined Islamic terrorist who expects to join Allah by killing some Americans."

The prevalence of suicide terrorism during the last two decades testifies to its gruesome effectiveness [see Table 17.1]. It has formed a vital part of several terror campaigns, including Hezbollah's successful operation against the Israeli invasion of Lebanon in the mid-1980s, the 1994–96 Hamas bus bombings aimed at stopping the Israeli–Palestinian peace process, and the 1995–99 Kurdistan Workers' Party (PKK) struggle against Turkey. The formation of special suicide units within the Liberation

*From Ehud Sprinzak, "Rational Fanatics," *Foreign Policy* (September/October 2000), pp. 66–73.

Table 17.1   Martyrdom's Global Reach

SUICIDE ATTACKS BY TERRORIST ORGANIZATIONS, 1983–2000

Liberation Tigers of Tamil Eelam	171
Lebanese Hezbollah and Amal	25
Other Lebanese groups	25
Palestinian Hamas	22
Kurdistan Workers' Party	21
Palestinian Islamic Jihad	8
Chechen separatists	7
Qaida (Osama bin Laden)	2
Kuwaiti Dawa	2
Egyptian Islamic Jihad	1
Egyptian Islamic Group	1
Algerian Armed Islamic Group	1

Sources: Yoram Schweitzer, "Suicide Terrorism: Development and Characteristics" (Herzliya: International Policy Institute for Counter-Terrorism, 2000); *Foreign Policy* magazine.

Tigers of Tamil Eelam (LTTE) army in Sri Lanka has added an atrocious dimension to the civil war on that devastated island. In addition to killing hundreds of civilians, soldiers, and high-ranking officers since 1987, LTTE suicide terrorists have assassinated two heads of state: Prime Minister Rajiv Gandhi of India in 1991 and President Ranasinghe Premadasa of Sri Lanka in 1993. Sri Lanka's current president, Chandrika Kumaratunga, recently lost sight in one eye following an assassination attempt that killed at least 24 people. The simultaneous 1998 bombings of the U.S. embassies in Kenya and Tanzania, which took the lives of nearly 300 civilians, were a brutal reprise of the 1983 tragedies in Lebanon.

Almost 20 years after its stunning modern debut, suicide terrorism continues to carry the image of the "ultimate" terror weapon. But is this tactic as unstoppable as it seems? The experiences of the last two decades have yielded important insights into the true nature of suicide bombers—insights that demystify their motivations and strategies, expose their vulnerabilities, and suggest ways to defeat what a se-

nior State Department official once called a "frightening" problem to which there are "no answers."

AVERAGE, EVERYDAY MARTYRS

A long view of history reveals that suicide terrorism existed many years before "truck bombs" became part of the global vernacular. As early as the 11th century, the Assassins, Muslim fighters living in northern Persia, adopted suicide terrorism as a strategy to advance the cause of Islam. In the 18th century the Muslim communities of the Malabar Coast in India, Atjeh in Sumatra, and Mindanao and Sulu in the southern Philippines resorted to suicide attacks when faced with European colonial repression. These perpetrators never perceived their deaths as suicide. Rather, they saw them as acts of martyrdom in the name of the community and for the glory of God.

Moreover, suicide terrorism, both ancient and modern, is not merely the product of religious fervor, Islamic or otherwise. Martha Crenshaw, a leading terrorism scholar at Wesleyan University, argues that the mind-set of a suicide bomber is no different from those of Tibetan self-immolators, Irish political prisoners ready to die in a hunger strike, or dedicated terrorists worldwide who wish to live after an operation but know their chances of survival are negligible. Seen in this light, suicide terrorism loses its demonic uniqueness. It is merely one type of martyrdom venerated by certain cultures or religious traditions but rejected by others who favor different modes of supreme sacrifice.

Acts of martyrdom vary not only by culture, but also by specific circumstances. Tel Aviv University psychologist Ariel Merari has conducted the most comprehensive study of individuals who commit acts of suicide terrorism. After profiling more than 50 [Muslim suicide bombers, he concluded that there is no single psychological or demographic profile of suicide terrorists. Furthermore, he maintains that no organization can create a person's basic readiness to die.] The task of recruiters is not to produce but rather to identify this predisposition in candidates and reinforce it. Recruiters will often exploit religious beliefs when indoctrinating would-be bombers, using their subjects' faith in a reward in paradise to strengthen and solidify preexisting sacrificial motives. But other powerful motives reinforce tendencies toward martyrdom, including patriotism, hatred of the enemy, and a profound sense of victimization.

Since suicide terrorism is an organizational phenomenon, the struggle against it cannot be conducted on an individual level. Although profiling suicide bombers may be a fascinating academic challenge, it is less relevant in the real-world struggle against them than understanding the modus operandi and mind-set of terrorist leaders who would never consider killing themselves, but opt for suicide terrorism as a result of cold reasoning.

THE CARE AND FEEDING OF A SUICIDE BOMBER

A suicide terrorist is almost always the last link in a long organizational chain that involves numerous actors. Once the decision to launch a suicide attack has been made, its implementation requires at least six separate operations: target selection, intelligence gathering, recruitment, physical and "spiritual" training, preparation of explosives, and transportation of the suicide bombers to the target area. Such a mission often involves dozens of terrorists and accomplices who have no intention of committing suicide, but without whom no suicide operation could take place.

In the cases of Hezbollah and Hamas, no permanent suicide units were formed, and bombers were recruited and trained on an ad hoc, conditional basis. But, in rare instances, some organizations adopt suicide terrorism as a legitimate and permanent strategy, harkening back to the Japanese kamikaze pilots of the Second World War. Currently, the Sri Lankan Tamil Tigers are the only example of this phenomenon. The "Black Tigers" launched their first attack in July 1987,

and since then suicide bombings have become an enduring feature of the LTTE's ruthless struggle. During the last 13 years, 171 attacks have killed hundreds of civilians and soldiers and wounded thousands more. The assassinations of two heads of state, political leaders, and high-ranking military officers have made it clear that no politician or public figure is immune to these attacks.

The Black Tigers constitute the most significant proof that suicide terrorism is not merely a religious phenomenon and that under certain extreme political and psychological circumstances secular volunteers are fully capable of martyrdom. The Tamil suicide bombers are not the product of a religious cult, but rather a cult of personality: Velupillai Prabhakaran, the brutal and charismatic LTTE leader who initiated the practice, appears to have been greatly influenced by the spectacular successes of Hezbollah in Lebanon. Fiercely determined to fight the repressive Sinhalese government until the Tamils achieve independence, Prabhakaran created the suicide units largely by the strength of his personality and his unlimited control of the organization.

The formation of the Black Tigers was greatly facilitated by an early practice of the organization's members: Since the early 1980s, all LTTE fighters—male and female alike—have been required to carry potassium cyanide capsules. A standard LTTE order makes it unequivocally clear that soldiers are to consume the capsule's contents if capture is imminent. The LTTE suicide units are essentially an extension of the organization's general culture of supreme martyrdom; the passage from ordinary combat soldier to suicide bomber is a short and tragic journey.

MAKING SUICIDE TERRORISTS PAY

The perceived strength of suicide bombers is that they are lone, irrational fanatics who cannot be deterred. The actual weakness of suicide bombers is that they are nothing more than the instruments of terrorist leaders who expect their organizations to gain tangible benefits from this shocking tactic.

. . . [O]nce it has been established that an organization has resolved to use suicide terrorism, security services can strike against the commanders and field officers who recruit and train the assailants and then plan the attacks. This counterterrorism effort calls for the formation of effective networks of informers, the constant monitoring of potential collaborators, and close cooperation among international intelligence services. Counterterrorist operatives must apply consistent pressure on the terrorist infrastructure through harassment and attacks. They must also seek ways to cut off the terrorists' sources of funding by depriving organizations of their financial resources (such as international bank accounts or "front" businesses). Regardless of the presence or absence of hard evidence for planned operations, it is essential to put potential terrorists on the run.

In fighting suicide bombers, it is important not to succumb to the idea that they are ready to do anything and lose everything. This is the same sort of simplistic reasoning that has fueled the widespread hysteria over terrorists acquiring weapons of mass destruction (WMD). The perception that terrorists are undeterrable fanatics who are willing to kill millions indiscriminately just to sow fear and chaos belies the reality that they are cold, rational killers who employ violence to achieve specific political objectives. Whereas the threat of WMD terrorism is little more than overheated rhetoric, suicide bombing remains a devastating form of terrorism whose complete demise is unlikely in the 21st century. The ongoing political instability in the Middle East, Russia, and South Asia—including Iran, Afghanistan, Chechnya, and possibly India and Pakistan—suggests that these regions will continue to be high-risk areas, with irregular suicide bombings occasionally extending to other parts of the globe. But the present understanding of the high costs of suicide terrorism and the growing cooperation among intelligence services worldwide gives credence to the hope that in the future only desperate organizations of losers will try to use this tactic on a systematic basis.

REVIEW QUESTIONS

1. What makes suicide bombers tick? Answer the question using at least two examples from Sarraj's and Sprinzak's articles.
2. Compare and contrast ancient and modern terrorism.

PART FIVE

SEXUAL AND FAMILY VIOLENCE

During the summer before her freshman year in college, Jennifer worked in a bakery, where she met Jack, a coworker. She got pregnant by him, and soon they were married. Jack turned out to be a heavy drinker and often subjected Jennifer to physical violence. Several times, she moved out then returned after Jack showed remorse. The abuse got worse. He would tie her up and vaginally and anally rape her, sometimes burning parts of her body with a cigarette. Finally, she bought a gun and killed him after suffering another episode of violence.[1]

Bibi, a young lower-caste woman in Pakistan, was also victimized. For an hour and a half, away from her home, four male members of a higher-caste family took turns raping her, then forced her to walk home naked. Now the men face the death penalty, and Bibi wants to see them hang. Apparently she feels the same way as Jennifer did toward her abuser. As she said, "I feel so enraged. If these people came in front of me, I would kill them."[2]

The family violence inflicted on Jennifer and the sexual violence inflicted on Bibi are relatively common. They typically result from the perpetrator being in a socially dominant position vis-à-vis the victim, a product of patriarchal, sexually inegalitarian society. Here we learn about various forms of sexual and family violence. In the first article, "How Women Construct Rape," Amy Chasteen presents data on how women define rape and what they think rape is like. In the second article, "'Giving In' to Unwanted Sex with the Husband," Kathleen Basile reports on her empirical study of how and why women have sex with their husbands even though they don't really want to. In the third selection, "Child Molesters: Denying Guilt," Carla van Dam discusses the common tendency among child molesters to provide various excuses to neutralize their guilt. In the fourth reading, "Female Genital Mutilation," Donald Barstow deals with a painful issue confronting mostly African societies.

1. Walter S. DeKeseredy and Martin D. Schwartz, *Contemporary Criminology* (Belmont, CA: Wadsworth, 1996).

2. Ian Fisher, "Account of Punjab Rape Tells of a Brutal Society," *New York Times,* July 17, 2002, p. A3.

HOW WOMEN CONSTRUCT RAPE

AMY L. CHASTEEN

As defined by Best (1999:103–116), the "contemporary ideology of victimization" that emerged ... in the post-1975 era has several key components, all of which relate to the reconstruction of sexual violence that has occurred over the past 30 years. First, in this new ideology, victimization is argued to be very common, and claims emphasize the large numbers of people affected (Best 1999:103). In the construction of any set of circumstances as a social problem, claims of widespread harm to large numbers of people are an integral part of framing the problem as serious and in need of public attention (Best 1990, 1999). Such claims routinely rely on the expansion of the problem's domain, which has occurred with rape. As Best (1999:104) noted,

> *The evolution of feminist thought on rape has led to increasingly broad standards for redefining the domain of sexual assault, including arguments that "no means no," that anything short of an explicit "yes" means no, and even that "women in our patriarchal culture can never freely consent to sex."*

A second component of the contemporary ideology of victimization involves framing victimization as highly consequential, with long-lasting damage (Best 1999:106). The characterizations of contemporary problems thus often involve terminology such as *syndrome* and *disorder*. In the case of sexual assault, the concept of "rape trauma syndrome" was developed to gesture to the lasting impact of a rape experience; this concept has become integrated into not only academic literature but also legal contests (Estrich 1987).

Third, in the new ideology, victimization is argued to be unambiguous, though it often goes unrecognized by both the public and the individuals involved (Best 1999). Although the definition of rape may be clear-cut—any violation of a woman's nonconsent—the reality is that various instances of rape may not be defined as such by the law or by the people involved; indeed, research has often indicated that women whose experiences meet the definition of rape used by researchers may well not regard those encounters as rapes (Warshaw 1988). Thus, as Best pointed out, another theme in the ideology of victimization is that "new victims" must learn to rename their experiences as victimization, so "advocates seek to teach individuals to recognize, acknowledge, and address their own victimization" (p. 111), through support groups, media tales, or college classrooms. Such education has been a priority for the feminist antirape movement. An additional component of the ideology is that anyone's "claim to the status of victim must not be challenged" (Best 1999:114). The notion that disbelieving a woman's account of rape is "blaming the victim" is a central element of feminist discourse. Finally, Best noted that many social movements around various

Source: Amy L. Chasteen, "Constructing Rape: Feminism, Change, and Women's Everyday Understandings of Sexual Assault," *Sociological Spectrum,* vol. 21 (April/June 2001), pp. 101–139. Reproduced by permission of Taylor and Francis, Inc., http://www.routledge-ny.com.

forms of victimization have argued that "the term 'victim' has undesirable connotations" (p. 116). This point is indeed true in feminist discourse, which favors the term *survivor* over *victim* as a more powerful and positive label (Kelly 1988).

In considering the social history of rape's meaning, it is clear that the feminist movement has sought to reframe rape as a "new crime," to use Best's (1999) terminology. By reconstructing the definition of rape, the character of the rapist, and the role of a rape survivor, feminist discourse has profoundly challenged traditional ideas about sex and violence. Legal, media, and academic discourse reflect the broadened definition of rape, newly discovered facts of rape's prevalence, and arguments about the ongoing deep trauma that sexual assault survivors must cope with (Brooks 1997; Donat and D'Emilio 1992; Freetly and Kane 1995; Ledray 1994; Plummer 1995). To what extent do these elements of the new ideology on rape filter into the everyday routine perceptions of women?

METHOD

The goal of this research was to explore the everyday definitions and interpretations of rape held by women. Because little research has been done on everyday constructions, this project was primarily exploratory in nature, designed to probe general definitions and meanings held by women. Rather than assuming a particular definition of rape or a specific meaning it holds for women, I sought to reveal the taken-for-granted assumptions about sexual violence held by a diverse group of women. These understandings are then compared with the feminist reconstruction of rape that has occurred over the past 30 years, allowing several key questions to be addressed: To what extent are broadened definitions of rape embraced by women in their everyday lives? Are concepts such as "no means no" integrated into respondents' explanations of their rape definitions? Is the notion of rape as a permanently devastating experience part of how women imagine what rape is like? Do women

share a unified "woman's perspective" on rape, or do significant points of diversity exist?

The methods used for this project were centered around obtaining a diverse sample and providing women with a forum to express their ideas about sexual assault. To explore the influence of differences among women, I developed a sampling methodology that would reach a wide variety of women. I wanted to include both students and nonstudents, women who had been raped and women who had not, older and younger women, and women of different racial groups. I elected to use a sample of [12] beauty salons in the Ypsilanti, Michigan, area as the base for soliciting participants to complete a series of written, open-ended questions regarding their definition and understanding of sexual assault.

The instrument used included four primary questions designed to elicit women's definitions and understandings of rape. The first two questions asked women to estimate the prevalence of rape. The first question was "What percentage of women do you think will be raped in their lifetime by a stranger?" The second question asked, "What percentage of women do you think will be raped in their lifetime by someone they know?" For each question, respondents were given five options for their answers—fewer than 10 percent, 11–20 percent, 21–33 percent, 34–50 percent, and more than 50 percent. These two questions were designed to elicit women's perception of rape's commonness and to gauge whether they thought strangers or acquaintances were the most frequent assailants.

The third question focused on women's definitions of rape. A sexual scenario was presented to the respondents to reveal what elements they focused on in deciding whether to label an encounter as rape. Other researchers have used vignettes to educe respondents' implicit definitions of rape and to consider how manipulation of certain variables (e.g., use of force) alters respondents' willingness to label an encounter as rape (Bourque 1989; Burt and Albin 1981; Freetly and Kane 1995). However, rather than altering the scenario to test variation in response, this instrument used a far more ambiguous sexual situation to see what percentage of women assumed a definition of rape that applied to such a situation. I chose a story that was not clear-cut in order to reveal differences among women in their everyday definitions of sexual assault. This story, referred to in this article as "Jane's Story," is presented here:

> Jane and her boyfriend haven't had sex in weeks. They are at home, and he doesn't try to have sex with her. She feels bad and thinks they might be about to break up. They go to bed. She wakes up in the middle of the night and feels one arm around her waist and another around her left leg. She feels something push inside her and realizes he's having intercourse with her. She stares at the wall and pretends to be asleep. She's 19 years old, and he's the second person she's had sex with. She doesn't like what's happening now, but she doesn't usually like sex with him so much. In a couple of minutes it's over, and he rolls away from her and goes to sleep. They both get up the next morning, and neither one mentions what happened the night before.

The story was followed by an open-ended question: "Do you think this is rape? Why or why not? What would you say to Jane or her boyfriend if they told you this story?"

The fourth and final question probed the meaning rape held for the women in the sample. Respondents were asked to generate analogies for sexual assault as a way of illustrating the understandings of rape they carried with them in their everyday lives. The question used was this:

> Imagine that someone came up to you and said, "I see the news and I know what rape is, but I don't know what rape is like for women when it actually happens to them." What is another experience or event that you think would be useful to illustrate what rape is like?

These four primary questions on the instrument were followed by a series of items asking the respondents to list their age, educational level, and marital status. I then asked them to identify their social class, sexual orientation, and race. The next three items were open-ended questions on religiosity, identification with feminism, and rape history.

FINDINGS

Rape's Prevalence

Women in this study estimated the lifetime risk of rape to be quite high, and no variation emerged in the rate estimated by women of different backgrounds or experiences. The most common responses were that 11–20 percent of women will be raped by strangers in their lifetime, and more than half of women will be raped by some they know. . . .

The responses of women in this sample to the question of rape's prevalence are thus in line with the highest estimates given by researchers and far higher than the estimates of the UCR [the FBI's Uniform Crime Reports] or NCVS [Bureau of Justice's National Crime Victimization Survey]. Women routinely assume that rape is extremely common and most often perpetrated by non-strangers; this central, once-radical argument of the feminist antirape movement is part of how the women in this sample viewed rape. However, women's estimates of the rape rate do not tell us how women define rape. And how do women understand the consequences of a rape experience? The two primary survey questions—the vignette and the analogies—addressed these points.

Jane's Story: How Women Define Rape

The reactions to Jane's Story were diverse and often very strong. Out of the 90 surveys collected, only six people left the question blank. Another eight women wrote comments without ever mentioning rape. The remaining 76 responses ranged from "yes, of course it's rape" to "no—what does this have to do with rape?" with 12 women stating that they "didn't know" because "it depends" on other factors (discussed below). The distribution of all 90 responses to Jane's Story is depicted in Table 18.1.

Table 18.1   Responses to Jane's Story: Was it Rape?

RESPONSES	%
Yes	44.4
No	26.7
I don't know/it depends	13.3
Written comments without mention of rape	8.9
No response	6.7

Approximately 44 percent of respondents stated that Jane's experience was rape—either a clear-cut case of rape or, as 10 percent of women stated, "a form of rape" in their definition, although perhaps not prosecutable. Consider the following responses:

Well, of course this was rape. He had sex with her without her consent. She wasn't even awake (so he thought). I would try to talk to the woman about why she didn't resist. My guess is that she was afraid to do so. . . . I don't know what to say to this man. Someone who would violate someone this way and then go to bed as though nothing unusual has happened is so far off the moral deep end that I doubt my talking to him would help. Sadly, my wish would be for him to drop dead and rot in hell.

Sexual intercourse that occurs without mutual consent is rape. The man needs to be told of and be held accountable for his unacceptable and criminal behavior.

Hell yes, anytime someone has sex without someone else's consent or permission and willingly forces him- or herself on somebody, that is rape. It doesn't matter if it was violent or not, the action was still rape. She was asleep, and he had sex against her will, which is an illegal act.

For these women, Jane was without a doubt the victim of rape. For another 27 percent of respondents, however, Jane was definitely *not* raped. Most commonly, these women cited Jane's silence as their reason for not defining the encounter as a rape. Some of their comments included the following:

If she didn't like it, why didn't she tell him to stop? If she had said anything, "No" "Stop"—I would consider it rape.

I do not think it was rape. Even though she didn't like what happened, she never said no. I'd say to her, "If you're not happy and do not like what has and probably will happen again, leave."

No, it is not rape because she did not tell him "no" or that she did not want to have intercourse.

When all responses to Jane's story were examined according to the variations in women's life experiences and backgrounds, some differences did emerge. The three factors that revealed the most variation in women's reaction to Jane's Story were race, age, and rape history. . . . Some racial differences between Black and White respondents can be seen. . . . White women were less likely to see Jane as a rape victim and were much more likely to report being uncertain about whether Jane was raped or not. Although 27 percent of White women reported that they didn't know whether Jane was raped, not a single Black respondent was uncertain. The age of respondents was also related to their response to Jane's Story: The 20–29 age group was the most likely to identify Jane as a rape victim; the majority of respondents in their twenties saw Jane as having been raped. All other age groups contained about a third of respondents who considered Jane a rape victim. . . .

The self-reported rape history of women and their responses to Jane's Story also revealed some interesting patterns. . . . [T]he two groups of women—those who had been raped and those who had not—were equally likely to see Jane as having been raped. . . . [R]oughly 48 percent of women who identified as rape victims and 45 percent of women who did not identify as rape victims saw Jane as having been raped. Women who had not been raped themselves, however, were more likely than rape victims to say that Jane had definitely not been raped

Clearly, the diversity of women's narrative responses to the ambiguous sexual scenario of Jane and her boyfriend indicate that women do not define rape in a uniform fashion. Rather, a wide range of ideas about and understandings of sexual assault exist among women in this sample. Some women considered any unwanted sexual contact to be rape; other women stipulated that a woman must aggressively fight back or that a woman cannot have an ongoing relationship with a man for a sexual act to constitute rape. Do similar differences emerge in the respondents' understandings of rape's meaning and consequence for women who are raped?

What Rape Is Like

[The women in this study held various views on what rape is like,] ranging from "getting your purse snatched" to "being drawn and quartered" to "having cancer." [These views can be divided into four categories]: personal destruction, theft, social status, and betrayal.

Personal Destruction. The most common [was the view that] the losses involved in rape were more than monetary or momentary; they were, as one respondent said, being "stripped of everything you ever had." One woman described rape in terms of someone "taking your emotions" and "thoughts and altering them so that you can never experience them for yourself." Another woman talked about a loss of identities, saying, "The closest analogy I can think of is having everything you own, everything you've earned, including jobs or titles, taken away." Thus, she imagined rape as an erasure of one's public roles—jobs, titles, everything. . . .

One woman described a gruesome scene:

> *You know what drawing and quartering is, don't you? Where they split you open and then they tie your, your insides, your intestines, to four different horses, then they slap the horses and they pull you into four pieces. That's what I think of when I think of rape.*

Theft. [Other women] described rape primarily in terms of robbery or burglary of something ma-

terial. Some women wrote things like "rape is like armed robbery—you steal something valuable" or talk about "the criminal act" of someone breaking into a house as similar to rape. The image of breaking and entering was used by several women, two of whom stated:

> *Rape is violence. It is similar to someone breaking into your home and taking or destroying something very important to you.*

> *[Rape is like] coming home from being out and finding your house broken into and all your most prized collections stolen.*

For other women, the object lost during theft was not that valuable. Two women mentioned getting your purse snatched or your billfold stolen as being similar to rape. Or, as one woman put it, rape is "like a bully stealing your lunch money, then beating you up."

Social Status. In a sharp narrative turn from tales of theft or personal destruction, some women provided images of rape as an event that propels one into a particular position in a social structure, similar to other stigmatizing events that place a person in a particular status in a larger, stratified system. Rape, in this view, is not about personal loss but about an ascribed status that affects others' perceptions and actions toward you. . . . One woman, for instance, simply stated that being raped was like being a slave in a plantation society, and another identified rape as similar to "the more general subjugation of the woman, in job situations, societal expectations, etc." that are seen in everyday society.

Other interviewees pointed to racial–ethnic stratification in the United States and analogized that being raped is a status much like being a racial minority:

> *A single incident of rape is like a lifetime of race and gender discrimination laid on your chest in one package. In a single instant, you are totally devalued; less than nobody. . . . You know that the burden is yours alone.*

Betrayal.   [Some women saw rape as betrayal. As one said,]

> *Put it like this, if you were standing in the middle of the street and a dog came up to you licking your hand and being friendly. You start to pet it and trust it and be nice to it. You develop a friendship and a relationship. You may even take it home with you. Then one day, all of a sudden, the dog attacks you for no reason, biting you, leaving a scar. You feel physically hurt as well as mentally hurt that your dog betrayed your trust, feelings, and friendship. Neither you nor the dog will have the same relationship or level of trust.*

For these women, rape was fundamentally about betrayal within the context of a trusting relationship. Clearly, the rape they described is an acquaintance rape, not sexual assault by a stranger. The assailant is presumed to be someone a woman knows and trusts who takes advantage of her faith to cause her harm.

Social Variations

Race, age, and rape history revealed interesting patterns in the analogies women gave. First, the most common 129response for Black women (36 percent) was the theme of personal destruction; for White women, the most common response was theft.

Second, those under age of 20 were most likely (33 percent) to use analogies to theft, those in their 20s most often used images of personal destruction (44 percent), those in their 30s most typically (38 percent) left the question blank, and women over 40 most frequently used images of social status (33 percent).

Third, women who reported being raped were 2.5 times as likely to use images of theft when describing sexual assault as women who said they had not been raped.

CONCLUSION

The research presented here reflects a sample of women's everyday constructions of rape. Most women agreed that rape is a common crime perpetuated most often by someone the woman knows; however, the everyday constructions of what rape is and what it means varied considerably among women in this sample. The female respondents in this study were a diverse group, and differences among the women in the sample resulted in variations in the answers they provided to questions on Jane's Story and analogies for rape.

REFERENCES

Best, Joel. 1990. *Threatened Children: Rhetoric and Concern about Child Victims.* Chicago: University of Chicago Press.

Best, Joel. 1999. *Random Violence: How We Talk about New Crimes and New Victims.* Berkeley: University of California Press.

Bourque, Linda Brookover. 1989. *Defining Rape.* Durham, NC: Duke University Press.

Brooks, Dianne L. 1997. "Rape on Soaps: The Legal Angle." Pp. 104–19 in *Feminism, Media and the Law,* edited by M. A. Fineman and M. T. McCluskey. New York: Oxford University Press.

Burt, Martha R., and Albin, Rochelle S. 1981. "Rape Myths, Rape Definitions, and Probability of Conviction." *Journal of Applied Social Psychology* 11:212–30.

Donat, Patricia L. N., and John D'Emilio. 1992. "A Feminist Redefinition of Rape and Sexual Assault: Historical Foundation and Change." *Journal of Social Issues* 48:9–22.

Estrich, Susan. 1987. *Real Rape.* Cambridge, MA: Harvard University Press.

Freely, Angela J. Hattery, and Emily W. Kane. 1995. "Men's and Women's Perceptions of Non-Consensual Sexual Intercourse." *Sex Roles* 33(11/12): 785–802.

Kelly, Liz. 1988. *Surviving Sexual Violence.* Minneapolis: University of Minnesota Press.

Ledray, Linda E. 1994. *Recovering from Rape.* 2d ed. New York: Henry Holt.

Plummer, Ken. 1995. *Telling Sexual Stories: Power, Change and Social Worlds.* London: Routledge.

Warshaw, Robin. 1988. *I Never Called It Rape.* New York: Harper & Row.

REVIEW QUESTIONS

1. How has the feminist movement sought to reframe rape as a "new crime"?
2. Answer the third question in the "Method" section of the article, and defend your answer.

"GIVING IN" TO UNWANTED SEX WITH THE HUSBAND

KATHLEEN C. BASILE

We as a society have taken steps to end unwanted sex that is physically forced on wives and girlfriends. The question that remains, though, is what are we doing to bring an end to coercive sex among intimates that is unwanted yet does not involve threats or even discussion between partners? The issue is confounded when examining unwanted sex among intimates when physical force is not involved, particularly when it occurs as a result of acquiescence on the part of the woman. These situations could occur because of the woman's perceived responsibilities as a spouse (i.e., the "wifely duty"), or could be due to threats of force and/or the woman's fear of force, among other things. How do we comprehend these more subtle forms of unwanted sex, particularly in the context of marriage, which is defined by ancient ideas of duty and obligation? More specifically, how does the idea of acquiescence fit into an understanding of sexual coercion in marriage? What are the different ways in which women "give in" to undesired sex with their partners? Furthermore, how do women make sense of their own reactions to the unwanted sex and other experiences within the relationships?

This article examines the ways in which women acquiesce to unwanted sex in marriage through in-depth analyses of 41 interviews with women who have experienced some form of unwanted sex in a marital or long-term intimate relationship. Various types of acquiescence are delineated and the contexts of these women's relationships within which these experiences occur are discussed. In addition, I examine the likelihood of women who use a given acquiescence type to believe that their experiences constitute rape.

REVIEW OF THE LITERATURE

Despite popular myths about rape, namely, that the perpetrator is primarily unknown to the victim and that wife rape is essentially impossible, physically forced sex by an intimate partner is recognized by some as rape (Hall, 1995; Ward, 1995). For instance, 72% of Finkelhor and Yllo's (1985) sample of women who survived sexual assaults by their husbands agreed that their experiences qualified as rape. More recently, Bergen (1996) found that one third of the women in her sample initially defined their experiences with their partners as rape, and others redefined their experiences as rape as their relationships progressed. Even the average citizen now acknowledges that wife rape is prevalent and chronic. A recent national poll found that 76% of the general public believes husbands use force to make their wives have sex, and 80% believe it occurs often or somewhat often (Basile, 1998).

Source: Kathleen C. Basile, "Rape by Acquiescence: The Ways in Which Women 'Give In' to Unwanted Sex with Their Husbands," *Violence against Women,* vol. 5 (September 1999), pp. 1036–1058. Reprinted by permission of Sage Publications, Inc.

It is harder to assign a name to experiences of unwanted sex where there is no physical force and no lack of consent. Begging, bothering, pressuring, or manipulating in some way the actions of your partner all fall into the subtle realm of coercion without being clear-cut enough to qualify as rape. Reminiscent of Betty Friedan's (1963) "problem that has no name," which typified the frustration of housewives in the 1950s, married women have for centuries been subjected to coercive sexual activity but have been unable to name it. It is clearly not rape in the eyes of popular culture, the legal system, or most wives who experience it, for the two critical components of rape, force and consent, are not at issue. The unwanted sex that occurs in these relationships happens as a result of the wife's acquiescence, and it is often never known to anyone, even her husband, that the sex was undesired. These kinds of sexual relations sit in the gray area that most women define as the inconveniences of being married.

These kinds of coercive sexual acts are illuminated by the work of Finkelhor and Yllo (1985). They identified four types of coercion: (a) social, (b) interpersonal, (c) threatened physical, and (d) physical. Social coercion involves the social and cultural expectations that go along with being a wife. For instance, a woman might feel obliged to be dutiful and have sex with her husband. Social coercion must be viewed within the framework of the institutions that perpetuate it: the legal system, religion, and the institution of marriage itself. Rules about how to be a good wife are learned by women early on through socialization. Interpersonal coercion, according to these authors, is sex that results from threatening behavior on the part of the husband. Interpersonal coercion is not violent but instead entails threats of things such as cheating, withholding money or other resources, or general anger or unkindness if sex is not given by the wife.

Finkelhor and Yllo's (1985) third and fourth types of coercion are most closely linked to what is commonly recognized as rape. Threatened physical coercion is that which specifically implies the use of physical force if sex is not performed. Physical coercion, as its name suggests, is the use of physical force (punching, holding down) to have sex. Finkelhor and Yllo argued that all four types of coercion would constitute forced sex, but only the last two types (threatened physical and physical coercion) could be considered rape.

Finkelhor and Yllo's (1985) conceptualizations of sexual coercion, particularly social and interpersonal coercion, will be used in this article as a springboard from which to better understand the gray arena of coercion that leads many women to give in to sex without threats or force. . . .

METHOD

This article is based on the results of semistructured, in-depth telephone interviews with 41 women previously involved in a national telephone poll of 1,108 randomly selected citizens. The national poll was conducted in the spring of 1997. The follow-up, in-depth interviews were conducted from June through October of 1997.

. . . To qualify for an interview, women were asked whether they had experienced unwanted sex with a husband or intimate partner. Women who answered yes were asked if they could be called back for a longer telephone interview. Of the 602 women polled, 204 or 34% had experienced unwanted sex, and 96 of those women agreed to be called back for a longer interview. Forty-one interviews were successfully completed. The remaining 55 women did not complete interviews due to disconnected numbers, their inability to be reached after five or more attempts, and subsequent refusals to participate.

Women who answered affirmatively to having had unwanted sex were also questioned about different sexual coercion scenarios to determine if they had ever experienced unwanted sex under one or more of the seven circumstances. These scenarios were designed to be of increasing severity. The initial question ascertaining the occurrence of unwanted sex and the seven scenarios are listed in [Table 19.1]. The first four scenarios are identified

Table 19.1   Sexual Coercion Items in the Spring 1997 National Telephone Poll

---

INITIAL QUESTION TO QUALIFY FOR STUDY:

Some women have had sex with a husband or intimate partner when they really did not want to, and others have never had this experience. Have you ever had sex with a husband or intimate partner when you really did not want to?

SEXUAL COERCION SCENARIOS:
Now I am going to present several circumstances. Please think of your current or most recent relationship in answering the following questions. Thinking of your current or most recent partner, have you ever had sex with that person when you really did not want to?

"LESS SEVERE" COERCION
1. when you thought your husband or partner expected sex from you in return for certain actions, like spending money on you for a gift or taking you out for a nice dinner
2. because you thought it was your duty to have sex with your husband or partner when he wants to have sex
3. after a romantic situation, like after a back rub or after intimately kissing
4. after your husband or partner begged and pleaded with you to have sex

"SEVERE" COERCION:
5. after your husband or partner said things to bully or humiliate you into having sex
6. after your husband or partner threatened to hurt you if you did not have sex
7. after your husband or partner used physical force on you in order to have sex

---

as less severe types of coercion, whereas the last three scenarios are considered to be severe forms of coercion. Women were also asked about the frequency of unwanted sex. In addition, women who responded "no" to a scenario were asked if it had ever happened with a past partner.

Participants were asked to give detailed descriptions of the incident(s) of unwanted sex in their marriages or intimate relationships, including when, where, and the circumstances under which it happened. They were asked why they thought the incident(s) happened and how they felt while the unwanted sex was occurring (i.e., what emotions they were feeling at the time). They were asked the circumstances under which they chose to stay with or separate from their spouses or partners. Finally, similar to Finkelhor and Yllo's (1985) and Bergen's (1996) research, women were

asked if they believe that they were raped. This was asked to see which of the women who have experienced unwanted sex at varying degrees of severity are willing to identify their experiences as rape. Given the harsh stigma associated with that word in our society, and the ambiguity related to marital relationships and rape, it is helpful to see which women use the term *rape* in describing their experiences.

FINDINGS AND DISCUSSION

The women's experiences with unwanted sex were varied. Approximately half of the sample described severe experiences involving verbal bullying, physical force, and/or threats of force (21 women), and most of the rest of the women described less severe situations, where physical force and threats were not involved (17 women). The remaining 3 women could not be categorized as having suffered from either severe or minor coercion, as they experienced a combination of both or one type in the present and the other type in the past. Those women whose experiences were severe tended to have suffered the full gamut of minor as well as severe forms of sexual coercion. Of the 21 women who described severe coercion, 19 of them were describing past relationships.

Types of Acquiescence

By virtue of being in the sample, all of the women admitted to having unwanted sex. The issue at hand is the way in which women become involved in the undesired sex act. Although the contexts in which they faced the unwanted sex varied, results show that their reactions were often similar; more than half of the women (24 women, or 59%) admitted to having given in to sex with their partners once or more during their relationships.

Through the course of the analyses, five types of acquiescence emerged. In this section, the types of acquiescence used by the women are described and examples of each are given in the words of the participants.

Unwanted Turns to Wanted. This type of acquiescence involves occasions when the women did not really feel up to sex initially but were able to enjoy it after a few minutes. It is perhaps the least severe way in which women gave in to undesired sex. These instances were usually the result of a romantic situation, where intimate kissing or a back rub preceded the sex act. Take, for example, the experience of Rita, a 27-year-old who describes sex that was initially unwanted with her current husband.

> Oh, let's see, just, you know, sometimes in the middle of the day or something and that's just not my time to have sex and they feel like it, and I guess kind of put you on a guilt trip if you don't want to, use things like, "you never want to when I do" or "you're always too tired," just stupid things, and

> so then you'll usually give in when initially you didn't feel like it and then afterwards, I was kind of glad that I did but initially I didn't feel like it.

Often the women ended up talking themselves into the sex, based on a feeling that they would be doing their partners a favor by making them feel good. The following quote is from Heidi, age 41, who spoke of her present husband:

> A lot of times if I don't really want to have sex and he does, sometimes after we start having sex it's like, it's okay, you know? It's like, well, yeah, you know. Okay, I can get into this too.

This type of acquiescence was used by 10% of the women. It occurred almost exclusively in relationships that were current and in relationships that were happy and healthy from the woman's perspective.

It's My Duty. This type of acquiescence is based on the idea of a wifely obligation inherent in the marital contract. This notion is bolstered by religious beliefs that women's role is to service their husbands. This was the most prevalent form of acquiescence among this sample. It occurred in current marriages and relationships that were defined as happy and healthy by the women, as well as in those past and present relationships that were filled with severe levels of physical abuse and/or physically forced sex. This method of acquiescence epitomized the "inconveniences of married life" for these women, but it was seen as an inherent responsibility of a wife and was virtually unchallenged. Denise, for example, was a 27-year-old who spoke about being pregnant a few months prior to the interview and having sex with her current husband because she thought it was her duty: "I felt like, you know, to be the dutiful wife, you know, you feel like you need to . . . I don't know . . . you just, kind of need to please him when he wants to, in order to keep everything happy."

As expressed in the above quote, the women saw their "wifely duty" as going hand-in-hand with "keeping peace" in the household. In this sense, their role as wife included being peacemaker, and sex was often the best route to peace. In addition, being a "dutiful wife" also gave many women the assurance that their husbands would not stray, which is suggested by Hillary, age 51, who spoke of her current marriage: "I think that it's your responsibility to, you know, to keep them satisfied so they don't look other places."

Of the 41 women who were interviewed for this study, 31 (76%) of them said that they sometimes had sex in their relationship because of a perceived wifely duty. Of the women sampled, 34% (or 14 women) saw a perceived wifely duty as the main reason they had unwanted sex.

Easier Not to Argue.   This method of acquiescence occurred when verbal or nonverbal behavior from a woman's partner became too much for her to stand and giving in to sex was the easiest way out of the situation. It was often connected to various forms of emotional manipulation, pressure, and, in some instances, control. Manipulation surfaced in the form of guilt trips, verbal abuse, withholding of attention or a general level of unkindness and ill will toward her if she withheld sex. In this way, the consequence of not having sex became worse than just giving in, doing it, and getting it over with. If she gave in, she did not have to hear him complain, pout, or, in some cases, become angry or unpleasant for extended periods of time as a form of punishment for her. There were differing degrees of severity to this category of acquiescence. For example, Rebecca, age 36, described her experiences with a former live-in boyfriend:

> I was sort of nudged and then pestered and, never like pinned down and forced but it was easier to just give in than to have to deal with this guilt tripping and nudging and pestering and poking and you know, all this kind of thing that would just go on and on and on and I would just want to go to sleep, or get out of this situation or whatever.

For some women, acquiescence because it was easier not to argue occurred in a context of complete emotional control. . . . Terri, a 32-year-old divorced woman, . . . spoke of an alcoholic ex-husband who commonly threatened her and emotionally manipulated her. In this way, putting up with sex was easier than dealing with the verbal abuse that would result if she did not give in. Having sex because it was easier not to argue occurred among 27% of the sample (11 women).

Don't Know What Might Happen If I Don't.   In this case, unwanted sex occurred due to fear of some negative reaction from the husband. In these cases, husbands commonly threatened their wives or acted in ways that were threatening and fearful to the wife, all in an effort to gain her complete acquiescence. These relationships were not usually characterized by physical force, just enough verbal threats to create an environment defined by fear and filled with the tension of wondering what might happen if she did not give in. Ellen, age 53, described why she always eventually acquiesced to her ex-husband:

> Oh, there was one point that he took out a gun, he had a little pistol, and uh, scared me half to death. I was shaking all over and he was looking for it and I had hidden it. He was looking through all my drawers and threw out everything from, you know, my bras and panties and things were all over the place, and he was looking for his gun. And so, after that episode, I just didn't dare, you know. I would just go through with it [sex], there was no way I was going to say no.

In another relationship, Nicole, age 31, suggests how she feared his potential reaction if she withheld sex: "The thing is, I didn't really fight it, but I think if I would have, that it probably would have gotten worse, not violent you know, but a little bit rougher for me so I would just give in." Although this type of acquiescence was less common than the others, it did occur among 7% of this sample. It was often a coping strategy employed after years of verbal threats and emotional control that culminated in the woman's complete acquiescence. As it involved more severe forms of emotional coercion, such as threats and bully-ing by the husband, it was most common among women who were no longer with the partner they discussed.

Know What Will Happen If I Don't. This form of acquiescence occurred in an effort to avoid any more of the prior experiences that they had with physical force and abuse from the partner. Similar to the previous type, women learned not to fight it and to essentially do whatever their husband or partner wanted because the women were totally controlled by them. However, unlike the previous type, the women in this category had firsthand ex-periences of physical abuse in their relationships and had frequently been physically forced to have sex with their partners. Agatha, age 74, described her acquiescence to her ex-husband in this way: "I guess you could say it was consensual when you feel like you are going to have your head beat so you feel like, why not?" Although not all women suffering from severe experiences fit into this cate-gory, 20% (or eight women) did acquiesce because they knew what would happen if they did not.

Most of these women (six women) experi-enced what Finkelhor and Yllo (1985) called bat-tering rape, where physically forced sex occurred in the context of a battering relationship. Holly, a 33-year-old divorced woman, described unwanted sex with her ex-husband in this way:

> When you're intimidated by someone and they want to have sex no matter what the reason or what the situation, you do it, otherwise, you get the hell beat out of you to be quite honest . . . you just let him do it. It's not him actually holding you down and forcing you but it is being forced be-cause you can't say no.

Physical force was also used by Holly's al-coholic ex-husband to have sex, and in those cases she did define it as rape. Ronnie, age 46, was willing to liken her acquiescence to her al-coholic, abusive ex-husband to rape: "Sex-wise, he never physically abused me. I didn't want sex. . . . I mean, you can call it rape, because I

didn't want it. But I wouldn't say no because I knew what would happen if I said no." As seen in the above quotes, this type of acquiescence usually occurred along with the presence of al-cohol, as 37% of the physically abusive husbands (15 in total) were described by the women as al-coholics. In addition, 5 women (12%) described drug-addicted husbands.

Calling It Rape

Which women were likely to identify their experi-ences as rape? Results of this study make it clear that most women define their experiences as rape only when there is the clear use of physical force and when they did not give consent. In the sample as a whole, 15 of the women (37%) conceded that they had been raped, whereas 23 women (56%) did not see themselves as rape victims due to their failure to say no, and 3 women (7%) were not sure. Although some of the women who described previous relationships disclosed that they did not recognize their situations as rape at the time that it occurred, they were able to redefine their pasts and call it rape. Two common threads connecting most of the women who identified their experiences as rape were that they were subjected to severe levels of physical violence in their relationships, and their experiences of unwelcome sex were chronic.

Some women viewed acquiescence as some-thing that they could not avoid, given the history of their relationship or the perceived consequen-ces of denying sex. The majority of women who did call it rape (13 out of 15) were referring to relationships that have long since dissolved. Given the politicalization of wife rape that has occurred in recent years due to cases such as Lorena Bobbitt's, which have made the reality of wife rape a public issue, perhaps more women are now willing to identify their experiences as rape (Wiehe & Richards, 1995). Some of the women were even willing to identify their "ac-quiescence" as rape, even if the recognition re-mained solely in their minds.

As stated earlier, more than half of the women in this sample . . . did not characterize their experiences as rape. This supports other studies that have consistently found that many women do not consider themselves raped when they experience unwanted sex with an intimate (Bergen 1996; Finkelhor & Yllo, 1985; Koss, 1993; Warshaw, 1988). Most women in the sample (56%) were not willing to call their experiences rape, but rather they considered them inconveniences that they gave in to, particularly if physical force was not involved. However, there were 5 women in the sample who described severe experiences that they did not call rape. Nicole, age 31, in negotiating in her own mind whether her experience with her ex-boyfriend was rape, said: "I didn't necessarily consent, but . . . I kind of gave in, I think if I wouldn't have given in and maybe fought it more . . . that it possibly could have turned into something that I would have called rape." Ellen, age 53, did not see her experience as rape: "I would have had to tell him no, right off the bat, right?"

If they do not define their experiences as rape, women who give in to unwanted sex with their husbands have no shared language with which to describe the incidents. It is as if the only available cultural labels are "rape" or "not rape," and this dichotomy leaves no room to acknowledge or label undesired sex of a less violent and physically coerced nature.

CONCLUSION

The central theme connecting the five types of acquiescence elaborated on here is the idea that they involved unwanted sex, therefore some level of coercion had to exist. These five types can be viewed as occurring in different marital contexts. Unwanted turns to wanted, the most seemingly innocuous of all the types of acquiescence, tended to occur in what the women defined as happy, non-coercive partnerships, and resulted in, as more than one woman put it, "the headache suddenly going away." Acquiescence as a result of a perceived marital duty, analogous to what Finkelhor

and Yllo (1985) called social coercion, can be seen as a product of a history of societal tradition that dictates proper behavior for women and perceived expectations of wives. Whether this type of acquiescence occurred in relatively happy or in severely abusive and unhappy relationships, all women shared the idea that sex was a responsibility of a wife. Inherent in both of these types of acquiescence is the societal notion that women should sexually service their partners.

The last three types, on the other hand, can be viewed as coping strategies used by the women. "Easier not to argue" occurred in a context of guilt, insecurity, and hostility wherein the clearest path to peace perceived by the women was acquiescence. Types four and five were seen as ways to avoid potential and real physical danger, respectively, while managing to survive the situation.

When negotiating and enduring unwanted sex with an intimate, the definition of rape becomes ambiguous when women's consent is given under societal conditions of dominance and inequality. This is due, in part, to the ways in which men are socialized to believe "no" sometimes means "yes" or "maybe" or at least "keep trying" (Searles & Berger, 1995). As MacKinnon (1983) points out, the difference between acquiescence and consent becomes unclear. The marital context makes this already ambiguous situation even more confused, as is evidenced in the words of many women in the sample who had a hard time making sense of their experiences. Time was the one variable that seemed to help these women define their situations. Indeed, the overwhelming majority of severe experiences were described by women who were no longer with the abusive partner but had previously been subjected to physical force. These women were often redefining the experiences as abuse, which was now possible because they were not still involved with the abuser and they were in a safer place to reconstruct what had happened. This is evidenced by the fact that many women said that they would call the experience rape at the time of the interview but would not have at the time of the relationship.

This article is an effort to recognize the varying degrees of force subsumed under the rubric of acquiescence. The processes and consequences of giving in to unwanted sex with an intimate have not been given as much attention as other forms of forced sex that have traditionally been identified as rape. Increased recognition of these more subtle forms of coercion is not suggested in an effort to dilute what is understood to be rape, a concern of Finkelhor and Yllo's (1985) that is well taken. The force or threat of force to gain sexual pleasures is a vicious and extremely damaging form of sexual assault that should not be compared or equated to the less severe forms of sexual coercion elaborated on in acquiescence types one, two, and three. However, types four and five, although they involved acquiescence on the part of the women, should be considered rape in the traditional sense, as they included threats and/or physical force. Indeed, each of the five types of acquiescence discussed in this article is a form of sexual coercion that has important implications.

It is useful to consider different paths to unwanted sexual contact on a continuum of severity. This helps us acknowledge the more subtle processes that result in women having undesired sex, while at the same time understanding the similarities of these subtle forms of coercion to the more severe forms that we recognize as rape. If we can make connections between subtle and severe experiences, we might make some headway in understanding the processes by which mildly coercive relationships become more coercive with time. We can also bring attention to and recognize the damage inherent in coercive experiences that have long been accepted by women as part of the marriage contract. All of this is done in an effort to come closer to the ultimate goal of feminist scholarship and all those working to end all forms of partner violence—to make intimate relationships equal for both partners.

REFERENCES

Basile, K. C. (1998). *Wife rape: Attitudes and experiences.* Unpublished manuscript.

Bergen, R. K. (1996). *Wife rape: Understanding the response of survivors and service providers.* Thousand Oaks, CA: Sage.

Finkelhor, D., & Yllo, K. (1985). *License to rape: Sexual abuse of wives.* New York: Free Press.

Friedan, B. (1963). *The feminine mystique.* New York: Norton.

Hall, R. (1995). *Rape in America: A reference handbook.* Santa Barbara, CA: ABC-CLIO.

Koss, M. P (1993). Detecting the scope of rape: A review of prevalence research methods. *Journal of Interpersonal Violence, 8*(2), 198–222.

MacKinnon, C. (1983). Feminism, Marxism, method, and the state: Toward feminist jurisprudence. *Signs, 8*(4), 635–658.

Searles, P., & Berger, R. J. (Eds.). (1995). *Rape and society: Readings on the problem of sexual assault.* Boulder, CO: Westview.

Ward, C. A. (1995). *Attitudes toward rape: Feminist and social psychological perspectives.* London: Sage Ltd.

Warshaw, R. (1988). *I never called it rape: The Ms. report on recognizing, fighting, and surviving date and acquaintance rape.* New York: Harper & Row.

Wiene, V. R., & Richards, A. L. (1995). Intimate betrayal: Understanding and responding to the trauma of acquaintance rape. Thousand Oaks, CA: Sage.

REVIEW QUESTIONS

1. What are the five types of reasons provided by women who give in to unwanted sex with their husbands?
2. How do women who do not initially define the unwanted sexual encounter as rape with their mate come to define the experience as rape?

CHILD MOLESTERS: DENYING GUILT

CARLA VAN DAM

To commit sexual offenses against children, the molester must overcome internal inhibitions (Finkelhor, 1984), which is done by Orwellian Newspeak. This occurs when the activities are reinterpreted in a different and seemingly more acceptable context. Such reinterpretations of reality range from denying the event, calling it social work, blaming the victim, or describing the abuse as an accident, to considering the problem to be with the rest of society. Many of the molesters, after developing some insight through treatment, refer to this as "grooming themselves."

The molesters' [often] admit to the behavior but blame the victim. Russell (1984) describes three rapists who said their victim "was only getting what she deserved for walking on the street without a man at night" (p. 153). One molester told Salter (1988) that "this behavior isn't immoral you know, it's just illegal" (p. 99). Many molesters reported that "if she's old enough to bleed, she's old enough to breed." Others placed the responsibility on the victim by describing how she "was really well-built," or believing that the girl's attire and stature was to blame "because she was wearing a revealing nightgown." A judge told a reporter that in most sexual assault cases, the assaults "occur when the woman is drunk and passed out. The man comes along, sees a pair of hips, and helps himself" (Halliday, 1995, p. 4).

Other molesters believe that their behavior is inevitable because "She was coming on to me," or "She was running around nude and she really wanted it." Explanations also include comments such as "This kid had been hanging all over me. She comes on with a lot of the guys in the neighborhood—what could I do? For a ten-year-old, she really knew it all" (in Sanford, 1980, p. 88). Interestingly enough, these rationales are also given when the victim is three years old. Some judges accept this reasoning, agreeing that a three-year-old victim is to blame for being sexually provocative and "coming on" to the adult (Halliday, 1995). In these cases, the molesters believe that each child's behavior is sexual, and that they are helpless in the face of such pressure.

Some molesters admit to the abuse and claim it was a simple mistake: "It only happened once. I said I'd never do it again, so I don't know what the big deal with the police is" (in Sanford, 1980, p. 88). These stories are often accepted by a number of adults in the community. For instance, one molester told a judge, "I just rolled over and tried to make love to the wrong girl," and was acquitted (Bavelas, Chovil, and Coates, 1993, p. 1), a line repeated verbatim by many of the molesters interviewed for this book.

Molesters also proudly proclaim their sexual involvement with children to be therapeutic. Writing in seemingly professional journals, they equate child sexual abuse to good social work. Brongersma (1991) refers to

several examples of social workers achieving miracles with apparently incorrigible young delinquents—not by preaching to them but by sleeping with them.

Source: Carla van Dam, *Identifying Child Molesters* (New York: Haworth Press, 2001), pp. 127–135. Reprinted with permission.

Affection demonstrated by sexual arousal upon contact with the boy's body, by obvious pleasure taken in giving pleasure to the boy, did far more good than years in reformatories. . . . I personally know of cases brought before [a certain judge]. In one, a boy who had been arrested several times for shoplifting, who had been a terror at home and a failure in school, suddenly turned over a new leaf, gave up crime, started getting good marks at school and became a national champion in his favorite sport. All of this occurred after a boy-lover had been asked officially to take care of him . . . likewise, in Berlin a test program was instituted in which young delinquents were put under the supervision of boy-lovers. The results were totally successful, but unfortunately the fear of public reaction soon closed the program down. (p. 160)

Molesters will use such terminology as "making love," which is also misleading and suggests a consensual affectionate act. Even using the term *sexual* in these cases helps create confusion. For instance, "If sex is stolen rather than willingly shared, then in a world in which sex was understood to be a truly consensual activity, stolen sex would not be sex. Yet the law obliges us to label what has been stolen as sexual" (Boyle, 1985, p. 104). This language problem allows judgments against molesters to be lenient because "at least there was no external violence committed upon her," thereby implying that the "accused simply had sex with the complainant" (Coates, Bavelas, and Gibson, 1994, p. 194). In criminal records, this is also exemplified with such modifiers as "no harm was caused to the victim." This is further exemplified in court cases. In one case, for instance, "a man pled guilty to sexually assaulting a young girl and boy. The judge remarked that the 'indecent assault against the young girl is less serious because it involved no violence' . . . again having the language facilitate the minimization of the event" (Coates, Bavelas, and Gibson, 1994, p. 194).

Carnes (1983) likens the molester's behavior to an addiction and describes how the "addictive system starts with a belief system containing faulty assumptions, myths, and values which sup-

port impaired thinking" (p. 16). In the case of child sexual abuse, as already mentioned, much of the impaired thinking echoes societal attitudes and beliefs to some extent. Many molesters also blame their wives, saying such things as "She wouldn't have sex with me anymore; she was unresponsive; she was cold." The sexual abuse of children to them is a logical response to their situation, since they believe their sexual needs must be met one way or another. Because this mirrors generally held beliefs that "boys will be boys," that the male sexual appetite must be satisfied, and that any subsequent molestation reflects family dysfunction, the responsibility for the abuse is placed on the child and/or the wife. Thus, the molester blaming the victim and the wife fits in neatly with society's prejudices.

In the professional literature, this same blaming occurs. Kempe and Kempe (1984) consider the wife responsible in many cases: "These men are often described as passive-aggressive personalities who frequently have wives who are dominant-dependent and demanding but ungiving within the marital relationship" (p. 30). They further state that the wife's failure to provide nurturing and intimacy to both her husband and her daughter drive them into an incestuous relationship: "For example, incest often occurs in a family in which not only the father receives little affection and sexual intimacy from his wife but in which the daughter may also receive little affection, nurture, or even attention from her mother" (p. 192).

Caplan (1993) describes this double bind created solely for mothers, "where mothers will be damned no matter what they do." For instance, they are supposed to be "endless givers of nurturance," which simultaneously means "that they drain the emotional energy of those around them" (p. 96). In the case of child sexual abuse, the mothers are responsible for the sexual abuse of their children because they were sexually unavailable to their spouses. In addition to being unavailable, they also are accused of deliberately setting up their child for the abuse. As Salter (1988) states, "there is nowhere in the literature the kind of animosity shown toward offenders that has repeatedly been expressed toward the victims and their mothers" (p. 34).

Yet although marital dysfunction is the most frequently cited cause for mothers being responsible for sexual abuse (Salter, 1988), such lack of access to sex does not explain the behaviors of child molesters (Groth, 1979):

> *In fact, the sexual encounters with children co-existed with sexual contacts with adults. For example, in the incest cases, we found that the men were having sexual relations with their daughters or sons in addition to, rather than instead of, sexual relations with their wives. Those offenders who confined their sexual activity to children did so through choice. There was no one for whom no other opportunity for sexual gratification existed. (p. 146)*

Various therapists and researchers have also demonstrated an affinity with the molester's view of the blame. Revitch and Weiss (1962) stated that "the majority of pedophiles are harmless individuals and their victims are usually known to be aggressive and seductive children" (p. 78). Gagnon (1965) described most incidents of child molestation as collaborative, since the victim "might have, in fact, been more provocative in the offense than the bare bones of the descriptions might allow" (p. 180). Weiss and colleagues (1955) felt the sexual assaults could best be understood by examining the victims' personality and believed most victims to have "participating" personalities. These personality traits were then described to cover most of the behaviors typically associated as evidence of the abuse. Mohr, Turner, and Jerry (1964) considered the child "a willing participant if not the instigator of a sexual act with an adult" (p. 34). Lukianowicz (1972) further used the subsequent propensity for victimized children to be sexually promiscuous with older men as evidence of their responsibility in the initial assaults, rather than evidence of the effect of such abuse on the developing personality. Virkkunen (1975) stated, "without doubt, the child victim's own behavior often plays a con-

siderable part in initiating and maintaining a pedophiliac crime" (p. 130).

Much of the research that reflects this perspective was obtained by interviewing child molesters. Unfortunately, this creates an alliance with the informant. Corroborating information from others was not obtained. Yet accepting information from molesters as independently reliable is fraught with difficulty, as it can be assumed that they will minimize, deny, and blame. This is a dilemma in both offender research and treatment programs.

In addition to blaming the wife and the victim, molesters minimize and rationalize their activities. One molester explained to the judge that a group of eight-year-old girls had asked him what a condom was. To best answer their question, he found it necessary to demonstrate. He further explained to the judge that to show them what a condom looked like required an erection, which he produced only to contribute to their education. He believed his activity to be educational and helpful (Halliday, 1985).

Groth (1979) considers appropriate sex education one of the best forms of protection parents can provide their children because it inoculates them from exactly this type of behavior. This was echoed by the advice of a number of molesters in Elliott, Browne, and Kilcoyne's (1995) study, who all confirmed the importance of parents teaching children about sex, different parts of the body, and right and wrong touches. "I used it to my advantage by teaching the child myself" (p. 590). The initial sex education provided by the molester quickly exceeds accepted boundaries of appropriateness.

According to a number of professionals, some offenders continue to deny the crime altogether (Ward, Hudson, and Marshall, 1995; Roys, 1995). This is also seen among the prison population. The defenses start to sound like clichés: "I could not have done it. . . . I have a bad back. . . . I work all the time. . . . My diabetes prevents me from getting erections anymore." The molesters also describe how the victim fabricated the story: "She made it all up. . . . She's obviously been abused by someone else. . . . She's the one who has been sexually abusing others." In each of their cases, the reason for the false conviction and subsequent prison sentence was because "I had poor legal representation. . . . I didn't understand the system. . . . Everyone was swayed by the victim's innocent act."

This response from molesters and their powerful allies contributes to letting child sexual abuse flourish undetected. In addition to the type of denial and minimization already discussed, there is also, among some molesters, another type of denial. This is the belief that sexualizing children is a healthy practice that benefits them. They consider their proclivities to be a "sexual orientation" and, through such organizations as North American Man-Boy Love Association (NAMBLA), the Rene Guyon Society, and the Childhood Sexual-ity Circle, have lobbied for legislative changes. They have marched in gay pride parades, representing themselves as another discriminated against and misunderstood sexual minority. Although they promote this behavior, they nevertheless keep their identities secret. "John Miller, the WNBC-TV correspondent who broke the story, said last week: 'We thought these guys were people who lurk around outside schools. What we found was, they lurk around inside the schools' " (Leo, 1993, p. 37). One high school science teacher is on the "NAMBLA steering committee and the editorial board of the NAMBLA Bulletin, which has offered advice on how to entice a child into sex—'leave a pornographic magazine someplace where he's sure to find it' " (Leo, 1993, p. 37). . . .

REFERENCES

Bavelas, J., Chovil, N., and Coates, L. 1993. "Language on sexual assault judgments." *Summary of a Project Funded by the B. C. Ministry of Women's Equality,* January–June. Report fran the University of Victoria.

Boyle, C. 1985. "Sexual assault and the feminist judge." *Canadian Journal of Women in the Law,* I, pp. 93–107.

Brongersma, E. 1991. "Boy-lovers and their influence on boys: Distorted research and anecdotal observations." *Journal of Homosexuality,* 20 (1/2), pp. 145–173.

Caplan, P. 1993. "Don't blame mother: Scapegoating and myths often keep natural allies apart." *Ms. Magazine,* 2 (12), September, p. 96.

Carnes, P. 1983. *The sexual addiction.* New York: Comp-Care Publications.

Coates, L., Bavellas, J., and Gibson, J. 1994. *Discourse and society.* London: Sage Publications.

Elliott, M., Browne, K., and Kilcoyne, J. 1995. "Child sexual abuse prevention: What offenders tell us." *Child Abuse and Neglect,* 19 (5), pp. 579–594.

Finkelhor, D. 1984. *Long-term effects of sexual abuse in child sexual abuse: New theory and research.* New York: The Free Press.

Gagnon, J. (1965). Female Child Victims of Sex Offenses. *Social Problems,* 13 (2), pp. 176–192.

Groth, N. 1979. *Men who rape: The psychology of the sex offender.* New York: Plenum.

Halliday, L. 1985. *Sexual abuse: Counseling issues and concerns.* Campbell River, BC: Ptarmigan Press.

Halliday, L. 1995. *Sexual abuse in Canada: An update.* Presented at the International Women's Day Conference at Comox, BC, by the British Columbia Teacher's Federation, May.

Kempe, R., and Kempe, H. 1984. *The common secret: Sexual abuse of children and adolescents.* New York: W. H. Freeman and Company.

Leo, J. 1993. "Pedophiles in the schools." *U.S. News and World Report,* October 11, p. 37.

Lukianowicz, N. 1972. "Incest I: Paternal incest." *British Journal of Psychiatry,* 120, pp. 301–313.

Mohr, J. W., Turner, R. E., and Jerry, M. B. 1964. *Pedophilia and exhibitionism.* Toronto, Ontario: University of Toronto Press.

Revitch, E., and Weiss, R. G. 1962. The pedophiliac offender. *Diseases of the Nervous System,* 23, pp. 73–78.

Roys, D. T. 1995. "Psychoeducation for incarcerated sex offenders in Georgia correctional institutions." *The Network,* 13 (1), pp. 53–57.

Russell, D. E. H. 1984. *Sexual exploitation: Rape, child sexual abuse, and workplace harassment.* Beverly Hills, CA: Sage Publications.

Salter, A. C. 1988. *Treating child sex offenders and victims.* Newbury Park, CA: Sage Publications.

Sanford, L. 1980. *The silent children: A parent's guide to the prevention of child sexual abuse.* New York: McGraw-Hill Book Company.

Virkkunen, M. 1975. Victim precipitated pedophilia offenses. *British Journal of Criminology,* 15 (2), pp. 175–180.

Ward, T., Hudson, S. M., and Marshall, W. I. 1995. "Cognitive distortions and affective deficits in sex offenders: A cognitive deconstructionist interpretation." *Sexual Abuse: A Journal of Research and Treatment,* 7 (1), pp. 67–84.

Weiss, J., Rogers, E., Darwin, M. R., and Dutton, C. E. 1955. "A study of girl sex victims." *Psychiatry Quarterly,* 29, pp. 1–27.

REVIEW QUESTIONS

1. What arguments put forth by researchers demonstrate an affinity with the molester's view of the blame?
2. Compare and contrast child molesters with other sexual deviants, such as gays, lesbians, and prostitutes.

FEMALE GENITAL MUTILATION

DONALD G. BARSTOW

Female genital mutilation (FGM), more commonly and less precisely referred to as female circumcision, is defined by the Council on Scientific Affairs of the American Medical Association as "the medically unnecessary modification of female genitals" (Council on Scientific Affairs, 1995, 274(21):1714–1716). The extensive physical, emotional, mental and sexual trauma which accompanies this procedure has resulted in the practice being labeled "barbaric [and] abhorrent" (Jordan, 1994, p. 94) and equated with torture by some authors (Davis, 1985; Joseph, 1996; Omer-Hashi, 1994). Lloyd DeMause (1998) considers the practice to be a form of incest. Winter asserts that the operation, whatever the stated reason, is "a direct attack on a woman's sexuality" (Jordan, 1994, p. 941). Research involving the short-term and long-term [aftereffects] that emerge from the experience indicate that many victims suffer the signs and symptoms of posttraumatic stress disorder. Opponents of the procedure urge that it be banned as an extreme form of child abuse. Proponents assert that it is an important cultural ritual of passage that must be preserved in order to maintain cultural identity.

Linda Burstyn (1995) has estimated that between 100 million and 130 million women (in at least 40 countries) have been subjected to FGM. The average number of females physically and psychologically coerced into undergoing this procedure on any given day is thought to be about 6000 (or about 2.2 million a year).

The first historical mention of FGM was in 450 BC by the Greek historian Herodotus. Other notables who made reference to it were Strabo (25 BC), Soramus (138 AD), and Aetius (502–575 AD). While the origins of the custom are obscure (Hastings, 1928), it was widely practiced by the ancient Egyptians. Medical examination of mummies has confirmed that FGM was common among the rich and powerful. One possible explanation has to do with the inheritance of property and title. For example, the early pharaohs are known to have inherited the right to the throne from their mother, not their father. As a consequence of this custom, the ruling male was required to marry either his mother or his sister in order to produce male offspring that legally qualified to ascend to the throne. Female circumcision may have been a principal measure of insuring the legitimacy of all claims to kingship. It may also have been adopted by wealthy men concerned with other legal or inheritance issues. A second interpretation may relate to the panhistorical male preoccupation with the sexual faithfulness of the wife. . . . Such preoccupation is well illustrated by the introduction of metal "chastity belts" in Europe during the Crusades. This latter form of enforced continence, in the Western world, may have led to a decline over time of the more invasive alternative of tough scar

Source: Donald G. Barstow, "Female Genital Mutilation: The Penultimate Gender Abuse," *Child Abuse and Neglect,* vol. 23, no. 5 (1999), pp. 501–510. Reprinted with permission.

tissue with all its implications for intercourse and childbirth.

Currently, FGM is reported to be widely practiced in [African] countries. . . . While many people in the Western world believe FGM to be a Muslim practice, this is certainly not the case (Jordan, 1994). This erroneous conclusion may have been drawn from the fact that the procedure is more widespread in those countries in which Islam is the principal religion (Gruenbaum, 1991). However, residents who identify themselves as Christians, Jews, or members of indigenous religions in these nations also practice the ritual (Toubia, 1994). Religious leaders tend to view FGM as a culture trait and not a theological dogma. A notable exception to this religious lassitude is to be found among the Jehovah's Witnesses who have imposed a worldwide ban on the practice since 1985 (Watchtower Bible & Tract Society, 1985, 1993).

PROCEDURES

There are four types of female genital mutilation. The first and most common is called sunna, and involves removal of the hood or prepuce of the clitoris. This is the simplest, least invasive, least mutilating form, and logically results in fewer untoward [aftereffects]. The second type entails a clitoridectomy, or total removal of the clitoris. The third type is referred to as excision, and signifies removal of the prepuce, clitoris, upper labia minora and perhaps the labia majora. The last, and most traumatic type is called infibulation (or Pharaonic), and includes removal of the prepuce, clitoris, the labia minora, and the labia majora.

Untrained midwives most often perform the surgery, which serves as a principal source of supplemental income. Victims can range in age from 1 week to 17 years (according to local custom), but most often the mutilation occurs at puberty. The initiates are generally restrained by two or more females who are often aunts or other family members. The procedure is most frequently performed without the aid of anesthetics (Jordan, 1994), antiseptics, analgesics, or antibiotics (Den-

ney & Quadagno, 1992). The instruments, which may have been used on multiple victims without being cleaned before, during or after the "surgery," include sharp stones (Gibeau, 1998), razor blades, broken glass, kitchen knives, scissors, or even the teeth of the midwife (Joseph, 1996). If the girl is to be infibulated, the edges of the raw flesh are approximated with sutures, thorns, adhesives made of eggs or sugar (Arbesman, Kahler, & Buck, 1993) or toothpicks. A match, twig, or straw may be inserted into the incision to leave a small hole through which urine and menstrual flow can pass. The legs may then be bound together to reduce hemorrhage (Arbesman, Kahler, & Buck, 1993). In some areas the victim may be forced to walk through the village to publicly demonstrate that she has undergone this rite of passage (Hirsch, 1981), dance (Joseph, 1996), or have intercourse with multiple partners. One can easily imagine the intensity and duration of the pain that accompanies these activities to say nothing of the risk for added trauma and infection.

DeMause (1998) classifies FGM as incest and a sadistic/sexual ceremony which, he suggests, is sexually exciting to observers. He notes that in some instances, the individual who performs the act is accompanied to the scene by prostitutes, since these occasions are often marked by heavy drinking and unrestrained sexual activity.

Personal accounts recorded by the victims themselves reveal the pain, terror, horror and humiliation associated with FGM (Davis, 1985; Joseph, 1996; Omer-Hashi, 1994; Toubia, 1994):

Once I was inside the hut, the women began to sing my praises, to which I turned a deaf ear, as I was overcome with terror. My throat was dry, and I was perspiring though it was early morning and not yet hot. "Lie down there," the excisor suddenly said to me, pointing to a mat stretched out on the ground. No sooner had I lain down than I felt my thin frail legs tightly grasped by heavy hands and pulled wide apart. I lifted my head. Two women on each side of me pinned me to the ground. My arms were also immobilized. Suddenly I felt some strange substance being spread over my genital organs. My heart seemed to miss a beat. I would have given anything at that moment to be a thousand miles away: then a shooting pain brought me back to reality from my thoughts of flight. I was already being excised: first of all I underwent the ablation [surgical removal] of the labia minor and then of the clitoris. The operation seemed to go on forever, as it had to be performed "to perfection." I was in the throes of endless agony, torn apart both physically and psychologically. It was the rule that girls of my age did not weep in this situation. I broke the rule. I reacted immediately with tears and screams of pain. I felt wet. I was bleeding. The blood flowed in torrents. Then they applied a mixture of butter and medicinal herbs which stopped the bleeding. Never had I felt such excruciating pain! (Joseph, 1996, pp. 3, 4)

Then they forced me, not only to walk back to join the other girls who had already been excised, but to dance with them. (Joseph, 1996, p. 4)

I realized that my thighs had been pulled wide apart, and that each of my lower limbs was being held as far away from the other as possible, gripped by steel fingers that never relinquished their pressure. I felt that the rasping knife or blade was heading straight down toward my throat. Then suddenly the metallic edge seemed to drop between my thighs and there cut off a piece of flesh from my body. I screamed with pain despite the tight hand held over my mouth, for the pain was not just a pain, it was like a searing flame that went through my whole body. (Davis, 1985, p. 332)

JUSTIFICATIONS

Proponents of FGM have offered the following as justification for continuing this traumatic practice: (1) it is required by the Koran or the Bible (in reality, neither of these Scriptures makes reference to, or requires, the procedure); (2) the clitoris is dirty; (3) the clitoris will grow like a penis and hang down between the legs if not removed; (4) a non-excised woman will be barren (FGM actually results in a high incidence of infertility); (5) the clitoris is evil; (6) the clitoris causes male impotence; (7) the clitoris contains a poisonous substance that kills babies during childbirth; (8) excision prevents the production of foul-smelling secretions; (9) circumcision aids fertilization (studies show that the opposite is true); (10) it insures virginity and chastity which Schroeder (1994) stresses are essential for the family's honor; (11) uncircumcised women are rejected as marriage partners which means they cannot fulfill their role, which is to provide heirs for their husbands, and therefore they have no social value (not uncommonly a serious suitor will demand to examine the infibulation of a prospective bride for reassurance concerning her virginity); (12) circumcised women do not make excessive or unreasonable sexual demands on their husbands; (13) the procedure increases a woman's femininity; (14) it is an important cultural trait; (15) it is an age-old tradition; (16) it prevents social ostracism, stigmatization, and scapegoating; (17) it is done for cosmetic reasons since the female genitalia are repulsive to look at; (18) it provides protection from temptations posed by the devil, and; (19) it provides tight vaginas for enhanced male satisfaction (Schrage, 1994).

It is obvious that the infibulation will need to be incised to allow for sexual intercourse. The laceration may be gradually enlarged, by penile thrusting, over a period of weeks or even months (Denney & Quadagno, 1992). In some cases the husband may use his fingers to break the adhesions. If this method fails, he may then resort to using a small knife, razor blade, or acid to open the scar (Arbesman, Kahler, & Buck, 1993). In some cases a midwife is called to make a mold of the bridegroom's penis in order that she may make an incision of "appropriate" size. Since this is done the night before the marriage, post-nuptial intercourse is a frightening and agonizing experience for the new bride.

When the pregnant wife is ready to deliver her child, she must be deinfibulated. Again, midwives, using unsanitary instruments, and without the benefit of medical knowledge, anesthetics (Jordan, 1994), antiseptics, analgesics, or antibiotics often perform this surgical procedure. After the baby has been delivered, the mother will frequently be reinfibulated. This cycle of infibulation, penetration, pregnancy, deinfibulation, and reinfibulation is repeated with each successive birth (Arbesman, Kahler, & Buck, 1993; Joseph, 1996; Mustafa, 1966). Reinfibulation may also occur following a divorce or death of the husband (Jordan, 1994). A major justified concern of adult infibulated females who move to Western nations is that health care personnel will not know how to provide for their needs, especially during childbirth (Brown, Calder, & Rae, 1989; Toubia, 1994). Health care providers should know that husbands will often demand to be present throughout the birth process to ensure that no breach of "sexual propriety" occurs. Personnel, in spite of personal values, must attempt to secure the husband's trust since he makes all decisions for his wife, including whether she receives medical care (Baker, Gilson, Vill, & Curet, 1993; Omer-Hashsi, 1994). If at all possible, doctors and nurses should be female (Baker et al., 1993).

How is such an invasive and debilitating procedure justified? Shaw (1985) writes that some anthropologists hypothesize that the practice may have originated in ancient times as a method of preventing evil spirits from entering the vagina. Today, a wide variety of reasons are offered. In some cultures it is said to distinguish respectable women from prostitutes and slaves (Denney & Quadagno, 1992; Lightfoot-Klein, 1989). Angela Davis (1985) asserts that the surgery is meant to prevent women from enjoying intercourse, thus reducing the probability of adulterous relationships. Akpaeti (1988, p. 590) has also labeled the practice a "promotion of chastity through the reduction or abolition of the clitoris." He adds that the practice is also justified as the celebration of a cultural or religious rite, and for enhancement of appearance. Beck and Reddie (1978) have pointed out that in the Middle East there exists a common stereotype of women as lacking in "mind and religion." Since these deficits could be used by the Devil to lead the unwary into sexual temptations and sin, FGM is viewed as a protection for salvation. This thought is supported by Lightfoot-Klein (1989), who states: "Women are assumed to be (by nature) sexually voracious, promiscuous and unbridled creatures, morally too weak to be entrusted with the sacred honor of the

family" (p. 379). Mustafa (1966) agrees, asserting that FGM is justified by proponents who assert that the practice "attenuates sexual desires in girls and protects their morals by removing the sensitive parts and constricting the introitus" (p. 303). . . . Infibulation certainly does preclude sexual penetration, thus preserving, at least physically, female chastity. Virginity is thus assured (Fourcroy, 1983). Additional justifications include protection from the HIV virus, elimination of seduction by pedophiles, prevention of forcible rape, and avoidance of abortion. Since the only value a girl has is her virginity, it must be preserved.

Masters, Johnson, and Kolodny (1988) state that the clitoris is often thought of as a miniature penis. Excision, therefore, makes a woman truly feminine. This was a common belief among the ancient Egyptians who regarded the prepuce of the clitoris as masculine, and the prepuce of the penis as feminine. To be "purely" masculine or feminine this tissue had to be removed.

This concept of bisexuality is reflected in the mythology of that time. Many Egyptian gods and goddesses are represented as being both male and female. How could they be "creators" unless they were blessed with the genitalia of both sexes? Statues of Hapi, the god of the Nile (a fertility deity), depict him with a pregnant abdomen and pendulous breasts, both of which symbolize fructuous reproductive abilities. It is not surprising, then, that both male and female "circumcision" was a common phenomenon.

Kluge (1993) writes that failure to undergo this procedure would be damaging to the female's self-esteem, cultural identity, and have an adverse impact on her social integration (Toubia, 1994). Jordan (1994) and Ladjali, Wrattray, & Walder (1993), confirm that uncircumcised women are stigmatized and avoided as marriage mates. As Lightfoot-Klein (1989, p. 375) has observed: " . . . an unmarried woman has virtually no rights, no status in the society and severely limited, if any, economic recourse. Without circumcision, a girl cannot marry and is thereby unable to fulfill her intended role, i.e., to produce legitimate sons to carry on her husband's patrilineage."

An additional reason for the practice proposed by Black & Debelle (1995) has to do with gender discrimination. They state (p. 590) that: "Female genital mutilation is supported and encouraged by men; indeed the operation can be regarded as an exercise in male supremacy and the oppression of women."

LEGAL, ETHICAL AND MORAL CONSIDERATIONS

Refugees and immigrants are bringing this belief system with them as they resettle in other countries. Some 7000 at-risk females move to the United States each year (Hirsch, 1981; Ziv, 1997), and these are old figures. Deaths from hemorrhage following FGM performed by midwives specifically imported for this purpose have been reported in Great Britain and Europe. Nations such as Belgium, Britain, Canada, Denmark, France, Sweden, and Switzerland have banned the practice. The World Health Organization, the International Planned Parenthood Foundation, the African Charter on the Rights and Welfare of the Child, the World Medical Association, the Vienna Declaration of the World Conference on Human Rights, [and] the Foundation for Women's Health, Research and Development have added their voices to the condemnation. In addition, the Inter-African Committee on Traditional Practices Affecting the Health of Women and Children has launched efforts directed toward the elimination of genital mutilation (Schroeder, 1994). While there is no such national proscription in America, a few individual states have taken steps to make FGM illegal.

Proponents of FGM argue that this procedure provides cultural identity, cultural cohesion, role clarification, and a sense of pride. At the same time it increases the desirability of the female as a prospective mate. They assert that pressures from outside the culture to abolish the practice are evidences of ethnocentrism, cultural imperialism, and cultural imposition. They point to invasive western cultural practices that are clearly designed to achieve the same results mentioned above: the promotion of female beauty, sexuality and attractiveness. Among the practices referred to are electrolysis, breast augmentation, stomach stapling, liposuction, piercing of the labia, lip, nose and/or eyebrow, and face lifts, all of which are "unnecessary medical modifications." In addition, they state, in the Western world, males engage in mutilating activities such as penis piercing and penis enlargement surgery. They suggest that opponents clean up their own act before attempting to impose their belief system on others.

The extent to which a government has the right to protect its citizens has been, and continues to be, a hotly debated issue. Laws requiring immunizations for children and domestic animals, and the use of seat belts and protective helmets, for example, have been widely challenged in the courts. There are laws regulating businesses that provide tattoos, ear piercing and body piercing which are intended to protect customers from disease. But what about scarification activities that are a basic practice among many groups, and which are viewed as an expression of personal identity and an enhancement of beauty? Should these be regulated? If so, where should the authority and responsibility be vested? What policies should be established by the overseeing agency? The list of potential questionable practices is nearly endless. And what is to be done with procedures involving religious beliefs such as male circumcision? Where does cosmetology end and mutilation begin? Where is the line to be drawn between individual choice, however variant, and the public good?

Can a case be made in favor of FGM if the environment in which the operation is executed is upgraded and, as a consequence, long-term [aftereffects] are virtually eliminated? Would ethical objections be satisfied if the procedure was to be performed by skilled professional surgeons, using anesthesia, sterile instruments and techniques, and adequate post-operative care? Not in the case of individuals determined by law to be minors, because they cannot grant legal "informed consent."

FGM is an act that, even under the best of circumstances, frequently results in permanent physical mutilation and alteration of body function. Therefore the potential consequences of any decision must be carefully reviewed and evaluated by the potential initiate. To this end individuals ought to be provided information that provides the opportunity for granting informed consent.

Informed consent is predicated upon five precepts. First, consent must be entirely voluntary. Second, the individual must have the mental capacity to understand the information provided. Third, the individual must receive adequate and accurate instruction (including the pros and cons) upon which to base the decision. Fourth, the person must not be physically or emotionally coerced into submission and fifth, the information must be presented in a language (frequently the mother tongue) that the client also speaks. It is obvious from the review of the literature that the vast majority of FGM victims are unable emotionally, intellectually or developmentally to provide informed consent. Therefore, altering the environment would do nothing to remove valid ethical objections.

Historically, some cultural practices and identities have been abolished, altered or "purified." The abolition of slavery has removed the stigma of being identified as a slave, and resulted in some degree of betterment of the human condition. The same can be said relative to the banning of the caste system in India, and outlawing the practice of suttee, the self-immolation of wives on the funeral pyre of their deceased husbands. Legal measures taken to eliminate footbinding in China (1949) and child marriages in India (1929) have not resulted in the death of these cultures. The eradication of head hunting, human sacrifice and cannibalism have undoubtedly had an impact on their respective cultures, but who would argue that these practices should be permitted solely in order to preserve cultural integrity?

FGM is internationally recognized as gender-specific child abuse, child exploitation and torture. Most of the countries in which it is practiced have passed legislation making the procedure a crime. However, a search of the literature reveals few, if any cases that have been prosecuted. Children have the right to be protected from acts that, without exception, result in mutilation and a compromised ability to participate fully in life. Concerned professionals have an obligation to be proactive in helping potential victims secure these rights. Many governments, as well as women's organizations, have concluded that the dissemination of information, emphasis on education and the realization of equal rights for women will ultimately prove more successful than legislation in bringing this custom to its long-deserved end (Jordan, 1994; Omer-Hashi, 1994; Winter, 1994).

REFERENCES

Akpaeti, J. I. (1988). Female circumcision in Nigeria. *World Health Forum, 9,* 590.

Arbesman, M., Kahler, L., & Buck, G. M. (1993). Assessment of the impact of female circumcision on the gynecological, genitourinary and obstetrical health problems of women from Somalia: Literature review and case studies. *Women & Health, 20,* 27–42.

Baker, C. A., Gilson, G. J., Vill, M. B., Curet, L. (1993). Female circumcision: Obstetrical issues. *American Journal of Obstetrics and Gynecology, 169,* 1616–1618.

Beck, L., & Reddie, N. (1978). *Women in the Muslim world.* Cambridge, MA: Harvard University Press.

Black, J. A., & Debelle, G. D. (1995). Female genital mutilation in Britain. *British Medical Journal, 310,* 1590–1592.

Brown, Y., Calder, B., & Rae, D. (1989). Female circumcision. *The Canadian Nurse,* April, 19–22.

Burstyn, L. (1995). Female circumcision comes to America. *The Atlantic Monthly,* October, 28–35.

Council on Scientific Affairs, American Medical Association. (1995). Council Report: Female genital mutilation. *Journal of the American Medical Association, 274,* 1714–1716.

Davis, A. (1985). *Women: A world report.* New York: Oxford University Press.

DeMause, L. (1998). The history of child abuse. *The Journal of Psychohistory,* 25, 216–236.

Denney, N., & Quadagno, D. (1992). *Human sexuality* (2nd ed.). St. Louis: Mosby Yearbook.

Fourcroy, J. L. (1983). L'eternal couteau: Review of female circumcision. *Urology,* XXII, 548–461.

Gibeau, A. M. (1998). Female genital mutilation: When a cultural practice generates clinical and ethical dilemmas. *Journal of Obstetric, Gynecologic and Neonatal Nursing,* January/February, 85–91.

Gruenbaum, E. (1991). The Islamic movement, development, and health education: Recent changes in the health of rural women in central Sudan. *Social Science Medicine,* 33, 637–645.

Hastings, J. (Ed.). (1928). *Encyclopedia of Religion and Ethics* (Vol. 3). New York, NY: Charles Scribner & Sons.

Hirsch, M. F. (1981). *Women and violence.* New York: Van Nostrand Reinhold Company.

Jordan, J. A. (1994). Female genital mutilation (female circumcision). *British Journal of Obstetrics and Gynecology,* 101, 94–95.

Joseph, C. (1996). Compassionate accountability: An embodied consideration of female genital mutilation. *The Journal of Psychohistory,* 24, 2–17.

Kluge, E. (1993). Female circumcision: When medical ethics confronts cultural values. *Canadian Medical Journal Association,* 148, 288–459.

Ladjali, M., Wrattray, T., & Walder, R. J. W. (1993). Female genital mutilation. *British Medical Journal,* 37, 460.

Lightfoot-Klein, H. (1989). The sexual experience and marital adjustment of genitally circumcised and in- fibulated females in the Sudan. *The Journal of Sex Research,* 26, 375–392.

Masters, W. H., Johnson, V., & Kolodny, R. C. (1988). *Human sexuality* (3rd ed.). Glenview, IL: Scott, Foresman and Company.

Mustafa, A. Z. (1966). Female circumcision and infibulation in the Sudan. *Journal of Obstetrics and Gynaecology of the British Commonwealth,* 73, 302–306.

Omer-Hashi, K. H. (1994). Commentary: Female genital mutilation: Perspectives from a Somalian midwife. *Birth,* 21, 224–226.

Shrage, L. (1994). *Moral dilemmas of feminism: Prostitution, adultery, and abortion.* New York: Routledge.

Schroeder, P. (1994). Female genital mutilation—a form of child abuse. *The New England Journal of Medicine,* 331, 739–740.

Shaw, E. (1985). Female circumcision. *American Journal of Nursing,* June, 684–687.

Toubia, N. (1994). Female circumcision as a public health issue. *The New England Journal of Medicine,* 33, 712–716.

Watchtower Bible & Tract Society. (1985). Female circumcision—Why? *Awake!,* 67, June 22, 24–27.

Watchtower Bible & Tract Society. (1993). Millions are suffering—Can they be helped? *Awake!,* 74, April 8, 20–23.

Winter, B. (1994). Women, the law, and cultural relativism in France. *Signs,* 19, 939–974.

Ziv, L. (1997). The horror of female genital mutilation. *Cosmopolitan,* May, 242–245.

REVIEW QUESTIONS

1. Name and discuss the four types of female genital mutilation.
2. Identify at least five justifications for continuing female genital mutilation.

PART SIX

SELF-TARGETED DEVIANCE

When she was only 14, Brianne Camilleri was so depressed that she wanted to die. She felt overwhelmed with a sense of hopelessness that, she says, "was like a cloud that followed me everywhere. I couldn't get away from it." She started drinking and using drugs. One Sunday she was arrested for shoplifting, and her mother came to pick her up. They were making their way home in what Brianne calls a "piercing silence." As soon as they walked in the door, Brianne went straight into the bathroom, where she swallowed all the Tylenol and Advil she could find. A few hours later, her mother found her vomiting all over the floor and rushed her to the hospital. After another failed suicide attempt several months later, Brianne was sent to one of the country's best mental-health facilities. Today, after three years of antidepressant medication and talk therapy, she is doing well as a sophomore at a university in Virginia.[1]

Depression among adolescents is much more common today than it was a decade ago. So is teen suicide. Here we take a closer look at these and other self-targeted deviances. In the first article, "A Teen Suicide in the Family," Thomas Cottle offers a close-up view of what it feels like to be a teenager who eventually commits suicide. In the second piece, "Being Sane in Insane Places," David Rosenhan reports a participant-observation study that shows how difficult it is for psychiatrists to tell the "sane" from the "insane," and also shows that once they label a sane person "insane" they treat him or her accordingly. In the third article, "The Emergence of Hyperactive Adults as Abnormal," Peter Conrad and Deborah Potter show how the medical diagnosis of hyperactivity in children has been expanded to apply to adults. In the fourth selection, "Tattoos Are like Potato Chips . . . You Can't Have Just One," Angus Vail looks into the social and subjective forces that lead some people to deface or adorn their bodies with many tattoos.

1. Pat Wingert and Barbara Kantrowitz, "Young and Depressed," *Newsweek,* October 7, 2002, pp. 52–60.

A TEEN SUICIDE IN THE FAMILY

THOMAS J. COTTLE

ADOLESCENT SUICIDE

Following accidents and homicides, suicide ranks as the third leading cause of death for people fifteen to twenty-four years of age, the actual rate being 11.3 deaths per 100,000 people (Berger and Thompson 1995). During the past two decades, suicide rates in this age group, have more than doubled; this finding occurs as well for children ages five to fourteen, where suicide rates tripled from 1980 to 1995.

It is estimated that almost 10 percent of the American adolescent population has attempted suicide, with white adolescents attempting far more often than African American adolescents (Garland and Zigler 1993; Crosson-Tower 1998). Generally, suicidal ideation is noted in girls more often than boys; hence, it is not surprising to discover that girls attempt suicide almost four times more frequently than do boys, although boys, because they employ more lethal methods, complete suicide about four times as often as girls (Garland and Zigler 1993). Girls contemplating suicide are not unique in expressing intense hopelessness along with their depression, even though many of them give the impression that they are able to handle loneliness and lowered self-esteem (Bellah 1999; Shneidman 1978).

Among those young people attempting and completing suicide, one discovers a familiar array of psychological traits and symptoms (Garland and Zigler 1993), such as relatively high rates of substance abuse, the presence of narcissistic traits, impulsive dramatic traits or low levels of impulse control, and most especially, mood disorders, particularly depression. Approximately 40 percent of adolescent suicide cases involve major depressions.

Significantly, adolescent suicide also involves factors related to family dynamics—many of them, actually, considered to be so-called predictors of adolescent suicide (Blumenthal and Kupfer 1988; Rubenstein et al. 1989). They include interpersonal loss or conflict (approximately 70 percent of adolescent suicides occur within one month following intense conflict with or separation from significant people), lack of family supports or cohesion (Curran 1987; Patterson, DeBaryshe, and Ramsey 1989), parental strictness (Dusek 1996), parent-child discord (Baumeister 1990), family histories of mood disorders, parental psychopathology (60 percent of adolescent suicide cases reveal parents with emotional disorders), and violence of any sort within the family. In sum, adolescent suicides often occur in families experiencing stress on an almost daily basis (Hauser and Bowlds 1990).

THE STUDY

The study to be presented [here] derives from life study research, which essentially is nothing more and nothing less than the collection of people's

Source: Thomas J. Cottle, "Mind Shadows: A Suicide in the Family," *Journal of Contemporary Ethnography,* vol. 29, no. 2 (April 2000), pp. 222–255. Reprinted by Permission of Sage Publications, Inc.

accounts of their own experiences (Cottle, forth-coming; Lightfoot and Davis 1997; Stake 1995). Research of this type is described by Woods (1986) as working "from within the group, and from within the perspectives of the group's members. It is their meanings and their interpretations that count" (p. 4). Life study research "allows the researcher to live with the characters of the story, then re-create the scenes and bring them to life by telling the story" (Roy, 1998, 45).

The data for the present work were collected during a period of several years as part of a larger study of teachers that students in various schools designated as being significant in their lives. Upon getting to know these teachers, a second list was drawn up of the students these teachers felt were significant in their own lives. Permission was then obtained to speak not only with the students but their families as well.

The data were derived from a series of visits within the homes with family members together as well as from visits with individual family members that might take place anywhere, focusing on the young people in question. Over time, in work of this type where researchers become implicated in the lives of families (Minuchin 1974), various family members become friends. Conversations therefore frequently contain the sort of personal information one normally reserves for one's intimates or even psychotherapists. Importantly, the family in this one life study perceived the researcher as just that, someone interested in their child and their family, someone attempting to describe the daughter's and the family's circumstances. The meetings with the family were not intended as therapy sessions.

In many respects, an examination of the account that follows tests the limits of life study research. The child and the family, or more precisely, the psychological state of the child and the social structure of the family are revealed in the descriptions and accounts. There is also the matter of the researcher's role. In many respects, the complexity of this account is captured by Frank (1998): "The most value laden areas to

study are mental states and social institutions; to study them together forces the researcher into the abyss of the subjective world" (p. 419). It is precisely this subjective world that the life study or autoethnographic research generally seeks to approach.

THE ACCOUNT

Sitting atop his younger brother, Timothy [Mansard] had him pinned down on the kitchen floor. He drove his knees hard into Jonathan's upper arms and then pounded him on the chest and stomach with his fists. Timothy was yelling, crying, and swearing. Periodically, he would blow out his breath, exhausted from the fight and clearly in some pain. [Their sister] Annie watched from her accustomed station in the doorway, half amused, half terrified.

Hearing her mother screaming at the boys, Annie described rushing into the living room. She heard her mother calling the boys horrible names. They were "ugly," "ferocious," "bestial," "idiots," "morons," "bastards." One minute she was screaming to her husband to stop them; the next minute she was urging them all to kill each other. If it meant that at last the house would know peace, then let them go all out. By now, Annie was picking out a record: Wagner, Beethoven, Shostokovitch. Everything seemed frenzied and bizarre. Everyone in the family was crying and screaming, while the music exploded from the living room speakers like a giant airplane revving its engine. Then Annie would rush back to the kitchen and witness the effects of her action. Holding her hands first over her mouth, then her ears, and jumping up and down, she watched her mother screaming at her to shut the music off.

It seemed as though Mrs. Mansard never stopped shouting during these horrendous sporting events: "All right, kill each other, but do it already! Annie, stop that damnable music! I don't understand you. I simply do not understand what's wrong with you. And them and all of us! Kill the house, burn it for all I care! I don't want anything to do with any of you anymore! Just once, I beg of you sick and rotten animals to stop it! All right, all right, that's it. I'm calling the police. That's it." And on one occasion she did reach for the phone and dial some numbers. Then she looked at her daughter and tried not to listen to the sounds of her husband and sons as they threw themselves over the hard stone floor, swearing, desperately trying to free their arms and legs. By now, the boys were drenched with perspiration, and Timothy was bleeding from the nose and mouth. Everyone was crying.

Annie reported that at times, Bill Mansard would hit one of his sons, since now he had lost interest in separating them and bringing peace. It appeared to her that in these moments, he wanted to destroy them. The boys would groan with pain, and Annie would see this sick and dazed look come over their faces and watch their bodies grow weak. They could not afford to lose consciousness. All the while, the boys were shrieking at the top of their lungs, "You animal bastard! You sick animal bastard!" And Annie would sense the music growing louder, which only fueled the fury.

In the doorway, Annie could be seen grimacing one moment, screaming the next. She would describe feeling a "sickly, empty sort of pain" inside, as if she were not there at all. Battle raging on the floor in front of her, she watched her mother dial the phone, waiting for it to be slammed down. Annie knew there was no way her mother would have policemen arrive at her home on a Saturday morning to quell a family fight as if this were some inner-city housing project. Her mother never followed through with her threats to call anyone. So Annie would grin derisively at her mother's helplessness, which only infuriated Jeanne, who now would run past Annie and turn off the music. This one sound, at least, she could control.

Yet with all this, she reported, there were still no feelings she could hold on to long enough to be able to define or control. Why, exactly, did she wish to dissect her emotions? Because that was what her mother did? Might she have been content

merely to have a feeling last long enough to allow her to define it before it leapt back into the shadows as if playing some trick on her? There was no mistaking those special feelings, the ones evoked by the fighting and the predictable final scene of her mother's spirit slowly breaking and her body folding forward as she trudged, the actress in anguish, across the kitchen floor toward the dining room. She wrote often of this in her diary. . . .

There is a story to be told of a happy day. Annie remembered it well. She had gone shopping at the sprawling complex of stores two towns west of her home. She, Gloria Brenning, Cynthia Ducksworth; there were others, but it is difficult to remember all the details of what one did at age twelve when almost four years have passed. The trip, Annie recalled, required the girls to go on a bus, which was always an adventure and not so much because one saw people—well, stared at people and usually laughed at them, although one hates to admit this. Trips on the bus or trolley rides into Boston were always more exciting than car trips with her family because she felt she was "getting out," being in the open world, and doing what others did or were supposed to be doing. It was action and activity, movement, the glory of movement.

The girls must have peered into a million store windows that one afternoon, although the jewelry stores were always the most tantalizing: tiny rings and bracelets and the earrings, always the earrings provoking the same conversations about finally getting one's ears pierced. The girls were standing in front of Hemion's Jewelry Store, its earring collection hanging in the window on fine wires like stars, when Annie abruptly made her decision. Inside the store, she found a tall blond woman who pierced ears. Best of all, if you had your ears pierced, you received a set of earrings as a gift. Some of the girls acted disgusted by the piercing, but Annie could sense their excitement. Some were already examining the display cases hunting for the appropriate gift. Cynthia chose a simple gold ring design. They were perfect.

The woman first used a liquid to clean the lobes and then took a small gadget that looked to be not unlike a paper hole punch to perform the minor operation. The girls crowded around Annie, who grimaced as though experiencing intense pain. There was a stinging sensation, but it was less frightening than she had imagined.

The woman had not spoken a word during the entire procedure. The girls, however, never stopped talking. Annie loved that they were so acknowledging of her courage. Finally, when they were outside in the colorful aisles of the mall, the girls admired how she looked. For an instant, the psychological nonsense, as she called it, was put aside. She loved what she saw reflected in every store window of the mall. She did look beautiful, with her thin straight nose and light brown hair with reddish glow barely falling over the new earrings. The girls had grown silent in admiration. All they could do was stare at her, their silence a tribute to her beauty.

Two hours later when she returned home, she was slapped across the face by her mother. Sentenced to her room, she was told she would not receive an allowance for one month and was denied the privilege of going anywhere for that month except to school or piano lessons. She was not to speak to any friends on the telephone unless the conversations involved schoolwork. All calls would be monitored. And she was never to wear the earrings again.

As she went to her room, tears cascading down her cheeks, she heard her mother telephoning the family physician and asking his nurse if the holes in recently pierced ears would automatically seal shut if earrings were never inserted. She was advised that infection was less likely to occur if something, even a small string, were placed in the lobes. But Mrs. Mansard did not abide by the nurse's instructions. Nor did she ever receive the little bracelet with the tiny bauble hanging from it that Annie had purchased for her. The bauble revealed a mother holding her baby's head on her shoulder. The gift was buried that same evening in one of the garbage cans along-

side the garage, still wrapped in its yellow and white striped box. That night in bed, when she reflected on the events of the day, Annie comforted herself with the thought that at least she had not wasted money on a card.

. . . Annie often used the word *absurd*. What the others called yucky or gross was for her absurd. Absurdity was like a disease. Starting slowly somewhere in the body, it came to light spreading its tendrils into everything, a metastasis of the absurd, with the effect that anything and everything could become absurd for her and then suddenly lose its meaning altogether. How satisfying this metaphor was for Annie. It grew to be another of those silencing mechanisms. When something became difficult or painful, she could obliterate it merely by labeling it absurd. Someone's question was absurd, changing underwear was absurd, so was combing one's hair and brushing one's teeth. And so were the conversations with her mother. The only things not absurd were her brothers' fights, especially when her father joined the battles. It was the sexual nature of the fighting, she decided, that kept them all alive. Neither her father nor Timothy had much going on the feeling side of the ledger. But when they fought, they were alive and vibrant. In those ugly moments, nothing about them could have been called absurd.

She shared a mother with her brothers. For that matter, she shared one woman with three men. All of them appeared to suffer from being alive at the same time as their mother. No one in the family would ever admit this to anyone and especially not to themselves; it was taken as a given. According to her daughter, Jeanne Mansard was breathing death into her family. She was polluting them and making them ill. Annie would laugh to herself, "Mother pollutes us to the tune of three packs a day. And she does not even have to inhale her own debris. She leaves it around for us to breathe and eventually drown in, although that is not her conscious plan." It may well have been unconscious, Annie debated on more than one occasion. Perhaps her mother really did wish for the family's destruction. There are many ways to murder people, but the perfect crime is the psychological destruction of the soul.

For Annie, it was not proper to go through a day without having some goal, some serious purpose. Clearly that was her parents talking. Every instant for them had to be a learning experience, or so she reported. They despised small talk, the meager descriptions of what happened at school, or the amusing things befalling a classmate in the cafeteria. The Mansards wanted grade talk, college talk, intellectual inquiry talk, and proper grammar talk. That was the worst for Annie. Could they not understand that sometimes, when one gets excited about something, one does not speak correctly, as especially her mother invariably demanded? It became a curse, the constant need to watch what she said—watch herself—in the presence of her parents. They appeared to be listening, but it was not the content of her communications to which they attended—it was her language.

"So anyway, me and Cynthia went out after—"

"Cynthia and I."

"Cynthia and I. We went to the caf and who's there but this kid."

"What kid?"

"I'm about to tell you." Her anger already was building. "There's like, this kid, Neil, you know."

"A kid, and no I don't know."

It went on like this until finally Annie, utterly frustrated, felt her energy reduced to nothing. But when she made a move to walk away, it was her parents who grew angry. The pattern repeated endlessly, and always she told herself these words, as if hoping they would conclude the exchange: "You'll see, someday I'm going to do one thing right." Later she would think, "Wouldn't it be wonderful to have something written on my gravestone that was grammatically incorrect? Those two would be so busy correcting it, they'd forget I died."

"Here me lies. Like, there ain't no 'nother one down here but I. Resting in pieces, sincerely yours."

Francine Cavanaugh remembers teaching her first class of Junior English at Bristol Town High School. She could see at once that her students were interested in books and curious about a variety of matters. Affluent looking, despite the overalls, work shirts, and sloppy jeans, most of Ms. Cavanaugh's advanced study Junior English students had completed most of the summer reading assignments. She remembered clearly the first discussion about the nature of the hero in literature. She remembered, too, the girl seated at the desk near the window, beneath the poster of Windsor Castle: Annie Mansard.

There was a special look about this studious young woman. She took notes, consulted her books, and communicated a host of gestures that signaled her attentiveness. Annie, she recalled, was one of the only students whose full names she had memorized by the end of class.

Francine Cavanaugh had to smile when she thought about her first Bristol Town classes: so many bright students but what burdens they lived under. Every one of them was getting pressured by parents. Many students had older siblings who had performed successfully, which meant that teachers approached them with still higher expectations. "You must be Timothy Mansard's sister." More pressure. Then there was the school itself, with its lofty standards and ideals, competitive test scores, and need to maintain an outstanding reputation in the state. It did not look good if graduates shunned college or the number of seniors admitted to prestigious colleges declined. More pressure.

Francine was the first to admit she was haunted by Annie's presence in the school. There was the student's fierce dedication to learning and gaining admission to one of the so-called better colleges and the fact that she could be so outstanding and still attract people to her. Annie was reading five times more than anyone else in the class—five times more than anyone she had ever taught. Always the good looks, and always the sadness. It seeped through the personality, Francine would say, as a slow but significant leakage. And it brought forth a message. Still, it was not her role, Francine believed, to intervene in the personal lives of students. After all, she was not a psychiatrist. If a student volunteered something, it was legitimate to talk it out. But teachers had to know their place as educators, not psychotherapists. Still, anyone could see that Annie needed help. With the whole world seemingly hovering about her, she displayed a deep sense of aloneness.

As best as she could recall, Francine met with Annie no more than six times during the student's final year in high school. No real friendship ever evolved. No matter, senior year for Annie was filled with tribulations, and Francine, now in her second year on the faculty, felt more a part of the institution and its rituals. Annie had her chums; Francine had a new class of eager students. No one in her classes was as compelling as Annie Mansard had been that first day of school a year before, but who was to say that the attraction to Annie had not derived from the fact that Annie was the first person to be noticed in the first class on the first day in a new school?

It is always sad, Francine would think, when friends separate or a friendship fails to materialize. Teachers, of course, are used to this, but Annie was different. But had Francine failed to notice the clues? Was that not what they always said about cases like this? There are always clues; it is just that the witnesses choose to look away. Yet she had not chosen to look away. Anyone could see she was not responsible.

Francine would take a leave of absence from the school the year after Annie's graduation and leave the state forever the following spring. On her final day in Bristol Town, she would pay a visit to the cemetery to have her last talk with the attractive young woman whom she first saw, face so alive and bright, although not without sadness, on a brilliantly clear morning, sitting so poised at the desk near the window, beneath the poster of Windsor Castle.

Six weeks after graduating from high school and with her family believing she was making plans to attend the prestigious university to which she had been accepted, Annie Katherine Mansard committed suicide. At the time of her death, she was eighteen years, one month, and three days old.

CONCLUSION

Like most significant social psychological phenomena, youth suicide typically does not come as a bolt out of the blue. To some, it may seem this way, but its signs, symptoms, and warnings—in most cases, although not all—have been evident for awhile. Suicide, furthermore, is not the result of one distinct event or experience. It is the result, usually, of long-standing day-in, day-out personal and social experiences that drive people's anger and despair to the point of self-destruction. Somehow, the child's anger gets directed at him- or herself; somehow the child's pain is more than he or she can endure. Anger is not the only emotion involved in suicide. Studies reveal depression to be a common companion of suicide (Novick 1984; Sabbath 1969). Still, no one emotion and no single event can explain an entire piece of human behavior, destructive or not. . . .

The term *broken home* seemingly describes so much it barely describes anything at all; hence, in the end it may not be useful for making sense of adolescent suicide. Yet if that term *broken* connotes a broken spirit, a broken will or esteem, then it may prove useful after all. Many suicidal youngsters feel that after years of taking a pounding of one sort or another—a pounding others may know little about and some of it, actually, self-induced—they finally feel something break. It may seem to an outsider as though one particular event brought down the house of cards, but having sustained a heavy bombardment for a long period of time, the house was ready to go.

From the outside, the Mansards were hardly what anyone would have designated a broken family. Neither Jeanne nor Bill Mansard ever spoke of divorce or ever thought of abandoning the family. They never engaged in physical fights between themselves. Bill drank every so often but never exhibited unusual behavior on those occasions. From the outside, the Mansards appeared to be a successful family: respected, attractive, liked, and surely well educated. But are we now combing through not superficial material exactly but the stuff of which so-called broken homes presumably are constructed? It is difficult indeed to follow a family, especially one that had its share of crises, and not reflect on the signs that may have been missed and the warnings overlooked, when later on a child decides to take her life. . . .

In the end, the Mansards were a broken family. They were broken by Annie's death at age eighteen, and as they would later recount, they were broken long before that.

REFERENCES

Baumeister, R. F. 1990. Suicide as escape from self. *Psychological Review* 97:90–113.

Bellah, M. 1999. *Tammy: A biography of a young girl.* Berkeley, CA: Aten Books.

Berger, K. S., and R. A. Thompson. 1995. *The developing person: Through childhood and adolescence.* New York: Worth.

Blumenthal, S. J., and D. G. Kupfer. 1988. Overview of early detection and treatment strategies for suicidal behavior in young people. *Journal of Youth and Adolescence* 17:1–23.

Cottle, T. J. Forthcoming. *At peril: Stories of injustice.* Amherst: University of Massachusetts Press.

Crosson-Tower, C. 1998. *Exploring child welfare: A practical perspective.* Boston: Allyn & Bacon.

Curran, D. K. 1987. *Adolescent suicidal behavior.* Washington, DC: Hemisphere.

Dusek, J. B. 1996. *Adolescent development and behavior.* Englewood Cliffs, NJ: Prentice Hall.

Frank, D. B. 1998. The live creature: Understanding the school and its passions. *Child and Adolescent Social Work Journal* 15(6):419–38.

Garland, A. R, and E. Zigler. 1993. Adolescent suicide prevention. *American Psychologist* 48:169–82.

Hauser, S. T, and M. K. Bowlds. 1990. Stress, coping and adaptation. In *At the threshold: The developing adolescent,* edited by S. S. Feldman and G. R. Elliot. Cambridge, MA: Harvard University Press.

Lightfoot, S. L., and J. H. Davis. 1997. *The art and science of portraiture.* San Francisco: Jossey-Bass.

Minuchin, S. 1974. *Families and family therapy.* Cambridge, MA: Harvard University Press.

Novick, J. 1984. Attempted suicide in adolescence: The suicide sequence. In *Suicide in the young,* edited by H. Sudak, A. B. Ford, and N. B. Rushford, 115–137. Boston: John Wright/PSG.

Patterson, S. J., B. D. DeBaryshe, and E. Ramsey. 1989. A developmental perspective on antisocial behavior. *American Psychologist* 44:329–35.

Roy, A. 1984. Family history of suicide. *Archives of General Psychiatry* 40: 971–74.

Roy, H. 1998, November 25. Inclusion: Voices from inside. EdD. dissertation proposal, Boston University.

Rubenstein, J. L., T. Heren, D. Housman, C. Rubin, and G. Stechler. 1989. Suicidal behavior in "normal" adolescents: Risk and protective factors. *American Journal of Orthopsychiatry* 59:59–71.

Sabbath, J. C. 1969. The suicidal adolescent—The expendable child. *Journal of the American Academy of Child Psychiatry* 8:272–89.

Shneidman, E. S. 1978. Suicide. In *Psychology.* 2d ed. Edited by G. Lindzey, C. S. Hall, and R. F. Thompson. New York: Worth.

Stake, R. E. 1995. *The art of case study research.* Thousand Oaks, CA: Sage.

Woods, P. 1986. *Inside schools: Ethnography in educational research.* New York: Routledge & Kegan Paul.

REVIEW QUESTIONS

1. What factors in Annie Mansard's life contributed to her decision to commit suicide?
2. What *one* factor appears to have been the final straw that pushed Annie to commit suicide?

BEING SANE IN INSANE PLACES

DAVID L. ROSENHAN

If sanity and insanity exist, how shall we know them?

The question is nether capricious nor itself insane. However much we may be personally convinced that we can tell the normal from the abnormal, the evidence is simply not compelling. It is commonplace, for example, to read about murder trials wherein eminent psychiatrists for the defense are contradicted by equally eminent psychiatrists for the prosecution on the matter of the defendant's sanity. More generally, there are a great deal of conflicting data on the reliability, utility, and meaning of such terms as "sanity," "insanity," "mental illness," and "schizophrenia." Finally, as early as 1934, Benedict suggested that normality and abnormality are not universal. What is viewed as normal in one culture may be seen as quite aberrant in another. Thus, notions of normality and abnormality may not be quite as accurate as people believe they are.

To raise questions regarding normality and abnormality is in no way to question the fact that some behaviors are deviant or odd. Murder is deviant. So, too, are hallucinations. Nor does raising such questions deny the existence of the personal anguish that is often associated with "mental illness." Anxiety and depression exist. Psychological suffering exists. But normality and abnormality, sanity and insanity and the diagnoses that flow from them; may be less substantive than many believe them to be.

At its heart, the question of whether the sane can be distinguished from the insane . . . is a sim-ple matter: do the salient characteristics that lead to diagnoses reside in the patients themselves or in the environments and contexts in which observers find them?

Gains can be made in deciding which of these is more nearly accurate by getting normal people . . . admitted to psychiatric hospitals and then determining whether they were discovered to be sane and, if so, how. If the sanity of such pseudopatients were always detected, there would be prima facie evidence that a sane individual can be distinguished from the insane context in which he is found. Normality . . . is distinct enough that it can be recognized wherever it occurs, for it is carried within the person. If, on the other hand, the sanity of the pseudopatients were never discovered, serious difficulties would arise for those who support traditional modes of psychiatric diagnosis.

This article describes such an experiment. Eight sane people [including the author] gained secret admission to 12 different hospitals. Their diagnostic experiences constitute the data of the first part of this article; the remainder is devoted to a description of their experiences in psychiatric institutions.

PSEUDOPATIENTS AND THEIR SETTINGS

The eight pseudopatients were a varied group. One was a psychology graduate student in his 20's. The

Source: David L. Rosenhan, "On Being Sane in Insane Places," *Science,* vol. 179 (January 19, 1973), pp. 250–258.
© 1973 "American Association for the Advancement of Science." Reprinted with permission.

remaining seven were older and "established." Among them were three psychologists, a pediatrician, a psychiatrist, a painter, and a housewife. Three pseudopatients were women, five were men.

The settings were similarly varied. In order to generalize the findings, admission into a variety of hospitals was sought. The 12 hospitals in the sample were located in five different states on the East and West coasts. Some were old and shabby, some were quite new. Some were research-oriented, others not. Some had good staff–patient ratios, others were quite understaffed. Only one was a strictly private hospital. All of the others were supported by state or federal funds or, in one instance, by university funds.

After calling the hospital for an appointment, the pseudopatient arrived at the admissions office complaining that he had been hearing voices. Asked what the voices said, he replied that they were often unclear, but as far as he could tell they said "empty," "hollow," and "thud." The voices were unfamiliar and were of the same sex as the pseudopatient. The choice of these symptom was occasioned by their apparent similarity to existential symptoms. Such symptoms are alleged to arise from painful concerns about the perceived meaninglessness of one's life. It is as if the hallucinating person were saying, "My life is empty and hollow." The choice of these symptoms was also determined by the *absence* of a single report of existential psychoses in the literature. . . .

Immediately upon admission to this psychiatric ward, the pseudopatient ceased simulating *any* symptoms of abnormality.

. . . [T]he pseudopatient behaved on the ward as he "normally" behaved. The pseudopatient spoke to patients and staff as he might ordinarily. Because there is uncommonly little to do on a psychiatric ward, he attempted to engage others in conversation. When asked by staff how he was feeling, he indicated that he was fine, that he no longer experienced symptoms. He responded to instructions from attendants, to calls for medication (which was not swallowed), and to dining-hall instructors. Beyond such activities as were avail-

able to him on the admissions ward, he spent his time writing down his observations about the ward, its patients, and the staff. Initially these notes were written "secretly," but as it soon became clear that no one much cared, they were subsequently written on standard tablets of paper in such public places as the dayroom. No secret was made of these activities.

The pseudopatient, very much as a true psychiatric patient, entered a hospital with no foreknowledge of when he would be discharged. Each was told that he would have to get out by his own devices, essentially by convincing the staff that he was sane. The psychological stresses associated with hospitalization were considerable, and all but one of the pseudopatients desired to be discharged almost immediately after being admitted. They were, therefore, motivated not only to behave sanely, but to be paragons of cooperation.

THE NORMAL ARE NOT
DETECTABLY SANE

Despite their public "show" of sanity, the pseudopatients were never detected. Admitted, except in one case, with a diagnosis of schizophrenia, each was discharged with a diagnosis of schizophrenia "in remission." The label "in remission" should in no way be dismissed as a formality, for at no time during any hospitalization had any question been raised about any pseudopatient's simulation. Nor are there any indications in the hospital records that the pseudopatient's status was suspect. Rather, the evidence is strong that, once labeled schizophrenic, the pseudopatient was stuck with that label. If the pseudopatient was to be discharged, he must naturally be "in remission"; but he was not sane, nor, in the institution's view, had he ever been sane.

The uniform failure to recognize sanity cannot be attributed to the quality of the hospitals, for, although there were considerable variations among them, several are considered excellent. Nor can it be alleged that there was simply not enough time to observe the pseudopatients. Length of hospitalization ranged from 7 to 52 days, with an average of 19 days.

Finally, it cannot be said that the failure to recognize the pseudopatients' sanity was due to the fact that they were not behaving sanely. While there was clearly some tension present in all of them, their daily visitors could detect no serious behavioral consequences—nor, indeed, could other patients. It was quite common for the patients to "detect" the pseudopatients' sanity. During the first three hospitalizations, when accurate counts were kept, 35 of a total of 118 patients on the admissions ward voiced their suspicions, some vigorously. "You're not crazy. You're a journalist, or a professor [referring to the continual note-taking]. You're checking up on the hospital." While most of the patients were reassured by the pseudopatient's insistence that he had been sick before he came in but was fine now, some continued to believe that the pseudopatient was sane throughout his hospitalization. The fact that the patients often recognized normality when staff did not raises important questions.

THE STICKINESS OF PSYCHODIAGNOSTIC LABELS

Beyond the tendency to call the healthy sick—a tendency that accounts better for diagnostic behavior on admission than it does for such behavior after a lengthy period of exposure—the data speak to the massive role of labeling in psychiatric assessment. Having once been labeled schizophrenic, there is nothing the pseudopatient can do to overcome the tag. The tag profoundly colors others' perceptions of him and his behavior. . . .

All pseudopatients took extensive notes publicly. Under ordinary circumstances, such behavior would have raised questions in the minds of observers, as, in fact, it did among patients. Indeed, it seemed so certain that the notes would elicit suspicion that elaborate precautions were taken to remove them from the ward each day. But the precautions proved needless. The closest any staff member came to questioning these notes occurred when one pseudopatient asked his physician what kind of medication he was receiving and began to write down the response. "You needn't write it," he was told gently. "If you have trouble remembering, just ask me again."

If no questions were asked of the pseudopatients, how was their writing interpreted? Nursing records for three patients indicate that the writing was seen as an aspect of their pathological behavior. "Patient engages in writing behavior" was the daily nursing comment on one of the pseudopatients who was never questioned about his writing. Given that the patient is in the hospital, he must be psychologically disturbed. And given that he is disturbed, continuous writing must be a behavioral manifestation of that disturbance, perhaps a subset of the compulsive behaviors that are sometimes correlated with schizophrenia.

The notes kept by pseudopatients are full of patient behaviors that were misinterpreted by well-intentioned staff. Often enough, a patient would go "berserk" because he had, wittingly or unwittingly, been mistreated by, say, an attendant. A nurse coming upon the scene would rarely inquire even cursorily into the environmental stimuli of the patient's behavior. Rather, she assumed that his upset derived from pathology, not from his present interactions with other staff members. Occasionally, the staff might assume that the patient's family (especially when they had recently visited) or other patients had stimulated the outburst. But never were the staff found to assume that one of themselves or the structure of the hospital had anything to do with a patient's behavior.

A psychiatric label has a life and an influence of its own. Once the impression has been formed that the patient is schizophrenic, the expectation is that he will continue to be schizophrenic. When a sufficient amount of time has passed, during which the patient has done nothing bizarre, he is considered to be in remission and available for discharge.

But the label endures beyond discharge, with the unconfirmed expectation that he will behave as a schizophrenic again.

POWERLESSNESS AND DEPERSONALIZATION

Eye contact and verbal contact reflect concern and individuation; their absence, avoidance and depersonalization. The data I have presented do not do justice to the rich daily encounters that grew up around matters of depersonalization and avoidance. I have records of patients who were beaten by staff for the sin of having initiated verbal contact. During my own experience, for example, one patient was beaten in the presence of other patients for having approached an attendant and told him, "I like you." Occasionally, punishment meted out to patients for misdemeanors seemed so excessive that it could not be justified by the most radical interpretations of psychiatric canon. Nevertheless, they appeared to go unquestioned. Tempers were often short. A patient who had not heard a call for medication would be roundly excoriated, and the morning attendants would often wake patients with, "Come on, you m——f——s, out of bed!"

Neither anecdotal nor "hard" data can convey the overwhelming sense of powerlessness which invades the individual as he is continually exposed to the depersonalization of the psychiatric hospital. It hardly matters *which* psychiatric hospital—the excellent public ones and the very plush private hospital were better than the rural and shabby ones in this regard, but, again, the features that psychiatric hospitals had in common overwhelmed by far their apparent differences.

Powerlessness was evident everywhere. The patient is deprived of many of his legal rights by dint of his psychiatric commitment. He is shorn of credibility by virtue of his psychiatric label. His freedom of movement is restricted. He cannot initiate contact with the staff, but may only respond to such overtures as they make. Personal privacy is minimal. Patient quarters and possessions can be entered and examined by any staff member, for whatever reason. His personal history and anguish is available to any staff member . . . who chooses to read his folder, regardless of their therapeutic relationship to him. His personal hygiene and waste evacuation are often monitored. The water closets may have no doors.

A nurse unbuttoned her uniform to adjust her brassiere in the presence of an entire ward of viewing men. One did not have the sense that she was being seductive. Rather, she didn't notice us. A group of staff persons might point to a patient in the dayroom and discuss him animatedly, as if he were not there. . . .

THE CONSEQUENCES OF LABELING AND DEPERSONALIZATION

. . . [W]e tend to invent "knowledge" and assume that we understand more than we actually do. We seem unable to acknowledge that we simply don't know. The needs for diagnosis and remediation of behavioral and emotional problems are enormous. But rather than acknowledge that we are just embarking on understanding, we continue to label patients "schizophrenic," "manic-depressive," and "insane," as if in those words we had captured the essence of understanding. The facts of the matter are that we have known for a long time that diagnoses are often not useful or reliable, but we have nevertheless continued to use them. We now know that we cannot distinguish insanity from sanity. It is depressing to consider how that information will be used.

Not merely depressing, but frightening. How many people, one wonders, are sane but not recognized as such in our psychiatric institutions? How many have been needlessly stripped of their privileges of citizenship, from the right to vote and drive to that of handling their own accounts? How many have feigned insanity in order to avoid the criminal consequences of their behavior, and, conversely, how many would rather stand trial than live interminably in a psychiatric hospital—but are wrongly thought to be mentally ill? How many have been stigmatized by well-intentioned, but nevertheless erroneous, diagnoses?

Finally, how many patients might be "sane" outside the psychiatric hospital but seem insane in it—not because craziness resides in them, as it were, but because they are responding to a bizarre setting, one that may be unique to institutions which harbor nether people? Goffman calls the process of socialization to such institutions "mortification"—an apt metaphor that includes the processes of depersonalization that have been described here. And while it is impossible to know whether the pseudopatients' responses to these processes are characteristic of all inmates—they were, after all, not real patients—it is difficult to believe that these processes of socialization to a psychiatric hospital provide useful attitudes or habits of response for living in the "real world."

SUMMARY AND CONCLUSIONS

It is clear that we cannot distinguish the sane from the insane in psychiatric hospitals. The hospital itself imposes a special environment in which the meanings of behavior can easily be misunderstood. The consequences to patients hospitalized in such an environment—the powerlessness [and] depersonalization . . . —seem undoubtedly countertherapeutic.

I do not, even now, understand this problem well enough to perceive solutions. But two matters seem to have some promise. The first concerns the proliferation of community mental health facilities, of crisis intervention centers, of the human potential movement, and of behavior therapies that, for all of their own problems, tend to avoid psychiatric labels, to focus on specific problems and behaviors, and to retain the individual in a relatively non-pejorative environment. Clearly, to the extent that we refrain from sending the distressed to insane places, our impressions of them are less likely to be distorted. (The risk of distorted perceptions, it seems to me, is always present, since we are much more sensitive to an individual's behaviors and verbalizations than we are to the subtle contextual stimuli that often promote them. At issue here is a matter of magnitude. And, as I have shown, the magnitude of distortion is exceedingly high in the extreme context that is a psychiatric hospital.)

The second matter that might prove promising speaks to the need to increase the sensitivity of mental health workers and researchers to the *Catch 22* position of psychiatric patient. Simply reading materials in this area will be of help to some such workers and researchers. For others, directly experiencing the impact of psychiatric hospitalization will be of enormous use. Clearly, further research into the social psychology of such total institutions will both facilitate treatment and deepen understanding.

I and the other pseudopatients in the psychiatric setting had distinctly negative reactions. We do not pretend to describe the subjective experiences of true patients. Theirs may be different from ours, particularly with the passage of time and the necessary process of adaptation to one's environment. But we can and do speak to the relatively more objective indices of treatment within the hospital. It could be a mistake, and a very unfortunate one, to consider that what happened to us derived from malice or stupidity on the part of the staff. Quite the contrary, our overwhelming impression of them was of people who really cared, who were committed and who were uncommonly intelligent. Where they failed, as they sometimes did painfully, it would be more accurate to attribute those failures to the environment in which they, too, found themselves than to personal callousness. Their perceptions and behavior were controlled by the situation, rather than being motivated by a malicious disposition. In a more benign environment, one that was less attached to global diagnosis, their behaviors and judgments might have been more benign and effective.

REVIEW QUESTIONS_____

1. What effects does a psychiatric label have on a person?
2. How was powerlessness evident in the psychiatric hospital?

THE EMERGENCE OF HYPERACTIVE ADULTS AS ABNORMAL

PETER CONRAD
DEBORAH POTTER

Over the past thirty years there has been keen sociological interest in the medicalization of deviance and social problems (Conrad 1992, 2000; Conrad and Schneider 1992; Zola 1972). By now, there are dozens of case examples of medicalization and a body of literature has accumulated that has loosely been called "medicalization theory" (see Williams and Calnan 1996). At this point, it is important to build on this corpus of knowledge to better understand different aspects of medicalization. Medicalization is, by definition, about the extension of medical jurisdiction or the expansion of medical boundaries. In different situations, medical professionals (Halpern 1990), political reformers (Haines 1989), lay activists (Schneider 1978), or social movements (Scott 1990) have promoted boundary expansion. Most medicalization studies focus on how nonmedical problems become defined as medical problems, usually as illnesses or disorders. But there has been less examination of how medicalized categories themselves can be subjects of expansion, thus, engendering further medicalization. . . .

This paper [focuses] on the emergence of the diagnosis of Attention Deficit-Hyperactivity Disorder (ADHD) in adults in the 1990s. How did hyperactivity, which was deemed largely a disorder of childhood, become adult ADHD? This research

follows on Conrad's study of the medicalization of hyperactivity published in the 1970s (Conrad 1975, 1976). Our interest here, however, is also to investigate this case as an example of how medicalized categories, once established, can expand to become broader and more inclusive. . . . After reviewing the state of childhood hyperactivity as a medicalized diagnosis in the 1970s, we trace the emergence of "adult hyperactives" among those whose childhood symptoms persisted into adulthood, and then examine how this was transformed into the category "ADHD adults." We show how lay, professional, and media claims helped establish the expanded diagnosis. We identify particular aspects of the social context that contributed to the rise of adult ADHD.

HYPERACTIVITY IN THE 1970S

The most significant criterion for diagnosis [of ADHD] was a child's behavior, especially at school. The emphasis in identification was on hyperactive and disruptive behaviors (Conrad 1976). The major treatments for hyperactivity were stimulant medications, especially Ritalin. During the 1960s, the disorder became increasingly well known, due, in part, to publicity it received concerning controversies about drug

Source: Peter Conrad and Deborah Potter, "From Hyperactive Children to ADHD Adults: Observations on the Expansion of Medical Categories," *Social Problems,* vol. 47, no. 4 (2000), pp. 559–582. © 2000 by The Society for the Study of Social Problems. Reprinted with permission.

treatment. By the middle 1970s, it had become the most common childhood psychiatric problem (Gross and Wilson 1974) and special clinics to identify and treat the disorder were established, although most children were diagnosed by their pediatrician or primary care physician.

THE EMERGENCE OF "ADULT HYPERACTIVES"

Beginning in the late 1970s, several cohort studies were published which followed children who had been originally diagnosed with hyperactivity a decade or more earlier and traced their development into adulthood. These studies established that for some hyperactive children, the symptoms persisted into adolescence and even into adulthood. Thus emerged the notion of what we call "adult hyperactives," hyperactive children who did not "outgrow" their symptoms and still manifested some problems as adults.

In [1987], two publications aimed at lay readers heralded a new category of "ADHD Adults"— adults who had not been diagnosed as children, but had suffered from symptoms. Although later claims would be made by those who could not trace their suffering to their youth, these early claims were made either by or for those who, retrospectively, could identify signs of ADHD in their childhood.

In 1987, Paul Wender, a longtime hyperactivity researcher, published a book that examined hyperactivity throughout the life span. Although the book was entitled, *The Hyperactive Child, Adolescent and Adult,* only one chapter described adults with ADHD symptoms. Nonetheless, the book targeted a lay audience and would be cited frequently in subsequent years.

The same year, Frank Wolkenberg (1987), a free-lance photographer and picture editor, wrote a first-person account in the *New York Times Magazine* about his discovery that he had ADHD despite his apparently successful life. When he sought treatment for depression and suicidal ideation, he was diagnosed with ADHD by a psy-chologist whose specialty was learning disorders. Wolkenberg then began reinterpreting several clues from early in his life (e.g., impulsivity, distractibility, disorganization, and emotional volatility) as signs of the disorder. This highly visible testimony of someone not previously diagnosed with ADHD as a child put the idea of "ADHD Adults" into the public realm. No one had diagnosed him as hyperactive as a child, yet now, he was attributing "seemingly inexplicable failures . . . all unnecessary and many inexcusable" (p. 62) to ADHD. He suggested it was a neurobiological dysfunction "of genetic origin," thus attributing his life problems to a chemical imbalance.

As the notion of ADHD in adulthood was filtering into the public, the psychiatric profession was also turning attention to this new problem. Clinics for adults with ADHD were established at Wayne State University in 1989 and two years later at the University of Massachusetts in Worcester (Jaffe 1995).

In 1990, Dr. Alan Zametkin of the National Institute of Mental Health and several of his colleagues published an often-cited article in the *New England Journal of Medicine.* Using positron-emission tomography (PET) scanning to measure brain metabolism, Zametkin demonstrated different levels of brain activity in individuals with ADHD compared to those without the disorder, providing new evidence for a biologic basis for ADHD. Because of the risks inherent in research involving radiologic images, the researchers used adult subjects who both had childhood histories of hyperactivity and were biological parents of hyperactive children. Although not their intention, Zametkin's work became one of the key professional sources cited by others to demonstrate the presence of ADHD in adults (e.g., Bartlett 1990; and *Newsweek,* December 3, 1990), since it appeared to bolster claims that ADHD could persist into or develop during adulthood. While the study made national headlines, additional follow-up studies which did not confirm the strength of the initial study's findings, received no widespread publicity from the professional and lay press.

Adult ADHD in the Public Sphere

By the early 1990s, several books written for a popular audience looking specifically at ADHD adults were published. Psychologist Lynn Weiss (1992) identified her adult subjects as those who were diagnosable with ADHD, not merely grown-up hyperactive children having remnants of the symptoms carried over from an earlier condition. Another popular book quickly followed with the provocative title of, *You Mean I'm Not Lazy, Stupid or Crazy?!* (Kelly and Ramundo 1993), emphasizing the shift in responsibility that being diagnosed with adult ADHD can bring. Thom Hartmann (1994), writing in a somewhat esoteric, but essentially sociobiological frame, associated ADHD with an evolutionary adaptation to the social environment. He likened those with ADHD to hunters (who are nomadic, scanning the environment for sustenance, seeking of sensation, reacting quickly and decisively) adapting to a more modern farming community (which requires greater stability and focus). This hypothesis, by its nature, supports the notion of ADHD adults.

Further support came from the television news media reports on the spread of ADHD in adults. Major news shows put their own spin on the prevalence of the disorder. For example, on "20/20," Catherine Crier attributed ADHD to a "biologic disorder of the brain" in adults (September 2, 1994). Dr. Timothy Johnson on "Good Morning America" (March 28, 1994) was quoted as saying that experts estimate as many as 10 million adult Americans may have ADHD (Vatz and Weinberg 1997, p. 77). The new face of the disorder was not limited to hyperactive children grown-up, but included a new group of "ADHD adults" who came to reinterpret their current and previous behavioral problems in light of an ADHD diagnosis.

The message was reiterated in popular magazines. A feature article in *Newsweek,* for example, described a 38-year old security guard who

held more than 128 jobs since leaving college after being enrolled in the academic institution for 13 years (Cowley and Ramo 1993). He finally "received a diagnosis that changed his life" at the adult ADHD clinic at the University of Massachusetts in Worcester. Similarly, an article in *Ladies' Home Journal* (Stich 1993) described a husband who would continually be fired from job after job, constantly interrupted his wife, and forgot details of conversations. Then "Two years ago, the Pearsons discovered there was a medical reason for Chuck's problems. After their son was diagnosed with attention deficit disorder (ADD) . . . they learned Chuck also had the condition" (Stich 1993, p. 74). The article does not mention the fact that Chuck, who was diagnosed at age 54, also went on to found the Adult Attention Deficit Foundation, which acts as a clearinghouse for information about adult ADHD (Wallis, 1994, p. 47).

Adult ADHD was given a great boost in 1994 with the publication of a best-selling book *Driven to Distraction* by Edward Hallowell and John Ratey (1994), two psychiatrists with prestigious organizational affiliations. Hallowell offered his own experience as the springboard for the book: although successful as a medical student, and later as a practicing psychiatrist, he came to believe he had ADHD. Ratey also stated he had ADHD. The book has become a crucial touchstone among the lay public. . . . Both remain very active in promoting their work in public circles. Their affiliation with Harvard Medical School gave them some academic legitimacy, but they came to the area of ADHD adults more as professional advocates than as scientific researchers. In a sense, they are moral entrepreneurs for the adult diagnosis (Leffers 1997).

The cover of July 18, 1994, *Time* magazine issued a clarion call for ADHD adults: "Disorganized? Distracted? Discombobulated? Doctors Say You Might Have ATTENTION DEFICIT DISORDER. It's not just kids who have it." The 9-page article disseminated the criteria and possibilities of ADHD in adults to a wide audience, including speculations that Ben Franklin, Winston Churchill, Albert Einstein, and Bill Clinton may have had the disorder (Wallis 1994).

Diagnostic Institutionalization

By 1994, DSM-IV [the official guide to psychiatric diagnoses] reflected the growing consensus that adults could be diagnosed with ADHD, provided they had exhibited symptoms as children before the age of seven. Two (out of the five) diagnostic criteria were clearly relevant to adults. First, DSM-IV required that "some impairment must occur in at least 2 settings." While for children, these settings usually mean school and home, the range of settings may be greater for adults and include home, school, work, and other vocational or recreational settings. Secondly and related, "there must be clear evidence of interference with developmentally appropriate social, academic, or occupational functioning." The inclusion of work environments in the criteria section of the manual reflected the central and relatively uncontroversial position that the diagnosis of ADHD in adults now occupied.

The new definition allowed for more variations of symptomatic behavior across and within settings. "It is very unusual for an individual to display the same level of dysfunction in all settings or within the same setting at all times" (APA 1994, p. 79). Adults who might be quite successful at work, but highly inattentive in particular interpersonal relationships and recreational activities, could now be diagnosed with ADHD. As the more expansive criteria in DSM-IV gained acceptance among mental health professionals, some advocated eliminating the requirement that adults be able to retrospectively reconstruct a history of ADHD (Barkley and Biederman 1997). This would permit even greater expansion of the adult ADHD category. Reports from the American Medical Association (AMA) and the National Institutes of Health (NIH) supported an expanded ADHD diagnosis. In 1997, the Council on Scientific Af-

fairs of the AMA issued recommendations for treating ADHD. . . .

[SELF-DIAGNOSIS]

One of the starkest contrasts to the earlier history of ADHD with children is the vast amount of self-diagnosis of ADHD among adults. Virtually all children were referred by parents or schools to physicians (Conrad 1976). Among adults self-referrals are the norm, and many patients come to physicians apparently seeking an ADHD diagnosis. Frequently, adults who encounter a description of the disorder, sense that "this is me" and go on to seek professional confirmation of their new identity. Another common path to self-diagnosis occurs when parents bring a child to a physician for treatment and remark, "I was the same when I was a kid . . . " and thus, begin to see themselves and their own difficulties through the lens of ADHD. While this trend appears to have been precipitated by some of the popular press (e.g., Hallowell and Ratey 1994), it continues with legitimization provided by support groups designed for adults with ADHD such as Ch.A.D.D.

Anecdotes in the popular literature suggest that adults who self-diagnose, may recognize the condition in a popular media article or book. Hallowell and Ratey (1994) tell of one woman who noted, "My husband showed me this article in the paper" (p. 26). Comments on Internet sites state directly that it was one of the books on adult ADHD that led individuals to physicians for a diagnosis. Diller (1997) relates that one of his patients came to self-diagnosis after reading *Driven to Distraction*. Diller points out that, while the physician who is presented with such a self-diagnosed patient may have difficulty establishing the existence of symptoms in their childhood (as opposed to a checklist of symptoms absorbed through reading), the self-diagnosis, itself, becomes an element that the professional diagnosis must take into account. One psychiatrist wrote a colleague, "Adult ADHD has now become the foremost *self-diagnosed* condition in my practice.

I fear that the condition allows a patient to find a biological cause that is not always reasonable, for job failure, divorce, poor motivation, lack of success, and chronic depression" (Shaffer 1994, p. 638).

Diagnosis-seeking behavior is an integral feature of the emergence of Adult ADHD. This kind of self-labeling, information exchange, and pursuit of diagnosis fuels the social engine medicalizing certain adult troubles. Without it, the spread of Adult ADHD would be seriously limited. . . .

THE SOCIAL CONTEXT FOR THE RISE OF ADULT ADHD

To the best of our knowledge, there were no breakthrough epidemiological or clinical studies that identified a population of adults as having ADHD who were not previously diagnosed in childhood. Yet it is clear that "adult ADHD" has become a more common and accepted diagnosis in recent years. What would bring adults to physicians seeking such a diagnosis and what spurs physicians to treat them? Several social factors appear to have contributed to the diagnostic expansion.

The Prozac Era

Since the introduction of chlorpromazine in 1955, there has been a psychopharmacological revolution in psychiatry (Healy 1997). Psychoactive medications played a major role in deinstitutionalization and became regular parts of physicians' treatment protocols for various life problems, especially anxiety (e.g., Valium). American psychiatrists preferred drugs that would be useful in office psychiatry, rather than medications limited to inpatient populations (Healy, p. 70).

In 1987, Prozac (fluoxetine) was introduced as a new type of medication to treat depression. This drug is a selective serotonin reuptake inhibitor that directly affected a different group of neurotransmitters with fewer unpleasant side effects than previous types of antidepressants. This drug quickly became a phenomenon in itself, and led to a whole new class of drugs for treating psychiatric and life problems. Peter Kramer's book, *Listening to Prozac* (1993) and the subsequent news media coverage (e.g., cover stories in *Newsweek* and *New York* magazines, and dozens of TV and radio appearances), piqued the public interest in this new drug. Prozac was increasingly depicted as a medication that was a psychic energizer and that could make people feel, in Kramer's terms, "better than well." Prozac was not seen as a medication only for the seriously disturbed, but was a formulation that could improve the lives of people with minor disturbances and distresses.

The introduction and popularity of Prozac (and a series of related medications) created a context whereby taking medications for life problems was more acceptable (cf., Diller 1996). Prozac was seen as a drug that was appropriate for a range of psychic difficulties, and whose use could even make an OK life better. It led numerous people to redefine their life woes in terms of mild depression and seek treatment. A person did not have to be severely disturbed to benefit from Prozac. Similarly, Ritalin was now available to adults who had not been diagnosed as hyperactive in childhood, but who were now redefining their life difficulties as related to "inattention," "impulsivity,' and "restlessness."

Genetics

Genetics is the rising paradigm in medicine and an increasing number of human problems are being attributed to genetic associations, markers, or causes (Conrad 1999). Some experts have long believed that there is a genetic component to ADHD and its predecessor, hyperactivity, but to date, evidence is only suggestive, even though the claims of inheritance date back at least 25 years (Cantwell 1975; Wender 1971; Wood, et al. 1976). . . . [But] the greater the medical and public acceptance of a genetic component of ADHD, the more adult ADHD becomes a social reality. If the disorder is genetic, then it is deemed an intrinsic characteristic of people with the gene. This supports the notion that ADHD is a lifelong disorder, and the position that adults could have the disorder, even though they were never diagnosed as children.

The Rise of Managed Care

Managed care affects all aspects of medicine, including psychiatry. Health insurance imposes strict limits on the amount of psychotherapy for individual patients. Psychiatrists, now, must make use of utilization review, participate in medication management, consultation, or administering "carve-out programs" (Domino, et al. 1998). Mental health advocates and some researchers argue that, under managed care, there is a growing reliance upon various forms of prescription therapies to treat all types of psychiatric and life problems (Johnson 1998). A recent study found that managed care might fuel growth in the pharmaceutical industry (Murray and Deardorff 1998). Undoubtedly, there are now greater incentives for psychiatrists and other physicians to treat all potential mental health problems with medication, rather with than some form of talking or psychotherapy. Managed care tends to replace psychiatrists with primary care physicians who are less versed in "talking therapies' (Stoudemire 1996), and, thereby, increasing the potential for relying on medication for treatment. . . . [T]here is some evidence that ADHD children are treated with stimulant medications to the exclusion of other "talking therapies" (Woolraich, et al. 1990). It is likely there are similar trends with adult ADHD. . . .

CONCLUSION

Adult ADHD offers a clear example of how a medicalized category can expand to include a wider range of troubles within its definition. ADHD's expansion was, primarily, accomplished by refocusing the diagnosis on inattention, rather than hyperactivity, and stretching the age criteria. This allowed for the inclusion of an entire population of people and their problems that were excluded by the original conception of hyperactive children. . . .

But in terms of diagnostic expansion, the ADHD case is not unique. We can point to other cases where medicalized categories, which were originally developed and legitimated for one set of problems, were extended or refrained to include a broader range of problems. Several examples come to mind. Post-Traumatic Stress Disorder (PTSD) was originally conceived of as a disorder of returning Viet Nam war veterans who suffered from the after effects of brutal combat experience (e.g., with flashbacks, sleep problems, intense anxiety, etc.) (Scott 1990; Young 1995). But in recent years, PTSD has been applied to rape and incest survivors, disaster victims, and witnesses to violence. Alcoholism was medicalized, in large part, due to the efforts of AA (Conrad and Schneider 1992), but the medicalization has expanded to include adult children of alcoholics, enablers, and especially "codependency" (Irvine 1999). Child abuse, which was originally limited to battering, has expanded to include sexual abuse and neglect, and to lesser extent, child pornography and exploitation (cf., Best 1990 and 1999) and, to a degree, spawned the larger domain of domestic violence (including woman battering and elder abuse). In 1972, multiple personality disorder was a rare diagnosis (estimated at less than a dozen cases in 50 years); by 1992, thousands of multiples were diagnosed (Hacking, 1995). . . .

REFERENCES

American Psychiatric Association, The Committee on Nomenclature and Statistics. 1994. *DSM-IV. Diagnostic and Statistical Manual of Mental Disorders,* Fourth Edition. Washington, DC: American Psychiatric Association.

Barkley, Russell A., and Joseph Biederman. 1997. "Toward a Broader Definition of the Age-of-Onset Criterion for Attention-Deficit Hyperactive Disorder." *Journal of the American Academy of Child and Adolescent Psychiatry* 36:1204–1210.

Bartlett, K. 1990. "Attention deficit: Scientists move toward understanding of brain disorder once thought limited to children." *Houston Chronicle* (December 2):6G.

Best, Joel. 1990. *Threatened Children: Rhetoric and Concern about Child Victims.* Chicago: University of Chicago Press.

———. 1999. *Random Violence: How We Talk about New Crimes and New Victims.* Berkeley: University of California Press.

Cantwell, D. P. 1975. "Psychiatric illness in the families of hyperactive children." *Archives of General Psychiatry* 27:414–417.

Conrad Peter. 1975. "The discovery of Hyperkinesis: Notes on the medicalization of deviant behavior." *Social Problems* 23:12–21.

———. 1976. *Identifying Hyperactive Children: The Medicalization of Deviant Behavior.* Lexington, MA: D.C. Heath.

———. 1992. "Medicalization and social control." *Annual Review of Sociology* 18:209–232.

———. 1999. "A mirage of genes." *Sociology of Health and Illness* 21:228–241.

———. 2000. "Medicalization, genetics, and human problems." In *The Handbook of Medical Sociology,* Fifth Edition, Chloe Bird, Peter Conrad, and Allen Fremont, eds., 322–333. Upper Saddle River, NJ: Prentice Hall.

Conrad, Peter, and Joseph W. Schneider. 1992. *Deviance and Medicalization: From Badness to Sickness,* Expanded Edition. Philadelphia: Temple University Press.

Cowley, Geoffrey, and Joshua Cooper Ramo. 1993. "The not-young and the restless." *Newsweek* (July 26):48–49.

Diller, Lawrence H. 1996. "The run on Ritalin: Attention Deficit Disorder and stimulant treatment in the 1990s." *The Hastings Center Report* (March–April): 12–18.

———. 1997. *Running on Ritalin.* New York: Bantam Books.

Domino, M. E., David S. Salkever, Deborah A. Zarin, and Harold Alan Pincus. 1998. "The impact of managed care on psychiatry." *Administration and Policy in Mental Health* 26:149–157.

Gross, Mortimer B., and William E. Wilson. 1974. *Minimum Brain Dysfunction.* New York: Brunner Mazel.

Hacking, Ian. 1995. *Rewriting the Soul: Multiple Personality and the Sciences of Memory.* Princeton, NJ: Princeton University Press.

Haines, Herb. 1989. "Primum non nocere: Chemical execution and the limits of medical social control." *Social Problems* 36:442–454.

Hallowell, Edward M., and John J. Ratey. 1994. *Driven to Distraction.* New York: Pantheon Books.

Halpern, Sydney A. 1990. "Medicalization as a professional process: Postwar trends in pediatrics." *Journal of Health and Social Behavior* 31:28–42.

Hartmann, Thom. 1994. *Attention Deficit Disorder: A Different Perception.* New York. Underwood Books.

Healy, David. 1997. *The Anti-Depressant Era.* Cambridge, MA: Harvard University Press.

Irvine, Leslie. 1999. *Codependent Forevermore: The Invention of Self in a Twelve Step Group.* Chicago: University of Chicago Press.

Jaffe, Paul. 1995. "History and overview of adulthood ADD." In *A Comprehensive Guide to Attention Deficit Disorder in Adults: Research, Diagnosis, and Treatment,* Kathleen G. Nadeau, ed. New York: Brunner/Mazel:3–17.

Johnson, Dale L. 1998. "Are mental health services losing out in the U.S. under managed care?" *PharmacoEconomics* 14:597–601.

Kelly, Kate, and Peggy Ramundo. 1993. *You Mean I'm Not Lazy, Stupid, or Crazy?! A Self-Help Book for Adults with Attention Deficit Disorder.* Cincinnati: Tyrell and Jerem Press.

Kramer, Peter. 1993. *Listening to Prozac.* New York: Penguin.

Leffers, Jeanne Mahoney. 1997. The Social Construction of a New Diagnostic Category: Attention Deficit Disorder in Adults (Medicalization). Unpublished Ph.D. dissertation, Brown University.

Murray, M. D., and F. W. Deardorff. 1998. "Does managed care fuel pharmaceutical industry growth?" *PharmacoEconomics* 14:341–348.

Newsweek. 1990. "A New View on Hyperactivity." (December 3):61.

New York Times. 1999. "For school nurses, more than tending the sick." *Late New York edition* (January 28):A20.

Schneider, Joseph W. 1978. "Deviant drinking as a disease: Alcoholism as a social accomplishment." *Social Problems* 25:361–372.

Scott, Wilbur J. 1990. "PTSD in DSM-III: A case of the politics of diagnosis and disease." *Social Problems* 37:294–310.

Shaffer, David. 1994. "Attention Deficit Hyperactivity Disorder in adults." *American Journal of Psychiatry* 151:633–638.

Stich, Sally. 1993. "Why can't your husband sit still?" *Ladies Home Journal* (September):74, 77.

Stoudemire, A. 1996. "Psychiatry in medical practice: Implications for the education of primary care physicians in the era of managed care. Part I." *Psychosomatics* 37:502–508.

Vatz, Richard E., and Lee S. Weinberg. 1997. "How accurate is media coverage of Attention Deficit Disorder?" *USA Today* 127 (July):76–77.

Wallis, Claudia. 1994. "Life in overdrive." *Time Magazine* (July 18):43–50.

Weiss, Lynn. 1992. *Attention Deficit Disorder in Adults: Practical Help for Sufferers and Their Spouses.* Dallas: Taylor Press.

Wender, Paul H. 1971. *Minimal Brain Dysfunction in Children.* New York: Wiley.

———. 1987. *The Hyperactive Child, Adolescent and Adult: Attension, Deficit Disorder Throughout the Lifespan.* New York: Oxford University Press.

Williams, Simon J., and Michael Calnan. "The 'Limits' of Medicalization: Modern Medicine and the Lay Populace in 'Late Modernity'." *Social Science and Medicine* 42:1609–1620.

Wolkenberg, Frank. 1987. "Out of a darkness." *New York Times* (October 11):62, 66, 68–70, 82–83.

Wood, D. R., F. W. Reimherr, Paul H. Wender, and G. E. Johnson. 1976. "Diagnosis and treatment of minimal brain dysfunction in adults." *Archives of General Psychiatry* 33:1453–1460.

Woolraich, Mark L., Scott Lindgren, A. Stromquist, R. Milich, C. Davis, and D. Watson. 1990. "Stimulant medication use by primary care physicians in the treatment of Attention Deficit Hyperactivity Disorder." *Pediatrics* 86:95–101.

Young, Alan. 1995. *The Harmony of Illusions: Inventing Post-Traumatic Stress Disorder.* Princeton, NJ: Princeton University Press.

Zametkin, Alan J., et al. 1990. "Cerebral Glucose Metabolism in Adults with Hyperactivity of Childhood Onset." *New England Journal of Medicine* 323 (November 15): 1361–1366.

Zola, Irving Kenneth. 1972. "Medicine as an institution of social control." *Sociological Review* 20:487–504.

REVIEW QUESTIONS

1. How is adult ADHD a "clear example of how a medicalized category can expand to include a wider range of troubles within its definition"?
2. Give another example of the expansion of a medicalized category to include a wider range of troubles.

TATTOOS ARE LIKE POTATO CHIPS . . . YOU CAN'T HAVE JUST ONE

D. ANGUS VAIL

The *Hartford Courant* (1997) recently reported the results from an American Business Information, Inc., survey listing the top six growth businesses in 1996. Along with the expected high-tech entries such as Internet service, a decidedly unexpected industry made the list: Tattooing. Similar attention has come to tattooing by way of recent *New York Times, New York Post,* and "All Things Considered" stories on the recent legalization of tattooing in New York City after a 37-year ban. In the following pages, I discuss how those who are largely responsible for tattooing's growth become "collectors"—heavily tattooed.

INTRODUCTION

People learn how to become deviant. How each individual learns his or her particular brand of deviance depends on the kind of deviance in which she or he participates. Professional thieves learn their trade from other professional thieves (Sutherland 1937), marijuana users learn how to smoke marijuana and how to interpret the drug's effects from other marijuana users (Becker 1963), and tattoo collectors learn how to interpret tattoos from those who wear them (Vail 1997).

That deviance is a learned process is well documented. Deviance theories have explained many expressions of deviance. One form of deviance not

yet examined in the sociological literature, however, is tattoo collecting. In the following pages, I examine how tattoo collectors learn to become collectors.

In discussing how one becomes a tattoo collector, I discuss how collectors learn about aesthetics appropriate for their body suits, what motifs appropriately and accurately convey their ideas, iconographies appropriate for those motifs, and how to choose artists to complete their collections. I frame this discussion in Matza's (1969) theory of affinity, affiliation, and signification and the phenomenology of Alfred Schutz (1962, 1967).

METHOD

Data for this article were collected through several ethnographic and auto-ethnographic methods. I conducted most interviews at a recent four-day tattoo convention in the southeastern United States. I conducted in-depth, semi-structured interviews with tattoo collectors and artists at the convention site. I also conducted formal interviews with artists and collectors in California and Connecticut.

Informal field conversations with tattoo artists and collectors (from Austria, Australia, France, Japan, Switzerland, California, Connecticut, Michigan, New Jersey, New Mexico, Ohio, Oregon, and Texas), participant observation at tattoo conventions, participation in the tattoo sub-

Source: D. Angus Vail, "Tattoos Are like Potato Chips? You Can't Have Just One: The Process of Becoming and Being a Collector," *Deviant Behavior,* vol. 20 (1999), pp. 253–273.

culture for the past 12 years, and over 150 hours getting tattooed have all provided me with preliminary data on which to base my suppositions. The data taken from these "less formal" observational techniques have been recorded in ethnographic field notes over the past four years.

I collected further secondary interview data from videos focusing on prominent "fine-art" tattoo artists from the San Francisco Bay area (Stearns 1988, 1990).

BECOMING AND BEING A COLLECTOR

Becoming a tattoo collector is a transformative experience in more ways than one. This transformation is physical (i.e., one actually alters skin pigmentation), psychological, and subcultural. Becoming a collector involves not only changing the way that light reflects off one's skin, but also the way that others view that skin and the person inside it. The images one chooses and the ways one combines them say a lot, not only about the person who has chosen them, but also about who has influenced those choices. For example, Ch_, an arborist, describes his collection as follows.

CH_: For my arm-band, I went out in the woods and cut a piece of branch with bittersweet around it . . . because . . . I climb trees and work outdoors . . . a lot doing tree removals and pruning and shit like that. . . . And this one over here . . . is sort of like . . . a protector. That's my climber line with my protecting dragons on either end. And then the third one [is] my back. . . . That design [a graphic depiction of a bare tree] came from . . . my belt buckle. . . . T_r did both of these pieces [on the lower legs]. This one here, I said, "I want some leaves in it. I want the Polynesian design, [Celtic] design, a band around by calf, but I want leaves in it." What he did was put in unfolding springtime ferns.

. . . American fine-art tattooing is, in many respects, a melting pot of motifs and aesthetics. The current tattoo renaissance encompasses such diverse styles as photorealism, cybertech, traditional Japanese style, neotribalism, and any number of combinations of the above. Artists have also made profound technical advances.

Although the meaning of specific tattoos is inherently individual, people learn how to build their collections from other people. It takes a great deal of research for one to become intimately familiar with a particular motif and the iconography appropriate to use within it. It takes still more comparative research to figure out what styles and/or motifs one will use in building one's collection. Some do this research using tattoo magazines and some learn through symbolic interaction with other collectors and artists. In the end, however, collectors learn how to become collectors.

Learning to Become a Collector: Affinity

Matza (1969) discussed the process of becoming deviant. Although tattoos are less a statement of deviance than they once were, becoming heavily tattooed still stands outside social norms. Becoming a collector requires devotion to a lifestyle that is more marginal than that associated with fraternities or "tasteful" flowers. In short, one must want to become a collector. This desire is what Matza (1969:90–100) called *affinity*. "[Affinity] may be regarded as a natural biographical tendency borne of personal and social circumstance that suggests but hardly compels a direction of movement" (p. 93). In essence, affinity refers to a person's *desire to become deviant*. Comments like the following were common among respondents both in formal interviews and in informal field conversations.

CH_: My wife's been collecting for about 20 years, off and on, small pieces. And I've always wanted one, I just, y'know, never came across the right idea or the right person to do it.

Ch_ is not alone in having always wanted a tattoo. However, not everyone who gets one tattoo becomes a collector.

To make the jump from having tattoos to being a collector, one must first have an affinity for being a collector. Here, I mean not only wearing tattoos (often, but not necessarily, many of them), but conceiving of oneself as tattooed.

> *Several of the people that I just talked to discussed becoming collectors in terms of starting with just one tattoo and building their collections from that starting point. The experience of getting several small, bad tattoos as a start seems to be a common one. It is only after they start to conceive of themselves as collectors, however, that they . . . begin to visualize their collections as conceptual and stylistic wholes. This becomes apparent by starting their collections by covering their old, small tattoos. This cover work tends to evolve in either geographic (i.e., specific areas of the body) or conceptual patterns. (field notes)*

This excerpt from my field notes speaks to how people express themselves differently once they have conceived of themselves as tattooed as opposed to wearing tattoos. The tattoos with which they started are pictures in their skin. The collections that they have started to build represent a new self-image: that of the tattoo collector. Part of what allows the collector to fully realize this transition is what Matza (1969) called *affiliation*.

Learning to Become a Collector: Affiliation

"Affiliation describes the process by which the subject is *converted* to conduct novel for him but already established for others" (Matza 1969:101). This process has also been analyzed by Sutherland (1937, 1939) as "differential association." According to both Sutherland and Matza, deviance is taught in symbolic interaction with successful deviants. "[Sutherland's] method of affiliation harbors an idea of conversion. . . . Unless one always was deviant, in which case little illumination is required, *becoming deviant* [emphasis added] depends on being converted" (Matza 1969:106–7). Thus, the collector learns how to feel good about becoming a collector, as well as learning where to place his or her tattoos. She or he learns how to become a collector *from other collectors and tattooers*.

As previously mentioned, for this conversion to be successful, one must want to be converted. Hence, affinity and affiliation work together in creating both deviance and deviants.

Respondents typically talked about tattooing as a desirable experience, the quality of which affected the perceived quality of the tattoo more than the crispness of lines or the boldness of the shading. In this way, collectors and artists alike see becoming collectors in terms of recruitment.

L_: What goes into a great tattoo is, I guess, is the experience, because it's like a personal album or something. . . . It's like a montage of your life. That's why the Japanese said I got tattooed for memories, and he got tattooed for a story. Some stupid fucking Japanese, Oriental story, he got tattooed for, y'know?

The pejorative "some stupid fucking Japanese, Oriental story" shows how L_ views the appropriate way to become tattooed. For L_, collectors should get tattooed to hold on to their memories. For him, the Japanese notion of getting tattooed for a story is inappropriate.

Other collectors view tattoos as a means of expression of personal spirituality and, thus, a moral enterprise.

SH_: For me to do a tattoo on somebody that runs against the grain of my philosophical life, it's impossible, it's just not going to happen. Y'-know, if somebody comes to me and says "I want a tattoo of dismembered babies" and whatever, I'm like, "Sorry."

In this statement, Sh_ shows how he goes about recruiting select people into his philosophical approach to tattooing. He not only is concerned with expressing himself artistically, he is concerned with teaching people that tattoos should be a means of positive self-expression. By turning away work that he finds indicative of destructive tendencies, he is not only strengthening the resolve of those he tattoos, he is also telling those whom he refuses to work on that their notion of what is acceptable for tattooing is flawed. In essence, he is recruiting "the right kind of people" into the tattoo world.

Sh_ also recruits through means other than tattooing or showing his collection. The following exchange shows how his beliefs of the appropriate reasons for becoming tattooed run counter to common misconceptions about the exhibitionistic tendencies of tattoo collectors. In essence, becoming a collector involves learning how to act like one.

DAV: Do you ever exhibit your collection?
SH_: No. Because they're real personal, my tattoos. I always get asked to take my clothes off, but I never do. And the line that I always give . . . is that when you start taking your clothes off, nobody listens to what you have to say. You lose credibility real fast.

Both tattooers and collectors teach other collectors about appropriate "use of the [body as a] canvas." Fine-art tattoos take into account musculature, size, shape, and texture of a given area of the collector's body. Fine-art "backpieces," for example, incorporate the breadth of the collector's shoulders and narrowness of his or her waist in the design. Another example is Filip Leu's watershed color portrait of Jimi Hendrix (Bannatyne 1992:52), done on my right thigh in 1992. Because the thigh is roughly the same size as a face and follows similar outlines (roughly oval), the portrait used all of the canvas, and used it appropriately.

[A] collector, Sa_, learned about appropriate use of the canvas [body] from her husband (a tattoo collector and motorcycle mechanic). Her collection, still in its initial stages, is of gargoyles.

Currently, she has four gargoyles, all of similar size and style. They begin on her left shoulder and descend down the center of her back. Eventually, they will finish on her right hip, connected by vines. She was not ready to get a full back piece, but she had seen other women's backs, tattooed in the same basic shape, in tattoo magazines. As she described it to me, the contours of the string of gargoyles accent her figure. Also, the design leaves two fairly large open canvases. (field notes)

Hence, Sa_ has learned about appropriate use of the canvas and has shown respect for its shape and possibilities. She learned about use and respect for the canvas from other collectors (her husband and collectors in tattoo-oriented publications) and from her artists.

These interviewees were recruited, and continue to recruit others, by learning and sharing what makes a tattoo (and/or a tattooer) good. Although every respondent talked about the artistic ability of his or her tattooer(s), 75 percent said that technique was less important than rapport. In a sense, then, collecting is based more on feeling a connection with an artist than acquiring "fine art." Now that they see themselves as collectors, they are going to make this self-applied label work for them. This is the final element of Matza's (1969) process of becoming deviant: *signification*.

Learning to Become a Collector: Signification

After one learns the techniques of being deviant, one often reconceptualizes one's life in terms of that deviance. In discussing "indication," Matza (1969:165) elaborated on this notion of identity building among professional thieves.

Quite different from consequence, indication points the subject to a consideration of himself; to the question of the unity of meaning of the various things he does and the relation of those things to what he conceivably is. To consider the possibility that the theft was important in the sense of being indicative of him puts the subject well into actively collaborating in the growth of deviant identity by building its very meaning.

In essence, once deviants have internalized their deviant labels, they reconceptualize their actions in terms of being appropriate for people who are "like that." Tattoo collectors see collecting as *appropriate for tattooed people.* This can have profound effects on how they view their collections as well as appropriate ways to display them.

As I said in the section on affiliation, once collectors begin to think of themselves as collectors, they often begin to plan how each new tattoo will work within the canvas. An aspect of collecting that exhibits signification is working around public skin. Co_ illustrates this point nicely.

Co_ is working on a full body suit, accompanied by facial piercings and satyr-horn implants on either side of his widow's peak at the hairline. The following excerpt from field notes shows how Co_ has planned his suit, at various stages, to *combine his tattooed identity with one that is acceptable to those outside the subculture.*

> *[Before] he became a full-time tattooer and piercer . . . his crew chief wouldn't let him work with any . . . tattoos showing. So, he had to get long-sleeved t-shirts to cover the tattoos that went to his elbow. He [has subsequently covered his arms] down to the wrists and is now going on to the tops of his hands. He said that he . . . is thinking about leaving the collar untattooed and, that way, he can take out the facial piercings and put on a hat and go out in public with a long-sleeved shirt and still look somewhat respectable.*

Thus, even though Co_ is obviously devoted to body modification, he still is concerned with getting along in normative society. By leaving open canvas at the collar, he will be able to pass (Goffman 1963; Garfinkel 1967) more easily. Other collectors are less concerned with passing than with planning their remaining space.

L_'s collection has been complete for about 20 years, but in the following excerpt from our interview he recalls when he realized what he had to do to finish the collection.

L_: Well, yeah. You look at yourself and you just, y'know, you see that there are these spaces that just need to be filled up. It's not that you're comparing yourself to someone else, or some kind or image, it's just that those spaces aren't complete. It's like you're on a course and you've gotta finish it. . . . Most tattoo suits fit within standard barriers. Some people go above and beyond, but the prescribed cover job is like, a neck band, ankle bands, wrist bands, put a cargo net underneath

your nuts and then just fill the rest of it up. So when it's done, you can tell.

Thus, L_ completed his collection within "standard barriers." He filled his canvas from those barriers into the body of the suit.

CONCLUSION

Collecting tattoos is both an individual and a collective journey. Collectors must choose their own designs for their own reasons. Yet, they learn how to incorporate those designs into collections from others who have been successful in building collections. Some have attempted to explain what these collections mean. I believe this is a fruitless endeavor. However, studying the tattoo collection process sheds light on several broader sociological and phenomenological issues.

Tattoo collecting incorporates all three of Matza's (1969) stages of becoming deviant (i.e., affinity, affiliation, and signification). As becoming a collector involves both considerable financial commitment and physical and stigmatic discomfort, it requires devotion to the process. In short, a collector's affinity must be strong.

Collectors must also learn how to become collectors. They must learn how to evaluate tattoos and tattooers. This involves learning how to evaluate technique and how to build rapport. Collectors must also learn how to best represent the tattoo subculture. This involves learning techniques of passing (Goffman 1963; Garfinkel 1967) and consensus building. They learn these things through affiliation with other collectors.

Finally, collectors, learn how to [confirm] their new master statuses (Becker 1963) as collectors, not just as people with tattoos. They begin to view their collections in the future-perfect tense (Schutz 1962, 1967), as collections that will-have-been-completed. This process of navigating signification from both within and without the tattoo world involves respecting the canvas as it is and as it will be.

In becoming tattooed, the collector learns not only how well-established members of the tattoo world conceive of "proper" use of form and iconography in building a collection, but also how to see him- or herself as a tattooed person. Although some may consider the distinction between those who have tattoos and those who are tattooed a semantic one, semantics, in this case, are important.

In discussing those who have tattoos, the analyst (be that person a sociologist, anthropologist, or psychologist) assumes a possessive relationship between the person and the dermographic embellishment that she or he has purchased. In essence, this person's tattoos are no different than the car she or he drives or the hair style she or he sports on any given day. Like these adornments, tattoos represent possessions that can be considered with or without the individual who wears them.

The collector, on the other hand, sees him- or herself as tattooed, not just as the owner of the pigments residing in the first layer of his or her dermis. The images that adorn the collector's canvas are, as L_ so colorfully stated earlier in this article, his or her memories made physical. To the collector, tattoos are not something one owns. Rather, they are a part of him or her, no less important than the color of his or her hair or skin and no more easily removed from his or her identity than

his or her deepest beliefs, most profound concerns, or idiosyncratic sense of humor. In short, the collector does not see himself as John who has tattoos but as John who is tattooed.

Because, for the collector, tattoos represent a master status, all of his or her actions, beliefs, fears, and hopes can be seen in his or her collection. How those personal characteristics become part of the collection only the collector knows. That they are there, however, is irrefutable. The fact that they are there affects not only the ways that collectors see themselves, but also the ways that others see them. In short, their tattoos have profound effects on their interactions with intimates and nonintimates alike.

The recent attention that the news media have paid to tattooing speaks volumes to the relevance of this topic. With tattoo shops being ranked among the six fastest growing industries in the nation (*Hartford Courant* 1997), and the recent legalization of tattooing in New York City (Hardt 1997; Kennedy 1997a, 1997b; National Public Radio 1997), we, as sociologists, have a unique opportunity to demystify the processes involved in enacting a cultural phenomenon that is rapidly losing its deviant status.

REFERENCES

Bannatyne, Bryce, ed. 1992. *Forever Yes: Art of the New Tattoo.* Honolulu, HI: Hardy Marks.

Becker, Howard S. 1963. *Outsiders: Studies in the Sociology of Deviance.* New York: Free Press.

Garfinkel, Harold. 1967. *Studies in Ethnomethodology.* Cambridge, MA: Blackwell.

Goffman, Erving. 1963. *Stigma: Notes on the Management of Spoiled Identity.* New York: Touchstone.

Hardt, Robert, Jr. 1997. "City Ends Tattoo Taboo Only Mom Could Love." *New York Post,* February 26, p. 4.

Hartford Courant. 1997. "Have You Heard?" March 1, p. F1.

Kennedy, Randy. 1997a. "Cappuccino with Your Tattoo? Try That on a Sailor." *New York Times,* July 27, pp. 31–2.

———. 1997b. "City Council Gives Tattooing Its Mark of Approval." *New York Times,* February 26, pp. B1, B5.

Matza, David. 1969. *Becoming Deviant.* Englewood Cliffs, NJ: Prentice-Hall.

National Public Radio. 1997. "All Things Considered." (Story on legalization of tattooing in New York City). March 16.

Schutz, Alfred. 1962. *Collected Papers.* Vol. I, *The Problem of Social Reality,* edited by Maurice Natanson. Boston: Martinus Nijhoff.

———. 1967. *The Phenomenology of the Social World.* Translated by George Walsh and Frederick Lehnert with an Introduction by George Walsh. Evanston, IL: Northwestern University Press.

Stearns, Michael O. 1988. *Tattooing Reality: Hardy & Associates Make Their Marks* (video). San Francisco: Metamorphosis II Productions.

———. 1990. *Frisco Skin and Tattoo Ink.* (video). San Francisco: Metamorphosis II Productions.

Sutherland, Edwin H. 1937. *The Professional Thief* Chicago: University of Chicago Press.

———. 1939. *Principles of Criminology.* 3d ed. New York: Lippincott.

Vail, D. Angus. 1997. "Angels and Dragons: The Social Meanings of Tattoos." Paper presented at the annual meeting of the Popular Culture Association, Arlington, Texas.

REVIEW QUESTIONS

1. How did the author gather data for this article?
2. Discuss David Matza's three-stage process of becoming deviant as it relates to this article.

PART SEVEN

VICTIMS OF STIGMA

A gay couple, Gary and Greg, both in their 30s, are known to neighbors simply as "the guys" in a small, fairly conservative town in central Pennsylvania. They call each other "honey" in the stores, and their straight friends call them "uncle" and "uncle." At their offices, their straight coworkers seem more familiar with gay issues than the gay couple themselves. As Gary says, "They realize we have the same worries they do. Now in tax season, they'll say, "That sucks, you can't put Greg on your return." All this friendliness shown by straights to Gary and Greg in a conservative town represents a significant progress in attitudes toward gays in the United States. Now, for the first time in U.S. history, only a minority (46 percent) of Americans consider homosexuality a sin. But at the same time a majority (57 percent) are still opposed to gay marriage, and more than thirty-two states have passed new laws banning same-sex marriages.[1] In this new century, then, U.S. society still has a long way to go toward treating gays the same as straights.

The continuing rejection of gays suggests that homosexuality is still a *social stigma,* something a person has or does that others see as bad in some way. A stigma is practically the same as deviance, so many deviances can be considered stigmas. It is a stigma to be a prostitute, a mental patient, a suicide, a child abuser, a murderer, a rapist, and so on. Some of these stigmas are *justifiable.* Murderers, rapists, and other nasty criminals, for example, deserve to get what is coming to them. But most stigmas are *unjustifiable* because people such as gays and lesbians, suicides, mental patients, the obese, and the tattooed do not hurt others yet are stigmatized—punished as victims of stigma. Here we focus on lesbians and other victims of unjustifiable stigma, including the obese, the deaf, and the mentally challenged.

In the first article, "Rejecting 'Femininity': Gender Identity Development in Lesbians," Margaret Cooper discusses how the lesbians she interviewed had rejected traditional femininity in their childhood. In the second article, "The Stigma of Obesity," Erich Goode explains why the obese are stigmatized in U.S. society and how this stigmatization affects the victims. In the third piece, "Deaf Culture's Opposition to Cochlear Implants," Bonnie Tucker discusses why some deaf people do not want to lose their disabilities. In the fourth selection, " 'You're Not a Retard, You're Just Wise,' " Steven Taylor shows why people labeled "retarded" by others may not see themselves that way.

1. John Leland, "Shades of Gay," *Newsweek,* March 20, 2002, pp. 46–49.

REJECTING "FEMININITY": GENDER IDENTITY DEVELOPMENT IN LESBIANS

MARGARET COOPER

The majority of social science research on homosexuality has been on men (see Oberstone and Sukoneck, 1976). Most nonfeminist work on lesbians has been of a quantitative nature, attempting to study the issue of lesbianism numerically. It has not allowed the women's experience to be quoted directly but to be interpreted solely for the reader by the researcher.

This study allows women to speak about their own gender identity development. The difference between "sex" and "gender" should be emphasized since it is a crucial distinction made in this article. Kate Millett (1970, p. 39) wrote of the "overwhelmingly *cultural* character of gender." She, along with others (Stoller, 1968), was active in distinguishing gender from the term "sex," which refers to one's anatomy and physiology. Robert Stoller (1968, pp. viii–ix) wrote that

gender is a term that has psychological or cultural rather than biological connotations. If the proper terms for sex are "male" and "female," the corresponding terms for gender are "masculine" and "feminine"; these latter may be quite independent of sex.

METHODS AND SAMPLE

Martin and Lyon (1972) felt surveys may not even be likely to include the respondents' true feelings, thereby forcing the respondent to fit into a category she or he might not otherwise. They were critical of quantitative methods in the study of lesbianism when they wrote:

Experience indicates that the questions are made up generally by heterosexuals and asked of homosexuals who very often find them irrelevant to their particular lifestyle. The questions, for the most part, are unanswerable by the required "yes" or "no" or multiple choice, and their only virtue is that they are easily computerized into instant (misleading) statistic (p. 2).

With feminist criticism of such studies in mind, a qualitative method, in-depth interviews, was chosen for this article. It allows for respondents to create their own categories rather than merely try to fit into those preconceived by a researcher. The validity of the qualitative method relates directly to the validity of the women's experiences.

Lesbians were identified and contacted through friendship associations. Fifteen women agreed to participate. All respondents were assured confidentiality and assigned pseudonyms. The interviews were conducted and analyzed according to the procedure suggested by Schwartz and Jacobs (1979) and Lofland and Lofland (1984). Rather than utilizing the statistical analyses of quantitative

Source: Margaret Cooper, "Rejecting 'Femininity': Some Research Notes on Gender Identity Development in Lesbians," *Deviant Behavior,* vol. 11 (1990), pp. 371–380. Reprinted with permission.

methods, the interview data were examined for emergent patterns of responses and descriptions.

The ages of the respondents ranged from 19 to 38, with the average age of 25.3 years. All of the women were born and reared in small towns and cities in the South and Midwest. All of them currently live in and around cities with a population of 50,000 or less in various towns in the central region of the United States.

Four of the women considered themselves to be feminists. The rest did not. One other woman had recently become involved with the gay rights movement. A few others expressed interest in the gay rights and feminist movements, but not from the standpoint of a participant.

Since the sample size of this study is small, no attempt will be made to say that this sample is reflective of all lesbians. However, this article is an honest account of the experience of the women who did take part in this study.

RESULTS

All of the women interviewed indicated a rejection of traditional femininity. Even as children, some even before they were consciously aware of same-sex attractions, had difficulty fitting into what they saw as the traditional female role. Apparently, even though these women might not have known what they wanted, they knew what they did *not* want. For them, it appears that the female gender role represented more than femaleness. It also represented heterosexuality:

That role is all sex-oriented. It's the dumb housewife image. If you really look at it, that's just the way it is. (Pat)

I remember as a very young child not identifying with the female role because it seemed like, and this was growing up in the sixties, that the female role was strongly attached to your role as a wife and mother and I knew I couldn't do that. So I felt more identified with the male role. When I was a kid, I would play the boy when we played house. And I wanted my mom to buy me "boy clothes." (Kate)

For Kate, this role rejection was directly linked, in her view, to her attraction to other girls. She was aware of this attraction at a very young age and she reported that she developed quite a "macho" image of herself by age seven. She explained it this way:

I used to think, as a kid, that you had to be masculine to get a woman. That women liked masculinity and men liked femininity. So I tried to convince every girl on the block that I was a boy. I even took a male name. And of course, it made perfect sense to me. I never understood when people's parents were flipping out.

The other women's responses fell into three categories: (1) taking the male role (like Kate's example), (2) being a "tomboy," and (3) rejecting items of dress and play associated with female children. These responses overlapped in all of the interviews.

Taking the male role was seen in both play and fantasy. Cindy said, "Kids would play house; and I was the one, when my cousins would come over, I'd play the boy. I'd always do the boy parts." This led her to believe that she might be gay. This also "concerned" her cousins, one of whom later said to her, "We was all worried about you, wondering about you because you always wanted to play the guy." Cindy said she wanted to respond by merely saying, "Take a hint." Anita's childhood fantasies often involved taking the male role. She described them by saying:

I might not have known what it was called when I was real young, I can remember going to see "James Bond" and like when . . . my imagination would run wild or I would have some kind of fantasy, I'd never fantasize as being one of the women. I was always "James Bond" . . . "Matt Dillon," you know.

Wolff (1971) found that many lesbians, as children, desired to be boys. She found lesbians were five times more likely to have expressed this desire than were heterosexual women. In a study by Fleener and reported by Lewis (1979), 82 percent of lesbians sampled had gone through a tomboy phase. In the sample for this article, all fifteen women told of their "tomboy" experiences as children. Not only did they engage in sports, tree-climbing, etc., many of them chose to play with boys. Robin said, "I was the only girl in my neighborhood my age when we moved here, so that was a lot of fun to hang around with the boys . . . I used to be a tomboy really bad." Barbara enjoyed "getting out and playing baseball with my brothers or basketball, things like that." This led her to conclude after some period of time, "I knew I was different. I just couldn't put my finger on it." . . .

Lewis (1979, p. 23) called the "rebellion against what is seen as being female and restrictive" that coincides with the desire for "those elements of male identity that carry independence . . . the first rite of passage into lesbian selfhood." The third set of responses involved this "rebellion against what is seen as being female." Carole said that she would "rather take a beating than put a dress on." Barbara not only disliked the frilly dresses her mother bought for her, she also hated the Barbie dolls. "I wanted to burn the Barbie dolls!" she laughed.

During the childhood years, the rejection of the female role is relatively risk-free. This begins to change in adolescence. The world again becomes the dichotomized place of girl/femininity and boy/masculinity, now with an additional imperative: heterosexuality, complete with its emphasis, for girls, on attracting the boys who will become their future protectors of social responsibility (Lewis, 1979). Lewis found that girls then began to lose their desire to be boys. Only 2 percent of her subjects wished to be boys after puberty. Most accepted female identities. However, most did not succumb to tradition, but sought to personally redefine what it meant to be female. As teenagers, sports became an outlet for many of them. Nine of the fifteen women in this study played in sports. This was enough to cause rumors to start. Two women explained it this way:

I played basketball and stuff, and you know, when you're an athlete and a woman, there's a lot of stereotypes. You know, "she's real bullish!" Or "she can really shoot that hard for a woman." Peo-

ple would say something and my sister heard about it and she'd go home and tell my mom. She would say, "I heard Stella's gay." (Stella)

If you were in athletics at that point in time when I was in high school, you were automatically stereotyped that you were gay because you were a big athlete. . . . You were automatically labeled. (Carole)

For Stella, these rumors were instigators of problems at home. The mere label of "lesbian" proved to be a threat to women. It was a warning that they were stepping outside the lines of acceptable gender behavior. Carole felt a lot of pressure from peers to disprove the rumors. She said, "It bothered me to a degree . . . it did put a little more pressure on me as to trying to prove myself not being that way as far as dating and stuff like that."

As teenagers, and for some even into adulthood, a rejection of feminine clothing was also a pattern. This rejection ranged from not wearing overtly feminine apparel to dressing in a way that was considered to be "mannish."

I went through that stage when I had to play a Dyke. Yeah, I had to ride a motorcycle and wear men's pants, men's clothes and I didn't wear women's stuff at all. Men's underwear even, you know. You go through this phase and it's one of those things. (Pat)

I don't know why I'm so butch, why I wear men's clothes. It's not that I want to be a man, because I don't. Because God knows, if I were a man, I wouldn't have been with some of the women that I've been with. (Anita)

For Pat, as with the rest of the women with the exception of Anita and Jennifer, it was just, as she said, a phase. Whether as a child, teenager, or adult, it did seem to serve, as previously stated by Lewis, as a "rite of passage." It is crucial to consider, as Anita articulated, that gay women do *not* want to be men. Instead, they had desired male privilege and access to women. They desired the freedom that men had; and *every* woman in the sample, whether or not she considered herself a feminist, found the female role restrictive.

Since adolescents undergo so much pressure concerning gender conformity, lesbian adolescents might experience confusion, frustration, and ridicule. Sasha Lewis (1979, p. 24) wrote, "The young lesbian realizes that she cannot be a boy, yet she realizes that she cannot be like her female peers and in many cases she feels a sense of intense isolation." Not understanding why such pressure to conform even exists, lesbians then must determine their own paths. For many, as Pat and Kate explained, the lack of role models dramatically increased their problems. The problem was not merely finding good or even adequate role models. It was finding *any* role models. The lack of visibility, on the part of lesbians reinforced their fears of being "freaks."

In what they perceived as a way to escape the constraints of female roles, two of the women had expressed a youthful intention to enter the military. Two more eventually did. Although the army did not satisfy either in her search for identity, both felt their reason for joining involved this rejection of traditional roles. Pat explained:

Why did I join the army? Because it was not a female role. To prove that I was just as good as they (men) were. That I could do anything they could do. . . .

CONCLUSION

While the issue of gender identity in lesbians calls for further research, this study does reveal some important points. Even at an early age, the women in this study were rebels where gender behavior was concerned. Many of them described experiences as "tomboys." They, as children, indicated they had no problem with this behavior but were forced by others to "wear dresses" or "play with dolls." Some did these willingly but rejected traditional femininity

when they saw it as representing heterosexuality. Most rejected the traditional female role, because even as children, they could not foresee themselves in the future portraying a heterosexual role. Some, in childhood fantasies, already perceived themselves in lives with women. Many of them saw a need to take the "male role" to achieve the relation to women that they desired. At the onset of adolescence, much more pressure existed from both peers and adults to abandon "tomboyish" behaviors. . . .

It should be reiterated that the women in this study found the traditional female role to be restrictive and constraining. Beginning as children, they began a journey of self-discovery usually without the assistance of role models or appropriate guidance from those they considered authorities. As adults, each reached her own conclusion on what it meant to be a woman and what it meant to be a lesbian. Risking the labels of "deviants" or worse, these women have chosen roles for which there were no scripts. Consequently, many feminists would consider their androgynous approach to selfhood to be much more well-rounded than those straining to conform to rigidly limited roles. In their paper on the psychological adjustment of lesbians and heterosexual women, Oberstone and Sukoneck (1976) concluded their analysis on gay women with the following:

Are they really more "masculine" in their behavior than their "normal" heterosexual counterparts, or are they more free to develop both their feminine and masculine and, in fact, their human potential? It is possible that, rather than being "masculine," the lesbian woman, by virtue of being an outlaw, has had to develop personality qualities that have been traditionally the domain of the male, such as independence, self-determination, competence, and aggression. (p. 185)

REFERENCES

Lewis, Sasha G. 1979. *Sunday's Women: Lesbian Life Today.* Boston: Beacon.
Lofland, John, and Lyn H. Lofland. 1984. *Analyzing Social Settings: A Guide to Qualitative Observation and Analysis.* Belmont, CA: Wadsworth.

Martin, Del, and Phyllis Lyon. 1972. *Lesbian/Women.* New York: Bantam.
Millet, Kate. 1970. *Sexual Politics.* New York: Ballantine.
Oberstone, Andrea, and Harriet Sukoneck. 1976. "Psychological Adjustment and Life Style of Single

Lesbians and Single Heterosexual Women." *Psychology of Women Quarterly,* I(no. 2): 172–188.

Schwartz, Howard, and Jerry Jacobs. 1979. *Qualitative Sociology: A Method to the Madness.* New York: Free Press.

Stoller, Robert J. 1968. *Sex and Gender.* New York: Science House.

Wolff, Charlotte. 1971. *Love between Women.* New York: St. Martin's.

REVIEW QUESTIONS_____

1. Cooper discovered four uniform responses given by the women in her study as they relate to the development of a lesbian identity. What are they?

2. Given the way that Cooper collected her data, why must her conclusions be treated cautiously?

THE STIGMA OF OBESITY

ERICH GOODE

Bertha was a massive woman. She weighed well over 400 pounds. Still, people enjoyed her company, and she had an active social life. One Friday night, Bertha and several of her friends stopped in a local Burger and Shake for a quick snack. Bertha disliked fast-food restaurants with good reason: Their seats were inadequate for her size. But, she was a good sport and wanted to be agreeable, so she raised no objection to the choice of an eating establishment. Bertha squeezed her huge body into the booth and enjoyed a shake and burger. A typical Friday night crowd stood waiting for tables, so Bertha and her companions finished their snack and began to vacate the booth so that others could dine. But Bertha's worst fears were realized: She was so tightly jammed in between the table and the chair that she was stuck.

Bertha began struggling to get out of the booth, without success. Her friends pulled her, pushed her, and twisted her—all to no avail. She was trapped. Soon, all eyes in the Burger and Shake were focused on the hapless Bertha and her plight. Onlookers began laughing at her. Snickers escalated to belly laughs, and the restaurant fairly rocked with raucous laughter and cruel, taunting remarks. "Christ, is she fat!" "What's the matter, honey—one burger too many?" "Look at the trapped whale!" "How could anyone get that fat!" Bertha's struggles became frenzied; she began sweating profusely. Every movement became an act of desperation to free herself from her deeply humiliating situation. Finally, in a mighty heave, Bertha tore the entire booth from its bolts and she stood in the middle of the floor of the Burger and Shake, locked into the booth as if it had been a barrel. The crowd loved it, and shrieked with laughter that intensified in volume and stridency, as Bertha staggered helplessly, squatting in the center of the room.

One of Bertha's friends ran to his car, grabbed a hammer and a wrench, came back in, and began smashing at the booth. He broke it into pieces that fell to the floor, freeing the woman from her torture chamber. Bertha lumbered and pushed her way through the laughing, leering crowd, and ran to her car, hot tears in her eyes and burning shame in her throat. The friend who freed her limply placed the pieces of the chair and table onto the counter. The employees, now irritated, demanded that he pay for the damaged booth, but he and Bertha's other companions simply left the restaurant.

After that incident, Bertha rarely left her house. Two months later, she died of heart failure. She was 31 years old.

THE OBESE AND THE THIN IDEAL

In contemporary America, obesity is stigmatized. Fat people are considered less worthy human beings than thin people are. They receive less of the good things that life has to offer, and more of

Source: Erich Goode, "The Stigma of Obesity," in Erich Goode (ed.), *Social Deviance* (Boston: Allyn and Bacon, 1996), pp. 332–340. Published by Allyn and Bacon, Boston, MA. © 1996 by Pearson Education. Reprinted by permission of the publisher.

the bad. Men and women of average weight tend to look down on the obese, feel superior to them, reward them less, punish them, make fun of them. The obese are often an object of derision and harassment for their weight. What is more, thin people will feel that this treatment is just, that the obese deserve it, indeed, that it is even something of a humanitarian gesture, since such humiliation will supposedly inspire them to lose weight. The stigma of obesity is so intense and so pervasive that eventually the obese will come to see themselves as deserving of it, too.

The obese, in the words of one observer, "are a genuine minority, with all the attributes that a corrosive social atmosphere lends to such groups: poor self-image, heightened sensitivity, passivity, and withdrawal, a sense of isolation and rejection." They are subject to relentless discrimination, they are the butt of denigrating jokes, they suffer from persecution; it would not be an exaggeration to say that they attract cruelty from the thin majority. Moreover, their friends and family rarely give the kind of support and understanding they need to deal with this cruelty; in fact, it is often friends and family who are themselves meting out the cruel treatment. The social climate has become "so completely permeated with anti-fat prejudice that the fat themselves have been infected by it. They hate other fat people, hate themselves when they are fat, and will risk anything—even their lives—in an attempt to get thin. . . . Anti-fat bigotry . . . is a psychic net in which the overweight are entangled every moment of their lives" (Louderback, 1970, pp. v, vi, vii). The obese typically accept the denigration thin society dishes out to them because they feel, for the most part, that they deserve it. And they do not defend other fat people who are being criticized because they are a mirror of themselves; they mirror their own defects—the very defects that are so repugnant to them. Unlike the members of most other minorities, they don't fight back; in fact, they feel that they can't fight back. Racial, ethnic, and religious minorities can isolate themselves to a degree from majority prejudices; the obese cannot. The chances are, most of

the people they meet will be average size, and they live in a physical world built for individuals with much smaller bodies. The only possibilities seem to be to brace themselves—to cower under the onslaught of abuse—or to retreat and attempt to minimize the day-to-day disgrace.

Our hostility toward overweight runs up and down the scale, from the grossly obese to men and women of average weight. If the hugely obese are persecuted mightily for their weight, the slightly overweight are simply persecuted proportionally less—they are not exempt. We live in a weight-obsessed society. It is impossible to escape nagging reminders of our ideal weight. Standing at the checkout counter in a supermarket, we are confronted by an array of magazines, each with its own special diet designed to eliminate those flabby pounds. Television programs and even more so, advertising, display actresses and models who are considerably slimmer than average, setting up an almost impossibly thin ideal for the viewing public. If we were to gain ten pounds, our friends would all notice it, view the gain with negative feelings, and only the most tactful would not comment on it.

These exacting weight standards not surprisingly fall more severely on the shoulders of women than on men's. In a survey of the 33,000 readers of *Glamour* who responded to a questionnaire placed in the August 1983 issue of the magazine, 75 percent said that they were "too fat," even though only one-quarter were overweight according to the stringent 1959 Metropolitan Life Insurance Company's height-weight tables. . . . Still more surprising, 45 percent who were *under*weight according to Metropolitan's figures felt that they were "too fat." Only 6 percent of the respondents felt "very happy" about their bodies; only 15 percent described their bodies as "just right." When looking at their nude bodies in the mirror, 32 percent said that they felt "anxious," 12 percent felt "depressed," and 5 percent felt "repulsed."

Evidence suggests that the standards for the ideal female form have gotten slimmer over the years. Women whose figures would have been comfortably embraced by the norm a generation or more ago are now regarded as overweight, even fat. The model for the White Rock Girl, inspired by the ancient Greek goddess Psyche, was 5'4" tall in 1894 and she weighed 140; her measurements were 37"-27"-38". Over the years, the woman who was selected to depict the "White Rock Girl" has gotten taller, slimmer, and she has weighed less. In 1947, she was 5'6", weighed 125 pounds, and measured 35"-25"-35". And today, she's 5'8", weighs 118, and measures 35"-24"-34". Commenting on this trend, in an advertising flyer the executives of White Rock explain: "Over the years the Psyche image has become longer legged, slimmer hipped, and streamlined. Today—when purity is so important—she continues to symbolize the purity of all White Rock products." The equation of slenderness with purity is a revealing comment on today's obsession with thinness: Weighing a few pounds over some mythical ideal is to live in an "impure" condition. Interestingly, today's American woman averages 5'4" and weighs 140 pounds, the same size as 1894's White Rock Girl.

Advertising models represent one kind of ideal; they tend to be extremely thin. . . . [F]ashion models typically border on the anorexic, and women who take them as role models to be emulated are subjecting themselves to an almost unattainable standard. It would be inaccurate to argue that all American women aspire to look like a fashion model, and it would be inaccurate to assert that women in all media are emaciated. Still, it is entirely accurate to say that the ideal woman's figure as depicted in the media is growing slimmer over the years. Even in settings where women were once fairly voluptuous, today's version has slimmed down significantly.

Prior to 1970, contestants in Miss America pageants weighed 88 percent of the average for American women their age; after 1970 this declined somewhat to' 85 percent. More important, before 1970 pageant *winners* weighed the same as the other contestants; after 1970, however, winners weighed significantly *less* than the contestants who didn't win—82.5 percent of the average for American women as a whole. Similarly, the weight of women who posed for *Playboy* centerfolds also declined between 1959 and 1978. Centerfolds for 1959 were 91 percent of the weight for an average American woman in her 20s; this declined to 84 percent in 1978.

The increasingly slim standards of feminine beauty represent the most desirable point on a scale. The opposite end of this scale represents undesirable territory—obesity. If American women have been evaluated by standards of physical desirability that have shifted from slim to slimmer over the years, it is reasonable to assume that during this same period it has become less and less socially acceptable to be fat. In tribal and peasant societies, corpulence was associated with affluence. An abundant body represented a corresponding material abundance. In a society in which having enough to eat is a mark of distinction, heaviness will draw a measure of respect. This is true not only for oneself but also for one's spouse or spouses, and one's children as well. With the coming of mature industrialization, however, nutritional adequacy becomes sufficiently widespread as to cease being a sign of distinction; slenderness rather than corpulence comes to be adopted as the prevailing esthetic standard among the affluent (Powdermaker, 1960; Cahnman, 1968, pp. 287–288). In fact, what we have seen is a gradual adoption of the slim standard of attractiveness in all economic classes for both men and women, but much more strongly and stringently for women. And while more firmly entrenched in the upper socioeconomic classes, the slim ideal has permeated all levels of society.

STIGMATIZATION AND ITS CONSEQUENCES

Not only is obesity unfashionable and considered unesthetic to the thin majority, it is also regarded as "morally reprehensible," a "social disgrace" (Cahnman, 1968, p. 283). Fat people are *set apart* from men and women of average size; they are isolated from "normal" society (Millman, 1980). Today, being obese bears something of a *stigma.* In the words of sociologist Erving Goffman, the stigmatized are "disqualified from full social acceptance." They have been reduced "from a whole and usual person to a tainted, discounted one." The bearer of stigma is a "blemished person . . . to be avoided, especially in public places." The individual with a stigma is seen as "not quite human" (Goffman, 1963, pp. i, 1, 3, 5).

Over the centuries, the word *stigma* has had two meanings—one good and the second, very bad. Among the ancient Greeks, a stigma was a brand on the body of a person, symbolizing that the bearer was in the service of the temple. In medieval Christianity, *stigmata* were marks resembling the wounds and scars on the body of Jesus, indicating that the bearer was an especially holy individual. [On the other hand,] [i]n ancient times criminals and slaves were branded to identify their inferior status; the brand was a stigma. Lepers were said to bear the stigma of their loathsome disease. As it is currently used, stigma refers to a stain or reproach on one's character or reputation, or a symbol or sign of this inferiority or defect. Anything that causes someone to look down upon, condemn, denigrate or ignore another can be said to be *stigmatizing.*

A stigmatizing trait is rarely isolated. Hardly anyone who possesses one such characteristic is thought to have only one. A single sin will be regarded as housing a multitude of others as well, to be the "tip of the iceberg." The one stigmatizing trait is presumed to hide "a wide range of imperfections" (Goffman, 1963, p. 5). . . . The one negative trait is a *master status*—everything about the individual is interpreted in light of the single trait. "Possession of one deviant trait may have a generalized symbolic value, so that people automatically assume that its bearer possesses other undesirable traits allegedly associated with it." Thus, the question is raised when confronting someone with a stigma: "What kind of person would break such an important rule?" The answer that is offered is typically: "One who is different

from the rest of us, who cannot or will not act as a moral human being and therefore might break other important rules." In short, the stigmatizing characteristic "becomes the controlling one" (Becker, 1963, pp. 33, 34).

To be stigmatized is to possess a *contaminated* identity. Interaction with nonstigmatized individuals will be strained, tainted, awkward, inhibited. While the nonstigmatized may, because of the dictates of polite sociability, attempt to hide their negative feelings toward the stigmatized trait specifically, or the stigmatized individual as a whole, and act normally, they are, nonetheless, intensely *aware* of the other's blemish. Likewise, the stigmatized individual remains self-conscious about his or her relations with "normals," believing (often correctly) that the stigma is the exclusive focus of the interaction.

> I am always worried about how Jane judges me because she is the real beauty queen and the main gang leader. When I am with her, I hold my breath hard so my tummy doesn't bulge and I pull my skirt down so my fat thighs don't show. I tuck in my rear end. I try to look as thin as possible for her. I get so preoccupied with looking good enough to get into her gang that I forget what she's talking to me about. . . . I am so worried about how my body is going over that I can hardly concentrate on what she's saying. She asks me about math and all I am thinking about is how fat I am (Allon, 1976, p. 18).

Highly stigmatized individuals, in the face of hostility on the part of the majority to their traits and to themselves as bearers of those traits, walk along one of two paths in reacting to stigma. One is to fight back by forming subcultures or groups of individuals who share the characteristics the majority rejects, and to treat this difference from the majority as a badge of honor—or at least, as no cause for shame. Clearly, the homosexual subculture provides an example of the tendency to ward off majority prejudices and oppression. This path is trod by those who feel that the majority's opinion of them and of the characteristic the majority disvalues is illegitimate or invalid—just plain wrong. Here, the legitimacy of the stigma is rejected. A trait, characteristic, a form of behavior that others look down upon, they say, is no cause for invidiousness. You may put us down, those who travel this path say, but you have no right to do so. What we are or do is every bit as blameless, indeed, honorable, as what you are or do.

The second path the stigmatized take in reacting to stigma from the majority is *internalization*. Here, stigmatized individuals hold the same negative attitudes toward themselves as the majority does. The stigmatized individual is dominated by feelings of self-hatred and self-derogation. Thus, those who are discriminated against are made to understand that they *deserve* it; they come to accept their negative treatment as *just* (Cahnman, 1968, p. 294). They feel that the majority has a *right* to stigmatize them. They may despise themselves for being who or what they are, for doing what they do or have done. As we see in testimony from fat people themselves, there is a great deal of evidence to suggest that the obese are more likely to follow the second path than the first. In fact, it might be said that in comparison with the possessors of all stigmatized characteristics or behavior, the obese most strongly agree with the majority's negative judgment of who they are.

WHY THE OBESE ARE STIGMATIZED

Negative feelings on the part of the majority have been directed at a wide range of different groups and categories. Prejudice and racism against minority groups—what Goffman calls "the tribal stigma of race, nation, and religion" (1963, p. 4)—is one type of stigma. In some all-white settings, Blacks will be stigmatized if they enter them. Likewise, in certain all-black settings, it is the reverse. Anti-Semitism is rife in some social contexts; in them, to be Jewish is to suffer discrimination. At the same time, gentiles will find themselves shunned and ostracized in specific Jewish settings or contexts. For racial, national, and religious groups, stigma may work both ways; what counts is which group has the most power and resources. Although racism, ethnic hostility, and prejudice are fascinating topics, they are not what we are concerned about here.

A second type of trait or characteristic that tends to attract stigma from the majority who does not share it is made up of individuals who possess those "blemishes of individual character," which include having a "weak will, domineering or unnatural passions, treacherous and rigid beliefs, and dishonesty." Behavior or tendencies that, to the majority, manifest these and other "blemishes of individual character" include "mental disorder, imprisonment, addiction, alcoholism, homosexuality, unemployment, suicidal attempts, and radical political behavior" (Goffman, 1963, p. 4). Sociologists commonly refer to these forms of behavior as behavioral deviance, deviant behavior, or simply deviance. The archaic notion that deviant behavior is abnormal, a product of a disordered, pathological personality, has been abandoned long ago within sociology. People who engage in disapproved behavior tend to be perfectly normal; psychological abnormality has nothing to do with the concept of deviance. In sociology, deviance simply means a departure from an approved norm, especially where this departure tends to be punished, condemned, or stigmatized. Behavioral deviance, then, is a type of stigma.

The third type of trait or characteristic that commonly attracts stigma from the majority includes what Goffman calls "abominations of the body—the various physical deformities" (1963, p. 4). While not as thoroughly or as strongly rejected or stigmatized as behavioral deviants, possessors of certain physical characteristics are not completely accepted by the majority, either. Many individuals without a physical handicap feel uncomfortable relating to or interacting with someone who has an obvious disability or disfigurement, and this feeling is translated into real-life behavior—most commonly, avoiding contact, especially if it is intimate, with the disabled. While most nondisabled individuals would state that they would or do treat those with a disability "the same" as those without one, the disabled report [from] their treatment at the hands of the majority

[that] this claim [is] fictional. In one study, only a small minority of the sample said that they would marry an amputee (18 percent), someone in a wheelchair (7 percent), a blind person (16 percent), or a stutterer (7 percent). While some might object and argue that marriage is a highly individual matter, having little to do with stigma, the same pattern prevailed in other areas of life. Only a shade over half said that they would have a deaf person as a *friend* (53 percent), and for the cerebral palsied, this was under four respondents in ten (38 percent)! Barely half (54 percent) said that they would live in the same *neighborhood* as a retardate (Shears and Jensema, 1969). Clearly, stigma is alive and well for the possessors of undesirable physical characteristics. The fact that they are involuntarily acquired is no protection against their stigmatization. Stigma is ubiquitous; no society exists in which all members are free of invidious feelings toward individuals with certain physical traits.

It is clear that much the same process of stigma occurs with the obese as with other traits, characteristics, and behavior that are regarded by the majority as undesirable. In fact, obesity is unique in at least one respect: It is considered by the "thin" majority as both a physical characteristic, like blindness and disabilities, and a form of behavioral deviance, like prostitution and alcoholism. The obese, unlike the physically disabled, are held *responsible* for their physical condition. Fatness, in the eyes of the nonobese majority, is viewed as both a physical deformity and as a behavioral aberration (Cahnman, 1968, p. 293; Allon, 1982, p. 130). Being fat is regarded as a matter of choice; the obese have gotten the way they are because of something they have done.

Overweight individuals "are stigmatized because they are held responsible for their deviant status, presumably lacking self-control and willpower. They are not merely physically deviant as are physically disabled or disfigured persons, but they [also] seem to possess characterological stigma. Fat people are viewed as 'bad' or 'immoral'; supposedly, they do not want to change the

error of their ways" (Allon, 1982, p. 131). Contrary to the strictly disabled, and contrary to individuals belonging to a race different from our own,

the obese are presumed to hold their fate in their own hands; if they were only a little less greedy or lazy or yielding to impulse or oblivious of advice, they would restrict excessive food intake, resort to strenuous exercise, and as a consequence of such deliberate action, they would reduce. . . . While blindness is considered a misfortune, obesity is branded as a defect. . . . A blind girl will be helped by her agemates, but a heavy girl will be derided. A paraplegic boy will be supported by other boys, but a fat boy will be pushed around. The embarrassing and not infrequently harassing treatment which is meted out to obese teenagers by those around them will not elicit sympathy from onlookers, but a sense of gratification; the idea is that they have got what was coming to them (Cahnman, 1968, p. 294).

The obese are overweight, according to the popular view, because they eat immodestly and to excess. They have succumbed to temptation and hedonistic pleasure-seeking, where other, more virtuous and less self-indulgent individuals have resisted. It is, as with behavioral deviance, a matter of a struggle between vice and virtue. The obese must therefore pay for the sin of overindulgence by attracting well-deserved stigma (Cahnman, 1968; Maddox et al., 1968). The obese suffer from what the public sees as "self-inflicted damnation" (Allon, 1973; Allon, 1982). In one study of the public's rejection of individuals with certain traits and characteristics, it was found that the stigma of obesity was in between that of physical handicaps, such as blindness, and behavioral deviance, such as homosexuality (Hiller, 1981, 1982). In other words, the public stigmatized the obese *more* than possessors of involuntarily acquired undesirable traits, but *less* than individuals who engage in unpopular, unconventional behavior.

This introduces a *moral* dimension to obesity that is lacking in other physical [characteristics. A trait such as being blind or deaf that is seen as beyond] . . . the individual's control, for which he or she is held to be not responsible, is seen as a misfortune. In contrast, character flaws are regarded in a much harsher light. Obesity is seen as the outward manifestation of an undesirable character; it therefore invites retribution, in much of the public's eyes.

So powerfully stigmatized has obesity become that, in a *New York Times* editorial (Rosenthal, 1981), one observer argues that obesity has replaced sex and death as our "contemporary pornography." We attach some degree of shame and guilt to eating. Our society is made up of "modern puritans" who tell one another "how *repugnant* it is to be fat"; "what's really disgusting . . . is not sex, but fat." We are all so humorless, "so relentless, so determined to punish the overweight. . . . Not only are the overweight the most stigmatized group in the United States, but fat people are expected to participate in their own degradation by agreeing with others who taunt them."

REFERENCES

Allon, Natalie. 1973. The stigma of overweight in everyday life. In G. A. Bray (ed.), *Obesity in Perspective.* Washington, D.C.: U.S. Government Printing Office, pp. 83–102.

Allon, Natalie. 1976. *Urban Life Styles.* Dubuque, Iowa: W. C. Brown.

Allon, Natalie. 1982. The stigma of overweight in everyday life. In Benjamin B. Wolman (ed.), *Psychological Aspects of Obesity: A Handbook.* New York: Van Nostrand Reinhold, pp. 130–174.

Becker, Howard S. 1963. *Outsiders: Studies in the Sociology of Deviance.* New York: Free Press.

Cahnman, Werner J. 1968. The stigma of obesity. *The Sociological Quarterly,* 9 (Summer), 283–299.

Dejong, William. 1980. The stigma of obesity: The consequences of naive assumptions concerning the causes of physical deviance. *Journal of Health and Social Behavior,* 21, 75–87.

Garner, David M., Paul E. Garfinkel, D. Schwartz, and M. Thompson. 1980. Cultural expectations of thinness in women. *Psychological Reports,* 47, 483–491.

Goffman, Erving. 1963. *Stigma: Notes on the Management of Spoiled Identity.* Englewood Cliffs, N.J.: Prentice-Hall/Spectrum.

Hiller, Dana V. 1981. The salience of overweight in personality characterization. *Journal of Psychology,* 108, 233–240.

Hiller, Dana V. 1982. Overweight as master status: A replication. *Journal of Psychology,* 110, 107–113.

Louderback, Llewellyn. 1970. *Fat Power: Whatever You Weigh Is Right.* New York: Hawthorn Books.

Maddox, George L., Kurt W. Back, and Veronica Liederman. 1968. Overweight as social deviance and disability. *Journal of Health and Social Behavior,* 9 (December 1968), 287–298.

Millman, Marxia. 1980. *Such a Pretty Face: Being Fat in America.* New York: W. W. Norton.

Powdermaker, Hortense. 1960. An anthropological approach to the problem of obesity. *Bulletin of the New York Academy of Medicine,* 36, 286–295.

Shears, L. M., and C. J. Jensma. 1969. Social acceptability of anomalous persons. *Exceptional Children,* 35 (1):91–96.

REVIEW QUESTIONS

1. What makes the obese different from other minorities?
2. What are some of the consequences the obese encounter because they are stigmatized?

DEAF CULTURE'S OPPOSITION TO COCHLEAR IMPLANTS

BONNIE POITRAS TUCKER

During the past decade, a growing concept of Deaf culture has taken root. Under this concept, people who cannot hear are viewed as either deaf (with a small d) or Deaf (with a capital D). Persons who view themselves as deaf are those who, although impaired in their ability to hear, have assimilated into hearing society and do not view themselves as members of a separate culture. People who call themselves "Deaf," however, view and define deafness as a cultural identity rather than as a disability for some purposes; they insist that their culture and separate identity must be nourished and maintained.[1]

A cochlear implant is a surgically implanted device that is capable of restoring hearing and speech understanding to many individuals who are severely or profoundly deaf. Numerous studies show both the ability of profoundly deaf individuals to hear speech with cochlear implants and the ability of implanted deaf children to develop age-appropriate spoken and receptive language skills.[2] As reported in May 1998 to the Advisory Council of the National Institute on Deafness and Other Communication Disorders: "It has now been demonstrated that the long-term benefits of cochlear implants in children are not limited to speech recognition but extend into dramatically improved language learning and language skills."[3] In a recent survey, parents of 176 implanted children perceived that: (1) 44 percent of the children had greater than 70 percent open speech discrimination (using sound alone with no visual dues), (2) 61 percent of the children had greater than 50 percent open speech discrimination, and (3) 84 percent of the children had greater than 40 percent open speech discrimination.[4]

DEAF CULTURE

Because cochlear implants have the potential to ameliorate or eliminate ramifications of deafness, they are opposed by Deaf culturists, who view efforts to "cure" deafness or ameliorate its effects as an immoral means of killing Deaf culture.

The theory of Deaf culture is primarily premised on a shared language—American Sign Language (ASL). Individuals who communicate via ASL clearly *do* speak a different language. American Sign Language is visual rather than spoken, with its own syntax and grammar. ASL is quite different from signed English, which involves signing each English word as it is spoken, using English grammar and structure. In addition, some members of the Deaf cultural community claim to be part of a separate culture as a result of attending segregated (often residential) schools for Deaf children,[5] or as a result of their participation in Deaf clubs or wholly Deaf environments in which they socialize or work.

Source: Bonnie Poitras Tucker, "Deaf Culture, Cochlear Implants, and Elective Disability," *Hastings Center Report,* vol. 28, no. 4 (1998), pp. 6–14. Reprinted with permission.

According to the leaders of the National Association of the Deaf (NAD), Deaf people like being Deaf, want to be Deaf, and are proud of their Deafness. Deaf culturists claim the right to their own "ethnicity, with [their] own language and culture, the same way that Native Americans or Italians [or blacks] bond together."[6] They claim the right to "personal diversity" which is "something to be cherished rather than fixed and erased." In short, they claim the right to their "birthright of silence."

Many members of the Deaf cultural community strongly desire to have Deaf children, who will be a part of their parents' Deaf culture. Some expectant Deaf parents visit geneticists for the purpose of determining whether their children are likely to be born deaf. As explained by Jamie Israel, a genetic counselor at Gallaudet University's genetic services center, "[m]any of our [Deaf] families are not interested in fixing or curing deaf genes . . . [m]any . . . couples come in and want . . . Deaf children."[7] If their children are *not* likely to be born deaf, Deaf parents may choose not to have children, or to abort children in gestation, just as hearing or deaf people who determine through genetic research that their children *are* likely to be born deaf may choose not to have children or to abort children in gestation.

Deaf culture advocates . . . are strongly opposed to research geared at "curing" deafness and are particularly opposed to placing cochlear implants in children. They assert that members of their minority group "are in no more need of a cure for their condition than are Haitians or Hispanics."[8] To many members of the Deaf cultural community, cochlear implants represent "the ultimate denial of deafness, the ultimate refusal to let deaf children be Deaf." As stated by Roz Rosen, former president of NAD, since "[h]earing is not a life or death matter . . . [it is] consequently not worth the medical, moral and ethical risk of altering a child."[9] In accord with this reasoning, Deaf culturists have strongly criticized the National Institute of Health's National Institute on Deafness and Other Communication Disorders, which gives federal grants for research geared at the prevention and treatment of deafness and other communication disorders.[10]

Gallaudet students and their families or friends have informed this author that cochlear implants are greatly frowned upon at Gallaudet, and that implanted individuals who attend Gallaudet are usually pressured (often by their peers rather than by staff or faculty members) to remove them or at least not to wear their processors. As one reporter succinctly stated:

> As anyone at Gallaudet knows, a student with a [cochlear implant] device . . . runs the risk of being shunned. "I have some friends with implants," says Scott Mohan, a sixth generation deaf senior at Gallaudet. "They just don't use them anymore."
>
> "You can understand why," says Keith Mullet, Executive Director of the League for the Hard of Hearing in New York City. "Kids who try to speak in deaf schools are ridiculed. And the greater their oral success, the more they are criticized."[11]

The hatred with which Deaf culturists view cochlear implants is expressed in the ASL sign for a cochlear implant, which contains a two-fingered stab to the back of the neck, indicating a "vampire" in the cochlea.

While vehemently proclaiming the right to preserve their Deaf cultural heritage and denouncing those who choose to alleviate—to the maximum extent possible—their deafness or their childrens' deafness, members of the Deaf cultural community are strong activists for the promulgation of laws protecting persons with disabilities, such as the Americans with Disabilities Act. They vigorously advocate for the provision of special services to alleviate the effects of deafness. The Deaf cultural community, for example, is opposed to educating children who are deaf in mainstream classrooms but insists that such children should be placed in segregated schools for the Deaf so that they may become full-fledged members of the Deaf cultural society.

BACKLASH AGAINST DISABILITIES

Today, there is a tremendous backlash against laws such as the ADA [Americans with Disabilities Act]. Some members of society, particularly the business sector, view the ADA as providing "special benefits" to people with disabilities;[12] those individuals and entities do not understand that the ADA is intended simply to level the playing field for people with disabilities, to allow them the opportunity to take part in mainstream society. The ADA does not provide "special benefits" for people with disabilities. For example, providing an interpreter or a special typewriter telephone (and a relay service) for an employee who is deaf is not a special benefit"; rather it is an accommodation (that must be provided only when it is reasonable for the employer to do so) to allow the deaf person to take part in the work force to the same extent that a hearing person is already able to do so (without accommodation).

The United Kingdom's recently enacted Disability Discrimination Act of 1995 (DDA) already recognizes this concept to some degree. Under the U.K.'s DDA, an individual is deemed to be disabled, even if the disability is controllable by medication or other medical treatment, if the disability would have a substantial effect on the individual's ability to carry out normal day-to-day activities without the medication or medical treatment. Practical exceptions are noted, however.

> *For example, this rule does not extend to those with impaired sight where the impairment is correctable by spectacles or contact lenses or by some other prescribed method,* whether or not those aids are in fact used. *This exception reflects the fact that the correction of impaired sight by spectacles and contact lenses is usually so effective that "people who wear spectacles or contact lenses would not generally think of themselves as disabled.[13]* (emphasis added)

The U.K.'s DDA provides that the Secretary of State may issue regulations making other exceptions (in addition to the exception dealing with certain vision impairments) to the rule dealing with disabilities and corrective medical treatment. The DDA's annotations offer one illustration of such a regulation that might be enacted:

> *For example, at the moment, people wearing hearing aids will be covered by the definition because hearing aids usually provide only a partial correction of a disability. Those people are still usually, and should be, seen as disabled. But if at some future date, as a result of improved technology, hearing aids became as completely effective as spectacles or contact lenses are today, it might be appropriate to exclude people in that situation from the general definition of disability.[14]*

The United States Equal Employment Opportunity Commission (EEOC), which is responsible for enforcing the employment section (Title I) of the ADA, also takes the position that the determination whether an individual's physical or mental impairment "substantially limits a major life activity" (as required to fall within the definition of a person with a disability under the ADA) should be made *without* considering the effects of medical treatment on the individual. The EEOC has not noted exceptions to that rule, as has the U.K.'s DDA. Nevertheless, even absent such exceptions, several courts have disagreed with the EEOC, and have refused, for practical reasons, to hold that a physical impairment that is correctable by medical treatment constitutes a disability under ADA Title I.

For example, the EEOC's regulations state that an insulin-dependent diabetic is disabled for ADA Title I purposes if the only way the individual can perform major life activities is with the aid of insulin (without insulin the individual would lapse into a coma). In *Coghlan v. H. J. Deinz Co.* the court disagreed with that reasoning, holding that the EEOC's interpretation contradicts the express language of the ADA, because "an insulin-dependent diabetic who takes insulin could perform major life activities, . . . would therefore not be substantially limited" in the ability to perform such activities, and is therefore not disabled within the meaning of Title I of the ADA.

Other courts have also disagreed with the EEOC's reasoning. These courts seem troubled by the need to give special protection to individuals whose physical or mental impairments (otherwise considered disabilities) are completely correctable, even though in the cases cited the plaintiffs *were* receiving appropriate medical treatment and were *not* seeking accommodations for problems alleviated by such medical treatment. Indeed, in at least one case a court held that an individual who refused to submit to surgery that would have remedied a physical impairment could not claim protection under ADA Title I. In *Pangalos v. Prudential Insurance* the court held that an individual's severe ulceritive colitis did not constitute a covered disability under the ADA because it could have been remedied by a colostomy, a surgical procedure the individual refused to have.

It seems likely that in the future more courts will hold that the law does not require that an individual with a physical impairment be provided with accommodations which would not be necessary if the individual would obtain reasonable medical treatment that would obviate the need for such accommodations.

CONCLUSION

It is impossible not to recognize the source and validity of the anger, hostility, and solidarity expressed by the Deaf culturists who choose to reject hearing society and who do not wish to be "hearing" to any degree. Any individual with any compassion who knows anything of the history of people who are deaf must understand how the concept of Deaf culture came into existence. Many people who are deaf continue to live as second class citizens, as indicated not only by the rejection of deaf people by most hearing people but by the facts that:

> *The average deaf person today reads at a fourth grade level. One in three drops out of high school. Only one in five who starts college gets a degree. Deaf adults make 30 percent less than the general population. Their unemployment rate is high, and when they are employed, it is usually in manual jobs such as kitchen workers, janitors, machine operator; tailors and carpenters, for which a strong command of English it not required . . .* [15]

Rejecting hearing society, technology that will alleviate the ramifications of deafness, and the potential eradication of most deafness, however, is not the solution to the problems of deaf people. Rather, deaf people with cochlear implants, particularly children, have a wealth of opportunities and potential life experiences available to them. To deny such opportunities based on theories of segregation is indeed illogical.

NOTES

1. For an article explaining the viewpoint of Deaf culture, see Edward Dolnick, "Deafness as Culture," *Atlantic* 272, no. 3 (1993): 37–53.

2. See, for example, Susan B. Waltzman, Noel L. Cohen, Railey H. Gomolin, Janet E. Green, William H. Shapiro et al., "Open-Set Speech Perception in Congenitally Deaf Children Using Cochlear Implants," *American Journal of Otology* 18, no. 3 (1997): 342–49.

3. Report of Dr. Robert E Naunton, Director, Division of Human Communications, National Institute of Deafness and Other Communication Disorders, 7 May 1998 (in the author's files).

4. Bonnie P. Tucker, *Cochlear Implants: A Handbook* (Jefferson, N.C.: McFarland & Co., 1998, forthcoming).

5. The vast majority of deaf children in the United States no longer attend such schools; the Individuals with Disabilities Education Act—enacted in 1973 for the purpose of providing children with disabilities with a free appropriate public education, primarily alongside children without disabilities—has resulted in sharp declines in special school enrollments. See, for example, Felicity Barringer, "Pride in a Soundless World: Deaf Oppose a Hearing Aid," *New York Times,* 16 May 1993.

6. Roslyn Rosen, "President Rosen on Cochlear Implants," *NAD Broadcaster,* December 1992, p. 6; see

also, "The President Signs On," *NAD Broadcaster,* January 1991, p. 3.

7. Abigail Traford, "The Brave New World of Genetic Planning," *Washington Post,* 15 November 1994.

8. Dolnick, "Deafness as Culture," p. 37.

9. Rosen, "President Rosen on Cochlear Implants."

10. The author is a member of the National Advisory Council to the National Institute on Deafness and Other Communication Disorders and has personal knowledge of such criticism.

11. M. Arana Ward, "As Technology Advances, a Bitter Debate Divides the Deaf," *Washington Post,* 11 May 1997.

12. See, for example, George Will, "Disabilities Act May End Up Granting Special Rights to Jerks," *Idaho Statesman,* 4 April 1996.

13. 1995 c.50 (United Kingdom), p. 50–8

14. 1995 c.50 (United Kingdom), p. 50–8, 9

15. Ward, "As Technology Advances."

REVIEW QUESTIONS

1. Why do Deaf culturalists view cochlear implants as undesirable?
2. If it can be demonstrated that a child of deaf parents could hear as a result of a cochlear implant, would you favor using this technology in spite of the parents' objection? Defend your answer.

"YOU'RE NOT A RETARD, YOU'RE JUST WISE"

STEVEN J. TAYLOR

This is a study of the social meaning of disability and construction of social identity in a family I will refer to as the Dukes. The immediate family consists of four members—Bill and Winnie and their two children, Sammy and Cindy—but has grown since I started my study to include Cindy's husband and her four young children. The Dukes are part of a much larger network of extended family members and friends. I have been following the Duke family and many of its kin and friends for the past ten years. . . . Bill, Winnie, and their two children have all been diagnosed as mentally retarded or disabled by schools and human service agencies, and a sizeable number of their kin and friends have been similarly diagnosed.

From a sociological or anthropological perspective, disability can be viewed as a social construct (Whyte and Ingstad 1995). Like other forms of social deviance, what we call disabilities—mental retardation, mental illness, Alzheimer's disease, blindness, deafness, mobility impairments—are not objective conditions but concepts that exist in the minds of people who attach those labels to others (Bogdan and Taylor 1994; Davis 1997; Gubrium 1986; Langness and Levine 1986; Mercer 1973; Murphy 1990).

Disability can serve as a master status (Becker 1963; Schur 1971) and can carry with it a stigma. A stigma is not merely a difference but a characteristic that deeply discredits a person's moral character (Bogdan and Taylor 1994; Goffman 1963; Langness and Levine 1986; Link et al. 1997). Numerous studies have demonstrated how people with disabilities are stigmatized and rejected by society. . . .

THE DUKE FAMILY

Bill and Winnie Duke live just outside of Central City, a medium-size city in the Northeast. Bill and Winnie have lived in and around Central City since they were married more than twenty-five years ago.

Bill

Bill, age fifty, describes himself as a "graduate of Empire State School," a state institution originally founded in 1894 as "Empire State Custodial Asylum for Unteachable Idiots." Born in a small rural community outside of Capital City, Bill was placed at the institution as an adolescent.

Bill was placed on "probation" and lived for a period of time in a halfway house in Central City, approximately 150 miles from his family's home. He was officially discharged from the institution in 1971.

Bill is on disability and receives government Social Security and Supplemental Security Income (SSI) benefits. Shortly after his release from

Source: Steven J. Taylor, " 'You're Not a Retard, You're Just Wise,' " *Journal of Contemporary Ethnography,* vol. 29 (February 2000), pp. 58–92.

the institution, he held several short-term jobs but has not worked in a regular, tax-paying job since the mid-1970s.

Winnie

Winnie, age forty-eight, runs the household, manages the family's finances, and negotiates relations with schools, government programs, and human service workers. Winnie acts very much like a typical wife and mother and performs the work associated with women in American families (DeVault 1991). Winnie was born and raised in Central City. She dropped out of school early to help raise her brother and stepbrothers and sisters, but she can read well and prides herself both on her memory and math skills.

Winnie has a speech impediment, which makes her very difficult to understand until one has known her for a while. She also has a host of medical problems. By her account, she had convulsions until she was nine years old and has arthritis, heart problems, and a clubfoot.

When I first met the Dukes, Winnie was on public assistance or welfare but was subsequently deemed eligible for SSI. She also previously received spouse's benefits from Bill's Social Security. She is eligible for vocational rehabilitation because she has "a disability which results in a substantial handicap to employment," according to her Individual Written Rehabilitation Plan, and she has participated in numerous job-training programs. She has worked twice at a large sheltered workshop for the disabled, Federated Industries of Central City. She took these jobs under the threat of losing her welfare benefits. Her last placement there in the early 1990s ended when Federated ran out of work and laid off most of its clients.

Sammy

Sammy, age twenty-seven, was born with cerebral palsy, which is not currently noticeable, a cleft palate, and heart problems. According to Winnie,

he has had more than ninety operations for hearing, heart, and other problems. As an infant, he had a tracheotomy and was fed through a tube in his stomach. Winnie proudly recalls how she learned to handle his tracheotomy. Sammy has a severe speech impediment and is extremely difficult to understand when he talks.

Sammy dropped out of school at age sixteen. He was enrolled in a special education program for students with multiple disabilities, and specifically mental retardation and hearing impairments. He receives SSI. Winnie is the representative payee for Sammy's SSI; that is, Sammy's check comes in Winnie's name, and she must periodically report how the funds are spent.

Sammy has never held a regular job, although he worked for a very brief period of time at a garage where his father worked for a month or so "under the table."

Since reaching adulthood, Sammy has lived off and on with his parents, one of his other relatives, or one of his "girlfriends." Whether or not he is living with Winnie and Bill, he has frequent contact with them. Sammy currently lives with his parents, although he says that he is looking for an apartment of his own.

Cindy

Cindy, age twenty-three, has epilepsy and receives SSI. Prior to dropping out of school at age seventeen, she was enrolled in an intensive special education class, and her federally mandated Individual Education Plan (IEP) indicated that she is "mentally retarded–mild" Both Bill and Winnie were proud of how Cindy was doing in school and disappointed when she dropped out.

One summer, while she was in high school, Cindy was placed at the Federated Industries sheltered workshop as part of a job-training program. Through her school program, she had volunteer job placements at fast food restaurants and a human service agency.

Cindy speaks very clearly but seems to have difficulty reading. Cindy has always been shy among strangers but is becoming less so as she grows older.

Since I started studying the Duke family, Cindy has changed from a girl to a young adult, wife, and mother. When Cindy was about seventeen, Bill and Winnie started to worry that she was becoming sexually active. Their fears were not unfounded. She became pregnant, broke up with her boyfriend, and then married a 26-year-old man, Vinnie, shortly afterward. Cindy's first baby, Mikey, was born in spring, 1993, and she has since had three additional babies. After the birth of her last child, Cindy agreed to be sterilized. Cindy and Vinnie's four children, all boys, are enrolled in an early intervention special education program.

Social Relations among Kin and Friends

Bill and Winnie not only come from sizeable extended families but also have a large and ever-expanding network of friends and acquaintances. The Dukes make friends easily and bring friends of friends, family of friends, and friends of family into their immediate social network.

Social relations within the Duke network are characterized by mutual support, on one hand, and arguments and feuds, on the other. . . . [T]he Dukes and their kin and friends depend on each other for help and assistance; mutual support networks are a means of coping with their marginal economic and social status. The Dukes as well as their relatives and friends take in homeless family members and friends, lend people food or money, and help each other out in other ways.

People within the Dukes's network also regularly complain about and argue with each other or become embroiled in all-out feuds. At any point in time, someone in the network is fighting with someone else. Hardly a month goes by when Bill and Winnie are not involved in a dispute with relatives or friends. Once an argument begins, other family members and friends are likely to be drawn into it.

Feuds can be emotionally charged and vehement but seldom last long. People can be bitter enemies one day and friendly to each other the next. For example, when I first met the Dukes, Lisa and Gary and their three children were staying with them since they were homeless. Bill and Winnie grew tired of Lisa and Gary and threw them out of their house. Within months, however, Lisa and Gary were once again close friends of the Dukes and frequent visitors to their home.

THE STUDY

When I first heard about the Duke family, I was interested in meeting them. Cindy's family support worker, Mary, had casually told me about the family and how each member had a disability. In particular, Bill's reported description of himself as a "graduate of Empire State School" fascinated me. My dissertation was based on an ethnographic study of a ward at Empire State School (Taylor 1977, 1987), and I had previously conducted life histories with former residents of Empire (Bogdan and Taylor 1976, 1994). Everything I knew based on my previous research led me to believe that people would avoid volunteering information about having lived at an institution for the mentally retarded. The longer this study has gone on, the more I have appreciated Gubrium and Holstein's (1990) notion of "listening in order to see."

Mary regularly collected used clothes, old appliances, and household items for the Dukes. I had an old portable TV and some electric heaters and asked Mary if she would arrange for me to drop them off at the Dukes. She agreed to do so, and I met the Duke family in February 1989. I have been studying the Dukes ever since that time.

From 1989 to the beginning of 1992, I recorded approximately 100 sets of field notes comprising more than 1,200 pages. Since that time, although visiting the Dukes less frequently, I have continued to maintain regular contact with them. In recent years, I have visited them four or five times a year and speak with them on the phone monthly, if not more often.

DISABILITY LABELS AND FAMILY CONSTRUCTIONS

Although Bill, Winnie, Sammy, and Cindy, as well as many of their kin and friends, have been labeled as disabled or might be considered disreputable in other ways, they do not attach the same meanings to disability labels as found in the broader society. Within the Duke family and to a large extent within their broader social network, disability labels are interpreted in nonstigmatizing ways. They are largely successful in insulating themselves from the messages received from programs, agencies, and schools . . . that they are handicapped, disabled, mentally retarded, and incompetent.

The disability labels of Bill, Winnie, Sammy, and Cindy are listed on plans, forms, and correspondence the family receives. *Mentally retarded, disabled,* and *handicapped* appear frequently on government paperwork; teachers and government officials have referred to Cindy's and Sammy's "mental problems" and "mental retardation" in discussions with Winnie. Their labels are not a matter of things said behind their backs but are thrown to their faces.

Yet, the Dukes, along with their friends and kin, attach social meanings to such labels that leave their social identities unscathed.

[In the Dukes's own opinion, they have only medical problems. As Winnie said]: Cindy has medical problems. She has epileptic seizures. . . . Sammy had medical problems when he was born. Bill has medical problems. He has seizures. And I have medical problems. We all have medical problems." Winnie explained that she and Bill were aware of each other's problems when they got married. . . .

Having medical problems is not something to conceal or to be ashamed of. Winnie volunteers this information to outsiders making their first visits to the home. Medical problems seems to represent a nonstigmatizing way of interpreting the messages received from the outside world. In the same way that a person's identity is not affected by having high blood pressure, allergies, or high cholesterol, the construct of medical problems avoids stains on a person's moral character.

Institutionalization

As Edgerton (1993) notes, institutionalization is itself stigmatizing and a biographical fact that people with mental retardation try to hide. The "cure" (being institutionalized) is worse than the "disease" (having an intellectual deficit).

When Bill discusses his institutional experience, he talks as though Empire State School were a reform school rather than an institution for the mentally retarded. According to Bill, Empire helped him "get my head together," and he is proud that he worked his way off "probation." Bill described his history:

> I was in Empire State School before I was married. I don't mind talking about that. I'm proud of it. I was there twenty-two years. Now I'm celebrating my eighteenth anniversary. I have a nice family, and I'm doing okay.

On another occasion, Bill commented that it would "straighten out" Sammy and Cindy if they were sent to institutions. Bill points to Sammy:

> Now it's too bad they don't have places like Empire today. I'll tell you, if you went to Empire, you wouldn't have the problems you have. I'll tell you. It was hard. You had to work hard scrubbing the floors. Then if you did something, they beat you with a stick or put your head in the toilet.

Retard, Retarded, Moron, Crazy, Weird, Dumb, and Stupid

As in other parts of society, *retard, retarded, moron, crazy, weird, dumb,* and *stupid* are used as general epithets and do not necessarily refer to intellectual deficits. People casually call each other these names. Bill often calls Sammy and Cindy "stupid" and "dumb" when they avoid doing something he has told them to do or when they irritate him. Bill turns the TV from a program to the VCR. Sammy complains, "Don't turn that. I'm watching it." Bill replies, "Stupid, that's almost over." Cindy says something about riding Sammy's bike. Bill says, angrily, "Stupid, there's bikes downstairs. Get one of them." When he is angry with family or friends, he also refers to them as "stupid." Both Bill and Winnie characterize his family as "crazy" and "weird." Bill told me the following story:

BILL: "I'll tell you, my family's crazy. They're all crazy. How's your stomach?"
ME: "Okay, I guess."
BILL: "I mean, do you have a weak stomach?"
ME: "No, go ahead."
BILL: "My sister Pam. . . . Well, she used to make macaroni salad, with cucumbers and everything. It was real good. This one time, I was over at her house, and she asked me if I wanted some macaroni salad, and I said, 'Sure. Yea.' Well. She gave me a dish, and I went to take a bite, and I looked down, and there were maggots in it. I said, 'Pam, there's maggots in there!' She took the macaroni and ate it, maggots and all. I'll tell you. She's crazy."

Although Bill often calls Sammy and Cindy "dumb" and "stupid," both he and Winnie also communicate to their children that they are not mentally deficient. Bill proudly showed me a TV on which Sammy had worked.

Everybody says Sammy's dumb, right? They all say he's dumb. Want to see something? (Bill points to a TV in Sammy's room.) I found that in the trash and brought it home. Sammy took the tube out and put another one in it from another TV I had. (Bill turns on the TV.) Look at that. Everybody says he's stupid, but look at that. He's not dumb.

The title of this article is a quote from Bill. One day when I was visiting the home, Bill was prodding Cindy to sweep the floor. Avoiding the job, Cindy would sweep for a minute or two and

then sit down. After being scolded repeatedly by Bill, she laughed and said, "I'm a retard." This is when Bill said, "You're not a retard, you're just wise." Cindy responded, "I'll be a retard if I don't do my homework." Bill's casual response, "You're not a retard, you're just wise," redefined her behavior in terms of being a smart alec and, hence, was normalizing. However, this exchange and other instances when Cindy called herself "stupid" indicate that she was aware of how she had been labeled at school, and this was problematic for her.

The Dukes simply do not internalize disability labels as a master status and, for this reason, avoid the stigma and spoiled identities associated with them. They do not attempt to pass as normal; they see themselves as normal.

SOCIAL IDENTITIES

The Dukes's kin and friends can be identified as disabled or disreputable in the context of schools, government programs, and human service agencies, but they have untainted identities, or images, within the family and social network.

Bill and Winnie describe themselves in terms of their family roles, interests, and skills. For both of them, their family relationships, gender roles, and responsibilities are especially important in the construction of identity. Bill is a husband, father, grandfather, uncle (who is looked up to by some of his nieces and nephews), son, and brother; and Winnie is a wife, mother, grandmother, aunt, daughter, and sister. Bill expresses pride about having a family, and Winnie prides herself on her child-rearing knowledge and skills. Winnie never passes up a chance to give me advice on raising my own children (six and eight years old) and will scold me if she thinks I am doing something wrong. Both Winnie and Bill like to remind me that I am a newlywed compared to them. Their anniversary, Mother's Day, and Father's Day are special holidays for Bill and Winnie and provide an opportunity to celebrate their status as marriage partners and parents.

When it comes to their children, Bill and Winnie have a way of turning labeling and stigmatizing experiences upside down and inside out. Their definitions of their children stand in stark contrast to how they have been defined by schools, government programs, and agencies. Winnie reports that Sammy was an "A-1 student" prior to dropping out. When I asked what Sammy "wants to be," Winnie answered, "A mechanic, maybe an artist."

When she was a full-time special education student, Cindy received constant reminders of her identity as being disabled or mentally retarded. Her IEP [Individual Educational Plan] mentioned her mental retardation, and Winnie attended what she called "Committee on the Handicapped" meetings on her behalf. Everything about Cindy's school program told her that she was handicapped and mentally retarded. She took a special education bus to and from school and had always been placed in a self-contained special education class. As her comments "I'm a retard" and "I'm stupid" indicated, Cindy was not oblivious to the messages she received from school, and she had to struggle to maintain an identity as a normal teenager. However, Bill and Winnie constructed an image of Cindy being a normal teenager.

Winnie boasted to family members and friends about Cindy's school achievements. One year, Cindy was awarded certificates of attendance and merit for participation in her special education program, and Winnie talked about her "making the honor roll." On the last day of class that year, Cindy's teacher gave out class awards. Cindy received one for "community service" and one for "student council" (three members of her special education class were among the sixty or seventy members of the school's student council). On the way home after Cindy's last day of class, Winnie commented, "That kid's bright. She'll graduate from high school."

For many, if not most, parents, marriage and child rearing would be out of the question for children with Sammy's and Cindy's limitations. For Winnie and Bill, raising a family is regarded as a natural part of growing up for Cindy and Sammy. Both Winnie and Bill are proud grandparents of Cindy's four children and expect Sammy to get married soon.

CONCLUSION

In the Duke family and broader network of extended family members and friends, people with obvious disabilities are not stigmatized, rejected, or necessarily viewed as disabled. Even when people's disabilities are recognized, as in the case of the handicapped, these disabilities do not represent a master status that controls interactions with them. That people can maintain positive identities while being subjected to labeling at the hands of government programs, human service agencies, and schools is no easy accomplishment. The Duke family experience shows that small worlds can exist that do not simply reproduce the broader social contexts in which they are embedded.

Four related factors seem to account for the Dukes's ability to avoid the stigma and stained identities associated with disability. First, the family stands between individual members and programs or agencies and provides a ready set of meanings and interpretations of their experiences. Reiss (1981) describes how families help members organize their experiences of situations in everyday life. According to Reiss, the family permits individuals to "select, highlight, and transform essential aspects of their experience and delete the rest" (p. 203). Culture, including the cultural meanings associated with disability and imparted by agencies, is interpreted in the context of the family's stock of shared knowledge and understandings.

Second, in the case of the Dukes, their family life world is shared and reinforced by an extensive network of kin and friends. Their extended social network appears to be much more influential than in the nuclear families described in much of the literature on family worlds (Hess and Handel 1995; Gubrium and Holstein 1990; Reiss 1981). Within the Dukes's social network, households are not necessarily identical with nuclear families and often are composed of members of different families. Furthermore, households and families within the network have a high degree of contact with one another.

Third, related to their roles within a family, none of the Dukes or members of the network are full-time clients of human service agencies. Institutions and community facilities engulf people in a separate subculture that provides them with scarce opportunities to define themselves as anything other than disabled (Bercovici 1983; Bogdan and Taylor 1994; Edgerton 1986). Bill's and Cindy's experiences are instructive in this regard. For Bill, the passage of time since being institutionalized has undoubtedly enabled him to establish a positive identity. In a follow-up study of "The Cloak of Competence," Edgerton and Bercovici (1976) found that ex-institutional residents' concern with stigma and passing became far less evident over time. Of all of the members of the Duke family and perhaps the network, Cindy seemed to struggle the most with an identity as a disabled or retarded person while she was in school. This suggests that the more enmeshed one is in disability programs—in Cindy's case, full-time special education classes—the more one has to contend with a negative identity.

Finally, competence is a relative concept (Goode 1994). Although the Dukes and other members of their network may not perform well on standardized tests, in school programs, or in traditional jobs in the mainstream marketplace, they are competent to meet the demands of day-to-day life as they experience it. Bill knows not only the best junking routes but also where to sell junk at the best price. Winnie knows where to turn for help when food is scarce. Sammy learned about junk [cars from his father. Cindy was very] aware and competent to function in stores and other settings within her immediate neighborhood.

Literacy and verbal agility are not requisite survival skills in the daily lives of the Dukes and other members of their social network. People within the network, therefore, are not defined based on such characteristics.

REFERENCES

Becker, H. S. 1963. *Outsiders: Studies in the sociology of deviance.* New York: Free Press.

Bercovici, S. M. 1983. *Barriers to normalization.* Baltimore: University Park Press.

Bogdan, R., and S. J. Taylor. 1976. The judged, not the judges: An insider's view of mental retardation. *American Psychologist* 31:47–52.

———. 1994. *The social meaning of mental retardation: Two life stories.* New York: Teachers College Press.

Davis, L. J. 1997. Constructing normalcy: The bell curve, the novel, and the invention of the disabled body in the nineteenth century. In *The disability studies reader,* edited by L. J. Davis, 1–28. New York: Routledge.

DeVault, M. L. 1991. *Feeding the family: The social organization of caring as gendered work.* Chicago: University of Chicago Press.

Edgerton, R. B. 1986. A case of delabeling: Some practical and theoretical implications. In *Culture and retardation: The histories of mildly mentally retarded*

persons in American society, edited by L. L. Langness and H. Levine, 101–26. Boston: D. Reidel.

———. 1993. *The cloak of competence revised and updated.* Berkeley: University of California Press.

Edgerton, R. B., and S. Bercovici. 1976. The cloak of competence: Years later. *American Journal of Mental Deficiency* 80:485–97.

Goffman, E. 1963. *Stigma: Notes on the management of spoiled identity.* Englewood Cliffs, NJ: Prentice Hall.

Goode, D. 1994. *A world without words: The social construction of children born deaf and blind.* Philadelphia: Temple University Press.

Gubrium, J. F. 1986. The social preservation of mind: The Alzheimer's disease experience. *Symbolic Interaction* 9:37–51.

Gubrium, J. F., and J. A. Holstein. 1990. *What is family?* Mountain View, CA: Mayfield.

Hess, R. D., and G. Handel. 1995. *Family worlds: A psychosocial approach to family life.* Lanham, MD: University Press of America.

Langness, L. L., and H. G. Levine. 1996. *Culture and retardation: Life histories of mildly mentally retarded persons in American society.* Boston: D. Reidel.

Link, B. G., E. L. Struening, M. Rahav, J. C. Phelan, and L. Nuttbrock. 1997. On stigma and its consequences: Evidence from a longitudinal study of men with dual diagnoses of mental illness and substance abuse. *Journal of Health and Social Behavior* 38:177–90.

Mercer, J. 1973. *Labeling the mentally retarded.* Berkeley: University of California Press.

Murphy, R. 1990. *The body silent.* New York: Norton.

Reiss, D. 1981. *The family's construction of reality.* Cambridge: Harvard University Press.

Schur, E. M. 1971. *Labeling deviant behavior: Its sociological implications.* New York: Harper & Row.

Taylor, S. J. 1977. The custodians: Attendants and their work at state institutions for the mentally retarded. Unpublished doctoral dissertation.

———. 1987. "They're not like you and me": Institutional attendants' perspectives on residents. *Child & Youth Services* 8:109–25.

Whyte, S. R., and B. Ingstad. 1995. Disability and culture: An overview. In *Disability and culture,* edited by B. Ingstad and S. R. Whyte, 3–32. Berkeley: University of California Press.

REVIEW QUESTIONS

1. What are some consequences for a deviant being medically labeled?
2. What does the title " 'You're Not a Retard, You're just Wise'" tell us about the study?

PART EIGHT

HETEROSEXUAL DEVIANCE

Jeanette Maier had worked for many years as a prostitute in New Orleans under various conditions. She had worked for pimps and sugar daddies as well as for strip joints and escort services. But she couldn't get rich. Then ten years ago she heard about the Circuit, a vast nationwide network of over 100 brothels run by madams who make enormous sums of money swapping hookers with one another. In her mid-30s in 1996, Maier opened her own brothel and tried to join the Circuit. She called the madams in various cities and offered to send them her "girls" if they sent theirs to her. Since then, Maier always has new faces in her bordello and has become fabulously rich. The prostitutes who work for her through the Circuit fly around the country and stay at one place for about a week. Clients love the variety and pay top dollar, sometimes spending thousands of bucks in one night. The women who temporarily work for Maier generally earn about $5,000 a week each, and she as their madam gets half of those earnings.[1]

This kind of prostitution, like any other way in which women sell sex to men, is an example of heterosexual deviance. Other examples include women showing off their naked breasts in a parade, dancing nude for pay in a club, and engaging in socially stigmatized sex. Here we take a look at these deviances. In the first article, "The Globalization of Sex Tourism," Nancy Wonders and Raymond Michalowski show how sex tourism has become globalized, flourishing in both developed and developing countries such as Netherlands and Cuba. In the second reading, "Parade Strippers: Being Naked in Public," Craig Forsyth discusses his research on women exposing their breasts at Mardi Gras parades in New Orleans. In the third selection, "Nude Dancing: Sexual Celebration in Conservative America," Frederick Schiff explores the world of nude dancing in the midst of a relatively conservative city in Texas. In the fourth article, " 'Everyone Knows Who the Sluts Are': How Young Women Get around the Stigma," Jennifer Dunn shows how sexually active college women try to avoid getting stigmatized as "sluts."

---

1. Arian Campo-Flores, "A Crackdown on Call Girls," *Newsweek,* September 2, 2002, p. 59.

THE GLOBALIZATION
OF SEX TOURISM

NANCY A. WONDERS
RAYMOND MICHALOWSKI

[The current era of globalization is characterized by unprecedented movement of material, information, finance, and bodies across borders. In this article, we examine how globalization facilitates the growth of sex tourism, as well] as the particular character of sex tourism in different locales. As others have already detailed (Opperman 1998), "sex tourism" is a protean term that attempts to capture varieties of leisure travel that have as a part of their purpose the purchase of sexual services. Clearly the concepts of "prostitution" and "tourism" are both central to an analysis of sex tourism, but neither term captures the full meaning of sex tourism. "Sex tourism" highlights the convergence between prostitution and tourism, links the global and the local, and draws attention to both the production and consumption of sexual services. The growth in sex tourism over the last two decades is well established (Kempadoo and Doezema 1998; Opperman 1998). In this article, we focus specifically on how the global forces shaping this growth connect the practice of sex work in two disparate cities with globalized sex tourism. . . .

Research provides compelling evidence that cities are strategic sites for observing the effects of globalization (Sassen 1998, 2000a, 2000b; Sassen and Roost 1997). In our analysis, we detail

the way that the global forces shaping the production and consumption of sex tourism impact two very different cities: Amsterdam and Havana. We explore the global connections that link sex work in these two cities with the forces associated with globalized sex tourism. Specifically, we argue that global forces impact sex work in both cities through four mediating institutions: (1) the tourism industry, (2) labor markets, (3) the localized sex industry, and (4) law and policy. As mediating institutions in these cities adjusted to the impact of global forces, they created opportunities for sex tourism to flourish.

It is important to our analysis that Amsterdam and Havana are very different cities. Many argue that global forces are easily discerned in "global cities" like Amsterdam (Sassen 2000a, 1998). Global cities are strategically positioned at the center of the global capitalist system as command points, key locations, and marketplaces for leading industries, and major sites of production. . . .

In contrast, Havana is located in Cuba, one of the last self-identified socialist states in the world. Cuba is a developing island nation struggling to find a foothold in the new global capitalist economy that will enable it to grow economically, while preserving its socialist accomplishments in

Source: Nancy A. Wonders and Raymond Michalowski, "Bodies, Borders, and Sex Tourism in a Globalized World: A Tale of Two Cities—Amsterdam and Havana," *Social Problems,* vol. 48 (2001), pp. 545–571. © 2001 by The Society for the Study of Social Problems. Reprinted with permission.

health, education, and social welfare (Dello Buono and Lara 1997).

Despite their differences, we illustrate that globalization's reach is evident in both Amsterdam and Havana. The specific responses to global forces differ, but comparison between these two cities reveals the impact of significant global connections on sex work in both locations.

SEX TOURISM IN AMSTERDAM, HOLLAND

In Amsterdam, the commodification of bodies has been perfected to the level of an art form. The red light district resembles the modern open-air shopping mall in the United States. Relatively clean streets, little crime, a neon atmosphere, and windows and windows of women to choose from—every size, shape, and color (though not in equal amounts). The red light district seems designed to be a sex tourist's Mecca. The range of services for the leisure traveler includes sex clubs, sex shows, lingerie and S&M clothing shops, condomories, and a sprinkling of porno stores. But the character of Amsterdam's red light district is different from most other sex tourist locations because it is centered in an historic district between the Oude Kerk (Old Church) and de Waag (an old weighing station)—two of the most spectacular cultural tourist sites in the city—and it is surrounded by an old, well established residential neighborhood. Indeed, walking through the red light district in the daytime is not so different from walking down any other shopping street in the city, though the area takes on a festival atmosphere at night. Crowds of men walk the street, stopping to gaze at the living merchandise in the window. The routine among men is much like the routine observed among women shopping for clothes, with plentiful commentary on the size, shape, color, and cost of the women on display. The smorgasbord of languages rising through the air reveals the international character of those shopping for bodies.

In describing the Amsterdam scene, it is important to make clear that women sex workers are far from passive in the shopping interaction. On quieter evenings and in the daytime, it is common for women to hover near the doorways of their small window booths, hooting and calling at men to "come here!" in a number of different languages. In an odd role reversal, one male friend commented to me after a walk through the district that: "I've never felt so objectified in my life. I felt like a piece of meat walking through there."

The Tourism Industry

. . . It has been well established that tourism, as a global force, has affected all of Western Europe. As Williams and Shaw (1998:20) note, "Europe dominates international movements of tourists. . . . Between 1950 and 1990, the number of international tourists in Europe increased 16 times." There is strong competition among European countries for international tourists, since they tend to spend more money than domestic tourists; additionally, starting in the 1970s, "international tourism income grew considerably faster than international merchandise trade" making it a market worth pursuing (Williams and Shaw 1998:36).

[Amsterdam] was among the top ten most popular European cities for tourism throughout the 1990s, currently ranking seventh (Dahles 1998). Amsterdam's positioning as a major tourist destination may be surprising to some. Although the city is filled with tree-studded canals and quaint narrow buildings, it lacks the tourist attractions characteristic of other tourist destinations in Europe; there is no cathedral, tower, or monument to draw visitors to the city. Yet, as one writer has noted, "foreign tourists have been attracted to the Netherlands in increasing numbers" and, within the country, "Amsterdam is overwhelmingly the dominant target for visitors from abroad. 1.7 million foreigners stayed in the city in 1995, one-third of them from outside Europe" (Pinder 1998:307). Dahles (1998:55) argues that: "The image of Amsterdam as a tourism destination is based on two major themes. The first is the image of the city as being dominated by the urban town design of the early modern period. . . . The second is the current popular image of Amsterdam, which was formed in the late 60s and is based on a youth culture of sexual liberation and narcotic indulgence." Pinder (1998:310) agrees with this assessment and adds that, "The city is renowned for the ready availability of soft drugs, and tolerance has also underpinned the rise of sex tourism as a niche market." . . . As tourism directed toward Amsterdam's cultural heritage stagnates, sex tourism plays an increasingly important role in keeping tourism dollars—and related tourism industry jobs—within the city.

The Labor Market

. . . By the late 1970s and 1980s, the reach of globalization became evident within the Netherlands in other ways as well, particularly in Amsterdam. Clearly, one of the most important global forces affecting sex work in the country was migration. Migration to the Netherlands during this period came from several sources. First, there was an influx of migrants from former Dutch colonies, particularly from Suriname and the Caribbean Islands. Additionally, like many other European countries, the Netherlands was affected by a surge of migrant guest workers from the Mediterranean area, most of whom were directed toward employment in undesirable, low-paying service sector jobs. Later in the 1980s and 1990s, another group of migrants arrived, including those escaping economic hardship in South America and Africa and the former Soviet bloc countries (Bruinsma and Meershoek 1999; de Haan 1997). Importantly, most of these migrant populations settled in the major Dutch cities, including Amsterdam. Almost half of the population of Amsterdam now consists of non-native Dutch residents making it, literally, a global city.

The presence of relatively large numbers of migrants within the city plays an important role in shaping local labor markets and the current char-

acter of the sex trade. For many female migrants, sex work is virtually the only employment available, particularly given the relatively high unemployment rate for ethnic minorities within the Netherlands (de Haan 1997). . . . One estimate put the current number of foreign prostitutes to be approximately 60% of all sex workers in the city (Marshall 1993), and a "repeated count by the Amsterdam police in 1994 and 1995 indicated that about 75% of all prostitutes behind windows in the Red Light District, De Wallen, are foreigners and that 80 percent of all foreign prostitutes are in the country illegally" (Bruinsma and Meershoek 1999:107).

Localized Sex Work

[Over the last two decades there has been] an important shift within the city from a focus on the individual providers of sexual services, "prostitutes," to a focus on the sex "industry." . . . [T]his shift is partly . . . a response to the global forces associated with the production and consumption of sex tourism. This shift is reflected in two areas: (1) organizational changes that reflect the growth of sex tourism as an industry and (2) the globalized character of sex tourists and sex workers.

In her analysis of prostitution policy in Amsterdam, Brants (1998:627) describes these changes in some detail:

> As conditions changed and opportunities for making money from the sex industry increased, ever more power became concentrated in the hands of a few not particularly law abiding citizens. Some of the pimps who had once controlled part of traditional window prostitution now also owned highly lucrative sex clubs and sex theaters. Prostitution had become big business with a huge and partly invisible turnover that was reinvested in gambling halls, sex tourism and more sex clubs.

This concentration of economic interests combined with consumer interest to create several organizations devoted to supporting sex tourism. Interestingly, some Dutch customers developed an organization to support the interests of the clients of prostitution; this organization is called the Men/Women and Prostitution Foundation. Although the number of active members in this organization is small (personal conversation with a member), it is symbolically important in legitimizing the sex industry as an important "industry" serving consumer desires. Members write articles that articulate client interests and the social benefits of prostitution (ten Kate 1995) and collaborate with other organizations interested in greater acceptance of prostitution.

Another organization that facilitates the sex trade is the Prostitute Information Centre (PIC). The Centre, which is located in the heart of the red-light district, serves as an information service for both tourists and prostitutes. Run by a former prostitute, the goals of the center are diverse—education around STD and AIDS prevention, information about prices for sex work, courses to prepare newcomers for sex work and information about how and where to sell sexual labor. For the casual tourist, the most amazing aspect of the PIC is its symbolic character and the way that it resembles a cross between a museum and a sex industry Chamber of Commerce, complete with a sample window brothel to tour (for an extra fee of course), copies of the local Sex Guide, and postcards to purchase.

A second global force shaping the sex industry in Amsterdam is the wide variety of sex tourists visiting the city. Currently, the sex industry is amazingly global in character; not just in terms of the providers of sexual services, but also in terms of the consumers. Sex tourists come to Amsterdam from around the world and vary depending, in part, on national holidays. The local *Pleasure Guide* notes, for example, that Italians are common in August. Although Dutch men are common customers, it appears that the Red Light District exists primarily to fulfill the desires of foreign, male, leisure travelers, often executives conducting business in this global city. Unlike tourists, Dutch consumers of the sex trade can frequent the mostly white

women in window brothels down less known side streets, or they can utilize the listings in the paper and obtain door-to-door service. It is important to appreciate that foreign tourists do not just pay for sex, they pay for accommodations, to eat at nice restaurants, and to attend cultural events. Indeed, the consumer behavior of sex tourists visiting this city helps to ensure that there will be many organized interests facilitating the continuation of sex tourism within the city.

Public Policy and Law

[Current policy does not appear to be strengthening the hand of sex workers. It appears that the full package of worker's rights are withheld from prostitutes for a variety of reasons (Brants 1998; van der Poel 1995).]

The presence of drug-addicted prostitutes makes it difficult for those advocating rights for prostitutes to argue for respectability. Perhaps, more importantly, the large and growing presence of non-native Dutch sex workers leads to local hostility toward sex work. One consequence of Dutch participation in the global economy is the inability of the state to continue to provide the extensive social welfare benefits it has provided to its citizens since the 1960s (de Haan 1997). . . . . Restrictive policies are creeping up everywhere, including in the sex industry. At least one motivation for this greater regulation is to restrict migrant women from engaging in sexual labor. As Raymond (1998:5) points out, "Third World and Eastern European immigrant women in the Netherlands, Germany, and other regulationist countries lower the prostitution market value of local Dutch and German women. The price of immigrant prostitution is so low that local women's prices go down, reducing the pimps' and brothels' cuts. . . ." To the extent that regulation is designed to keep non-native Dutch women out of sex work, it fosters a two-tiered hierarchy of sex work within the city that leads to even greater impoverishment and risk for migrant women.

. . . Significantly, legislation legalizing brothels was approved by the Dutch Parliament and Senate in 1999 (Brewis and Linstead 2000); this is a radical move in the Netherlands, where sex workers were historically only considered "workers" when "self-employed." Until recently, third party involvement in sex work was considered a crime resulting in the oppression and even enslavement of sex workers. Some argue that the legalization of brothels is a first step toward their ultimate regulation, a situation that could improve the working conditions for some sex workers (Brants 1998; Visser 1997). However, it seems that the focus of regulation is increasingly on improving the "merchandising" environment for the sex industry and for consumers, and reducing disruption to local citizens. Currently local officials are attempting to identify who owns the buildings that house window brothels and sex clubs so that some standards can be imposed on facilities where sex is sold. Brothels that pass government inspection would receive special certification, serving as a kind of quality control for sex tourists (Visser 1997). Regulations are growing and include strange new guidelines that limit how long clients can be tied up during purchased sadomasochistic acts. A new "red light district manager" will facilitate the implementation of the new regulations. To many, including de Rood Draad, the rights of sex workers have taken a back burner (Visser 1997). The proliferation of new regulations has caused some to argue that the red light district is becoming "the red tape district" (Reiland 1996:29).

. . . [I]t is interesting to note current proposals to impose price controls on the sex industry. At first glance, this policy appears to be a move toward protecting the wages of sex workers. However, it also serves primarily as a way to discourage price-cutting by illegal immigrants engaged in the sex trade. . . . This policy is reflective of growing Dutch concern about immigration; like many other European countries under global migration pressures, the Dutch tend to close doors to gainful employment by outsiders rather than open them.

SEX TOURISM IN HAVANA, CUBA

Havana, like so many other places in the Caribbean, is a sensuous and social city. Warm nights, humid sea breezes laden with the complex perfume of flowers, diesel exhaust, and restaurant odors, music everywhere, bodies unencumbered by layers of cold-weather clothing, and a culture of public interaction that brings tourists and locals into easy contact. This is the context for Havana's particular soft-sell sex trade. Since the reemergence of sex tourism in the 1990s, the following scene has become relatively common in Havana's tourist districts: A woman, usually decades younger than the object of her immediate interest, approaches a foreign tourist. Brandishing a cigarette, she asks for a light, or maybe points to her wrist and asks for the time. The opening gambit leads to other questions: Where are you from? Where are you going? For a walk? Would you like me to walk with you? Have you been to such-and-such disco? Would you like me to take you there? If the mark seems interested, the woman turns the subject to sex, describing the pleasures she can give, often with no mention of price unless the man asks. If they agree to go off to a disco or for a drink, the subject of sex may not even be openly discussed. Instead, both the *jinetera* ["hustler"] and her mark proceed as if they are on a date. Who knows? Maybe this one will be around for a few days, a week, even a month, providing steady work and freedom from having to continually find new customers. Whether the liaison lasts for a night or a month, the tourist will leave something to be remembered by—maybe money or a few nice new dresses, perhaps some jewelry— something that makes the sex and the attention provided worth the effort. This is not the hard sell of commodified bodies typical of sex tourism in Amsterdam. This is a more subtle trade. A trade where local, rather than immigrant women, make themselves available as sex partners and companions to privileged men from North America and Europe who can give them access to the currency of globalization, U.S. dollars. . . .

The Tourism Industry

[In the late 1960s, the emergence of relatively] affordable jet service created a new era of Caribbean island vacations (Patullo 1996:16). Between 1970 and 1994, the number of stay-over visits to Caribbean islands increased six-fold (Caribbean Tourism Organization 1995). Just as this boom in Caribbean tourism was beginning, the U.S. embargo against Cuba sent Cuban tourism into a steep decline that bottomed out with a mere 15,000 visitors in 1974. From that point forward, however, Cuba began to reorient its development plans to include investments in the tourist industry (Mesa-Lago 1981). Although some development was focused on internal tourism by Cubans, by 1979, foreign tourism had grown to 130,000 stay-over visits. A decade later, 300,000 foreign tourists visited the island, more than in any year prior to the Revolution (Triana 1995). Moreover, only 18 percent of these tourists were from Soviet-bloc countries. Forty percent came from Canada, 15 percent from Western Europe, 15 percent from Latin America, and—despite the embargo—another 12 percent from the United States (Miller and Henthorne 1997:8).

The most spectacular growth in Cuban tourism came in the 1990s (Robinson 1998). During this period, the Cuban government intensified its investment in tourism as part of a broader search for development strategies that would enable the country to survive in the face of post-Soviet economic and political forces determined by a now-worldwide capitalist market (Castro 1999). Between 1994 and 1999, Cuba doubled the number of hotel rooms from 23,500 to just under 50,000 (Miller and Henthorne 1997:98). This translated into a five-fold increase in the number of stay-over visits from 300,000 in 1989 to an estimated 1.7 million in 2000. Revenue gains were

even greater. Between 1990 and 1998, gross revenue from tourism increased seven-fold, from 243 million in 1990 to 1.8 billion, while the share of the country's GDP contributed by tourism grew from 1.1 percent to 6.9 percent. This growth made Cuba . . . a significant force in Caribbean tourism. At 1.8 billion dollars, Cuba's tourism earnings for 1998 were second only to the 2.1 billion tourism dollars earned by the Dominican Republic, and well ahead of the Bahamas and Jamaica, which respectively earned 1.4 billion and 1.1 billion in tourist revenues (Association of Caribbean States 2001).

The Labor Market

[As the socialist world crumbled between 1989 and 1993,] Cuba underwent a dramatic reversal of fortune that forced a radical reorganization of economic life (Azicri 1992; Landau and Starratt 1994). The disappearance of Cuba's socialist trading partners created what Cuban sociologist Elena Diaz González (1997a) characterized as the worst crisis in the history of Cuban socialism. Between 1989 and 1993, the Cuban GDP fell between 35 and 50 percent, importation of Soviet oil declined by 62 percent, overall imports fell by 75 percent, and the domestic manufacture of consumer goods fell by 83 percent (Diaz González 1997a; Espinosa 1999).

As Cuba struggled to reconstruct its trade and financial relations to meet the hard-currency demands of the new capitalist world order, many Cubans found themselves facing a significantly altered labor market (Eckstein 1997). As in other former socialist bloc countries, the Cuban government could no longer provide the extensive employment and social-welfare package it once sought to establish as a universal birthright for all Cubans (Koont 1998; Verdery 1996). By 1999, although Cubans continued to benefit from state subsidies in the areas of food, housing, transportation, health-care, and education, many desired goods could increasingly only be purchased in dollar stores for prices roughly equivalent to those found in the United States for the same goods (Michalowski 1998). It was at this very moment that international tourism to Havana began to increase significantly, with a concomitant growth in tourist-sector jobs—jobs where it was possible to earn at least some portion of one's salary in hard currency. As a consequence, a growing number of high school and college students in Havana began orienting themselves toward tourist-sector employment rather than state-sector jobs, while some Habaneros [Havana natives] already employed in professional careers abandoned them to work in tourism as well (Randall 1996).

The impact of expanding tourism in a city with a shrinking state-sector labor market was also cultural. As youth in Havana were increasingly exposed to the growing number of tourist-oriented nightclubs, restaurants, and beachside hotels, and the clothes, jewelry, and the new model rental cars enjoyed by foreign visitors, some began to feel dissatisfied with their own lack of access to these luxuries. Faced with declining returns from routine labor and rising material desires, some Cuban women (and a smaller number of Cuban men) began making themselves sexually available to foreign tourists. By the late 1990s, a sex worker in Havana could earn forty dollars for providing one night of sex and companionship—double the *monthly* salary of a Cuban university professor (Michalowski 1998). While most young Cubans resisted the temptations created by such disparities, enough succumbed to create a pool of available bodies to serve the desires of sex tourists (Diaz González 1997b).

Localized Sex Work

[Although the growth of Havana's tourist industry resulted in a subsidiary increase in sex tourism to the island, so far, this sex] trade has not become the province of the organized syndicates—whether legal or illegal—that typically control sex work in many other nations. During her fieldwork in Cuba in 1995, O'Connell Davidson (1996:40) observed

that there was "no network of brothels, no organized system of bar prostitution: in fact, third party involvement in the organization of prostitution is rare. . . . Most women and girls are prostituting themselves independently and have no contractual obligations to a third party."

Even though the practice of prostituting for sex tourists in Havana is largely independent and entrepreneurial, it is nevertheless embedded in a globalized market for sex services. To compete in a worldwide capitalist marketplace, every local industry needs a global market niche. The sale of what Hochschild (1983) termed "emotional labor" to accompany a sexually commodified body is that niche for many of Havana's *jineteras* serving the male tourist trade. For many male sex tourists from Italy, Spain, England, and Canada, the particular attraction of Cuba is their expectation that *jineteras* will treat them not as customers, but as pseudo-boyfriends. This means acting as a dinner "date" in a restaurants or a dance partner at a disco, serving as a local (and seemingly loving) guide on sightseeing tours, or perhaps spending a few days or even weeks at a seaside resort as bedmate, playmate, and companion.

One Italian sex tourist summarized his attraction to Cuban *jineteras* by saying he came to Cuba because "the women here are really sweet. They make you feel like they really care. They are always trying to do whatever makes you feel good, not just sex, but everything else too." A pair of expatriate American men currently living in Costa Rica echoed this sentiment: "The Cuban women don't act like professional whores, 'here's the sex, now give me the money.' They are really kind. They want to spend time with you, be your friend." As experienced sexual tourists, they bemoaned the growth of sex tourism in Costa Rica because it "ruined" Costa Rican sex workers: "Now they act just like whores in the States. They just do it for the money and when it's over, they want to move on to the next customer. It wasn't like that in the 60s when there were hardly any tourists. Then they were really nice like the Cuban women are today. Things will probably change here [in Cuba], too. So we thought we'd enjoy it while it lasts." Another appeal of sex tourism in Havana is its price. In 1999, a sex tourist could spend as little as ten dollars for a quick sexual encounter, and between thirty and forty dollars for a companion for the entire evening. This means that for between one hundred and two hundred dollars a day, including the meals, the tours, and other "gifts," European, Canadian, and American men in Havana can spend days or even weeks in the company of young, seemingly-exotic women who appear to be providing them with loving attention, all at a price they can afford. In this way, for a short time, they can enjoy a level of class privilege available only to wealthier men in their home countries.

There are several other important elements of the emotional simulacra consumed by sex tourists in Havana that draw them there. . . . One is the opportunity that sex tourism in Havana provides for men who are forty, fifty, or older to receive both sex and sexualized companionship from women thirty or more years younger than themselves. This gratifies the Western male sexual ideal of continuing access to the bodies of young women, regardless of one's own age. Another is the appeal of gaining sexual access to the body of the non-white "other." In the racialized world of the North American and European male sexual fantasy, mixed-race Cuban women provide the ideal, the fetishized combination of the imaginary "hot" Latin and the equally imaginary sexually insatiable African (O'Connell Davidson 1996; Sanchez Taylor 2000). Thus, it is little surprise that the majority of the women visibly searching for clients in the tourist areas of Havana in 1999, were typically of the "cafe" or "carmelita" skin tones signifying this highly desired racialized "other."

Public Policy and Law

[In 1993, the government legalized the possession of foreign currency, and began allowing] citizens

to legally exchange dollars for *pesos* at banks and government-run, street kiosks known as *cadecas.* Between 1992 and 1994, the Cuban government promulgated a number of other legal changes that would indirectly help create an infrastructure for sex tourism in Havana. These included: (1) permitting the private rental of rooms, apartments, and houses; (2) expanding the arena of self-employment; (3) legalizing the establishment of privately-owned restaurants, colloquially known as *paladares;* (4) expanding the licensing of private vehicles as taxi-cabs; and (5) opening "dollar" stores where Cubans could purchase a broad range of items including food, appliances, furniture, clothes, jewelry, and many other items for U.S. currency (Gordon 1997).

Structurally, these changes facilitated sex-tourism in several ways. The legalization of the U.S. dollar meant that sex workers could obtain hard currency payment from foreign clients without violation of currency laws, and the opening of dollar stores meant they could spend their earnings without having to enter into black market exchanges. Legalizing the rental of private rooms and houses created new opportunities for commercial sexual transaction by eliminating the rules that required tourists to stay in hotels, while prohibiting Cubans from visiting foreigners in their hotel rooms. The legalization of private restaurants provided places where sex workers and tourists could meet and spend non-sex time. Meanwhile, the legalization of private taxis became an important conduit through which some cab drivers could help sex tourists find their way to prime locations for meeting sex workers, or work as pimps by directing their fares to specific sex workers.

CONCLUSION

[The contemporary growth and character of sex tourism is intimately linked to significant global forces. These global forces, which include tourism, migration, and commodification, are not just] abstract concepts; they can be observed within grounded contexts as a variety of local mediating institutions respond to global pressures. In the cases of Amsterdam and Havana, our research suggests that global forces have altered particular institutions in these cities in ways that expand the possibilities for sex tourism. Our work supports Sassen's (1998) view of cities as strategic sites for globalization. . . . At a theoretical level, we contend that the global forces of tourism and migration stimulate the production of sex workers, while the increasing commodification of bodies ensures a steady stream of clients who desire to consume sexual services. Within the cities we analyzed, these global forces find concrete expression at the institutional level, specifically in the changing character of the tourism industries, labor markets, sex work, and laws and policies.

As we have described in some detail, in both Amsterdam and Havana, the tourism industry has become a noticeable sector of the local economy as a by-product of efforts by these cities to secure a share of the burgeoning market created by global tourism. This competition is necessitated by a world in which global markets dominate and determine local fortunes for countries and cities. Additionally, in both of the cities we analyzed, labor markets changed in ways that increased the attractiveness and, for some women, the necessity of sex work. This is particularly true among certain populations of women, such as immigrants in Amsterdam seeking jobs in an environment hostile to migrant workers, or young Cuban women in Havana for whom the globalization has meant that they can earn more dollars and go to more exciting places by selling sex and companionship than they can through more routine employment.

REFERENCES

Association of Caribbean States. 2001. "Statistical database." Available at www.acs-aec.org/Trade/DBase/DBase_eng/dbaseindex_eng.htm.

Azicri, Max. 1992. "The rectification process revisited: Cuba's defense of traditional Marxism-Leninism." In *Cuba in Transition: Crisis and Transformation,* Sandor Halebsky and John M. Kirk, eds., 37–54. Boulder, CO: Westview.

Brants, Chrisje. 1998. "The fine art of regulated tolerance: Prostitution in Amsterdam." *Journal of Law and Society* 25, 4:6211–6235.

Brewis, Joanna, and Stephen Linstead. 2000. *Sex, Work and Sex Work: Eroticizing Organization.* London: Routledge.

Bruinsma, Gerben J. N., and Guus Meershoek. 1999. "Organized crime and trafficking in women from Eastern Europe in The Netherlands." In *Illegal Immigration and Commercial Sex: The New Slave Trade,* Phil Williams, ed., 105–118. London: Frank Cass.

Caribbean Tourism Organization. 1995. "Statistical report: 1994 edition." Barbados, WI: Caribbean Tourism Organization.

Castro, Fidel. 1993. Quoted in "Villalba." *Cuba y el Turismo.* Havana: Editorial de Ciencias Sociales.

———. 1999. *Neoliberal Globalization and the Global Economic Crisis.* Havana: Publications Office of the Council of State.

Dahles, Heidi. 1998. "Redefining Amsterdam as a tourist destination." *Annals of Tourism Research* 25:55–69.

de Haan, Willem. 1997. "Minorities, crime and criminal justice in The Netherlands." In *Minorities, Migrants and Crime: Diversity and Similarity across Europe and the United States,* Ineke Haen Marshall, ed., 198–223. Thousand Oaks, CA: Sage.

Dello Buono, Richard A., and Jose Bell Lara, eds. 1997. *Carta Cuba: Essays on the Potential and Contradictions of Cuban Development.* La Habana: FLACSO-Programa Cuba.

Diaz González, Elena. 1997a. "Introduction." In *Cuba, Impacto de Las Crises en Grupos Vulnerables: Mujer, Familia, Infancia,* Elena Diaz, Tania Carmen León, Esperanza Fernández Zegueira, Sofía Perro Mendoza, and María del Carmen Abala Argüeller, eds., 3–8. Habana: Universidad de La Habana.

Eckstein, Susan. 1997. "The limits of socialism in a capitalist world economy: Cuba since the collapse of the Soviet bloc." In *Toward a New Cuba?: Legacies of a Revolution,* Centeno and Font, eds., 135–150. Boulder, CO: Lynne Rienner Publishers.

Espinosa, Luis Eugenio. 1999. "Globalización y la economia de Cuba." Interview, Havana, January 23.

Gordon, Joy. 1997. "Cuba's entrepreneurial Socialism." *The Atlantic Monthly* 279, 1:18–30.

Hochschild, Arlie Russell. 1983. *The Managed Heart: Commercialization of Human Feeling.* Berkeley: University of California Press.

Kempadoo, Kamala, and Jo Doezema, eds. 1998. *Global Sex Workers: Rights, Resistance and Redefinition.* London: Routledge.

Koont, Sinan. 1998. "Cuba's unique structural adjustment." Unpublished paper presented at the Latin American Studies Association annual meeting, Chicago, IL.

Landau, Saul, and Dana Starratt. 1994. "Cuba's economic slide." *Multinational Monitor* (November 15) 10:7–13.

Marshall, Ineke Haen. 1993. "Prostitution in the Netherlands: It's just another job!" In *Female Criminality,* Concetta C. Cullive and Chris E. Marshall, eds., 225–248. New York: Garland.

Mesa-Lago, Carmelo. 1981. *The Economy of Socialist Cuba.* Albuquerque: University of New Mexico Press.

Michalowski, Raymond. 1998. "Market spaces and socialist places: Cubans talk about life in the post-Soviet world." Unpublished paper presented at the Latin American Studies Association, Chicago.

Miller, Mark M., and Tony L. Henthorne. 1997. *Investment in the New Cuban Tourist Industry: A Guide to Entrepreneurial Opportunities.* Westport, CT: Quorum Books.

O'Connell Davidson, Julia, and Jacqueline Sanchez Taylor. 1996. "Fantasy islands: Exploring the demand for sex tourism." In *Sun, Sex, and Gold: Tourism and Sex Work in the Caribbean,* Kamala Kempadoo, ed., 37–54. Lanham, MD: Rowman and Littlefield Publishers.

Opperman, Martin. 1998. *Sex Tourism and Prostitution: Aspects of Leisure, Recreation, and Work.* New York: Cognizant Communication Corporation.

Patullo, Polly. 1996. *Last Resorts: The Cost of Tourism in the Caribbean.* London: Cassell.

Pinder, David. 1998. "Tourism in The Netherlands: Resource development, regional impacts and issues." In *Tourism and Economic Development: European Experiences,* Allan M. Williams and Gareth Shaw, eds., 301–323. New York: John Wiley and Sons.

Randall, Margaret. 1996. "Cuban women and the U.S. blockade." *Sojourner* 22, 3:10–11.

Raymond, Janice G. 1998. "Violence against women: NGO stone-walling in Beijing and elsewhere." *Women's Studies International Forum* 21, 1:1–9.

Reiland, Ralph. 1996. "Amsterdam's taxing issue: Wages of sin." *Insight on the News* (June) 12, 21:29.

Robinson, Linda. 1998. "Castro gives tourism a try: The Pope and 1.4 million other people are expected to visit Cuba this year." *U.S. News and World Report* (Jan. 12) 124, 1:32–36.

Sanchez Taylor, Jaqueline. 2000. "Tourism and 'embodied' commodities: Sex tourism in the Caribbean." In *Tourism and Sex: Culture, Commerce, and Coercion,* Stephen Clift and Simon Carter, eds., 41–53. New York: Pinter.

Sassen, Saskia. 1998. *Globalization and its Discontents: Essays on the New Mobility of People and Money.* New York: The New Press.

———. 2000a. *Cities in a World Economy.* Thousand Oaks, CA: Pine Forge Press.

———. 2000b. "Women's burden: Counter-geographies of globalization and the feminization of survival." *Journal of International Affairs* 53, 2: 503.

Sassen, Saskia, and Frank Roost. 1997. "The city: Strategic site for the global entertainment industry." In *The Tourist City,* Dennis R. Judd and Susan S. Fainstein, eds., 143–154. New Haven, CT: Yale University Press.

ten Kate, Niel. 1995. "Prostitution: a really valuable asset." Paper distributed by the Mr. A. de Graaf Stichting, Amsterdam: The Netherlands.

Triana, Juan C. 1995. "Consolidation of the economic reanimation." *Cuban Foreign Trade* 1:17–24.

van der Poel, Sari. 1995. "Solidarity as boomerang: The fiasco of prostitutes' rights movements in the Netherlands." *Crime, Law, and Social Change* 23: 41–65.

Verdery, Katherine. 1996. *What Was Socialism, and What Comes Next?* Princeton, NJ: Princeton University Press.

Visser, Jan. 1997. "Dutch preparations for a different prostitution policy." Mr. A. de Graaf Foundation: Institute for Prostitution Research. Amsterdam, The Netherlands (January).

Williams, Allan M., and Gareth Shaw. 1998. *Tourism and Economic Development: European Experiences.* New York: John Wiley and Sons.

REVIEW QUESTIONS_____

1. Compare and contrast how sex tourism emerged in Havana and Amsterdam.
2. What makes Havana's sex tourism market attractive to foreigners?

PARADE STRIPPERS:
BEING NAKED IN PUBLIC

CRAIG J. FORSYTH

This article is concerned with the practice of exposing the female breasts in exchange for "throws" (trinkets and glass beads thrown from floats) from Mardi Gras parade floats in the New Orleans area. It has become so commonplace that the term "beadwhore" has emerged to describe women who participate in this activity. This phenomenon can be compared to other related practices: nude sunbathing, nudism, mooning, and streaking [which many other researchers have studied].

BEING NAKED IN PUBLIC

As a topic for research, being naked in public can be discussed under the broad umbrella of exhibitionism or within the narrow frame of fads or nudity (Bryant 1977). In general, exhibitionism involves flaunting oneself in order to draw attention. In the field of deviance the term exhibitionism may also refer to behavior involving nudity for which the public shows little tolerance (Bryant 1977, p. 100; Bartol 1991, p. 280). This research, however, focuses on a form of public nudity that has a degree of social acceptance.

An extensive sociological study of public nudity was *The Nude Beach* (Douglas et al. 1977). Weinberg's (1981a, 1981b) study of nudists represents another type and degree of public nakedness. Other research has addressed the topics of streaking (running nude in a public area) (Toolan et al. 1974; Anderson 1977; Bryant 1982) and mooning (the practice of baring one's buttocks and prominently displaying the naked buttocks out of an automobile or a building window or at a public event) (Bryant 1977, 1982). Both streaking and mooning were considered fads. One question considered by sociological research on nakedness is when and why it is permissible, appropriate, or acceptable to be naked in public (Aday 1990). Researchers have also addressed some possible motivations or rationales for public nudity. Toolan et al. (1974, p. 157), for example, explain motivations for streaking as follows:

> *While streaking is not in itself a sex act, it is at least a more-than-subtle assault upon social values. Its defiance serves as a clarion call for others to follow suit, to show "the squares" that their "old hat" conventions, like love, marriage, and the family, are antiquated.*

Both Bryant (1982) and Anderson (1977) say that streaking began as a college prank that spread quickly to many campuses. As a fad, it still retained parameters of time and place. Bryant (1982, p. 136) contended that it was one generation flaunting their liberated values in the faces of the older, more conservative generation. Anderson (1977, p. 232) said that it embodied the new

Source: Craig J. Forsyth, "Parade Strippers: Being Naked in Public," *Deviant Behavior,* vol. 13 (1992), pp. 391–403. Reprinted with permission.

morality and thus was "perceived by many to be a challenge to traditional values and laws."

Mooning, like streaking, was considered a prank and an insult to conformity and normative standards of behavior. Neither streaking nor mooning had any erotic value (Bryant 1982). Unlike streaking, mooning is still relatively common on college campuses.

Nudism in nudist camps has had little erotic value. Indeed, nudity at nudist camps has been purposively antierotic. Weinberg (1981b, p. 337) believes that the nudist camp would "anesthetize any relationship between nudity and sexuality." One strategy used by nudist camps to ensure this was to exclude unmarried people.

> Most camps, for example, regard unmarried people, especially single men, as a threat to the nudist morality. They suspect that singles may indeed see nudity as something sexual. Thus, most camps either exclude unmarried people (especially men), or allow only a small quota of them (Weinberg 1981b, p. 337). . . .

Nude sunbathing incorporates many rationales from voyeurism to lifestyle and in many cases has a degree of erotic value. The sexuality of the nude beach has been evaluated as situational.

> Voyeurism . . . poses a dilemma for the nude beach naturalists, those who share in some vague way the hip or casual vision of the nude beach. . . . voyeurs have become the plague of the nude scene. . . . The abstract casual vision of the beach does not see it as in any way a sex trip, but the casual vision of life in general certainly does not exclude or downgrade sex (Douglas et al. 1977, pp. 126–27).

Similar to the nudist in the nudist camp, nude beachers expressed contempt for the "straight" voyeur.

> Sometimes I really feel hostile to the lookers. Obviously you can't look at people that way even if they are dressed . . . it really depends on your attitude in looking. I've even told a couple of people to fuck off . . . and some people to leave. I was thinking this would be the last time I would come down

> here . . . there were too many sightseers . . . it sort of wrecks your time to have someone staring at you (Douglas et al. 1977, p. 130). . . .

[What about parade stripping, the most recent phenomenon of being naked in public, as practiced on Mardi Gras day in New Orleans?]

MARDI GRAS: DEVIANCE BECOMES NORMAL

On Mardi Gras day in New Orleans many things normally forbidden are permitted. People walk around virtually nude, women expose themselves from balconies, and the gay community gives new meaning to the term outrageous. Laws that attempt to legislate morality are informally suspended. It is a sheer numbers game for the police; they do not have the resources to enforce such laws. . . .

The celebration of carnival or Mardi Gras as it occurs in New Orleans and surrounding areas primarily involves balls and parades. These balls and parades are produced by carnival clubs called "krewes." Parades consist of several floats, usually between fifteen and twenty-five, and several marching bands that follow each float. There are riders on the floats. Depending on the size of the float, the number of riders can vary from four to fifteen. The floats roll through the streets of New Orleans on predetermined routes. People line up on both sides of the street on the routes. The float riders and the viewers on the street engage in a sort of game. The riders have bags full of beads or other trinkets that they throw out to the viewers along the route. The crowds scream at the riders to throw them something. Traditionally, the scream has been "throw me something mister." Parents put their children on their shoulders or have ladders with seats constructed on the top in order to gain some advantage in catching some of these throws. These "advantages" have become fixtures, and Mardi Gras ladders are sold at most local hardware stores. It is also advantageous if the viewer knows someone on the float or is physically closer to the float. Another technique is to be located in temporary stands constructed along the parade route that "seat" members of the other carnival krewes in the city or other members of the parading krewe.

In recent years another technique has emerged. Women have started to expose their breasts in exchange for throws. The practice has added another permanent slogan to the parade route. Many float riders carry signs that say "show me your tits"; others merely motion to the women to expose themselves. In some cases, women initiate the encounter by exposing their breasts without any prompting on the part of the float rider.

The author became aware of the term "bead-whore" while viewing a Mardi Gras parade. There were several women exposing their breasts to float riders. I had my 3-year-old son on my shoulders and I was standing in front of the crowd next to the floats. I am also a tall person. All of these factors usually meant that we caught a lot of throws from the float riders, but we caught nothing. Instead, the float riders were rewarding the parade strippers. As we moved away to find a better location, a well-dressed older woman, who had been standing behind the crowd, said to me:

> You can't catch anything with those beadwhores around. Even cute kids on the shoulders of their fathers can't compete with boobs. When the beadwhores are here, you just need to find another spot.

The term was also used by some of the interviewees [in this research].

METHODOLOGY

Data for this research were obtained in two ways: interviews and observations in the field. Interview data were gotten from an available sample of men who ride parade floats ($N = 54$) and from women who expose themselves ($N = 51$). These interviews ranged in length from 15 to 45 minutes. In the interviews with both float riders and parade strippers an interview guide was used to direct the dialogue. The guide was intended to be used as a probing mechanism rather than as a generator of specific responses. Respondents were located first through friendship networks and then by snowballing. Snowball sampling is a method through which the researcher develops an ever-increasing set of observations (Babbie 1992). Respondents in the study were asked to recommend others for interviewing, and each of the subsequently interviewed participants was asked for further recommendations. Additional informal interviews were carried out with other viewers of Mardi Gras.

Observations were made at Mardi Gras parades in the city of New Orleans over two carnival seasons: 1990 and 1991. Altogether, 42 parades were observed. The author assumed the role of "complete observer" for this part of the project (Babbie 1992, p. 289). This strategy allows the researcher to be unobtrusive and not affect what is going on. The author has lived a total of 24 years in New Orleans and has been a complete participant in Mardi Gras many times. Observations were made at several different locations within the city.

FINDINGS

The practice of parade stripping began in the late 1970s but its occurrence sharply increased from 1987 to 1991. During this study, no stripping occurred in the daytime. It always occurred in the dark, at night parades. Strippers were always with males. Those interviewed ranged in age from 21 to 48; the median age was 22. Most of them were college students. Many began stripping during their senior year in high school, particularly if they were from the New Orleans area. If from another area, they usually began in college. All of the strippers interviewed were in one location, a middle-class white area near two universities. Both riders and strippers said it was a New Orleans activity not found in the suburbs, and they said it was restricted to only certain areas of the city. One float rider said:

In Metairie [the suburbs] they do it rarely if at all, but in New Orleans they have been doing it for the last ten years. Mostly I see it in the university section of the city during the night parades.

Parade strippers often attributed their first performances to alcohol, to the coaxing of the float riders, to other strippers in the group, or to a boyfriend. This is consistent with the opinion of Bryant (1982, pp. 141–42), who contended that when females expose themselves it is usually while drinking. Alcohol also seemed to be involved with the float riders' requests for women to expose themselves. One rider stated:

Depending on how much I have had to drink, yes I will provoke women to expose themselves. Sometimes I use hand signals. Sometimes I carry a sign which says "show me your tits." If I am real drunk I will either stick the sign in their face or just scream at them "show me your tits."

Data gained through both interviews and observation indicated that parade stripping is usually initiated by the float riders. But many of the women indicated that they were always aware of the possibility of stripping at a night parade. Indeed, some females came well prepared for the events. An experienced stripper said:

I wear an elastic top. I practice before I go to the parade. Sometimes I practice between floats at parades. I always try to convince other girls with us to show 'em their tits. I pull up my top with my left hand and catch beads with my right hand. I get on my boyfriend's shoulder. I do it for every float . . . I'd show my breasts longer for more stuff and I'll show both breasts for more stuff.

Other parade strippers gave the following responses when asked, "Why do you expose yourself at parades?"

I'm just a beadwhore. What else can I say?

I expose myself because I'm drunk and I'm encouraged by friends and strangers on the floats.

I get drunk and like to show off my breasts. And yes they are real.

Basically for beads. I do not get any sexual gratification from it.

I only did it once. I did it because a float rider was promising a pair of glass beads. When I drink too much at a night parade, I turn into a beadwhore.

It's fun.

I exposed myself on a dare. Once I did it, I was embarrassed.

Only one woman admitted that she did it for sexual reasons. At 48, she was the oldest respondent. When asked why she exposed her breasts at parades, she said:

Sexual satisfaction. Makes me feel young and seductive. My breasts are the best feature I have.

One woman who had never exposed herself at parades commented on her husband's efforts to have her participate during the excitement of a parade.

We were watching a parade one night and there were several women exposing their breasts. They were catching a lot of stuff. My husband asked me to show the people on the float my breasts so that we could catch something. He asked me several times. I never did it and we got into an argument. It seemed so unlike him, asking me to do that.

Float riders often look on bead tossing as a reward for a good pair of breasts, as the following comments show:

The best boobs get the best rewards.

Ugly women get nothing.

Large boobs get large rewards.

When parade strippers exposed themselves they were not as visible to people not on the float as one would think. Strippers were usually on the shoulders of their companions and very close to the float. For a bystander to get a "good look" at the breasts of the stripper was not a casual act. A person had to commit a very deliberate act in order to view the event. Those who tried to catch a peek but were either not riding the floats or not among the group of friends at the parade were shown both pity and contempt.

I hate those fuckers [on the ground] who try to see my boobs. If I'm with some people they can look. That's ok. But those guys who seek a look they are disgusting. I bet they can't get any. They probably go home and jerk off. I guess I feel sorry for them too. But I still don't like them. You know it's so obvious, they get right next to the float and then turn around. Their back is to the float. They are not watching the parade. We tell them to "get the fuck out of here asshole" and they leave.

Like a small minority of nude sunbathers who like to be peeped at (Douglas et al. 1977, p. 128), there are strippers who like the leering of bystanders. Our oldest respondent, mentioned earlier, said she enjoyed it. "I love it when they look. The more they look the more I show them," she remarked.

Parade strippers most often perform in the same areas. Although parade stripping usually involves only exposing breasts, three of the interviewees said they had exposed other parts of their bodies in other public situations.

Strippers and their male companions tried to separate themselves from the crowds; they developed a sense of privacy needed to perform undisturbed (Sommer 1969; Palmer 1977). Uninvited "peepers" disturbed the scene and were usually removed through verbal confrontation.

Most strippers and others in attendance apparently compartmentalized their behavior (Schur 1979, p. 319; Forsyth and Fournet 1987). It seemed to inflict no disfavor on the participants, or if it did they seemed to manage the stigma successfully (Gramling and Forsyth 1987). . . .

CONCLUSION

Parade stripping seemed to exist because trinkets and beads were given; for those interviewed, there was no apparent sexuality attached except in one case.

Parade stripping is probably best understood as "creative deviance" (Douglas et al. 1977, p. 238), deviance that functions to solve problems or to create pleasure for the individual. Many forms of deviance, however, do not work in such simplistic ways.

Most people who go to a nude beach, or commit any other serious rule violation, do not find that it works [emphasis added] for them. They discover they are too ashamed of themselves or that the risk of shaming by others is too great, so they do not continue. Other people find it hurts them more (or threatens them) or, at the very least, does not do anything good for them. So most forms of deviance do not spread (Douglas et al. 1977, p. 239).

Some forms of deviance apparently do "work," and parade stripping is one of them. The beadwhore engages in a playful form of exhibitionism. She and the float rider both flirt with norm violation. The stripper gets beads and trinkets and the float rider gets to see naked breasts. Both receive pleasure in the party atmosphere of Mardi Gras, and neither suffers the condemnation of less creative and less esoteric deviants.

REFERENCES

Aday, David P. 1990. *Social Control at the Margins.* Belmont, CA: Wadsworth.

Anderson, William A. 1977. "The Social Organizations and Social Control of a Fad." *Urban Life* 6:221–40.

Babbie, Earl. 1992. *The Practice of Social Research.* Belmont, CA: Wadsworth.

Bartol, Curt R. 1991. *Criminal Behavior: A Psychosocial Approach.* Englewood Cliffs, NJ: Prentice-Hall.

Bryant, Clifton D. 1977. *Sexual Deviancy in Social Context.* New York: New Viewpoints.

Bryant, Clifton D. 1982. *Sexual Deviancy and Social Proscription: The Social Context of Carnal Behavior.* New York: Human Sciences Press.

Douglas, Jack D., Paul K. Rasmussen, and Carol A. Flanagan. 1977. *The Nude Beach.* Beverly Hills, CA: Sage.

Forsyth, Craig J., and Lee Fournet. 1987. "A Typology of Office Harlots: Party Girls, Mistresses and Career Climbers." *Deviant Behavior* 8:319–328.

Gramling, Robert, and Craig J. Forsyth. 1987. "Exploiting Stigma." *Sociological Forum* 2:401–415.

Palmer, C. Eddie. 1977. "Microecology and Labeling Theory: A Proposed Merger," pp. 12–17 in *Sociological Stuff,* edited by H. Paul Chalfant, Evans W. Curry, and C. Eddie Palmer. Dubuque, IA: Kendall/Hunt.

Schur, Edwin M. 1979. *Interpreting Deviance.* New York: Harper & Row.

Sommer, Robert. 1969. *Personal Space.* Englewood Cliffs, NJ: Prentice-Hall.

Toolan, James M., Murray Elkins, and Paul D'Encarnacao. 1974. "The Significance of Streaking." *Medical Aspects of Human Sexuality* 8:152–165.

Weinberg, Martin S. 1981a. "Becoming a Nudist," pp. 291–304 in *Deviance: An Interactionist Perspective,* edited by Earl Rubington and Martin S. Weinberg. New York: Macmillan.

Weinberg, Martin S. 1981b. "The Nudist Management of Respectability," pp. 336–345 in *Deviance: An Interactionist Perspective,* edited by Earl Rubington and Martin S. Weinberg. New York: Macmillan.

REVIEW QUESTIONS

1. What factors influenced women to expose their breasts during Mardi Gras parades?
2. What do you think about the city of New Orleans suspending some of its laws during Mardi Gras? Are there other events where cities should follow New Orleans's lead in suspending laws? If yes, what are they and why? If no, why not?

NUDE DANCING: SEXUAL CELEBRATION IN CONSERVATIVE AMERICA

FREDERICK SCHIFF

In the long cultural war against a puritan and patriarchal establishment, nude dance clubs are outposts on the frontier of the current conflict. At first glance, the spectacle constitutes an anomaly in allowing anonymous men to have a series of close but public encounters with the most intimate and normally concealed parts of a woman's body. The legalization and commercialization of nude dancing arguably represents a new social ethos that did not exist even after the sexual revolution of the 1960s and 1970s. Nude dancing illustrates the oppositional nature of the unstable neo-puritan legacy.

Eric Widmer, Judith Treas, and Robert Newcomb characterize the United States as one of the four most sexually conservative Western industrialized nations. Americans strongly disapprove of all types of non-marital sex, according to the 1994 International Social Survey Program, which sampled the opinions of 33,590 respondents from 24 countries. Americans are among the least permissive about extramarital, teenage, and homosexual sex, and their opinions about premarital sex are more divided than in other countries. The "sexual regime" in the United States is most like that in Poland, Ireland, and Northern Ireland, where public opinion supports conservative Catholic norms,

said the authors. For example, the Irish and the Americans are polarized between strong approval and strong disapproval of premarital sex. Among industrialized countries, the survey evidence seems to suggest a distinctive and conservative sexual regime with a degree of unresolved conflict. Indeed, the United States seems to be in a transitional period of cultural conflict, demonstrated in part by the appearance, rise, and commercialization of nude dancing in public places. Live sex exhibitions are a significant extension of explicit portrayals in pornographic magazines, film, and video that have been legalized and popularized since the 1960s.

Volkmar Sigusch uses the term "neosexual revolution" to characterize the radical but gradual sexual recoding of the 1980s and 1990s. He uses the prefix "neo" to suggest both the creative and innovative as well as the dying and retrospective changes that differentiate the contemporary sexual ethos from the sexual revolution of the late 1960s and from the repressive sexuality of the 1950s. Sigusch distinguishes between the old sexuality "based primarily upon sexual instinct, orgasm, and the heterosexual couple" (331) from the contemporary period when sexuality revolves predominantly around gender

Source: Frederick Schiff, "Nude Dancing: Scenes of Sexual Celebration in a Contested Culture," *Journal of American Culture,* vol. 22 (Winter 1999), pp. 9–16. Reprinted by permission of Taylor & Francis, Inc., http://www. routledge–ny.com

difference, spectacle, self-gratification, and prosthetic substitution. Sex is no longer mystified positively as the potential for human pleasure and happiness. Sex has a diminished and negative significance as the source and scene of oppression, inequality, violence, abuse, and deadly infection. Rather than the promise of paradisiacal sexual communion and an imagined universal of oceanic good will, Sigusch describes three empirical tendencies that epitomize the current period: (1) The sexual sphere of life has been radically separated from reproduction and from experiential response. He lists his evidence as matters of common knowledge: Pregnancy can be prevented or induced. The fetus can be autonomous and viable apart from the female body. Mothers are not biologically or economically dependent on fathers. Prostheses and stimulants allow sexual performance without sexual desire. Personal want ads, telephone sex, faked climaxes, and cybersex are considered adequate substitutes for closeness, joy, tenderness, excitement, pleasure, affection, and comfort. (2) Sex is fragmented, packaged, and commercialized. Rather than one primary sexual urge, there are a range of gender choices and identities. Again, Sigusch argues by enumerating the products and services of commercial culture. Sexual experiences and lifestyle paraphernalia like labia piercing, dolphin-shaped clitoral vibrators, surgically implanted penis pumps, and sex toys are all saleable commodities. Media self-exposure, flirting schools, partner brokerage services, sex tourism, and trade in human embryos are normalized as commercial exchanges. Child prostitutes and online pedophilia are widely available in post-industrial Europe, not just in the developing world. Sexual spectacle is now amplified in public, online, through broadcasting, by cable, via satellite, and on videotape, so that previously considered abnormalities, perversions, and fetishes tend to become isolated, smaller, almost benign issues. (3) Intimate relationships are diverse. The male-dominated nuclear family is no longer the privileged and preferred site of emotional attachment and psycho-sexual identity. Sigusch

simply lists the mundane features of everyday life that have been deregulated: rigidly defined social roles, self-constructed psychic identities, enduring family bonds, presumed natural instincts, enforceable inhibitions, and so-called eternal values. Sigusch argues that mainstream socio-sexual norms have changed radically:

> *Direct, external controls have given way to indirect, internal ones. . . . People today are expected to manage intimate experiences and relationships in a self-determined, self-reliant [and self-interested] manner, free of the corset of the old, powerful moral institutions. . . . [T]oday's emotional and behavioral codes are more variable and more highly differentiated. (350–51)*

He says the liberating goal of the 1960s and 1970s was an impossible contradiction arising from the same philosophic idea but resulting in incompatible social practices—setting one's natural drives free and at the same time bringing spontaneity and decency into balance.

Sigusch seems to suggest that the legacy of sexual revolution is a sort of techno love for neosexuals who are responding to the absence of sexual norms and to a culture without an acceptable general model of an equally stimulating and harmonious intimate relationship. If sexual dysfunction, child abuse, the absent father, sexualized violence, and the recurrent leitmotif of performance sex are part of the neosexual ethos, so too is detached, cool, scientific sexology.

Nude dancing is clearly sexual, directly intended to arouse prurient interests, sexual desires, and fantasy. Dancers and cabaret managers are minimally concerned about the aesthetics of movement or choreography. The core product is a fleeting but close-up gaze at the details of female genitalia. Nude dancing shares the three characteristics that Sigusch calls neosexual. (1) It is for display with little or no corporeal contact or experiential release for the spectator. (2) It is commercialized, packaged in the form of on-stage routines and table dances, and fragmented with the focus of attention on female body parts. (3) It allows for a diversity of intimate relationships, which vary from dancers acting as non-professional, extra-marital "therapists" for their regular customers, to drive-time clients surreptitiously getting a liability-free legal look at intimate but unknown vaginas, clitorae, labia, and so on. If Sigusch is correct, the pendulum of social change seems to have swung from reform to reaction to a new cultural stasis with its own unstable contradictions. What, if anything, then, does the existence and prevalence of nude dancing reveal about the nature of normative sexual expectations and fundamental change in American culture?

The legacy of the 1960s sexual revolution may not be the psychological liberation of sexual participants as much as a novel repressive form of sexual spectatorship. Commercialized sexual display might be seen as "repressive desublimation," terms used by Herbert Marcuse, a leading philosopher of the Frankfurt School. At the height of the sexual revolution, Marcuse described repressive desublimation as substituting the satisfactions of private, personal permissiveness for the deferred and more constrained gratifications of social and sexual conformity while leaving the real engines of repression in the society entirely intact ("Repressive" 114–15). His example was the pop psychology movement known as self-actualization; the case here is the commercialization of explicit sexual display. Arguably, both are instances of repressive tolerance. In any case, Marcuse considers cultural movements and artistic forms to be domains of struggle.

In the present period, the cabarets offer the most explicit sexually oriented performances that are both mass marketed and unmediated in the United States. The sex clubs in San Francisco, for instance, may be more extreme, but the oppositional significance of the nude cabarets is national. From the dialectical point of view in *Eros and Civilization,* in which Marcuse critiques Freud, nude cabaret dancing is both liberating and repressive. Minimally, the exclusive mandates of procreative sexuality, heterosexual monogamy, and institutionalized male domination

are being displaced by widespread, ritualized sexual display.

My purpose here is primarily to offer an ethnographic description of a relatively novel and largely unnoticed socio-sexual phenomenon. Secondarily, I will highlight features of nude dance shows that seem to challenge or support the dominant sexual regime and might result in everyday practices that may be more liberating or more repressive. My sources were dancers, managers, and owners at nude cabarets. I leave to other researchers the study of the uses of nude performances by and effects on audience members. The point of view is from those who produce the sexual spectacle rather than from the gaze of the spectators.

UNBUCKLING THE SEXUAL SCENE IN THE BIBLE BELT

Nude dancing clubs are widespread from Las Vegas, Nevada, to Centerville, Ohio, from Beverly, Massachusetts, to Portland, Oregon, from Appleton, Wisconsin, to Dade County, Florida, from Los Angeles to New York City. Houston, however, is a particularly revealing case because of its sexual politics. Houston is the fourth largest U.S. city in a consolidated metropolitan statistical area (CMSA) with a population of 4.3 million in 1997. It has eight licensed nude dance cabarets and at least three illegal "butt naked" dancing places. While there are more than 40 topless bars in town, nude dancing is no longer exotic in the sense of being rare nor is it considered extreme.

Houston is cosmopolitan, ranking only behind Los Angeles in ethnic diversity among the top 10 CMSAs (*Houston Metropolitan Study* 21). The city often touts itself as the energy capital of the world, an aerospace gateway, the third largest harbor in the country, and a world-class medical center renowned for cardiac transplants and breast implants. The Montrose district houses the third largest gay community in the country. The city is surrounded by smaller cities in the Southwest in the Bible belt, which is staunchly

Methodist and Southern Baptist. Waco, 209 miles north-northwest, was the scene of the fire-bombing and mass killing of the polygamous Branch Davidian cult. For years, Texas school districts have led the country in the number of banned book titles. Texas is the home of leading Christian conservatives in the U.S. House of Representatives and survivalists in the militias. Nevertheless in 1992 in Houston, the Mustang became the first night club that went from topless to totally nude. The owner, who converted the Mustang and three other topless clubs to all nude in Houston, discovered a loophole in the law that allowed nude performances as long as alcoholic beverages were not served. Though the Mustang was raided numerous times, it was never closed and the staff were never arrested.

The legal and regulatory regime makes for unanticipated contradictions: The topless bars serve alcohol and so admission is limited to patrons who are 21 years old or older. Nude cabarets do not serve liquor and so are open to 18-year-olds. Nude cabarets allow patrons to bring in (and take out) their own alcoholic beverages, and so they tend to get rowdier on the weekends than the topless bars.

On April 2, 1997, a new city ordinance took effect licensing all dancers and managers at nude cabarets. Police records (Chandler) indicate that by the end of 1999 most of the 5,000 dancers in the city were no longer performing. According to Robert Birmingham, general manager of Scores Cabaret, many "girls" started up their own escort and out-call services and at least 20 were forced back into street prostitution—just one unanticipated and contradictory consequence of an ordinance to improve public morals. From the point of view of a woman, exposing herself is obviously less invasive and cleaner than having sexual intercourse.

The club managers note that the April ordinance to clean up the city had another unexpected irony: Unable to find enough licensed dancers, many topless bars had the women wear full-back bikini bottoms and cover their nipples with see-through latex. Since a bikini bar is not considered a sexually oriented business, the ordinance does not apply. Patrons and bikini dancers are free to touch and grope each other although they are still restrained by the same public lewdness statute.

An indication of resistance to the growth of explicit sex shows is the fact that three topless bars burned down within a week. One owner said at least eight of 53 sexually oriented businesses have been burnt down by their owners. According to a manager at a different cabaret, owners anticipated that the supply of dancers would disappear, their businesses would no longer be profitable, and their fire insurance would expire before they could recoup their capital investment. After the April ordinance took effect, door receipts dropped 30 to 40 percent, he said. Another manager said the clubs make too much money to close themselves down. Whether the club burnings are an indication of a violent cultural politics or economic opportunism remains unclear. A spokesman for the Bureau of Alcohol, Tobacco and Firearms agency in Washington, D.C., confirmed that arson was the cause of four of the fires.

In nude cabarets, the sex scenes occur on stage and at "table dances." Nude dancing is obviously more explicit than the live performances at topless bars and lingerie shows. On stage, the first dance number is usually performed partially or fully clothed for the general club audience. Dancers who often do not wear panties flash their customers. Before or during the second song, the woman completely disrobes. Customers seated around the edge of the stage lay dollar bills in front of them to tip the dancer, who goes from one client to the other exposing her vagina or rectum or both for his narrow, close-up view. A woman may lie on her back, spread her legs, separate the folds of her labia and massage her clitoris. A dancer may turn around and bend over or kneel down in front of a client. Lying on her side, she may pull her buttocks apart to open her anus to better view. Some dancers do skits and features. A favorite trick of one particularly "wet" dancer is to steal a baseball cap off the head of a stage-side client and wipe it between her legs. Before the ordinance, one buxom dancer used to knock patrons in the head with her breasts. Besides the ubiquitous spiked super-high platform shoes, some dancers use wardrobe to suggest role plays, like "Ginger" at Fantasy North who has a little girl outfit or "Chloe" who likes to get dressed up with a hat and gloves. Most of the stages have a central pole where dancers do sexually revealing athletic tricks. Climbing to the top, a dancer wraps her legs around the 10-foot pole and slowly lets herself slide down, torso first. One floor stunt is for a woman to do the splits and rhythmically dilate and contract her vagina. The interactive scenes between customers and nude performers are in public view, unlike traditional prostitution or the new array of escort services, amateur photography studios, and massage parlors. Nude dancing is a live, public exhibition with the performers often a few feet and sometimes a few inches from audience members, whereas the sex scenes on videocassettes are usually viewed in separate booths in video arcades or in private homes. The cabarets do rent their space for private bachelor parties.

Another symbol of the oppositional status of the cabarets is that many nude dancers have "alternative" body styles. Nude dancers do not match the standards set at the topless bars. Their breasts are often small or sometimes flaccid compared to topless performers in a city famous for breast augmentation in a state where the unofficial "party" philosophy is "Bourbon, blondes and boobs." Ron McGuinness, day manager at Fantasy North, said, "Tits don't matter in a nude bar. Customers pay to look at tweedies. The big bush of the '70s is gone." Most nude dancers shave their pubic hair; many shave smooth. According to Birmingham, the women at Scores could not dance at an upscale topless bar like the Men's Club before the April law because its mainstream, glamour-magazine standards were too high. Overweight women with large thighs are often popular. Also body piercing and tattoos, which are common

among the nude dancers, were not permitted at the upscale clubs.

In nude cabarets, women are more in charge than in traditional prostitution or even in topless bars. At Fantasy South on a chance weekday night, a birthday boy is brought up on stage; his pants and underwear are pulled to his ankles; and he is tied to a chair. All the dancers take turns massaging and rubbing up against him, and wax is dripped on his exposed penis. Giving him an erection is part of getting a laugh out of his friends. The ritual illustrates how the man is objectified and equalized in the exposed but safe environment of newly legal public nudity.

FANTASY GRATIFICATION

The fantasy element in the sex scenes produced by nude dancers is paramount. Nude dancing is a live exhibition that does not lead to copulation, fondling, or even touching. Nude dancing is a form of erotic fantasy formation. Clubs do not permit masturbation in public. Nevertheless, the primary psychological function of the show is similar in a way to the experience that Carol Queen describes of suddenly discovering she could have multiple orgasms at a Jack-and-Jill-Off party inside a San Francisco safe-sex club. A client's wholesale exposure to numerous sex scenes with a parade of women provides a storehouse of imaginative fantasies for later masturbatory self-consumption.

Many clients are not attractive, young, wealthy, or assertive. For many men, having a series of close encounters with attractive women is outside the reality of their everyday lives. For many a client, such a woman might barely look at him, normally never talk to him, and certainly never expose herself to him. Even on stage in a crowded room, the dancer gives each tipping customer a narrow, close-up view of her genitalia, thereby promoting his fantasies of having a romantic or sexual relationship with an otherwise unattainable woman. Furthermore, the client can focus on the woman he chooses to tip on stage or to pay for an individual table dance. For men in ongoing relationships that include sexual intercourse, spectatorship may heighten later arousal through fantasy. For males without sexual partners, however, the connection between spectatorship and masturbation may seem pretty obvious.

If fantasy offers the psycho-symbolic material for later self-gratification, it also fulfills more immediate personality needs. The dancers and managers describe many of their "regulars" as lacking in self-esteem. According to Birmingham, an ex-bail bondsman with a degree in criminal justice, dancers who make the most money are not necessarily the best looking. "They have great personalities. They're really untrained psychologists," said Birmingham. Dancers typically sit and talk at length with customers who have paid, or who might pay, for table dances. In a society where successful men often obtain trophy wives, the social status of a man is partially enhanced by the demonstrable, socially standardized, and competitively superior good looks of his romantic partner. Nude dancers seem to offer their clients an alternative way to enhance their own self-esteem, a customer service in a hospitality industry.

WORKING-CLASS AUDIENCE

The contested nature of nude dancing is partially reflected in the clientele. Customers at topless bars are mostly white-collar middle-class men over 29 years of age. Customers at the nude cabarets are mostly blue-collar men under the age of 29. The customers often wear blue jeans and baseball caps backwards; some have long hair; pickup trucks are prominent in the parking lots. The nude clubs are frequently patronized by Hispanics and African Americans.

The club owner who started nude dance cabarets in Houston was a fireman for 20 years. He got the idea for a cabaret from an incident in a topless club when a waitress said a $10 bill wasn't enough to cover two $5.75 drinks. He said average working guys can't afford the high-dollar topless clubs that cater to businessmen with credit cards.

On rainy days when nearby construction crews shut down, groups of guys in hard hats and cowboy boots bring in six-packs and fill Fantasy South to its seating capacity of 290. Part of its working-class policy is that there is no "cooler fee" or "uncorking fee."

In Houston's large and established black bourgeois community, Scores serves as an "alternative elite" black men's club. The primary activity consists of men socializing with each other, not with men observing or interacting with the women. The nude club scene has become the place to be seen by "everybody who is anybody or who wants to be somebody [in the black community]," according to Raymond Leslie, floor manager at Scores. "Being somebody" in this context is reserved to men and is presumably privileged by watching women expose themselves.

Cabaret owners, like the porn industry in general, share the class and race biases of the larger society (Hamamoto). Two white self-described "honkie" managers switched Scores from being white-oriented to a black club. The white owners objected until the club turned a profit within a month. When they started playing more rap and soul music, the owners "jumped on us," according to the general manager, Birmingham. "[Scores] is 'the' elite black club in Houston, especially after hours." The two began sneaking in more African-American dancers and stationed lookouts in the parking lot to warn them of the owners' approach to switch the music. They listened to one of their customers, a rapper named Mister P, who made the slowest night, Monday, into a "players' night." On one full-house Monday in November, coming through the door were black celebrities, sports stars, and local music millionaires, including the founder of Suave House Records, supposedly worth $85 million.

There are distinct types of clients, according to McGuinness. Most are blue collar. (1) The "kids" (those under 21 years old) come in on weekends and during the summer. (2) The businessmen and older gentlemen stop by in the afternoon, get two or three table dances and spend an hour at most. (3) The "regulars" follow individual dancers from club to club. (4) The "lookers" come with two, three, or four friends and "camp out" all evening. Many cabarets open to attract middle-class business during the 4 P.M. drive-time traffic crunch, but the peak crowd arrives after 10 P.M. or after the bars close.

The fact is that nude cabarets are cheaper. Older and middle-class men are more likely to be able to afford the topless bars. The nude clubs are the preferred venue for younger and blue-collar males, who are relatively marginal to the entertainment market because of their more limited discretionary income.

REGULATORY REGIME

How to regulate the boundary between spectators and participants is one of the most central issues about managing and maintaining puritan pieties. The new ordinance insisted that dancers stay at least three feet away from their clients. In fact, a nude dancer will often bend over and put her exposed vagina within inches of a client's nose. Nude places, however, do not allow touching at all. Patrons are not allowed to fondle the dancers, who often sit in their patrons' laps. Meanwhile, at the bikini bars, sexually oriented rules do not apply. One vice squad investigator admits he does not know how to react to the new legal loophole. The dilemma is yet another instance of the unintended contradiction between capitalist deregulation and retro puritan morality.

The regulatory regime at the nude clubs forbids (1) lap grinding, which refers to a woman rubbing or gyrating her buttocks against a man's crotch; (2) body slides, which occurs when a nude woman slides down the front of a man seated before her; (3) fondling; and (4) solicitation. Dancers are not supposed to touch their clients or themselves. The new regime has meant that dancers no longer kiss their clients on the cheek or allow them to put dollar bills in their garters. In the past, a

man might lie face-up on the edge of the dance floor with a dollar bill in his teeth as a dancer would lower herself to take the bill with her vagina. Managers enforce the vice squad rules to avoid being raided. The first time "Uncle Ray" Leslie, 36, finds a violation, the dancer is fined $20, the second time $30, and the third time she is fired. If a patron ignores a warning to not fondle or touch a dancer, both the patron and dancer may be ejected. Birmingham said a woman can be arrested for not having a license, lewd dancing, or solicitation. She can't get a license if she has a criminal record for prostitution, rape, sex with a minor, or moral turpitude.

The oppositional character of the nude clubs is also reflected in the admission policy. In an era of court-ordered equal access, no unescorted woman is allowed in the club, supposedly to protect male clients from their romantic partners or wives. Boyfriends of nude female dancers are kept out, asked to wait outside or made to sit in the back, depending on the club.

The continued existence of nude and topless clubs is being contested. Nelson Hensley, a lawyer who represents most of the cabarets, says all of the nude clubs but one have had their licenses suspended while a class-action suit against the city is pending before the 5th U.S. Circuit Court of Appeals. In the only large city in the country without zoning, sexually oriented businesses (known as SOBs) are not restricted or confined to designated zones. Yet the April ordinance requires that an SOB cannot be within 1500 feet of a school, church, day-care center, public park, home, or residence. The clubs claim the city is trying to put them out of business by creating provisions so restrictive as to discriminate unequally against one category of legal (corporate) persons. One owner estimated that more than half the clubs would close if the suit fails. The biggest issue is whether the existing clubs will be grandfathered in.

A club often has a full-time attorney who regularly checks with the vice division about rules changes. Leslie hobnobbed at vice headquarters two days prior to my visit. The managers say there have been several rules changes and most clubs have had several managerial overhauls. The vice squad is issuing no more SOB licenses for cabarets in Houston. Most significantly, the surrounding cities in Harris County are passing similar restrictive anti-SOB ordinances.

ECONOMIC INDEPENDENCE OF DANCERS

For working-class women, who are often single mothers and have no more than a high school education, the ability to enter the labor force and to make excellent wages honestly with their self-respect intact is a major liberating development.

Aspen—a thin 20-year-old club star in day-glow yellow hot pants with small pointed breasts that poke through her diaphanous jumpsuit—takes home an average of $500 to $600 a night. She has no savings and no investments, but she is the one who pays for an apartment she shares with her boyfriend and she just bought a $27,000 Acura. She says she is "burnt out" after two years but can't resist the money. Another woman reported that an average dancer on an average night makes $250 although another dancer said she averaged $100 a night. Estimates for an average week ranged from $1600 over three days to $500 over five days. As with salespeople elsewhere, remuneration for the personal services the dancers offer seems to vary widely. Notable is the fact that a young single mother with little education can make $25,000 to $75,000 a year without actually prostituting herself.

On peak Friday and Saturday nights, 30 or 35 women may be dancing; on the off nights 7 to 15 dancers show up. Typically, 4 to 8 dancers work the day shift. The managers expect dancers to stay six to eight hours, especially because many of the clients come in after 2 A.M. A dancer must have two licenses, one worn on her body at all times, usually tied to her shoe, and the other on deposit in the office. Cabarets may have 40 to 50 licenses of dancers on hold, and another 25 or so dancers who take their site licenses with them

when they leave each night. Dancers sign a release as independent contractors, freeing the club from liability, and making the dancers subject to surprise drug tests and locker checks by the cabaret management.

Dancing is expensive, however. One dancer says she spends $1,000 a month on personal hygiene, clothes, accessories, makeup, and the almost obligatory super-high-heeled shoes. The total for a dance license, including the cost of driver's license, photos and parking, is about $65. Dancers have to pay the club a "tip out" or "floor fee" to dance. The tip out is typically $20. Depending upon the club and the time the dancers show up to work, it varies from no floor fee when the club opens at 4 P.M. to $55 after 11 P.M. More important, dancers pay their own Social Security and income taxes, though at least one club figures the amounts for the women.

Part of the oppositional nature of nude dancing is that it empowers women financially. Nevertheless, it is probably true that older dancers are still exploited by their own lack of financial discipline to capitalize the wealth they could accumulate in their prime earning years. Their long-term independence is also compromised because after only a few years, dancers say they are burned out.

SUBJECTIVE EXPERIENCES
OF THE DANCERS

The meaning of any cultural activity largely depends on the point of view of its participants. I have described how dancers consider their clients, but what is their subjective experience and how do the women think of themselves?

Kathy Brady, 28, who has danced for 10 years under the stage name "Chloe," and who was damp all over after just coming off stage at Fantasy South, described the joy of dancing. She said she gets as emotionally involved with her customers as they are with her.

Money is the primary motivation for dancing nude. Marisa, 24, a dancer at Fantasy North who has an 8-year-old and an 8-month-old by different men, said she doesn't enjoy dancing or find it sensual, but it is easy and fast money. She tried working assembly line at Compaq for $210 a week until she was laid off. She came back to dancing and makes $200 to $400 a night, spends $300 a month on canned baby formula and contributes rent to her boyfriend, who is buying his house. She refuses to make eye contact with her clients.

For dancers, romantic relationships are often transient. One dancer on break seemed alternately defiant, sad, and disappointed as she recounted why yet another boyfriend had just dumped her. Brady, who has had one three-year relationship on and off in 10 years as a dancer, says keeping a boyfriend is hard because a lot of men feel intimidated and insecure.

Managers said on average, dancers are between 18 and 21 years old, although I talked to women in their mid and late 20s. "Black," a psychology major at a local college and a former floor manager at a black club called Harlem Nights, said that dancers often have low self-esteem and few job skills. McGuinness, who has a bachelor's degree in emergency medicine and seven years in the cabaret business, portrayed the dancers: a lot are single mothers supporting their children; hardly any are married; often they are from dysfunctional families; they have no credit and no higher education. Their outlook is cash and carry. My interviews suggest few dancers have savings and even fewer have investments.

FINANCIAL IMPERATIVES

Finally, the reality of running a nude club is financial. In the history of U.S. capitalism, entire cultural industries like vaudeville have arisen and disappeared. Many news organizations and entertainment forms have lost their competitive market advantages, or never developed a commercial base and hence the political clout to survive: for example, the working-class partisan press after the 1840s and independent amateur radio operators after the 1920s. Besides the long-term uncertainty

about whether nude cabarets can rely on a permissive legal environment, their continued short-term existence depends on whether they are profitable commercial ventures. All estimates were obtained from the owners and managers or calculated on the basis of information from them.

The most important startup cost is "building out" the club, which may mean renovating the space, building a stage, installing a sound system, and buying furniture. Only a few topless or nude clubs own their own buildings, but rental of commmercial property in Houston is relatively cheap at about $1 to $2 per square foot. The largest variable costs are payroll and advertising for the first year or two. A medium-sized club may have four to six managers plus two D.J.s and weekend security, but again in the Southwest, salaries are lower than elsewhere in the country. Managers usually receive a fixed base pay plus a percentage of the tip outs with no benefits and no tax deductions. Retaining a full-time lawyer is considered a necessary business expense to keep the club open.

The managers agree that getting dancers who attract regular clients is the key to the success of a club. The main income source is the take at the door, which depends on the night. At peak times, seating capacity is also a limitation. Since cabarets allow clients to bring their own liquor, the bar is a break-even operation. Tip outs are typically used for lawyers' fees and renovation. Break-even supposedly requires two or three years. In hearings about amortizing the city's "taking" of the clubs, the city council claimed that most of the clubs had already recouped their total investment or could do so within one year. Note that at least five nude cabarets failed in Houston, and another three were burned down in 1998. Furthermore, no surviving club has been in business for more than five years.

Nude cabarets are entrepreneurial gambles. Many of the initial owners were Greek, according to one manager, although nowadays Anglo-Saxon surnames are mixed with those from Mediterranean, Arabic, and Persian origins. The high risk and the uncertainty about the city ordinance, regulatory enforcement, and the pending judicial review reflect the prolonged conflict.

Not only do the laws and rules change, ownership and management of the nude clubs change. The owners recurrently take on additional partners or sell out their interests. No one ownership group predominates, although Fantasy had four locations at one time. Rick's, which has three topless clubs (two in Houston and one in Minneapolis), opened up XTC nude cabarets in Houston and San Antonio; and went public in 1994. Scores has had three sets of managers in its two-year history. One club replaced its entire management staff for stealing, that is, for kickbacks for letting in non-paying patrons. After seven years, McGuinness, who is married with two children, says he doesn't like the drunken patrons and whining dancers. Turnover is high, with many managers confessing to getting into the business as "titty bar whores." So, compared to other businesses, nude cabarets have moderate startup costs and their break-even points come early. Despite volatility in personnel and the legal uncertainty at this initial entrepreneurial stage of development, clubs seem to achieve a sufficient return on investment to recoup total costs within one to three years.

CONCLUSION

A variety of considerations lead to the conclusion that nude dancing constitutes a symbolic form of class opposition to the dominant neo-puritan norms. There is the intensifying downward class pressure on undereducated dancers, some of whom would otherwise make their livings by engaging in naked penetration rather than nude performance. The audience consists mostly of working-class and younger men as opposed to the more middle-class and middle-aged patrons at topless bars. In Houston in the Bible belt where there is strong Methodist and Baptist sentiment, an ordinance was passed in the name of middle-class Southern righteousness to put 90 percent of the sexually oriented businesses out of business. Arsonists have burned down at least three of the eight nude clubs since the ordinance took effect in early 1998. The nude cabaret owners have found a highly profitable new business model and are actively working to defend their interests in court and through their lobbying efforts. Nearby cities subsequently modeled ordinances after the one crafted in Houston. Finally, the anti-SOB rhetoric and media coverage surrounding the ordinance focused on "titty bars" that are bigger and glitzier, when the more extreme and explicit challenge would seem to be posed by the BYOB "pussy palaces." The politicians seem almost unwilling publicly to recognize the problematic existence of totally nude dancing, preferring instead to direct their mass-marketed appeal to the popular imagination excited by the villainy of the exposed breast. At the turn of the twenty-first century in America, nude dancing in commercial public places seems to represent the most widespread and direct challenge to puritan proprieties. Houston is a particularly interesting case because it is such a large and cosmopolitan city deep in the conservative heartland. Given the symbolic and financial interests at stake, the political, popular, and judicial struggle may be protracted and uneven.

WORKS CITED

Chandler, Roy B., Vice Division Captain, Houston Police Department. Interview and letter in response to a freedom of information request. 19 Oct. 1999.

Hamamoto, Darrell Y. "The Joy Fuck Club: Prolegomenon to an Asian American Porno Practice." *New Political Science* 20.3 (1998): 323–45.

The Houston Metropolitan Study: An Entrepreneurial Community Looks Ahead. Houston: U of Houston Center for Public Policy and Rice U Baker Institute for Public Policy, 1998.

Marcuse, Herbert. *Eros and Civilization: A Philosophical Inquiry into Freud.* Boston: Beacon, 1966.

———. "Repressive Tolerance." *A Critique of Pure Tolerance*. Robert Paul Wolff, Barrington Moore Jr., and Herbert Marcuse. Boston: Beacon, 1968. 81–123.

Queen, Carol. *Real Live Nude Girl*. Pittsburgh: Cleis, 1997.

Rick's Cabaret International, Inc. *Annual Report*. Houston. 1996, 1997, 1998.

Sigusch, Volkmar. "The Neosexual Revolution." *Archives of Sexual Behavior* 27.4 (1998): 331–59.

Widmer, Eric D., Judith Treas, and Robert Newcomb. "Attitudes Toward Nonmarital Sex in 24 Countries." *Journal of Sex Research* 35.4 (1998): 349–58.

REVIEW QUESTIONS

1. Compare and contrast the clientele of the topless bars and the nude cabarets.
2. How have socio-sexual norms changed over time?

"EVERYONE KNOWS WHO THE SLUTS ARE": HOW YOUNG WOMEN GET AROUND THE STIGMA

JENNIFER DUNN

When deviance from a group's expectations is profound, the person who violates the norm can come to have what the sociologist Erving Goffman (1963) called a stigma. People with a stigma have a "spoiled" identity, because we have discovered that they are not who they claim to be or they act in ways contrary to how we think people like them should act. Goffinan said that we carry around stereotypes of people, and when people don't match up—when there is a "discrepancy" between what we expect and what we get—we look down on the stigmatized person and treat him or her accordingly (1963, p. 5). Not only do we demean such persons, but we treat them as unworthy of our respect and regard, and in this way, Goffman said, "we effectively, if often unthinkingly, reduce [their] life chances" (1963, p. 5).

This article is about how becoming sexually active in the wrong ways can be deeply discrediting for young women, and what young women do to avoid or repair the stigma of being a "slut." It is based on interviews of 22 undergraduate women, individually and in an exploratory focus group, who were asked about their reasons for becoming sexually active or for refraining from sexual activity. Even though adolescents face a variety of pressures to have sex, and almost half (48.4 percent) of teenagers between 15 and 17 are sexually active (Risman and Schwartz, 2002), girls in partic-

ular are not free to be sexual as often as, or with whomever, they please. Instead, it is common for young women to be ascribed the "slut" identity if they are perceived as becoming active too young, having too many partners, choosing inappropriate partners, or having intercourse under the influence of alcohol or other drugs.

The young women I interviewed constructed their own "image" and "reputation" by telling me about other despised girls; they adamantly did not want themselves to be seen as a "slut." All but one of the women spoke in these terms. "Susan" (all of the names I use are pseudonyms), for example, discussed her feelings after an alcohol-induced "one-night fling" this way:

> *I felt as oh my god what's going to happen to my image . . . before in high school, I was known as Miss Virgin and I dated a lot of guys in high school, but I was never . . . you know how some girls who date a lot of guys in high school are considered a tease? But I know, 'cause I've talked to some of my ex boyfriends, I was never considered a tease. I was just considered a girl who would never put out.*

Susan explained about different types of women, describing the valued image of the respected virgin and contrasting it to the more sexual "tease"—an identity that does not fit the "nice girl" stereotype

Source: Written specifically for this reader.

of virtue and chastity. Susan went on to explain that she was afraid she would be seen as one of the "slutty girls"—that is, "girls who go to parties and then have sex with men they meet there."

Darla was able to describe this other, stigmatized identity in some detail for me. "Sluts" were the girls who were "popular among the guys" for the "wrong reasons," who called men all the time and were sexually aggressive, and who "forced themselves" on men who, she explained, would rather be left alone. Darla had a friend who would do "anything" to get the approval of men:

> *She's the kind of person . . . if she likes someone, she would call them all the time, do everything to get their attention, all the time . . . and it was like she would even have sex with them, just to like, get their attention.*

"I could never be a person who dates casually and has casual sex," Susan told me, a remark that reflected the consensus among the women I interviewed.

Several of the women I interviewed reported feeling "slutty" as a consequence of a decision to have sex outside the context of a committed relationship. None were more profoundly affected than Valerie, who used the language of stigma to describe the experience with multiple partners she had in high school. After she told me about her self-described decision to trade sex for intimacy, I asked her how she felt about that choice. "I'm still trying to get over that," she acknowledged, "because it gave me, like, the slut complex . . . [I thought] that maybe it was just an inherent personality trait, that I was just a slut, that I slept around."

Valerie took the expectations of her peers, and her deviance from their norms, very seriously. It led her to have intensive counseling, and she claimed to be only just beginning to feel recovered at the time of our interview. Goffman describes shame as a "central possibility" for the person who sees the possession of an attribute as "defiling," and Valerie was extremely conscious of how she thought other people saw her (1963, p. 7). Sally said that at her high school, "everyone knows who the sluts are; it gets around," and she was careful to distinguish herself from these women, who were friends but not the people she chose to spend much time with. When I asked her what she meant by "sluts," she defined them as "people who were easy and just had sex whenever they went on a date."

It appears that pregnancy and sexually transmitted diseases are not the only hazards associated with becoming sexually active. Young women also run the risk of acquiring the stigmatized identity of the "slut." In their concern for their reputations, the women I interviewed seem to invest sex with what Ehrenreich, Hess, and Jacobs (1986) refer to as "old meanings," understandings of sex that predate the sexual revolution, in which amorous sex is approved and casual sex is condemned. Only one of the women I interviewed spoke of her own pleasure in any kind of sex; the majority were far more likely to describe their feelings as shamed or valued, depending on whether they encountered or avoided the stigma attached to their decisions. Even though the sexual revolution has so changed our thinking about sex that sex divorced from love, marriage, or reproduction has arguably "become a mainstream American value" (Risman and Schwartz, 2002:23), these women still take into account traditional values that censure the uninhibited expression of female sexuality. In this view, sex that is "purely about play and pleasure" (Risman and Schwartz, 2002, p. 22) is something that "sluts," not girls with "self-respect," engage in. Sex for fun is a deviation from social norms, violating what Goffman (1963) called a "normative expectation" and thus incurring stigma.

Is there any way out of this dilemma? After all, almost all American teenagers are sexually active by the end of their teen years, and our culture is "highly sexualized" (Risman and Schwartz, 2002, p. 22). How can a young woman follow her desires, or conform to significant historical, cultural, and peer pressures to have sex, yet still preserve her reputation? The contradictory features of this social structural situation present a dilemma. It is a kind of "identity bind" (Lofland, 1995). How do you face conflicting expectations and still keep from spoiling your image?

The answer, it turns out, is to simultaneously avoid a stigmatized, discredited identity and acquire a valued one by being in a "relationship"—taking on a "coupled" identity by having a boyfriend. Indeed, having a boyfriend was tremendously important to the young women in this study. For example, Felicia described how important it was for her friends to have a relationship: "All my friends have said, 'God, I want a boyfriend.' It's like, I want a boyfriend so I can feel and have that self-esteem, you know, to feel good about myself." Valerie, too, was eloquent in her description of her need to be coupled:

> I was destroyed on a regular basis, and then I had to build myself up so I could go on with daily living, but daily living felt like an existence, not, not like I was living, just like I was going through the motions. Until I found a man, and then the man kind of made the life thing worthwhile.

Tessa said that she and her boyfriend had been "joined at the hip," meaning always together. She matter-of-factly described herself as "consumed with him" and as envisioning herself married, saying she would have married him unless she had met someone else. This is how she described being coupled:

> My whole life just revolved around him, I was always with him. Just completely, any time, any spare time that I had was with him, and there was never time to myself, it was always with him. We were always together. We were married, I mean, that was the way we acted, that was the way people—it was never Tessa, it was always Tessa and Kyle [she laughs]. We were always together.

For these young women, being in a relationship enables them to be sexually active while at the same time avoiding the stigma of the "slut" identity. By carefully choosing their partners and the circumstances of coitus, they conform to the stereotype that most young people are no longer

virgins by their senior year in high school (in fact, only 25 percent of women and 10 percent of men are still virgins at age 20, according to the survey cited by Risman and Schwartz). Thus, it is "normal" to have sex, but deviant to have "casual" sex, especially if you are female (Risman and Schwartz, 2002). The discrepancies in these expectations, and the possible stigma, are avoided by confining sex to "boyfriends." Goffman might say that the girlfriend identity manages to meet the normative expectations to be both virtuous and sexual.

The interviews support this interpretation. In an adolescent subculture these women understand as valuing sexual experience and chastity, they talk about the importance of forming committed monogamous relationships and what they are willing to do in order to achieve the valued identity attached to such relationships. Susan, for example, said that her "bad experiences" with men who did not maintain relationships with her after sexual encounters had taught her to appreciate the importance of a relationship:

> Well, does this guy really care about me, you know? . . . I think if a person really cares about you, they're not going to even try to sleep with you on the very first night. . . . And I think I've learned more of what types of guys to look for, you know, if I went out on a date and a guy just seemed interested in trying to sleep with me rather than trying to get to know me, then, I would probably never see him again. Because I don't want to get involved with a person that goes from relationship to relationship.

Corinne has also learned about the same thing from the failed relationships in her life. When she meets a new male, she says, "I can sit back now, because of this incident, and say, what is this person going to offer me? I just go whoa, does he fulfill all this that I want, and if he doesn't, then that's it. I can't waste my time and risk getting hurt." These understandings are completely consistent with the idea that women who have casual sex are "sluts" and are stigmatized for sexual behavior in a way that "girlfriends" are not. They support these women's decisions to form particular types of relationships in order to be sexually active. In today's world:

> *Teens and adults have sex before, during, and after marriage with a variety of partners over their life course. . . . For most people, a sexual life begins during adolescence and is likely to include all kinds of sexual behaviors, including coitus, before people reach the legal age for drinking alcohol. (Risman and Schwartz, 2002, p. 23)*

In conclusion, as Goffman would have anticipated in 1963 (just prior to the sexual revolution), there are normative expectations for young women today and different ways of violating them, some of which may lead to stigma and, because of it, being treated badly. On the one hand, it is now pretty "normal" for young women to be sexually active even before they graduate from high school. But such women risk being stigmatized as a "slut." On the other hand, young women who remain as virgins even in their senior year may be afraid of being stigmatized as a "tease." Thus many tend to be sexually active but get around the "slut" stigma by seeking out relationships to have sex in them. Even so, there is no guarantee the stigma will be avoided, because after all, "Everyone knows who the sluts are."

REFERENCES

Ehrenreich, Hess, and Jacobs, 1986. Re-making Love: *The Feminization of Sex.* Garden City, New York.: Anchor/Doubleday.

Goffman, E. 1963. *Stigma.* New York: Simon and Schuster.

Lofland, L. 1995. Personal communication.

Risman, B., and P. Schwartz. 2002. "After the sexual revolution: Gender politics in teen dating." *Contexts,* 1:16–24.

REVIEW QUESTIONS

1. How do women get around the stigma of being defined as a slut?
2. Do you agree or disagree with the statement "Everyone knows who the sluts are"? Defend your answer by providing concrete examples in defense of your position.

PART NINE

SUBSTANCE ABUSE

Linda McCaffrey, a regular smoker in Toronto, Canada, was shocked the first time she saw pictures of rotting gums and diseased lungs on her pack of cigarettes. Working in a law firm as a paralegal, she recalls how she felt then. She says, "I thought, 'Oh, my God, I really have to quit smoking.' " In 2001 the Canadian government began requiring tobacco companies to put horrifying health warnings on cigarette packs. So nowadays just before they light up, Canadian smokers can see a damaged brain with the warning about strokes or a limp cigarette with the message "Tobacco Use Can Make You Impotent." Such warnings seem to have worked, reducing the rate of smoking in Canada. Now the U.S. Justice Department wants to use similar tactics to fight smoking and has asked a judge to force cigarette makers to cover half of their packs with "graphic health warning labels."[1]

There is an obvious reason why the Canadian and U.S. governments have become more aggressive in fighting smoking. The use of cigarettes is more prevalent than the use of any other legal or illegal drugs, such as cocaine, marijuana, and alcoholic beverages. Smoking also costs considerably more lives than any other form of substance abuse. Over 430,000 Americans die from cigarette use every year, compared to, for example, 5,000 to 10,000 who die from illegal drugs. In addition to this problem, though, over the last decade, a new type of substance abuse has increased sharply: the illegal use of prescription drugs such as Percocet, OxyContin, and other painkillers.

Here we focus on the use of illicit and licit drugs. In the first reading, "Using Illegal Drugs: Sociological Factors," Steve Sussman and Susan L. Ames discuss how four social factors influence the use of illegal drugs. In the second article, "Playing with Painkillers," Claudia Kalb describes and explains the surge of prescription drug abuse in the United States. In the third selection, "Binge Drinking and the College Environment," Richard Keeling reviews research findings on binge drinking on U.S. campuses. In the fourth piece, "Predictors of Smoking among College Students," Karen Emmons and her colleagues discuss their empirical study on why some college students are more inclined than others to smoke.

1. Keith Naughton, "Gross Out, Smoke Out," *Newsweek,* March 25, 2002, p. 9.

USING ILLEGAL DRUGS:
SOCIOLOGICAL FACTORS

STEVE SUSSMAN
SUSAN L. AMES

Four types of [sociological] factors are correlated with, or predict, drug use and abuse: *demographic, environmental, cultural,* and *social* influences.

DEMOGRAPHIC INFLUENCES ON DRUG USE

Gender

Drug use generally is more prevalent among males than females (Barbor 1994; Johnstone 1994). For example, in most surveys and studies of problematic opiate use, males outnumber females by a ratio varying around 2:1 to 4:1 (Grant 1994). Gender *per se* is a description of group differences, not an explanation of why these group differences exist. Gender differences in drug use might be explained by a consideration of sex-role expectations and differential stigma associated with drug use.

Males are often taught to deal with problems by engaging in goal attainment (instrumental orientation), rather than by talking about difficulties (expressive, nurturing or nurture-seeking orientation). Taking drugs might be one way for men to take action to cope with stress. Women, on the other hand, might be more likely to seek out social support. The magnitude of gender differences currently observed may change among younger cohorts of more recent decades, given changing sex-role expectations. As females pursue more instrumental goals and decrease in tendency towards expressiveness (for example seeking social support), drug use and abuse may increase in prevalence as a maladaptive coping option.

. . . Women who are drug abusers are different from men who are drug abusers in at least three ways. First, among women in drug abuse treatment, 70 per cent report having been sexually abused in their lifetimes. This is a much higher prevalence of sexual abuse than in the general population. Sexual abuse appears to be a risk factor that affects drug initiation and maintenance of drug use among women. Additionally, female drug users are more likely to be subject to physical victimization than their male counterparts (Brooner *et al.* 1997).

Age

Teenage drug abuse differs from adult drug abuse in several ways (see Sussman *et al.* 1997). First, regular use may or may not be considered abuse in adults, whereas it might be considered abuse in youth because of the potential of such use to interfere with developmental growth and adjustment tasks. Second, adolescents may exhibit less physical dependence and fewer physical problems

Source: Steve Sussman and Susan L. Ames, *The Social Psychology of Drug Abuse* (Philadelphia: Open University Press, 2001), pp. 57–68. Reprinted with permission.

related to use . . . and consume a lower quantity overall. . . . Third, high-risk situations may differ between adolescents and adults. In particular, adolescents may be relatively likely to use drugs in situations in which they are not responsible for the care taking of others; that is, aside from serving as car drivers (in which they are at highest risk among age groups for fatal accidents). Finally, adolescents have a higher likelihood of suffering social consequences specific to adolescence (for example problems at school, statutory difficulties and truncated development such as early involvement in family creation and divorce: Newcomb and Bentler 1988).

Ethnicity

In the United States, several researchers have found White ethnicity to be associated with relatively greater drug use among adolescents and adults (Newcomb and Earleywine 1996; Galaif *et al.* 1998; Johnston *et al.* 1999). Perhaps Whites achieve less extended familial support, leading to greater drug use as a means of coping. On the other hand, among those with a lifetime history of dependence, African Americans are significantly more likely than Whites to report twelve-month dependence duration. Possibly, once dependent on drugs, disadvantaged minorities have less access to health care, leading to a more sustained period of drug dependence.

These data are not as simple to interpret as they may seem. Ethnicity also interacts with other demographic variables such as age and gender in predicting prevalence of drug abuse. For example, the prevalence of use of alcohol, marijuana, hallucinogens and cocaine among adolescents in the United States tends to be highest among Latino and White males, followed by Latino and White females, then African American males, and then African American females. . . . Also, across genders among adults, rates of current use of cocaine are approximately 1.4 per cent for African Americans, 0.8 per cent for Latinos and 0.6 per cent for

Caucasians. Perhaps taking on, or giving up, key adult responsibilities (jobs, parenthood) may be associated with such apparently complex patterns of drug use.

ENVIRONMENTAL INFLUENCES ON DRUG USE

Environmental antecedents describe the influence of an individual's physical surroundings, including geographical location, dwelling contexts and changes occurring in these contexts (for example disorganization, modernization). Environmental influences that are associated with, and perhaps motivate, experimentation with drugs include neighbourhood disorganization, economic deprivation and availability of drugs (Hawkins *et al.* 1992).

Neighbourhood disorganization refers to a lack of centralized authority, or rapid changeovers of authority, such as to produce insufficient methods or degree of monitoring and regulating behaviours in the community. In a disorganized neighbourhood, one is relatively likely to be exposed to unsanctioned instances of social disobedience, such as public drunkenness, drug dealing and gang-related activities (Skogan and Lurigio 1992). Building structures that provide many enclosed public areas (lack of defensible space), as well as abandoned buildings, lend themselves to a greater incidence of crime perpetration and drug use, and tend to be prevalent in dense, urban, disorganized neighbourhoods.

Adverse socio-economic conditions may limit access to prosocial recreational opportunities (for example money for cinema tickets). Additionally, adverse environmental conditions might also expose one to relatively greater drug-related criminal activity, such as drug sales, as an alternative means of generating income. Relatively low socioeconomic status (SES) tends to be associated with greater drug use among adults (Wills *et al.* 1996). For example, the use of crack cocaine is prevalent among economically deprived groups and ethnic minorities who reside in large metropolitan areas. There exists a perennial question: does drug abuse lead to lower SES (downward drift) or does lower SES lead to drug abuse (alternative income . . .)? Among adolescents, influences such as family dynamics and peer group association may affect the relative importance of socio-economic influences on drug use. One may conjecture that familial and other social influences protect children from pro-drug influences. However, as young people grow older, these protective influences fade. As adults, lower SES may be associated with a myriad of challenges to self-worth and security. Some young adults may seek out means of self-medication under these disadvantaged circumstances. Conversely, young adults who are successful economically may be able to afford to purchase large quantities of expensive drugs, may become addicted, and then may suffer a rapid descent in SES. Probably, both self-medication and downward drift operate as explanations of the relations of SES with drug abuse.

The *availability* of drugs in a person's environment includes ease of distribution, access and acquisition. *Ease of distribution* refers to the establishment of a 'business' structure, with relatively little resistance to transporting drugs in and out of a location. *Access* refers to an individual's knowledge on where to tap drug supplies along the distribution route. Finally, ease of *acquisition* refers to someone's ability to obtain the drug (for example through establishment of trust, provision of services, or through money). An obvious example of availability would be the presence of drug use in an apartment upstairs from where one lives. Near proximity of drugs in an individual's environment may result in frequent exposure, and may suggest means to acquire the drugs. As a second example, observed regional variation in drug use prevalence has been found within the United States. In particular, residents of communities in the Northeast or West are more likely to use drugs than residents of the Midwest or South (Adams *et al.* 1989; Almog *et al.* 1993; Warner *et al.* 1995).

It is likely that differences in use frequency are related to distance from major points of drug distribution (for example New York City and Los Angeles).

CULTURAL INFLUENCES ON DRUG USE

Cultural precursors of behaviour include intergenerational, geographically derived group differences that impact their members. Examples of cultural antecedents that might affect drug use include life habits and rituals that are important and meaningful to the group, normative structures and expectations (cultural morality), and beliefs and attitudes about reasons for drug use and drug effects. Culture might help determine which drugs are available, preferable and highly valued at a given time, whether experimentation is acceptable, and what one's expectations about the effects of a drug might be (Heath 1999).

An example of a "life habit" and "normative structure" is the regular use of wine with meals in France. Some children in France learn that wine is a food rather than merely an alcoholic beverage; they learn to drink wine with meals and are able to buy wine in stores. On the other hand, in the United States, it is illegal for individuals less than 21 years old to buy alcohol and children are not supposed to drink any alcohol. Another example of a normative structure pertains to the acceptance, availability and recreational use of marijuana and hashish in the Netherlands . . . , whereas in the United States even the medical use of marijuana is highly controversial. As an example of a "ritual" which involves "beliefs pertaining to drug use," one unique cultural influence is the use of peyote, a hallucinogen, by certain groups of Native Americans in the Church for Spiritual Enlightenment (in the United States: Julien 1998). Cross-culturally, looking across several countries, a defining characteristic of whether or not people suffer from drug abuse appears to be their ability to perform their culturally specific roles. If they are viewed as unable to carry out their life roles because of drug use, they are considered to be a drug abuser (Quintero and Nichter 1996).

Another important cultural construct is acculturation (Diaz-Guerrero 1984). This construct pertains to *changes* in cultural rituals, norms or beliefs. New cultural influences may interface with a person's native culture, or the person may move to a location that provides a new host culture. Generally, acculturation is defined as the degree to which individuals adopt or prefer a culture to which they are more recently exposed. The degree to which a group or individuals distance themselves from their native culture increases as more time is spent in the environment of a different culture (that is acculturation can be construed as a social learning process: Szalay *et al.* 1993). Level of acculturation in the new environment can affect drug use through exposure to cultural attitudes towards use or expectations of drug effects. Drug use or abuse might also occur when individuals are separated from traditional cultural groups that might discourage drug use. Alternatively, the stress resulting from failure to bond successfully to a new culture may increase the probability of drug use.

Finally, an important macro-level sociocultural influence affecting drug use initiation and experimentation is the increasing role of the media and worldwide access to information. The worldwide web now provides incredible access to information about drugs of abuse and means of producing these drugs. Different cultures may influence others' beliefs regarding drug use to the extent that they use a shared language on the web (for example www.legalize.org/global/). Also, television and films may inadvertently promote drug use by conveying images of role models or idols, such as rock stars, romancing heroin addiction, models who are tough chain smokers, film stars happily addicted to alcohol, or rappers who like to sing about marijuana (Sussman *et al.* 1996). Cinema images, in particular, are likely to be viewed internationally, and influence the host culture within which they are viewed. Even if an individual does not attend to images portrayed by

the media, the *mere exposure* to these images has been shown to affect preferences for objects (for more about the mere exposure effect and preference literature, see Kunst-Wilson and Zajonc 1980; Zajonc 1980).

SOCIAL INFLUENCES ON DRUG USE

Social antecedents of drug use include the characteristics of the people in an individual's support system, and describe the various effects the group has on the individual. The values and behaviours of parents, siblings, friends, peers and role models affect the learning experiences of individuals. *Social support* pertains to the assistance that people in social networks give each other. *Social networks* describe connections among individuals—that is, different relationships (for example friends, colleagues). There are various types of social support individuals can offer each other (for example companionship, instrumental, conformity, informational), all of which may be important in the development of drug use and abuse. For example, observing friends who seem to be enjoying drug use may make one more curious about drug use; friends may provide an "informational" type of support. Also, one may want to use drugs in order to have others with whom to spend time ("companion" type of support). Alternatively, social support may directly influence an individual's behaviour (for example peer pressure to use drugs; "conformity" type of support; drugs may be purchased by friends or family; "instrumental" support).

Differential socialization refers to the channelling of the development of beliefs, intentions, expectations, perceptions and modelling of social behaviours. For instance, socialization processes may lead to beliefs and perceptions that drug use is tolerable by others in one's social environment (Akers *et al.* 1979). This may affect an individual's intention to initiate use. Family conflict, poor supervision or drug-use tolerance by parents, family modelling of drug-using behaviour and deviant peer group association are processes of differential socialization that have been found to be influential in experimental drug use (for review, see Hawkins *et al.* 1992).

Researchers in social psychology report two main types of pressure the peer group exerts on its members (see Sussman *et al.* 1995). First, normative social influence is described as wanting members to act consistently with the group to gain or maintain acceptance of other group members. Second, informational social influence is described as wanting members of the group to share similar attitudes about the frequencies of various behaviours and their social meanings. In turn, for yielding to normative or informational social influence attempts, the group provides social reinforcers. These reinforcers are various social supports. Researchers have consistently demonstrated that one of the strongest predictors of drug use among teens is friend and peer use of drugs (Barnes and Welte 1986; Kandel and Andrews 1987). The deviant peer group tends to use drugs, will offer drugs at times, and will role model drug use. Social influence is especially important as a predictor of drug use and abuse among teens.

CONCLUSION

[We have] addressed a variety of [sociological,] extrapersonal influences that contribute to drug use—demographics, environmental factors, cultural factors and social factors. Many of these extrapersonal influences overlap. And, while exposure to numerous extrapersonal influences might place an individual at risk for use, they alone cannot explain why some individuals who use drugs go on to abuse them and others do not. Disentangling the aetiologic web of drug use and abuse, understanding the diversity and various levels of influence of correlates and predictors, is a daunting task. The need to continue exploring prediction models of use and abuse, and to identify at-risk individuals among diverse populations, exists because of the implications for the health and well-being of individuals and society.

REFERENCES

Adams, E. H., et al. 1989. "Epidemiology of substance abuse including alcohol and cigarette smoking." *Annual New York Academy of Science,* 562: 14–20.

Akers, R. I., et al. 1979. "Social learning and deviant behavior: A specific test of a general theory." *American Sociological Review,* 44: 636–55.

Almog, Y. J., et al. 1993. "Alcohol and heroin use patterns of narcotics addicts: gender and ethnic differences." *American Journal of Drug and Alcohol Abuse,* 19: 291–38.

Barbor, T. F. 1994. "Overview: demography, epidemiology, and psychopharmacology—making sense of the connections." *Addiction,* 89: 1391–6.

Barnes, G. M. and Welte, J. W. 1986. "Patterns and predictors of alcohol use among 7–12th grade students in New York State." *Journal of Studies on Alcohol,* 47: 53–62.

Brooner, R. K., et al. 1997. "Psychiatric and substance use comorbidity among treatment-seeking opioid abusers." *Archives of General Psychiatry,* 54: 71–80.

Diaz-Guerrero, R. 1984. "Behavioral health across cultures." In J. D. Matarazzo et al. (eds.), *Behavioral Health: A Handbook of Health Enhancement and Disease Prevention.* New York: Wiley.

Galaif, E. R., et al. 1998. "Depression, suicidal ideation, and substance use among continuation high school students." *Journal of Youth and Adolescence,* 27: 275–99.

Grant, B. F. 1994. "ICD-10 harmful use of alcohol and the alcohol dependence syndrome: prevalence and implications." *Addiction,* 88: 413–20.

Hawkings, J. J., et al. 1992. "Risk and protective factors for alcohol and other drug problems in adolescence and early adulthood: implications for substance abuse prevention." *Psychological Bulletin,* 112: 64–105.

Heath, D. B. 1999. "Culture." In P. J. Ott et al. (eds.), *Sourcebook on Substance Abuse, Etiology, Epidemiology, Assessment, and Treatment.* Needham Heights, MA: Allyn and Bacon.

Johnston, L. D., et al. 1999. *National Survey Results on Drug Use from the Monitoring the Future Study, 1975–1998,* vols. 1 and 2. Rockville, MD: US DHHS (NIH Publication nos. 99–4660 and 99–4661).

Johnston, B. M. 1994. "Sociodemographic, environmental, and cultural influences on adolescent drinking behavior." In National Institute on Alcohol Abuse and Alcoholism (NIAAA) *The Development of Alcohol Problems: Exploring the Biopsychosocial Matrix on Risk,* Research Monograph 26, Rockville, MD: US DHHS.

Julien, R. M. 1998. *A Primer of Drug Action.* New York: W. H. Freeman.

Kandel, D. B. and Andrews, K. 1987. "Processes of adolescent socialization by parents and peers." *International Journal of the Addictions,* 22: 319–42.

Kunst-Wilson, W. R. and Zajonc, R. B. 1980. "Affective discrimination of stimuli that cannot be recognized." *Science,* 207:557–8.

Newcomb, M. D. and Bentler, P. M. 1989. "Substance use and abuse among children and teenagers." *American Psychologist,* 44: 242–8.

Newcomb, M. and Earlywine, M. 1996. "Intrapersonal contributors to drug use: the willing host." *American Behavioral Scientist,* 39: 823–37.

Quintero, G. and Nichter, M. 1996. "The semantics of addiction: moving beyond expert models to lay understandings." *Journal of Psychoactive Drugs,* 28: 219–28.

Skogan, W. G. and Lurigio, A. J. 1992. "The correlates of community antidrug activism." *Crime and Delinquency,* 38: 510–21.

Sussman, S., et al. 1995. *Developing School-based Tobacco Use Prevention and Cessation Programs.* Thousand Oaks, CA: Sage.

Sussman, S., et al. 1996. "Marijuana use: current issues and new research directions." *Journal of Drug Issues,* 26: 695–733.

Sussman, S., et al. 1997. "The correlates of substance abuse and dependence among adolescents at high risk for drug abuse." *Journal of Substance Abuse,* 9: 241–55.

Szalay, L. B., et al. 1993. "Vulnerabilities and cultural change: drug use among Puerto Rican adolescents in the United States." *International Journal of the Addictions,* 28: 327–54.

Warner, L. A., et al. 1995 "Prevalence and correlates of drug use and dependence in the United States: results from the National Comorbidity Survey." *Archives of General Psychiatry,* 52: 219–29.

Wills, T. A., et al. 1996. "Large-scale environmental risk factors for substance use." *American Behavioral Scientist,* 39: 808–22.

Zajonc, R. B. 1980. "Feeling and thinking: preferences need no inferences." *American Psychologist,* 35: 151–75.

REVIEW QUESTIONS

1. Why do researchers believe white ethnicity is associated with greater drug use among adolescents and adults?
2. Discuss the two main types of peer pressure discussed in the article.

PLAYING WITH PAINKILLERS

CLAUDIA KALB

It all started innocently enough. Three years ago, when Michelle Brown got pregnant, her doctor wrote her a prescription for Lortab, a potentially addictive painkiller similar to Vicodin, for relief from migraine headaches. Her migraines eventually got worse; the Lortab made her life bearable. But it had a devastating side effect: "Slowly," says Brown, who is from Sanford, Maine, "I started to get addicted." She became a classic "doctor shopper," hopping from one physician to the next to get multiple prescriptions. She discovered Percocet, and soon she was mixing Lortab with OxyContin, a new, superstrength painkiller she got through a dealer. By early last year, Brown, 25 years old, and the mother of two small children, worked up the nerve to commit fraud. Pretending to be phoning from her doctor's office, she called her local pharmacy, read her physician's identification number off a prescription bottle and won, she says, "my key to the palace."

For millions of Americans, painkillers are a godsend. Cancer patients suffer the agony a little bit more easily. People battling severe arthritis can, for the first time, take walks and play with their grandchildren. Realizing that for years doctors neglected to include pain management in patient care, the medical establishment has, over the past decade, taken a new, more aggressive approach to treating pain. In January a national accrediting board issued new standards requiring doctors in hospitals and other facilities to treat pain as a vital sign, meaning that they must measure it and treat it as they would blood pressure or heart rate. Even Congress has gotten into the act, last fall passing a law declaring the next 10 years the "Decade of Pain Control and Research."

In this environment, pharmaceutical companies are experimenting with new formulations of painkillers, and existing painkillers themselves are more widely distributed than ever before. While the pharmaceutical market doubled to $145 billion between 1996 and 2000, the painkiller market tripled to $1.8 billion over the same period. Yet at the same time, the incidence of reported first-time abuse of painkillers has also surged. Many of these painkillers aren't new, and "there's not necessarily something wrong with" the increase in controlled substances, says Michael Moy in the Drug Enforcement Administration's Office of Diversion Control. "But once you put something into the food chain, someone's going to want to bite."

Although there are no perfect statistics on how many people misuse or abuse prescription drugs, in 1999 an estimated 4 million Americans over the age of 12 used prescription pain relievers, sedatives and stimulants for "nonmedical" reasons in the past month, with almost half saying they'd done so for the first time. According to the DEA, the most-abused prescription drugs include

Source: Claudia Kalb, "Playing with Painkillers," *Newsweek,* April 9, 2001, pp. 45–48.

the oxycodone and hydrocodone types of painkillers, which contain potentially addictive opioids (the two drugs differ slightly in chemical structure, but both work similarly on the body). And emergency-room data suggest that certain drugs have seen dramatic spikes in abuse in recent years. ER visits involving hydrocodone medications like Vicodin and Lortab jumped from an estimated 6,100 incidents in 1992 to more than 14,000 in 1999, oxycodone painkillers like Percodan and OxyContin rose from about 3,750 to 6,430 and the anti-anxiety drug Xanax (including generic formulations) increased from 16,500 to more than 20,500. Illegal drugs, abused in much higher numbers, also increased: cocaine from 120,000 to 169,000 and heroin and morphine from 48,000 to 84,400.

Reports of painkiller abuse from Hollywood catch the attention of the public more than any statistic ever will. In the last six months, Melanie Griffith and Matthew Perry each checked into rehab, publicly acknowledging their addiction to prescription painkillers. TV shows fill their scripts with the problem: on *ER,* Dr. John Carter gets hooked on painkillers after he's stabbed, and on the new show, *The Job,* Denis Leary plays a detective who takes painkillers on a stakeout. Even Homer Simpson battles a compulsion for the drugs in a season-ender where he's catapulted into a surreal celebrity existence. After looking at the data and following the news reports, the National Institute on Drug Abuse (NIDA) will announce next week a major public-health initiative about prescription-drug abuse. "Once you get into millions of people [abusing]," says Dr. Alan Leshner, NIDA's director, "you have a serious public-health issue on your hands."

Addiction to prescription drugs is not a new problem. Remember *Valley of the Dolls*? The uppers, the downers, the sleeping pills? But some of today's drugs are far more sophisticated than anything Jacqueline Susann could have envisioned. OxyContin, which hit the market in 1996, is by far the most powerful: it's a 12-hour time-release in-

carnation of the molecular compound oxycodone, the active ingredient in older drugs like Percodan and Percocet. Unlike drugs in the hydrocodone category, OxyContin and several other oxycodones don't contain acetaminophen, which can damage the liver in high doses and limits the extent to which those drugs can be safely used. OxyContin allows patients to swallow fewer pills, and offers pain relief three times longer than earlier versions. But when the drug is crushed and snorted, eliminating its time-release feature, it's a huge narcotic rush to the brain. "You feel vitalized, like you can do whatever you want," says Eric, 38, of Portland, Maine, who has spent as much as $525 a week buying the drug from a street dealer. Abuse of OxyContin has gotten so bad that in some areas users are robbing pharmacies to get the drug—just last month, Hannaford, a major chain in Maine, decided that "for the safety of our associates and customers," it would no longer stock the drug on its shelves.

When it comes to prescription painkillers, there is no typical abuser. Police departments say they've seen every variety, from teenagers to stay-at-home moms to executives who started taking drugs for their tennis elbow. Particularly at risk are chronic substance abusers who may divert to prescription drugs when their preferred poisons, like heroin, run out. In Hollywood clubs, cocaine and ecstasy still dominate, one 30-year-old actor says, but people also share Vicodin, Xanax and Valium, then wash them down with alcohol. Health-care professionals, with easy access to drugs, often succumb. Among arrests in Cincinnati, which carefully tracks prescription-drug abuse, 30 percent of cases involve medical employees. Landon Gibbs, a Virginia state police officer, says his department arrested a doctor last year who would "write a prescription, drive that person to the pharmacy and then split the pills."

Prescription painkillers are appealing in part because users think of them as "safe." They're FDA approved, easy to take on the sly and don't have the same stigma as illegal drugs. Cindy

Mogil started taking Valium at 20 to ease the trauma after a car accident, and "liked the feeling of euphoria." As a manager in a health clinic, she had easy access to sample pills, then found her way to Vicodin and Percodan, visiting different doctors to get her supply. "Boy, it's so easy," says Mogil, who lives in suburban Atlanta. "I'd walk in and tell them I had a migraine; that's all I had to say." Her family never questioned the pills: "They think you're taking it for medical reasons." Finally, after two decades of abuse, Mogil collapsed—her face numb, her speech slurred—and checked into rehab. "I was no better than a street addict," she says.

All pain passes through the brain. Pills like Vicodin and OxyContin lock onto a cell receptor called *mu,* found most prominently in the brain, spinal cord and gut. When the drug connects to the receptors in the spinal cord, pain signals from nerves are blocked; in the brain, the receptors seem to promote an overall sense of well-being; in the gut, they have the unfortunate side effect of constipation. While any patient who takes an opioid painkiller or any other addictive drug over a long period will develop a physical dependence—meaning the body adjusts to the chemicals now swirling about and thinks that's normal—that dependence can be properly managed. When it's time to go off the drug, a good physician will taper the prescription so there's no withdrawal or rebound effect. But a genetic tendency, an underlying mental illness, a history of substance abuse or a combination of factors may lead a small group of patients to go beyond just physical dependence. They become compulsive about taking the drug, even when it threatens their health or social and professional lives.

Once you're hooked, getting more becomes an obsession. Many abusers, like Michelle Brown, become doctor shoppers. Others buy their fix on the street: one Vicodin goes for about $6, Percocet and Percodan, up to $8, and an 80mg OxyContin for as much as $80. Tales of cunning and desperation abound—the weekend visits to the ER

claiming a toothache, the stolen prescription pads. Dr. Sheila Calderon, an internist in Dallas, says a former employee used her name to call in a prescription for Vicodin (she was never charged). Cathy Napier, a former Percodan addict and now head of the chemical-dependency program at Presbyterian Hospital in Dallas, says she knows women who go to real-estate open houses, "then go through the medicine cabinets and steal the Lortab."

So who's to blame for the misuse of these drugs? Many abusers point the finger at doctors, who they say tend to prescribe medications too quickly without warning patients that certain drugs can be highly addictive. But once patients begin deceiving doctors and pharmacists by phoning in fake scripts or seeking prescriptions from multiple doctors, they become the culprits. Seventeen states currently have prescription-monitoring programs, which vary widely—some track drugs like OxyContin (a schedule II drug, deemed "high potential for abuse"), but not Vicodin (schedule III, "some potential"). But many states don't dedicate resources to full-time oversight. Nor does the DEA, which is largely watching out for abuse by health professionals. If abusers are caught, they're charged with fraud—a misdemeanor in some states and a felony in others. Brown says she is "so thankful" for the DEA agent who handled her case after a suspicious pharmacist called the police. "He knew I needed help. He told my family everything. And it just blew open from there." Now, says Brown, she's in treatment, taking methadone to ease her off her addiction and finally "learning how to live a normal life."

With all the focus on abusers, pain specialists worry that legitimate patients will suffer. Too many doctors succumb to "opiophobia," fear of prescribing much-needed medications for appropriate patients who suffer moderate to severe pain, says Dr. Russell Portenoy, chair of pain medicine at New York's Beth Israel Medical Center. Dr. Kenneth Pollack, a pain specialist in Des Moines, Iowa, says he recently prescribed

OxyContin for a woman who had suffered painful nerve tumors in her feet for 11 years and could barely stand up. Last time Pollack saw her, "she was practically in tears," he says. "She said, 'Thank you for giving me my life back'." Says David E. Joranson, director of the Pain & Policy Studies Group at the University of Wisconsin: "My fear is that some patients and doctors are going to start looking at this stuff like it's nuclear material. There is a real risk of losing recent gains made in pain management."

Pharmaceutical companies acknowledge that misuse is a problem. Pharmacia, which manufactures Xanax, says "all of our peer-group companies realize there is a potential for abuse here." They say they educate as many people as possible about the importance of taking the drug safely under a doctor's care; the drug is also marketed generically by other companies. Abbott Labs, which manufactures Vicodin, offers symposiums for prescribers and pharmacists to teach about abuse potential. And Purdue Pharma, which manufactures OxyContin, has been actively addressing the problem through education sessions and meetings with the DEA and the FDA.

Maryann Timmons, 51, says she needs her medication. After lifelong ear infections and a broken eardrum, Timmons, 51, of Concord Township, Ohio, takes Vicodin to dull the pain. Initially, she says, her doctor didn't want to prescribe the pills; he ultimately did, but told Timmons to use them sparingly because of their addictive potential. "I felt like a criminal," she says. "It shouldn't be a battle to get help with pain relief." Pain relief and criminal activity. The new challenge for doctors and public-health officials is to provide one without advancing the other.

REVIEW QUESTIONS

1. What is the relation between painkiller abusers and chronic substance abusers?
2. Why do prescription drugs not have the same stigma as illegal drugs?

BINGE DRINKING AND THE COLLEGE ENVIRONMENT

RICHARD P. KEELING

Taken together, the 3 major articles on college drinking in this issue of the *Journal [of American College Health]* disallow complacency, forbid shallow analysis, and demand renewed commitments. These are extensive national studies of drinking patterns and programs at hundreds of institutions, involving many thousands of students, and conducted over as many as 8 years. They provide an essential, if bracing, view of trends and a cautious assessment of what we, in our binary way of thinking, call our successes and failures. There is nothing in them that should make us feel even briefly comfortable; neither should they paralyze us. We discover most what surprises few of us: that the work has just begun.

The key findings include these:

• The prevalence of binge drinking at 4-year colleges did not change between 1993 and 2001, despite the combined influences of task forces, changes in public and institutional policy, augmented and more diverse prevention programs, elevated fear of liability, and demands for greater accountability. The Harvard School of Public Health's College Alcohol Study (CAS), now conducted 4 times (1993, 1997, 1999, and 2001), continues to show that 40% to 45% of college students binge drink. This matters a great deal be-cause it is binge drinking specifically—as opposed to drinking in general—that causes most of the alcohol-associated harm that occurs on campuses and in students' lives. Binge drinking is at once the most important public health problem on our campuses and a critical challenge to institutional mission.

• The trends identified in earlier reports from the CAS were maintained through 2001: modest increases in the percentages of abstainers and frequent binge drinkers (therefore a progressive polarization of drinking patterns); moderate reductions in the percentage of college students who reported binge drinking when they were in high school; and a greater frequency of extreme drinking styles, including drinking for the purpose of getting drunk.

• An increase in the prevalence of frequent binge drinking (from 5.3% in 1993 to 11.9% in 2001) among women enrolled in all-women's colleges and a lesser, but still significant, increase of the same behavior for women in coeducational schools.

• Although students' attendance and heavy drinking at fraternity and sorority parties each decreased significantly between 1993 and 2001, there was, in parallel, an increase in attendance and heavy drinking at off-campus parties. This

Source: Richard P. Keeling, "Binge Drinking and the College Environment," *Journal of American College Health,* vol. 50 (March 2002), pp. 97–201. Reprinted with permission.

finding verifies the despairing belief that reducing controlling drinking in one setting only stimulates its increased appearance in another.

• Over the 4 CAS reporting periods, there were modest increments in the percentage of students who reported being somehow sanctioned for alcohol-related offenses—but fewer than 10% of frequent binge drinkers experienced any disciplinary actions resulting from their drinking.

• The prevalence of drinking among underage students is lower (77.4%) than that among 21- to 23-year-old students (85.6%). In addition, underage students drink less frequently than do their "legal age" peers, and the percentage of underage students who binge drink (43.6%) is lower than that of students who are over the age of 21 who do (50.2%). But more underage students reported being drunk on 3 or more occasions in the past 30 days, more said that getting drunk was an important motivation for drinking, and more reported that their usual mode of drinking was binge drinking. Underage students consumed almost exactly half of the alcohol drunk by all the students in the CAS sample during the 30 days prior to the survey.

• Half of the underage students who were studied reported obtaining alcohol easily; other students are their primary source, whether those student sources are of legal age (71.6% in 2001) or also underage (42.2%). But since 1993, the use of fake identification cards to obtain alcohol illegally has declined, whereas the role of parents as providers of alcohol to underage students has increased.

• Support among underage students for "cracking down on underage drinking" varies by the students' drinking styles. Seventy-seven percent of students under 21 who do not binge drink indicated such support—but only 29% of underage binge drinkers agreed.

• Having more laws restricting underage drinking or governing the volume of sales and consumption of alcohol in effect is associated with less drinking among underage students.

Two issues demand our attention first as we review these articles, make sense of their results, and determine how to apply their conclusions in our work. First, what do they tell us about the value and effectiveness of the broad spectrum of alcohol-prevention programs, services, activities, and policies used on our campuses for the past decade (it has been as Wechsler et al. note in the very title of the 2001 CAS report, "a period of increased prevention efforts")? Second, what do they reveal about the patterns and practices of drinking on campus that may inform new or better efforts in the future?

The stability of the most important indicator—the binge-drinking rate—from 1993 to 2001 suggests that we have not solved the problem of excessive drinking. We may (or may not) justly take credit for some increase in the prevalence of abstention from alcohol—but, if we do, we also have to accept responsibility for a similar increase in the prevalence of frequent binge drinking. Whatever we have done (and we have done a great deal), we have not yet significantly changed the dominant patterns of dangerous drinking—not with peer educators; not with social marketing; not with "social norming"; not with "dorm talks"; not with student assistance programs; and not with the arrayed forces of grants, campus–community coalitions, and concerned leaders. An optimistic reader can detect in the current articles evidence of our work: some increase in the proportion of students who report being disciplined for alcohol-related offenses, growing support among students for stronger campus alcohol policies, a protective effect of substance-free housing, modest declines in binge drinking among residents of fraternity and sorority houses, and some success with strategies that involve students actively or take advantage of traditional academic systems (such as the curriculum itself). But, if we are honest with ourselves, we must say that there have also been negative trends: more frequent binge drinking among women, an increase in the prevalence of binge drinking by underage students, and more alcohol-related problems for students under 21. . . .

Taking [various] studies into joint consideration, we learn more than anything else about the importance of properly and accurately defining the object of our work and of figuring out how best to work with that object. The object is not our students; demonizing, blaming, demeaning, and bemoaning them, either one by one, or in their networks and groups, is unbefitting and unworkable, and has been unsuccessful. Students can be—should be—partners in our efforts. They have real experience and real ideas. Just as our colleagues in the classroom have come to regard students as collaborators in the creation of knowledge, so we should involve them as authentic partners in solving one of the most complicated and difficult of campus social, cultural, and public health problems.

With forceful clarity, we learn that the right object of our efforts is embedded so intricately in everything that is college that separating the two—or even adequately telling them apart—is frustratingly difficult; this object is as behemoth and miniscule, as entrenched and ephemeral, and as pervasive and variable as culture itself. We call this object, often, *the environment*. But that term externalizes rather too much a concept that should instead be conveyed in ways that emphasize our collective responsibility and accountability. Once again binary, we think too easily of the environment as something surrounding, but not involving, us. We assign to the environment all the things we fear we cannot influence or control (eg, the multimedia marketing of alcohol to students); the people and organizations we con. sider to be part of the problem (bars, taverns, and their owners and leagues; returning alumni who want to party; members of governing boards who have links to the alcohol industry); and well-established (read: thought to be impervious to change) campus traditions, customs, rituals, and celebrations. "The environment" can sound, and seem, both intractable and vaporous—not of us, not in our

hands, not housed anywhere. But it is of us, in our hands, and housed among us.

Aaron M. Brower . . . writes persuasively and simply about this: "College problem drinking is a product of the college environment." Remember Wechsler's comment about the persistence of high rates of binge drinking despite the influence of certain protective factors: "other factors are keeping overall binge-drinking rates in college at these high levels." Those "other factors" must very likely be features of the college environment that Brower describes; as he notes, "this [college binge drinking] is a pattern that is strongly determined by living in a college environment and by the developmental life stage of being a college student."

The 3 reports, aggregately, underscore some pertinent and pressing points about the environment of college drinking:

• That environment is of human, social construction; it is not governed by divine or natural law, and it is not immutable.

• The sphere of the environment is capacious; it includes not only the slipperiest of social concepts (cultural norms) and the most boisterous (special events and celebrations), mysterious (group-based traditions and rituals), and provocative (alcohol advertising) elements of the college experience, but also the infrastructure of regulation, policy, and law that restricts certain features of the sale or consumption of alcohol. The sociocultural and regulatory components of the environment are joined, of course, in the determination and deployment of various patterns of enforcement. Customs dictate, in other words, the alacrity and vigor with which policies and laws come to have real effect in the lives of real students—or real members of the faculty, staff, and community.

• More, and more restrictive, policies and laws, and more energetic enforcement thereof, do, in fact, affect drinking behavior among students. Some of those changes are associated with positive outcomes (eg, the finding by Wechsler's group that underage students in states with more extensive laws restricting underage drinking and high-volume drinking were less likely to drink and to binge drink); others are negative (Wechsler and associates' more general finding that underage students drink alcohol less frequently but are more likely to drink to excess when they drink—an observation that resonates with the common complaint of underage students that the minimum legal drinking age forces them to drink a lot in a hurry "before the cops come").

• At the same time, involving students in a serious and legitimate way seems to be associated with greater success in almost any environmental program model, from volunteer service to classroom-based leaning, from developing educational strategies to serving on committees or task forces with responsibility for policy, from determining how to provide alternative events that meet students' social and relational needs without centering on alcohol to reaching a campus consensus about delivering economical, equitable, and consistent enforcement.

Let us not, then, be parsimonious or exclusive in our investigation of environmental manipulations. . . . The CAS articles show that students themselves—with the exception of binge drinkers—are more likely than not to favor more stringent policies and enforcement. At the same time, students—like most of us—will react defensively and angrily to actions taken "against" them, especially when they are not consulted in a meaningful way in the process. "Regulation without representation' is a surefire ticket to unrest, disenfranchisement, and, ultimately, disengagement. But to suggest that any restrictive statutes or policies—devices to control access, reduce the volume of alcohol consumed, or demand accountability for harm done—are by their nature onerous and unwarranted is ridiculous (as foolish as letting binge drinkers, or the alcohol industry, control the debate about the definition of binge drinking).

There are a lot of "environmental" things to try: alternative late night events and activities (imagine: keeping college facilities open, and staffed, until 3 or 4 AM!), keg registration, legislation to limit or eliminate drink specials, reducing the density of alcohol-serving establishments through control of licenses, new approaches to orientation to college that accept the challenge of producing a healthier transition experience, out-front leadership by officers and trustees, restrictions on alcohol advertising, banning alcohol in stadiums, student leadership development programs, and many more. They have in common what Aaron Brower calls a focus on the campus and community, rather than the drinking of individual students. They call us, though, to remember what the environment is and where we can find it: it is of us, in our hands, and housed among us. And if we can also remember that students are also of us, in our hands, and housed among us—and honor their assets and contributions, as much as we note their vulnerabilities—we may, together, reduce the prevalence of binge drinking.

REVIEW QUESTIONS

1. What are some ways in which binge drinking among college students can be reduced? Provide more than a listing; include enough specifics to demonstrate comprehension of suggested alternatives.
2. Can students aid in the reduction of binge drinking on college campuses and the community? If yes, how so? If not, why not?

PREDICTORS OF SMOKING AMONG COLLEGE STUDENTS

KAREN M. EMMONS
HENRY WECHSLER
GEORGE DOWDALL
MELISSA ABRAHAM

The overall smoking prevalence in the United States has been reduced considerably over the past 20 years; however, there have been only minimal reductions in smoking prevalence among adolescents and young adults. Recent data from the National Health Interview Survey suggest that . . . [a]mong college students, the prevalence of use of cigarettes within the previous 30 days has been reported as 24.5%. Interestingly, 40% of all college students have used cigarettes at least once during the previous 12 months, suggesting that considerable experimentation with smoking occurs during the college years. Although smoking among adolescents and young adults is associated with socioeconomic status and educational achievement, determinants of smoking among college students are largely unknown.

The health behaviors of young adults are important because this group is in a transition between adolescence and early adulthood, a time during which unhealthy behaviors developed during adolescence may be malleable or may be consolidated into lifetime patterns.[1-4] Because of both the health and lifestyle risks facing college smokers, it is important to understand the characteristics associated with smoking in this population and the factors that might be used to influence students' smoking behavior. The purpose of this paper is to explore the predictors of smoking among a large, representative national sample of students enrolled in American 4-year colleges. Identification of the characteristics associated with smoking among this population may lead to more effective intervention efforts.

METHODS

The data used in this study were obtained from a representative national sample of 140 four-year colleges. A random sample of 25,627 undergraduate students received a study survey; 17,592 students responded, yielding an overall response rate of 69% (response rate range = 60% to 80%). Details of the sampling procedure and the characteristics of the participating colleges have been described elsewhere.[5-7] Comparison of the nonparticipating schools with the 140 schools included in the final sample revealed that the only statistically significant difference was in enrollment size. Proportionately fewer small colleges (fewer than 1000 students) participated in the study; however, these colleges were oversampled,

Source: Karen M. Emmons, Henry Wechsler, George Dowdall, and Melissa Abraham, "Predictors of Smoking among U.S. College Students," *American Journal of Public Health,* vol. 88 (1998), pp. 104–107. Reprinted with permission.

and thus sufficient numbers were available for statistical analyses.

The purpose of the parent project, the Harvard School of Public Health College Alcohol Study, was to examine binge drinking among college students. The study survey provided detailed information about drinking behavior, as well as information about smoking, illicit drug use, demographic characteristics, family characteristics, living arrangements, lifestyle choices, and academic performance. Smoking status was based on self-reported use of cigarettes within the preceding 30 days.

RESULTS

. . . In this sample, 22.3% of the full-time students at 4-year colleges had smoked during the previous 30 days, and 25% were classified as former smokers (16% abstinent for at least 12 months, 9% abstinent for 1 to 12 months). Among the smokers, 33.7% smoked half a pack per day or more; 14% smoked one pack per day or more. Smoking prevalence was not related to year in college. No gender differences in smoking prevalence were found.

[Univariate analyses showed the following variables as likely to cause smoking:]

Precollege Drinking Behaviors. The primary measure of precollege drinking behavior was participation in binge drinking during high school. This variable had a strong relationship with smoking status and was found to raise the likelihood of smoking in college more than threefold. . . .

College Lifestyle Choices. As a broad indicator of college lifestyle choices, students rated their participation in and attitudes toward several types of activities (e.g., community service, academics, religion, athletics, arts, leisure activities). Several lifestyle choices predicted smoking status, including not participating in intercollegiate athletics (men only), considering athletics to be not very important, considering religion to be not very im-

portant, endorsement of parties as important or very important, and level of participation in leisure activities. An index of nonparticipation in productive activities was also related to smoking status. Being a member of a fraternity or sorority increased the likelihood of a student being a smoker, as did residing in a coed dorm (women only).

High-Risk Behaviors. The co-occurrence of health-threatening behaviors was demonstrated by . . . current marijuana use and binge drinking. . . . Gender differences were noted, particularly in terms of marijuana use. In addition, having two or more sex partners in the previous month increased the likelihood of smoking among men and almost tripled the likelihood of smoking among women.

Self-Reported Unhappiness. Overall unhappiness with life was related to smoking status. Dissatisfaction with one's education was found to be a moderate predictor of smoking status.

[Multivariate analyses showed the following factors as predictors of smoking after other variables were taken into account:] . . . [G]ender emerged as a predictor of smoking, with men less likely to smoke than women. Race/ethnicity was not related to smoking status. The high-risk behavior variables were the strongest predictors of smoking status. Using marijuana and binge drinking during college both independently raised the likelihood of smoking substantially. . . . In addition, high school binge drinking moderately increased the likelihood of smoking in college, as did having multiple sex partners in college. Not participating in athletics was a predictor of smoking status. Participation in leisure activities and dissatisfaction with education were also predictors of smoking.

DISCUSSION

This representative national sample provided a unique opportunity to examine the predictors of smoking behavior among college students.

Lifestyle characteristics clearly emerged as important predictors of smoking behavior. The results suggest that other high-risk behaviors, such as using marijuana, drinking heavily, and having multiple sex partners, are the strongest correlates of smoking status among this population. Other characteristics of a hedonistic lifestyle were also predictive, such as endorsement of parties as important and participation in leisure activities. These relationships were stronger for women. Engaging in binge drinking in high school increased the likelihood of smoking in college. This may indicate that smoking among college students is part of a risk-taking lifestyle initiated well before college.

Nonparticipation in athletics increased the likelihood of smoking. This is in contrast to previous findings suggesting that binge drinking is associated with active participation in athletics.[5–7] Such findings have important implications for health education and health promotion interventions among college populations, which often assume that a similar message must be delivered regardless of the substance being discussed.

These results may be useful for consideration in the development of interventions designed to target smoking and other substance use behavior among college students. There are several intervention implications of these findings. First, students who were not involved in the productive aspects of university life and who were dissatisfied with their educational experience were more likely to be smokers. Efforts to engage these students in academic or other types of college-based activities may be an important part of helping them to develop healthier lifestyles. Second, the likelihood of smoking was greatly increased among students who engaged in other high-risk behaviors. Intervention efforts need to take into account co-occurrence of smoking with use of alcohol and other substances, and the possibility that students may have developed dependencies on multiple substances. Third, the gender differences in these results are particularly interesting. Young women who adopt more risk-taking lifestyles are more likely to smoke. The college period offers a number of unique opportunities for intervention with this group. For example, residence halls and sonorities may provide a strategic channel for development and modification of social norms around health behaviors. In addition, residence advisors and academic advisors often develop ongoing relationships with students and, with proper training, could provide interventions addressing these important health behaviors. Helping these at-risk students to develop more productive lifestyles may be an appropriate role for college personnel.

These results suggest that college may present an important opportunity to intervene with smokers in regard to multiple health risk factors. The development of effective interventions and substance abuse policies for colleges and universities is likely to help reduce the long-term morbidity and mortality related to smoking facing this large population of young smokers.

REFERENCES

1. Schorling JB, Gutgesell M, Klas P, Smith D, Keller A. Tobacco, alcohol and other drug use among college students. *J Subst Abuse.* 1994;6:105–115.

2. Gray NL. The relationship of cigarette smoking and other substance use among college students. *J Drug Educ* 1993;23:117–124.

3. Gray NL, Donatelle RL. A comparative analysis of factors influencing smoking behaviors of college students: 1963–1987. *J Drug Educ.* 1990;20:247–255.

4. Martin CS, Clifford PR, Clapper RL. Patterns and predictors of simultaneous and concurrent use of alcohol, tobacco, marijuana, and hallucinogens in first-year college students. *J Subst Abuse.* 1992;4:319–326.

5. Wechsler H, Davenport A, Dowdall G, Moeykens B, Castillo S. Health and behavioral consequences of binge drinking in college: a national survey of students at 140 campuses. *JAMA* 1994;272:1672–1677.

6. Wechsler H, Dowdall GW, Davenport A, Castillo S. Correlates of college student binge drinking. *Am J Public Health.* 1995;85:921–926.

7. Wechsler H, Dowdall GW, Davenport A, Rimm EB. A gender-specific measure of binge drinking among college students. *Am J Public Health.* 1995;85:982–985.

REVIEW QUESTIONS

1. Identify three factors that are linked to the smoking behavior of college students.
2. The authors provide three intervention strategies to reduce smoking behavior among college students. What are they?

PART TEN

DEVIANCE IN CYBERSPACE

Six years ago Christopher Klaus, then only 19, started his company, Internet Security System (ISS), out of his grandmother's house. Since then, he has earned well over $200 million. He and his young employees help numerous corporations ward off hackers who try to break into their computer systems. The Internet security provided by ISS and similar companies has turned into a highly lucrative business because the security measures in most computers are so "laughably inadequate" that they "often fail to stop intruders armed only with the most rudimentary skills." Not surprisingly, as a survey has shown, among even top corporations and government agencies, 30 percent said that their systems had been penetrated by outsiders and 55 percent reported unauthorized access by insiders.[1]

There is no way to know how many hackers exist in cyberspace, but there are clearly enough to attract the attention of law enforcement. Most hackers are relatively innocent and harmless; they break into various computer systems strictly for the challenge and tell system administrators how they broke in. A few are downright criminal, and they are called "crackers." Crackers use their computer skills for malice, such as disabling a telephone company's computer network to knock out the phone service for an entire city. Law enforcers, because of their relative lack of computer knowledge, often confuse harmless hackers with destructive crackers. As a result, many hackers end up being treated like criminals.[2]

Hackings and crackings are products of the computer revolution. The same revolution has also brought about other kinds of cyberdeviance. Here we take a look at various forms of cyberdeviance. In the first article, "The Proliferation of Cyber-Crimes," Brian Hansen discusses the nature of cyber-crimes as well as the implications of cyber-crimes for consumers, merchants, and software companies. In the second article, "Let Your Fingers Do the Talking: Sex on an Adult Chat Line," Diane Wysocki shows how the computer network has lured some people into chat rooms for sexual purposes. In the third selection, "Child Porn on the Net: Perpetuating a Cycle of Abuse," Ethel Quayle and Max Taylor offer research data on the various ways some people use child pornography on the Internet. In the fourth reading, "On-Line Accounts of Unrepentant Pedophiles," Keith Durkin and Clifton Bryant reveal how the Internet has made it possible for pedophiles to spread their view that pederasty is harmless and acceptable behavior.

1. Brendan I. Koerner, "Can Hackers Be Stopped?" *U.S. News & World Report,* June 14, 1999, pp. 46–52.
2. Paul Taylor, "The Social Construction of Hackers as Deviants," in Alex Thio and Thomas C. Calhoun (eds.), *Readings in Deviant Behavior,* 2nd ed. (Boston: Allyn and Bacon, 2001), pp. 283–292.

THE PROLIFERATION
OF CYBER-CRIMES

BRIAN HANSEN

Carlos Salgado Jr. walked into San Francisco International Airport carrying a tote bag containing an ordinary CD-ROM disk and Mario Puzo's popular Mafia novel *The Last Don*. He passed through security without incident and strolled clown the concourse to a passenger lounge near Gate 67. But Salgado, 36, wasn't there to catch a plane.

The freelance computer technician had stolen more than 100,000 credit-card numbers by hacking into several e-commerce databases on the Internet. It was an easy heist for Salgado, who simply used a ready-made computer-intrusion program that he found on the Web. Using a pirated e-mail account to conceal his identity, Salgado arranged to sell the information to an online fence for $260,000. The exchange was set for May 21, 1997.

As a precaution, Salgado put the stolen data on a CD-ROM, but with Hollywood-like flair he encoded the information based on a passage in Puzo's novel. Salgado's story, too, would someday make good reading: He was about to pull off one of the largest cyber-crimes in the Internet's short history. All told, the bank data that Salgado had electronically liberated from the Internet had a combined credit line of more than $1 billion.

Unfortunately for Salgado, he was walking into an FBI sting operation. The bureau had started monitoring Salgado's online machinations after being tipped off by an alert technician at one of the companies Salgado had pilfered. Initially, the FBI knew Salgado only as "SMACK," his online "handle." But when he handed over the encrypted CD to an undercover agent, the feds finally had their man. Salgado pleaded guilty to breaking into a computer network and trafficking in stolen credit cards. He was sentenced to two and a half years in prison.

[WHAT ARE CYBER-CRIMES LIKE?]

Few cyber-attacks are as serious as Salgado's. Nonetheless, experts say unauthorized incursions into government and private computer systems are part of a larger—and growing—cyber-crime trend.

"This is the 21st-century equivalent of the armored-car robbery," says Computer Security Institute (CSI) Editorial Director Richard Power. "Why should the bad guys bother dealing with armored cars and police with machine guns when they can knock off a [network] server and get tens of thousands of live credit cards? This is happening all the time now. The Salgado case was just the beginning."

Riptech, Inc., an Internet security firm in Alexandria, Va., verified 128,678 cyber-attacks on just 300 of the companies it serves in the last six months of 2001.[1] To be sure, only a small fraction

Source: Brian Hansen, "Cyber-Crimes," *CQ Researcher,* vol. 12 (April 12, 2002), pp. 307–314, 323–324. Reprinted by permission of CQ Press, a division of Congressional Quarterly, Inc.

of these attacks successfully breached the organizations' front-line security measures. Still, 41 percent of Riptech's clients had to patch holes in their computer-security systems after "critical" attacks. And nearly one in eight suffered at least one "emergency" attack requiring some form of data-recovery procedure.

An annual survey conducted by the FBI and CSI confirms the explosion of cyber-crime to epidemic proportions. More than 91 percent of the corporations and U.S. government agencies that responded reported a computer-security breach in 2001, and 64 percent acknowledged financial losses because of the attacks.[2]

Some cyber-crimes, like Salgado's caper, are committed primarily for money. Others are "inside" jobs perpetrated by disgruntled employees like Timothy Lloyd, a revenge-minded network administrator in New Jersey. After being demoted and reprimanded in 1996, he wrote six lines of malicious computer code that caused $10 million in financial losses for the Omega Engineering Corp.

Lloyd was convicted of sabotaging the company's computer network and last February was sentenced to 41 months in prison and ordered to pay more than $2 million in restitution. At Lloyd's trial, an Omega executive said the firm "will never recover" from the attack.[3]

Many computer attacks are essentially on-line vandalism. Hackers have defaced countless Web pages, greatly embarrassing major corporations and government agencies. Hackers sometimes act to advance social or political views. Last year, Chinese hackers defaced a host of U.S. government Web sites after a Chinese pilot died in a collision with an American spy plane over the South China Sea. American hackers retaliated by defacing 2,500 Chinese sites. Similar cyber-warfare broke out between American and Middle Eastern hackers after the Sept. 11 terrorist attacks.

To be sure, not all hackers are viewed as criminals. So-called ethical or white-hat hackers who try to break into computer systems at the behest of security-conscious companies are often lauded for advancing the state of computer technology. But "black-hat" hackers, or "crackers," seek to wreak havoc or illegally profit from their cyberspace forays. . . .

Con artists, meanwhile, are using the Web to perpetrate various types of fraud schemes in record numbers, according to law-enforcement officials. "The number of [fraud] complaints has increased steadily over the last two or three years," says Timothy Healy, director of the Internet Fraud Complaint Center (IFCC), operated by the FBI and the National White Collar Crime Center.

Internet auction fraud was the most frequently reported type of complaint handled by the IFCC last year, according to Healy. Fraudsters can rig Internet auctions in a number of ways, such as using skills to drive up the bidding process. Con men also use the Internet to perpetrate a wide variety of investment scams, bogus e-commerce opportunities and confidence rackets. "It's amazing what's out there," Healy says.

One of the most prevalent and insidious Internet-assisted scams is identity theft—stealing credit card and Social Security numbers and other personal information. Some identity thieves hack into e-commerce Web sites to pilfer such data. Others set up bogus Internet sites of their own to dupe unwitting consumers into revealing their credit-card numbers.

Armed with stolen identities, thieves can perpetrate a variety of crimes, from opening bogus bank accounts and writing bad checks to taking out car loans and mortgages in their victims' names.

Under federal law, consumers who use credit cards are liable only for the first $50 of fraudulent charges made on their accounts, and many credit-card companies even waive that amount. Still, identity-theft victims typically incur more than $1,000 in out-of-pocket expenses trying to restore their mangled credit ratings, according to the Federal Trade Commission. (Debit-card purchases do not receive automatic fraud protection.)[4]

Lenders are hit even harder. Identity theft cost financial institutions some $2.4 billion in direct losses and related mopping-up expenses in 2000, according to Celent Communications, a Boston consulting firm.[5]

Controversies abound over how best to deal with Internet hucksters, hackers and virus writers. Some policymakers, wary of Internet-facilitated terrorist attacks, are calling for tough new laws to prevent computer crimes—including life sentences for some offenses. Others fear that such initiatives will trample on civil liberties. Still others want legislation to make software companies such as Microsoft liable for damages caused by computer-security failures.

As the debate rages, here is a closer look at some of the key questions being asked:

IS IT SAFE FOR CONSUMERS AND MERCHANTS TO DO BUSINESS ONLINE?

Only about 40 percent of all adult Internet users in the United States use the Web to shop or pay bills, according to the Census Bureau.[6] Many Americans eschew online shopping, banking and other types of Internet commerce because they fear having their credit card or Social Security numbers stolen, numerous studies have found. For example, 85 percent of die Internet users polled recently by Washington-based SWR Worldwide cited security as the biggest deterrent to e-commerce. A poll by GartnerG2, a Stamford, Conn., firm, put die number worried about security at 60 percent.[7]

According to Gartner, U.S. e-commerce fraud losses in 2001 exceeded $700 million, constituting about 1.14 percent of the $61.8 billion in total online sales. That ratio was 19 times higher than the fraud rate for traditional in-store transactions, which hovered at less than one-tenth

of 1 percent during the same time period, Gartner said. Since the e-commerce era began in the mid-1990s, Gartner estimates that one in every six online consumers has been victimized by credit-card fraud, and one in 12 has been hit with identity theft.

"We're not going to see low fraud rates like we have in the brick-and-mortar world until we make some serious changes in the way that online business is conducted," says Avivah Litan, Gartner's vice president for research. "There are some big issues to deal with."

For merchants, the Internet is a double-edged sword. While they can broaden their customer bases and increase their revenues by going online, merchants also expose themselves to cyber-criminals.

Some law-enforcement officials concede that they can't keep pace with the number of e-commerce fraud scams already on the Internet. "There's no way that we can police the entire Web with the small staff that we have at this agency," says an official at the FTC, which investigates Internet fraud. "We go after things that are particularly egregious or pernicious, but we really have to strategically target our limited resources."

Other experts downplay the risks associated with online commerce. "I think we're doing quite well in terms of protecting buyers and sellers in the virtual marketplace," says Emily Hackett, executive director of the Internet Alliance, a Washington-based trade group. "The vast majority of online transactions are carried out without any problems at all."

Consumers can protect themselves when shopping online (as well as in traditional brick-and-mortar stores) by using a credit card. Under federal law, consumers are liable for only the first $50 of fraudulent charges made on their credit-card accounts, and many card issuers waive that amount. Users of debit cards, checks or other payment methods are not necessarily protected. Consequently, more than 95 percent of all e-commerce transactions are made with credit cards, Gartner says.

Credit-card companies are liable for fraudulent in-store transactions accompanied by signed (albeit forged) receipts. However, merchants are typically on the hook for any transactions they process without validating the purchaser's signature—which is rarely done over the Internet. Consequently, merchants—not consumers or credit-card companies—bear most of the costs of e-commerce fraud.

Most Internet merchants utilize a fraud-prevention program. But programs vary widely in effectiveness and customer convenience. Many small merchants screen their online orders manually, flagging those with unusually high dollar volumes, suspicious billing information or other indicators of fraud. Large merchants' often use sophisticated computer software programs to identify potentially fraudulent transactions. Best Buy Co., a consumer electronics retailer, can program its system to red-flag or automatically reject any online orders that originate from countries with high fraud rates. . . .

SHOULD SOFTWARE COMPANIES BE LIABLE FOR INTERNET SECURITY BREACHES?

Hackers and virus writers frequently launch attacks over the Internet by exploiting security flaws in commercial software. The Boston consulting company @Stake found that 70 percent of the security gaps that plagued its customers' computer networks last year were due to software bugs.[8]

Many computer-security experts say that software manufacturers know about most of these flaws before they put their products on the market. Mark Minasi, an investigative journalist who specializes in technology issues, claims that 90 percent of the bugs that consumers report to software vendors were already known to the vendors at the time of release.[9] Yet, many studies have found that businesses and government agencies that have been attacked via these types of software security gaps have incurred billions of dollars in damages.[10]

There are no laws requiring software vendors to manufacture hack-proof or virus-resistant products. Likewise, no software company has ever been held responsible for damages stemming from a known security flaw in a product. Software vendors have long avoided this type of liability by inserting disclaimers in the so-called end-user licensing agreements (EULAs) that customers must consent to before using a product. In general, EULAs require users to assume all risks associated with the product. The EULA for Microsoft's Windows 2000 operating system is typical of this type of liability waiver. It states, in part:

"In no event shall Microsoft or its suppliers be liable for any damages whatsoever . . . arising out of the use of or inability to use the software product, even if Microsoft has been advised of the possibility of such damages."[11]

Given the crucial role that software plays in the modern world, many computer-security experts say it's high time that software companies take responsibility for producing hack-prone products.

"Software is deployed in places where it's absolutely critical for safety, like in much of our infrastructure," says Hunger of SecurityFocus. "It's totally unreasonable to give software vendors immunity from liability when every other industry— the Fords and the Boeings of the world—are held to a much, much higher standard."

Some legal experts predict that consumers will use the courts to force software vendors to accept liability for unsafe products, as occurred with the tobacco industry. "I think where you're going to see reform come is through lawsuits," said Jeffrey Hunker, dean of the H. John Heinz III School of Public Policy and Management at Carnegie Mellon University in Pittsburgh. "So much of our economic structure depends on computers that it's unsustainable to hold software companies blameless."[12]

Microsoft continues to oppose efforts to make software vendors liable for security breaches.

However, CEO Bill Gates says security is now the company's highest priority. In a Jan. 15 e-mail to all Microsoft employees, Gates launched the company's "trust-worthy computing" initiative, which he described as "more important than any other part of our work. Our products should emphasize security right out of the box, and we must constantly refine and improve that security as threats evolve. Eventually, our software should be so fundamentally secure that customers never even worry about it."[13]

"Issuing a statement doesn't solve any problems," said Schneier of Counterpane Internet Security. "Microsoft is notorious for treating security as a public-relations problem. Gates said all the right words. If he does that, it will be a sea change. I'd like to believe him, but I need proof."[14]

NOTES

1. "Internet Security Threat Report," *Riptech, Inc.,* February 2002. For related coverage, see Brian Hansen, "Cyber-Predators," *The CQ Researcher,* March 1, 2002, pp. 169–192, and Ellen Perlman, "Digital Nightmare," *Governing*, April 2002, pp. 20–24.

2. "Computer Crime and Security Survey 2001," Computer Security Institute (CSI) and Federal Bureau of Investigation (FBI), January 2002.

3. Quoted in Linden MacIntyre, "Hackers," PBS *Frontline,* Feb. 13, 2001.

4. Top 10 Consumer Fraud Complaints of 2001, Federal Trade Commission, Jan. 23, 2002.

5. "Identity Theft and Its Effect on the Financial Services Industry," Celent Communications, September 2001.

6. U.S. Census Bureau, *Current Population Survey,* September 2001.

7. GartnerG2, "Privacy and Security: The Hidden Growth Strategy," August 2000.

8. From "The Injustice of Insecure Software," @Stake white paper, February 2002.

9. Mark Minasi, *The Software Conspiracy: Why Companies Put Out Faulty Software, How They Can Hurt You and What You Can Do about It* (1999).

10. See, for example, CSI and FBI, *op. cit.,* and "Security Review 2002," Computer Economics Inc., 2002.

11. From "End-User License Agreement for Microsoft Software," as posted on Microsoft's Web site.

12. Quoted in Dennis Fisher, "Software Liability Gaining Attention," *Eweek,* Jan. 14, 2002.

13. Bill Gates, "Trustworthy Computing" memo, Jan. 15, 2002, as posted on Microsoft's Web site.

14. Quoted in Kristi Helm and Elise Ackerman, "Gates Makes Security Top Focus," *The San Jose Mercury,* Jan. 17, 2002.

REVIEW QUESTIONS

1. Some would argue that some computer-related crimes should carry a life-in-prison sentence. Do you agree or disagree with this suggestion? Defend your answer.

2. Discuss three types of cyber-crimes.

LET YOUR FINGERS DO THE TALKING: SEX ON AN ADULT CHAT LINE

DIANE KHOLOS WYSOCKI

Interpersonal relationships have changed at a dramatic rate during the late twentieth century, with the advancement of technology and the emergence of the "information society" (Ryan, 1997). The increased availability of technological products such as computers, modems, computer bulletin boards (BBS), and the Internet, along with their declining prices, have had a dramatic effect on social life as we have known it. While in the comfort of home or office, social networks have increased, new online communities have emerged, individuals have met their spouses or partners, and even fulfilled their deepest sexual fantasies.

The purpose of this paper is twofold: to examine . . . why individuals participate in sexually explicit computer bulletin boards; and to see if sex on-line is a way of *replacing* face-to-face relationships or a way of *enhancing* them. This analysis focuses on the social construction of love and sexuality and uses a sexually explicit computer BBS that I have called *Pleasure Pit* as the source for contacting individuals who combine their technological abilities with their sexual desires. . . .

MOTIVES FOR ON-LINE SEXUAL ACTIVITY

Five basic reasons were reported by the respondents of this study for using sexually explicit BBS.

As shown in Figure 39.1, the reasons most commonly given for taking part in sex on-line were due to the need for anonymity, time constraints in their personal life, the ability to share sexual fantasies with other people, to participate in on-line sexual activity, and to meet other people with similar sexual interests.

Anonymity

As expected, respondents stated they participated in sexually explicit BBS because they were able to take on whatever persona they liked. . . . In other words, individuals using computer BBS have the opportunity to be whoever they want to be because the computer "provides ample room for individuals to express unexplored parts of themselves" (Turkle, 1995: 185). The users can take on a different identity and portray themselves as that person or persons. If they are too shy and/ or are unable to be comfortable meeting people face-to-face, the computer provides the physical barrier and anonymity which enables the users to meet new people and communicate from a distance. For instance, a 29-year-old female, states that

they [other BBS users] can get to know me, faults and all, and vice versa, without too much pressure.

Source: Diane Kholos Wysocki, "Let Your Fingers Do the Talking: Sex on an Adult Chat Line," *Sexualities,* vol. 1 (1998), pp. 425–452. Reprinted with permission.

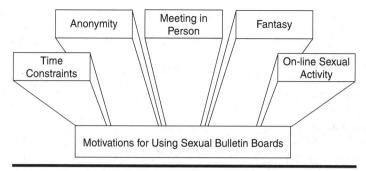

FIGURE 39.1   Motivations for Using Sexual Computer Bulletin Boards

It is also a great way to weed out the scary ones [individuals] . . . no one can hide behind their words for long . . . I have met more people on-line than through traditional methods.

According to Goffman (1963), when individuals possess attributes that discredit them in the eyes of others, it can greatly affect their self concept of themselves and the way they interact with other people. The anonymity of the BBS is one way in which individuals can conceal themselves in order to avoid receiving the negative reaction of others. The computer provides the perfect shield against stigma. A single male wrote that since he was shy, e-mail "provided a curtain to hide behind." Similarly, Fred stated he has had more opportunities to talk to people on-line than he does off-line. In fact, he said:

I am a little more shy face-to-face, but I'm working on it. On-line, you can talk to someone without worrying about how you are dressed or undressed, what you look like. All the other person can see is what you want them too. I'm very open on the boards [BBS] . . . for some it's just a fantasy life and the people aren't usually anything like they are in person. I am, I'm just the same, just a little more shy in person.

Some respondents, especially women, mentioned they felt they were fat and undesirable in person. On the BBS, they stated they felt completely different; they felt young, wanted, slim, and sexual.

Too Many Time Constraints

Another reason respondents stated they used sexually explicit BBS was due to the many time constraints in their lives. Some mentioned they had very little time in their busy schedules to pursue friendships or sexual contacts on a face-to-face basis. Traditional face-to-face relationships of any kind develop through a pool of "eligibles" who are involved in close proximity to one another (Michael et al., 1994). However, there are many constraints to finding a person with similar sexual ideas and desires within close social networks. According to Michael et al. (1994: 153) it is "difficult to find a sexual partner who, right off the bat, has the same sexual preferences as you have. If you desire anything but vaginal sex or, perhaps, oral sex, it will be hard to find a partner with your tastes." The respondents in this study stated the same thing. They believed it took too much time and was almost impossible to meet people with similar sexual interests and therefore the computer was the best way to handle this dilemma. A 41-year-old married man said he uses e-mail and BBS to meet people for sex because of the "immediacy of sexual conversation. Real life sexual relationships require a lot of small talk first." Paula, a single female who said she was in a face-to-face relationship with a man, considered the BBS as the "preliminary foreplay leading to real sex with swinging heterosexual couples who are real and sensitive." Paula was interested in trying new sexual behaviors, such as having sex with other couples, engaging in sex with women, and watching other people having sex. Paula believed she would not have found couples who shared her similar interests if she had not been on-line looking for sexual sharing.

Sharing Sexual Fantasies

The views most commonly held about sex are formed at a very early age and are dependent upon the dominant views held by groups we associate with and society as a whole (Rubin, 1990). Any sexual activity that is not heterosexually oriented and geared towards reproduction traditionally has been considered to be against the *ideal* norms of society (D'Emillio and Freedman, 1988), which makes it difficult for some to share sexual fantasies and interests with those in the *face-to-face* world. David stated he would never be the type to go to bars hoping to find some kind of (sexual) action, but wanted a friend with whom he could talk and have sex. He also said he had some sexual fantasies he was unwilling to share with his wife and had found the BBS was a safe way to ask for what he was really interested in. David was very specific about what he was looking for:

I want a special woman who can understand and handle it when I want to wear nylons, panties, etc. . . . one who would not mind strapping on a dildo and say giving me a work-out . . . one who would let me watch her please herself as well as watch me put on a show for her . . . also a male who would like to try a few safe fantasies together . . . no strings attached . . . just pure pleasure. . . .

A bisexual male stated that his:

on-line friends are safe and we should all be able to have fun with no guilt feelings . . . if people have fantasies and their spouse doesn't want to hear them or do them . . . well what's the harm if we do it on the BBS . . . we are all adults.

On-Line Sexual Behavior

Sexually explicit material, such as videos, books, or magazines, are just a few of the outlets for people to find out about new sexual acts and develop new fantasies and ideas. Traditionally, this material has been geared towards the heterosexual male and has included scantily dressed or nude women in all kinds of poses or sexual acts; now sexual material has been made available for people with all kinds of sexual interests. Reading stories and looking at sexually explicit pictures typically has been known as "material to masturbate by." Whereas masturbation used to be considered dangerous and apt to "destroy both the body and the mind" of the individual (D'Emillio and Freedman, 1988:69), it is currently taught as an accepted practice and takes place on a regular basis for many individuals (Michael et al., 1994).

With all this in mind, it should be no surprise that computers, e-mail, and various BBS have provided outlets for people interested in fulfilling their sexual fantasies. It is easier than meeting someone face-to-face and trying to decide if that person would experience the same sexual interests. For instance, if two people meet on a BBS conference for bondage, they already know that each has some interest in that kind of sexual activity and are able to divulge their fantasies early in the "relationship." If they like one another, they could then act out their sexual fantasy on-line.

On *Pleasure Pit,* one of the most common ways sex on-line happened was that the individuals went into chat mode and in "real time" typed out a fantasy with each other or a group of people.

The sex act was accomplished by typing out in detail what each person could be doing to the other. Nate, a man who is getting married and whose significant other knows about his on-line escapades, stated he had sex on-line and "loved it." It began with "me and this lady talking and she then called my computer, and we told each other what we looked like and then we started with . . . well, what we wanted to do with each other and then acted it out with words." Nate said he didn't masturbate during this because he "loves the real thing, but it was fun to role play."

Most often the act of having "sex" on-line involved masturbation for the users and ended usually in an orgasm. One female stated that she had "sex" on-line quite frequently and she said:

> I love it when the guy gets off . . . it starts with teasing and flirting . . . leads to more . . . I usually rub my clit and we eventually get off . . . I most often am wearing a mini skirt or nude and it goes from there . . . it is planned sometimes, most often not . . . usually the men are on-line for a hot chat and wanting to cumm [sic]. . . .

Meeting the Sexual Fantasy Person of Your Dreams

Meeting the perfect sexual partner is not always easy. If individuals were looking for someone who could fulfill their sexual fantasies off-line, they needed to be able to meet someone who expressed similar sexual interests. It was also difficult for most people to discuss sexual fantasies with someone face-to-face because it meant risking rejection (Culbert, 1968). . . .

On the other hand, relationships that develop over BBS appear to be much easier for people. They are able to get to know one another without inhibitions and share their sexual fantasies with their on-line partners. They meet on "conferences" where they are more likely to have similar sexual interests. Sexually explicit BBS discussions tend to move very quickly since both people divulge their fantasies early in the "relationship." . . .

After meeting on-line and finding they have similar sexual interests, the individuals decide whether to meet one another face-to-face. If they meet, the physical characteristics are then revealed and the individuals decide whether to continue or discontinue the relationship based on the physical characteristics they display. If they decide not to meet one another on a face-to-face basis, they still have the option of continuing to correspond via computer. . . .

Many of the respondents stated they were quite willing to meet and have sex with another willing partner either over BBS or in person if the chance arose. Over 57 percent stated they had already met someone face-to-face with whom they became involved as a result of meeting through *Pleasure Pit*. Most stated the experiences went well for them. A single man who claimed to be bisexual went to the park and met his on-line friend, but said "nothing happened" after that. A woman, who was married and claimed to be heterosexual stated that she met "many nice couples and single males." Another male who stated he was bisexual and married met people from the BBS and "had at one time a bi encounter . . . that was great [and] would do it again with the right person . . . would like to meet an understanding female for special encounters." Another single female found that "2 guys were WONDERFUL! nice, good-looking, funny, friendly, great." However, she also found "two guys were fat, lied about [their] looks, shy, 1 of them is obsessed with me and the rest (8 or 9) are normal, everyday nice people." . . .

SIGNIFICANT OTHERS

Although most spouses or partners knew their significant other had been using the computer, very few knew exactly what their partners were doing and that the computer was being used as a sexual outlet. One respondent stated he communicated with other people sexually at work or when his wife was not at home. Others logged on after their partners went to bed at night. Another respondent stated he had a laptop and "unless you're looking straight at it is hard to see." This same respondent said he was "hoping to get lucky and of course I don't want her to know." Yet another respondent said he "does all my BBS work at the office . . . don't want the headaches of explaining my fantasies to my wife."

Other times, the significant other knew their partner was on-line, but not that so much time and money was being spent on the X-rated BBS. One respondent stated his wife and he

> were married young and no matter what we really haven't been able to relax with each other. . . . I'm always told she has no fantasies and she has never masturbated. I've tried a couple of times to relax her and masturbate her, but it just seems like it can't be. . . . I'm sure it's not what I'm doing cause I've done this with other women and both have enjoyed it . . . also phone sex with my wife . . . we used to do it when I was gone or working the all day shifts, but that too has stopped . . . she is going through a lot of changes and guess maybe I am also . . . but the bottom line is that I do need and want sex, either on phone or in flesh with a special friend. . . .

Jan, a 30-year-old married female, stated:

> just access the BBS when he [her husband] is not here or sleeping, Why? Because of our relationship. I don't want him to have the access to the email. I have little sexual contact with my husband. I want to look at pics of naked men for some stimulation.

The mass media commonly has stories about love and lust on-line and about couples who have gone off to live happily ever after (Kerr, 1993; Edwards, 1994). However, the other side of these stories is that some individuals spent endless amounts of time on-line, withdrew themselves from communicating at home, and became involved in a cybersexual romance with someone other than their partner. Some respondents stated they were having trouble with their face-to-face relationships because of their sexual computer use. One man stated his ex-wife met some friends on *Pleasure Pit,* and then their relationship broke up. . . .

SUMMARY

. . . [T]his study of adult sexual relationships over a sexually explicit BBS found people used it for many different reasons. The most common reason given was that the respondents had specific fantasies and desires that were not being fulfilled in their relationships off-line. Some of the respondents stated they did not have the time it took in off-line relationships to get to know one another and see if they had similar sexual interests. It became much easier to go to a "conference" set up for specific pleasures, such as S&M, and know that the people participating in that "conference" have some interest in the subject or they probably would not be there.

The anonymity of the BBS also seemed to be an attraction to many of the users. They felt they could be more open and direct without having face-to-face interactions. Many stated they could say things to other people about their sexual needs and fantasies that they would not think of saying to someone they knew face-to-face or even to their spouse or significant other. Computer BBS just seemed to make self-disclosure much easier, and therefore reversed the order of the relationship. When people first meet in face-to-face relationships they look at the character of the individual to see how they are displayed (clothing, ethnicity, class) and then they decide whether to continue. In on-line relationships, the order is reversed. Once the BBS users had developed a relationship on-line, even if it was relatively new, the people involved sometimes met to have "real" sex. Ultimately individuals got to know each other much better and quicker, based on actual characteristics. Rather than face-to-face relationships being replaced by computers, the computer BBS has worked as a way of enhancing the face-to-face relationships in some cases. Often the ultimate goal of meeting on-line for many individuals on this BBS was to meet in person. Therefore, the BBS and face-to-face encounters work together in a common enterprise to enhance interpersonal relationships.

REFERENCES

Culbert, Samual Alan (1968) *The Interpersonal Process of Self-Disclosure: It Takes Two to See One.* New York: Renaissance Editions.

D'Emillio, John, and Freedman, Estelle (1988) *Intimate Matters: A History of Sexuality in America.* New York: Harper & Row.

Edwards, Cliff (1994) "Computer Dating: New Bar Scene in Your Own Home," *Santa Barbara News Press* (23 Jan.): D4.

Goffman, Erving (1963) *Stigma: Notes on the Management of Spoiled Identity.* Englewood Cliffs, NJ: Prentice-Hall.

Kerr, Robert (1993) "Digital Age Couples Meet via On-Line Dates," *Rocky Mountain News* (16 Nov.): 5D.

Michael, Robert, Gagnon, John, Laumann, Edward, and Kolata, Gina (1994) *Sex in America: A Definitive Survey.* New York: Warner Books.

Rubin, Lillian (1990) *Erotic Wars: What Happened to the Sexual Revolution.* New York: Farrar, Straus & Giroux.

Ryan, Alan (1997) "Exaggerated Hopes and Baseless Fears: Technology and the Rest of Culture," *Social Research* 65 (3): 1167–91.

Turkle, Sherry (1995) *Life on the Screen: Identity in the Age of the Internet.* New York: Simon & Schuster.

REVIEW QUESTIONS

1. Identify and discuss three of the five reasons for online sex given by the people Wysocki interviewed.

2. What are some strategies used by the subjects in this article to hide their behavior from significant others?

CHILD PORN ON THE NET: PERPETUATING A CYCLE OF ABUSE

ETHEL QUAYLE
MAX TAYLOR

The ways that people use pornography on the Internet have largely focussed on sexual gratification, as a tool in molestation, as a means of locating children, and as a social consolidation mechanism (Durkin 1997). This paper seeks to examine the accounts of those convicted of downloading pornography in order to further our understanding of the complex relationship between those who are sexually interested in children and the Internet. What are explored are the different discourses that emerge when these respondents talk about child pornography, and the role that the Internet plays in such discourses. Above all, this study recognizes the central significance of meaning for the individual in understanding the role of child pornography.

. . . The data is drawn from semi-structured interviews with 13 men, all of whom had been convicted of possessing illegal and obscene images of children on their computers (see Taylor et al. 2001 for further discussion of this). While preferences were shown for certain images over others, all participants had viewed similar images (as identified by forensic evidence). Of these men, four also were convicted of assault on children, three had been involved in assaults prior to accessing pornography on the Internet, and two had produced pornographic pictures of children which had not been traded. The men came from a variety of demographic backgrounds and varied in terms of both current judicial status and engagement with treatment programs. The respondents were accessed through probation, police, social work, and voluntary agencies. All were approached prior to the interview, were given information about the study, and gave their consent. The data set is part of a much larger, ongoing series of interviews and was chosen because the subjects had all used the Internet to download child pornography. The interviews, each lasting approximately two hours, were recorded using a mini-disc system and then transcribed. All identifying names were removed or changed to ensure anonymity and the transcripts were kept in a secure environment. The first author both interviewed the respondents and transcribed the data.

. . . Six principal discourses relating to the ways that respondents used child pornography emerged during the analysis, and are discussed below under discourse headings.

CHILD PORNOGRAPHY AND SEXUAL AROUSAL

The most dominant discourse to emerge in the analysis was that of child pornography as a means

Source: Ethel Quayle and Max Taylor, "Child Pornography and the Internet: Perpetuating a Cycle of Abuse," *Deviant Behavior,* vol. 23 (2002), pp. 331–361. Reproduced by permission from Taylor and Francis, Inc., http://www.routledge–ny.com.

of achieving sexual arousal. Some (but not all) of the pictures that were accessed were used for masturbatory purposes, and respondents were selective in the pictures they used. Such selectivity might relate to specific age groups, physical types, gender of the child, or to a particular sexual activity. For example,

> Developing girls . . . just starting to get pubic hair and just starting to develop breasts . . . my preference was for younger people (O.K.).

Such pictures were used as an aid to fantasy:

> Fantasies . . . it would basically run like I take a young girl on a date . . . and then we'd go home and then she'd we'd . . . you know the stuff that adults do which would lead to sex and would involve her masturbating me and then me giving her oral sex (Q.H.).

This invariably, but not exclusively, involved masturbation to the fantasies:

> Because if I was on-line for an hour or so I actually would be masturbating on and off for an hour . . . and wanting to . . . maintain the sense of arousal . . . trying not to come (I.I.).

Claims were made that masturbation to child pornography was a substitute for abuse:

> Our main aim in collecting the child pornography is that we weren't involved with kids . . . it was helping . . . I didn't feel the urge as strongly as I do now to try and start something with a child . . . when I was on-line with the child porn . . . because when I felt that urge I'd look at the child porn I'd masturbate or I'd read the stories more often and masturbate . . . and it was under control (E.I.).

CHILD PORNOGRAPHY AS COLLECTIBLES

The discourse of collecting and its importance for respondents overlapped with but was not subsumed by discourses of arousal. Pleasure was obtained from collecting pictures as part of a series,

even when the material was not attractive or sexually arousing:

> Some of them I didn't much care for at all . . . but as I say they were part of a series or they were there for other people or they were just to see what was out there . . . I mean it gets to a stage also where you're just collecting to see how many different ones you can get and this sort of thing and you're not . . . necessarily aroused or turned on by all the pictures that are coming in . . . (O.K.).

Such pictures were often talked about in a very dispassionate way with no reference made to the fact that they were pictures of children. This is seen both in comparisons made to other kinds of collections and in terms used to describe the pictures themselves:

> We were trading pictures . . . it's, as much as it pains me to say . . . kinda like trading baseball cards (Q.H.).

> And there was also the thrill in collecting them. You wanted to get complete sets so it . . . was a bit like stamp collecting as well (E.I.).

Comparisons between baseball cards and stamps also served to normalize the activity, and made it appear innocent in its intent. When talking about the pictures, invariably no reference was made to the content as being child pornography.

CHILD PORNOGRAPHY FACILITATING SOCIAL RELATIONSHIPS

. . . When on-line, those who traded images inevitably came into social contact with others similarly engaged, and clearly this was very important to some respondents:

> Pornography was there almost as much to facilitate the on-line relationship as an end in itself (I.I.).

Clearly such [relationship] was reinforced by having material to trade, by behaving correctly, and by following the rules for trading. Once status had been achieved through membership of the group, trading reduced and, instead, the social function of the on-line exchanges and the ability to be on the inside and obtain special photographs was more important:

> *There was less and less trading going on because a lot of us by now had most of what we were interested in from each other's collections. And there were very few new people or producers. I mean Paul was one and I was one of the few people he trusted enough to give everything that he was making with his kids (E.I.).*

E.I.'s friendship with Paul gave him status but it also allowed him to access new pictures as they were being produced as well as giving him contact with Paul's children. The latter served to enable his sexual fantasies. The notion of community in relation to the pornography was reinforced by the metaphor of club or bar with reference to virtual space:

> *I mean the times when I would . . . stay up all night swapping pics with people were long gone. All I did, basically, I was a bartender . . . I was serving drinks and what not (Q.H.).*

This analogy is an interesting one because it emphasized the idea of the community as a club, giving people what they wanted and ensuring that everything was running smoothly. Again, we have the idea of child pornography as having some equivalence with alcohol—a commodity to enable social exchange. . . .

CHILD PORNOGRAPHY AS A WAY OF AVOIDING REAL LIFE

It is interesting that for many respondents, linking up with others on the Internet provided important social support that often replaced unsatisfactory relationships in the real world:

> *I wanted sex all the time . . . and you know I had a very high sex . . . and I wasn't getting as much sex as I want off my wife (D.X.).*

Accessing child pornography on the Internet became part of a bid to create a secret and separate world:

> *It was a little fantasy world for me . . . and it was so different from the mundane existence I'd been leading. Here was something that was dangerous . . . it was exciting . . . it was new (I.I.).*

Clearly this cyber world had many qualities that were unobtainable in the real world and allowed escape from many unpleasant realities:

> *I think it mattered to the extent that it shut out the . . . part of my life that I was finding difficult to deal with . . . it was sort of my time, it was my space . . . I got to the stage where I started to feel . . . annoyed if I felt . . . other people were intruding on that (M.Q.).*

This could be taken in a very literal way in that M.Q. was able to physically remove himself into the room where they kept the computer and where he could access his own files. He was also able to emotionally shut himself off from a situation that was becoming increasingly aversive and achieve pleasure and escape through sexual arousal and masturbation.

ACCESSING CHILD PORNOGRAPHY AS THERAPY

. . . Some respondents made claim to actively seeking pornographic images as a way of controlling their interests:

> *I really wanted to find out about myself as well . . . in a sense I wanted to know . . . what I was about . . . what was it that I . . . that actually turned me on and . . . perhaps in the process deal with it . . . accept it and then move on (M.Q.).*

What was prioritized were his needs, his feeling of wanting to explore the nature of the problem. The children in the pictures had a function only in so far as they were meeting this need. They are almost incidental to the process. The idea of self-exploration was also seen in talk about examining the "dark side" of one's personality.

At its most extreme, accessing child pornography was seen as a form of personal survival:

I was aroused by some of the pictures . . . some of the images I wasn't aroused by . . . you know I was just desperate to find some way of getting out of the shit life that I was in (K.Q.).

It was the only thing that was remotely keeping me alive at that point cause I could escape on it. I could play games and look at child porn (E.I.).

Child pornography was a way of dealing with emotions, such as anger, that had no other outlet:

I think certainly they precipitated it yeah . . . and I started downloading child pornography . . . one it was getting the anger out of my system and saying "up yours" to the police . . . and two it was a way of relieving the pressure (O.T.).

CHILD PORNOGRAPHY AS EASILY ACCESSIBLE VIA THE INTERNET

. . . It is clear that the Internet facilitated access to photographs, whether adventitiously or purposefully:

The children side of it came into being when I discovered this stuff on the Internet (K.Q.).

Accessing such material was possible because the Internet as a medium was anonymous and because there was an enormous variety of pornography freely available:

So I then got into this kind of regime of finding hard core porn . . . the sort that if I had . . . the nerve I would have bought a magazine that showed this kind of material in a shop, but then there'd be the problem of sneaking the magazine back into the house and then accessing that material privately (I.I.).

A chain of responses also was associated with the Internet, leading to more and more extreme material, even when that material was not kept for personal collections or for trading:

It seemed to be getting younger and younger . . . as the more I got into the sites and more I diversified the more you could . . . you know . . . the harder the pornography got . . . seemed to be getting harder and harder (D.X.).

What we see here is the use of the passive voice in relation to the Internet, as if the responsibility lies with it as a medium. What is apparent is that with the Internet access is rapid and for those interested, child pornography can be found very quickly (which would not be the case from more conventional sources). Inevitably, the more the respondent used the computer as a means of accessing pornography, the more skillful he became in finding material and getting round any security checks.

CONCLUSION

What emerged from these accounts is that child pornography downloaded from the Internet does act as a means of sexual arousal and is used as an aid to masturbation both on and off-line, and that for the majority of respondents in this sample it resulted in an increase in masturbatory behavior. This is similar to the findings of Hamman (1996) in the context of cybersex on the Internet. Respondents were highly selective in the material they chose, seeking out content that was arousing for them and which fit with individual fantasies. . . . Again, one aspect of Internet use is that respondents could largely ensure privacy, which may facilitate immediate sexual behavior. Given the scope of child pornography available on the Internet, none of the respondents had difficulty in finding material that met their sexual proclivities.

The Internet clearly plays an important role in collecting behavior related to child pornography, and here we see a function that overlaps with that of sexual arousal. Material is often collected even when it has no arousing properties for the individual but because it is part of a series or is new. Collections can be correspondingly large, because the bulk of child pornography on the Internet is free and also because respondents often acquired the technological skills to use software that allowed them to download without them having to be physically present. . . .

Discourse about child pornography and social relationships is almost exclusively seen in the context of trading and using [Internet chat]. Such social relationships are bound by rules and have all the qualities of community outlined by Linehan et al. (in press). Pornography played a role in such communities because status was reflected in volume, having parts of missing series, and distributing these and new images through the Internet. Social relationships allowed respondents to normalize their activities, consolidating a body of accounts which allowed others to justify or legitimize their orientation and behavior (Durkin and Bryant 1999). Such legitimizing activity is also heightened by the metaphor of the Internet as a physical space, a bar, or a museum, where the commodity is pornography rather than alcohol or art.

Morahan-Martin and Schumacher (2000) talk about the Internet as providing an attractive alternative to a mundane or unhappy life. Certainly, for these respondents, accessing child pornography on the Internet was often used as a way of creating a private and intensely arousing world, where it was possible to go beyond normal limits. Such a world was often associated initially with feelings of regaining control, but this quickly changed and was followed by frequent reference to loss of control and addiction.

At its most benign, the Internet facilitates access to a wide variety of child pornography. Tate (1990) suggests that the particular advantage of the Internet to the pedophile is its security, as a lifetime's collection can be hidden on a small amount of electric gadgetry, stacking the odds heavily against discovery. The Internet also functions in such a way that there are constant links to other sites, some of which are signaled by the word "illegal," and that these in turn act as a discriminative stimulus for accessing more and more extreme material. Frequent reference was made by respondents to the pictures being of younger and younger children, or of more extreme activities. It may be that the quest for newness and difference and the rapidity of habituation is exaggerated on the Internet because of the shear volume of material available and the amount of time that downloaders spend with it.

REFERENCES

Durkin, K. 1997. "Misuse of the Internet by Pedophiles: Implications for Law Enforcement and Probation Practice." *Federal Probation 61*(2): 14–18.

Durkin, K., and C. Bryant. 1999. "Propagandizing Pederasty: A Thematic Analysis of the On-Line Exculpatory Accounts of Unrepentant Pedophiles." *Deviant Behavior* 20: 103–27.

Hamman, R. 1996. "Cyborgasms: An Ethnography of Cybersex in AOL Chatrooms." Master's dissertation, University of Essex. Available: http://www.cybersoc.com

Linehan, C., E. Quayle, G. Holland, and M. Taylor. (in press). "Virtual Paedophile Communities." *The Journal of Sexual Aggression.*

Morahan-Martin, J., and P. Schumacher. 2000. "Incidence and Correlates of Pathological Internet Use among College Students." *Computers in Human Behaviour* 16: 13–29.

Tate, T. 1990. *Child Pornography.* St. Ives: Methuen.

Taylor, M., E. Quayle, and G. Holland. 2001. "Child Pornography, the Internet and Offending." *Isuma* 2(2): 94–100.

REVIEW QUESTIONS_____

1. After reading "Our main aim in collecting the child pornography is that we weren't involved with kids . . . it was helping . . . I didn't feel the urge as strongly as I do now to try and start something with a child," do you think that child pornography can serve as a substitute for abuse?
2. Do you believe that men should be convicted of a crime just for possessing obscene pictures of children on their computers? Why or why not?

ON-LINE ACCOUNTS OF
UNREPENTANT PEDOPHILES

KEITH F. DURKIN
CLIFTON D. BRYANT

Adults who engage in sexual activity with children, or possess such a sexual orientation, are considered to be among the most serious deviants in our society. Such contacts are illegal everywhere in the United States. Pedophiles, unlike some other varieties of deviants, enjoy almost no social support. None of the 2,753 respondents to a recent national survey indicated that they believed it was "normal" or "all right" for adults to have sexual contact with children (Janus and Janus 1993). The prospect of adults engaging in sexual activity with children "inspires an innate disgust in most people" (Finkelhor 1979:693). Pedophiles are "considered to be among the most degenerate" of all deviants (Bryant 1982:332). In fact, they are even disvalued by other deviants. In prison, "pedophiles occupy the lowest rung of the inmate social system" (Heitzeg 1996:325). The especially strong societal condemnation of pedophilia raises an important sociological question: How do pedophiles manage such a disvalued identity?

Currently, there is a growing societal concern over the use of the Internet by pedophiles. These individuals are using this computer network to transmit child pornography, to locate children to molest, and to communicate with other pedophiles (Durkin 1997). There have also been reports of adult men masquerading as children and entering computer chat rooms that are frequented by youngsters to engage in sexually oriented discussions or "cybersex" with these children (Lamb 1998). Although the use of the Internet by pedophiles presents serious social problems, it also provides new possibilities for sociological investigations of pedophilia.

Pedophilia has been the topic of a plethora of studies conducted by psychologists, psychiatrists, sociologists, sexologists, and criminologists. However, this previous research has been widely criticized on methodological grounds. Critics have pointed to the fact that not even a single investigation has used a potentially representative sample of pedophiles (Okami and Goldberg 1992). These studies typically used samples of individuals who were incarcerated for committing sexual offenses or who were receiving mental health treatment. However, those samples are biased and lack generalizability. The subjects included in those studies constitute "at most a very tiny and unrepresentative sample" of all pedophiles (Finkelhor 1986:138). Therefore, there are a large number of pedophiles about whom little is known.

The data for this study were gathered from a Usenet discussion group composed of pedophiles, alt.support.boy-lovers. Scott and Lyman's (1968)

Source: Keith F. Durkin and Clifton D. Bryant, "Propagandizing Pederasty: A Thematic Analysis of the On-line Exculpatory Accounts of Unrepentant Pedophiles," *Deviant Behavior,* vol. 20 (1999), pp. 103–127. Reproduced by permission of Taylor & Francis., Inc., http://www.routledge–ny.com.

classic formulation of accounts served as the conceptual framework for this study. The guiding research question was this: How do pedophiles who use the Internet account for their deviance? The accounts framework affords an effective conceptual tool for examining pedophiles and the attitudes that they hold in regard to their deviant orientation and behavior. . . .

METHOD

The data were gathered from a Usenet newsgroup composed of pedophiles, alt.support-boy.lovers. Users of this newsgroup can read and post messages. These postings are organized in an archival fashion. These messages can be downloaded to a personal computer and sent directly to a printer. Consequently, messages can be printed for content analysis. There are approximately 5 to 10 new messages posted daily. There are between 150 and 200 messages posted to the newsgroup each month. These postings range in length from several sentences to several paragraphs.

We performed content analysis on all of the postings to the Usenet newsgroup alt.support.boy-lovers for a period of one month. There were a total of 154 postings from 80 individuals that appeared on the newsgroup during this time period. Ninety-three of these postings were contributed by 41 users who are admitted pedophiles. These 93 postings constituted the data that were analyzed for this undertaking. Slightly more than half (51 percent) of the individuals who posted to the newsgroup during the month were admitted pedophiles. These individuals contributed 60 percent of the postings for this time period. The unit of analysis for this undertaking was the individual pedophile (i.e., the posters). The postings of each of the admitted pedophiles were examined to determine the presence or absence of [the following accounts]:

Account offered—the posting contains some type of explanation offered in defense of pedophilia or adults having sexual contact with children.

Condemnation of condemners—the poster attempts to shift the focus from pedophiles and their behavior to the actions of those who condemn them. Targets of condemnation may include law enforcement officers, social workers, psychologists, psychiatrists, and others.

Denial of injury—the poster claims that adults engaging in sexual contact with children does not cause harm to children. It may involve a claim of benefit assertion.

Claim of benefit—this particular account is an extension of the denial of injury account. The poster goes a step beyond simply asserting that adult–child sex does not harm the child and claims that such behavior is actually beneficial for the child involved.

Appeal to loyalties—the poster attempts to justify pedophilia and adult–child sex by claims of an allegiance to "children's liberation" or "children's rights."

[Basking in reflected glory of others]—the poster makes the assertion that "great men" have also been pedophiles.

Polythematic account—the posting contains an appeal to more than one defensibility. It includes any combination of the following accounts: condemnation of condemners, appeal to loyalties, denial of injury, and [basking in reflected glory of others].

RESULTS

The number and percentage of pedophiles in this sample who offered each of the various accounts are reported in Table 40.1. Slightly more than one half (53.7 percent) of these 41 pedophiles proffered some type of account in defense of pedophilia or adults engaging in sexual activity with children. The most common type of account offered by the pedophiles in this sample was denial of injury. Thirty-nine percent provided this type of account which consisted of the assertion that sexual contact with adults does not cause harm to children. For instance, one poster, who was

Table 40.1 Number and Percentage of Pedophiles Offering Each
of the Various Types of Accounts

ACCOUNT	NUMBERING OFFERING	PERCENTAGE OFFERING
Any type of account	22	53.7
Denial of injury	16	39.0
Condemnation of condemners	13	31.7
Polythematic account	10	24.4
Basking in reflected glory	6	14.6
Claim of benefit	4	9.8
Appeal to loyalties	2	4.9

speaking of his sexual relationships with boys, wrote, "The experiences were always mutual and I don't feel/think those [boys] were mentally damaged by this as many people believe." Another pedophile asserted that: "I don't see anything wrong with a teenager having a sexual relationship with an adult providing both are consenting and that there is some sort of friendship for this closeness to be based on."

The next most popular account, condemnation of condemners, was offered by nearly one third (31.7 percent) of the pedophiles in this sample. This involved shifting the focus from pedophiles to those who would condemn them, such as law enforcement officers, social workers, mental health professionals, and parents. Interestingly, gay men were also the target of condemnation. Some of the pedophiles who use this newsgroup had apparently argued that they were an oppressed sexual minority similar to homosexual men. They had made these claims on computer newsgroups dedicated to discussions of homosexuality. In response, several gay men had posted messages on alt.support.boy-lovers claiming that the behavior of pedophiles is aberrant and has nothing to do with homosexuality. One of the pedophiles responded,

Oh wow, you're a good homosexual. You should be accepted by society. And in many countries you will indeed. You might even find yourself integrated in society as being a homosexual.

No, you don't want to be classified in the same category as those nasty, tasteless, and horrible pedophiles. You don't like the young boys so you don't even want to think about those pedophile bastards. Come on you guys! What was the situation about half a century ago? Homosexuals were in the same position as pedophiles are nowadays. People looked upon homosexuals as being nasty, tasteless, and horrible bastards. Now YOU are doing the same towards another group. You're right: pedophiles aren't in the same group, but a little bit of understanding is the least pedophiles could expect from previously repressed groups.

Approximately 15 percent of the pedophiles in the sample offered a ["basking in reflected glory"] account. This involved the claim that great men have also been pedophiles. For example, one poster wrote,

A favorite pastime of boy lovers is collecting pictures of boys, and those boy lovers who have no desire to break the law usually make excellent photographers. An example is the German photographer Hermann List, who is internationally renowned as one of the finest photographers of the first half of this century.

Another maintained,

some of the more famous lovers of boys throughout history include the following: Alexander the Great. The Greek philosophers Socrates and Plato. Plato was 13 when the two met. The Greek poets Anacreon, Alcaeus, Meleager, Strato, and many others far too numerous to mention . . . Oscar Wilde, commonly thought to be the "father of the modern gay movement." In fact, he loved boys, not men. Allan Ginsberg, the beatnik poet of the '60s, and his literary guru William S. Burroughs (of "Naked Lunch" fame).

The claim-of-benefit account, which consisted of the contention that sexual contact with an adult is beneficial to children, was offered by 9.8 percent of the pedophiles in the sample. This justification is an extension of the denial of injury account. Speaking of the boys that he was sexually involved with, one pedophile remarked,

In all cases the boys had a noticeable improvement in their self-esteem, their grades in school went up, they became more stable emotionally, and in one case I pulled a boy back from the drug/school dropout scene and he is now an officer in the Army.

Another poster wrote, "I feel that a consensual intergenerational relationship can be a learning experience for people that want to get involved in one."

The least popular account among these pedophiles was an appeal to loyalties, which was only offered by 4.9 percent of the sample. One pedophile briefly spoke of his support for the "sexual rights of minors" in a posting. Another individual always concluded his posting with the statement "in liberation," which was obviously an allusion to the so-called "children's liberation movement."

Nearly one quarter (24.4 percent) of the pedophiles in this sample offered a polythematic account that appealed to more than one defensibility. They included some combination of denial of injury, condemnation of condemners, [basking in reflected glory], and appeal to loyalties. Some of these accounts were quite lengthy and presented detailed arguments. For example, one pedophile contributed a polythematic account that combined a denial of injury account with a condemnation of condemners account:

A child is a sexual being. Therefore, children should have the right to explore any aspect of sexuality they desire to engage in. Why do parents,

politicians, and police (the 3 p's) feed guilt into children that are sexually active? The guilt and shame put on the child's senses does a major amount of damage to the child. The majority of damage comes when the parents press charges and the boy lover goes to jail and the boy has to deal with the fact that the relationship which was consensual has put this guy away for a long time. There is no doubt that children can and do have the ability to decide for themselves what they want. . . . Children that are sexually active should be left to themselves to decide who should be their sex partner. . . . Consensual sex is justified in all forms, so there should not be a tag of criminal placed on intergenerational sex.

CONCLUSION

Caution should be exercised in the interpretation of these results. First, these findings cannot be generalized to the entire population of pedophiles who use the Internet with any certitude. They are reflective of admitted pedophiles who participate in the Usenet newsgroup alt.support.boy-lovers. There is no way to know how the users of this particular group are similar to or different from pedophiles who participate in other computer forums (e.g., America Online). Second, these findings are probably not generalizable to pedophiles in the general population. Pedophiles who use this newsgroup are probably of higher socioeconomic status than other pedophiles because they have the resources necessary to access expensive computer and telecommunications equipment. Although there are some limitations associated with the generalizability of the results of this research, this study has significant import nonetheless inasmuch as it represents the first substantive data on pedophiles who use the Internet. Furthermore, a major problem associated with previous research on pedophiles is the fact that the samples used were drawn from clinical and correctional populations. Accordingly, the current undertaking can serve as a useful supplement to the extant body of knowledge on pedophilia.

The overall tone and demeanor of this newsgroup may contribute to the management of the deviant identity of pedophile. Semantic manipulation would appear to be a major mechanism of both self- and public image enhancement. In the context of this newsgroup, pedophiles are referred to as "boy lovers." In fact, this newsgroup is named alt.support.boy-lovers. Sex between adults and children is called "love." However, in the context of the larger society, pedophiles are referred to with such pejorative appellations as *pervert* and *child molester.* [Sociologists have] observed a similar tendency in some occupations. They noted that trash collectors call themselves *sanitation engineers,* undertakers refer to themselves as *funeral directors,* and dog catchers use the term *animal control officer* in a self-descriptive fashion. This technique has implications not only for the self-concept of the practitioners of these occupations but also for the public perceptions of these vocational endeavors. Although it is highly unlikely that the use of the term *boy lover* will have any impact on public perceptions of pedophiles, it nonetheless may have important implications for the self-concept of pedophiles. Rather than conceiving of themselves as child molesters or perverts, these pedophiles can more comfortably conceptualize themselves as adults who have a "romantic" interest in boys.

REFERENCES

Bryant, Clifton D. 1982. *Sexual Deviancy and Social Proscription: The Social Context of Carnal Behavior.* New York: Human Sciences Press.

Durkin, Keith F. 1997. "Misuse of the Internet by Pedophiles: Implications for Law Enforcement and Probation Practice." *Federal Probation* 61(3): 14–8.

Finkelhor, David. 1979. "What's Wrong with Sex between Adults and Children?" *Journal of Orthopsychiatry* 49:692–97.

———. 1986. *A Sourcebook on Child Sexual Abuse.* Beverly Hills, CA: Sage.

Heitzeg, Nancy A. 1996. *Deviance: Rulemakers and Rulebreakers.* New York: West.

Janus, Samuel, and Cynthia Janus. *The Janus Report on Sexual Behavior.* New York: John Wiley & Sons.

Lamb, Michael, 1998. "Cybersex: Research Notes on the Characteristics of the Visitors to On-Line Chat Rooms." *Deviant Behavior* 19:119–33.

Okami, Paul, and Amy Goldberg. 1992. "Personality Correlates of Pedophilia: Are They Reliable Indicators?" *Journal of Sex Research* 29:297–328.

Scott, Marvin B., and Stanford Lyman. 1968. "Accounts." *American Sociological Review* 31:46–62.

REVIEW QUESTIONS

1. Discuss three types of accounts offered by the subjects in this study.
2. Durkin and Bryant identify two major methodological problems with their study of pedophiles. What problems do they identify? Identify at least one problem with the study not mentioned by Durkin and Bryant.

PART ELEVEN

PRIVILEGED DEVIANCE

As the boss of the worldwide conglomerate Tyco, Dennis Kozlowski made tons of money for his corporation and himself. In the 1990s, he went on a frenzied shopping spree, spending more than $60 billion to buy 200 major corporations and hundreds of smaller ones. As a result, Tyco, once a relatively small industrial-parts manufacturer with $3 billion in yearly sales, turned into a global colossus that annually pulled in $36 billion, selling practically everything from diapers to fire alarms. For that feat, Kozlowski rewarded himself with more than $300 million in total compensation for the three years before the good times ended. He further acquired for himself, among other things, three Harley-Davidson motorcycles, a 130-foot sailing yacht, a private plane, and lavish homes in four states. Unfortunately for him, in the summer of 2002, he was charged first with failing to pay $1 million in sales tax on art purchases and then with stealing $600 million from Tyco.[1]

What Kozlowski was charged with is an example of privileged deviance, a highly profitable deviance that characteristically involves privileged people—the relatively wealthy, powerful, or well educated. Here we take a look at different aspects of privileged deviance. In the first article, "Living Rich," Shawn Tully presents what it is like to be Marc Rich, a U.S. millionaire fugitive living it up in Europe while faced with many legal problems for his criminal activities in the United States. In the second article, "Political Deviance: Two Case Studies," Don Liddick examines two incidents of public officials selling their accessibility and influence to private entrepreneurs and power brokers. In the third article, "Psychotherapists' Accounts of Their Professional Misdeeds," Mark Pogrebin and his colleagues show how psychotherapists, who are relatively well educated, try to mitigate the wrongfulness of their sexual exploitation of clients by offering excuses, justifications, and apologies. In the fourth selection, "Situational Ethics and College Student Cheating," Emily LaBeff and her colleagues report on their study of how relatively well-educated youth—college students—rationalize their cheating on tests and homework assignments without rejecting the norm of honesty.

---

1. Daniel Eisenberg, "Dennis the Menace," *Time,* June 17, 2002, pp. 46–49; Andrew Hill, "Ex-Tyco Chairman Free on $10m Bail," *FT.com,* September 27, 2002.

LIVING RICH

SHAWN TULLY

"When the gods wish to punish us they answer our prayers." So wrote Oscar Wilde more than 100 years ago. He could have been referring to Marc Rich.

Until Jan. 20, [2001,] when Rich was pardoned by President Clinton during his final hours in office, the world's most pampered fugitive was enjoying a safe, sumptuous life in Switzerland and Spain. The 66-year-old commodities trader, who fled the U.S. in 1983 to avoid prosecution for oil profiteering and tax evasion, thumbed his nose at those who wanted to bring him to justice. He entertained the Swiss elite at his mansion crammed with Dalis and Picassos on the Lake of Lucerne. He threw parties on the roof of Lucerne's avant-garde concert hall, which his philanthropy had helped build. He dined at his $9.5 million Moorish villa in glitzy Marbella with Placido Domingo and other celebrities. And he showed off his trophy wife, Gisela, 48, a six-foot-tall exercise fanatic whom he wooed on the ski slopes of St. Moritz.

Even more galling to some, exile hardly crimped Rich's success in the commodities business. After selling his stake in Marc Rich & Co. AG for more than $500 million in 1994 (the firm, now known as Glencore, is the largest metals and oil commodities company in the world), he's back with a new venture, called Novarco in the U.S., that has revenues of $7 billion and trades oil out of offices in White Plains, N.Y., a few miles from the Manhattan courthouse where Rich once faced a 325-year prison term.

Rich seemed sure to live out his days in plush exile, a dimly remembered figure in the U.S., far from the reach of its laws. So why bother to push for a pardon? Though Rich isn't talking, friends and former associates say he wanted to regain his freedom to travel. As a fugitive, Rich couldn't set foot in America—he wasn't allowed to visit one of his daughters, who died of leukemia in 1996—or any other country friendly to the U.S. for fear of being captured, extradited, and sent to jail. "The local authorities were looking for him in airports all over the world," says a former U.S. marshal who pursued Rich for more than a decade.

But now that Rich is free to stroll down Fifth Avenue or the Champs-Elysées, it's hardly a moment of triumph. Indeed, getting a pardon may prove to be the worst trade of his career. It set off a firestorm that has already singed a President who bypassed the normal pardoning process to exonerate a man whose ex-wife happened to be a major Democratic Party fundraiser. It has turned up the heat on Rich's partner and fellow fugitive Pincus Green, who was pardoned as well. And it threatens to engulf Rich in more litigation, including claims for back taxes that could exceed $100 million and criminal charges for embargo-busting commodities deals.

Source: Shawn Tully, "Living Rich," *Fortune,* February 19, 2001, pp. 130–132. Reprinted with permission.

At issue is whether Rich is a U.S. citizen. If he is—and the evidence is overwhelming, even though Rich and his attorneys claim he abandoned his citizenship years ago—then he is liable for back taxes for the 18 years he has been living abroad as a fugitive. And, given the level of outrage over the pardon, chances are excellent that the government will pursue Rich wherever he's vulnerable. "If Rich hasn't paid his liability in full, he should be called upon to pay it," says former IRS Commissioner Donald Alexander. "If I were back in the tax shop, I'd do my best to make a civil fraud case against him."

The cosmopolitan, Belgian-born Rich and the homespun, Brooklyn-bred Green got into trouble in the West Texas oil patch in the early 1980s. The two had bolted Philipp Brothers commodities house in 1973 in a dispute over bonuses and started their own company, Marc Rich & Co. Though the firm was based in Zug, Switzerland, Rich and Green worked in New York. In 1980 and 1981, according to a 65-count indictment, the two men exploited the government's complex energy regulations by buying price-controlled Texas crude for as little as $6 a barrel, relabeling the barrels to make them look like decontrolled supplies, then selling them for as much as $40 on the open market—a scam that generated $105 million in illegal profits. They allegedly used sham transactions to ship the profits to offshore subsidiaries that paid no taxes. And they were accused of profiting from the Iran hostage crisis by purchasing $200 million of Iranian crude, a violation of the U.S. embargo against Tehran.

In 1983, Rudolph Giuliani, then U.S. Attorney in Manhattan, brought criminal charges against Rich, Green, and two of their companies for tax fraud, racketeering, tax evasion, and trading with the enemy. At the time it was the biggest tax-evasion case in U.S. history: The government accused the companies of failing to pay $48 million due on their illegal profits and charged Rich and Green personally with orchestrating the scam. If convicted on all counts, each would have faced 325 years in prison. In late 1984 their companies

agreed to settle all charges for $171 million. The deal allowed Marc Rich & Co., or any company owned by Rich and Green, to trade freely in the U.S. But it did nothing to settle the criminal case. Instead of negotiating a plea bargain as they had done for their companies, or fighting the charges in court, Rich and Green chose exile. Just before the indictments came down, they fled to Zug. Swiss authorities, arguing that tax evasion is not a crime in their country, refused to extradite them.

Now a stroke of the presidential pen has ended the criminal case. But how much Rich and Green still owe the U.S. remains a matter of considerable confusion. Even Clinton may not have understood the situation fully. On the evening of Jan. 19, as he was finalizing his pardon list, the President told Jack Quinn, his former White House counsel and the attorney representing Rich, that he would grant the pardon on one condition. He requested, and received later that night, a letter promising that Rich and Green wouldn't use the statute of limitations to duck any civil claims connected to the original case that the government might bring.

Clinton's demand is perplexing because the $171 million settlement covered everything. "They've paid in full, through their companies," says Martin Auerbach, a former assistant U.S. attorney who worked on the case. "Please ask Jack Quinn what civil damages he's talking about." Quinn didn't respond to requests for comment.

But neither the $171 million payment, nor the pardon, prevents the U.S. from bringing charges for tax evasion or other misdeeds that Rich and Green may have committed as fugitives—assuming they're still citizens. The State Department won't comment on their citizenship status, citing privacy laws. But former law enforcement officials insist that the two are U.S. nationals. "In my view, they never properly renounced their citizenship," says Howard Safir, the former New York City police commissioner who pursued Rich as head of the U.S. Marshals Service in the 1980s.

A 1991 U.S. appeals court ruling supports Safir. Rich had argued in a 1988 breach-of-contract suit filed against him in New York that the U.S. courts didn't have jurisdiction since he had become a Spanish citizen in 1982 by taking an oath in Madrid. At the same ceremony, Rich claimed, he had relinquished his U.S. citizenship. The appeals court said that swearing you're no longer a U.S. citizen isn't enough. The person renouncing must also show that he's doing so with the right intentions, which includes surrendering the rights and benefits of being an American.

The court found that Rich flunked the test. He had acted like an American long after he supposedly ditched his citizenship, using his U.S. passport to travel in 1983. And, when it benefited him, Rich swore in a lawsuit in Switzerland that he was a U.S. citizen.

If Rich is still a citizen, he would be liable for back taxes on his worldwide income. Expatriates get a credit for any tax they pay in their country of residence. But if the U.S. tax is higher—certainly the case in Switzerland, where there are no capital gains taxes—they owe Uncle Sam the difference. Rich's income isn't known, but he told *Fortune* in 1986 that he and Green earned salaries of about $1 million a year. And it's safe to estimate that his capital gain on the sale of Marc Rich & Co. was more than $200 million. With interest and penalties, Rich could easily owe the IRS $100 million.

Rich and Green could also be charged with violating U.S. embargoes. A 1986 antiapartheid law made most trading with South Africa a crime. But Rich and Green, industry sources say, were supplying South Africa with oil into the 1990s. Then there's Cuba. According to Jose Oro, a former director at the Ministry of Basic Industries who defected to the U.S. in 1991, Rich advanced cash to the money-strapped Castro regime in the late 1980s to import mining equipment and raw materials. In exchange he got minerals, primarily gold and nickel, which he traded on world markets. "Rich was looking for a quick buck," says Oro, who estimates Rich was doing tens of millions of dollars a year in business with Cuba, despite a long-standing U.S. embargo.

"U.S. citizens who participated in trading with Cuba could face criminal prosecution under the Trading with the Enemy Act," says Hal Eren, a former Treasury official and an attorney with Clifford Chance Rogers & Wells.

Government officials won't say if they're pondering fresh investigations. But if they do choose to pursue Rich, it's a safe bet he'll remain elusive. A surprise call that a U.S. law enforcement officer made to Pinky Green during the Gulf War may provide a clue as to the former fugitives' intentions. He traced Green to the King David Hotel in Jerusalem and called his room. "Hey, Pinky," he crowed, "I'm watching CNN, and it looks like you're getting pounded by Scuds. Why don't you give yourself up and come home? You'd be safer!" Green slammed down the phone. Now that missiles are flying again—Congressional hearings on the pardon are set for this week—it's unlikely either man will find it safe enough to come home.

REVIEW QUESTIONS

1. Are Marc Rich and Pincus Green deviant? Defend your answer.
2. Do you think that the authorities should pursue Rich and Green despite President Clinton's pardon?

POLITICAL DEVIANCE:
TWO CASE STUDIES

DON LIDDICK

The raising of campaign contributions in and around the 1996 elections involved a wide variety of crimes perhaps best described as organized criminality. Although typically framed by many politicians and pundits as relatively minor technical violations of statutes governing campaign finance, a close examination of the case studies provided in this article demonstrates that political fund-raisers committed a variety of more serious crimes and did so in a coordinated fashion. The purposes of the article are (a) to describe two of the lesser known campaign fund-raising episodes associated with the 1996 scandal [and] (b) to suggest that these crimes should be viewed as a breed of organized criminality (a category of behaviors in which so-called white-collar crimes would fall). . . .

ROGER TAMRAZ

In the mid 1990s, Roger Tamraz, an international fugitive wanted on bank fraud and embezzlement charges, attempted to obtain U.S. government support for an oil pipeline project that would cross the Caspian Sea region. Tamraz's efforts included using his past relationship with the CIA and making political donations to the Democratic Party to gain access to mid-level and upper level U.S. government officials, including the vice-president and president of the United States. Al-

though Tamraz did not get U.S. support for his pipeline project, . . . the events surrounding this case study exemplify the widespread practice of purchasing access to government officials and, conversely, the great lengths some officials will go [to,] to ensure that contributions are made and access granted.

In the spring of 1995, a National Security Council (NSC) interagency group on Caspian Sea oil pipeline policy, headed by Sheila Heslin, became aware that Tamraz was promoting himself in the Caspian Sea region as a deal maker and that the substance of his pipeline proposal ran contrary to U.S. policy. Despite his flawed proposal and his shady background in Lebanon, . . . Heslin and the NSC group decided that Tamraz at least deserved a hearing in front of his government to assess his proposal. NSC and CIA officials subsequently met with Tamraz in May and June of 1995 to discuss the proposed Caspian pipeline. Prior to a June 2 meeting between Heslin and Tamraz, CIA officials from both the Directorate of Intelligence (DI—analysis of information) and the Directorate of Operations (DO—gathering of information) informed Heslin that they would send her a report. Heslin testified before the Senate Governmental Affairs Committee in 1997 that the DI report contained primarily negative information about Tamraz, whereas the DO report was

Source: Don Liddick, "Political Fund-Raising, Patron–Client Relations, and Organized Criminality," *Journal of Contemporary Criminal Justice,* vol. 17 (November 2001), pp. 346–357. Reprinted by permission of Sage Publications, Inc.

completely positive. A CIA agent in the DO, identified only as "Bob" at committee hearings, began to contact Heslin and push for a White House meeting between President Clinton and Tamraz in early June 1995, a lobbying effort that continued through October. . . .

Efforts to arrange access to the White House on Tammz's behalf were not limited to "Bob" at the CIA. . . . After the NSC interagency group led by Heslin indicated to Tamraz that his pipeline proposal would not gain White House support, Tamraz testified before the Senate Governmental Affairs Committee that "they kicked me from the door, I will come through the window." Tamraz's passage through the window began in July 1999, when he became a major contributor to the Democratic Party. Between July and October 1995, Tamraz contributed $220,000 to various Democratic entities, including the Virginia Democratic Party, the Louisiana Democratic Party, the Democratic National Committee (DNC) Federal Account, the DNC, and the Richard Molpus for Governor of Mississippi campaign. Check-tracking forms obtained by the Governmental Affairs Committee listed DNC chairman Donald Fowler as the solicitor of Tamraz's donations. . . . Denied top-level access by the NSC, Tamraz came in through the DNC window.

The culpability of the DNC and DNC chairman Donald Fowler in soliciting and taking money from Tamraz is beyond dispute. Before and after Fowler's July 1995 meeting with Tamraz, DNC staffers warned Fowler about the dubious nature of Tamraz's pipeline proposal as well as his troubles in Lebanon. . . . Despite the warnings, Fowler, DNC finance director Richard Sullivan, and other fund-raisers at the DNC not only solicited and accepted Tamraz's donations but also went to great lengths to arrange access and provide him the political leverage he sought. . . .

[Ultimately,] Tamraz, through his DNC and Democratic Party donations, was permitted to attend six events with President Clinton from September 1995 through June 1996. The events included the following:

1. A reception for the DNC's Business Leadership Forum on September 11, 1995.
2. A DNC dinner on September 15, 1995.
3. The DNC chairman's holiday reception on December 13, 1995.
4. A DNC trustee's dinner on March 27, 1996.
5. A presidential coffee on April 1, 1996.
6. A buffet dinner and private screening of the film *Independence Day* on June 22, 1996. ("Investigation of Illegal or Improper Activities in Connection with 1996 Federal Election Campaigns," 1998, ch. 21)

Having successfully purchased access to President Clinton, Tamraz proceeded to pursue his ultimate goal of changing U.S. foreign policy and influencing the president to endorse his pipeline project to the governments of the Caspian region. Tamraz pitched his proposal to President Clinton at a March 27, 1996, DNC dinner and an April 1, 1996, White House coffee; the president expressed interest, and the matter was referred to Counselor to the President Thomas "Mack" McClarty for investigation. McClarty delegated the investigation of the merits of the pipeline proposal to the Associate Deputy Secretary for Energy, Kyle Simpson, who in turn enlisted the help of his Energy Department colleague Jack Carter. Because the NSC's interagency task force on Caspian region matters was the only real obstacle to Tamraz's objective, Carter subsequently called the beleaguered Sheila Heslin on April 4, 1996. Heslin testified before the Senate committee in 1997 that Carter pressured her to change the position of the task force, invoking the clout of Mack McClarty and Tamraz's sizable campaign contributions. Carter also inferred that her job could be in jeopardy if McClarty ever became energy secretary and informed her that she should not be "such a girl scout." Moreover, Heslin recalled that Carter quoted a $200,000 contribution figure, a number essentially equal to the $205,000 total recorded in a memoranda compiled for Tamraz by the DNC within 24 hours of Tamraz's March 27, 1996, discussion with President Clinton about his pipeline proposal. Tamraz's support for the DNC and the Democratic Party was effectively communicated from the president through Mack McClarty to officials at the Energy Department, who attempted to pressure a national security official to change official U.S. foreign policy.

In April 1999, the 515 mile Baku-Supsa pipeline opened and was hailed by Azerbajani officials because it avoided Russian territory and thus contributed to Azerbaijan's economic independence. However, the Baku-Supsa line is expected to handle only 10% of Caspian Sea production, and 12 energy companies (including U.S.-based Penzoil, Unocal, McDermott and Exxon, and Amoco/British Petroleum) have formed a $7.5 billion consortium . . . that favors another pipeline route from Baku northward through Chechnya to the Black Sea port of Novorossiysk. By October 1998, [the consortium] had completely rejected the Baku-Ceyhan route pushed by Roger Tamraz and the Clinton State Department, a friction that was viewed by some as a loss of U.S. credibility on the pipeline issue. Of course, whether Roger Tamraz's relatively paltry $300,000 influenced U.S. foreign policy is debatable, but the sale of access to the White House and the undue political pressure placed on a U.S. foreign policy formulator is beyond doubt.

THE CHEYENNE AND ARAPAHO TRIBES

In March 1997, media accounts revealed that the Cheyenne and Arapaho tribes of Oklahoma had donated $107,000 to the DNC in 1996 with the understanding that the contributions would help them reacquire the Fort Reno tribal lands (the federal government had seized the 9,500 acre parcel in 1883, and it was now believed that significant oil and gas deposits lay beneath it). Staff for the Senate Governmental Affairs Committee interviewed tribal leaders in August and September 1997 . . . , uncovering a series of events in which Democratic fund-raisers attempted to fleece the tribes out of additional contributions, legal fees, and land development fees. . . . The story is one of blatant influence peddling that at one point sank as low as attempted extortion.

Prior to 1996, the tribes had aggressively pursued their claims to the Fort Reno lands, contacting both the Departments of Interior and Agriculture in 1994 and 1995. Frustrated by these attempts, tribal leaders hired Michael Turpen, a former attorney general of Oklahoma, to lobby on their behalf. Turpen set up meetings with Washington officials and accompanied tribal representatives to Washington, D.C., in early 1996 and wrote a letter to presidential aide Mack McClarty seeking his assistance. During this time period, Tupen was also a top fund-raiser in Oklahoma for the Democrats and Clinton–Gore '96, so he soon informed the tribes that the way to get heard in Washington is to make political donations, typically in the six-figure range. The tribes eventually agreed to donate $100,000 and were soon invited to attend a luncheon with President Clinton in the White House. On June 17, 1996, two tribal leaders, Surveyor and Todd, dined with the president and a small group of people in the White House. Surveyor and Todd left the meeting uplifted, for as they remember it, the president had told them something to the effect that "we'll look into it and see what we can do."

Because the tribes had not actually delivered the $100,000 at or prior to the luncheon, a flurry of phone calls from Turpen and Jason McIntosh (Turpen's contact at Clinton–Gore '96) ensued, pressing the tribes for payment. Turpen called June 20, insisting that the tribes pay the DNC immediately, and McIntosh placed several calls beginning June 24 that became increasingly "aggressive" in tone. On June 26, 1996, the tribes wired a contribution to the DNC totaling $87,671.74, representing the entire sum in the tribal bank account. Sometime in July, Turpen called the tribe and reminded them that they were still $13,000 short and suggested that they donate $20,000 to help host President Clinton's 50th birthday party. The tribal leaders agreed and donated the $20,000 through Turpen's firm. . . .

By December 1996, the tribes had grown restless because they had seen no progress in their quest to regain the Fort Reno lands. Apparently, the only tangible result of their $107,000 donation was additional solicitations from Democratic fund-raisers. . . . [When the tribes refused, the deal] was dead in the water. The Cheyenne Arapaho did not get the Fort Reno lands back because of their $107,000 donation. But this case does at the very least embody a classic example of influence peddling. If asked, Roger Tamraz would have likely told tribal representatives that they should have contributed more if they really wanted results.

CONCLUSION

The two case studies provided here embody what has become intrinsic in the American political process—the purchasing of access, the peddling of influence, and all too often, the brazen sale of political office. Moreover, it seems perfectly legitimate to frame these behaviors as organized criminality, in which public officials, private entrepreneurs (both licit and illicit), and assorted power brokers engage in complicated reciprocal exchange relations. In the present examples, these complex relationships mesh legal, quasi-legal, and illegal behaviors and utterly blur the lines dividing legitimate political processes from what is commonly referred to as white-collar crime.

REFERENCES

[Major sources of material for this article:]

Investigation of Illegal or Improper Activities in Connection with 1996 Federal Election Campaigns. (1998). Chapter 21: The Saga of Roger Tamraz (Final Report of the Senate Committee on Governmental Affairs, 105th Congress, 2nd session, 1998). Washington, DC: Government Printing Office.

Investigation of Illegal or Improper Activities in Connection with 1996 Federal Election Campaigns. (1998, March 10). Chapter 24: The Cheyenne and Arapaho Tribes (Final Report of the Senate Committee on Governmental Affairs, 105th Congress, 2nd session, 1998). Washington, DC: Government Printing Office.

REVIEW QUESTIONS

1. Why are these two case studies considered political deviance? Support your answer using one or more theories of deviance.
2. Do you think that white-collar criminals should be treated the same as violent criminals in the court of law?

PSYCHOTHERAPISTS' ACCOUNTS OF THEIR PROFESSIONAL MISDEEDS

MARK R. POGREBIN
ERIC D. POOLE
AMOS MARTINEZ

Intimate sexual relationships between mental health therapists and their clients have been increasingly reported in recent years (Akamatsu, 1987). In a survey of over 1400 psychiatrists, Gartell, Herman, Olarte, Feldstein, and Localio (1987) found that 65 percent reported having treated a patient who admitted to sexual involvement with a previous therapist. National self-report surveys indicate that approximately 10 percent of psychotherapists admit having had at least one sexual encounter with a client (Gartell, Herman, Olarte, Feldstein, and Localio, 1986; Pope, Keith-Spiegel, and Tabachnick, 1986). It is suggested that these surveys most likely underestimate the extent of actual sexual involvement with clients because some offending psychotherapists either fail to respond to the survey or fail to report their sexual indiscretions (Gartell et al., 1987). Regardless of the true prevalence rates, many mental health professional associations explicitly condemn sexual relations between a therapist and client. Such relationships represent a breach of canons of professional ethics and are subject to disciplinary action by specific licensing or regulatory bodies. . . .

Since 1988 [in Colorado] sexual intimacy between therapists and clients has been explicitly and formally recognized as one of the most serious violations of the professional–client relationship, subject to both regulatory or administrative and criminal penalties. Yet, between August 1, 1988, and June 30, 1990, 10 percent ($n = 33$) of the 324 complaints filed with the State Grievance Board involved allegations of sexual misconduct. Given the implications that these sexual improprieties raise for both the client as victim and the therapist as offender, we wish to examine the written accounts submitted to the board by psychotherapists who have had complaints of sexual misconduct filed against them. . . .

METHOD

To the 33 complaints of sexual misconduct filed from August 1988 through June 1990, 30 written responses from psychotherapists were submitted to the State Grievance Board. Twenty-four therapists admitted to sexual involvement with clients; six denied the allegations. In the present study we examine the statements of the 24 therapists who provided accounts for their sexual relations with clients. Twenty-one therapists are men; three are women.

The analytical method utilized in reviewing therapists' accounts was content analysis, which

Source: Mark R. Pogrebin, Eric D. Poole, and Amos Martinez, "Accounts of Professional Misdeeds: The Sexual Exploitation of Clients by Psychotherapists," *Deviant Behavior,* vol. 13 (1992), pp. 229–252. Reprinted with permission.

"translates frequency of occurrence of certain symbols into summary judgments and comparisons of content of the discourse" (Starosta, 1984, p. 185). Content analytical techniques provide the means to document, classify, and interpret the communication of meaning, allowing for inferential judgments from objective identification of the characteristics of messages (Holsti, 1969).

The 24 written responses ranged in length from 2 to 25 pages. Each response was assessed and classified according to the types of explanations invoked by therapists in accounting for their acknowledged sexual relations with clients. We employed Scott and Lyman's (1968) classic formulation of accounts (i.e., excuses and justifications) and Goffman's (1971) notion of the apology as conceptual guides in organizing the vocabularies of motive used by our group of therapists to explain their untoward behavior. . . .

FINDINGS

Accounts are "linguistic device[s] employed whenever an action is subjected to valuative inquiry" (Scott and Lyman, 1968, p. 46). An important function of accounts is to mitigate blameworthiness by representing one's behavior in such a way as to reduce personal accountability. This involves offering accounts aimed at altering the prevailing conception of what the instant activity is, is well as one's role in the activity. Excuses, justifications, and apologies all display a common goal: giving a "good account" of oneself.

Excuses

Appeal of Defeasibility. In an appeal of defeasibility, one accounts for one's behavior by denying any intention to cause the admitted harm or by claiming a failure to foresee the unfortunate consequences of one's act, or both. . . . In the following account, the therapist claims ignorance of

professional rules of conduct governing relations with clients:

> *I did not know that seeing clients socially outside of therapy violated hospital policy . . . [I]f I realized it was strictly forbidden, I would have acted differently . . .*

In the following example, a therapist admits that she simply misinterpreted her own feelings and did not consciously intend to become sexually involved with her client:

> *It was after a short period of time that I first experienced any sexual feelings toward her. I did excuse the feelings I had as something which I never would act on. Unfortunately, I did not understand what was happening at the time.*

Similarly, another therapist seeks to diminish culpability by attributing his sexual indiscretion to a misreading of his client's emotional needs:

> *I experienced her expressions of affection as caring gestures of our spiritual bond, not lust. And I had no reason to suspect otherwise from her, since I had been so clear about my aversion to romantic involvement. We had sexual intercourse only once after termination. I am not promiscuous, neither sexually abusive nor seductive. . . .*

Scapegoating. Scapegoating involves an attempt to blame others for one's untoward behavior. Scapegoating is available as a form of excuse in the professional–client relationship because of the contextual opportunity for the therapist to shift personal responsibility to the client. The therapist contends that his or her actions were the product of the negative attributes or will of the client, for example, deceit, seduction, or manipulation. The therapist in the following example recognizes the wrongfulness of his behavior but deflects responsibility by holding the client culpable for her actions:

> *I am not denying that this sexual activity took place, nor am I trying to excuse or justify it. It was wrong. However, the woman who complained about me is a psychologist. She was counseling me as well, on some vocational issues. So if anyone*

had cause for complaint under the regulations, it seems it would be me.

Another example of an account where the therapist attempts to "blame the victim" for the improper sexual activity reveals the focus on his diminished personal control of the relationship:

That I became involved in a sexual relationship with her is true. While my actions were reprehensible, both morally and professionally, I did not mislead or seduce her or intend to take advantage of her. My fault, instead, was failing to adequately safeguard myself from her seductiveness, covert and overt.

Here we have a therapist recognizing the impropriety of his actions yet denying personal responsibility because of the client's overpowering charms. The message is that the therapist may be held accountable for an inadequate "self-defense" which left him vulnerable to the client's seductive nature, but that he should not be culpable for the deviant sexual behavior since it was really he who was taken in and thus "victimized." The therapist's account for his predicament presumes a "reasonable person" theory of behavior; that is, given the same set of circumstances, any reasonable person would be expected to succumb to this persuasive client.

Justifications

Sad Tale. The sad tale presents an array of dismal experiences or conditions that are regarded—both collectively and cumulatively—as an explanation and justification for the actor's present untoward behavior. The therapists who presented sad tales invariably focused on their own history of family problems and personal tribulations that brought them to their present state of sexual affairs with clients:

Ironically, her termination from therapy came at one of the darkest periods of my life. My father had died that year. I had met him for the first time when I was in my twenties. He was an alcoholic. Over the years we had worked hard on our relationship. At the time of his dying, we were at peace with one

another. Yet, I still had my grief. At the time I had entered into individual therapy to focus on issues pertaining to my father's alcoholism and co-dependency issues. I then asked my wife to join me for marriage counseling. We were having substantial problems surrounding my powerlessness in our relationship. Therapy failed to address the balance of power. I was in the worst depression I had ever experienced in my entire life when we began our sexual involvement.

Therapists who employ sad tales admit to having sexual relations with their clients, admit that their actions were improper, and admit that ordinarily what they did would be an instance of the general category of the prohibited behavior. They claim, however, that their behavior is a special case because the power of circumstance voids the defining deviant quality of their actions. This type of account is similar to Lofland's (1969, p. 88) "special justification," where the actor views his current act as representative of some category of deviance but does not believe it to be entirely blameworthy because of extenuating circumstances. One therapist outlines the particular contextual factors that help explain his misbehavior:

The following situations are not represented as an excuse for my actions. There is no excuse for them. They are simply some of what I feel are circumstances that formed the context for what I believe is an incident that will never be repeated.
(1) Life losses: My mother-in-law who lived with us died. My oldest son and, the next fall, my daughter had left home for college.
(2) Overscheduling: I dealt with these losses and other concerns in my life by massive overscheduling.

Other therapists offer similar sad tales of tragic events that are seen to diminish their capacity, either physically or mentally, to cope with present circumstances. Two cases illustrate this accounting strategy:

In the summer of 1988, my wife and I separated with her taking our children to live out-of-state. This was a difficult loss for me. A divorce followed.

Soon after I had a bout with phlebitis which hospitalized me for ten days.

My daughter, who lived far away with my former wife, was diagnosed with leukemia; and my mother had just died. Additional stress was caused by my ex-wife and present wife's embittered interactions. . . .

Sad tales depict individuals acting abnormally in abnormal situations. In short, their instant deviance is neither typical nor characteristic of the type of person they really are, that is, how they would act under normal conditions. They are victims of circumstance, for if it were not for these dismal life events, their sexual improprieties would never have occurred.

Denial of Injury.   Denial of injury is premised on a moral assessment of consequences; that is, the individual claims that his or her actions should be judged as wrong on the basis of the harm resulting from those acts. Again, the actor acknowledges that in general the behavior in which he or she has engaged is inappropriate but asserts that in this particular instance no real harm was done. This type of account was prevalent among the therapists who had engaged in sexual relations with clients following the termination of therapy.

A good therapy termination establishes person-to-person equality between participants. Blanket condemnations of post-therapy relationships also are founded on a belief that such relationships invariably cause harm to the former patient. I defy anyone to meet Gerry, interview her, and then maintain that any harm was done to her by me. . . .

Apology

. . . Two consequences of an accused wrongdoer's action are guilt and shame. If wrongful behavior is based on internal standards, the transgressor feels guilty; if the behavior is judged on external normative comparisons, the person experiences shame. Shame results from being viewed as one who has behaved in a discrediting manner. In the

following three cases, each therapist expresses his remorse and laments his moral failure:

I find myself in the shameful position that I never would have thought possible for me as I violated my own standards of personal and professional conduct.

I feel very badly for what I have done, ashamed and unprofessional. I feel unworthy of working in the noble profession of counselling.

I entered into therapy and from the first session disclosed what I had done. I talked about my shame and the devastation I had created for my family and others.

Schlenker and Darby (1981) observe that the apology incorporates not only an expression of regret but also a claim of redemption. An apology permits a transgressor the opportunity to admit guilt while simultaneously seeking forgiveness in order that the offending behavior not be thought of as a representation of what the actor is really like. One therapist expresses concern for his actions and proposes a way to avoid such conduct in the future:

I continue to feel worry and guilt about the damage that I caused. I have taken steps I felt necessary which has been to decide not to work with any client who could be very emotionally demanding, such as occurs with people who are borderline or dependent in their functioning.

This account seems to imply that one's remorse and affirmative effort to prevent future transgressions are sufficient remedies in themselves, preempting the need for others to impose additional sanctions. . . .

DISCUSSION

The consequences of deviant activity are problematic, often depending on a "definition of the situation." When a particular definition of a specific situation emerges, even though its dominance may be only temporary, individuals must adjust their behavior and views to it. Alternative definitions of problematic situations routinely arise and are usually subject to negotiation. Thus, it is incumbent upon the accused therapist to have his or her situation defined in ways most favorable to maintaining or advancing his or her own interests. When "transformations of identity" are at stake, such efforts become especially consequential (Strauss, 1962). The imputation of a deviant identity implies ramifications that can vitally affect the individual's personal and professional life. As noted earlier, the negotiation of accounts is a negotiation of identities. The account serves as an impression-management technique, or a "front," that minimizes the threat to identity (Goffman, 1959). If the therapist can provide an acceptable account for his or her sexual impropriety—whether an excuse, justification, or apology—he or she increases the likelihood of restoring a cherished identity brought into question by the deviant behavior.

There is a close link between successfully conveying desired images to others and being able to incorporate them in one's own self-conceptions. When individuals offer accounts for their problematic actions, they are trying to ease their situation in two ways: by convincing others and by convincing themselves. An important function of accounts is to make one's transgressions not only intelligible to others but intelligible to oneself. Therapists sought to dispel the view that their deviation was a defining characteristic of who they really were; or, to put it another way, they attempted to negate the centrality or primacy of a deviant role imputation. The goal was to maintain or restore their own sense of personal and professional worth notwithstanding their sexual deviancy. In a way, laying claim to a favorable image in spite of aberrant behavior means voiding the apparent moral reality, that is, the deviance-laden definition of the situation that has been called to the attention of significant others (Grievance Board) by a victim-accuser (former client).

Goffman (1959, p. 251) maintains that individuals are not concerned with the issue of morality of their behavior as much as they are with the amoral issue of presenting a moral self;

Our activity, then is largely concerned with moral matters, but as performers we do not have a moral concern with them. As performers we are merchants of morality.

The presentation of a moral self following deviance may be interpreted as an attempt by the individual to reaffirm his commitment to consensual values and goals in order to win the acceptance of others (Tedeschi and Riorden, 1981). The demonstration of shared standards of conduct may also be seen as consistent with the wish to redeem oneself in the eyes of others and to preserve self-respect. The desire for self-validating approval becomes more important when circumstances threaten an individual's identity. In these instances an actor will often make self-presentations for purposes of eliciting desired responses that will restore the perception of self by others that he or she desires. If discredited actors can offer a normal presentation of self in an abnormal situation, they may be successful in having their instant deviant behavior perceived by others as atypical, thus neutralizing a deviant characterization.

Individuals seek a "common ground" in accounts of their deviant behavior, explaining their actions in conventional terms that are acceptable to a particular audience. These accounts should not be viewed as mere rationalizations. They may genuinely be believed in. . . .

Finally, it should be noted that, as retrospective interpretations, accounts may have little to do with the motives that existed at the time the deviance occurred. In this case accounting for one's deviant behavior requires one to dissimulate, that is, to pretend to be what one is not or not to be what one is. As Goffman (1959) asserts, social behavior involves a great deal of deliberate deception in that impressions of selves must be constantly created and managed for various others. Thus, it is not logically necessary that one agree with others' moral judgments in order to employ accounts. Even where no guilt or shame is consciously felt, one may offer accounts in the hope of lessening what could be, nonetheless, attributions of a deviant identity. When used convincingly, accounts blur the distinctions between "appearance and reality, truth and falsity, triviality and importance, accident and essence, coincidence and cause" (Garfinkel, 1956, p. 420). Accounts embody a mixture of fact and fantasy. As shown in the accounts provided by therapists, what is most problematic is determining the mixture best suited for a particular situational context.

REFERENCES

Akamatsu, J. T. 1987. "Intimate Relationships with Former Clients: National Survey of Attitudes and Behavior among Practitioners." *Professional Psychology: Research and Practice* 18:454–458.

Garfinkel, H. 1956. "Conditions of Successful Degradation Ceremonies." *American Journal of Sociology* 61:420–424.

Gartell, N., J. Herman, S. Olarte, M. Feldstein, and R. Localio. 1986. "Psychiatrist–Patient Sexual Contact: Results of a National Survey. I: Prevalence." *American Journal of Psychiatry* 143:1126–1131.

Gartell, N., J. Herman, S. Olarte, M. Feldstein, and R. Localio. 1987. "Reporting Practices of Psychiatrists Who Knew of Sexual Misconduct by Colleagues." *American Journal of Orthopsychiatry* 57:287–295.

Goffman, E. 1959. *The Presentation of Self in Everyday Life.* Garden City, NY: Doubleday.

Goffman, E. 1971. *Relations in Public: Microstudies of the Public Order.* New York: Basic Books.

Holsti, O. R. 1969. *Content Analysis for the Social Sciences and Humanities.* Reading, MA: Addison-Wesley.

Lofland, J. 1969. *Deviance and Identity.* Englewood Cliffs, NJ: Prentice-Hall.

Pope, K. S., P. Keith-Spiegel, and B. G. Tabachnick. 1986. "Sexual Attraction to Clients: The Human Therapist and the (Sometimes) Inhuman Training System." *American Psychologist* 41:147–158.

Schlenker, B. R., and B. W. Darby. 1981. "The Use of Apologies in Social Predicaments." *Social Psychology Quarterly* 44:271–278.

Scott, M. B., and S. M. Lyman. 1968. "Accounts." *American Sociological Review* 33:46–62.

Starosta, W. J. 1984. "Qualitative Content Analysis: A Burkean Perspective," pp. 185–194 in *Methods for Intercultural Communication Research,* edited by W. Gudykunst and Y. Y. Kim. Beverly Hills, CA: Sage.

Strauss, A. 1962. "Transformations of Identity," pp. 63–85 in *Human Behavior and Social Processes: An Interactional Approach,* edited by A. M. Rose. Boston: Houghton Mifflin.

Tedeschi, J. T., and C. Riorden. 1981. "Impression Management and Prosocial Behavior Following Transgression," pp. 223–244 in *Impression Management Theory and Social Psychological Research,* edited by J. T. Tedeschi. New York: Academic Press.

REVIEW QUESTIONS

1. What are the differences between "excuses" and "justifications"? Give an example, not mentioned in the article, of each.
2. What are some methodological problems with the data used in this article?

SITUATIONAL ETHICS AND COLLEGE STUDENT CHEATING

EMILY E. LᴀBEFF
ROBERT E. CLARK
VALERIE J. HAINES
GEORGE M. DIEKHOFF

Studies have shown that cheating in college is epidemic, and some analysts of this problem estimate that 50 percent of college students may engage in such behavior. . . . Such studies have examined demographic and social characteristics of students such as age, sex, academic standing, major, classification, extracurricular activity, level of test anxiety, degree of sanctioned threat, and internal social control. Each of these factors has been found to be related, to some extent, to cheating although the relationship varies considerably from study to study. . . .

In our freshman classes, we often informally ask students to discuss whether they have cheated in college and, if so, how. Some students have almost bragged about which of their methods have proven most effective including writing notes on shoes and caps and on the backs of calculators. Rolling up a tiny cheat sheet into a pen cap was mentioned. And one student said, he had "incredibly gifted eyes" which allowed him to see the answers of a smart student four rows in front of him. One female student talked about rummaging through the dumpsters at night close to final examination time looking for test dittos. She did find at least one examination. A sorority member informed us that two of her term papers in her freshman year were sent from a sister chapter of the sorority at another university, retyped and submitted to the course professor. Further, many of these students saw nothing wrong with what they were doing, although they verbally agreed with the statement that cheating was unethical. . . .

The concept of situational ethics might well describe this college cheating in that rules for behavior are not considered rigid but dependent on the circumstances involved (Norris and Dodder 1979, p. 545). Joseph Fletcher, in his well-known philosophical treatise, *Situation Ethics,* defines it as the notion that any action is good or bad depending on the social circumstances. In other words, what is wrong in most situations might be considered right or acceptable. . . . Central to this process is the idea that situations alter cases, thus altering the rules and principles guiding behavior (Edwards 1967).

[Situational ethics seems to be the core of what Sykes and Matza (1957) call "neutralization," the process of justifying violation of accepted rules. Neutralization takes five forms]: denial of responsibility, condemnation of condemners, appeal

Source: Emily E. LaBeff, Robert E. Clark, Valerie J. Haines, and George M. Diekhoff, "Situational Ethics and College Student Cheating," *Sociological Inquiry,* vol. 60 (1990), pp. 190–198. Reprinted with permission.

to higher loyalties, denial of victim, and denial of injury. In each case, individuals profess a conviction about a particular law but argue that special circumstances exist which cause them to violate the rules. . . .

METHODOLOGY

The present analysis is based on a larger project conducted during the 1983–1984 academic year when a 49-item questionnaire about cheating was administered to students at a small southwestern university. The student body (n = 4950) was evenly distributed throughout the university's programs with a disproportionate number (27 percent) majoring in business administration. In order to achieve a representative sample from a cross-section of the university student body, the questionnaire was administered to students enrolled in courses classified as a part of the university's core curriculum. Freshmen and sophomores were overrepresented (84 percent of the sample versus 60 percent of the university population). Females were also overrepresented (62 percent of the sample versus 55 percent of the university population).

There are obvious disadvantages associated with the use of self-administered questionnaires for data-gathering purposes. One problem is the acceptance of student responses without benefit of contest. To maximize the return rate, questionnaires were administered during regularly scheduled class periods. Participation was on a voluntary basis. In order to establish the validity of responses, students were guaranteed anonymity. Students were also instructed to limit their responses regarding whether they had cheated to the current academic year.

Previous analysis (e.g., Haines et al. 1986) focused on the quantitative aspects of the questionnaire. The present analysis is intended to assess the narrative responses to the incidence of cheating in three forms, namely on major examinations, quizzes, and class assignments, as well as the perceptions of and attitudes held by students toward cheating and the effectiveness of de-

terrents to cheating. Students recorded their experiences in their own words. Most students (87 percent) responded to the open-ended portion of the questionnaire.

RESULTS

Of the 380 undergraduate students who participated in the spring survey, 54 percent indicated they had cheated during the previous six-month period. Students were requested to indicate whether cheating involved examination, weekly quizzes, and/or homework assignments. Much cheating took the form of looking on someone else's paper, copying homework, and either buying term papers or getting friends to write papers for them. Only five of the 205 students who admitted cheating reported being caught by the professor. However, seven percent (n = 27) of the students reported cheating more than five times during the preceding six-month period. Twenty percent (n = 76) indicated that most students openly approved of cheating. Only seventeen students reported they would inform the instructor if they saw another student cheating. Many students, especially older students, indicated they felt resentment toward cheaters, but most also noted that they would not do anything about it (i.e., inform the instructor).

To more fully explore the ways in which students neutralize their behavior, narrative data from admitted student cheaters were examined (n = 149). The narrative responses were easily classified into three of the five techniques [of neutralization] described by Sykes and Matza (1957).

Denial of Responsibility

Denial of responsibility was the most often identified response. This technique involves a declaration by the offenders that, in light of circumstances beyond their control, they cannot be held accountable for their actions. Rather than identifying the behavior as "accidental," they attribute wrongdoing to the influence of outside forces. In some instances, students expressed an inability to withstand peer pressure to cheat. Responses show a recognition of cheating as an unacceptable behavior, implying that under different circumstances cheating would not have occurred. One student commented:

> I was working forty plus hours a week and we had a lot to read for that day. I just couldn't get it all in. . . . I'm not saying cheating is okay, sometimes you just have to. . . .

Other responses demonstrate the attempt by students to succeed through legitimate means (e.g., taking notes and studying) only to experience failure. Accordingly, they were left with no alternative but to cheat. One student commented:

> . . . even though I've studied in the past, I've failed the exam so I cheated on my last test hoping to bring a better grade.

Another student explained his behavior in the following manner:

> I studied for the exam and I studied hard but the material on the test was different from what I expected. . . . I had to make a good grade. . . .

In addition, some students reported accidentally seeing other students' test papers. In such instances, the cheaters chastised classmates for not covering up their answer sheets. As one student wrote, such temptation simply cannot be overcome:

> I studied hard for the exam and needed an A. I just happened to look up and there was my neighbor's paper uncovered. I found myself checking my answers against his through the whole test.

Appeal to Higher Loyalties

Conflict also arises between peer group expectations and the normative expectations of the larger society. When this occurs, the individual may choose to sacrifice responsibility, thereby maintaining the interest of peers. Such allegiance allows these individuals to supercede moral obligations when special circumstances arise.

Students who invoke this technique of neutralization frequently described their behavior as an attempt to help another. One student stated:

> I only cheated because my friend had been sick and she needed help . . . it (cheating) wouldn't have happened any other time.

Another student denied any wrongdoing on her part as the following statement illustrates:

> I personally have never cheated. I've had friends who asked for help so I let them see my test. Maybe some would consider that to be cheating.

These students recognize the act of cheating is wrong. However, their statements also suggest that in some situations cheating can be overlooked. Loyalty to a friend in need takes precedence over honesty in the classroom. Another student described his situation in the following manner:

> I was tutoring this girl but she just couldn't understand the material. . . . I felt I had to help her on the test.

Condemnation of Condemners

Cheaters using this technique of neutralization attempt to shift attention from their own actions to the actions of others, most often authority figures. By criticizing those in authority as being unfair or unethical, the behavior of the offender seems less consequential by comparison. Therefore, dishonest behavior occurs in reaction to the perceived dishonesty of the authority figure. Students who use this technique wrote about uncaring, unprofessional instructors with negative attitudes who were negligent in their behavior. These incidents were said to be a precursor to their cheating behavior. The following response illustrates this view:

> The teachers here are boring and I dislike this school. The majority of teachers here don't care about the students and are rude when you ask them for help.

In other instances, students cite unfair teaching practices which they perceive to be the reason for their behavior. One student stated:

Major exams are very important to your grade and it seems that the majority of instructors make up the exams to try and trick you instead of testing your knowledge.

In this case, the instructor is thought to engage in a deliberate attempt to fail the students by making the examinations difficult. Also within this category were student accounts which frequently express a complaint of being overworked. As one student wrote:

One instructor assigns more work than anyone could possibly handle . . . at least I know I can't, so sometimes cheating is the answer . . .

Denial of Injury and Denial of the Victim

Denial of injury and denial of the victim do not appear in the student accounts of their cheating. In denial of injury, the wrongdoer states that no one was harmed or implies that accusations of injury are grossly exaggerated. In the second case, denial of the victim, those who violate norms often portray their targets as legitimate. Due to certain factors such as the societal role, personal characteristics, or lifestyle of the victim, the wrongdoer felt the victim "had it coming."

It is unlikely that students will either deny injury or deny the victim since there are no real targets in cheating. However, attempts to deny injury are possible when the one who is cheating argues that cheating is a personal matter rather than a public one. It is also possible that some students are cognizant of the effect their cheating activities have upon the educational system as a whole and, therefore, choose to neutralize their behavior in ways which allow them to focus on the act rather than the consequences of cheating. By observing

their actions from a myopic viewpoint, such students avoid the larger issues of morality.

CONCLUSION

The purpose of this report was to analyze student responses to cheating in their college coursework. Using Sykes and Matza's model of neutralization, we found that students rationalized their cheating behavior and did so without challenging the norm of honesty. Student responses fit three of the five techniques of neutralization. The most common technique is a denial of responsibility. Second, students tend to "condemn the condemners," blaming faculty and testing procedures. Finally, students "appeal to higher loyalties" by arguing that it is more important to help a friend than to avoid cheating. The use of these techniques of neutralization conveys the message that students recognize and accept cheating as an undesirable behavior which, nonetheless, can be excused under certain circumstances. Such findings reflect the prevalence of situational ethics.

The situation appears to be one in which students are not caught and disciplined by instructors. Additionally, students who cheat do not concern themselves with overt negative sanctions from other students. In some groups, cheating is planned, expected, and often rewarded in that students may receive better grades. That leaves a student's ethical, internalized control as a barrier to cheating. However, the neutralizing attitude allows students to sidestep issues of ethics and guilt by placing the blame for their behavior elsewhere. Neutralization allows them to state their belief that in general cheating is wrong, but in some special circumstances cheating is acceptable, even necessary. . . .

REFERENCES

Edwards, Paul. 1967. *The Encyclopedia of Philosophy, #3,* edited by Paul Edwards. New York: Macmillan Company and Free Press.

Fletcher, Joseph. 1966. *Situation Ethics: The New Morality.* Philadelphia: The Westminster Press.

Haines, Valerie J., George Diekhoff, Emily LaBeff, and Robert Clark. 1986. "College Cheating: Immaturity, Lack of Commitment, and the Neutralizing Attitude." *Research in Higher Education* 25:342–354.

Norris, Terry D., and Richard A. Dodder. 1979. "A Behavioral Continuum Synthesizing Neutralization Theory, Situational Ethics and Juvenile Delinquency." *Adolescence* 55:545–555.

Sykes, Gresham, and David Matza. 1957. "Techniques of Neutralization: A Theory of Delinquency." *American Sociological Review* 22:664–670.

REVIEW QUESTIONS

1. What are the researchers' major findings about college students cheating?
2. Identify and define the five types of neutralization described in the article.

PART TWELVE

UNDERPRIVILEGED DEVIANCE

As a young man, Mani Chulpayev came to New York from Russia with his family in 1989. He first worked with his father, who owned several food carts, selling pretzels and sausages. Then he quit because, he said, "I was driven by greed." He went into extortion rackets with several immigrants from his home country. They made as much as $500 a week shaking down owners of furniture stores, restaurants, bakeries, and travel agencies. Chulpayev used pistols, knives, and stun guns to enforce payments from the victims. He also pimped prostitutes, two or three at a time, importing them from Moscow on six-month contracts. His luck finally ran out in 1998 when he was arrested after a furniture store proprietor complained to the F.B.I. about extortion. At the time, Chulpayev was in Los Angeles delivering a prostitute to a group of Russian doctors.[1]

As a participant in organized crime, Chulpayev can be said to engage in underprivileged deviance. Such a deviance typically occurs among underprivileged people—the relatively poor, powerless, or inadequately educated. It is also distinguishable from privileged deviance in being less profitable or—if not so, as in the case of successful organized crime—more disreputable and more liable to be punished and punished severely.

Here we take a look at various forms of underprivileged deviance. In the first article, "Burglary: The Offender's Perspective," Paul Cromwell reports from his study of thirty burglars what they think they should consider in order to commit their crime successfully. In the second article, "Interactional Dynamics in Robbery," Andy Hochstetler finds from his study of twenty-two robbers how they interact with other criminals in order to enjoy partying and decide on whether and how to commit robbery. In the third reading, "Cockfighting: The Marketing of Deviance," Donna Darden and Steven Worden find that although the illegality of cockfighting—popular in poor rural communities—can be expected to encourage cheating and other related deviances, cockfighters strive to establish their reputation for honesty and trustworthiness. In the fourth selection, "The World of Dogfighting," Rhonda Evans and Craig Forsyth show a similar paradox about another favorite sport of the rural poor: despite the deviant status of dogfighting, the "dogmen" consider themselves respectable and endeavor to make their transactions with each other as respectable as conventional business dealings.

---

1. Bill Berkeley, "Code of Betrayal, Not Silence, Shines Light on Russian Mob," *New York Times,* August 19, 2002, pp. A1, A14.

295

BURGLARY:
THE OFFENDER'S PERSPECTIVE

PAUL CROMWELL

Burglary is easy, man. I've done about 500 [burglaries] and only been convicted one time.
—Billy, a juvenile burglar

Why am I a burglar? It's easy money. . . . Beats working!
—Robert, a 20-year-old burglar

These burglars are essentially correct in their appraisal of the benefits and risks associated with burglary. Burglary constitutes one of the most prevalent predatory crimes, with an estimated 5.1 million burglary offenses committed in 1990, resulting in monetary losses estimated to be more than $3.4 billion annually. Yet only about one-half of all burglaries are even reported to the police (Bureau of Justice Statistics, 1991). More alarming still, U.S. Department of Justice statistics reveal that less than 15 percent of all reported burglaries are cleared by arrest. Consequently, burglary has been the subject of a great deal of research in the hope that understanding will lead to the development of effective prevention measures and ultimately to reduction in the incidence of burglary (Lynch, 1990).

THEORETICAL PERSPECTIVE

Here I will report findings from a study of burglars and burglary as seen through the perspective of the offenders themselves. The study addresses several issues critical to the understanding of burglary and to the consequent development of burglary prevention and control strategies. Among these are: (1) How do residential burglars choose targets? and (2) What determines a burglar's perception of a particular site as a vulnerable target?

Such issues are based on the theory that the commission of a crime is primarily a product of opportunity. Thus, how burglars choose targets and make other relevant decisions has much to do with the opportunity for carrying out burglary. In fact, several researchers have concluded that the majority of burglaries result from exploitation of opportunity rather than careful, rational planning (Scarr, 1973; Rengert and Wasilchick, 1985, 1989; Cromwell, Olson, and Avary, 1991). The assumptions are that offenders develop a sensitivity to the opportunities in everyday life for illicit gain and that burglars see criminal opportunity in situations where others might not. This "alert opportunism"

Source: Written specifically for this reader, with portions drawn from *Breaking and Entering: An Ethnographic Analysis of Burglary* (Newbury Park, CA: Sage, 1991) by Paul Cromwell, James N. Olson, and D'Aunn W. Avary. Reprinted with permission.

(Shover, 1971) allows them to rapidly recognize and take advantage of potential criminal opportunities. Their unique perspective toward the world results from learning experiences that have sensitized them to events ignored by most. Just as an architect looking at a house notes its functional, technological, and aesthetic qualities, burglars perceive it in terms of its vulnerability to break-in and potential for gain. They do not simply see an open window, but the chance for covert entry and a "fast buck." These perceptual processes are almost automatic and are as much a part of the tools of the burglar as a pry bar or a window jimmy.

METHOD

The Sample

Thirty *active* burglars in an urban area of 250,000 population in a southwestern state were recruited as research subjects (hereinafter referred to as informants) using a snowball sampling procedure. They were promised complete anonymity and a "referral fee" of $50 for each active burglar referred by them and accepted for the study. They were also paid a stipend of $50 for each interview session. The initial three informants were introduced to the researchers by police burglary detectives who had been asked to recommend "burglars who would be candid and cooperate with the study."

The final sample consisted of 27 men and 3 women, of whom 10 were White, 9 Hispanic, and 11 African American. The mean age of these informants was 25 years with the range 16 to 43.

Procedure

The procedure consisted of extensive interviews and "ride alongs," during which informants were asked to reconstruct burglaries they had previously committed and to evaluate sites burglarized by other informants in the study. During these sessions, previously burglarized residences were visited, evaluated, and rated on their attractiveness as burglary targets. Informants were also asked to select sites in the same neighborhood that they considered too risky as targets and to explain why they were less vulnerable than those previously burglarized. At each site informants were asked to rate the "hypothetical" vulnerability of the site to burglary on a scale of 0 to 10. A rating of "0" meant "Under the circumstances that are present now, I would not burglarize this residence." A rating of "10" meant "This is a very attractive and vulnerable target and I would definitely take steps to burglarize it right now." Informants were told that a rating of "5" was an "average" score. At the conclusion of the study, informants had participated in as many as nine sessions and had evaluated up to thirty previously burglarized and high-risk sites. Four hundred sixty previously burglarized and high-risk sites were evaluated. Each session was tape recorded and verbatim transcripts were made.

FINDINGS

Motivation

Almost every informant used some of his or her proceeds from burglary to buy food or clothing and to pay for shelter, transportation, and other licit needs. However, the greatest percentage of proceeds went toward the purchase of drugs and alcohol and for the activity the burglars loosely labeled "partying." In fact, most informants stressed their need for money to fulfill these needs as the *primary* motivation for their burglaries. Only one informant reported a primary need for money to purchase something other than alcohol or drugs or for partying.

Second in importance was the need for money to maintain a "fast, expensive life." Keeping up appearances was stressed by many as a critical concern. One young burglar reported:

> *The ladies, they like a dude that's got good clothes. You gotta look good and you gotta have bread. Me, I'm always looking good.*

Katz (1988) has noted that young people may find certain property crimes (joyriding, vandalism, burglary, shoplifting) appealing, independent of material gain or esteem from peers. He categorized these as "sneaky crimes that frequently thrill their practioneers" (p. 53). Similarly, in the present study, almost every informant mentioned excitement and thrills; however, only a few would commit a burglary for that purpose only. Like Reppetto (1974), we concluded that the younger, less experienced burglars were more prone to commit crimes for the thrill and excitement.

Time of Burglary

Rengert and Wasilchick (1985, 1989) found that burglars work during periods when residences are left unguarded. We found the same thing. Our informants stated they preferred to work between 9:00 and 11:00 A.M. and in mid-afternoon. Most organized their working hours around school hours, particularly during the times when parents (usually mothers) took children to school and picked them up after school. Several told us that they waited "until the wife left to take the kids to school or to go shopping." Most stated that they did not do burglaries on Saturday because most people were home then. Only a small number (*n* = 3) of burglars in our study committed burglaries at night. Most preferred to commit their crimes during hours when they expected people to be at work and out of the home. Those who did night-time burglary usually knew the victims and their schedules or took advantage of people being away from home in the evening.

Inside Information

Burglars often work with "inside men" who have access to potential targets and advise the burglar about things to steal. They may also provide such critical information as times when the owner is away and of weaknesses in security. One female burglar reported that she maintained close contact with several women who worked as maids in affluent sections of the community. She would gain the necessary information from these women and

later come back and break into the house, often entering by a door or window left open for her by the accomplice. Others gained information from friends and acquaintances who unwittingly revealed information about potential burglary targets. One told us:

> I have friends who mow yards for people and work as maids and stuff. When they talk about the people they work for, I keep my ears open. They give me information without knowing it.

Information about potential targets is frequently gained from "fences." Because many fences have legitimate occupations, they may have knowledge of the existence of valuable property from social or business relationships. They can often provide the burglar with information about the owners' schedules and the security arrangements at the target site.

People involved in a variety of service jobs (repair, carpet cleaning, pizza delivery, lawn maintenance, plumbing, carpentry) enter many homes each day and have the opportunity to assess the quality of potential stolen merchandise and security measures taken by the residents. Burglars will often establish contact with employees of these businesses for purposes of obtaining this "inside" information. One informant said:

> I know this guy who works for [carpet cleaning business]. He sometimes gives me information on a good place to hit and I split with him.

Occupancy Probes

Almost all burglars avoid selecting houses that are occupied as targets. Only two informants stated that they would enter a residence they knew was occupied. Therefore, it is important that the burglar develop techniques for probing the potential target site to determine if anyone is at home. The most common probe used by our informants was to send one of the burglars to the door to knock or ring the doorbell. If someone answered, the prober would ask directions to a nearby address or for a nonexistent person, for example, "Is Ray home?" The prospective burglar would apologize and leave when told that he or she had the wrong address. A female informant reported that she carried her two-year-old child to the target residence door, asking for directions to a nearby address. She reported:

I ask them for a drink [of water] for the baby. Even when they seem suspicious they almost always let me in to get the baby a drink.

Several informants reported obtaining the resident's name from the mailbox or a sign over the door. They would then look up the telephone number and call the residence, leaving the phone ringing while they returned to the target home. If they could still hear the phone ringing when they arrived at the house, they were sure it was unoccupied.

Burglar Alarms

In general, burglars agreed that alarms were a definite deterrent to their activities. Other factors being equal, they preferred to locate a target that did not have an alarm instead of taking the additional risk involved in attempting to burglarize a house with an alarm system. More than 90 percent of the informants reported that they would not choose a target with an alarm system. Most were deterred merely by a sign or window sticker stating that the house was protected by an alarm system. As Richard, an experienced burglar, stated:

Why take a chance? There's lots of places without alarms. Maybe they're bluffing, maybe they ain't.

Although several informants boasted about disarming alarms, when pressed for details, almost all admitted that they did not know how to accomplish that task. One informant stated that while she could not disarm a burglar alarm, she was not deterred by an alarm. She stated that once the alarm was tripped, she still had time to complete the burglary and escape before police or private security arrived. She explained that she never took more than 10 minutes to enter, search, and exit a house. She advised:

Police take 15 to 20 minutes to respond to an alarm. Security [private security] sometimes gets there a little faster. I'm gone before any of them gets there.

Locks on Doors and Windows

Past research has been inconsistent regarding the deterrent value of locks on windows and doors. A few studies have reported that burglars consider the type of lock installed at a prospective target site in their target selection decision. Others did not find locks to be a significant factor in the selection process.

The majority of informants in the present study initially stated that locks did not deter them. However, during burglary reconstructions, we discovered that given two potential target sites, all other factors being equal, burglars prefer not to deal with a deadbolt lock. Several told us that they allowed themselves only one or two minutes to effect entry and that a good deadbolt lock slowed them down too much.

The variation in findings regarding security hardware appears related to the burglar's level of expertise and experience. To the extent to which burglars are primarily opportunistic and inexperienced, locks appear to have deterrent value. The opportunistic burglar chooses targets based on their perceived vulnerability to burglary at a given time. Given a large number of potential targets, the burglar tends to select the most vulnerable of the target pool. A target with a good lock and fitted with other security hardware will usually not be perceived to be as vulnerable as one without those items. The professional or "good" burglar chooses targets on the basis of factors other than situational vulnerability and conceives ways in which he or she can overcome impediments to the burglary (such as the target site being fitted with a high-quality deadbolt lock). Thus, to the extent that burglars are skilled and experienced, deadbolt locks have limited utility for crime prevention. However, our findings support the deterrent value of deadbolt locks. Seventy-five percent of the burglaries reconstructed during our research were opportunistic offenses. Many of those burglaries would have been prevented by the presence of a quality deadbolt lock. *It is important to note that nearly one-half of the burglary sites in the present study were entered through open or unlocked windows and doors.*

Dogs

Almost all studies agree that dogs are an effective deterrent to burglary. Although there is some individual variation among burglars, the general rule is to bypass a house with a dog—any dog. Large dogs represent a physical threat to the burglar and small ones are often noisy, attracting attention to a burglar's activities. We found that although many burglars have developed contingency plans to deal with dogs (petting, feeding, or even killing them), most burglars prefer to avoid them. When asked what were considered absolute "no-go" factors, most burglars responded that dogs were second only to occupancy. However, approximately 30 percent of the informants *initially* discounted the presence of dogs as a deterrent. Yet, during "ride alongs," the sight or sound of a dog at a potential target site almost invariably resulted in a "no-go" decision. As Richard said:

> I don't mess with no dogs. If they got dogs, I go someplace else.

Debbie reported that she was concerned primarily with small dogs:

> Little dogs "yap" too much. They [neighbors] look to see what they are so excited about. I don't like little yapping dogs.

Opportunity and Burglary

The "professional burglars" among our informants tended to select targets in a purposive manner, analyzing the physical and social characteristics of the environment and choosing targets that they knew from experience were ideally vulnerable. But by far the greater proportion of the informants were opportunistic. The targets they chose appeared particularly vulnerable *at the time.* Thus,

most burglaries in the jurisdiction studies seem to result from the propitious juxtaposition of target, offender, and situation.

Our findings suggest that a burglar's decision to "hit" a target is based primarily on environmental cues that are perceived to have immediate consequences. Most burglars appear to attend only to the present; future events or consequences do not weigh heavily in their risk-versus-gain calculation. Drug-using burglars and juveniles are particularly oriented to this immediate-gain and immediate-risk decision process. Non-drug-using and experienced burglars are probably less likely to attend only to immediate risks and gains. Our informants, though experienced burglars, were all drug users, and tended to have a "here and now" orientation toward the rewards and costs associated with burglary.

Exploiting opportunity characterized the target selection processes in more than 75 percent of the burglaries reconstructed during our research. Even professional burglars among our informants often took advantage of opportunities when they arose. Chance opportunities occasionally presented themselves while the professional was "casing" and "probing" potential burglary targets chosen by more rational means. When these opportunities arose, the professional burglar was as likely as other burglars to take advantage of the situation.

IMPLICATIONS FOR CRIME PREVENTION

This study suggests burglars may be much more opportunistic than previously believed. The opportunistic burglar chooses targets based on their perceived vulnerability to burglary at a given time. Given a large number of potential targets, the burglar tends to select the most vulnerable of the target pool. The burglar does not, however, choose targets on the basis of situational vulnerability alone. He also considers how to overcome impediments to the burglary.

Programs designed to prevent burglary must be based on valid assumptions about burglars and burglary. Measures designed to combat the relatively small population of high-incidence "professional" burglars tend to overemphasize the skill and determination of most burglars. These measures are expensive, complex, and require long-term commitment at many levels. However, the typical burglar is not a calculating professional against whom complex prevention tactics must be employed. In fact, most burglars are young, unskilled, and opportunistic. This suggests that emphasis should be directed at such factors as surveillability, occupancy, and accessibility. More specifically, dogs, good locks, and alarm systems deter most burglars. Methods that give a residence the "illusion of occupancy" (Cromwell, Olson, and Avary, 1990) deter almost all burglars and are maintained with little effort or cost. Our study suggests that these simple steps may be the most cost-efficient and effective means for residents to insulate themselves from victimization by burglars.

REFERENCES

Bureau of Justice Statistics. October 1991. Criminal Victimization 1990. *Bulletin.* Washington, DC: U.S. Department of Justice.

Cromwell, Paul, James N. Olson, and D'Aunn Avary. 1991. *Breaking and Entering: An Ethnographic Analysis of Burglary.* Newbury Park, CA: Sage.

Katz, Jack. 1988. *Seductions of Crime.* New York: Basic Books.

Lynch, James P. 1990. Modeling Target Selection in Burglary: Differentiating Substance from Method. Paper presented at the 1990 annual meeting of the American Society of Criminology, Baltimore, Maryland.

Rengert, G., and J. Wasilchick. 1985. *Suburban Burglary: A Time and a Place for Everything.* Springfield, IL: Charles C. Thomas.

Rengert, G., and J. Wasilchick. 1989. *Space, Time and Crime: Ethnographic Insights into Residential Burglary.* A report prepared for the National Institute of Justice. (Mimeo).

Reppetto, T. G. 1974. *Residential Crime.* Cambridge, MA: Ballinger.

Scarr, H. A. 1973. *Patterns of Burglary.* Washington, DC: U.S. Government Printing Office.

Shover, Neal. 1971. *Burglary as an Occupation.* Ph.D. Dissertation, University of Illinois. Ann Arbor, MI: University Microfilms, 1975.

REVIEW QUESTIONS

1. Of what value are "inside men" to someone who wants to engage in burglary?
2. What are some factors that encourage a burglar to pick one house instead of another?

INTERACTIONAL DYNAMICS IN ROBBERY

ANDY HOCHSTETLER

In this paper I apply an interactionist approach to investigating the processes by which offenders subjectively interpret and define situations in choosing to commit crime. I draw on interviews with 22 robbers who committed their crime with others. Analysis of these interviews reveals some common patterns of interpersonal dynamics, rooted in street activities, that contribute to situational construction of criminal opportunity. By communicating their emerging preferences or by referring to target characteristics, offenders negotiate a shared sense of opportunity. Interaction can reduce the appeal of law-abidingness to group participants and make developing criminal opportunity difficult to refuse. In addition, co-offender interaction can act as a catalyst for crime by increasing access to illicit pathways and easing the pursuit of criminal objectives.

STREET ACTIVITIES

[Robbers'] descriptions of decision making contrast with depictions of crime choice that cast it as calculating and purposeful. Many robbers report that they do not plan their crimes or spend only a few minutes planning. Robbers often ignore and can put out of mind consequences of being caught while considering a crime. In this study, several subjects exhibited an extreme lack of concern with

consequences by choosing to commit crimes in which they were sure to be suspects. Some pawned goods using accurate identification, loitered or aimlessly drove their cars near the scene of recently committed robberies, robbed victims they knew, or indifferently allowed themselves to be photographed during an offense.

The hallmark of street life, as a style of living, is pursuit of pleasure and status through conspicuous leisure and consumption "with minimal concern for obligations and commitments that are external to the immediate social setting" (Shover and Honaker, 1992:283). Street-offenders live for the moment. . . .

[Robbers] share their chaotic lifestyles and parties with compatible friends and a loose network of associates who live similarly. Expensive drug and alcohol habits, fighting, shoplifting, writing bad checks, and amassing debt to drug dealers, lawyers, and other creditors are normal in their circles of friends. Street-offenders often sleep in cheap motels or on associates' couches or move from party to party with little idea of where they will rest next (Wright and Decker, 1997:38). Curtis, a heroin addict, explains that a continuous and mobile party allowed him to maintain his drug habit by reciprocal sharing with others. His lifestyle made locating criminal opportunities effortless and led him to his robbery co-offender, a man that he scarcely knew.

Source: Andy Hochstetler, "Opportunities and Decisions: Interactional Dynamics in Robbery and Burglary Groups," *Criminology,* vol. 39 (2001), pp. 737–763. Reprinted with permission.

. . . Small groups of friends intent on "partying," a word unambiguously meaning drug consumption and action-seeking to offenders, comprise most theft groups. In this sample, 44 subjects were drinking or under the influence of controlled substances during their crime. Levels of consumption on the day of the crime were extreme even by the standards of men who construct their lives around drug use and drinking. A robber reports: "I drank a lot. After my divorce, I drank a lot. But, on that day I drank more. We was drinking a *whole lot* on that day!" A robber currently serving his third sentence for the crime describes the occasion preceding his last offense:

> *Well, it more or less started out like most of them do: getting high with my buddy there and riding around drinking. Stopped off to get a few Valiums, and we was just riding around here and there. You know, stopped at a buddy's here. It was an all day thing, drinking and driving, driving and drinking . . . I was in and out [of consciousness]. I would get so drunk he would drive, and then he would get so drunk I would drive while he was sleeping. And just more or less the whole day went on like that.*

Offenders encounter many people during their extended parties. As a result, the composition of a group often changes as it proceeds toward crime. Some participants excuse themselves from company suspected to be on a criminal course, whereas others are quick to volunteer. A persistent robber remembers the outcome of his group's plan to rob a gas station: "[t]he other guys backed out, didn't show . . . just me and the guy that worked at the station, we carried out the plan." Continued participation in a scene already construed by others as potentially criminal conveys approval of a criminal course. Restraining influences on a group diminish as those wary of crime and less committed to the party depart.

INTERACTIONAL DYNAMICS

Subjects described three general styles of interaction that made illicit opportunity apparent and readily accessible.

Incremental Signaling

In many cases, small decisions and incremental actions made more or less intentionally and by multiple participants alter situations and perceptions until criminal choice is attractive. [This is] what I term *incremental signaling.*

Deliberation begins ambiguously, but escalates quickly. Typically, someone in the group mentions an apparent need for money. The context makes it clear that a suggestion is being made that the group has the potential for acquiring money illegally. Next, a participant mentions a specific type of crime or target.

. . . Two robbers recall definitive progressions in verbal deliberation:

> *Yeah, it went, "we need some damn money" and then here he sat and told us all. Well, we were all sittin' there, and he was telling us about robberies or whatever, and he told us how to do it.*

> *We was riding around gettin' high, and I was telling them that I needed to make some money for Christmas. They kinda looked at each other and started laughin'. They pretty much said, "you need some easy money, you're with the right people." I said, "that's what I'm talking about." When they said fast and easy, I didn't know they meant armed robbery.*

Criminal proposals are provisional but are often made by those participants who have established a relatively firm definition of a situation. One thief reported that his drug habit did not allow him to be selective about criminal opportunity. When conversations turn to crime, he immediately directs the group toward action with a challenge: "let's go then . . . if they are for real, if they really want to do something, then they will do it right then cuz there ain't no sense talking about it." Because criminal conversations often begin with ambiguous or exploratory statements, the influence of people who speak tersely and forcefully during decision making is substantial. . . . An offender remembers how an outspoken participant influenced his group's decision making:

> *He wanted them how he wanted them, and he was the main one who hollered at people to get things*

done. He said, "let's go do this!" And I tell you, he had a way of talking you into it. He had this way, "oh come on pussy" and this and that and the other. There was one that was real dominant.

Target Convergence

Some groups reach criminal decisions when participants mutually and instantaneously recognize an appealing target, what I term *target convergence*. These groups seemingly converge on a target with only the slightest communication between offenders. The eight subjects whose groups clearly reached their decisions in this manner had participants with extensive criminal experience and exposure to street life. However, none of these groups had committed a robbery . . . together previously. The groups did not discuss crime because they did not set out to commit one, but when an opportunity appeared, talk was not necessary. Appealing targets trigger a group's partially formed and contingent criminal frame of a situation. Targets stand out against a recently constructed backdrop of illicit potential.

Many spontaneous robbers find conspicuous contrast between their situational understandings and ignorant victims who, without realizing the danger, "flash their money around" or "play [the robbers] for punks" or who simply are "somewhere they don't belong." In these situations, deliberative communication with robbery partners is limited to abrupt gestures, nods, or a few words. A robber recalls that his crime began when an older group of men challenged his friends to a fight. When the younger men did not balk, the groups made a frail peace by mentioning mutual associates and sharing a bottle. The newfound allies, apparently on edge from the averted fight, assaulted a stranger who entered the scene minutes later:

We were just sitting there chillin', and I asked one of the guys do he got a cigarette . . . About this time, he says "nah," and he says "but I bet you this dude got one coming down the street." So, I went over there and, you know, asked the dude for a cigarette. One of them dudes comes runnin' across the parking lot and hit him—just Boom! So, when he

hit him, [he] hit the ground, and just immediately we started kicking him. While we was beating him, others was going in his pockets gettin' everything he got.

Establishing Identity

Criminality can be a group identity or a mental device shared by participants for organizing events and predicting group action. Participants' knowledge of others in the group, whether gained in first-hand experience or by reputation, frames how a group sees its potential. The characters inhabiting street scenes often have reputations for criminal capability that precede them. These reputations play a significant part in turning group participants' heads toward illicit opportunity.

Most group offenders have first-hand knowledge of co-offenders' criminal potential. . . . [S]ubjects from [these] experienced groups report that their group interaction began and proceeded with the potential for crime in participants' minds. Shared criminal experiences are especially salient in ascribing criminal potential to a group. Several subjects knew others in their group for years before committing a felony together, but stole every time they were together after the first offense. Although individual criminal careers are usually diverse, crime groups often specialize in method and target selection. This shared specialization suggests that participants associate assembly of the practiced group with particular opportunity (Warr, 1996).

INTERPERSONAL INFLUENCE

To this point, I have described how offenders cooperatively negotiate shared recognition of criminal opportunity. Indeed, most subjects took care to assert that crime participants mutually influence each other and that each offender exercises considerable agency in crime choice. Nevertheless, as the preceding discussion of interactional dynamics implies, some participants have more influence on a group's behavior than do others. Almost all subjects readily identified the most influential person(s) in their group's decision. Nine interviewees identified themselves as leaders and several more viewed themselves as instigators in their last offense.

Directives made to a group have the greatest influence when participants attribute relevant expertise or experience to the speaker. Offenders sometimes ascribe expertise to partners with a paucity of information, however. Subjects cite co-offenders' age, toughness, confident demeanor, and criminal reputations as sources of influence. Partners' presumed and proven criminal abilities not only lead others to look toward criminal opportunity, but also define power relations in the group.

In some groups, offenders provide drugs and alcohol to reduce fear of criminal participation (Cromwell et al., 1991:64). A severe alcoholic reports that when he refused a criminal proposal, his partner bought more liquor in an attempt to "get me drunk . . . to where I didn't give a damn." Collecting and displaying weapons or other facilitating hardware also elicits criminal ideas and shapes the behavior of others (Carlson et al., 1990; Lofland, 1969:69–72). A young man recalls his surprise when his partners suddenly presented tools needed to stage a robbery: "the guns was theirs; they had them and some ski masks already in the car."

Most subjects reported that at least one group participant contemplated or made some preparation for their crime before the group assembled. The consistent finding that many thieves keep a store of potential targets in mind until they need them or an opportune situation arises supports their claim. Six subjects said that before discussing specific criminal plans their group arrived at a target that was preselected by another participant. A home invasion robber contends that until he saw the target, he thought his group's plan was to intimidate a nonpaying drug customer as his partners had implied:

> I mean, as soon as we pulled up—and they had gone in and come out to get me—and when I got inside, that's when I first knew. I mean, they didn't tell me outside before I went in; that's the part I couldn't understand about it. All I knew is that the people in there [a wealthy attorney's home] wouldn't mess with these two guys.

Offenders who are the most hesitant or uninformed often become acutely aware of the influence of others on their actions in the instant before they offend. When confronting a target, they realize that their previous decisions and the actions of co-offenders constrain their options. The most motivated offenders in a group often turn from subtle to overt means of influence in an attempt to overcome this late hesitation.

CONCLUSION

Understanding why people who are not determined to commit a crime one minute become so the next requires attention to the immediate situations that link street life and criminal decisions. This paper shows that interaction with other people in distinctive compositional settings and organizing activities conditions criminal choice. Findings support portrayals of criminal decision making as complex, bounded by the desperate circumstances of offenders' lives, and framed by the pursuit of an escapist party. Moreover, findings suggest that examining offenders' fallible perceptions of costs and benefits or their commitment to conduct norms of street life only begins to capture complexity in criminal decision making.

Many investigators portray criminal motivation either as an enduring predisposition or else as an attraction to offending that remains dormant until an encounter with a target (Jacobs and Wright, 1999:164). Criminological theories suggest models of overdetermined individuals who are driven to crime and waiting for a chance to satisfy their preferences. However, conceptual distinctions between opportunity and motivation blur when ethnographers and situational analysts examine decisions and interaction preceding crime (Athens, 1997; Short and Strodtbeck, 1965; Wolfgang, 1958). . . . [R]obbers construct criminal opportunity by comparing recently formulated understandings with developing events and adjusting situations to make events and understanding correspond. Criminal choice "blends indiscriminately into the flow of practical activity" as offenders improvise action and expectations to suit ever-shifting circumstances in informal situations (Emirbayer and Mische, 1999). Some crime groups are more goal directed than are others, but only a few pursue determined and consistent ends known equally to all; more typically, the rational path mutates as options open and close and as participants interact to make sequential choices. Participants in this study contend that the immediate allure of crime is incomprehensible without considering preparation, cajoling, encouragement, and other enabling and constraining action by others.

Qualitative and interactionist studies of crime have great potential. This paper, however, is not a call for a particular methodology, but for empirical attention to "immediate background and context of offenders' action" (Katz, 1991:167). Examining event characteristics may support well-worn theories and improve specification of established models. For example, offenders without biographical characteristics correlated with street crime may offend when their lives take a short-term turn for the worse or when they are in the company of those who clearly are at risk of offending. Reducing the accessibility of targets may deter groups without experience. Groups that have committed many crimes may be willing to take on greater risks or only be displaced by a challenging target. In methodologies that examine crime as an outcome of individual offenders' characteristics, potential sources of variation escape notice. Group crimes are an intersection of participants' pathways in which [actors] and their characteristics meld and interact with environments to shape events.

REFERENCES

Athens, Lonnie H. 1997. *Violent Criminal Acts and Actors Revisited.* Chicago, Ill.: University of Chicago Press.

Carlson, Michael, Amy Marcus-Newhall, and Norman Miller. 1990. Effects of situational aggression cues: A quantitative review. *Journal of Personality and Social Psychology* 58:622–633.

Cromwell, Paul F., James N. Olson, and D'aunn Wester Avary. 1991. *Breaking and Entering: An Ethnographic Analysis of Burglary.* Newbury Park, Calif.: Sage.

Emirbayer, Mustafa, and Ann Mische. 1998. What is agency? *American Journal of Sociology* 103: 962–1023.

Jacobs, Bruce A., and Richard T. Wright. 1999. Stickup, street culture, and offender motivation. *Criminology* 37:149–174.

Katz, Jack. 1991. The motivation of persistent robbers. In Michael Tonry (ed.), *Crime and Justice: An Annual Review of Research* 14:149–173. Chicago, Ill.: University of Chicago Press.

Lofland, John. 1969. *Deviance and Identity.* Englewood Cliffs, N.J.: Prentice-Hall.

Short, James F., and Fred Strodtbeck. 1965. *Group Process and Gang Delinquency.* Chicago, Ill.: University of Chicago Press.

Shover, Neal, and David Honaker. 1992. The Socially Bounded Decision Making of Persistent Property Offenders. *Howard Journal of Criminal Justice* 31:276–290.

Warr, Mark. 1996. Organization and instigation in delinquent groups. *Criminology* 34:11–37.

Wolfgang, Marvin E. 1958. *Patterns in Criminal Homicide.* Philadelphia: University of Pennsylvania Press.

Wright, Richard T., and Scott Decker. 1997. *Armed Robbers in Action.* Boston, Mass.: Northeastern University.

REVIEW QUESTIONS

1. What conditions criminal choice, according to Hochstetler's paper?
2. List and describe the three general styles of interaction identified in this study.

COCKFIGHTING:
THE MARKETING OF DEVIANCE

DONNA K. DARDEN
STEVEN K. WORDEN

Then one day I was driving through a small town . . . and I noticed one of the nicest set-ups for gamefowl that I have ever seen. I stopped . . . and gazed. . . . About that time an old man came out of his house and started towards me. . . . He said he remembers seeing me . . . buying fowl off a friend of his. The same man who got me started in this sport. . . . I was talking to probably the toughest, most honest and complete rooster man alive today, at least I think so. Anyway, we introduced ourselves and he told me about how he had tried to locate me about a year ago. I asked Sal why he tried to find me of all people and he said because he needed a partner. Well, when he said that, I about fell out of my shoes. Sal then explained that he had just moved to Oklahoma a few years ago and that he wanted someone who was a beginner in this sport, willing to learn what fifty years of cockfighting had taught him. (Whitney, 1991, p. 150)

Prus (1989a, 1989b) has shown us the close relationship which can exist between sociology and much of marketing. [That is,] the ethnographic study of marketing in action—the observation of salespeople selling, for example—can add to our knowledge of sociology. Here, we use a qualitative approach to the marketing of game fowl and the sport of cockfighting to illuminate problems which may be common in the deliberate spread and diffusion of other deviant activities, and we note the gamefowl world's attempts at solutions.

Cockfighting is a hobby and sport for all of its practitioners, and a business venture for the many who sell gamefowl and accessories. Like any small business person, the entrepreneurial cockfighter faces a different set of problems from those that General Motors and IBM contend with, yet he too must work within a set of forces which shapes his activities. We look here at the market forces which affect entrepreneurial cockfighters and the solutions they find as they and their consumers construct the marketing of a deviant sport and the fighting cock as a commercial object.

Source: Donna K. Darden and Steven K. Worden, "Cockfighting: The Marketing of Deviance," *Society and Animals,* vol. 4, no. 2 (1996), pp. 211–231. Reprinted with permission of White Horse Press.

After a brief description of cockfighting, we will describe our research and discuss how cockfighters market their questionable sport. We will show how marketing deviance differs from more conventional marketing.

COCKFIGHTING

Cockfighting is a very old sport—some even claim "the oldest" (Dundes, 1994, p. vii). In 386 Saint Augustine used a description of a cockfight in his "De Ordine" to illustrate evil in the world. Although cockfighting is not universal, it may be the closest to a universal sport, occurring almost everywhere that chickens live. There are cultural nuances to the fights which occur in different places, some differences larger than nuances (bare-spurred versus the "slasher" fights, for example, see below), but the elements are fairly standard, owing to the inherent elements of pitting two roosters against each other to fight.

A cockfight consists of several rounds of putting weight-matched pairs of specially bred roosters against each other in a pit. Depending on the circumstances, they usually fight until one is dead. The birds are often brightly colored, and, again depending on the circumstances, a fight may be awesomely savage and, in its way, beautiful, although bloody. Spectators usually make bets on the birds, in any of several fashions, frequently calling out bets even as the fight progresses. Birds may fight bare-heeled (rarely) or with knives ("slashers") or gaffs (slender, pointed spurs) attached. The knife fight is quicker and bloodier, and more rounds are held during a session. During the gaff fight, it is normal for both birds to be wounded and exhausted but still living, so they may be dragged to a pit where they lie near each other. One or the other will usually rise up one last time to peck at the other, evidencing the quality of "deep gameness," and winning the fight. They may stay in the drag pit for an hour or more. During that time, other birds are fighting in the main pit. Most of the people involved in cockfighting are men, although there are some women in-

volved. The settings for the fights are usually rural, and range from the informal fight in a farmer's yard to the formal, specially constructed pits in a few areas of the country such as the Neighbors Game Club in Cibola, Arizona, which seats 350 people.

Most often, a cockfight is like other rural small town events, such as a rodeo or a high school ballgame. Although as Bryant and Capel (1974) have pointed out, cockfights attract people from all levels of the stratification system, our data show that people from the high-end of the social hierarchy are underrepresented: rural poor, construction workers and agriculturists predominate at most cockfights. People wear levis, overalls, camo outfits, and the occasional sport shirt. They generally sit on wooden benches or mill around. There is often a sign posted saying, "No Profanity, Alcohol, or Gambling." During daylight fights, there is usually gambling, but the alcohol and profanity are less obvious than they are at night fights, which can go on all night. Behavior at these fights can get rough, so that there may be as much fighting in the stands as in the pits. During daylight fights, children run around, men stand around and tell tales, women talk. There is little unanimity in the crowd. For a person who does not have money riding on a particular fight, the scene can grow boring. The fighting of the roosters often looks more like a pair of robins arguing over turf in one's front yard than a WWF scene, a lot of wing flapping and little more. If the ground is red clay, such as in the area we studied, and the birds both brightly colored, one may see little or no blood, just a lot of dust. The smells and sounds resemble a rodeo more than anything else. The atmosphere is rather like that of a secret club. Cockers do not believe that outsiders and those who oppose the sport know anything about it, but they do not want video pictures taken or newspaper accounts given. They feel like they are "in on something."

Referees are usually cockfighters themselves, men who are not fighting birds at this particular event. They are chosen and paid by the house, and ratified by the people in attendance. If people do not trust them, they will not return to that pit. Most are trusted by the crowd; Worden attended one fight where a referee's wife was fighting, but everyone believed him to be impartial. Referees are most important when the birds are dragged to the pit; they may be accused of counting fast or slow at these occasions.

BACKGROUND

Like marrying your cousin, cockfighting is illegal in most states in this country and frowned upon in the rest. Schiff (1995) called it a "degraded gladiatorial spectacle," categorizing it with professional wrestling, a comparison students often made for us in classroom discussions, except that students ranked it much lower than wrestling, in a league sometimes with wife-beating. There can be no arguing its disvalued status in much of our society. How do people get involved in such a disvalued activity, especially one that is inherently social, shared with others, rather than a type of secretive deviance? Some cockfighters got into their sport through the propinquity that must also assist people in falling in love with their cousins, as the novelist Harry Crews describes in a short story:

> [I been a cocker] all my life. My daddy given me my first chicken when I was twelve year old. Most rooster men that's any good been in it that long. It don't take but a lifetime to learn it. (Crews, 1979, p. 35)

One informant, for example, told us that before he knew about organized cockfighting, he used to shut two roosters in his bathroom and let them fight it out. Cocks do fight each other without human intervention, and people do fall in love without social approval and sanction. However, most cockfighters do not learn the sport from watching their chickens.

Most cockers get involved with the sport through deliberate diffusion instigated by the entrepreneurial cockers. The informant who fought chickens in his bathroom later introduced a friend to the sport this way. The friend, now a cocker too,

said that he had not even known that chickens fought before watching in the bathroom pit. Tales such as the archetypal anecdote about Sal with which we begin this article, about how old men pick young men, beginners, give them their first birds, and train and encourage them in the sport of cockfighting and the care and raising of fowl, are quite common. Obituaries are usually written by sons, protégés, and admirers of the men who have died, rather than colleagues and peers. As we will show, old men recruit new ones in order to promote the sport and to ensure their own immortality, and young men turn to old ones as the only trustworthy people available in an ambiguous, probably disreputable, world. This gives a distinctively gerontocratic aspect to both the sport and the marketing efforts.

In order to continue the sport, old cockfighters must market it, recruit new cockfighters, sell or give them birds, and encourage them in the sport, and they must do so in a relatively covert manner because of the widespread disvalued nature of the sport and the illegality of it in most parts of the country. In order to sell chickens, they must establish their reputations as honest and knowledgeable old men engaged in an illegal activity, whose only vested interest seems to be in continuing the sport for its own sake.

METHOD

This paper is based upon research into cockfighting which began in the spring of 1989 and continued intensively for about three years. The data were obtained through participant observation, intensive interviewing, and analysis of secondary materials. Our naturalistic study took place along the border region of Eastern Oklahoma and Western Arkansas. Worden did the primary research and observation, with Darden's role mostly limited to locating respondents and secondary research. This is not a sport where middle class female college professors are warmly greeted and introduced to the nuances of meaning and behavior. Although there are a few women cockers, some men's wives attend some fights, and "sew-up girls" may repair injured birds, this is a mostly male world. The editor of *The Gamecock,* however, is a woman.

Worden has observed formal and informal cockfights at varied settings. Interviews with main informants and informal conversations with many different participants were carried out over a period of nineteen months. Finally, an informant (who has since died, allegedly shot by his ex-wife's new boyfriend) read and commented on some of our material and corroborated its major conclusions, as well as our interpretations of supporting data.

For this study, we also concentrated on 24 issues of magazines devoted to cockfighting: *The Gamecock* (various issues ranging from May 1967 to May 1991), *Grit and Steel* (several issues from 1991), and *The Feathered Warrior* (several from 1991). For comparison, we read the June 1992 and January 1993 issues of *Bird Talk,* a magazine devoted to exotic bird keeping, and talked with a number of owners of such birds and one former breeder. Darden also attended the 1993 Annual Rattlesnake Roundup in Whigham, Georgia, and we looked closely at the program from that event.

MARKETING DEVIANCE

Since we are talking about marketing, it is useful to use paradigms established in that discipline to shape our discussion of the spread of cockfighting and selling gamefowl. Kotler's (1991) version of marketing is one of the most used and best accepted; we will adapt his major concepts for our project. While the models of the conventional marketing process that Kotler (1991) and others present may describe the processes by which mass marketers and many smaller businesses operate, we wonder if they work for the entrepreneur engaged in marketing dangerous or illegal activities: marketing deviance? When, for example, the environment is more than merely hostile, and threatens to arrest the seller and destroy his product and production facilities, can one of these models explain that situation and help the seller to make decisions? How do you sell something illegal, to people who know it is illegal?

Studies of drug sales, prostitution, and other vices help in this connection, but only to an extent. Many studies (Adler & Adler, 1983) have described the various techniques of drug-dealing. Two major differences between drug-dealing and cockfighting are the relative ephemerality of drug dealing compared to cockfighting and chicken-raising, and the relative visibility of the contraband which the owner must hide or disguise.

Although the small, local drug dealer may continuously maintain possession of a large enough amount of drugs to send him or her to prison, the bigger dealer usually maintains possession for a very limited amount of time, if any, before distributing the product to others who will merchandise it in smaller amounts to others. People who grow chickens, however, have committed themselves to several years' worth of labor, possession, and visibility. An airplane full of illegal drugs is extremely visible, but it is also portable and soon emptied. A pound of cocaine or marijuana will fit in an easily carried container. A couple of acres of loud and brightly colored roosters tied to little sheds is also very visible, not portable, and relatively permanent. Law enforcement uses specially trained animals to sniff out drugs, but anyone who knows what to look for can spot a rooster yard.

Prostitutes face the visibility problem from a slightly different perspective. Call-girls, masseuses, and others at the higher end of the profession may have normal, conventional marketing problems, but the street hooker has to be out and available to customers without attracting the attention of law enforcement. This is a tricky act, with various solutions. Some women rely on the portability idea, moving frequently, from corner to corner, which makes repeat sales difficult. Some believe (wrongly) that they can hide or deny their activity by "passing" as dates if they do not mention money first. Some rely on pimps or other forms of word-of-mouth, and likely others pay law enforcement people to ignore them. Again, though, the chicken farmer's size and visibility present problems which prostitutes can handle with relative ease.

Still, cockfighters have not thought of themselves as outlaws, but as little guys who have fallen victims to big guys, little guys who are maintaining a noble tradition with a long and respectable history, including George Washington and Abraham Lincoln, and other notable chicken men of their times—in face of terrific odds. These odds include not only "the many crazy laws that are trying to be passed" (Abacherli, 1991, p. 171) and the animal rights activists, but the "big money men" who fight in the knife fight variation which runs costs up beyond the reach of the average little guy. In this form of cockfighting matches are over rapidly and many more cocks are destroyed (Worden & Darden, 1992).

How do these people continue to think of themselves as embattled practitioners of a noble sport which is illegal? Most believe that the birds will fight anyway, that birds just do fight. Many say that birds do not feel pain, owing to their simple nervous systems. Hearne (1994) would likely disagree with this point. In her essay on "Parrots and Philosophers," for example, she says, " . . . even a cat isn't as good at keeping control of a conversation as a parrot is" (1994, p. 4). Barber (1993) would definitely disagree with the notion that birds are too simple to feel pain. In his book *The Human Nature of Birds,* he demonstrates that birds are intelligently aware. While breeders of exotic birds generally take a position somewhere between Barber's and that of cockfighters, owners of pet exotics emphatically agree with Barber, finding their pets not only intelligent but cuddly, lovable, and loving. Cockers, of course, may admire their birds and love their sport, but they do not love their birds. It is a rare rooster who even gets a name. Exotic bird breeders usually leave the naming of birds to the people who will buy and love them, as do dog breeders. Some particularly courageous and game roosters do get names. Pigeons are never named; they all receive numbers and are identified by their numbers only (Worden, 1992).

In defending their sport, cockers also point out that nature itself is bloody. If a poultry farmer has 100 chicks, for example, and eight live, the farmer is doing well. For the cockfighter, who has watered, fed, trained, and tended these birds for at least two years, the argument is simple: these birds get treated better than do those raised for food, and they may die with the dignity that nature intended for them, in a fight. Others ignore the whole question of animal rights by believing that chickens are fowl, not animals. The illegality issue they nullify by saying that the government is overreaching itself, getting into issues that are none of its concern, that the government has no right to regulate a group of gentlemen making wagers.

With the outlawing of the sport, however, and the often highly publicized efforts of both law enforcers and animal rights activists, cockfighting has in recent years attracted adherents who do think of themselves as outlaws. "Just tell me something is illegal, and I'll do it," one informant said. While the "fraternity of cockers," as they often call themselves, probably contains no armed robbers or hit men, many cockers probably grow and sell marijuana on some scale or own illegal weapons. The story circulated among some of our informants that two men had tried unsuccessfully to set up a "clean" pit, and when it failed, they sold out to people rumored to be big drug-dealers in the area. It is likely that at least some drug money is laundered through cockfighting, since cash is the usual standard of exchange.

Kotler uses several core concepts of marketing to look at the processes of conventional marketing, and we will adapt these to look at our data and describe the selling of deviance. These concepts are: needs, wants, and demands; product; value; exchange; and market (1991, p. 4).

Needs, Wants, and Demands

According to Kotler, needs are basic and biological. Wants are ways of satisfying needs, and demands are elaborated satisfiers. Consider food, bread, and croissants. While the idea of needs is a little too psychological and too motivational for us, we are willing to talk about wants and desires/demands here. Conventional marketers protest, perhaps rightly, that they engage in satisfying existing wants rather than creating new ones. The case of gamefowl is largely an exception, as the established chicken men must depend on finding new chicken men and getting them to want chickens. Cockfighters talk about wanting entertainment and wanting to continue the traditions of the "great sport" of cockfighting. The novice and the more experienced chicken man who buy chickens want to win money in the pits.

Although marketers usually consider sellers' long-range goals to be the obvious financial profit, those who sell chickens have an additional long-range goal. The epitome of the sport consists of becoming a legend whose fighting record is attested to by having his name attached to the stock which will be preserved by those who come after him.

Sandy Hatch may well not recognize the fowl that bear his name today as having much of a connection with the fowl that he had way back when. The important thing would be that he would be so extremely proud that his name and legend had lived on and was passed down to today's fowl, who contain little true old-time Hatch blood. His name is synonymous with the tenacious, game, powerfully enduring fowl for which his fowl were known for. The qualities of endurance and power liken today's hatch type fowl to those from the hands of the originator himself. (Warbird, 1991, p. 29)

Most cockers want to become trustworthy old men who can choose younger men to train and entrust with their fowl (Prus 1989b, pp. 102–130). Immortality is the ultimate desire/demand of the chicken man, seller and buyer. In the short run, this reputation as a trustworthy old man helps to sell chickens, too, and it is often a deliberate construction on the part of the seller.

Products

Product includes services, and refers to satisfying needs, wants, and desires. Here, the major prod-

uct is a chicken. Since fighting the chickens is illegal in most states, and shipping animals across state lines for the purposes of fighting is against federal law, most sellers sell brood stock, and the buyers experiment with crossbreeding the fowl to produce battlecocks for fighting. As with drugs and prostitution, there is no product stability or standardization with chickens. The best breeding chickens are usually considered to be the pure lines with the original breeders' names attached.

I continue to read with interest the arguments against pure this or pure that. Well, if anyone is so shallow or nitpicking as to condemn such a practice by those of us that purchased fowl under this premise, whether we think them to be pure as the original breeder bred them or not, it still remains our right to call them what we want! If anyone wants to nitpick such a trivial difference with you, then tell them to stick it and walk away. You will have done yourself a favor. (Warbird, 1991, p. 29)

If there ever were pure lines of chickens, the resurgence of cockfighting in this country after World War II probably ended them. Whether there once were or not, the establishing of a chicken as a pure breed today is a social constriction. One cannot look at a chicken and know from its physical characteristics that he is a Hatch or a Kelso. Color, comb size, leg color, and other features once distinguished the various breeds, but they no longer do. There are many arguments over the ostensible breeds of specific chickens. The chicken that is sold as a "White Hatch" is a socially constructed product in that only through the claims that the breeder makes and the breeder's reputation and fighting record can the buyer form any idea of what he is purchasing. The features of a bird which breeders and buyers stress are things such as muscle and the quality of his conditioning. A desirable bird has just the right amount of muscling in his legs. Too much muscle makes a bird unable to act: he can't "cut" (is too slow and cannot aim). A bird that can "cut" can aim his gaff or knife, a skill which comes from an inbred instinct, cockers believe. The bird that cannot cut just flails away in the direction of his opponent. Superb conditioning results in rock-hard strong legs and wings. A bird with "bottom," probably a genetic feature, is one that can sustain punishment. "Gameness" is the key to a superior bird, that ability to persevere in the face of obstacles, to peck his opponent with his last dying gasp, to "hang in there" until the end. Stories are told about cockers who come with birds in polished wooden cages, put their birds in the pit with those of guys who bring their birds in paper bags, with mites crawling all over them, and lose to the mite-infested bird that is "deep game." A bird that is ready to fight, genetically superior and in condition, will swagger and cut his wings side to side before a fight. Handlers say that they can feel the tension in the birds and tell when the birds are ready. They also believe that the birds can feel the confidence and courage that the good handlers impart to them through holding them before a match. They also say that a good handler can feel the electricity go out of a bird during a match, when the handlers separate the birds. Advantages that some handlers are said to use include strychnine, which can cause a bird to attack even his handler, and steroids. Such chemicals are considered invasions on the pure sport by most cockers.

The cheapest fowl probably come from Mexico or the Philippines, but most American and Spanish cockers currently prefer to "Buy American," particularly fowl from the Arkansas–Oklahoma area where it is believed that the cold winters produce birds with fewer parasites and the "ground" is superior. The ground refers to just that, the portion of earth the chicken uses, but it has become a bit mystified among cockers and includes in its meaning the climate and weather, the other living things which share it, such as parasites, and other uncontrollable forces of nature. There is a fad element to choosing birds, in that at various times and places, one breed will be "in" and others "out." Being in results from winning, or being thought to win, at derbies and other fights. Instability of the chicken as product also results from biological factors. Genetics and breeding are always a gam-

ble and when the birds are kept outside, available to predators and other natural elements, with parentage often unknown, the risks become quite high. A breeder may find his "nick," the absolutely best fowl, in a set of brothers, but may never be able to reproduce them. It takes two years to raise, train and fully test a battlecock. By the time a breeder is certain that he has a superior battlecock, the parents (if he knows which birds they were) are two years older, a long and significant time in the breeding life of a chicken. The care, feeding, and training also matter, so that genetic perfection may not prove out in the pits for an inexperienced owner. This product instability makes the breeder's reputation as a trustworthy, winning old man even more critical and problematic. Sellers offer services, too. A typical display ad in *The Gamecock* offers:

> SPECIAL—*With the purchase of fowl you may spend 1 week at my expense seeing how we take care of our fowl and go to a derby with us to watch our roosters perform. (Think about it.) SPECIAL CONSIDERATION GIVEN TO BEGINNERS!!!*

Videotapes, magazines, books, personal phone calls, all back up the chicken seller and offer advice on feeding, training, keeping, and handling birds. Often these include strange advice: "A ounce of cure is worth a pound of remedy" according to Long Spur (1991, p. 77). This follow-up service is particularly crucial because the young guys are thought not to know what they are doing. Like new guys in any endeavor, new guys, beginners, in cocking must pay their dues (thus enabling the old guys to fleece them from time to time), but not to the point of driving them out:

> *To misinform beginners or purposely mislead someone can probably do more harm to this sport than some other more often talked about enemies. (Roberts 1991, p. 24)*

> *His customers are experienced cockers that know ace battlecocks. Not beginners that don't know a good cock from a bad one. (Fulldrop Jr., 1991, p. 136)*

In closing, I have a word for all the beginners out there. Keep with it and be as strong-willed as the gamest cock alive! So often I read short articles about beginners being involved in raw dealings. I have been very fortunate in not being involved in many. I would just like to tell you there are plenty of experienced cockers that are willing to guide and help the beginners. The beginner only needs one prerequisite, to be strong-willed. (Whitehackle Haven, 1991, p. 87)

If they do not recruit and keep the young guys, the sport will not continue and there will be no one to trust with their immortality. More importantly, they cannot make money in the pits. Much of the money that changes hands in the pits goes from beginners who bet without sufficient knowledge of the real variables—the trainers and handlers— to the more knowledgeable, experienced men.

There is other equipment available for breeding and fighting birds. Breeding equipment is pretty basic and seldom used by cockfighters. Incubators for hatching eggs, for example, are expensive and not thought to be worth the money. Medications are sold as for any other kind of livestock, so that one bypasses the veterinarian as often as possible. Worming medications, feed supplements, and other sorts of medications are usually as much related to lore passed down and around as to any sort of scientific research that a veterinarian may have access to and charge a lot of money for. In contrast, *Bird Talk*, a magazine for exotic bird keepers and breeders, has a column written by a veterinarian. Other paraphernalia, such as tie-downs, are also sold. Some breeders tie each rooster to his own little shed, to keep the birds from fighting with each other, wandering away, or getting into any other kind of trouble. Tied-down birds cannot be carried away by predators such as hawks.

The equipment for fighting the fowl, the knives and gaffs, is probably, next to the birds themselves, the single most important item available to the cocker (Worden & Darden, 1992). The world of cockers is divided into those who fight with the gaff, the traditionalists, and those who fight with the more deadly knife. A large variety of these instruments is available, as are cases for containing them. Some men make their own elaborate wooden cases. Attaching the gaff to the bird is considered an art by many, and is often done in secret. It involves wrapping the gaff with tape to attach it to the bird's heel.

The chicken, then, is the major product, other than the sport itself. As we have suggested, the chicken may represent a man's hopes for financial gain and even immortality, but he remains basically a chicken. He is not a pet. He is not beloved, although he may be admired. He is not cuddled or named, only trained, tended, and bred. Pictures of winners with trophies are published in cockfighting magazines, whereas *Bird Talk* pictures pets with Santa Claus and with favorite toys. He is a product.

Values, Cost, and Satisfaction

Values are "the consumer's estimate of the product's overall capacity to satisfy his or her needs" (Kotler, 1991, p. 6), and are usually expressed in terms of price.

There is very little price competition among gamefowl sellers. The value of chickens at the time of sale is established by the breeder's record in the pits and his reputation.

I have to put in a good word for Papa Buck. Both Tom Johnson and myself have gotten the Brown Reds from Buck. Both of us have had the very best success with them. They are not only agile and able fighters, but have the bottom to hang in there just as long as it takes and then some . . . not a trait for which Brown Reds are known for. (Warbird, 1991, p. 30)

Because the line of chickens a man produces does not stop at the man's death, especially if he has passed his stock and lore on to a younger man, his obituary may even become part of his reputation and of someone else's promotional material. Probably for these reasons, the obituaries in the magazines tell more about a man's chickens than about the man and his life; perhaps, in this instance, his chickens are his life:

> *MSGT. Milton M. Hall, U.S. Army Air Corps, born July 24, 1915, died March 23, 1990. Services were held at Cochran Mortuary in Wichita, Kansas. A veteran of World War II, he passed away at home. He was known for his Canadian Mugs, which he had won numerous derbies at different pits in Kansas. Before his death he tied a 33 derby at BJ's in Ponca City, Oklahoma. Winning a hack and four in a row. He leaves a wife, son, and daughter. We will miss him. (Bert White, 1991, p. 214)*

In conventional market arenas, where a buyer can rely on sellers' reputations, histories, credit ratings, and so forth, buying still involves "uncertainties, risks and dilemmas" (Prus 1989a, p. 135).

> *Despite attempts to make purchasing more "professional" . . . buying remains a gamble. Not only does buying entail strategies and gaming, trust and cooperation, and deception and competition, but buying activity takes place within a setting of shifting uncertainties and reflects dependencies on others outside the immediate transaction. (Prus, 1989a, p. 139)*

Buyers of fighting chickens, quite naturally, fear "phony chicken-peddlers." The real secret to obtaining value in buying chickens lies in the old man who spots a promising youngster, what Prus (1989a) describes as a "seeker," and gives him his chickens. All other deals are suspect:

> *Mr. KinCannon is the only major breeder that I know that does sell super blood lines (when he does sell fowl). His word is his bond and he sells out every year to repeat customers. (Fulldrop, Jr. 1991, p. 136)*

Many informants asked, "Why would a guy sell his best chickens to someone he may meet later in the pits?" Their answer is that most will not, leaving anyone who offers fowl for sale open to the charge of being a "phony chicken peddler." "However a small percentage [of beginners] get hooked up with an *honest cocker* and tries to learn and goes ahead to make an excellent cocker," according to RWN (1991, p. 30). Sometimes people buy

out of state, figuring that a seller who lives at a distance might be willing to sell good chickens, but they know that sellers often fight out of state, too, so they cannot depend on that method of finding a trustworthy seller. The second best method is to buy from a pure line (in conventional marketing, an established brand), but you can never be sure that you are doing that. Our observations confirm the dubiousness of the pure line; on several occasions Worden watched a breeder stroll through his yard, pick up eggs and put them unmarked into his pocket, so that he had no way of knowing which chickens produced which eggs.

Some deny the importance of the brood fowl, saying that the stock is less important than the regimen of care and training.

> *I'm sure many of you cockers have read this best selling book on nutrition and I'm going to try to emphasis to you as a game fowl feeder that it is just as important to fowl as it is to a human being. I think we under emphasize feed and proper nutrition and over emphasize the importance of paying large amounts of money for a trio. (Dutcher, 1991, p. 148)*

These people offer their secrets, again backed up by pit records and reputations, either free through letters and columns in the magazines or by purchase as books, pamphlets, or video tapes:

> *The purple powder is a strong grease cutting biodegradable detergent that you can buy at a wholesale outlet store for around $2.50 to $3.00 a gallon. If you can find the orange powder, it is the strongest (Long Spur, 1992. p. 76)*

Customer satisfaction is defined very simply: "When you don't kill 'em." Chickens are usually sold with the admonition. "If you do not like them, kill them." Sellers do not want buyers to give away unsatisfactory chickens, because doing so might dilute the purity of the blood lines. Chickens can be battletested, i.e., pitted against each other unarmed in controlled circumstances to observe their parent abilities as fighters, at 6 months as "baby stags," and at one year as stags. If owners are not pleased by the chickens' performances at these ages, they usually kill the chickens. (And, of course, the full-grown 2-year-old or older battlecock who loses in the pit usually dies, too.) A man who keeps the chickens he has bought, then, is a satisfied customer, as is, obviously, a repeat customer.

Exchange, Transactions, and Relationships

This refers to obtaining products we want, offering resources in exchange for them. The epitome here is "relationship marketing," wherein the seller tries to build up long-term trusting relationships with customers (Bigus, 1972; Prus & Irini, 1988). Advertising, promotion, sales force training, distribution, and repair service are all methods of effecting exchange and developing relationships in conventional marketing.

Word-of-mouth is still the most effective means of advertising and promoting in all forms of marketing. For the cockfighter/chicken seller, this extends to winning in the pits and constructing and maintaining a reputation as a good chicken man: usually honest, religious, sometimes considerate and caring, a man of integrity.

> *Maybe the most important thing, by all means, be honest in all your dealings. This is probably the most important as you can get a bad reputation much quicker than an honest one. I have birds, thru friendship and small amounts of cash, that wasn't for sale at any price. (Cogburn, 1991, p. 158)*

Personal sales, where the buyer and seller jointly define the chickens as breeders of potential winners from proven lines, without any or much third-party intervention, account for most sales. Cantrell and Brannan, Ohio cockers, invite potential buyers to "bring two of the best cocks you have or can acquire and we will be more than glad to show you [ours] in action" (Whitney, 1991, p. 18). Many people buy mail-order chickens, a process which most chicken men agree is absurd. The idea is to find those honest chicken sellers who will sell good chickens out of state and not have to face those chickens in a nearby pit. Most mail-order buyers are disappointed.

The major third-party intermediary or facilitator in the marketing of fighting chickens is the magazine. Although professionally printed, all three seem to be the results of desktop publishing of one sort or another. *The Gamecock* reports a circulation of 13,000. Spelling, grammar, and punctuation vary from poor to awful, as does the quality of photographs and their reproduction. The content is about 50% advertising, much of it informal and folksy in tone. The editorial content is about 40% letters and 60% columns, articles, and notices. Most of the editorial content is informational, about choosing and caring for chickens. There are some letters asking for help, but most letters are gratuitous offers of expert information from old cockers with secrets to share, what Prus (1989a, p. 205) might call "cultural entrepreneurship." These likely have the effect, and perhaps the intention, of boosting the writer's reputation:

> *After several requests, I have written a Cocker's Guidebook. . . . I hope it will be helpful to many cockers, especially beginners. . . . I have been so blessed in my life that I feel the least I can do is share with those less fortunate. (Roberts, 1991, p. 24)*

The information is welcomed by all of the cockfighters we know.

> *I thank The Feathered Warrior people for publishing a fine magazine, month after month, for the benefit of many. Good information is there to read each month. It seems that it is getting better as time goes on. The many pictures published each month are appreciated by cockers worldwide. (Roberts, 1991, p. 24)*

These are the only magazines many cockers read, although some also read *Field and Stream,* and, interestingly, *The Pigeon Journal.* Most readers relate to the magazine very personally, as if they knew the editor, the authors, and the other readers.

> *I enjoy your magazine and the articles by Bill Roberts. He is one good man and doesn't mind helping you in any way he can, and also Sleepy. I went to see him and his better half, they are just as nice as can be. I enjoyed the coffee and chicken*

talk. They make you feel welcome and at home, and ask if there is any way he can help you. (Trull, 1991, p. 156)

Many of the authors use only their nicknames: Long Spur, Whitehackle Haven, the Traveller. The magazines form the core of a community for most cockers. The relationship is so intense and personal for many that we heard comments such as, "I'm gonna cut his [the editor's] balls off for letting that guy advertise his phony chickens."

Relationships among cockfighters show a great deal of respect and deference. Good friends will tease and interact informally, using nickname, but acquaintances call each other "Mr." Mr. is usually an honorific, implying an older, respected, experienced man. The articles in the magazines use Mr. and use specific names only when they have something good to say about a person. Perhaps in response to the possibility of slander or castration, an author who has something bad to say about another person usually avoids mentioning that person's name.

Many of the ads in the magazines play on the "old man" theme:

After 31 years of raising, selling and fighting gamecocks, I am ready to slow down a little and take it easy. (Whitney, 1991, p. 34)

The story among our informants is that one man ran the same ad saying he was old and ready to retire for 20 years.

The idea of vicarious competition is implicit in much of the magazine content and in cockers' conversations. Many cockers are rural, poor, aging athletes, disabled, and overweight—they cannot themselves compete physically, so they enjoy the competition among their birds. Although it is perhaps peripheral, it is worth noting that in every society in which men fight gamecocks, at least one word referring to the birds is also a slang reference to the penis. (Dundes, 1994)

Another theme obvious in the magazines and conversations is death. Fighting birds is about death, equanimity in the face of death, stoicism, physical courage, and an unflinching acceptance of pain. These are old agricultural and masculine values, so it is not surprising to find them here. These values combine easily, too, with the theme of the God-fearing older man who is the hero of the sport and of most of its stories.

Markets

For chicken sellers, the potential market is mostly younger guys, beginners, since older guys usually have their stock or will know whose stock they want and often get it free. The younger guys are seen as naive if not stupid, and in need of a lot of help and advice. The market is crucial, of course, as it always is, but perhaps even more so because it also offers posterity, the ultimate reason many of the chicken men are in the sport.

Kotler (1991) presents the model in Table 48.1 of the relationships among the various factors in the conventional market:

Table 48.1 Kotler's Models of Conventional Marketing Processes

STARTING POINT	FOCUS	MEANS	ENDS
Factory	Products	Selling and promotion	Profits through sales volume
	(a) The selling concept		
Market	Consumer	Coordinated needs marketing	Profits through satisfaction
	(b) The marketing concept		

This overall picture shows that marketing deviance differs considerably from conventional marketing. Instead of being an example of one of Kotler's two contrasting strategies (the marketing concept or the selling concept), selling gamefowl appears to be a hybrid of the two, the deviant marketing concept (shown in Table 48.2). There are fewer steps in the process of marketing deviance. The factory, as Dutcher (1991, p. 149) says, is often the producer. The product is unstable and unstandardized. The producer is the seller, who has only the one intermediary/facilitator (the magazines) to worry about. There are no wholesalers or sales forces. Distribution is usually from one hand to another, although occasionally interstate shipments are made, which legally limits the kinds of fowl which can be sold. Word-of-mouth is a strong determinant of sales and is highly dependent on building a reputation as an honest competitor; but the seller as competitor is suspect. Marketing efforts are so uncoordinated as to be fragmented. Profits are made in an ancillary fashion through betting in the pits and through taking advantage of the people the trustworthy old man must convince of his trustworthiness. And this entrepreneur works within a particularly hostile environment (not so hostile, perhaps, as the drug-dealer or the prostitute, who may be killed): given the size of the setup required to keep and raise chickens, and its obvious signs, the gamecock breeder's operation is extremely visible and relatively permanent. In some places there is probably collusion with authorities, since a drive down many secondary highways in this country yields the obvious signs of fighting chickens being kept.

The threat to destroy the product is particularly harsh for the chicken man, since his product is also his factory. While the drug-dealer may face huge financial loss if his or her stock and other possessions are confiscated, these things can be replaced. Most arrests for prostitution result in fines, some in jail terms; either way, the prostitute has lost only time and money, not her product. When the law destroys the last of Mr. Smith's Hatches, however, there are no more. And Mr. Smith loses his shot at immortality.

CONCLUSIONS

We have described the processes involved in the marketing of a deviant activity, cockfighting. Cockfighting is illegal in most states in this country, and yet the breeding and selling of fighting chickens is legal, and the traditions and history attached to cockfighting maintain that the sport is old, honorable, and gentlemanly, descended from such figures as George Washington and Abraham Lincoln. We have found that those engaged in marketing the sport and its paraphernalia, including the chickens, must conduct their activities in ways which differ from the marketing activities of more conventional businesses, as described in the marketing literature. We have found that there is an apparent paradox involved, in that while the participants usually consider themselves fine, upstanding citizens, they trust each other only slightly, knowing that they may well end up pitting their birds against each other. This results in the necessity for establishing one's reputation as an honest, trustworthy person who is engaged in illegal and stigmatized activities. Since the organization of the marketing efforts is very loosely structured, with no sales force and only one third-party medium for advertising, the most effective form of advertising and marketing is word-of-mouth, which can spread rapidly through this community of mostly rural people who communicate through their magazines and through face-to-face encounters at fights and in

Table 48.2 The Deviant Marketing Concept

STARTING POINT	FOCUS	MEANS	ENDS
Producer as factory	Reputation of product	Word of mouth, uncoordinated activities	Profits through side activities (i.e., gambling), immortality

informal meetings. Having winning birds and winning honestly, without taking advantage of neophytes, is the best method of establishing one's reputation for honesty and trustworthiness. Winning, however, can sometimes come at a cost of the honesty reputation.

The marketing of fighting chickens, because of this deviant nature and stigmatized tradition, has a distinctly gerontocratic aspect. As the stories, perhaps myths, of the old man giving his chickens and his blessing to the promising youngster demonstrate, a chicken man can never trust an opponent. Yet, in order to keep the sport going, to insure that there is a history for a man to go down in, chicken people must recruit new chicken people, who become opponents. The only trustworthy

person is the old man who no longer competes (cf. Adler & Adler, 1983). As Whitney (1991, p. 150) concludes:

> So to all you other beginners out there, when your driving around and see some old man out tending his birds, stop and introduce yourself. Maybe you're what he's looking for. If not then, good luck.

Does this gerontocratic aspect characterize the marketing of other deviant activities? It probably does to a greater degree than researchers have noticed. The smart drug buyer, for example, tries to maintain an established, trustworthy source: prostitution is stratified in terms of trustworthiness. This gerontocratic aspect of the marketing of deviance deserves further attention.

REFERENCES

Abacherli, L. (1991, May). Defense Fund Committee. *The Gamecock,* 172.

Adler, P., & Adler, P. (1983). Relationships between dealers: The social organization of illicit drug transactions. *Sociology and Social Research, 67,* 260–278.

Barber, T. X. (1993). *The human nature of birds.* New York: Penguin.

Bigus, O. (1972). The milkman and his customers. *Urban Life and Culture, 1,* 131–165.

Bryant, C., & Capel. W. (1974, November). Profiles of the American cocker. *Grit and Steel,* 33.

Cogburn, R. (1991, May). Letter to the editor. *The Gamecock,* 157–8.

Crews, H. (1979). Cockfighting: An unfashionable view (pp. 35–41). *Florida frenzy,* Gainesville, FL: University Presses of Florida.

Dundes, A. (1994). *The cockfight: A casebook.* Madison: University of Wisconsin Press.

Dutcher, M. (1991, May). You are what you eat! *The Gamecock,* 148–149.

Fulldrop, Jr. (1991, May). Super bloodlines part 2. *The Gamecock,* 136–137.

Hearne, V. (1994). *Animal Happiness.* New York: HarperCollins.

Kotler, P. (1991). *Marketing management.* Englewood Cliffs, NJ: Prentice Hall.

Long Spur (1991, May). Bubblefoot cure. *The Gamecock,* 76–77.

Prus, R. (1989a). *Pursuing customers: An ethnography of marketing activities.* Newbury Park: Sage.

Prus, R. (1989b). *Making sales: Influence as interpersonal accomplishment.* Newbury Park: Sage.

Prus, R., & Irini, S. (1988). *Hookers, rounders, and desk clerks: The Social organization of the hotel community.* Salem, WI: Sheffield.

Roberts, B. (1991, May). Tools of the trade. *The Gamecock,* 68–69.

RWN (1991, February). Beginners only. *Grit and Steel,* 30.

Schiff, S. (1995, April 5). Geek shows. *The New Yorker,* 9–10.

Trull, J. (1991). Letter to the editor. *The Gamecock,* 156.

Warbird. (1991, July). A few thoughts. *The Feathered Warrior,* 29–30.

White, B. (1991, July). Obituary for M. M. White. *The Gamecock,* 214.

Whitehackle Haven (1991, May). Reminiscence of Doc Tuttle. *The Gamecock,* 86–87.

Whitney, R. (1991, May). Beginner's luck. *The Gamecock,* 150.

Worden, S., & Darden, D. (1992). Deviant behavior. Knives and gaffs: Definitions in the deviant world of cocking. *Deviant Behavior, 13,* 271–289.

Worden, S. (1992). *Fighting chickens and racing pigeons: Animalistic extensions of identity.* Mid South Sociological Association, Chattanooga, TN.

REVIEW QUESTIONS_____

1. How do cockfighters justify their involvement in this activity?
2. How did the authors gather their data for this article?

THE WORLD OF DOGFIGHTING

RHONDA D. EVANS
CRAIG J. FORSYTH

It is believed that dogfighting was transported to the United States by European dog breeders who were looking for a new market for their product and by the Irish immigrants who had also enjoyed a long tradition of baiting sports in their homeland (Atyeo, 1979). There is evidence that baiting sports were being practiced in this country as early as 1726, if not earlier.

The baiting sports faced opposition in the United States, much like they had in Europe. Early laws pertaining to baiting sports varied from state to state and often from county to county within the states. New York passed legislation in 1856, which made dogfighting, cockfighting, and ratting illegal (Matz, 1984)....

The next serious attempt to stop dogfighting did not emerge until 1976 when the federal government passed legislation making it a felony to transport dogs across state lines with the intent to fight them (Atyeo, 1979; Semencic, 1984). This legislation was in part a reaction to efforts by Humane Societies to bring baiting sports to the attention of the general public by use of the media. Despite continued efforts at legislative reform, not to mention the ever increasing social stigma associated with dogfighting, participation continues. Dogfighting is now illegal in all 50 states and a felony in at least 36 states.

METHODOLOGY

This article examines the world of dogfighting, through the use of thick descriptions (Geertz,

1973). The data, for this study, were obtained through field research, using interviews with and observations of people who fight dogs. Our technique was to let the responses speak for themselves, thus presenting the world of dog fighting in full vivid detail and then to offer both summarization and interpretation. This method, which is called interpretative interaction (Denzin, 1978), is concerned with the study and imputation of meaning, motive, emotion, intention, and feeling as life events are experienced and organized by interacting individuals. This method is in stark contrast to thin description, which consists solely of statistical explanation and abstraction. Our purpose was to capture the essence of dogfighting from those who have experienced it.

Interviews were conducted with 31 individuals who fight and breed pit bulls. All of the participants had been involved in dogfighting for several years. Three interviews were conducted with former breeders and fighters of pit bulls who no longer participate in the sport. Interviews ranged from 2 to 4½ hours. These interviews were conducted at the pre-fight meetings, at the fights or at the homes of dogfighters. Several informal interviews were also conducted with spectators and the wives of men who participate in dogfighting. Additional data were obtained from interviews with SPCA officials, veterinarians, and local sheriff's officers. Observations took place at 14 formal dogfights. Spectators were represented by all races, ages, and both sexes. In the United States, formal

Source: Rhonda D. Evans and Craig J. Forsyth, "The Social Milieu of Dogmen and Dogfights," *Deviant Behavior,* vol. 19 (1998), pp. 51–71. Reprinted with permission.

dogfighting is a sport dominated by White men. Although the participation of Black males is on the rise, they make up only a small percentage of the participants within the sport. Women for the most part are there as spectators, but do have an active role in gambling. Women rarely handle dogs. The research took place in several parishes of Louisiana and counties in Mississippi. The authors also examined newspaper accounts of dogfighting.

The goal of this research was to describe the world of the dogfighter so that subsequent researchers will be able to recognize its components and proceed with their own research based upon knowledge gained from this study. This is, indeed, the test of validity of qualitative research (Forsyth, 1986).

Both of the authors have relatives who are engaged in dogfighting. Additional respondents were identified through a snowball method. Each respondent was questioned regarding several aspects of dogfighting: the reasons they engage in dogfighting and how they started dogfighting; techniques of breeding and training; the negotiation of a contract; the fight, the setting, and the choice of a setting for the fight; the types of dogs in general and great fighting dogs of the past; changes in dogfighting; and the career of a fighting dog. Additional questions were intended to elicit responses regarding the rationalizations and motivations used by dogmen for their continuance in these illegal activities, and their confrontations with residents, law enforcement and/or humane society officials, or other dogfighters.

In our interviews with dogmen they continually referred to themselves as a fraternity. McCaghy and Neal (1974) also used the term fraternity in describing the informal association of cockfighters. We will also use the term fraternity in describing dogmen. All the names of dogmen used are pseudonyms.

FINDINGS

Breeding

Breeding [pit bulls] to participate in the sport of dogfighting is the most crucial function within the fraternity of dogmen. It is the facet on which every other element within the sport is based and without it the sport could not exist. Thus, breeders hold the most prestigious positions within the fraternity.

The following responses were from experienced dogmen regarding the importance of breeding and the various techniques employed in breeding.

> . . . Now you got certain bloodlines, if you're a breeder you just don't choose dogs at random. They've got to have a background behind them. Sometimes you have athletes that come up that are just freaks. Those idiots that don't know anything about breeding they start breeding into them. He's not the one who made that fighting dog; it's his daddy and his mama. Hell the people don't know that, they want to breed to that dog because he's a good dog. That's not where it's at. If it's not a line of production of good dogs I don't want him. (INTERVIEW)

> It's the bloodline you go by. Just cause a dog won't fight doesn't mean he won't throw good dogs. The genes are still in that dog. (INTERVIEW)

As indicated in these statements . . . breeding is perhaps the most important aspect of dogfighting. Another critical facet of the game is the training of the dog.

Training

When these dogs reach a certain age, anywhere from a year old to 18 months, they are rolled (briefly put against a proven dog) a few times to test their ability and gameness. If the owner determines that the dog is ready for the pit, he then puts out a wager that is open to anyone. The amount of the wager is usually anywhere from a couple hundred dollars to as much as $100,000.

Once the wager is accepted and a contract is drawn up it is time to prepare for the fight. The dogs undergo from 6 weeks to 3 months of rigorous training to prepare for the fight. They must be brought down to their pit weight, which is considered the optimal weight at which a dog can fight. This training seeks to build wind and stamina in the dogs so that they can fight for long periods of time if need be.

Various methods are used in the conditioning of a dog such as a treadmill, flirtpole and sometimes even swimming, The dogs are also fed special lean diets at this time. The following responses were from accomplished dogmen regarding the relevance of training and the sundry of methods utilized.

> It takes a lot of time and money to get these dogs ready for the pit. They don't just throw their dogs into the pit and hope for the best. They go through a lot of trouble to make sure their dogs are in the best condition possible for the fight. They invest in all kinds of equipment to aid in the conditioning of the dogs. They have treadmills, flirtpoles, and turntables that are made just for the dogs. As a matter of fact, there's a man out in Scott, LA that makes dog treadmills, for a living . . . The object is to make sure that your dog can go the distance in the pit. If your dog is not conditioned properly he won't be able to maintain his wind in the pit. Hell, these fights can last anywhere from 30 minutes to 4 or 5 hours. That's why the conditioning is so important. (INTERVIEW)

> Around 19 months to 2 years old, if his attitude is right then I will school him out. I'll roll him a few times with different types of dogs to teach him different types of fighting. I'll do that 4 or 5 times. I decide how far to push the next time by what he shows me at each roll. The last time I roll him, I would game check him by putting some time on him and a better dog on him. You let him see the bottom. You make sure he gets some of the worst end of the deal. A lot of people put 2 or 3 dogs on him, one after the other. I find it easier to put him on a jenny or a mill and blow all his air out of him and then put a dog on him for 30 minutes. You see what kind of attitude he has then. When you match a dog he will never have to fight against more than one dog. He only has to whip one dog at a time. (INTERVIEW)

As demonstrated in these accounts, experienced dogmen are very cognizant of the significance of proper training. Matches sometimes continue for 4 hours (there is no time limit). Dogs must be trained so they will have the stamina to endure the match. Individuals who place bets also

put a lot of weight on the reputation of the dog's trainer.

Negotiating a Contract

When a member of the fraternity has a dog he is ready to fight, he puts out his conditions such as the weight of the dog, sex of the dog, and the amount he wants to bet on the fight. These facts are advertised either in the underground journals or by word of mouth. Once another dogman accepts the conditions and the wager a contract is drawn up.

The process of matching dogs has become a normative process. The owner "puts out a weight," which means they have a dog at a particular weight that they wish to fight.

> First thing people do is put a weight out there. They agree upon a weight, like 46 lb. male. They agree on a purse and a forfeit. A forfeit means that if a dog comes in over weight his owner must pay the other owner the agreed upon amount and negotiate a new contract. A match is set at a specific amount of money, let's say three thousand dollars, that is the purse. The forfeit will be set at let's say five hundred dollars. If your dog comes in over weight, you have to pay a $500 forfeit then negotiate a new contract. The first fight was canceled. The man with the dog that was over weight will lay odds. He might agree to pay $3,500 because his dog is over weight, which puts the other dog at a disadvantage. (INTERVIEW)

Although not as critical to the fight itself as training and breeding, and not as monetarily important as the contract, planning and selecting the location is critical. Because dogfighting is illegal, participants are very secretive about the date and location of the event.

Planning and Selecting the Location of the Fight

Dogfights are most commonly staged in secluded rural areas such as barns or fields. There is a national network, consisting of members of the dogfighting fraternity, which facilitates the planning of locations for these events. When a contract is drawn up for a fight, the participants decide on a central location. They then contact a dogman in that area to make arrangements to have the fight at a location that he provides. The following are comments about finding a location.

The location of the fight is usually kept secret until the afternoon of the fight with only the two owners and the man providing the location knowing where it will take place. This is done in order to protect themselves against possible raids. When the time arrives for the event to take place everyone is then informed of the location. The people leave the initial location at separate times so as not to attract attention and all meet at the location of the fight.

> When Rick and L. G. agreed to fight their dogs, they called Mike to help them plan a location for the event. They wanted to meet somewhere in between Florida and Arizona so Mike agreed to have the fight here in North Louisiana. There's a whole network of dogmen who aid one another in finding locations for the fights. They're the only three people who actually know where the fight will be. They keep the location a secret until the night of the fight in order to avoid raids. Once Mike lets everybody know where the fight will take place, we leave his house one vehicle at a time so as not to attract attention. We have to be careful these days with the Humane Society breathing down our necks and pressuring the cops to bust up dogfighting. I don't know why those damned people don't just mind their own business. They act like we're hard core criminals or something. We're not hurting anybody and the dogs love to fight, so what's the harm. (INTERVIEW)

Dogmen realize that keeping this veil over the circumstances of the fight, until immediately before the event, is necessary for the survival of dogfighting. A successful raid can push those marginal dogmen and spectators out of the sport. Dogmen face fines, confiscation of dogs, and in some states prison time. A sport supported by such a small fraternity cannot afford to lose any peers.

The Meeting of Dogmen and Dogs

The Pre-Fight.   On the day of the fight the participants and the spectators, usually members of

the fraternity, which tends to be almost exclusively male, meet at a dogman's house near the location where the fight will take place. Here they will converse for hours before the fight about such things as the history of champion bloodlines, recent fights that they have attended, breeding and conditioning practices, and a vast array of other issues pertaining to their sport. This gathering of the fraternity before the event is a very important element of the dogmen subculture. It is at this time that the social status of the fraternity members is most evident. In these conversations the old timers do most of the talking and the newcomers listen like obedient students eager to learn all that they can. It should be noted that even though dogfighters are seen as deviant by society, they did not have deviant self-concepts.

The following is both a vivid description and summarization of the meeting before a dogfight took place. The fight had been planned for months, The following interview took place during the trip in a car to the pre-fight meeting.

> We're almost there now . . . just a little further up the road. Everyone who is anyone, in the dog game, will be at the fight tonight. They've been planning this event for months and people from all over the country will be there. Most of the old timers will be there. Man, they are awesome. They can teach you anything you want to know about the game and the dogs. They know all the champion bloodlines and every champion dog that ever walked on the face of this earth. Well hell, they're the ones that put most of the champion dogs on the ground. Those guys know what the hell they're talking about when it comes to anything having to do with dogfighting. It's important that you listen to them and show them the respect they deserve. If those guys don't accept you, you are not going anywhere in this game. They decide who is going to move in this circle, so don't piss them off. (INTERVIEW)

The following interview took place at the pre-fight meeting that was held in the home of a dogman.

> We'd better head over to Norman's place; we don't want to miss the beginning of the fight. When we get there, park as close as you can to the road and

turn your car facing the road. You never know when we might need to make a fast get away. Just remember if the cops ever show up at a fight, always be prepared to leave fast. If they ever catch you, you didn't see or hear anything about dog-fighting. Always be loyal to the fraternity and don't ever rat out anybody else. If they catch you they'll try to get a confession out of you. Don't give it to them. (INTERVIEW)

These pre-fight comments reveal the loyalty of dogmen to their sport. Their need for secrecy and loyalty is why the ranks of dogmen are difficult to invade. Although the viewing of these fights was certainly more stirring, the pre-fight meetings were more informative. At these meetings one learns about all aspects of the dogmen and their pit bulls.

The Fight.   There are two types of dogfights: formal and informal. The informal fight is when two dogs are fought without any contract. There may be only a few people present, it may take place in the streets, is usually engaged in by teenagers and arises spontaneously. Formal fights are defined as organized events in which a contract exists (stating the terms of the fight—amount of the wager, the weight at which the dogs will be fought, the amount of the forfeit and the sex of the dogs). In addition, there is a sub-culture that maintains it. Our research was only concerned with the formal dog fight. Formal fights were classified as either conventions or private matches.

There used to be conventions, now it's turned into private matches. A convention you might have up to 6 or 7 fights that night. At private matches the most you will have is 2 fights and with the same people . . . at conventions there were up to 300 people. The fights may go on all night into the morning. Law enforcement could catch us at conventions because there are so many people there and you cannot check them all out. In a private match the owner of the place where the fight takes place checks everyone out before they get there. (INTERVIEW)

Prior to the fight the dogs are weighed in and washed to make sure they are free of any noxious substances that could interfere with the dogs' ability to fight.

The dogfight is a staged event in which two dogs are placed into a pit, much like a boxing ring, and fight until one opponent either quits or dies, at which time the other is declared the winner. There is a referee and two handlers present in the pit with the dogs and many spectators viewing the event. The fight begins when the referee tells the handlers to pit their dogs; at which time the dogs are released and attack one another. Once the fight begins the spectators begin placing bets with one another on which dog will win. . . .

The owners are bringing the dogs to their corners of the pit. Tile pit is about 20 feet by 20 feet, and this one is surrounded by 3-feet-tall wooden sides. Both of the dogs look eager to fight.

Norman [the referee] says sternly, "gentlemen pit your dogs." The handlers [Rick and L. G.] release their dogs and Snow and Black lunge at one another. Snow rears up and overpowers Black, but Black manages to come back with a quick locking of the jaws on Snow's neck. The crowd is cheering wildly and yelling out bets. Once a dog gets a lock on the other, they will hold on with all their might. The dogs flail back and forth and all the while Black maintains her hold. It looks like Black is hung up so Norman motions for the handlers to separate the dogs. They approach the dogs and L. G. pries Black's mouth open with a breaking stick. The dogs are returned to their corners and sponged down with water.

Once again Norman calls for the dogs to be pitted. This time Snow must scratch to [attack] Black and make contact with her within 10 seconds. Snow races toward Black and is not going to let Black get the best of her. Snow goes straight for the throat and grabs hold with her razor sharp teeth. Almost immediately, blood flows from Black's throat. Despite a severe injury to the throat Black manages to continue fighting back. They are relentless, each battling the other and neither willing to accept defeat. This fighting continues for an hour. Finally, the dogs [stop biting] and Norman gives the okay for them to be handled. He gives the third and final pit call. It is Black's turn to [attack] and she is severely wounded. Black manages to crawl across the pit to meet her opponent. Snow attacks Black and she is too weak to fight back. L. G. realizes that this is it for Black and calls the fight. Snow is declared the winner.

Rick collects his money. L. G. then lifts Black from the pit and carries her out back. Her back legs are broken and blood is gushing from her throat. A shot rings out barely heard over the noise in the barn. Black's body is wrapped up and carried by her owner to his vehicle.

There are four possible ways in which the fight may end: a dog's failure to [attack], the owner calling the fight (this is analogous to the manager of a boxer throwing the towel into the ring that signals that the fighter has quit), the death of one or both dogs, or one of the dogs jumping the pit.

The failure to [attack the] opponent upon command of the referee . . . is the most common way in which fights will end. A less common ending is the death of one of the opponents.

The least common ending is for one of the dogs to jump the pit, which means they literally jump out of the pit in order to escape their opponent. This is very rare because a dogman will not bring a cur dog (coward) to a fight at the risk of facing humiliation. If a dog does jump the pit it will surely result in his death at the hands of his owner.

Within the dogfighting fraternity, the most admirable quality is gameness, that can be described as continued willingness to fight and never stop fighting as long as one is physically and mentally able to continue. The canine opponents employed in these dogfights are expected to show this quality of gameness as long as there is breath left in their bodies. A dog that exhibits this quality in extreme measures is considered to be dead game (some call this a killer dog) and therefore he will be seen as the ultimate canine warrior. So important is this quality that it is the goal of every dogman to own a dog who is dead game.

DISCUSSION

The sport of fatal fighting (Enquist and Lelmar, 1990) in America primarily involves two animals: the fighting cock and the pit bull dog. There is very little literature on dogfighting and little academic interest in the topic. The literature that does exist on fatal fighting is primarily concerned with the fighting cock (Bryant, 1982; McCaghy and Neal, 1974; Worden and Darden, 1992). The efforts of law enforcement have taken their toll on the dogmen fraternity. In the past, large meets called conventions took place, now these events have been reduced to private matches.

. . . Dogmen have developed norms that govern conduct between their deviant associates, therefore planning and precautions have assumed law-like importance to them. The organization of dogmen, although deviant and secret, resembles respectable transactions. The dogfight has become an ordered, yet deviant activity, by respectable people.

When one views a staged dogfight between pit bulls for the first time, the most macabre aspect of the event is that the only sounds you hear from these dogs are those of crunching bones and cartilage. The dogs rip and tear at each other; their blood, urine, and saliva splatter the sides of the pit and clothes of the handlers. This is the American Pit Bull Terrier at work in a role they have been performing for over a century. The emotions of the dogs are conspicuous, but not so striking, even to themselves, are the passions of the owners of the dogs. Whether they hug a winner or in the rare case, destroy a dying loser, whether they walk away from the carcass or lay crying over it, their fondness for these fighters is manifest. Whether it produces admiration or disdain, you will be overwhelmed by the game and the connection between the true dogman and his fighting dog.

The meaning that this sport has for these men can only be gotten from listening to the accounts of dogmen who are willing to share several generations of knowledge and experience. The loyalty and secrecy are important components of subcultural maintenance. This article has conveyed these subcultural pieces so that the reader will better understand the complete world of the dogmen. This world is indeed much more than a dogfight. More research is needed into this much-maligned arena of sport. Hopefully this research will serve as a heuristic device for further study on this topic.

DOGFIGHTING: VICTIMLESS CRIME?

There are two broad research perspectives in the understanding of deviant behavior. Understanding deviance involves studying both those who make the rules and those who break the rules (Becker, 1963; Little, 1995). These two perspectives are both evident if we look at cases of deviance in which there is objective rule breaking but there is not consensus in society, as to the deviance of the act. In other words, there is a law against the behavior but many times when the law is broken the rule breaking is treated as though it were not deviant at all (Little, 1995). Becker (1963) called such behavior secret deviance, meaning that it is so well hidden nobody sees it and if it is seen nobody seems to do anything about it. Closely related to this category of deviance in some respects is the idea of victimless crime.

Victimless crimes (Schur, 1965) refer to the willing exchange among adults of goods and services. These goods and services are legally proscribed, but are strongly demanded by the adult public. Homosexuality, illegal gambling, drug misuse, abortion, prostitution, and pornography are examples of victimless crimes. The primary characteristics of so called victimless crimes is a transaction between two participants, both of whom choose to enter into a relationship. Because neither individual in the relationship desires to make a complaint, laws against these exchanges are difficult to enforce. Most activities of this sort go on with little intrusion from law enforcement (Little, 1995). . . .

[Dogmen and their supporters see dogfighting as a victimless crime, but] the impediment to these victimless events comes from moral entrepreneurs. The presumption is that they serve the community by protecting its virtue and its members. Dogfighting involves two forms of deviance: gambling and the violation of animal protection laws. Because gambling is widely accepted in the areas where dogfighting takes place (horse racing, casinos, lottery), it is not this aspect that has brought on the concern of moral entrepreneurs. Dogfighting has been labeled as deviant because moral entrepreneurs consider the dog a victim. . . . In addition, dogfighting is in conflict with the new environmental sensitivity. Animals have arisen as a highly visible and logical subset of this new environmental awareness/sensitivity and greater respect is accorded them as a somewhat incidental beneficiary in this cultural wave of animal rights (Palmer and Forsyth, 1992). Dogfighting agitates this cultural swell, hence dogmen can expect a persistent storm of moral challenge.

REFERENCES

Atyeo, D. (1979). *Blood and guts, violence in sports.* New York: Paddington Press.

Becker, H. S. (1963). *Outsiders.* New York: Free Press.

Bryant, C. D. (1982). Cockfighting in sociohistorical context: Some sociological observations on a socially disvalued sport. *The Gamecock, 45,* 65–70, 80–85.

Denzin, N. (1978). *The research act.* New York: McGraw-Hill.

Enquist, M., & Leimar, O. (1990). The evolution of fatal fighting. *Animal Behavior, 39,* 1–9.

Forsyth, C. (1986). Sea daddy: An excursus into an endangered social species. *Maritime Policy and Management: The International Journal of Shipping and Port Research, 13,* 53–60.

Geertz, C. (1973). *The interpretation of cultures: Selected essays.* New York: Basic Books.

Little, C. B. (1995). *Deviance and control.* Itasca, IL: Peacock Publishers.

Matz, K. S. (1984). *The pit bull fact and fable.* Sacramento, CA: De Mortmain Publishing.

McCaghy, C. H., & Neal, A. G. (1974). The fraternity of cockfighters: Ethical embellishments of an illegal sport. *Journal of Popular Culture, 8,* 557–569.

Palmer, C. E., & Forsyth, C. (1992). Animals, attitudes, and anthropomorphic sentiment: The social con-

struction of meat and fur in postindustrial society. *International Review of Modern Sociology, 22,* 29–44.

Schur, E. (1965). *Crimes without victims.* Englewood Cliffs, NJ: Prentice-Hall.

Semencic, C. (1984). *The world of fighting dogs.* Neptune City, NJ: T. F. H. Publications.

Worden, S., & Darden, D. (1992). Knives and gaffs: Definitions in the deviant world of cockfighting. *Deviant Behavior, 13,* 271–289.

REVIEW QUESTIONS

1. Describe the methodology that Evans and Forsyth used.
2. If someone is interested in dogfighting and wants to join that fraternity, what steps would he take to become a member of that fraternity?

PART THIRTEEN

CONTROL AND RESISTANCE

In October 2002, U.S. Marine Antonio Sledd and his buddies were taking a break from a military exercise in Kuwait by playing baseball on a makeshift diamond. Suddenly two Kuwaiti men ran toward third base and opened fire, killing Sledd and wounding another Marine. When the assailants turned their weapons toward home plate, they were gunned down. They were later identified as members of Al Qaeda, the terrorist group that directed the September 11 attack on the United States. Before and after the attack in Kuwait, there were other attacks, including the explosion that hit a French oil tanker near Yemen and the bombing of a nightclub on the Indonesian island of Bali that killed nearly 200 people, many of them Westerners.[1]

These terrorist acts represent a response to the war the United States and its allies wage against Al Qaeda. Such a response is one of the common ways deviants react to the conventional society's attempt to control them. It involves *rejecting, resisting,* or *fighting* the conventional society. Examples include gays, lesbians, and people with disabilities rejecting negative conventional views about them and fighting for better treatment by conventional others. Another common way deviants react entails *accepting, reconciling with,* or *surrendering to* the society's negative view and treatment of them. Such a reaction can be seen, for example, from many overweight U.S. women who agree with their society that they are unattractive and therefore feel unhappy because they are "fat."

On the other side, the social control used by conventional society against deviants can be divided into two types: formal and informal. Formal controls are carried out through killing, imprisonment, expulsion, or surveillance by the government and its law-enforcement agencies, the military, and business companies and other civilian organizations. Informal controls come from relatives, neighbors, peers, and even strangers through discipline, criticism, ridicule, or dirty looks.

Here we take a look at the formal control of deviants and at resistance by deviants. In the first article, "Why Do They Hate Us? What to Do," Fareed Zakaria explains the importance of fighting Al Qaeda on three fronts: military, political, and cultural. In the second piece, "Everyday Surveillance in Postmodern Society," William Staples discusses how today's society seeks to control deviants and everybody else by surveilling them. In the third selection, "Social Movements of People with Disabilities," Sharon Barnartt and her colleagues provide a history of how Americans with disabilities fought for better treatment in U.S. society.

---

1. Daniel Klaidman and Rod Nordland, "No Time to Stand Down," *Newsweek,* October 21, 2002, p. 38.

WHY DO THEY HATE US? WHAT TO DO

FAREED ZAKARIA

For most Arabs, relations with the United States have been filled with disappointment.

While the Arab world has long felt betrayed by Europe's colonial powers, its disillusionment with America begins most importantly with the creation of Israel in 1948. As the Arabs see it, at a time when colonies were winning independence from they West, here was a state largely composed of foreign people being imposed on a region with Western backing. The anger deepened in the wake of America's support for Israel during the wars of 1967 and 1973, and ever since in its relations with the Palestinians: The daily exposure to Israel's iron-fisted rule over the occupied territories has turned this into the great cause of the Arab—and indeed the broader Islamic—world. Elsewhere, they look at American policy in the region as cynically geared to America's oil interests, supporting thugs and tyrants without any hesitation. Finally, the bombing and isolation of Iraq have become fodder for daily attacks on the United States. While many in the Arab world do not like Saddam Hussein, they believe that the United States has chosen a particularly inhuman method, of fighting him—a method that is starving an entire nation.

There is substance to same of these charges, and certainly from the point of view of an Arab, American actions are never going to seem entirely fair. Like any country, America has its interests. In my view, America's greatest sins toward the Arab world are sins of omission. We have neglected to press any regime there to open up its society. This neglect turned deadly in the case of Afghanistan. Walking away from that fractured country after 1989 resulted in the rise of bin Laden and the Taliban. This is not the gravest error a great power can make, but it is a common American one. As F. Scott Fitzgerald explained of his characters in *The Great Gatsby,* "They were careless people, Tom and Daisy—they smashed things up and creatures and then retreated back into their money, or their vast carelessness . . . and let other people clean up the mess." America has not been venal in the Arab world. But it has been careless.

Yet carelessness is not enough to explain Arab rage. After all, if concern for the Palestinians is at the heart of the problem, why have their Arab brethren done nothing for them? (They cannot resettle in any Arab nation but Jordan, and the aid they receive from the gulf states is minuscule.) Israel treats its 1 million Arabs as second-class citizens, a disgrace on its democracy. And yet the tragedy of the Arab world is that Israel accords them more political rights and dignities than most Arab nations give to their own people. Why is the focus of Arab anger on Israel and not those regimes?

The disproportionate feelings of grievance directed at America have to be placed in the overall context of the sense of humiliation, decline and

Source: Fareed Zakaria, "Why Do They Hate Us? What to Do," *Newsweek,* October 15, 2001, pp. 36–40. Reprinted with permission.

despair that sweeps the Arab world. After all, the Chinese vigorously disagree with most of America's foreign policy and have fought wars with U.S. proxies. African states feel the same sense of disappointment and unfairness. But they do not work it into a rage against America. Arabs, however, feel that they are under siege from the modern world and that the United States symbolizes this world. Thus every action America takes gets magnified a thousandfold. And even when we do not act, the rumors of our gigantic powers and nefarious deeds still spread. Most Americans would not believe how common the rumor is throughout the Arab world that either the CIA or Israel's Mossad blew up the World Trade Center to justify attacks on Arabs and Muslims. This is the culture from which the suicide bombers have come.

America must now devise a strategy to deal with this form of religious terrorism. As is now widely understood, this will be a long war, with many fronts and battles small and large. Our strategy must be divided along three lines: military, political and cultural. On the military front—by which I mean war, covert operations and other forms of coercion—the goal is simple: the total destruction of Al Qaeda. Even if we never understand all the causes of apocalyptic terror, we must do battle against it. Every person who plans and helps in a terrorist operation must understand that he will be tracked and punished. Their operations will be disrupted, their finances drained, their hideouts destroyed. There will be associated costs to pursuing such as strategy, but they will all fade if we succeed. Nothing else matters on the military front.

The political strategy is more complex and more ambitious. At the broadest level, we now have a chance to reorder the international system around this pressing new danger. The degree of cooperation from around the world has been unprecedented. We should not look on this trend suspiciously. Most governments feel threatened by the rise of subnational forces like Al Qaeda. Even some that have clearly supported terrorism in the past, like Iran, seem interested in re-entering the world community and reforming their ways.

We can define a strategy for the post-cold-war era that addresses America's principal national-security need and yet is sustained by a broad international consensus. To do this we will have to give up some cold-war reflexes, such as an allergy to multilateralism, and stop insisting that China is about to rival us militarily or that Russia is likely to re-emerge as a new military threat. (For 10 years now, our defense forces have been aligned for everything but the real danger we face. This will inevitably change.)

The purpose of an international coalition is practical and strategic. Given the nature of this war, we will need the constant cooperation of other governments—to make arrests, shut dawn safe houses, close bank accounts and share intelligence. Alliance politics has become a matter of high national security. But there is a broader imperative. The United States dominates the world in a way that inevitably arouses envy or anger or opposition. That comes with the power, but we still need to get things done. If we can mask our power in—sorry, work with—institutions like the United Nations Security Council, U.S. might will be easier for much of the world to bear. Bush's father understood this, which is why he ensured that the United Nations sanctioned the gulf war. The point here is to succeed, and international legitimacy can help us do that.

Now we get to Israel. It is obviously one of the central and most charged problems in the region. But it is a problem to which we cannot offer the Arab world support for its solution—the extinction of the state. We cannot in any way weaken our commitment to the existence and health of Israel. Similarly, we cannot abandon our policy of containing Saddam Hussein. He is building weapons of mass destruction.

However, we should not pursue mistaken policies simply out of spite. Our policy toward Saddam is broken. . . . [The economic sanctions imposed on Iraq are]—for whatever reason—starving Iraqis and he continues to build chemical and biological weapons. There is a way to reorient our policy to focus our pressure on Saddam and not his people, contain him militarily but not harm common Iraqis economically. Colin Powell has been trying to do this; he should be given leeway to try again. In time we will have to address the broader question of what to do about Saddam, a question that, unfortunately, does not have an easy answer. (Occupying Iraq, even if we could do it, does not seem a good idea in this climate.)

On Israel we should make a clear distinction between its right to exist and its occupation of the West Bank and Gaza. On the first we should be as unyielding as ever; on the second we should continue trying to construct a final deal along the lines that Bill Clinton and Ehud Barak outlined. I suggest that we do this less because it will lower the temperature in the Arab world—who knows if it will?—than because it's the right thing to do. Israel cannot remain a democracy and continue to occupy and militarily rule 3 million people against their wishes. It's bad for Israel, bad for the Palestinians and bad for the United States.

But policy changes, large or small, are not at the heart of the struggle we face. The third, vital component to this battle is a cultural strategy. The United States must help Islam enter the modern world. It sounds like an impossible challenge, and it certainly is not one we would have chosen. But America—indeed the whole world—faces a dire security threat that will not be resolved unless we can stop the political, economic and cultural collapse that lies at the roots of Arab rage. During the cold war the West employed myriad ideological strategies to discredit the appeal of communism, make democracy seem attractive and promote open societies. We will have to do something on that scale to win this cultural struggle.

First, we have to help moderate Arab states, but on the condition that they embrace moderation. For too long regimes like Saudi Arabia's have engaged in a deadly dance with religious extremism. Even Egypt, which has always denounced fundamentalism, allows its controlled media to rant crazily about America and Israel. (That way they don't rant about the dictatorship they live under.) But more broadly, we must persuade Arab moderates to make the case to their people that Islam is compatible with modern society, that it does allow women to work, that it encourages education and that it has welcomed people of other faiths and creeds. Some of this they will do—Sept. 11 has been a wake-up call for many. The Saudi regime denounced and broke its ties to the Taliban (a regime that it used to glorify as representing pure Islam). The Egyptian press is now making the case for military action. The United States and the West should do their own work as well. We can fund moderate Muslim groups and scholars and broadcast fresh thinking across the Arab world, all aimed at breaking the power of the fundamentalists.

Obviously we will have to help construct a new political order in Afghanistan after we have deposed the Taliban regime. But beyond that we have to press the nations of the Arab world—and others, like Pakistan, where the virus of fundamentalism has spread—to reform, open up and gain legitimacy. We need to do business with these regimes; yet, just as we did with South Korea and Taiwan during the cold war, we can ally with these dictatorships and still push them toward reform. For those who argue that we should not engage in nation-building, I would say foreign policy is not theology. I have myself been skeptical of nation-building in places where our interests were unclear and it seemed unlikely that we would stay the course. In this case, stable political development is the key to reducing our single greatest security threat. We have no option but to get back into the nation-building business.

It sounds like a daunting challenge, but there are many good signs. Al Qaeda is not more powerful than the combined force of many determined governments. The world is indeed uniting around American leadership, and perhaps we will see the emergence, for a while, of a new global community and consensus, which could bring progress in many other areas of international life. Perhaps most important, Islamic fundamentalism still does not speak to the majority of the Muslim people. In Pakistan, fundamentalist parties have yet to get more than 10 percent of the vote. In Iran, having experienced the brutal puritanism of the mullahs, people are yearning for normalcy. In Egypt, for all the repression, the fundamentalists are a potent force but so far not dominant. If the West can help Islam enter modernity in dignity and peace, it will have done more than achieved security. It will have changed the world.

REVIEW QUESTIONS

1. Zakaria says, "Our strategy must be divided along three lines." Discuss the purpose of each strategic line. Is one more important than the others? Defend your answer.

2. Choose a theoretical perspective discussed in earlier chapters and apply it to Zakaria's article.

51

EVERYDAY SURVEILLANCE IN POSTMODERN SOCIETY

WILLIAM G. STAPLES

Throughout the U.S., thousands of criminals are placed under "house arrest," their movements monitored electronically by a transmitter attached to their ankle. In many states, criminal defendants and judges carry out proceedings on video monitors. In Arizona, a "welfare" mother has a court-ordered contraceptive device surgically implanted in her arm. In New York, a high-tech courtroom collects a myriad of information about a single defendant that is kept in an electronic file folder. Most "clients" in community corrections programs are subjected to random drug and alcohol testing.

At the same time:

Sixty-seven percent of major U.S. employers engage in some form of electronic monitoring of workers. In New York City, more than two thousand private surveillance cameras are taping citizens on public streets. In California, every citizen wishing to be issued a driver's license must have their thumbprint computer scanned. In Massachusetts, a company tracks the Web surfing habits of more than thirty million Internet users. Nearly 90 percent of U.S. manufacturers are testing workers for drugs.

The preceding examples illustrate a blurring distinction between the practices of the official justice system and the everyday lives of ordinary people. How are we to understand these developments? Are they simply "advances" in our struggle against illegal, deviant, or "troublesome" behavior, or do they signal the rise of what might be called a "culture of surveillance"? What kind of society has produced these practices, and why do we appear so willing to adopt them? The purpose of this [article] is to explore these and other questions about the emergence of new forms of social control in contemporary society.

Recently, I sat in the "café" section of a large, suburban bookstore talking with a friend. She asked me what I was working on these days, and I told her that I was writing . . . about social control in contemporary life. At this she said, "You mean about crime and prisons?" "No," I said, "not really. More like the issue of surveillance." "Oh," she replied, "so you are looking into how the FBI spies on people?" To many of us, including my friend, issues of discipline, social control, and surveillance tend either to revolve around the criminal justice system or to invite the image of George Orwell's notorious Big Brother. Yet as important as the prison system and the activities of domestic "spying" organizations are, I am more interested here in the relatively small, often mundane procedures and practices—the Tiny Brothers if you will—that are increasingly present in our daily lives. These techniques exist in the shadow of large institutions such as prisons; they are not ushered in with dramatic displays of state power such as the Branch

Source: William G. Staples, *Everyday Surveillance: Vigilance and Visibility in Postmodern Life* (Lanham, MD: Rowman & Littlefield, 2000), pp. 1–11, 158–159. Reprinted with permission.

Davidian standoff in Waco, Texas, nor do they appear as significant challenges to constitutional democracy such as the FBI's COunterINTELligence programs of the 1960s and 1970s. The techniques I mean are the more commonplace strategies used by governmental and, increasingly, private organizations to "keep us in line," monitor our performance, gather knowledge or evidence about us, assess deviations, and, if necessary, exact penalties. For it is these daily activities that involve many more, if not all, of us than does life in a state prison or the latest FBI "sting" operation.

THE CONTINUUM OF SURVEILLANCE

The techniques I have in mind range along a continuum. They begin with the "soft," seemingly benign and relatively inconspicuous forms of monitoring such as those used in the very bookstore where I sat with my friend. In that business, as in thousands across the United States, a security system monitored our interaction with video cameras, while the store's spatial arrangement was designed for optimal surveillance of customers and employees alike. Computerized checkout stations kept track of inventory, calculated store performance figures, assessed the credit worthiness of patrons through remote data banks, collected personal information about customers so they could be targeted for marketing campaigns, monitored the log-on and log-off times of employees, and calculated the average number of customers those employees processed per hour. All this was accomplished "behind the scenes" as it were, without disruption to the manufactured ambiance of soft leather chairs, melodic Muzak, and the sound and smell of cappuccino making.

At the "hard" end of the spectrum are the more obtrusive and confrontational practices that often begin with the assumption of guilt and are designed to uncover the "truth," to test an individual's character, and, more generally, to make people consciously aware that they are indeed being watched and monitored. Of course, this element was also evident at the corporate bookstore I visited with my friend, as they had "tagged" all the merchandise so

that both of us could be electronically "frisked" as we walked through the sensor gates at the exit. These are what I call "surveillance ceremonies." They include random drug and alcohol testing, the use of lie detectors, pre-employment integrity tests, and "sobriety checkpoints" in the streets. They also include the practices of electronically monitored "house arrest," adolescent curfews, and the use of metal detectors.

Between these soft and hard types of social control lies a vast array of techniques and technologies—exercised on and by people both inside and outside the justice system—that are designed to watch our bodies, to regulate and monitor our activities, habits, and movements, and, ultimately, to shape or change our behavior. These procedures are often undertaken in the name of law and order, public safety, the protection of private property, or simply "sound business practice"; other procedures are initiated for an individual's "own good" or benefit. But no matter what the stated motivation, the intent of social control is to mold, shape, and modify actions and behaviors.[1]

The subject of this [article], then, is the cultural practices that I will call "meticulous rituals of power." Most generally, I include those microtechniques of social monitoring and control that are enhanced by the use of new information, communications, and medical technologies. These are knowledge-gathering activities that involve surveillance, information and evidence collection, and analysis. I call them meticulous because they are "small" procedures and techniques that are precisely and thoroughly exercised. I see them as ritualistic because they are faithfully repeated and are often quickly accepted and routinely practiced with little question. And they are about power because they are intended to discipline people into acting in ways that others have deemed to be lawful or have defined as appropriate or simply "normal."

THE CHARACTERISTICS OF POSTMODERN SURVEILLANCE

"OK," you may say, "so what is really new here? Hasn't society always had ways of keeping people in line? Aren't these meticulous rituals just newer, perhaps more effective ways of doing what we have always done to ensure social order?" In some ways, yes, they are logical extensions of "modern" solutions to the problems of crime, deviance, and social control, and they may indeed be more efficient. Yet, at the same time, they have qualities that make them fundamentally new, and, I want to argue, *post*modern in design and implementation, and I think it's important that we come to understand the implications of their use. I see at least four defining characteristics that set these practices apart from more traditional methods. In the first place, consider the following. In the past, the watchful eyes of a small shopkeeper may have deterred a would-be shoplifter; her surveillance was personal, not terribly systematic, and her memory, of course, was fallible. She was more likely to know her customers (and they her), to keep a "closer eye" on strangers, and to "look the other way" when she saw fit (and to make a call to the offending juvenile's parents later). This kind of "personal" social control was once typical of small communities or close-knit societies where people certainly watched one another very closely and where fear of ridicule or exclusion was a powerful inducement to conformity.

By contrast, the part-time, non-owning employees of the large corporate bookstore where I sat with my friend have less interest in watching for thieves; their huge number of customers is an anonymous crowd. So here, the store management relies on the hidden, faceless, and ever-ready video security camera. The videocam—one of the defining features of postmodern society—projects a hyper-vigilant "gaze," randomly scanning the entire store day or night, recording every event, and watching *all* the customers, not just the "suspicious ones." The cameras are also positioned to watch the vast number of employees, who must now be monitored both as "productive" workers and as potential thieves. In this way, surveillance and discipline have become oddly democratic; everyone is watched, and no one is trusted.

So the first characteristic of postmodern social control is that it tends to be systematic, methodi-

cal, and automatic in operation. It is likely to be impersonal in that the observer is rarely seen and is anonymous; further, the "observer" is likely to be a computer system, a videocam, a drug-testing kit, or an electronic scanner of some kind. Once more, the data that these devices collect may become part of a permanent record in the form of a videotape, a computer file, or some other digital format.

Second, these new meticulous rituals of power often involve our bodies in new and important ways, and I want to distinguish two primary tactics of bodily social control. I agree with Donald Lowe when he states: "As living beings, we are more than body and mind, more than the representations and images of our body. We lead a bodily life in the world."[2] These bodily lives are shaped, manipulated, and controlled by a set of ongoing practices that compose our daily lives as workers, consumers, and community members.

The first tactic I want to distinguish has to do with types of monitoring and surveillance that enhance our visibility to others. We seem to be entering a state of permanent visibility where attempts to control and shape our behavior, in essence our bodies, are accomplished not so much by the threat of punishment and physical force but by the act of being watched—continuously, anonymously, and automatically. This kind of watching happens when people engage in such diverse activities as clipping on a company beeper, using a credit card to purchase something at a store, or parking their car in a garage with a security camera. These instances signify different forms of "visibility": the beeper enables an employer to remotely "check up" on and monitor an employee; the credit card purchase leaves an electronic paper trail of a person's activities and whereabouts; and the security camera identifies to the police, or anyone else who gains access to the tape, that a particular individual was indeed parked in that garage on a particular day at a certain time. The methodical, technology-driven, impersonal gaze, I argue, is quickly becoming a primary mechanism of surveillance and, by extension, social control in our society, and it is fixed on our bodies and their movements.

A second tactic of bodily surveillance and social control relates to new developments in science, technology, and medicine. These intersecting fields are making the human body infinitely more accessible to official scrutiny and assessment. This means that the ability of organizations to monitor, judge, or even regulate our actions and behaviors through our bodies is significantly enhanced. It also means that it becomes less important to trust suspects to "speak the truth" or convicted offenders to "mend their ways." Rather, it is the individual's body that will "tell us what we need to know," as in indicating that someone is using drugs or was at the scene of a crime or even has "deviant desires." In this way, the body is treated as an "object" that contains the evidence of any possible deviance. For example, on the soft side of our spectrum of social control, we see that corporations are using medical data collected on employees in their "wellness" and exercise clinics to confront the "unhealthy lifestyles" of those not conforming to prevailing standards (about, for example, tobacco use or obesity). Meanwhile, on the hard side, DNA samples are being systematically collected and stored and are increasingly presented as evidence in courtroom proceedings. The body, I contend, is a central target of many postmodern surveillance techniques and rituals.

The third defining characteristic of postmodern social control relates to a shift in the location of social control and surveillance and which behaviors are the subject of it. Since the early nineteenth century, our primary method of dealing with lawbreakers, those thought to be insane, other deviants, and even the poor has been to isolate them from everyday life—as in the case of the modern prison, mental asylum, poorhouse, and reformatory. Yet the kinds of practices I am most concerned with here attempt to impose a framework of accountability on an individual in everyday life. While, obviously, removing "troublesome" people from society is still a significant means of formal social control (after all, in the United States, we institutionalize more people than any other Western country does), this approach is increasingly considered, by various experts, to be an inefficient, ineffective, and undesirable practice. This is particularly true if we consider the idea that as a society we seem to be engaged in a far-reaching attempt to regulate not only the traditional crimes of person and property but also the behaviors, conditions, and "lifestyles" of substance (ab)use, alcohol and tobacco consumption, "eating disorders," forms of sexual expression and sexual "promiscuity" and "deviance," teenage pregnancy, out-of-marriage births, domestic violence, child abuse, "dysfunctional" families, various psychological or psychiatric disorders and other "medical" conditions such as "attention deficit disorder," and such diseases as AIDS. How can we possibly institutionalize and control everyone that falls into these rapidly expanding categories of "troublesome" individuals?

Given these conditions, it would appear that the segregative or quarantine models of social control of the nineteenth century are an invention whose time has simply passed. The incentive now is to develop new ways to control and "keep an eye on" what appears to be an increasing number of "deviants" through an expanding network of formal "community corrections" programs; regulatory welfare, health, and social service agencies; and even schools, workplaces, and other community institutions. New developments in the forensic, medical, and computer and information sciences—generated by corporate research and development departments and the post–Cold War military–industrial complex (which I believe is being converted rapidly into a "security–industrial complex")—are creating more remote, more flexible, and more efficient ways of making this happen.

Finally, as new forms of social control are localized in everyday life, they are capable of bringing wide-ranging populations, not just the official "deviant," under their watchful gaze. As I indicated earlier, trust is becoming a rare commodity in our culture. The notion of "innocent until proven guilty" seems like a cliché these days, when people are apt to be subjected to disciplinary rituals and surveillance ceremonies simply because statistics indicate that they have the potential for being offenders (for example the police tactic known as "racial profiling" as a justification for stopping motorists). Data generated through surveillance techniques produce "types" or whole classes of individuals who are deemed "at risk" for behavior, whether any one particular individual has engaged in such behavior or not. These data, of course, are then used to justify even closer surveillance and scrutiny of this group, thereby increasing the likelihood of uncovering more offenses; and so it goes. In the context of these changes, social control becomes more about predicting and preventing deviance—always assuming that it will, indeed, happen—rather than responding to a violation after it has occurred.[3] Therefore, when put in place, ritualistic monitoring and surveillance ceremonies often blur the distinction between the official "deviant" and the "likely" or even "possible" offender. Indeed, what separates the convicted felon, the college athlete, or the discount store cashier if each is subjected to random drug screening? One consequence of this blurring is that we may be witnessing a historical shift from the specific punishment of the individual deviant to the generalized surveillance of us all. . . .

[In short], postmodern surveillance practices have four characteristics:

1. They are increasingly technology-based, methodical, automatic, and sometimes anonymously applied, and they usually generate a permanent record as evidence.
2. Many new techniques target and treat the body as an object that can be watched, assessed, and manipulated.
3. The new techniques are often local, operating in our everyday lives.
4. Local or not, they manage to bring wide-ranging populations, not just the official "deviant," under scrutiny.

WHAT TO DO ABOUT IT?

All this sounds pretty bleak, doesn't it? Now that we have arrived at the crumbling edge of the cliff,

it's time to turn to me and say, "OK, now what? You brought us here; what do we do about it?"

. . . One strategy is to simply drop out of the culture entirely. This is the tactic of many that have retreated to remote areas as part of the so-called radical survivalist movement. Interestingly, these predominately right-wing "counterculture" groups characterize themselves as living "off the grid" of credit cards, television, public utilities, and the consumer society. While these folks appear to be alert to some of the issues I have raised, their often racist attitudes and rampantly conspiratorial Big Brother paranoia about the government miss the mark completely, and this makes them quite an unattractive lot to sign on with.

An alternative position, however, is one of active resistance. If we accept the premise that much of the exercise of this kind of power takes place in the form of "local" micropractices that are present in our everyday lives, then the sites of opposition are right before us. They are in our own homes, workplaces, schools, and communities. We don't need, necessarily, to form a counterinsurgency movement to storm Washington, D.C. Rather, when some school board members in your community assert that student athletes should be tested for drugs, demand that they demonstrate that drug abuse is indeed a problem. Next time you telephone a business and a recording tells you that your call is being monitored "for your protection," ask to speak to a supervisor, and tell that person that you disapprove of the practice. When your state legislature debates the merits of fingerprinting drivers license applicants, call your representative's office and ask her or him to vote against it. The next time someone carries on about the wonders of the latest digital gadget, acknowledge its potential benefits but remind the speaker that there may be privacy or surveillance implications to the product's use. Talk with your kids, openly and honestly, about both the allure and the dangers of drug use. In fact, turn off the television, log off the computer, unclip the beeper, and take your kid for a walk around the block. Wave to your neighbors. Well, you get the point.

NOTES

1. The term *social control* has a long history in the sociology. See Jack Gibbs, *Norms, Deviance, and Social Control: Conceptual Matters* (New York: Elsevier, 1981); Stanley Cohen and Andrew Scull, *Social Control and the State* (New York. St. Martin's Press, 1983); and Donald Black, *The Social Structure of Right and Wrong* (New York: Academic Press, 1999).

2. Donald Lowe, *The Body in Late Capitalism USA* (Durham: Duke University Press, 1995).

3. This perspective is rooted in recent "neo-liberal" models of managing the "risk society" where, as Ericson puts it, "deviance gives way to risk as the concept for the understanding of how dangers are both identified and responded to technologically. The concern is less with the labeling of deviants as outsiders, and more on developing a knowledge of everyone to ascertain and manage their place in society." This perspective strikes me as positively frightening. See Richard V. Ericson's review of an earlier edition of this book in *Social Forces* 76, no. 3 (1998): 1154, as well as his, *Policing the Risk Society* (Toronto: Toronto University Press, 1997).

REVIEW QUESTIONS

1. Identify and discuss the four characteristics of postmodern surveillance that set it apart from traditional methods.

2. Compare and contrast the social control mentioned in Staples's article with Travis Hirschi's control theory (see selection 7, pp. 44–46).

SOCIAL MOVEMENTS OF PEOPLE
WITH DISABILITIES

SHARON BARNARTT
KAY SCHRINER
RICHARD SCOTCH

While disability movements have formed in many nations around the world, the movement in the United States is probably the most extensive and the one with the longest and broadest history of contentious disability politics. This [article] presents empirical results from a study by Barnartt and Scotch (forthcoming) of protests in the disability community from 1970 to 1999. That study used media and other reports of 646 specific instances of protest activity by disability activists in the United States. The reports were compiled from 4 newspapers of national scope, which covered the entire period; more than 100 newspapers with more limited geographical or temporal scope; and some non-newspaper sources, including books, disability periodicals, and disability-related e-mail discussion lists. The published media reports were identified by the use of Internet search engines as well as other methods (see Barnartt and Scotch [forthcoming] for further methodological details). Using event history analysis, this research focuses on the actual protest event, not on protesters or social movement organizations. Variables that represented characteristics of the protests, such as location, date, target, and issue, were created, and the data were coded and entered into computer files for quantitative analysis.

Here we examine patterns of movement that political action has taken over time [and] changes in types of issues over time. . . .

No reports of protests could be located for 1971 or 1972. From 1972 through 1987, the number of reported protests fluctuated between 4 (1978) and 18 (1977). After 1987, contentious political activity began to explode, with at least 18 protests every year. In 1987, there were 10 reported protests, but the next year, there were 41. The highest levels of protest were in 1991, 1992, and 1997, with 55, 57, and 80 protests, respectively.

What made protest activity begin in 1972, and how do we explain the fluctuations in the numbers of protests in subsequent years? Even when the social stage is set for collective action, as seemed to be the case by the end of the 1960s, collective action is unlikely to occur without some proximate cause. There must be the emergence of some specific grievance that sparks collective action. According to our database, the central political issue that provoked protests by disability activists from 1972 to 1977 was the struggle to pass and implement the Rehabilitation Act of 1973, particularly the provision in that law that prohibited discrimination on the basis of disability in federally supported programs, Section 504 (Scotch 1984).

Source: Sharon Barnartt, Kay Schriner, and Richard Scotch, "Advocacy and Political Action," in Gary Albrecht, Katherine Seelman, and Michael Bury (eds.), *Handbook of Disability Studies* (Thousand Oaks, CA: Sage, 2001), pp. 430–449. Reprinted with permission of Sage Publications, Inc.

These highly visible protests were conducted by a broad cross-disability coalition, a somewhat new development in the disability movement. In 1972, protests in New York and Washington focused on President Nixon's two vetoes of earlier versions of this law. Many protests in 1976 and particularly 1977 urged the release of federal regulations implementing Section 504, which had been held up for several years by cautious federal officials (Scotch 1984). Although the officials involved denied any connection, after a delay of more than three years, the Section 504 regulations were issued following these widely publicized disability protests. The apparent success of the protestors fueled the growth of the movement.

The Rehabilitation Act success contributed to a growing willingness in the disability community to plan and participate in disruptive collective action. In 1981, protests occurred in response to cuts in social programs by the Reagan administration.

However, at least two other issues showed up in the early 1980s that might have been expected to attract disability protests but did not. One was the controversy over the so-called Baby Doe regulations. These regulations related to the extent to which hospitals must keep babies with several physical impairments alive or, alternatively, when a hospital could let such an infant die. The other was a controversy over the right of a woman named Elizabeth Bouvia, who had severe physical impairments, to take her own life. This controversy also involved the extent to which hospitals should or could keep someone alive—by force, if necessary—who did not want to stay alive. There were no protests identified by the searching mechanisms used here that focused on either of these cases. However, the organization Not Dead Yet refers to this situation as the basis for its establishment.

The surge in protest activity that began in 1988 does not have a single cause. Rather, there seems to be several factors at work. One cause may have been the success of the Deaf President Now (DPN) protests at Gallaudet University. Gallaudet, a university in Washington, D.C., serving deaf students, had never been led by a deaf president, and students demanded that the university trustees select one in a series of large-scale demonstrations (Christiansen and Barnartt 1995). Partly as a result of that protest, there appears to have been a change in political culture regarding disability around that time, which resulted in more sympathy and empathy for disability issues in Congress than had heretofore been seen (Altman and Barnartt 1993). This change in political culture may have brought with it an opening up of the political opportunity structure (Tarrow 1994), which was supportive of the introduction of the Americans with Disabilities Act (ADA) into Congress. The responsiveness of the American government to disability protests also may have increased with the transition from the Reagan to the Bush administration, which included more officials with some connection to disability (Altman and Barnartt 1993). This opening of the political opportunity structure may have been perceived by activists as something to be exploited with increased protest activity.

In addition, the introduction of the first version of the ADA in Congress in 1988 probably spurred some protest activity; it clearly provided a target for some protests. Although there is little evidence of a huge increase in protests specifically aimed at the ADA, some of the protests between 1988 and 1990 were aimed at its issues. A few protests had demanded one or more of the provisions that were eventually included in the law, especially the transportation provisions, but the numbers of these protests are smaller than one might have expected. Between the introduction of the ADA into Congress and the fact that there was now also a track record of widely publicized and successful protests, we have the beginnings of an explanation for the rise in the numbers of protests.

The large numbers of protests in 1992 and 1993 may be explained in part by protests against telethons that many disability advocates consider demeaning and exploitative of disability as tragic and catastrophic. In 1992, there were 18 such protests, and in 1993, there were 10. The large numbers of protests in 1997 are partially explained by the events of August 9, 1997. On this day, ADAPT sponsored protests against Greyhound in 40 cities across the country ("Protesters Serve Notice" 1997). Although the number of protests in 1998 decreased somewhat, the number of protests for the first half of 1999 suggested that protest activity has not begun to die down.

Analysis of the specific protest issues does not tell us enough about why the levels of protest waxed and waned or why they increased overall during this period. To do that, we examine changes over time in several other factors. Some disability movement researchers (e.g., Longmore 1997; Young 1998) claim that the current disability movement is more cross-disability than it had been in the past because of the presence of cross-disability organizations such as the American Coalition of Citizens with Disabilities (ACCD),

which was founded in 1974. They further imply that this is one reason for the increasing number of protests during this time. Longmore (1997) states that current disability protests exemplify "an ecumenical ideology of disability issues and an inclusive definition of disability identity" (p. 97).

While mainstream research in politics has traditionally tended to view protests and other nonelectoral political activities as ineffective, social movement research suggests that protest activity, particularly when it is disruptive, may be successful in influencing public policy (Gamson 1990; Piven and Cloward 1979). [As the study reported here suggests,] disability movements appear to be influential in securing short-term policy goals and in charting the terms of the larger debate over how government and society at large ought to address the role of people with disabilities.

REFERENCES

Altman, Barbara, and Sharon N. Barnartt. 1993. "Moral Entrepreneurship and the Passage of the ADA." *Journal of Disability Policy Studies* 4 (1): 21–40.

Barnartt, Sharon, and Richard Scotch. Forthcoming. *Social Movements in the Disability Community.* Washington, DC: Gallaudet University Press.

Christiansen, John B., and Sharon N. Barnartt. 1995. *Deaf President Now!: The 1988 Revolution of Gallaudet University.* Washington DC: Gallaudet University Press.

Gamson, William. 1990. *The Strategy of Social Protest.* 2d ed. Belmont, CA: Wadsworth.

Longmore, Paul. 1997. "Political Movements of People with Disabilities: The League of the Physically Handicapped, 1935–1938." *Disability Studies Quarterly* 17 (2): 94–98.

Piven, F. F., and R. Cloward. 1979. *Poor People's Movements: Why They Succeed, How They Fail.* New York: Random House.

"Protesters Serve Notice on Greyhound." 1997. *Ragged Edge* (September/October):6.

Scotch, Richard K. 1984. *From Good Will to Civil Rights: Transforming Federal Disability Policy.* Philadelphia: Temple University Press.

Tarrow, S. 1994. *Power in Movement: Social Movements, Collective Action and Politics.* New York: Cambridge University Press.

Young, Jonathan. 1998. "The President's Committee on the Handicapped and the Origins of Cross-Disability Organizing." Paper presented at the annual meeting of the Society for Disability Studies, June, Oakland, CA.

REVIEW QUESTIONS

1. What needs to be present to motivate collective action from the disability community?
2. Are the disability movements effective? Support your answer with evidence from the study.

Murray, M. D., 159
Mustafa, A. Z., 134

Napier, Cathy, 241
Naunton, Robert E., 186n.
Neal, A. G., 323, 327
Nettler, Gwynn, 3
Newcomb, M. D., 234
Newcomb, Robert, 216
Nichter, M., 235–236
Nixon, Richard M., 344
Norris, Joel, 91
Norris, Terry D., 290
Novick, J., 146
Nuttbrock, L., 188

Oberstone, Andrea, 171, 174
O'Connnel Davidson, Julia, 205, 206
Ogle, Robbin, 66
Okami, Paul, 270
Olarte, S., 284
Olson, James N., 297, 302, 306
Omer-Hashi, K. H., 131–134, 136
Opperman, Martin, 199
O'Reilly-Fleming, T., 94
Oro, Jose, 279
Orwell, George, 337

Pakulski, Jan, 74
Palmer, C. Eddie, 214, 328
Paternoster, Raymond, 67
Patterson, S. J., 141
Patton, Michael Quinn, 21
Patullo, Polly, 204
Perlman, Ellen, 257n.
Perry, Matthew, 240
Pfohl, Stephen C., 9, 11–14, 73
Phelan, J. C., 188
Pincus, Harold Alan, 159
Pincus, Jonathan H., 91
Pinder, David, 200, 201
Pitcher, Richard, 51
Piven, F. F., 345
Plummer, Ken, 112
Pogrebin, Mark R., 275, 284–289
Pollack, Kenneth, 241–242
Pollner, Melvin, 19
Polsky, Ned, 21
Poole, Eric D., 284–289

Pope, K. S., 284
Portenoy, Russell, 241
Potter, Deborah, 139, 154–161
Powdermaker, Hortense, 178
Powell, Colin, 335
Power, Richard, 253
Prabhakaran, Velupillai, 107
Prentky, R. A., 89
Prus, R., 308, 313, 316, 317
Puente, Dorothea, 93

Quadagno, D., 132–134
Quayle, Ethel, 251, 264–269
Queen, Carol, 220
Quinn, Jack, 278
Quinney, Richard, 51, 59–63
Quintero, G., 235–236

Rada, Richard, 79
Rae, D., 134
Rahav, M., 188
Ramo, Joshua Cooper, 156
Ramsey, E., 141
Ramundo, Peggy, 156
Randall, Margaret, 205
Rasmussen, Paul K., 210, 211, 214
Ratey, John J., 156, 157
Raymond, Janice G., 202
Reagan, Ronald, 105, 314
Reddie, N., 134
Rees, Matt, 77n.
Reiland, Ralph, 203
Reimherr, F. W., 158
Reiss, D., 193
Rengert, G., 297, 299
Reppetto, T. G., 299
Ressler, R. K., 90, 91, 94
Revitch, E., 128
Rhodes, W., 92
Rich, Marc, 275, 277–279
Richards, A. L., 123
Rimm, E. B., 250n.
Riorden, C., 288
Risman, B., 227–230
Ritzer, George, 72
Roberts, B., 314, 317
Robinson, Linda, 204
Rogers, E., 128
Rohner, Ronald P., 80

Ethics
  and cheating in school, 290–294
  of female genital mutilation, 135–136
  political influence and, 277–279, 280–283
  of psychotherapist relationships with patients,
    284–289
  of researcher intimacy with informants, 27–29
Ethnicity. *See* Race/ethnicity
Excision, genital, 132, 134
Exhibitionism, 210

Family violence. *See* Sexual and family violence
Federal Bureau of Investigation (FBI), 253, 254,
    337–338
Federal Trade Commission (FTC), 254–255
Female genital mutilation (FGM), 131–137
  dangers of, 133–134, 135
  ethical considerations in, 135–136
  history of, 131–132
  justifications for, 133–135
  legal considerations in, 135–136
  moral considerations in, 135–136
  procedures used in, 132–133
Feminist theory, 64–69
  critique of male bias, 64–65
  deconstructionist criminology and, 73
  gender identity development in lesbians, 171–175
  gender-neutral theory and, 67–68
  patterns of lawbreaking, 67–68
  quality of female offenses, 65–67
  rape and, 112
  treatment of deviant women, 66–67
Field research. *See also* Participant observation
  researcher intimacy with informants, 25–31
First Amendment rights, 102–103
Fluoxetine (Prozac), 158
Fort Reno tribal lands, 282–283
Fraud, Internet, 254–257
Free will, 5–6
Fugitives from justice, 277–279, 280–282

Gallaudet University, 184, 344
Gangs. *See* Juvenile gangs
Gender. *See also* Feminist theory; Sexual and family
    violence
  dogfighting and, 323
  female genital mutilation and, 131–137
  female prostitution, 67, 197, 199–209, 219,
    311–312

obesity stigma and, 176–182
and physical violence, 79–86
rape and, 111–125
of researcher, and violence, 27
substance abuse and, 233, 248, 249
teen suicide and, 141
tobacco use and, 248, 249
Gendered crime, 68
Gendered lives, 68
Gendered pathways to lawbreaking, 68
Gender identity development. *See also* Masculinity
  lesbian, 171–175
Gender-neutral theory, 67–68
Gender ratio of crime, 68
Genetics
  deafness and, 184
  hyperactive adults and, 158–159
Grounded theory, 19
Guatemala, 13
Gulf War (1991), 11

Hackers, 251, 253–257
  computer safety and, 255–256
  nature of, 253–255
  software company liability for, 256–257
Hamas, 107
Handicapped persons. *See* Disabilities and
    stigmatization
Harvard School of Public Health College Alcohol
    Study (CAS), 243–246, 248
Hate crimes, 97–103
  biblical bigotry and, 98–100
  from a distance, 98
  militia movement and, 100–101, 219
  organized groups and, 97–98, 101–103
  White supremacy and, 97–103
Havana, Cuba, 199, 203–206
  labor market in, 204–205
  localized sex work in, 205–206
  public policy and law in, 206
  tourism industry in, 204
Heterosexism, 14
Heterosexual deviance, 197–230
  adult chat lines, 258–263
  female promiscuity, 227–230
  female prostitution, 67, 197, 199–209, 219, 311–312
  nude dancing, 216–226
  parade strippers, 210–215
  sex tourism, 199–209

Hezbollah, 107
Hillside Strangler, 90, 93
History of Sexuality, The (Foucault), 29
Homeless population, research strategies with,
    18–24
Homicide
    female deviance and, 66–67
    hate crimes, 97–103
    serial murder, 87–96
    suicide bombers, 77, 104–108
Homosexuality and homophobia, 171–175
    gender identity development in lesbians, 171–175
    stigmatization and, 169, 179–180
Hyperactive adults, 154–161
    books on, 155, 156, 157
    diagnosis of, 154–155, 157–158
    emergence of, 155–157
    social context for, 158–159
    treatment of, 158
Hyperactive Child, Adolescent, and Adult, The
    (Wender), 155
Hyperreality, 72–73

Identity Church, 98–99
Identity theft, 254–255
Incest
    child molestation, 126–130
    female genital mutilation (FGM) as, 131, 132
India, 136
Individual Education Plan (IEP), 189, 193
Individual Written Rehabilitation Plan, 189
Infibulation, 132, 133–134
Influence peddling, 280–283
Informational social influences, 237
Informed consent, 136
Innovation, in individual adaptation, 38
Insanity
    pseudopatients in mental wards and, 148–153
    serial killers and, 89
Inside information, burglary and, 299
Institutionalization
    of mentally challenged persons, 191, 194
    pseudopatient study of mental wards, 148–153
    as stigmatizing, 191, 194
Interactionism
    robbery and, 303–307
    symbolic, 74
Interdependency, in shaming theory, 47–49
Internalization, of stigmatization, 180

Internet
    adult chat lines, 258–263
    e-commerce, 254–257
    hackers and, 251, 253–257
    hate crimes and, 102–103
    on-line child pornography, 264–269
Internet Alliance, 255
Internet Fraud Complaint Center (IFCC), 254
Internet Security System (ISS), 251
Intertextuality, 72
Intimacy with informants, 25–31
Involvement, in control theory, 45
Iraq, 11
Islam
    Arab resistance to U.S. policies, 333–336
    female genital mutilation and, 132, 133
    suicide bombers and, 77, 104–108
Israel, 77
    Arab resistance to U.S. policies, 333–336
    suicide bombers and, 77, 104–108

Jehovah's Witnesses, 132
Justice system, and female versus male offenders,
    65–67, 66–68, 68
Juvenile gangs, 13
    female involvement in, 56, 64–66, 68

Kenya, 106
Khazarian Legend, 99–100
Kingdom of Khazarian, 99–100
Ku Klux Klan, 97, 98, 101
Kuwait, 105, 331

Labeling, 1–2, 3–4
    depersonalization and, 149–152
    of disability and family constructions, 191–192
    of hyperactive adults, 154–161
    of lesbians, 173
    of mentally challenged persons, 191–192
    pseudopatients and, 149–152
    of rape, 123–124
    stickiness of, 150–151
Labeling theory, 53–55
Language, power of, 72
Las Vegas, Nevada, 72, 73
Lebanon, 105
Legal agents, 59, 60
Lesbianism, gender identity development, 171–175
Liberation Tigers of Tamil Eeelam (LTTE), 105–107